ENCYCLOPEDIA OF CATHOLIC DEVOTIONS AND PRACTICES

ENCYCLOPEDIA OF CATHOLIC DEVOTIONS AND PRACTICES

ANN BALL

Introduction by Rev. Neil Roy, S.T.L., Ph.D

Our Sunday Visitor Publishing Division
Our Sunday Visitor, Inc.
Huntington, Indiana 46750

Nihil Obstat: Rev. Michael Heintz
Censor Librorum

Imprimatur: ✠ John M. D'Arcy
Diocese of Fort Wayne-South Bend
March 27, 2003

The *nihil obstat* and *imprimatur* are official declarations that a book or pamphlet is free of doctrinal or moral error. No implication is contained therein that those who have granted the *nihil obstat* or *imprimatur* agree with the content, opinions, or statements expressed.

This volume is dedicated to all employees of Our Sunday Visitor, who are the real heroes, the ones responsible for turning a lowly author's work into a book, and especially to retired OSV editors John Laughlin and Henry O'Brien with gratitude and laughter. May God bless them for making my job fun. I would also like to dedicate this in memory of my friend Arcadio Saenz, in whose home I first met *Santo Niño*.

— *The editor*

☙

A Word of Thanks

To Robert P. Lockwood, Msgr. Francis Mannion, and Michael J. Walsh, my editorial board, I extend my thanks for keeping me on track. And to my editors, Jackie Lindsey, Julianne Will, Bill Dodds, Henry O'Brien, and Lisa Grote, what can I say but "I love you!" Thank you all for believing I could handle a project this big.

A very special thank you to my "writer" friends: Alejandro Bermúdez, who assisted me in translations; Matt Bunson, Joan Cruz, and Roy Varghese for answering a million questions; and Leo Knowles, who always came through in a pinch. They have put up with my incessant e-mails for information on minor points cheerfully and competently.

I extend a prayerful thanks to my "heavenly" assistant, Father Francis X. Weiser, whom I feel has been looking over my shoulder, and prodding me to more and careful research, from his place in Our Father's mansion as I worked on this project. Thanks to Rev. Neil J. Roy, S.T.L., Ph.D., for his careful review and valuable additions to this text. And to the following who have been treasure-houses of information and assistance: Rev. Ray Bucko, Creighton University, The Jesuweb web list members, the Hagiomail web list members, Robert Brideau, Erv Grafe, Ben Lytz, Susan Tassone, John Thavis, David A. Flory, Eduardo Schmidt, S.J., Rossana Goni, Father Eugene Carrella, Patrick Nugent, Bob Seguin, C.S.B., David Birchall, S.J., Mary Talamini, Father Jack Walsh, Tom Sepulveda, C.S.B., Pat Hunt, Peter Martinez, Daniel J. Lynch, Maureen Tilley, Father Thomas Neulinger, S.J., Michael Perigo, Byron Bullock, Pat Rensing, Roy Hammerling, the Franciscan Sisters of Manila, Mary Ann Olivier, Barbara Spear, Chuck Thompson, and Mr. and Mrs. Tom Keppler. If I have inadvertently left off the name of any others who should have been included, I leave it to Our Blessed Mother to give my gratitude to them.

And, of course, my friend Karin Murthough, who puts up with me and my writing projects daily at the office.

Sincerely in Christ,
Ann Ball

Table of Contents

∽∾∽

Introduction / 9

Preface / 17

Contributors / 19

Entries, A-Z / 23

Appendix A, Patron Saints / 673

Appendix B, Shrines and Places of Historic Interest in the U.S. / 683

Appendix C, Emblems of the Saints / 693

Appendix D, Sacred Symbols / 697

Selected Bibliography / 701

Index / 707

Introduction

∽▰▰▰∾

Lifelong Catholics well-versed in the teachings of their childhood catechism will recall, perhaps word for word, the answer to the question,
"Why did God make you?" *God made me to know Him, to love Him, and
to serve Him in this world and to be happy with Him forever in the next.*[1]
For all its simplicity of expression, the answer to this question is really
quite profound. We are called by God to be co-heirs with Christ of the
heavenly Kingdom;[2] and our participation in that Kingdom depends on
our knowledge, love, and service of God in this life. We can scarcely serve
with fidelity and perseverance someone whom we do not love and respect; nor can we love someone whom we do not know. Hence the need
for us to learn in this life as much as we can about God, to grow daily in
our love for Him, and to express this love by worshiping Him "in Spirit
and in truth."[3]

If we have grasped the import of this elementary teaching of Catholicism, then we understand that God is calling us, both individually and as
a Church, to be holy. The Second Vatican Council (1962-65) called the
entire People of God to a profound — indeed radical — renewal. Perhaps the most fundamental legacy of the Council remains its stress on
the universal vocation to holiness. In simple terms, this means that God
calls us to be saints. The vocation to holiness, or sanctity, is not reserved
for those in either holy orders or religious vows. Married couples, singles,
the widowed, children, professionals, trades people, politicians, prisoners, public servants, entertainers, domestic engineers, entrepreneurs, film
producers, students — in short, all people — are called to holiness, which is
achieved, under grace, through the knowledge, love, and service of God.

The foremost service that the Church renders to God is liturgical worship. Yet, the Church's liturgy is more than just a privileged act of divine

---

[1] *The Penny Catechism,* or *A Catechism of Christian Doctrine, American Edition* (South Bend,
Ind.: Marian Press, 1973; reprinted Rockford, Ill.: TAN Books, 1982), question 2, p. 3.

[2] See Romans 8:17.

[3] John 4:23-24. Scriptural citations are all from the *Revised Standard Version* (Catholic Edition).

service. The fathers of Vatican II drew attention to the centrality of the liturgy in the very life and mission of the Catholic Church. In the words of the Constitution on the Sacred Liturgy *Sacrosanctum Concilium*, "Liturgy is the summit toward which the activity of the Church is directed; it is also the fount from which all her power flows."[4] More recently, Pope John Paul II has underscored the Eucharist as the principal source of the Church's vitality. The title of his most recent encyclical letter, *Ecclesia de Eucharistia*, expresses quite strikingly the beautiful reality that the Church derives her very existence from the sacrament which contains Christ himself. Without the Eucharist there would be no Church.

One of the chief strengths of the liturgy is its objective character. Despite the personal sentiments experienced by individual Christians at times of prayer, the liturgy prays in the words of the Church. The liturgy gives voice to the love of the Church for her divine Bridegroom. In liturgical worship, God is glorified and humanity in turn is sanctified. "From the liturgy, therefore, and especially from the Eucharist, grace is poured forth as from a fountain, and the sanctification of men in Christ and the glorification of God to which all other activities of the Church are directed, as toward their end, are achieved with maximum effectiveness."[5]

Nevertheless, the Constitution acknowledges that the spiritual life is not limited to participation in the liturgy.[6] Indeed, Christians, called to pray without ceasing,[7] must cultivate, by an interior life of prayer, a personal relationship with the Persons of the Holy Trinity, as well as with the Blessed Virgin, the angels, and the saints. Spiritual reading, or *lectio divina*, is an essential component of growth in the spiritual life because it nourishes prayer and meditation. In the selection of spiritual reading, Sacred Scripture naturally enjoys pride of place because the Bible contains the inspired Word of God. The writings of the saints, doctors of the

---

[4] Vatican Council II, Constitution on the Sacred Liturgy *Sacrosanctum Concilium*, 10. Excerpts from *Sacrosanctum Concilium* are taken from *Vatican Council II. The Conciliar and Post Conciliar Documents*, study edition, ed. Austin Flannery (Dublin, Ireland: Dominican Publications and Newtown, NSW, Australia), new revised edition, 1992.

[5] *Sacrosanctum Concilium*, 10.

[6] See *Sacrosanctum Concilium*, 12.

[7] "Pray at all times in the Spirit, with all prayer and supplication" (Ephesians 6:18). "Rejoice always, pray constantly, give thanks in all circumstances; for this is the will of God in Christ Jesus for you" (Thessalonians 5:17).

Church, mystics, and approved spiritual authors likewise provide food for mental prayer. Even meditation on Christian doctrine, as the Venerable John Henry Newman shows in his *Meditations and Devotions*, is profitable to the inner life of the soul and fosters spiritual growth.[8]

In addition to private prayer undertaken in the secrecy of one's inner chamber,[9] Christians may likewise derive immense spiritual profit from praying with others both in small groups and in large assemblies. Paraliturgical and devotional services celebrated in common fulfill a keenly felt need on the part of the faithful to respond to the Holy Spirit's promptings to pray "at all times" in various ways and in the various circumstances of the local community. Eucharistic adoration outside Mass, communal recitation of the Rosary, and Stations of the Cross are but a few of the many expressions of popular piety long approved by the Church and still practiced by communities of the faithful.

Far from discouraging the practice of devotions and communal prayer, the fathers of Vatican II heartily endorsed both universal and local expressions of piety: "Popular devotions of the Christian people, provided that they conform to the laws and norms of the Church, are to be highly recommended, especially when they are ordered by the Apostolic See."[10] Since the Middle Ages, the popes have encouraged participation in such devotions as Eucharistic worship outside Mass, the Rosary, and the Stations of the Cross. The Council further upheld the dignity of devotions proper to individual churches, provided, of course, that these are undertaken at the direction of the bishops and in accordance with lawfully approved customs and books.[11]

The relationship between devotions and the sacred liturgy, however, remains clear. Devotions and pious customs are subordinate to the Church's liturgical prayer. No devotion or pious practice, however worthy and spiritually beneficial to the faithful, can rival or equal in excel-

---

[8] This spiritual classic was first published in 1903 by Longmans, Green, and Co., London and New York. A new edition, enriched by *The Devotions of Bishop Andrewes* and Newman's own *Verses on Various Occasions*, has been published under a new title: *Prayers, Verses, and Devotions* (San Francisco: Ignatius Press, 2000).

[9] "But when you pray, go into your room and shut the door and pray to your Father who is in secret; and your Father who sees in secret will reward you" (Matthew 6:6).

[10] *Sacrosanctum Concilium*, 13.

[11] See *Sacrosanctum Concilium*, 13.

lence the official prayer of the Church. The Constitution on the Sacred Liturgy reminds Catholics, "Such devotions should be so drawn up that they harmonize with the liturgical seasons, accord with the sacred liturgy, are in some way derived from it, and lead the people to it, since in fact the liturgy by its very nature is far superior to any of them."[12]

This is not to deny the influence of devotion and popular piety on the liturgy. Some of the most beautiful solemnities on the Church's liturgical year derived from popular piety. Trinity Sunday, for example, emerged in the Carolingian era out of the desire of priests newly ordained on the Saturday after Pentecost to celebrate their first Mass in honor of the Blessed Trinity. In the thirteenth century, devotion to the real presence of Christ in the Eucharist gave rise to the feast of Corpus Christi, still marked today in many places by processions with the Blessed Sacrament exposed in highly ornamented monstrances. The feast of the Sacred Heart of Jesus, though dating only from the seventeenth century, owes its origin to the devotion of religious, lay people, and priests to the merciful and self-sacrificing love of Christ. This love finds particular expression in that Heart which was pierced by the soldier's lance as the Savior hung on the cross.[13] The various Marian feasts that punctuate the Roman calendar, most of which were imported from the East, likewise testify to the influence of popular piety on liturgical observance. It must be acknowledged that the spirit of devotion that inspired and popularized these feasts sprang from the Church's reflection on the deposit of the Christian Faith. This devotion and the liturgical feasts that developed under its influence frequently aimed at asserting the Church's accepted beliefs against systems and strains of thought that resisted or rejected Christian orthodoxy. In this sense, popular devotion has played a significant role in both the cultivation of liturgy and the general adherence to authentic Christianity.

Despite the generous endorsement of piety and devotions by the fathers of Vatican II, the decades immediately following the Council witnessed, in some places, the decline of pious practices in favor of an almost exclusive reliance on Mass as a means of worship. Devotional prayer forms of long standing and venerable custom were disparaged or even aggres-

---

[12] *Sacrosanctum Concilium*, 13.

[13] See John 19:34.

sively opposed, regardless of their proven pastoral effectiveness and the support of saints and popes alike. Such a narrow insistence on liturgy to the active discouragement of devotions finds no sanction in the conciliar or post-conciliar documents. North America saw various praiseworthy attempts to accommodate traditional devotions to the renewed liturgy and thereby to preserve them in pastoral practice; but such popular works enjoyed only limited success.[14] Where policies hostile to devotion and pious customs were implemented, younger Catholics and converts admitted to the Church as adults may not have been introduced to practices and devotions that constitute a lively part of the Church's rich spiritual patrimony. These newer members of the faith are entitled to all the spiritual goods of the Church and ought to have access to their rightful heritage as Catholics.[15]

On the other hand, there are areas where unapproved devotions may have been exaggerated to a point where superstition or unhealthy fear exercised undue influence in patterns of prayer. The circulation of "chain letters" in the form of a prayer that must be reprinted and distributed at the expense of each recipient is such an abuse. The notion that burying a statue of St. Joseph on one's property will guarantee the sale of a house likewise is an example of a superstition that has gained currency, even among non-Catholics, in some cultures and social classes. The practice of hanging rosary beads on the clothesline to ward off rain on one's wedding day is yet another example of superstition that overlooks the whole point of a prayer as beautiful and profound as the Rosary. Anything that hints of superstition or a mechanical manipulation of divine power with a view to achieving a specific end is alien to authentic Christian piety.

Devotions which lack the official approval of the Church or which, in some cases, even stray from accepted Christian teaching are best discarded in favor of those which, endorsed by ecclesiastical authority, harmonize well with the liturgy and lead one to a deeper union with God. The

---

[14] See for example Walter Kern, *New Liturgy and Old Devotions: Explanations and Prayers,* Canfield, OH: Alba House Communications, 1979.

[15] "The Christian faithful have the right to receive assistance from the sacred pastors out of the spiritual goods of the Church, especially the word of God and the sacraments" (Canon 213, *New Commentary on the Code of Canon Law. An Entirely New and Comprehensive Commentary by Canonists from North America and Europe, with a Revised English Translation of the Code,* eds. John P. Beal, James A. Coriden, and Thomas J. Green (Mahwah, NJ: Paulist Press, 2000) p. 267.

advice of a competent spiritual director is desirable, perhaps even necessary, particularly in cases where the source or the aim of a given pious practice is unclear. It is the mark of genuine sanctity, and altogether consonant with the Catholic spirit, to submit one's private judgment to the mind of the Church as manifested in the authoritative pronouncements of her legitimately appointed leaders.

The publication of the *Encyclopedia of Catholic Devotions and Practices* could scarcely have come at a more favorable time. Its appearance in autumn 2003, forty years after the release of *Sacrosanctum Concilium*, follows closely upon the release of John Paul II's encyclical on the Eucharist[16] and coincides with the culmination of the Year of the Rosary.[17] Less than two years ago, on December 17, 2001, the Congregation for Divine Worship and the Discipline of the Sacraments issued its *Directory on Popular Piety and the Liturgy*.[18] The Vatican's English translation of the *Directory* became available on the Vatican web site in August 2002 and constitutes an appendix of this work.

Why, it may be asked, has the Vatican shown such interest in devotions and popular piety that it has issued the recent *Directory*? Without ignoring the ongoing interest of the Holy See in specific aspects of popular devotions and piety, expressed periodically by such papal documents as *Mense Maio* (1965), *Marialis cultus* (1974), and *Vicesimus quintus annus* (1988), as well as by curial instructions such as *Varietates legitimae* (1994), a possible answer may be suggested. The promulgation in 2001 of the *Martyrologium Romanum* marked an end to the post-Vatican II revision of all the liturgical books.[19] Indeed the approval on Maundy Thursday 2002 of the third typical edition of the 1970 *Missale Romanum* testifies to the considerable progress accomplished in the renewal of the liturgy mandated by the Second Vatican Council.[20] Once the monu-

[16] John Paul II, Encyclical Letter *Ecclesia de Eucharistia* (Vatican: Libreria Editrice Vaticana, 2003).

[17] John Paul II, Apostolic Letter *Rosarium Virginis Mariae* (Vatican: Libreria Editrice Vaticana, 2002).

[18] Congregation for Divine Worship and the Discipline of the Sacraments, *Directory on Popular Piety and the Liturgy: Principles and Guidelines* (Vatican: Libreria Editrice Vaticana, 2002).

[19] *Martyrologium Romanum* (Vatican: Libreria Editrice Vaticana, 2001).

[20] *Missale Romanum ex decreto sacrosancti oecumenici Concilii Vaticani II instauratum auctoritate Pauli Pp. VI promulgatum Ioannis Pauli P. II cura recognitum.* 3rd ed. (Vatican: Libreria Editrice Vaticana, 2002).

mental task of reforming the Western Church's liturgical books had been completed, the Holy See could turn its attention more fully to devotional life and popular piety. Hence the timeliness of the present volume.

This encyclopedia aims to provide, at the popular level, a handy reference to many of the devotional exercises, religious customs, and pious practices that mark the lives both of individual Catholics and of Catholic communities. Families, parishes, religious houses, schools, confraternities, and sodalities traditionally have provided the context for growth in the life of devotion. Each has the potential to foster in its members an ever deeper love of God and of one's neighbor. This, of course, is the chief goal of devotion: an increase in the love of God and the sanctification of the human. Each group, whether home, church, school, or religious association, enjoys its own particular ways of transmitting this love and of nurturing piety.

The widespread popularity of certain devotions such as the Rosary, first Fridays and Saturdays of the month, and the Stations of the Cross underscores the catholicity or universality of the Church. On the other hand, the plethora of particular forms of piety or devotional expression reflects the quite varied experience of the Church in different places and in different periods of history. Some devotions, particularly those honoring the Virgin Mary under various titles, are restricted to regional and national communities. Other customs, such as the serving of specific meals or beverages on certain feast days, prevail among various language groups and appeal to age-old traditions of a beloved homeland. This encyclopedia serves as a guide to the many examples of popular piety and spirituality that have found and continue to find expression in the lives of Catholics.

For actual collections of prayers and devotional practices, particularly those enjoying the approval of ecclesiastical authority, interested readers do well to consult the appropriate manuals of piety.[21]

Like the liturgy itself, popular piety both shapes culture and in turn is

---

[21] See for example Sacred Apostolic Penitentiary, *Enchiridion of Indulgences. Norms and Grants*, authorized English edition, trans. William T. Barry from the second revised edition of the *Enchiridion Indulgentiarum*, with English supplement (New York: Catholic Book Publishing Co., 1968). This is an updated version of the much fuller *Raccolta* or a *Manual of Indulgences, Prayers, and Devotions enriched with indulgences in favor of all the faithful in Christ or of certain groups or persons and now opportunely revised,* eds. Joseph P. Christopher, Charles E. Spence, and John F. Rowan (New York and elsewhere: Benziger Brothers, 1952).

influenced by the surrounding culture. Pope John Paul II, throughout his pontificate and indeed since his very youth, has demonstrated a keen awareness of this reality and has urged not only his native Poland but all the countries of Europe to rediscover and to revitalize their cultural roots in the fertile soil of the Christian religion, without prejudice to those of other faiths. The Pope's recent apostolic letter on the Rosary, and his earlier letter on the observance of Sunday as the Lord's Day,[22] serve to remind all Catholics of their obligation to pray not only as individual members of the Church but also as the whole Body of Christ hierarchically arranged, head and members, around the local bishop.

Clearly devotions and popular piety continue to play a vital role in the spiritual development of Christians the world over. It is hoped, then, that this encyclopedia will afford readers an accurate and interesting compendium of the many devotions and practices that continue to inform and enhance the Catholic experience as the Church moves forward with joyful hope into the third millennium.

Rev. Neil J. Roy, S.T.L., Ph.D.
The Catholic University of America
Washington, DC 20064

June 27, 2003
Solemnity of the Sacred Heart of Jesus

---

[22] John Paul II, Apostolic Letter *Dies Domini* (Vatican: Libreria Editrice Vaticana, 1998).

Preface

Since my book on sacramentals was published in 1991, I have received so many letters with questions and suggestions for practices not discussed in the book that I hoped one day to do a revision of that book. When I was invited to be the editor of this present work, I realized that the revision of the previous book would lie within these pages: the revision and more!

At first it seemed a daunting and impossible task: to collect in a single volume the entire treasure of Catholic devotion. As indeed it is. When I began work on the sacramentals book I foolishly dreamed of writing about all of the sacramentals in existence. I had the happy notion that there must be, somewhere deep in the Vatican archives, a tidy little list of them. Thank heaven that, as I began my research, my good friend Father Michael Miller, C.S.B., explained why that is an impossible task. While the right to establish official sacramentals belongs to the Holy See, the pope does not hesitate when an individual bishop or bishops' conference asks to establish a sacramental appropriate to specific cultures and situations. This means there are probably tens of thousands of sacramentals — far too many to include in a single book. For example, I included twenty-six chaplets in the sacramentals book; I promptly received a list from a lady who had collected over a hundred different ones.

This current volume, then, does not begin to contain all of the beautiful devotions that have existed throughout the history of our Church. Instead, I have tried to include as many as possible of those that are common and popular today, as well as a smattering of some historical practices that may well see a return in popularity. I have also included a number of the beautiful Hispanic devotions that are popular in my own area and that are beginning to spread throughout the United States.

To do this, I have culled books, brains, and my correspondence since 1991. Certainly, I will have left out some reader's favorite. If so, I encourage him or her to write to me. Who knows, one day I may find myself doing a revision of this book. At the least, I hope the reader will find some old favorites, and that young Catholics will find some devotions they don't know but wish to acquire for their own.

Contributors

Following is a list of individuals who have been instrumental in making this work possible. Their contributions — whether in providing text, information, moral support, or a combination of these — were invaluable.

Eldon Ball works for Penwell Publishing in Houston, Texas. A graduate of the school of journalism at the University of Texas in Austin, Ball has worked in a wide variety of newspaper, magazine, corporate communications, and technical writing assignments for more than thirty years.

Alejandro Bermúdez writes from Lima, Peru, where he is director of the Latin American Catholic News Agency (ACI-PRENSA) and Latin American correspondent for a number of American periodicals including *Our Sunday Visitor.*

Matthew Bunson is the author or co-author of over thirty books, including *Our Sunday Visitor's Encyclopedia of Catholic History, Pope John Paul II's Book of Saints, The Encyclopedia of Saints,* and *The Angelic Doctor: The Life and World of St. Thomas Aquinas.* He also serves as general editor of *Our Sunday Visitor's Catholic Almanac.* Born in Germany and raised in Hawaii, he has a B.A. in history and an M.A. in theology.

Enrique de la Vega is an artist whose works are found throughout the United States, Mexico, and Europe. He holds a Master of Fine Arts degree from the Los Angeles County Art Institute. He lives in Prescott, Arizona.

Brent Devitt is the principal of Ascension Catholic Elementary School in Kettering, Ohio. He holds a master's degree in educational administration. An avid collector of holy cards, he maintains a website for card collectors.

Rev. Dennis D. Evenson is a priest of the archdiocese of Minneapolis-St. Paul, Minnesota. Since college, he has worked in Spanish-English ministry in parishes and prisons. For many years he has been a strong promoter of devotion to Our Lady of Guadalupe as the Mother of all the Americas.

Sister Mary Jeremiah Gillett, O.P., is a cloistered Dominican nun at the Monastery of the Infant Jesus in Lufkin, Texas. She holds degrees from the University of Dallas and the Pontifical University of St. Thomas Aquinas in Rome. She has written extensively for Catholic publications in the United States, Canada, India, and Italy.

W. Doyle Gilligan is the publisher of Lumen Christi Press in Houston, Texas, and the author of several devotional books. Gilligan is an alumnus of Northwestern University and did graduate work in English at the University of Chicago.

Leo Knowles has written extensively for Catholic periodicals in the United States and the United Kingdom and is the author of a number of Catholic books on the lives of the saints. He lives in Manchester, England.

Tom Kreitzberg is the editor of *The Short Order*, the newsletter of the Short Mystery Fiction Society. His short stories and articles have appeared in a variety of print and online markets. A member of the Dominican Laity, Kreitzberg lives in Maryland.

Daniel J. Lynch is an active promoter of devotion to Jesus, King of All Nations. Mr. Lynch is a judge, retired lawyer, author, video producer, and public speaker. He lives in St. Albans, Vermont.

Rev. J. Michael Miller, C.S.B., is president of the University of St. Thomas in Houston. From 1992 to 1997 he served in the Secretariat of State of the Holy See. Father Miller is the author of several books, including *The Shepherd and the Rock: Origins, Development, and Mission of the Papacy*, and *The Encyclicals of John Paul II*, both published by Our Sunday Visitor, Inc.

Gerald Muller, C.S.C., has been a Holy Cross Brother for more than fifty years. He holds degrees from the University of Notre Dame and VanderCook College of Music in Chicago. He is chair of the music department at St. Edward's University in Austin, Texas. Brother Gerald has written more than a hundred books for children and adults.

Anne C. Phelan is a writer, editor, researcher, and craftswoman in Cary, North Carolina. She holds a Bachelor of Arts degree in political science from Manhattanville College in Purchase, New York.

David Scott is an associate with the St. Paul Center for Biblical Theology in Steubenville, Ohio. The former editor of *Our Sunday Visitor* newspaper, he has an advanced degree in religion with a specialization in biblical studies. His books include *Weapons of the Spirit: The Selected Writings of Father John Hugo,* which he co-authored with Mike Aquilina, and *Praying in the Presence of the Lord with Dorothy Day*; both were published by Our Sunday Visitor.

Thomas J. Serafin is a professional photographer in Los Angeles. In 1993, he began the Saints Alive apostolate to promote veneration of saints' relics. He is also the founder of the International Crusade for Holy Relics.

Rev. Dr. Kevin Thomas Shanley, O. Carm., serves at the Carmelite Spiritual Center in Darien, Illinois. Father Shanley is the director of the Carmelite News Service and the Celtic News Service and a columnist for the *Irish American News.*

Robert A. Stackpole is the director of the John Paul II Institute of Divine Mercy in Stockbridge, Massachusetts, and the author of a study in Christology titled *Jesus, Mercy Incarnate.* He holds degrees from Williams College, Oxford University, and the Angelicum in Rome.

Roy Abraham Varghese is the editor and author of several books on the relationship of science, philosophy, and religion. He lives in Dallas, Texas.

Michael Walsh served as librarian of Heythrop College, University of London. Among his publications are *The Dictionary of Christian Biography* and *A Dictionary of Devotions.*

Raven Wenner writes on pre- and post-Reformation English Catholicism. She is an instructor at the Institute of Catholic Culture at Our Lady of Walsingham (Anglican Use) Church and Shrine, Houston, Texas.

Mary L. Wilson is president of the Dallas Comitium of the Legion of Mary. She has a Bachelor of Arts degree in English and theology from St. Mary College in Leavenworth, Kansas, and a Master of Arts in English literature from the Catholic University of America. Wilson works for the Environmental Protection Agency.

Mark and Louise Zwick founded a center for refugees, Casa Juan Diego, in Houston, Texas, in 1980. They edit and publish the *Houston Catholic Worker*, and have studied and published extensively on the philosophical and theological sources of the Catholic Worker Movement.

A

AACHEN

A city in what is now Germany.

It served as the capital for the Emperor Charlemagne and remained so for the Holy Roman Empire until the middle of the sixteenth century. Aix-La-Chapelle, the city's famous pilgrimage shrine, was built by Charlemagne and holds a number of famous relics, including those said to be the crown of thorns and the swaddling clothes of Jesus. The relics are shown on the average of once every seven years.

(See also **RELICS**.)

ABANDONMENT

The spiritual practice of yielding in trust and acceptance to God's loving providence in every event and experience of daily life.

The recommendation of this practice was a characteristic feature of the spiritual teaching of the French Jesuit Jean-Pierre de Caussade (1675-1751). The practice is meant to engender attitudes of peace, spiritual tranquility, and the allaying of anxiety.

Aachen

ABBA

An Aramaic word meaning "father."

Abba appears in the New Testament (see Mark 14:36, Romans 8:15, and Galatians 4:6). In the Old Testament, God is often identified as a father to Israel (see Jeremiah 31:9) and as father to the anointed king (see Psalm 89:27). Although the Aramaic word *abba* itself is found only infrequently, the New Testament frequently refers to God as Father. Many scholars believe that Semitic usage underlies the opening words of the Lord's Prayer, "Our Father who art in heaven" (see Matthew 6:9) and "Father" (see Luke 11:2).

ABSTINENCE

Voluntarily going without, especially food.

In the Catholic Church, it came to be identified with not eating meat on Fridays and certain other days of the Church's calendar as a form of penance. In the early Church, the laws of abstinence were very severe and included milk products and eggs. The rules governing abstinence have steadily been modified, and according to the 1983 Code of Canon Law, adults are required to fast and abstain on Ash Wednesday and Good Friday. Other days of fasting and abstinence are left to the local conferences of bishops. In the United States, abstaining is required on the Fridays of Lent.

(See also **FASTING**.)

ACHIROPOETOS (ACHIROPOETA)

From the Greek for "not made by a [human] hand."

The term is used to designate the archetype of icon, Jesus Christ himself, the Incarnate Son of God. The appearance of God-in-the-flesh is the underpinning for the justification of the use of sacred images. The Second Council of Nicaea (787) taught that the honor given to sacred images is referred to the original they represent, so that by kissing, kneeling before, or venerating them, the faithful adore Christ and honor his saints. Examples include Veronica's veil and the image of Our Lady of Guadalupe.

ACOEMETI

Certain Eastern Church nuns or monks who kept perpetual prayer.

They were called "sleepless monks" because they chanted the Divine Office in relays day and night without interruption.

ACOLOUTHIA

From the Greek for a "sequence" or "ordering."

Acolouthia is the arrangement of all the Divine Praises, except for the Divine Liturgy itself, in the liturgical offices of the Eastern churches, particularly the Byzantine Rite. The sequence begins with Vespers introducing the day to come (before sunset) and is followed by the office of Compline at midnight, and Matins at dawn. Four "hours" are given over to a numerical sequence: First, early morning; Third, mid-morning (usually 9:00 A.M.); Sixth, early afternoon (usually 12:00 noon); and Ninth, midafternoon (usually 3:00 P.M.). The Divine Praises are structured for public liturgical celebration and usually take place in a public context, although, for reasons of personal piety, the Divine Praises may be privately read.

(See also DAY HOURS.)

ACT OF ACCEPTANCE OF DEATH

The expressed intention of accepting calmly and gladly the manner of death God may give a person.

One form is:

O Lord my God, I now, at this moment, readily and willingly accept at your hand whatever kind of death it may please you to send me, with all its pains, penalties, and sorrows. Amen.

ACT OF CONTRITION

A prayer expressing sorrow for sin coupled with a purpose of amendment.

One common form is:

O my God, I am heartily sorry for having offended you, and I detest all my sins because of your just punishment, but most of all because I have offended you, my God, who are all good and deserving of all my love. I firmly resolve, with the help of your grace, to sin no more and to avoid the near occasions of sin. Amen.

ACT OF DEDICATION TO CHRIST THE KING — See DEDICATION TO CHRIST THE KING, ACT OF.

ACTA SANCTORUM — See ACTS OF THE SAINTS.

ACTS OF FAITH, HOPE, AND CHARITY

Traditional prayers asking God for the three theological virtues.

Among the most popular are:

O my God, I firmly believe that you are one God in three divine Persons, Father, Son, and Holy Spirit; I believe that your divine Son became man and died for our sins; and that he shall come to judge the living and the dead. I believe these and all the truths that the holy Catholic Church teaches, because you have revealed them, who can neither deceive nor be deceived.

O my God, relying on your almighty power and infinite mercy and promises, I hope to obtain pardon for my sins, the help of your grace, and life everlasting, through the merits of Jesus Christ, my Lord and Redeemer.

O my God, I love you above all things, with my whole heart and soul, because you are all-good and worthy of all my love. I love my neighbor as myself for the love of you. I forgive all who have injured me and ask pardon of all whom I have injured. Amen.

ACTS OF THE MARTYRS

A term applying to a large and disparate collection of writings in which are detailed the events surrounding the martyrdom of many of the Church's earliest saints.

The great Bollandist Delahaye categorized these writings into several types, consisting especially of official court records of Christian trials, passions written or narrated by witnesses to the events, and edited materials composed some time after the death of the saints. The earliest recognized parts of these collections are the accounts of the martyrdom of Justin Martyr and his six brethren in the year 164.

ACTS OF THE SAINTS

In Latin: *Acta Sanctorum*; an extensive and very well-known collection of saints' lives compiled by the Bollandists.

The study is a significant one in the critical studies of ancient Church literature and is an ongoing project. Although references to it are often made in translated lives of the saints, it is published only in Latin.

AD LIMINA APOSTOLORUM

The requirement placed on bishops to visit Rome to report on their dioceses.

Latin for "to the thresholds of the Apostles," the expression was used in the early Church to signify a pilgrimage to the tombs of the Apostles Peter and Paul in Rome. Today the Code of Canon Law says bishops must make an *ad limina* visit every five years.

ADONAI

An Old Testament Hebrew term for God, meaning "Lord" or "my Lord."

It was used as a substitution for the unspeakable name "Yahweh," in order to demonstrate profound reverence.

ADORATION

The form of love and worship owed to God alone. Also known as *latria*.

Adoration before the Blessed Sacrament and the adoration of the cross during the solemn liturgy of Good Friday are both indulgenced actions.

(See also **DULIA; INDULGENCE; DEVOTION.**)

ADORATION OR VENERATION OF THE CROSS — See **CROSS, ADORATION OR VENERATION OF THE**.

ADORATION, NOCTURNAL

The practice of keeping watch in adoration of the Blessed Sacrament during the night hours.

An ancient custom in the houses of religious orders, nocturnal adoration has been adopted in a number of parishes in the United States.

ADVENT

The Church season that begins the liturgical year and precedes and prepares for Christmas.

Advent starts on the Sunday closest to the Feast of St. Andrew, November 30, and lasts four weeks or slightly less. The earliest evidence of this season comes from the end of the fourth century, when Gaul and Spain observed a period of preparation for the newly inaugurated Feast of Christmas. The length and emphasis of the season varied in the early Church. The Council of Saragossa (380) commanded the Christian faithful to gather each day from December 17 to January 6. In sixth-century Gaul, Advent lasted as long as Lent and assumed a penitential character. Because the season began on November 11 and entailed fasting three days a week, it was known in Gaul as "St. Martin's Lent." Rome began to celebrate an Advent liturgy only toward the middle of the sixth century. Pope St. Gregory the Great (d. 604) reduced the number of Advent Sundays to four.

Advent assumed a twofold significance: first, it marked a preparation for the Feast of the Lord's Birth; second, it was a time of waiting for Christ's second coming. Both themes became interwoven in the prayers and readings. Since the twelfth century, the season has been regarded as a time of "joyful penance."

ADVENT CALENDAR

A seasonal scene on cardboard with "windows" or "doors" to be opened each day during Advent.

Behind each is a picture or symbol that points to Christmas. On December 24, the main "door" is opened, revealing a Nativity scene. The custom originated in Germany in the nineteenth century.

ADVENT CANDLE

A candleholder covered with white silk and a large candle used to symbolize Mary, the mother of the Light of the World.

A German custom, the Advent candle is lit in the evening during family prayers.

ADVENT PLAYS

Catechetical skits with a Nativity theme.

In Germany, *Herbergsuchen*, "Search for an Inn," shows the Holy Family's efforts to find suitable lodging in Bethlehem. In Spain, Latin America, and the Philippines, *Las Posadas* (The Inns) tells the same story. In the Spanish tradition, Mary and Joseph travel through town (or neighborhood), stopping and knocking at the doors of homes along the way. In many areas, it is traditional to enact the *Posadas* for nine successive nights in the form of a novena. They typically include a fiesta. *Pastorelas* (The Shepherdesses) is another form of Advent play that, historically, was used for evangelization.

(See also **NOVENA**.)

ADVENT WREATH

A wreath of evergreen boughs with four candles lighted successively during the four weeks of Advent.

Originally a Lutheran custom that began in Germany in the Middle Ages and used by Catholics and Lutherans by the year 1500, the Advent wreath uses light to symbolize the coming feast celebrating the birth of Christ, the Light of the World. Popular in homes as well as churches, the wreath typically has three purple candles as signs of penance and one rose candle for upcoming joy. They are lighted at the beginning of the third week of the season, starting on Gaudete (Latin for "rejoice") Sunday. Since ancient times a wreath has symbolized victory. It also refers to the eternal love of God who has no beginning and no end. The green symbolizes our hope in God's never-ending love.

AESTHETICS

The study of the principles underlying the perception of beauty in nature and in the arts.

Critical judgments can concern landscapes, paintings, sculpture, architecture, literature, drama, dance, etc. St. Thomas Aquinas thought that the primary ingredients of beauty were: integrity of form, proportion or harmony, and radiance (brilliance, as of color). The aesthetic value of beauty can also be applied to the nobility of moral attitudes and actions as well as to the supernatural beauty of God himself.

AETERNA CHRISTI MUNERA

The oldest known hymn for the feasts of martyrs. Literally, "[Let us sing of] the eternal gifts of Christ."

Generally attributed to St. Ambrose (c. 340-397) it was divided, possibly in the tenth century, to provide hymns for other feast days and for Matins.

(See also LITURGY OF THE HOURS.)

AFFECTIONS

Emotional responses of delight or revulsion to particular objects of sense perception.

Spiritual life involves the discipline of affection or training of the heart in order to cultivate an ordered response to the good things of life and to grow in virtue.

AFFECTIVE PRAYER

The lifting of the heart to God in words and silent longings expressive of loving devotion.

Some types of affective prayer can be heartfelt prayers such as, "Jesus, Mary, Joseph, save souls"; the repetition, out of love, of holy words as in the "Jesus Prayer" or the Rosary; "praying in tongues" by means of this charismatic gift; or a simple quiet opening of the heart to God's presence. Such prayers lead to closer union with God and perfecting of the virtue of love. They can be a prelude to contemplative prayer.

AFRICAN LITURGY

An extinct Latin Rite liturgy in use in North Africa prior to the Arab invasion in the seventh century.

AGAPE

Greek for "love" or "love feast." Used for the meal of fellowship eaten at some gatherings of early Christians.

The Agape was celebrated by the early Christians as a symbol of their mutual charity and union in one family. The practice of holding such common meals, or "love feasts," seems to have been borrowed from pagan custom. A sacramental meal was a familiar feature of many ancient religions. At first, the Agape preceded the eucharistic celebration, and the interval was filled with readings from Scripture, prayers, and the singing of Psalms. Toward the beginning of the second century, the Agape was separated from the Mass, which was normally celebrated in the morning while the Agape took place in the evening and was seldom celebrated on Sunday. The Agape was held in private homes or in churches, with a bishop, presbyter, or deacon presiding. According to Hippolytus, the host provided the meal, invited the guests including the poor and needy, and expected the guests to pray for him in return. From Tertullian we learn that the meal was begun and ended with prayer. After eating, each one present sang a hymn or psalm and possibly prophesied.

The Agape was supposed to promote Christian fellowship and love and to unite those participating in closer relationship with Christ, who was considered to be the unseen head of the table. Increasingly the meal became a charity supper or a memorial to the departed. When the faithful began to multiply, it became increasingly difficult to arrange these affairs, and abuses such as drunkenness and gluttony crept in. By the eighth century, these "love feasts" had practically disappeared. In modern times, the Agape in one form or another was revived by the Moravians, Mennonites, Dunkards, Methodists, and some other sects. A remnant of the Agape is found in the Cursillo movement.

Agnus Dei

AGNUS DEI

Latin for "Lamb of God."

Agnus Dei is a title for Christ (see John 1:29), as the victim of the sacrifice on Calvary and at the Mass. This is also the name of the prayer said at Mass before the reception of Holy Communion. It was first used as a Mass prayer around 700.

As a sacramental, an *Agnus Dei* is a round Paschal candle fragment that has been blessed by the pope. One side features the impression of a lamb, the other has any number of symbols, such as the image of a saint or the reigning pope's coat of arms. The sacramental may have originated in Rome in the fifth century and was first definitively mentioned in the early ninth.

(See also **SACRAMENTALS**.)

AKATHIST HYMN

The most profound and famous expression of Marian devotion in churches of the Byzantine Rite.

The hymn has twenty-four sections, half relating to the Gospel of the Infancy and half to the mysteries of the Incarnation and the virginal motherhood of Mary. The Akathist Hymn is sung in part in

Byzantine churches on the first four Saturdays of Lent and *in toto* on the fifth Saturday. It is also recited in private devotion. Of unknown origin prior to 626, it gained popularity as a song of thanksgiving after the successful defense and liberation of Constantinople, which had been under siege by Persians and Avars. Its name (Greek for "without sitting") indicates that the hymn is recited or sung while standing. In 1991, Pope John Paul II granted a plenary indulgence to the faithful of any rite who recite the hymn in a church or oratory, as a family, in a religious community, or in a pious association.

(See also **INDULGENCE**.)

ALABANZA

A chanted poem or song of praise, customarily used in Hispanic Catholic celebrations.

ALEXANDRIA, SCHOOL OF

Once flourishing school in Alexandria.

Christian thinkers of the caliber of Cyril, Clement, and Athanasius combined to place the ancient city at the center of Catholic scholarship. It was acclaimed for its pioneering catechetical techniques, but the best known work of its academicians was the Septuagint version of the Bible, named for the team of some seventy scholars who contributed to it. With the lapse of the city into various heresies, its schools and academic reputation slowly disintegrated.

ALEXANDRINE LITURGIES

Three liturgies in use in the Coptic Church: those of St. Cyril, St. Gregory Nazianzen, and St. Basil.

The ancient liturgy of St. Mark survives today only in the *anaphora* (Greek for "offering") of the liturgy of St. Cyril.

ALL SAINTS' DAY

A holy day of obligation, November 1, commemorating all the blessed in heaven; intended particularly to honor those who have no special feasts.

In the fourth century, groups of martyrs, and later other saints, were honored on a common day in various places. In 609 or 610, the Pantheon, a pagan temple in Rome, was consecrated as a Christian church in honor of Mary and the martyrs and, later, all saints. In 835, Pope Gregory IV fixed November 1 as the date of the observance.

ALL SOULS' DAY

The annual commemoration of all the faithful departed, November 2.

The dead were prayed for from the earliest days of the Church. By the sixth century, Benedictine monasteries customarily held commemorations for departed members at Pentecost. A common commemoration of all the faithful departed on the day after All Saints' Day was begun in the Abbey of Cluny by St. Odilio in 998. Five years later, it was recommended and approved by Pope Sylvester II, and from the eleventh to the fourteenth centuries the feast gradually spread throughout Europe.

In the Western Church, All Souls' Day was set for November 2 so that the memories of all the souls, both of the saints in heaven and the souls of those in purgatory, could be celebrated on two successive days. In this way, the Christian belief in the communion of saints could be more clearly expressed. In Eastern Rites, commemorations for the souls in purgatory are celebrated during the Easter season.

Throughout the world, numerous customs and pious traditions were associated with the celebrations in honor of the dead. Almost all ethnic traditions include special prayers, decorations, foods, lights, and the visiting and maintenance of graves. Some groups distribute food to the poor on this day, and others visit graves of the "forgotten," plots that would otherwise remain neglected and unadorned.

ALLEGORICAL INTERPRETATION (BIBLICAL)

A method of interpretation of Sacred Scripture whereby persons, places, events, and things are seen as signifying other persons, places, events, and things, usually with a spiritual significance.

Though found in the New Testament and rabbinic literature, it was especially popular among the patristic writers of both East and West. Richard of St. Victor made popular in the twelfth century the interpretation of Noah's ark as an allegory of the Church, also described as the "bark of Peter." The blessing of Easter water alludes to a number of allegories for the saving waters of baptism, among them the waters after the flood, the Red Sea parted by Moses, and the water that came from the rock at his touch.

ALLELUIA

An expression of joy or thanksgiving, derived from the Hebrew for "praise God."

Used by the earliest Christian communities, it entered the Mass during the time of Pope St. Damasus (r. 366-384). First said only at Easter, by the fifth century its use expanded to include the whole Easter season. Under the pontificate of St. Gregory the Great (r. 590-604), the Alleluia became part of the Mass throughout the year except during penitential seasons.

ALMS

Money or gifts given to the needy as a corporal work of mercy.

Almsgiving has been a devotional practice from the earliest days of the Church. Clement of Rome (d.c. 100) wrote that it was better than either fasting or prayer as a penance for sin.

(See also **CORPORAL WORKS OF MERCY**.)

ALPHA AND OMEGA

The first and last letters of the Greek alphabet, signifying that the beginning and end of all things is God, the Creator (see Revelation 1:8).

They are also used as a monogram for Christ (see Revelation 22:13).

ALPHABETIC PSALMS

Psalms in which the various parts of a single Psalm begin consecutively with one of

Alpha and Omega

the twenty-two letters of the Hebrew alphabet.

These parts may be verses, half-verses, or strophes. Examples include: Psalms 9, 25, 34, 37, 111, 119, and 145. The form is also found in Sirach 51:13-30, Proverbs 31:11-31, and Lamentations 1-4. This artificial device apparently was used simply as an aid to memory and had no theological meaning.

ALTAR

A consecrated table on which the sacrifice of the Mass is offered; from the Hebrew for "place of Sacrifice."

The altar symbolizes Christ, who is both the priest and the victim. Placing a gift on the altar symbolizes handing it over to God.

Early Christians met for the "breaking of the bread" in private homes, where a table was used for the altar. Beginning about the fourth century, Mass was often celebrated over or under the tombs of the martyrs, leading to the custom of having a saint's relics under or in every altar. By the sixth century, Mass was celebrated in churches, and the Holy Sacrifice was offered on altars of stone.

In early churches, the altar was freestanding. In Rome, churches were built so the main door and celebrant's chair faced east. Early references to this custom note that humanity began in the east, in

Eden. Later it was said that, from the cross, Jesus looked toward the west and it was from the east that he would come for the Last Judgment. When the celebrant stood at the altar, he faced the people. From the fifth century, the Eastern custom of having the apse (the semicircular vaulted end of the building) and its altar face east gained popularity in the West. After that, altars tended to be built against the apse wall with the celebrant's chair (or bishop's seat) on the side. This arrangement remained the norm until an instruction prepared by a special liturgical commission established by Pope Paul VI for the implementation of the decrees of the Constitution on the Sacred Liturgy of Vatican Council II declared: "It is proper that the main altar be constructed separately from the wall, so that one may go around it with ease and so that celebration may take place facing the people."

Today, fixed altars (those permanently attached to the floor) are consecrated by a bishop. Movable altars (which no longer require an altar stone with relics enclosed) are simply blessed.

(See also DOMESTIC CHURCH [HOME CHURCH].)

ALTAR LINENS
Cloths used for the Mass.

The corporal, purificator, and pall have been called "holy cloths." All are made of white linen. A finger towel is used by the priest after washing his fingers following the Offertory. This towel has no special significance. The corporal is a large square piece of linen folded inward, first lengthwise, then widthwise, into a square to catch any fragments that might fall from the host. The purificator is an oblong linen folded into a ceremonial towel and used to cleanse the chalice after use. The pall is a stiff square linen that rests over the cup of the chalice to prevent dust and other foreign matter as well as insects from getting into the chalice.

ALTAR STONE
The permanent, or immovable, table of the altar made of one piece or slab of natural solid stone into which are deposited the relics of martyrs or other saints.

It can also mean the smaller stone slab, containing relics, which is mortised or imbedded into a larger altar table or (formerly) carried about for the celebration of Mass outside a sacred place.

ALTAR, STRIPPING OF
The removal of the altar cloth (or cloths) following Holy Thursday's evening Mass of the Lord's Supper and Good Friday's Communion rite during the "Celebration of the Lord's Passion."

It was accompanied by the chanting

of Psalm 22 prior to the liturgical reforms of 1970 but is now performed in silence and without ceremony.

AMBROSIAN CHANT

A simple chant in the iambic dimeter style.

These melodies were composed by St. Ambrose or his followers for use in the Ambrosian or Milanese Rite. Over the centuries many of the rhythmic values of the chants have been lost. In recent years the syllabic form of these chants has been adapted to the vernacular with some success. The Ambrosian chants themselves were part of the development of Gregorian chant.

AMBROSIAN HYMNS

Hymns composed by St. Ambrose or one of his followers in classical style, yet readily accepted by the populace of his own day.

The hymns presented Christian beliefs to those who were being evangelized by them. They also created a new school of hymnody.

AMBROSIAN RITE

The rite of the Mass and Divine Office prevailing for centuries in the territory of the archdiocese of Milan and attributed to St. Ambrose.

After the reform of the liturgy mandated by Vatican Council II, the Ambrosian Rite was brought into conformity with the Roman Rite (1976) but in a way that respected its traditions. Certain variations in the Divine Office and the Mass (notably the Offertory procession before the Profession of the Creed) continue.

AMBRY

A wall cupboard for the reservation of altar bread and wine, sacred vessels, liturgical books, holy oils, relics, or the Eucharist itself.

AMBULATORY

An aisle extension, generally forming an arc, behind the high, or main, altar, used for processions.

Also, the covered walkway between the main church and auxiliary buildings or along the sides of a cloister.

AMEN

Hebrew for "truly" or "it is true." Also means "so be it."

In the Gospels, Christ used "Amen" to add a note of authority to his statements. In other New Testament writings, as in Hebrew usage, "Amen" was the concluding word to doxologies. As the concluding word of prayers, it expresses assent to and acceptance of God's will.

AMICE

A rectangular linen cloth with long strips of linen tape attached at two corners.

It is designed to be worn under the alb at liturgical functions if the alb does not completely cover street clothing at the neck.

AMIENS

A city in northern France renowned during the Middle Ages as the home of the relic of the head of St. John the Baptist, which was transported there from Constantinople in 1206.

Amiens is traditionally the place where St. Martin of Tours cut his cloak in half to clothe a freezing beggar. One tradition holds that the beggar was Jesus.

(See also **RELICS**.)

ANAGOGICAL SENSE (BIBLICAL)

From the Greek word *anagein*, meaning "to raise" or "lead up."

The spiritual sense of Scripture that foreshadows or otherwise anticipates the blessings hoped for and to be realized in the beatific vision. For example: Paul refers to the earthly city of Jerusalem as the heavenly city that is our mother, thus the anagogical anticipation of the heavenly reality.

ANALECTA

The gathering of various excerpts or fragments of texts into one collection.

ANAMNESIS

Greek word meaning "remembrance," "commemoration," or "memorial."

It refers specifically, in the Latin Rite, to the prayer that follows the institution narrative and memorial acclamation, and it commemorates the death and Resurrection of the Lord.

ANASTASIS

Greek word for "resurrection."

It is used to refer to the Church of the Holy Sepulcher in Jerusalem.

ANATHEMA

A Greek word with the root meaning of "cursed" or "separated" and the adapted meaning of "excommunication," used in church documents, especially the canons of ecumenical councils, for the condemnation of heretical doctrines and of practices opposed to proper discipline.

ANAWIM

In the prophecies of Zephaniah, he predicted impending punishment and judgment for the people of Jerusalem.

However, he also prophesied that a holy remnant of the people, the anawim, would be spared. The anawim are also mentioned in the book of Amos.

ANCHOR

A symbol of hope from earliest Christian times (see Hebrews 6:19).

An anchor was frequently used in the catacombs and sometimes associated with another common symbol, the fish. Although the cross was not used in early Christian art, the crosspiece and shaft of the anchor were sometimes drawn in such a way as to suggest a cross.

ANCHORITE

A hermit, one who has withdrawn from the world.

In common usage, however, a hermit is someone who withdraws physically to some distance from another habitation while an anchorite lives with close links to a community. In the Middle Ages, anchorites sometimes lived in cells built along the sides of churches.

ANGELIC SALUTATION — See AVE MARIA.

ANGELS

Spiritual beings created by God who are personal and immortal.

Intelligent and having free will, they glorify God without ceasing and serve as messengers of his saving plan. The word comes from the Greek translation of the Hebrew word for "messenger."

The *Catechism of the Catholic Church* notes: "From its beginning until death, human life is surrounded by their watchful care and intercession. 'Beside each

Angels in Adoration

St. Michael the Archangel

believer stands an angel as protector and shepherd leading him to life' " (n. 336).

The New Testament features seven classes of angels: angels, powers, and virtues (see 1 Peter 3:22); principalities, dominions (see Ephesians 1:21; 3:10); thrones (see Colossians 1:16); and archangels (see 1 Thessalonians 4:16). The Old Testament adds two more: cherubim (see Genesis 3:24) and seraphim (see Isaiah 6:2).

From early Church times, the tradition has been to group the nine angelic choirs into three sections, each with three subsections.

Cherub

The supreme hierarchy consists of the cherubim, seraphim, and thrones; the intermediate consists of the dominations, powers, and virtues; the lowest is that which includes the principalities, archangels, and angels. The three angels named in the Bible are Michael, Gabriel, and Raphael. The feast of these three archangels is celebrated on September 29. October 2 is the Feast of the Guardian Angels.

Michael, a name meaning "who is like God," was honored by the Church in a particular way with a prayer commonly said immediately following Mass:

St. Michael the Archangel, defend us in battle; be our safeguard against the wickedness and snares of the devil. May God rebuke him, we humbly pray, and may you, prince of the heavenly hosts, by the power of God, cast into hell Satan and all the fallen angels who wander through the world seeking the ruin of souls. Amen.

(Satan and his demons are "fallen angels," who radically and irrevocably rejected God and his reign.)

Gabriel, a name that means "the Power of God," announced the Incarnation of the Son of God to the Blessed Virgin (see Luke 1:26-38) and appeared to Joseph in a dream. Raphael, a name meaning "healing medicine of God," plays a key role in the Old Testament book of Tobit.

In the Gospels, angels announced the birth of Christ, worshiped him, ministered to him after his temptation in the desert, and came to his aid in his agony in the Garden of Gethsemane.

St. Raphael the Archangel

They were witnesses of the risen Christ on Easter and at his Ascension.

Christ is in heaven "and is at the right hand of God, with angels, authorities, and powers subject to him" (see 1 Peter 3:22).

ANGELS OF DEATH

Spiritual entities usually assumed to be present when death comes to individuals.

From earliest centuries, tradition has assigned St. Michael the Archangel the role of protector of Christians against the devil, especially at the hour of death, by leading the soul to God.

In medieval iconography, he is often depicted carrying a balance scales and weighing the souls of the dead. In some

St. Gabriel the Archangel

An Angel Taking a Soul to Heaven

votive pictures he appears as the protector of those who have struggled with evil, and gained a victory; his foot is on a dragon or he holds a dragon's head in his hand.

Tradition held that Michael is not only protector of the Christians on earth, but of those in purgatory as well. After assisting the dying, he accompanies the souls to purgatory and afterward presents them to God at their entrance into heaven. A contemporary thread of this tradition is the folk song "Michael, Row the Boat Ashore." Tradition assigns Gabriel the task of announcing the arrival of the souls in heaven.

One of the legends of the Virgin Mary tells that it was St. Michael who announced to her the time of her death. The pictures of this announcement bear a strong resemblance to those of the Annunciation except that these have the symbols of a palm on a lighted taper in the hand of the angel instead of the lily of the Archangel Gabriel.

Michaelmas day, September 29, was celebrated as a feast in his honor from the sixth century. In 1970, the feast was combined with feasts of St. Raphael and St. Gabriel and is still celebrated on that day.

"Mourning" angels appear more frequently in sculpture than in painting and have been commonly used for cemetery monuments. In cemetery art, angels are traditionally among the most popular motifs. The cherubim as chubby infants without bodies and with two wings often found on the gravestones of babies and children date from the Renaissance. This portrayal differs radically from the Bible's description in the vision of Ezekiel of cherubim as beings with four wings and "full of eyes."

Carved images of a death angel known as *Dona Sebastiana* or *Nuestra Comadre Sebastiana* (Our Godmother Sebastiana) are still commonly seen in the folk art of the southwestern United States. This is possibly the New World remnant of the renaissance theme of the triumph of death.

(See also **MEMENTO MORI; DOÑA SEBASTIANA**.)

ANGELS, OUR LADY OF THE

A Marian title since the early Church. There are a number of famous shrines dedicated to Mary under this title including the Basilica of Santa Maria degli Angeli at Assisi, where the great St. Francis recognized his vocation; the church in Rome built on the ruins of Diocletion which was designed and executed by Michaelangelo; the shrine of St. Mary of the Angels in Engeberg, Switzerland; Notre Dame du Angles near Lurs, France; the shrine dedicated to Our Lady of Boulogne, in France; the Church of Our Lady of the Angels in London, England; and the Mission of Our Lady of the Angels in Los Angeles.

Our Lady of the Angels

ANGELUS

A prayer traditionally repeated three times daily, morning, noon, and evening, at the sound of a bell.

The practice of reciting the three Hail Marys in honor of the Incarnation was introduced by the Franciscans in 1263. Though the form of the three verses and the Hail Marys first appeared in the mid-sixteenth century, the version as it is now recited does not appear before the second decade of the seventeenth. At about that time, the substitution of the *Regina Caeli* for the *Angelus* during the Easter season was recommended and finally became the standard practice.

V. The angel of the Lord declared unto Mary;

R. And she conceived by the Holy Spirit.

Hail Mary . . .

V. Behold the handmaid of the Lord.

R. Be it done unto me according to your word.

Hail Mary . . .

V. And the World was made flesh,

R. And dwelt among us.

Hail Mary . . .

V. Pray for us, O holy Mother of God,

R. That we may be made worthy of the promises of Christ.

Let us pray:

Pour forth, we beseech you, O Lord, your grace into our hearts, that we, to whom the incarnation of Christ, your Son, was made known by the message of an angel, may by his passion and cross be brought to the glory of his Resurrection, through the same Christ our Lord. Amen.

(See also **REGINA CAELI LA-ETARE.**)

ANIMA CHRISTI

A prayer commonly, though inaccurately, attributed to St. Ignatius of Loyola (1491-1556).

Although Ignatius quotes and recommends the *Anima Christi* in his *Spiritual Exercises*, the earliest references to it appear to be from Germany in the mid-fourteenth century. The prayer may be older and possibly from a Dominican source. It is an indulgenced prayer:

> Soul of Christ, sanctify me.
> Body of Christ, heal me.
> Blood of Christ, drench me.
> Water from the side of Christ,
>   wash me.
> Passion of Christ, strengthen me.
>
> Good Jesus, hear me.
>
> In your wounds shelter me.
> From turning away keep me.
> From the evil one protect me.
> At the hour of my death call me.
> Into your presence lead me,
> to praise you with all your saints
> for ever and ever. Amen.

ANIMA SOLA

A popular devotion, especially in Latin countries.

The *Anima Sola* (Lone Soul) is the most neglected soul in purgatory, who is depicted as a beautiful young woman with manacled hands, incarcerated in a grilled cell engulfed in flames, or as an old man in fetters also engulfed in flames. The *Anima Sola* is one of the most important images of the cult of the souls in purgatory.

From the seventeenth to the early twentieth century, prayers for souls in purgatory became the most widespread and popular devotion of the Catholic Church. In churches large enough to have more than one altar, a chapel was set aside for this devotion and was often maintained by a specialized confraternity. Over the altar there was usually a painting showing the souls burning in flames below, with their eyes raised toward paradise from whence deliverance will come. Above, heaven is open with an image of Christ or the Virgin and Child on one side and one of the popular intercessors on the other side. Among these popular intercessors are Our Lady of Mt. Carmel, St. Agatha, St. Dominic, St. Simon Stock, and St. Francis. A group of angels sprinkles consolation in the form of drops of water from a watering can. The tradition of the anonymous souls has been present at least from medieval times, and was popularized in certain traditions from southern Europe from the seventeenth century. In Santa Maria delle Anime del Purgatorio in Naples, it was a custom for people to take one of the skulls from the charnel house, choosing it at random, and take it into a

46

Anima Sola

in the prayers for the rest of the souls. Even today, many of the churches of Mexico have a bust representation of *Anima Sola,* and prayers in front of the image are popular.

In the devotion of *Anima Sola*, prayers are said both for and to the lonely and abandoned souls. In the prayers for the *Anima Sola*, God is asked through the merits of the Precious Blood, through Divine Mercy, to grant relief and rest to the souls and to conduct them to eternal light.

Unfortunately, like a number of other valid devotions, the devotion to *Anima Sola* has at times been corrupted and used in spiritualist and Santeria cults. In Puerto Rico, she has become something of a boogeyman, and mothers tell their children she is the soul of a mother who has lost her children. Any child who does not go to bed on time may be taken away by the *Anima Sola* to replace her lost children. In Colombia, a folk tale about her says that there was a woman in Jerusalem who was to carry drinks to those who were executed by crucifixion. The afternoon of Holy Friday, this was a girl named Celestina Abdenago. From her urn, she gave a drink to Dismas and Gesta (the two thieves crucified with Christ), but she scorned the

crypt transformed into a mortuary chapel. One visited one's skull periodically to keep the candles lighted and to say prayers, hoping that the unknown soul thus favored would be promptly delivered from purgatory.

The *Anima Sola* was a frequent subject of the Mexican *retablos,* or devotional tin paintings. According to a popular custom dating back to France in the 1600s, many artists included the names of dead family members, patrons, or friends in their paintings or *retablos* of the souls in purgatory in order that they might be included

47

Savior, and for this she was condemned to suffer the thirst and the heat of Purgatory forever. Candles and magical charms depicting the *Anima Sola* abound in botanicas who cater to the magical cults. The corruption of this devotion is sad because it is a "holy and pious thing to pray for the dead," and those souls who have no one left to pray for them are in need of prayers.

(See also **PURGATORY; ALL SOULS' DAY.**)

ANNUNCIATION

A solemnity observed on March 25 commemorating the announcement of the angel to the Virgin Mary that she would become the mother of Christ (see Luke 1:26-38).

The feast was held in the Eastern Church as early as the fifth century and introduced into the West during the sixth and seventh centuries. In many churches in Spain, the feast was held on December 18 until the eleventh century, when they adopted the Roman date but retained their own feast. In the eighteenth century, the December commemoration was re-placed with a feast of the "Expectation of Birth of the Blessed Virgin Mary." Until 1918, the feast was a public holiday in many Catholic countries.

In the early Church, March 25 was observed in a special way as the Day of the Incarnation, and tradition claimed that it was also the date of the crucifixion. By the Middle Ages, the anniversaries of

The Annunciation

several other events in salvation history were placed on this date.

It was an ancient custom of the papal curia to start the year on March 25 in all documents, calling it the Year of the Incarnation. The practice was adopted by civil governments for the legal dating of documents, and the Feast of the Annunciation, called "Lady Day," marked the beginning of the legal year in England until 1752.

In the Greek Church, the feast was called *Evangelismos* (Glad Tidings); Eastern Rite Slavs referred to it as *Blagovescenije Marii* (Glad Tidings of Mary); and for Arabic Christians it was *Id Al-bishara* (Feast of Good News). Central Europeans knew it as the Feast of Swallows because of the general belief that the first swallows returned from their migration on or about this day.

The scene of the Annunciation used to be represented in mystery plays, and in some places Mass was followed by processions or elaborated with the lowering of a boy dressed as an angel from the Holy Ghost Hole in the top of the church. In Rome at the end of the Middle Ages, a colorful procession on the feast was held and, after a pontifical Mass, the pope would distribute fifty gold pieces to each of three hundred deserving poor girls for a dowry. The feast returned to its Christological orientation by the reform of the calendar in 1969.

ANNUNCIATION BREAD

The Russian custom of priests blessing large wafers of wheat flour and giving them to the faithful.

In the home, a father would hand a small piece of the wafer to each member of the family and to the servants who received it with a bow and ate it in silence. Later, they would take the crumbs of the Annunciation bread into the fields and, with pious superstition, bury them in the ground as a protection against blight, hail, frost, and drought.

In a similar tradition in central Europe, farmers put a picture of the Assumption in the seed grain while asking Our Lady's help with the crop.

ANOINTING OF THE SICK

One of the sacraments of the Church.

It can be administered to any member of the faith who has reached the age of reason and is in danger of death. The priest anoints and prays over the sick person, conferring on the individual not only grace but the remission of venial sins and inculpably unconfessed mortal sins, together with at least a portion of the temporal punishment due for the sins; sometimes an additional benefit of this sacrament is the alleviation of the person's condition.

Anointing of the sick may be received more than once, as in the case of new or continuing stages of a serious illness. It should be given in cases of doubt as to whether the person has reached the age of reason, is dangerously ill, or dead.

ANTICHRIST

The principal antagonist of Christ in a final war of cosmological proportions that will occur immediately prior to Christ's Second Coming and the final judgment of the world.

The term appears only in 1 John 2:18, 22; 4:3; 2 John 7. The Gospels speak of false prophets (see Matthew 24:5-26; Mark 13:21-23) and Paul speaks of the man of lawlessness (see 2 Thessalonians 2:3-12).

ANTICIPATE

A liturgical term meaning "to observe a feast or to celebrate an office earlier than the time officially appointed."

Examples of this include Sunday Mass on Saturday evening and the Office of Readings or Vigils on the evening before the feast.

ANTIMENSION (ANTIMENSIUM)

Greek term meaning "that which replaces the table."

It is the linen cloth imprinted with an icon of Christ's burial and into which is sewn the relic of a saint.

ANTIOCHENE LITURGY

An ancient liturgy represented today in East Syrian (Chaldean and Malabarese) and West Syrian (Syrian and Malankarese) liturgies.

The third-century *Didascalia Apostolorum* provides a glimpse of the ancient Antiochene liturgy. In the fourth century, elements of the Jerusalem liturgy (e.g., the prayer of St. James) were incorporated at Antioch.

ANTIPHON

A short verse or text, generally from Scripture, recited in the Liturgy of the Hours before and after Psalms and canticles.

Any verse sung or recited by one part of a choir or congregation in response to the other part, as in antiphonal or alternate chanting. Antiphons also occur during Mass, specifically at the entrance of the ministers (Introit, Entrance Antiphon) and at Holy Communion (Communion Antiphon).

(See also **LITURGY OF THE HOURS**.)

ANTIPHONARY

A book containing antiphons with accompanying melodies.

(See also **ANTIPHON**.)

ANTITYPE

The Old Testament anticipation of a New Testament "type" whereby a person, event, or thing foreshadows or prepares the way for a corresponding one that will come later.

In typological interpretation, Christ is seen as the type anticipated by such figures as Moses and David; Mary is the type prefigured by Eve; the Eucharist is the type for which the manna is the antitype.

APARECIDA, OUR LADY

A Marian title.

In 1717, fishermen found a three-foot dark wooden statue of Mary in the Paraiba River at the Port of Itaguacu, Brazil, and named it *Nossa Senhora Aparecida*, Portuguese for "Our Lady Who Appeared."

A shrine built in her honor near São Paulo became a major center of devotion, and in 1930 Pope Pius XII named her the principal patroness of Brazil. The Feast of Our Lady of Aparecida is October 12.

(See also **PATRON SAINTS**.)

APOCALYPTICISM

A movement that was widespread in the Jewish world between 600 B.C. and 200 A.D., which attempted to discern God's intention for the immediate future.

With its roots in Old Testament proph-

ecy, apocalyptic literature is preoccupied with the power of sin and its hold on the world. It prophesies impending catastrophic war of a cosmic nature, a final and climactic conflict between God and evil, in which God wins and creation is restored to its preternatural state. It can also mean a cluster of beliefs, expectations, and practices recurring in Church history up to the present.

APOCALYPTIC NUMBER

The number 666, also known as the "number of the beast."

It is from Revelation 13:18, which is commonly thought to refer to the Antichrist.

APODEIPNON

From the Greek for "after the evening meal."

A term used to refer to the concluding office in the liturgical cycle for the day in the Byzantine Church, that is, the midnight (Compline) service.

APODOSIS

The conclusion of the period of time during which a feast is observed in the Byzantine Church.

An example would be the Nativity of the Mother of God, September 8, which has its apodosis on September 12. In the West, it is called an octave.

APOLOGETICS

The theological discipline concerned with the defense of the Christian faith.

The principal functions are defending against those who challenge the reasonability of the faith and persuasion of those who are potential converts to the faith. Although apologetics works from general principles, it is most effective when it is developed with reference to specific objections or difficulties.

APOLOGIA

Latin for "apology."

A Christian literary genre, characterized by the effort to defend or vindicate the Christian faith against standard or specific objections. The earliest examples of such writings are the words of Christian writers known as apologists (notably Justin Martyr), who defended Christianity against the pagan objectors of late antiquity.

APOLYSIS

A dismissal prayer.

It is said by the priest at the conclusion of a liturgical ceremony in the Eastern Church.

APOLYTIKION

From the Greek for "dismissal."

A liturgical term in the Byzantine Church that describes the portion of a liturgical ceremony at which the congregation is dismissed and the ceremony concludes. More specifically, the *apolytikion* refers to the final prayer or hymn terminating a liturgical service.

APOSTLE SPOON

A medieval baptismal gift with the image of an Apostle carved on the handle.

Wealthy godparents gave a child a set of twelve. Because the child of wealthy parents did not need the gift, he was said to have been "born with a silver spoon in his mouth." This is a vestige of infant communion in the West. Once the chalice was withdrawn from the laity in the eleventh century, infant communion died out soon thereafter.

APOSTLES'CREED — See **CREED, APOSTLES'**.

APOSTLESHIP OF PRAYER

An association begun in 1844 by Father Francis Xavier Gautrelet, S.J., in the seminary in Le Puy, France.

Now worldwide, the Apostleship of Prayer promotes the glory of God and the salvation of souls through constant prayer, particularly to the Sacred Heart. The association is headquartered in Rome with secretariats in most countries. Members daily make an offering and pray for the particular intentions of the pope.

(See also **MORNING OFFERING**.)

APOSTLESHIP OF THE SEA

An international organization for the moral, social, and spiritual welfare of seafarers and those involved in the maritime industry.

Founded in Glasgow, Scotland, in 1920, it was formally instituted by the Holy See in 1952 (apostolic constitution *Exul Familia*). It is a sector of the Pontifical Council for Migrants and Itinerant Peoples. In some areas it is known as the Stella Maris Program for Seafarers. (*Stella Maris*, Latin for "Star of the Sea," is a Marian title.)

(See also **STAR OF THE SEA**.)

APOSTOLATE

In Catholic usage, a broad term for a variety of work and endeavors for the service of God and the Church and the good of its people.

Apostolic works are not limited to those done within the Church or by specifically Catholic groups, although some apostolates are officially assigned to certain persons or groups and are under the direction of Church authorities.

APOSTOLATE OF THE SICK, PIOUS UNION OF THE

A group founded in the diocese of Haarlem, Holland, in 1925.

This society seeks to unite Catholics who are sick with the person of Christ carrying his cross so that they may learn to suffer with Christ, and so that their suffering may be to the glory of God and the salvation of souls.

APOSTOLATE OF SUFFERING

A pious association founded in 1926 through the inspiration of Father Mateo Crawley-Bovey, SS.CC.

The association strives to inculcate, especially in the terminally and chronically ill, a sense of the Christian meaning of suffering.

Those who are chronically ill or handicapped or afflicted with mental suffering who wish to offer their sufferings, disappointments, and struggles as very special prayers to assist priests in bringing people and families to the Sacred Heart of Jesus may become members of the Apostolate of Suffering by writing to the headquarters for the Enthronement of the Sacred Heart.

APOSTOLIC BLESSING

A form of blessing given by the pope on solemn occasions.

All bishops may give such a blessing on occasion, and all priests may administer one to the dying.

APOSTOLIC UNION

An association of diocesan priests initiated by Venerable Benedict Holzhauser and begun in Bavaria in the seventeenth century. Its members follow a rule of life intended to enhance their spiritual and pastoral activities.

APPARITION

An appearance to people on earth of a heavenly being, such as Christ, the Blessed Mother, an angel, or a saint.

Within the Church, a distinction is made between an apparition during apostolic times and one following the end of public revelation with the death of the last Apostle. A Catholic is not required to believe in an apparition that is a "private revelation," even one the Church judges "worthy of belief" (e.g., revelations made to St. Margaret Mary Alacoque, St. Bernadette at Lourdes, and the children at Fátima).

An extraordinary and paranormal experience, "apparition" refers primarily to the object of one's perception. It remains something that is outside the viewer. "Vi-

sionary" refers to the person who perceives the apparition (the "vision").

Phenomena such as apparitions and visions do not constitute an essential element of Christian holiness, and they are not proof of the holiness of the visionary. Some reported visions (and "locutions," which are attributed to inner voices) can be the result of hallucination or an unknown natural cause. Because it is not permissible to presume that a cause is supernatural, cases require careful investigation and discernment.

In a vision, a body is not objectively present, although, for example, an angel who appears in a vision will "assume" a body. In an apparition, a person is present at a definite location in space and time and is visible (in some instances to more than one witness).

Throughout the history of the Church following the end of public revelation, there have been reports of apparitions, but few have been judged "worthy of belief." When called to evaluate a given claim, the Church has considered the facts of the phenomenon itself (the ecstasy, the visionary), the doctrine that emerged, and the spiritual and other fruits. These three central themes have been systematized into sets of positive and negative criteria by the Congregation for the Doctrine of the Faith:

Positive Criteria

1. That there be a moral certitude or a

high probability that the facts are consistent with what has been claimed.

2. That the persons involved be psychologically balanced, honest, living a good moral life, sincere, and respectful toward Church authority.
3. That there be immunity from error in theological and spiritual doctrine.
4. That there be sound devotion and spiritual fruits, such as the spirit of prayer, testimony of charity, and true conversion.

Negative Criteria

1. That there be no manifest error regarding the facts of the event.
2. That there be no doctrinal errors attributed to God, Mary, or a saint.
3. That there be no evidence of material or financial motives connected with the event.
4. That there be no gravely immoral acts by the person on the occasion of the revelations or apparitions.
5. That there be no psychopathic tendency in the person that might enter into the alleged supernatural event, and no psychosis or collective hysteria of some type.

(See also **FÁTIMA, OUR LADY OF; GUADALUPE, OUR LADY OF; LOURDES, OUR LADY OF; SACRED HEART OF JESUS**.)

APPETITE

A philosophical term designating the capacity of a thing to seek its good (and to avoid evil things).

In human beings, appetite is both sensitive (passions or emotions) and intellectual (the will). In addition to natural appetites (the basic tendency to be and to function according to one's nature), there are elicited appetites that respond to awareness or knowledge of certain objects of desire or avoidance. Appetite is understood to follow upon knowledge — according to the maxim "you can't love what you don't know."

Among sensitive appetites, one group is called "concupiscible" (e.g., love, desire, hatred, and sorrow), whose object is the simple sense-perceptible good. Another group is called "irascible" (e.g., hope, anger, and courage), whose object is the difficult sense-perceptible good. Scholastic philosophy introduced the notion of appetite into Christian tradition, and it remains central to all discussion of the principles of the moral life.

AQUILEIAN RITE

The rite of the ancient patriarchal see of Aquileia in northern Italy, superseded by a variant of the Roman Rite during the Carolingian period, and finally suppressed in 1597.

ARACOELI, HOLY CHILD OF

A crowned, jeweled, life-size figure of the Child Jesus venerated in a special chapel at the Basilica of Santa Maria of Aracoeli in Rome.

The statue is world famous, and pilgrims venerate it, owing to many reported miracles, favors, and answered prayers. An ancient legend tells that the Emperor Augustus saw a vision of the Blessed Virgin standing on an altar of heaven, hence the name *Ara Coeli*.

The statue of the Holy Bambino dates back to the end of the fifteenth century.

The Holy Child of Aracoeli

It was carved from the wood of an olive tree from the Mount of Olives by a pious Franciscan friar. One of several quaint traditions says that the friar did not have the necessary paints to complete his work, and that the statue was miraculously finished by an angel.

Pope Leo XIII ordered its coronation, which took place with a solemn ritual in 1897.

Pregnant women often visit the Holy Bambino to receive a special blessing, and many return bringing their infants to be consecrated to the Christ Child. Often the statue has been divested of its golden trappings and carried to the bedside of the sick faithful.

At Christmas, a special crèche is erected in the church. Throughout the season, the children of Rome come to sing, recite poems, and perform plays for the Infant King. At dusk on the Feast of the Epiphany, in a special ceremony, a blessing is given to the pilgrims gathered there. In the early 1990s, the statue of the Holy Bambino was abducted by the Mafia and held for ransom. The friars refused to pay this ransom and a copy was made for the veneration of the faithful.

ARCA

A box, or pyx, in which the Eucharist was reserved by early Christians in their homes for daily communion outside Mass.

ARCHANGELS — See **ANGELS**.

ARCHCONFRATERNITY — See **CONFRATERNITY**.

ARCHCONFRATERNITY OF CHRISTIAN MOTHERS

An association founded as an archsodality in Pittsburgh, Pennsylvania, in 1881.

Its aim is to foster Catholic family life, especially through the intercession of Our Lady of Sorrows. Its headquarters remain in Pittsburgh, and it is under the direction of the Capuchins.

ARCHCONFRATERNITY OF THE HOLY GHOST

A group founded in Paris in 1884.

Members pray for the grace of the Holy Spirit on the pope and on the Church's missionary activity. The group is under the direction of the Holy Ghost Fathers, or Spiritans. The archconfraternity was established in the United States in 1912.

ART AND DEVOTION

Artistic creations used in conjunction with devotion among the faithful.

The earliest forms of Christian decoration can be found in the Roman catacombs, the burial chambers of the early Christian community. Both carved and painted images and symbols depict the life of Christ, biblical scenes, and the death of martyrs. Here, art was used to console and encourage the early Christians during the persecution in Rome.

The freedom of the Church guaranteed during the reign of the Emperor Constantine in the fourth century led to new forms of art and more obvious Christian symbols. With the building of churches came the use of mosaic, sculpture, and icons.

Early in the history of the Church there was opposition to the religious use of holy images. The use of these images was a part of religious worship. Those who opposed the use of these images did so for reasons of assumed idolatry. Iconoclasm flourished throughout Asia Minor during the eighth and ninth century; but was rejected at the Second Council of Nicaea. The iconoclastic controversy resulted in the change of religious expression of images by Byzantine artists toward a more spiritual and less natural approach. The Nicaean Council of 787, was convened by the Byzantine Empress Irene and called to refute iconoclasm. The council declared that images ought to be venerated but not worshiped, and ordered them restored in churches. Practically the only Western delegates were the papal legates, but popes have confirmed the conciliar canons. It is the last council accepted by both the Roman Catholic

Church and the Orthodox Eastern Church as ecumenical.

Iconoclasm was revived during the Reformation with the belief of Catholic idolatry of religious images, and to this day many Protestants believe that Catholics worship the image rather than what the image represents.

The Middle Ages produced an explosion of creative expression ranging from incredible architectural triumphs in cathedral designs to sculpture, mosaics, stained glass, manuscripts, and music that set the tone of transition into the Renaissance and beyond.

Throughout the late and post Renaissance, art and architecture became more secularized as the ecclesiastical arts ascended in technique and descended in spiritual value which has continued to decline, more or less, to the present time as man has become impressed with his own accomplishments and less concerned with the spiritual and the devotional values; art in search of itself and not for the divine.

The best Christian art is designed to educate as well as to inspire. The *Catechism of the Catholic Church* notes: "*Sacred art* is true and beautiful when its form corresponds to its particular vocation: evoking and glorifying, in faith and adoration, the transcendent mystery of God — the surpassing invisible beauty of truth and love visible in Christ.... This spiritual beauty of God is reflected in the most

holy Virgin Mother of God, the angels, and saints. Genuine sacred art draws man to adoration, to prayer, and to the love of God" (n. 2502).

Art reveals, in a human way, the beauty of God and his creation and sensually defines and defends truth. The human expression of God's truth and creation in diverse ways by the artist, reflects dimly the fullness of Divine beauty as it is applied both emotionally and intellectually. When art is weak and insincere then beauty and truth suffers and the body of Christ suffers; but when art becomes invigorated, it will brighten the way of faith in devotion. "Authentic Christian art is that which, through sensible perception, gives the intuition that the Lord is present in his Church, that the events of salvation history give meaning and orientation to our life, that the glory that is promised us already transforms our existence. Sacred art must tend to offer us a visual synthesis of all dimensions of our faith" (Pope John Paul II).

The artist and the craftsman reflect the image of God and his creation in revelation of his work as image maker that leads men to God through devotion. Beauty in visible form inspires devotion as it stirs the senses and tickles the intellect in reaching toward the mystery and awe of the divine. The Church is in need of the artist and his art. As the Holy Father stated in his "Letter to Artists," in 1999: "In order to communicate the message entrusted to her by Christ, the Church needs art. Art must make perceptible, and as far as possible attractive, the world of the spirit, of the invisible, of God.... In the history of human culture, all of this is a rich chapter of faith and beauty. Believers above all have gained from it in their experience of prayer and Christian living. Indeed for many of them, in times when few could read or write, representations of the Bible were a concrete mode of catechesis. But for everyone, believers or not, the works of art inspired by Scripture remain a reflection of the unfathomable mystery which engulfs and inhabits the world."

(See also **ICON; SYMBOL**.)

ARTES MORIENDI
Medieval books on the technique of dying well.

Each page of text was illustrated with a woodcut picture so that not even the illiterate could misunderstand the meaning. The rising printing trade multiplied the books by the thousands, and illustrations from it were commonly hung in homes.

ASCENSION
A movable observance held forty days after Easter; a holy day of obligation and solemnity.

The Ascension of the Lord celebrates Christ's ascending into heaven forty days after his Resurrection from the dead (see Mark 16:19; Luke 24:51; Acts 1:2,9). While there is documentary evidence that the feast dates from the early fifth century, it was observed long before then in connection with Pentecost and Easter.

Page from the Artes Moriendi

During the tenth century, some dramatic details were added to the liturgical procession on the Ascension in central and western Europe. From the eleventh century on, the procession was gradually omitted in most countries, and a pageant, performed in church, took its place. The plays never received liturgical status or official approval from Rome.

By the thirteenth century, a fairly common practice was to enact the Ascension by hoisting a statue of the risen Christ until it disappeared through an opening in the ceiling of the church. While the image moved slowly upward, the people rose and stretched out their arms, acclaiming the Lord in prayer and hymns. In Bavaria, this raising of the image was accompanied by a number of actors dressed as Apostles, the Virgin, and angels. As the image of Christ ascended, some images of angels holding lighted candles descended to meet it. A few moments after the image of the Savior disappeared, a shower of roses and other flowers and large wafers in the shape of hosts fell on the congregation. The children scrambled to collect the flowers and wafers as cherished souvenirs.

During the Middle Ages, it became a custom widespread in Europe to eat fowl on Ascension because Christ "flew" to heaven. In Germany, bakers and innkeepers gave their customers pieces of pastry made in the shapes of various birds. In England, the feast was celebrated with games, dancing, and horse races. In central Europe, families went hiking and on picnics.

ASCETICISM
The practice of self-discipline.

In the spiritual life, asceticism is motivated by love of God and contributes to growth in holiness. This may be accomplished by personal prayer, meditation, self-denial, works of mortification, and outgoing interpersonal works.

ASHES — See LENT.

ASPERGES
The celebrant's blessing and sprinkling with holy water of the congregation and concelebrants before Mass.

The *Asperges* gets its name from the Psalms: "Purge me with hyssop, and I shall be clean; / wash me, and I shall be whiter than snow" (Psalm 51). Hyssop is a plant referred to in the Bible as being used for sprinkling water. Originally, the sprinkling in the church was done with a plant or leafy branch. The *aspergillum*, a bulbed wand with a hollow handle for holding water, was not in common use until almost the end of the eleventh century, although the custom of sprinkling the congregation was certainly in use by the seventh century. During the Easter season, Psalm 51 is replaced by the *Vidi Aquam*, an antiphon drawn from Ezekiel 47 with the first verse from Psalm 118.

(See also **WATER, HOLY**.)

ASPIRATION

A short exclamatory prayer.

ASSOCIATION OF THE LIVING ROSARY — See **LIVING ROSARY, ASSOCIATION OF THE**.

ASSUMPTION

A holy day of obligation in the United States but not in all English-speaking countries.

August 15 is a solemnity commemorating Mary being taken into heaven, body and soul, at the end of her life on earth. A truth of faith, it was proclaimed infallibly as dogma by Pope Pius XII in 1950.

By the fifth century, a feast called the Memorial of Mary was already being celebrated on August 15 in the Eastern Church. Over time it came to be known as the "falling asleep," or, in Latin, the *dormitio*. Early Christians believed Mary "fell asleep" at death and rested until she awoke in heaven.

Emperor Mauricius Flavius (r. 582-602) decreed the Feast of the Dormition would be celebrated on August 15 throughout the Byzantine Empire. A basilica in Gethsemane marked the spot where, according to popular belief, she had died. Today in Eastern liturgies, the feast is more commonly called the Assumption or "Journey of the Blessed Mother of God into Heaven."

Rome adopted the feast in the seventh century and its title became Assumption. In the West, from the very beginning, it focused on Mary's bodily assumption into heaven. During the sixteenth century, the Assumption became the greatest of the Marian liturgical celebrations and one of the most prominent of the Church year.

In Hungary, there is a tradition that the first Hungarian king, St. Stephen (d. 1038), offered his royal crown to Mary and made her the patroness of the country. Pageants, parades, and rejoicing marked their annual celebration of the Assumption. Delegates from all parts of the country brought gifts from their harvest to Budapest. In Poland, a similar presentation included bringing *wieniec*, or harvest wreaths, to the president in Warsaw. A traditional play was performed in France where a flowery platform with figures of angels was lowered within the church to a flower-covered sepulchre and was raised with a statue of the Virgin while boys dressed as angels played and the people sang Marian hymns. In

Austria, the people processed through the fields led by the priest who asked God's blessing on the harvest. Processions in honor of the day were held in most of central Europe, France, Spain, Italy, and in South America.

In the Italian procession, a statue of Mary was carried through the streets of the town until it was met by a statue of Christ. Three times, the images were inclined toward each other as if bowing, then the Christ conducted his mother back to the parish church for benediction. The procession is called *Candelieri* in Sardinia because huge candles of wax are carried through the streets to her shrine in fulfillment of a promise made in 1580 when a deadly plague was stopped on August 15 after prayers to the Virgin.

Herbs picked in August were said to have particular healing power. In central Europe during the Middle Ages, the Church elevated a popular belief of pre-Christian times and made it a Christian rite with deep meaning by holding the "Blessing of Herbs" on Assumption Day. This practice remained in effect until recent reforms. The Eastern Rites had similar blessings. The Syrians even celebrated a special Feast of Our Lady of Herbs on Mary 15. The Armenians brought the first grapes to church on Assumption Day to have them blessed. The Sicilians kept a partial abstinence from fruit during the first two weeks of August and on the feast

day had all kinds of fruit blessed in church to be served at dinner. Baskets of fruit were a customary gift for the Feast of the Assumption. In the German sections of Europe, the time from August 15 to September 15 was called "Our Lady's Thirty Days," and many of the medieval shrines show the statue of Mary clad in a robe covered with grain. A robe of grain is still a popular feature of Assumption decorations in many places.

Another old and inspiring custom on the Assumption was the blessing of the elements of nature as the source of human food. In many parts of Europe, the priests blessed the fields, orchards, and farms on that day. In the French Alps, the priest rode from pasture to pasture with an acolyte sitting behind him holding the holy water. At each meadow, the priest blessed the animals which were gathered around a large cross decorated with flowers. In the Latin countries, especially Portugal, the ocean and the boats of the fishermen were blessed. This custom is popular today in the United States in a number of coastal towns.

ATOCHA, OUR LADY OF

A popular devotional figure of Mary and the Christ Child.

Our Lady of Atocha traces its history to medieval Spain, where Atocha is a Madrid suburb. Tradition says devotion to Our Lady of Atocha originated in Antioch, and that St. Luke the Evangelist was the sculptor of the first mother-and-child image. Thus, Atocha could be a corruption of Antiochia. The devotion spread rapidly, and by 1162 had spread to Spain. The statue was in Toledo in the Church of St. Leocadia. In 1523, Charles V of Spain paid for an enormous temple, and placed the statue under the care of the Dominicans. The image of the Divine Child was detachable, and devout families would borrow the image of the infant when a woman was about to give birth to her child.

The legend of the miraculous nature of the statue begins in Spain during the dark years of the Moorish invaders. The Spanish were persecuted for their faith. In Atocha, many of the Spanish men were thrown into Moorish dungeons. As the Moors did not feed their prisoners, food was taken to them by their families. During one persecution, an order went out from the caliph in Atocha that no one except children twelve years old and younger would be permitted to bring food to the prisoners. Those with young chil-

Our Lady of Atocha

dren would manage to keep their relatives alive, but what of the others?

The women of the town went to the parish church where there was a statue of Our Lady of Atocha holding the baby Jesus which had been venerated for many years. They begged Our Lady to help them find a way to feed their husbands, sons, and brothers. Soon the children came home from the prison with a strange story.

Those prisoners who had no young children to feed them were being visited, and fed, by a young boy. None of the children knew who he was, but the little water gourd he carried was never empty, and there was always plenty of bread in his basket to feed all of the hapless prisoners without children to bring them their food. He always came at night, slipping past the sleeping guards, or smiling politely at those who were alert. Those who had asked the Virgin of Atocha for a miracle began to suspect the identify of the little boy. As if in confirmation of the miracle they had prayed for, the shoes on the statue of the child Jesus were worn down. When they replaced the shoes with new ones, these, too, were worn out.

ATOCHA, SANTO NIÑO DE

Literally, "The Holy Child of Atocha."

The Infant Jesus, in this depiction, carrying a basket of bread, wears the clothing of a medieval pilgrim to the shrine of St. James. When the devotion to Our Lady of Atocha came to Mexico with the miners, the image of the Child Jesus was detachable, and it is known as a "traveler," since it is often carried out to visit devotees and also sometimes travels to other towns including those in the American Southwest. The shrine at Fresnillo, Zacatecas, is the third most important shrine in Mexico. There is also an American shrine

to Our Lord under this title in Chimayo, New Mexico.

After Ferdinand and Isabella drove the Moors from Spain in 1492, the Spanish people continued to invoke the aid of Our Lady and her Holy Child under the name of Our Lady of Atocha They especially asked help for those who were in jail, and those who were "imprisoned" in the mines.

When the Spanish came to the New World, they brought along the devotions of their native regions. Those from Madrid naturally brought their devotion to Our Lady and her miracle-working, pilgrim infant. In 1540, silver mines were found in Mexico, and mineworkers migrated there. In Plateros, a tiny village near the mines of Fresnillo, a church was built in honor of El Niño de Santa Maria de Atocha. Here the Holy Child continued his miracle-working for those who appealed to him, through his mother, for help. Soon the shrine became a major place of pilgrimage. The original statue in the shrine was donated by a rich mine owner.

The statue made was a duplicate of the one in Spain. It, too, had a removable infant which could be borrowed. The infant at one time was lost, and when a replacement was carved to size to be affixed to the original statue, the new babe had Indian features. Those whose prayers were answered left *retablos*, devotional tin paintings, in thanksgiving (*retablos* here

Santo Niño de Atocha

date from the 1500s to present day). In Mexico, a land of many churches, only the shrine of Our Lady of Guadalupe has more of these thanksgiving plaques. Through a century of revolution, Mexico has provided many prisoners for the Holy Child to aid. Annually, other miraculous cures and escapes are reported here.

In the 1800s, a man from New Mexico made a pilgrimage to Fresnillo and took back with him a small statue of the Holy Child. This statue was enshrined in Chimayo, near Santa Fe.

Some of the first American troops to see action in World War II were from the New Mexico National Guard. They fought bravely on Corregidor, with its underground tunnels and defenses. The Catholics remembered that the Santo Niño de Atocha had long been considered a patron of all who were trapped or imprisoned. Many of them made a vow that if they survived the war, they would make a pilgrimage from Santa Fe to Chimayo in thanksgiving. At the end of the war, two thousand pilgrims, veterans of Corregidor, the Bataan death march, and Japanese prison camps, together with their families, walked the long and rough road from Santa Fe to Chimayo. Some walked barefoot to the little adobe shrine. The prayers and novenas to the miracle-working little Child Jesus all begin with prayers to Our Lady of the Atocha. As Jesus is shown as a small child, first his visitors have to ask his mother's permission for him to go to their aid. As in all true Marian devotions, the Holy Virgin is begged for her intercession.

(See also **ATOCHA, OUR LADY OF**.)

ATONEMENT, OUR LADY OF THE
A Marian title.

The Rosary League of Our Lady of the Atonement was formed in 1901 "to pray and work for the restoration of Mary's Dowry, England, to our Virgin Queen, the

Holy Mother of God." Later, the object of the league became more extensive and included not only the conversion of England but the entire world. The league was formed by Father Paul Wattson and Mother Lurana Mary Francis White, members of the Anglican communion until they, with fifteen others, were received into the Catholic Church in 1909. The community grew, and is now popularly known as the Franciscan friars and sisters of Graymoor. In 1919, Pope Benedict XV gave his approval and apostolic recognition to the title of Our Lady of the Atonement.

Our Lady of the Atonement shows Mary with a red mantle, symbolizing the Precious

Our Lady of the Atonement

Blood of which she was the immaculate source, and by which she was made immaculate. She wears a blue inner tunic, and she holds the Infant Jesus in her arms.

AUGUSTINIAN ROSARY — See CORONA OF OUR MOTHER OF CONSOLATION.

AVE MARIA

The title of a Marian prayer (from the Latin for "Hail, Mary").

The Hail Mary is made up of the words addressed to Mary by the Archangel Gabriel at the Annunciation, Elizabeth's greeting at the Visitation, and a concluding petition.

The first two salutations were joined in Eastern Rite formulas by the sixth century, and were similarly used at Rome in the seventh century. The insertion of the name of Jesus at the closing of the salutations was probably made by Urban IV about 1262. The present form of the petition was incorporated into the breviary in 1514:

Hail, Mary, full of grace, the Lord is
    with you;
blessed are you among women,
and blessed is the fruit of your womb,
    Jesus.
Holy Mary, Mother of God, pray for
    us sinners,

now and at the hour of our death.
Amen.

AVE MARIA SALUTATION

A Marian prayer written by St. John Eudes in the seventeenth century.

A copy of the prayer was found in a book belonging to St. Margaret Mary Alacoque after her death. The prayer was strongly promoted by Father Paul of Moll, O.S.B. (1824-1896), of Belgium.

Hail Mary! Daughter of God the Father.
Hail Mary! Mother of God the Son.
Hail Mary! Spouse of God the Holy Spirit.
Hail Mary! Temple of the Most Blessed Trinity.
Hail Mary! Pure Lily of the Effulgent Trinity, God.
Hail Mary! Celestial Rose of the Ineffable Love of God.
Hail Mary! Virgin pure and humble, of whom the King of Heaven willed to be born and with your milk to be nourished.
Hail Mary! Virgin of Virgins.
Hail Mary! Queen of Martyrs, whose soul a sword transfixed.
Hail Mary! Lady most blessed! Unto whom all power in Heaven and earth is given.
Hail Mary! My Queen and my Mother, my life, my sweetness and my hope.
Hail Mary! Mother most amiable.
Hail Mary! Mother most admirable.
Hail Mary! Mother of Divine Love.
Hail Mary! Immaculate! Conceived without sin.
Hail Mary, full of grace. The Lord is with you. Blessed art you among women and blessed is the fruit of your womb, Jesus.
Blessed be your spouse, St. Joseph.
Blessed be your father, St. Joachim.
Blessed be your mother, St. Anne.
Blessed be your guardian, St. John.
Blessed be your holy angel, St. Gabriel.
Glory be to God the Father, who chose you.
Glory be to God the Son, who loved you.
Glory be to God the Holy Spirit, who espoused you.
O glorious Virgin Mary, may all men love and praise you.
Holy Mary, Mother of God, pray for us and bless us, now and at death, in the name of Jesus, your divine Son.

AVE MARIS STELLA

Latin for "Hail, Star of the Sea"; the title of a hymn used at Vespers on feasts of the Virgin Mary.

This song was probably first intended for use on the Feast of the Annunciation. Considered one of the greatest of the Marian hymns, it is unique from most of the early hymns of the breviary in that it has remained in its original form. Its author is unknown.

Hail, thou star of ocean, portal of the
    sky,
Ever virgin Mother, of the Lord Most
    High.

Oh, by Gabriel's *Ave* , uttered long
    ago
Eva's name reversing, 'stablished peace
    below.

Break the captives' fetters, light on
    blindness pour,
All our ills expelling, every bliss
    implore.

Show thyself a Mother, offer Him our
    sighs,

Who for us incarnate did not thee
    despise.

Virgin of all virgins, to thy shelter
    take us,
Gentlest of the gentle, chaste and
    gentle make us.

Still as on we journey, help our weak
    endeavor,
Till with thee and Jesus, we rejoice
    forever.

Through the highest heaven, to the
    almighty Three,
Father, Son and Spirit, one same
    glory be.

B

BADGE

A small cloth emblem pinned on the clothing or hung around the neck on a string.

Popular badges have included those for the Sacred Hearts and the Precious Blood Heart.

(See also **SACRED HEARTS BADGE; PRECIOUS BLOOD HEART**.)

BAMBINA — See **DIVINA INFANTITA**.

BANNEUX, APPARITIONS OF

The eight appearances of the Blessed Virgin Mary to Mariette Beco of Banneux, a tiny Flemish village near Liège, Belgium.

The twelve-year-old girl received the apparitions in her family's garden between January 16 and March 2, 1933. Our Lady identified herself as the "Virgin of the Poor" and promised to relieve the sickness of the poor throughout the world. She appeared dressed in white with a blue sash and had a rosary draped over her right arm. In 1942, the Holy See approved public devotion to Our Lady of Banneux, while the bishop of Liège gave final authorization in 1949 to the devotion to Mary as "Our Lady of the Poor, the Sick and the Indifferent."

Today, several million persons honor Our Lady of Banneux by belonging to the International Union of Prayer, by visiting the shrine near Liège, and by attending any of the more than one hundred shrines dedicated to her under this title.

BAPTISM

One of the seven sacraments of the Church.

It consists of pouring water upon a person, or immersing the person in water, and using the words "I baptize you in the name of the Father, and of the Son, and of the Holy Spirit." In doing so, the one baptized is cleansed of original sin and (in the case of one who has reached the age of reason) of actual sins, is incorporated into Christ, and is made a member of his Body the Church. The baptized individual is infused with sanctifying grace and receives the gifts of the Holy Spirit and the theological virtues of faith, hope, and charity. The ordinary minister of baptism is a bishop, priest, or deacon. In an emergency anyone can baptize validly. A person must be baptized in order to receive any of the other sacraments effectively.

BAPTISMAL CANDLE

A candle used at baptism.

Lighted from the Easter candle, it signifies Christ has enlightened the new Christian. In Jesus, those who have been baptized are "the light of the world" (see

Matthew 5:14; Philippians 2:15) and are called on to share Christ's light with others.

In some cultures there is the pious custom of keeping the candle received at baptism as a treasured sacramental and lighting it on birthdays or the feast day of one's patron saint and at First Communion.

(See also **CANDLES; EASTER CANDLE; SACRAMENTALS.**)

Baptismal Candle

BAPTISMAL VOWS OR PROMISES

The promises made by a person to renounce Satan and serve God faithfully and are a part of the baptismal ritual.

They were restored to the Easter Vigil in 1951 and are a part of all Masses on the day itself (replacing the Creed). After renouncing Satan, as well as his pomps and works, the person to be baptized (or the parents speaking for the infant) then professes the faith in a threefold affirmation of the Creed in question-and-answer fashion, much as the actual rite of baptism was conferred in the early Church.

BASIL, LITURGY OF

A Eucharistic liturgy.

The basic structure of this liturgy is most likely the work of St. Basil the Great (c. 330-379), although it has undergone certain modifications from the date of the earliest manuscript (c. ninth century). Apart from some of the prayers, it is quite similar to the Liturgy of St. John Chrysostom. The Liturgy of St. Basil is used by some Eastern Orthodox churches and by Catholics of the Byzantine Rite on certain appointed days of the liturgical year. Some scholarly opinion holds that this anaphora was actually the work of Pope St. Gregory the Great.

BASILICA

From the Greek term for "royal hall."

Originally applied to an official building in Roman times, it is now a title assigned to churches because of their antiquity, dignity, historical importance, or significance as centers of worship.

There are two types of basilicas: major (or patriarchal) and minor. Among the major basilicas in Rome are St. Peter, St. John Lateran, St. Mary Major, and St. Paul Outside-the-Walls. Major basilicas have the papal altar (used only by the pope or his delegate) and a holy door, which is opened at the beginning of a Jubilee Year.

A minor basilica has special privileges associated with it, including certain indulgences. It features the emblem of the *ombrellino*, a red-and-yellow striped umbrella signifying papal and senatorial colors (in former times the *ombrellino* was carried over the pontiff when he traveled by horseback on official visits); a bell on a staff (formerly used to announce the pontiff was approaching); and the papal coat of arms in the sanctuary or above the front door.

(See also **INDULGENCE; JUBILEE YEAR**.)

BATTLE OF LEPANTO — See **LEPANTO, BATTLE OF**.

BAY LAUREL — See **LAUREL**.

BEAUPRÉ, SHRINE OF

A basilica dedicated to St. Anne at Beaupré in Quebec.

In 1650, when the French colony of Quebec in Canada was just beginning, a group of Breton sailors built a tiny frame church in honor of Mary's mother, where the town of Beaupré now stands. The seamen had been caught in a vicious storm and had vowed that if St. Anne's intercession would bring them to safety, they would build her a sanctuary at the spot where their feet first reached shore. Eight years later, the people began the construction of a larger church, and the first claim of many reported miraculous cures took place. The present basilica was dedicated in 1976.

BEAURAING, OUR LADY OF

A Marian title.

In 1932, it was reported that Mary appeared a number of times to five Belgian children at Beauraing, about sixty miles southeast of Brussels. They described Our Lady walking over a viaduct and beneath a hawthorn tree in a convent garden. Although the Virgin appeared numerous times, she spoke little. Her words, which are considered the great promise of Beauraing, were, "I will convert sinners."

The woman appeared as a young woman of about nineteen or twenty. She had

Beauraing Visionaries

Our Lady of Beauraing

beautiful deep blue eyes, and appeared smiling. Rays of light came from her head. She was dressed in a long, white, heavily pleated gown without a belt. She generally held her hands together in a prayerful attitude during most of the apparition, but parted them just before she disappeared. In the later apparitions, she carried a rosary over her arm. On her chest, a heart of gold, surrounded by glittering rays appeared. All five of the children who witnessed the apparitions grew up and married.

In 1935, the diocese appointed an episcopal commission to investigate the events. Public devotions to Our Lady of Beauraing were authorized in 1943. In 1949, the bishop wrote to the clergy of his diocese: "We are able in all serenity and prudence to affirm that the Queen of Heaven appeared to the children of Beauraing during the winter of 1932-33 especially to show us in her maternal heart the anxious appeal for prayer and the promise of her powerful mediation for the conversion of sinners."

BEES OF ST. RITA

Insects associated with the holy Italian mystic who died in 1457.

Biographers report that when St. Rita was an infant, a swarm of tiny white bees was seen around her mouth. After the death of her husband and children, Rita became an Augustinian nun at Cascia. Some two centuries after her death, tiny white bees built a hive in a wall of her fifteenth-century monastery and have remained. These bees remain in hibernation for ten months of the year and emerge during Holy Week. The bees are never seen to leave the convent enclosure. After a few weeks of activity about the gardens of the convent, they return to the wall, after the Feast of St. Rita, and seal themselves into holes they have made themselves. The sisters of the convent of Cascia do not consider their presence to be anything other than a natural occurrence which by an unusual coincidence occurs in the walls of their convent.

The bee has long been a symbol of wisdom as well as industry. The story of the swarm of bees hovering over the cradle of a saint is common in hagiography and is associated with St. Ambrose and St. Dominic, among others.

BEFANA

From the Italian for "old lady."

In Italian folklore and culture, when the Three Wise Men (or Kings or Magi) were on their way to visit and pay homage to the Infant Jesus, they passed through the Italian peninsula. There they were in need of assistance and sought the hospitality of an old lady, *La Befana*. The old lady, however, was not hospitable at all, and thus

God punished her. From that time on she would have to perform good deeds in memory of the Three Kings on the Feast of the Epiphany by bringing toys, candy, and tasty morsels to all the children of Italy. To this day, Italian children expect a visit from the old witchlike hag, *La Befana*, on the sixth day of January and, without fail, she keeps her due appointment, to make up for her mistreatment of those who were on their way to worship the King of Kings and Prince of Peace.

Sometimes this term is used as a synonym for the Feast of the Epiphany, also called "the Feast of Children."

BEGUINES AND BEGHARDS

Associations of laywomen and laymen founded in the thirteenth century.

They followed the religious rule of St. Dominic or St. Francis but did not take vows. They were suppressed because of heresy, but remnants of them still exist.

The women, beguines, were widowed or unmarried and had a communal prayer life. It is thought their name comes from the Flemish *beghen*, meaning "to pray." The men were known as beghards. The communities were called beguinages.

BELL, BOOK, AND CANDLE

An excommunication ritual.

In the Middle Ages, to signify that a

major excommunication had been formalized, three symbolic actions were performed. The church bell was tolled as at a funeral, symbolic of the spiritual death of the excommunicated party. The book of the Gospels was solemnly closed to signify that the heart and ears of the excommunicated individual were similarly closed to the message contained therein. As the Paschal candle was lighted at baptism to symbolize the light of Christ burning brightly in the soul of the baptized, a candle was snuffed out to symbolize that the faith was now similarly extinguished.

BELLS

Metallic devices apparently not often used in a Christian context until the sixth century.

Bells rang to call people to church services, to summon crowds, and to wake religious community members for the saying of the office and other duties. The use of a bell to announce that a monk or nun was at the point of death became particularly prominent, and was extended to laypeople. In the Celtic tradition, bells were treated with particular reverence. By the eighth century, bell towers began to be built to house a church's bells, and blessings were instituted for them. Beginning in medieval times, bells were pealed for the *Angelus*.

The ringing of a bell during the canon of the Mass seems to have begun when the elevation became part of the ritual in the early thirteenth century. In many places, it was the large church bell that was rung at this point in the Mass. The custom of using a small handbell at the elevation apparently began in England.

(See also **ANGELUS**.)

BENEDICTION

A devotional service to Christ in the Eucharist.

The Blessed Sacrament is put in a monstrance that is placed on an altar and incensed. (A monstrance, from the Latin *monstrare*, meaning "to show," is a portable receptacle designed so that the host, enclosed in it, can be seen.) Benediction can include scriptural readings, silent prayer, and hymns, traditionally the *O Salutaris Hostia* and *Tantum Ergo*. The priest celebrant blesses the people with the monstrance.

Benediction began in the Middle Ages with the increased desire by the lay faithful to see the consecrated host. At a time when lay reception of communion was infrequent, Benediction gained popularity. In the current rite, the Blessed Sacrament is not exposed just for Benediction, but the service can follow the conclusion of Eucharistic exposition or Mass.

BIBLE

Sacred Scripture, the books containing the truth of God's revelation.

The Bible (from the Greek and Latin for "book" or "collection of books") was composed by human authors under the inspiration of the Holy Spirit. Ancient tradition holds that one can distinguish between two senses of Scripture: the literal and the spiritual. The Old Testament is made up of forty-six books; there are twenty-seven in the New Testament. The Church discerned the canon (list) for each Testament by apostolic tradition. The earliest extant copy of the present canon of Scripture dates from 367, when St. Athanasius, bishop of Alexandria (c. 296-373), issued the list in an Easter letter.

The Old Testament records the history of salvation from creation through the old covenant, or alliance, with Israel in preparation for the coming of Christ as Savior of the world. The New Testament, written in apostolic times, has Jesus (his life, teachings, Passion, and glorification, and the beginnings of his Church) as its central theme. The promises and God's mighty deeds in the old covenant, reported in the Old Testament, prefigure and are fulfilled in the New Covenant established by Christ and reported in the writings of the New Testament.

The reading of Sacred Scripture (or listening to its proclamation) has been both a central devotion and a key element of the Mass since apostolic times.

(See also **MASS**.)

BIBLE SOCIETIES AND STUDY GROUPS

Groups that have been fairly common from the time of *Divino Afflante Spiritu*, the encyclical of Pope Pius XII, which first encouraged Catholics to become informed regarding the Scriptures.

This effort was further fostered by the Second Vatican Council in *Dei Verbum*. These groups generally meet informally for a discussion of the Scriptures and an attempt to relate their message to the daily lives of the participants. Since the Church is responsible for the interpretation of Sacred Scripture, these groups must be under the direction of a competent authority, ideally the parish priest or one with solid Catholic training in the meaning and interpretation of the Sacred Scriptures.

BIBLICAL HARMONY — See HARMONY, BIBLICAL.

BIBLICAL INTERPRETATION — See INTERPRETATION, BIBLICAL.

BLACK CHRIST OF ESQUIPULAS — See ESQUIPULAS, BLACK CHRIST OF.

BLACK FAST

A day or days of penance on which only one meal is allowed, and that in the evening.

The prescription of this type of fast not only forbids the partaking of meats, but also of all dairy products, such as eggs, butter, cheese, and milk. Wine and other alcoholic beverages are forbidden as well. Only bread, water, and vegetables form part of the diet for one following such a fast. In former times, the Latin Rite practiced this type of fast, but it has long since disappeared. It is still the general custom of the Orthodox Churches as well as some Eastern Rite Catholics. In the Latin Rite, some religious orders of strict observance have maintained such a fast.

BLACK MADONNA, THE

The title of a Marian painting in Czestochowa, Poland; patroness of that country. Also known as Our Lady of Jasna Gora.

According to pious legend, St. Luke painted the image on a cedar wood table at which Mary had eaten. Little else is told about its early history until 326, when it was found by St. Helen. She gave it to her son, the Roman Emperor Constantine, who had a shrine built for it in Constantinople. Over the centuries it was given as a gift to royal families and credited with miraculously saving cities during battles.

For the last six centuries, it has been at the Pauline monastery and church in Jasna Gora (Polish for "Bright Hill"). The painting was damaged several times including, again according to legend, during a siege when an arrow was shot into Mary's throat and again during an attempted robbery, when a thief slashed her right cheek twice with a sword. Those "scars" remain visible today.

Art historians say the icon displays a Byzantine style from the thirteenth or fourteenth century. There are several explanations given for the dark skin of Mary and the Child Jesus: it is characteristic of that style during the period in which it was painted; during a restoration it was painted darker than it had been originally; centuries of smoke from candles and incense pots, as well as church fires (from which it was miraculously spared), "darkened" the original paint.

In modern times, Our Lady of Czestochowa increased in popularity worldwide because of Pope John Paul II's devotion to her. Her intervention was credited with helping end communist rule in Poland and the collapse of the Soviet Union.

BLACK MADONNAS

Images of Mary that portray her as dark-skinned.

Among the better known pilgrimage sites that have Black Madonnas are Altotting, Germany; Czestochowa, Poland;

Einsiedeln, Switzerland; Loreto, Italy; and Montserrat, Spain. In some cases, the pigmentation is unintentional and owing to discoloration through age and grime. In others, the dark hue is simply the color of wood from which the statue was made. There are also Madonnas whose facial characteristics and skin color match a particular, dark-skinned indigenous population, such as Our Lady of Guadalupe.

(See also **BLACK MADONNA, THE;** **GUADALUPE, OUR LADY OF; MONTSERRAT.**)

Our Lady of Czestochowa,
Black Madonna of Poland

BLACK SCAPULAR (PASSION)

A small black-and-white cloth reproduction of the habit worn by members of the Passionist Order.

The front panel has the Passionist symbol: a heart with three nails below it and a cross with the inscription *Jesu XPI Passio* (Latin and Greek for "The Passion of Jesus Christ") above it. The back panel features an image of Christ crucified. In the corners are the instruments of Jesus' Passion: the chalice of Gethsemane, Veronica's veil, the crown of thorns, and the stone column at which he was scourged. On the lower half of each panel are the Latin words *Sit Semper in Cordibus Nostris*, "May it [the Passion of Jesus Christ] be always in our hearts." The two panels of the scapular are joined with black strings.

Those who are enrolled in the Black Scapular share in all the spiritual graces and indulgences of the Congregation of the Passion. Apparently originally intended for, and restricted to, the members of the Confraternity of the Passion, the privilege of being enrolled in the scapular was extended to all the faithful by Pope Pius IX in 1861. The members of the confraternity are not required to be enrolled with this scapular, although it is strongly recommended.

(See also **CONFRATERNITY; SCAPULAR**.)

BLACK SCAPULAR (SEVEN SORROWS OF THE BLESSED VIRGIN MARY)

A black cloth scapular featuring an image of Our Lady of Sorrows on the front panel.

The back panel may also have a Marian theme. The Servite Order is the trustee of this devotion.

According to tradition, the Servite Order was founded in the early thirteenth century and received the habit through private revelation made to seven noblemen of Florence who were later canonized. Popular accounts say that on Good Friday, 1240, the brothers were praying in their oratory, when suddenly they received a vision of the Mother of God surrounded by a radiant light. She was clad in a long black mantle and was holding a black habit in her hands. In this same vision, she gave the founders the name "Servants of Mary" and presented them with the rule of St. Augustine, telling them that their black habit would serve as a reminder of the sorrows she endured.

Soon after Pope Alexander IV sanctioned the Servite Order, many of the faithful began to associate themselves with it in confraternities honoring the Seven Sorrows of Mary. In later times, confraternity members began wearing a black scapular.

(See also **SAINTS, CULT OF THE; SCAPULAR; SEVEN SORROWS Of MARY**.)

BLAISE, BLESSING OF — See BLESSING OF THROATS.

BLESS ONESELF

To make the sign of the cross on oneself.

BLESSED CANDLES — See CANDLES.

BLESSED DRESSES

A pious custom in the 1950s and 1960s.

Young women wore blessed dresses as a promise or to obtain some special favor. The most commonly used blessed dresses were those in honor of Our Lady of Lourdes, Our Lady of Sorrows, the Immaculate Conception, Our Lady of Mount Carmel, Mary Help of Christians, and those of St. Anthony or of St. Joseph. The color of the dress indicated in whose honor it was worn. For example: the dress of

Our Lady of Lourdes was white with a blue sash tied in front. That of Our Lady Help of Christians was coral pink with a powder-blue sash tied in a bow at the left side. All blessed dresses were to be modest with long sleeves and closed necklines.

BLESSED MAGNOLIA LEAF

A pious custom among those of French descent in Louisiana.

A blessed magnolia leaf, two blessed candles, and holy water are kept on a shelf near the family shrine where night prayers are said.

BLESSED ROSES

A pious custom in Dominican and other churches on the Feast of the Holy Rosary, October 7.

The rose symbolizes the Rosary. The leaves represent the joyful mysteries; the thorns, the sorrowful; and the flowers, the glorious.

The formula in the Roman Ritual for the blessing of roses reads:

O God, Creator and Preserver of mankind, deign to pour out Thy heavenly benediction upon these roses, which we offer to Thee through devotion and reverence for Our Lady of the Rosary. Grant that these roses which are made by Thy Providence to yield an agreeable perfume for the use of men and women, may receive such a blessing by the sign of Thy holy cross that all the sick on whom they shall be laid and all who shall keep them in their houses may be cured of their ills; and that the devils may fly in terror from these dwellings, not daring to disturb Thy servants.

BLESSING

The placing of a person, place, or thing under God's care.

Blessings have been a form of prayer since Old Testament times. The simplest Catholic blessings are sacramentals and are made with the sign of the cross, sometimes accompanied by the sprinkling of holy water.

A liturgical blessing is one that uses a prescribed formula or ceremony and is given by a priest. At ordination, the bishop anoints and blesses the hands of the new priest, saying, "May it please you, O Lord, to consecrate and sanctify these hands … that whatever they bless may be blessed, and whatever they consecrate may be consecrated in the name of our Lord Jesus Christ."

Some liturgical blessings are reserved to the pope or to bishops. The official blessings of the Church are contained in the *Roman Ritual.* At one time there were special blessings for all facets of life; but abuse and superstition, especially in the late Middle Ages, led Pope Paul V in 1614 to publish the official *Roman Ritual* as a model for other dioceses.

The revised *Book of Blessings*, confirmed by the Apostolic See in 1989, has a wide variety of blessings for persons, places, and things.

(See also **SACRAMENTALS**.)

BLESSING BEFORE MEALS — See GRACE AT MEALS.

BLESSING OF ANIMALS

A pious custom.

In all Christian countries before the Reformation, the clergy traditionally blessed the countryside, including its farms, orchards, fields, gardens, and livestock.

In the Alpine areas, the parish priest rode from pasture to pasture on Assumption (August 15) with an acolyte sitting behind him on the horse, holding the holy water vessel. In every meadow a blessing was given to the animals gathered around a large cross decorated with branches and flowers. In Latin countries, the ocean and the fishermen's boats were blessed.

Tradition says St. Francis of Assisi (1181 or 1182-1226) began the widespread custom of being especially kind to animals at Christmas. He encouraged farmers to give their stock extra feed "for reverence of the Son of God, whom on such a night the blessed Virgin Mary did lay down in the stall between the ox and the ass." In modern times parishes bless animals, including pets, on his feast day, October 4.

The revised *Book of Blessings* from the *Roman Ritual* has an order for the blessing of animals: "According to the providence of the Creator, many animals have a certain role to play in human existence by helping with work or providing food and clothing. Thus when the occasion arises, for example, the feast of some saint, the custom of invoking God's blessing on animals may be continued."

BLESSING OF CHALK AND INCENSE

A pious custom also known as "The Blessing of the Three Kings."

Among certain nationalities, the blessing is still faithfully carried out at Epiphanytide. With chalk blessed for the occasion, the priest writes "CMB" between the second and third numbers of the year at the top of the door of the house (e.g., 20 CMB 03). The three letters stand for the traditional names of the three kings: Caspar, Melchior, and Balthasar. The number changes annually and indicates the year the blessing was given. Incense is used in the ceremony, possibly in remembrance of the incense offered by the three kings.

BLESSING OF EASTER BASKETS

A popular Easter tradition.

In Slavic countries, baskets of food, especially decorated eggs, are taken to the church to be blessed. In other regions, priests go from house to house to bless the Easter foods. All visitors are given a decorated egg.

In Ukraine, the blessing of the traditional Easter foods is called *Sviachenia*. Each of the foods in the basket (eggs, meat, cheeses, bread, horseradish, herbs, and salt) has a symbolic meaning.

In Russia, the tradition had been that, after the midnight Benediction, the people carried their *paska* (Easter bread) to the priest to be blessed and then took it home and gave it a place of honor on the Easter breakfast table. Easter was that country's great day for gift-giving. It was as Easter presents for his family that Czar Nicholas had the artist Fabergé create jeweled eggs.

BLESSING OF GRAPES

A pious custom in Armenia.

The first grapes of the season were taken to Mass and blessed. Another custom was that all women named Mary entertained their friends on this day in mid-August.

BLESSING OF HORSES

A pious custom.

St. Stephen, the first Christian martyr, is the patron of horses, and they have figured prominently in the celebration of his feast, December 26. His patronage may be based on the fact that in pre-Christian times horses were sacrificed at the winter solstice among the Germanic nations. A tenth-century poem pictures the saint as the owner of a horse that is miraculously cured by Our Lord.

In Italy, chestnuts are roasted and bread shaped like horseshoes are baked on that day. In many rural sections of Europe, it was, and sometimes still is, customary to bless horses in front of the church on this day. Formerly, water, salt, oats, and hay were also blessed. These would be kept by the farmers and fed to the horses in case of sickness.

BLESSING OF THE FLEET

Every year in fishing villages around the world, fishermen and other commercial boat operators ask the Church to perform the ceremony of the Blessing of the Fleet. Its purpose is to ask God's protection for the safety of the vessel and the crew and for good harvests and a successful season. The ceremony is tied to the beginning of the local fishing season, or in some areas such as the Louisiana and the Texas Gulf Coast, where shrimp fishing is a major industry, to the beginning of the shrimp season.

Wherever it is practiced, the Blessing of the Fleet shares several common traits: 1) One or more priests perform the blessing; 2) Fishermen or boat owners gather in their highly decorated vessels to receive the blessing; and 3) Friends and family members join in making preparations for the event.

Although the exact beginnings of the ceremony are unknown, it is believed to have originated in Italy or Portugal hundreds of years ago, and perhaps as early as biblical times. In some localities, it is preceded by festivals that may last for several days. The festivities vary from one location to another. In Viana Do Costelo, in the Portuguese Province of Minho, the blessing is preceded by a three-day festival. There are daily parades, each with a different theme. The first day showcases artisans and their wares, the second has a biblical theme, and the third focuses on the history of relations between Spain and Portugal. At midnight on the third day, the road from the church to the pier is closed and following an age-old custom, the road is decorated for the procession that will occur the following day.

In San Francisco, the Blessing of the Fleet has been held the first weekend in October for more than sixty years. The celebration is named for Madonna del Lume, the Mother of the Light. The ceremony begins with a memorial Mass for fishermen and seamen lost at sea, followed by a fishing boat parade and memorial ceremony at sea. The next day, a high Mass dedicated to the "Mother of the Light" is celebrated with liturgy in Italian. It is followed by a procession led by marchers holding the painting of the Madonna del Lume, a replica of the original in Porticello. The blessing of the fleet follows, accompanied by traditional Sicilian music. A dinner concludes the three-day celebration.

The tradition of blessing the shrimp fleet in Biloxi, Mississippi, began in 1929, and now takes place annually in a colorful procession in the Mississippi Sound. The ceremony begins with the dropping of an evergreen wreath into the Sound in remembrance of fishermen who have been lost at sea. A procession of shrimp boats files past the anchored "blessing boat" from which the officiating priest sprinkles holy water on each of the boats and pronounces a blessing for each one.

As with most blessing-of-the-fleet ceremonies, other events have been added, such as a cook-off and dinner, dance, and coronation of the Shrimp King and Queen. The Shrimp King and Queen join the priest as he conducts the blessing. St. Michael's Catholic Church, the central sponsor of the ceremony through the years, reflects the town's fishing heritage in its architecture: a scalloped-shaped roof resembling a huge clam shell and stained glass windows that depict the Apostles as fisherman. Here, the background of shrimp and oyster fisherman has changed with the years. Originally largely central European immigrants, many now are Vietnamese who began working in the canning plants and later bought their own boats.

BLESSING OF THROATS

A pious custom celebrated on the Feast of St. Blaise, February 3.

The centuries-old tradition has been adopted by the Church as one of its official blessings. The priest crosses two candles against the head or throat of the person and says, "Through the intercession of St. Blaise, bishop and martyr, may the Lord free you from evils of the throat and from every other evil." In some parts of Italy, instead of using the blessed candles, the priest touches the throat with a wick dipped in blessed oil while he pronounces the invocation.

(See also **ST. BLAISE.**)

BLESSING OF A WOMAN AFTER CHILDBIRTH — See CHURCHING OF WOMEN.

BLESSINGS FOR THE CEMETERY

An invocation used for a new cemetery.

The Church considers a cemetery to be a holy place and strongly suggests new ones be blessed and a cross erected as a sign to all of Christian hope in the resurrection of the body. Visiting a cemetery is also a practice encouraged by the Church. The *Book of Blessings* has special prayers for both occasions.

Throughout the centuries, Catholics have always preferred that their dead be buried in consecrated ground. In the Soviet Union, when the priest could not bless the cemetery, it became customary for people to take dirt from their loved ones' plots and have it blessed by a priest.

BLIND CHILD JESUS (NIÑO CIEGUITO)

An image venerated in the Church of the Capuchins in the city of Puebla, Mexico.

Following Mexican custom, the small statue is dressed and has a wig of human hair. A tiny throne and a golden crown symbolize his royalty. In his right hand he holds a golden crucifix; in his left he holds a scepter to which are affixed a pair of eyes. A sign at the church door tells visitors "sacrilegious hands made this image blind." (*Niño cieguito* in Spanish is literally "little blind boy.") Each Wednesday the church has a special healing Mass for the sick.

Devotees come in reparation for the outrage; the eyes of the image were gouged out during the Mexican persecutions of the Church. They pray to be liberated

Blind Child Jesus

explicable transformation in the physical and observable appearance of the consecrated Host or the consecrated "wine" and/or b) a singularity in which the Host or the "wine" are observed to transcend a law of nature (for instance, the law of gravity).

Eucharistic miracles may be classified under the following categories:

- Transformation of the Host into flesh
- Appearance of blood on the Host
- Transformation of the consecrated "wine" into blood
- Preservation of the Host or Hosts over centuries
- Host or Hosts that transcend gravity or other laws of nature
- Visions of Jesus witnessed by the congregation during the consecration of the Host
- Lifetime subsistence on the Host

Drilling deeper, the "hard facts," facts that may be deemed indisputable, in the historical miracles are the following:

- Continued preservation of Hosts that have turned to flesh
- Continued preservation of Hosts with streaks of blood
- Continued preservation of Hosts involved in other supernatural phenomena

Clearly, claims of miracles of the Eu-

from eternal blindness of their souls. The indulgenced prayer to the little blind Jesus reads, in part: "O Sacred Child Jesus, because of the patience you had in suffering the outrages that a cruel and inhuman man did to your holy image, I pray you to liberate me from my sins.

BLOOD MIRACLES

The phrase "blood miracles" is understood here to refer to what are called "eucharistic miracles."

A miracle of the Eucharist refers to a) any phenomenon involving a naturally in-

charist cannot be dismissed as hallucinations because the subjects of some of these miracles — Hosts that have turned to flesh — are even today available for tangible observation

Like it or not, then, even the skeptics have to go along with two starting points: 1) various Hosts and fragments of flesh have been preserved over long periods of time and 2) reliable reports of the conversion of Hosts into flesh and blood continue to this very day and in certain cases these conversions have been accurately recorded.

That there is something extraordinary about the preservation of Hosts and particles of flesh and blood over centuries, cannot be denied for the following reasons:

In the case of the flesh, scientific analysis in the main instances has shown that the object in question is human flesh. How this flesh could retain its original characteristics over hundreds of years despite exposure to physical, biological, and atmospheric contaminants is inexplicable on a purely natural level.

In the case of the blood, again scientific analysis has confirmed that we are dealing with human blood — in fact, blood with the sero-proteic make-up of fresh blood and containing all the minerals present in normal blood. It is well known that blood loses its chemical properties within an hour of being shed and blood from a dead body decays almost immediately. In the case of Lanciano, Trani, Santarem, Florence and others, the samples of blood have been preserved for literally hundreds of years, without any preservatives present. This pattern of retaining the external and chemical characteristics of blood is true not just of the drops of blood preserved in their original state but also in those instances, like Daroca and Bolsena, where bloodstains continue to remain on corporals (the cloth on which the Host and the chalice are placed during Mass).

The preservation of the Hosts is noteworthy because these Hosts are made from unleavened bread which can at best retain its original properties over a period of five to ten years. But the Hosts on display from the various miracles have maintained their original color and remained fresh over centuries, this without being kept in sterile conditions or in an airtight environment. Those that have been chemically analyzed were found to be edible and to retain the same starchy composition as bread. Dr. Siro Grimaldi, a professor of chemistry at the University of Siena and director of the Muncipal Chemical Laboratory, noted that the preservation of the Hosts in Siena represents "a singular phenomenon that inverts the natural law of the conservation of organic material."

The most famous Eucharistic miracle — and the first of the miracles that left us with continuing tangible evidence — was the miracle of Lanciano, Italy. In 700 A.D., a Basilian priest had begun to doubt the Real Presence of Christ in the Eucharist. Then one day, during the consecration at Mass, the bread and the wine turned to actual human flesh and blood. On witnessing this, he turned to the congregation and said, "O fortunate witnesses to whom the Blessed God, to confound my disbelief, has wished to reveal Himself in this Most Blessed Sacrament and to render Himself visible to our eyes. Come, brethren, and marvel at our God so close to us. Behold the Flesh and Blood of our most Beloved Christ."

Samples of the flesh and blood were subjected to clinical studies in 1970 by Odoardo Linoli, a specialist in anatomy and pathological histology and in Chemistry and Clinical Microscopy, and Ruggero Bertelli, a specialist in human anatomy. Their March 4, 1971 report noted (among other things) that:

- The Flesh is real Flesh. The Blood is real Blood.

- The Flesh consists of the muscular tissue of the heart (myocardium).
- The Flesh and the Blood belong to the human species.
- The Flesh and the Blood have the same blood-type (AB).

Starting with this miracle, Italy became the single most prominent location for Eucharistic miracles, with miracles reported in every century from the eleventh through the eighteenth. Most of these miracles left tangible footprints available for contemporary inspection. Other significant sites of Eucharistic miracles in the second Christian millennium included France, Germany, Austria, Belgium, Holland, Portugal, Spain, Czechoslovakia and Poland. In the twentieth century, Eucharistic miracles were reported in Korea, Venezuela, Ecuador, Japan, Germany, and the U.S. Although it is not possible to identify the cause of a miracle, most of the transformation miracles took place in the context of unbelief, negligence, or sacrilege.

In the twentieth century, two remarkable women reputedly lived on the Eucharist alone for extended periods: Alexandrina da Costa of Spain for thirteen years and Theresa Neumann of Konnersreuth, Germany, for thirty six years. During this time, both were placed under periods of round-the-clock medical surveillance while their physiological activities were monitored.

(See also **MIRACLES; JANUARIUS, MIRACLE OF ST.**)

BLUE ARMY, THE

A lay organization founded in 1947 by Father Harold Colgan in fulfillment of a promise to make Fátima better known if he were granted a cure.

The American priest called it the Blue Army in contrast to the Russian "Red" army, and because blue is the color associated with the Virgin. Today it is a worldwide organization with international headquarters in Fátima, Portugal. Members accompany a "pilgrim statue" of Our Lady of Fátima and promote the messages of repentance, devotion to the Rosary, and personal holiness.

BLUE SCAPULAR (IMMACULATE CONCEPTION)

A scapular associated with Venerable Ursula Benincasa (1547-1618), foundress of the Theatines of the Immaculate Conception.

The small scapular is worn in honor of the Immaculate Conception for the conversion of sinners. It usually bears a symbolization of the Immaculate Conception on one side and the name of Mary on the other.

The scapular was approved by Pope Clement X in 1671. In 1894, a confraternity of the Immaculate Conception of the Blessed Virgin and Mother of God, Mary, was erected in the Theatine Church of Sant' Andrea della Valle in Rome. Members are invested with the blue scapular.

(See also **CONFRATERNITY; SCAPULAR.**)

BOLLANDISTS

The Dutch Jesuits who edit the *Acta Sanctorum* (*Acts of the Saints*), named for the founder and first editor, Reverend John Bolland (1596-1665).

Héribert Rosweyde (d. 1629) began to organize a mammoth and critical edition of the lives of the saints but died before any of the material was published. His work was continued by Father Bolland who, with an assistant, visited the archives, libraries, and collections of religious houses to study carefully all information and useful sources they might provide, and to organize and edit the huge collection of materials dealing with the lives of the early saints. The first volume was published in 1643. After Father Bolland's death, the project continued with strong support from several popes. A museum was established in Antwerp to house the material that had been gathered for the *Acts*. The work of the Bollandists was suspended when the Jesuits were suppressed in Belgium in 1773, but began again around 1837 and continues to the present. A supplement,

Rev. John Bolland

the *Analecta Bollandiana*, has been published since 1882.

BOOK OF BLESSINGS

An English translation of *De Benedictionibus.*

This official Latin edition of the section of the Roman Ritual contains the blessings of persons, places, and things. It has all the major blessings of the Church.

(See also **BLESSING**.)

BOOKS OF HOURS

Popular medieval devotional books.

To be distinguished from the Liturgy of the Hours, these were devotional books used by laypeople who could not participate in the celebration of the Liturgy of the Hours (because the liturgy was in Latin or because they lived far from a church or oratory where the hours were observed). Such books were popularized during the thirteenth century and were frequently commissioned by rather wealthy people. The resulting books contained prayers of popular devotion to be recited at the seven canonical hours of the day. They were also usually works of fine calligraphy and artistic illumination. Chief among the persons revered in these prayers and in the artwork of these books is the Blessed Virgin Mary. Books of hours played a significant role in late medieval popular piety, as well as in the fabric of medieval social life.

BOOK OF LAMENTATIONS — See LAMENTATIONS, BOOK OF.

BOWING

A liturgical gesture.

In this particular practice, either the head or the whole body from the waist is inclined to give reverence to a sacred object or to some person, such as a bishop or the principal celebrant of a liturgical service. Bowing has replaced genuflection in Japan.

BOXING DAY

A British observance based on an ancient Roman custom.

On December 26, the Feast of St. Stephen, gentry would give gifts, usually money, to servants and other workers. The presents were known as Christmas boxes. Also, a box was taken aboard vessels that sailed out of port near Christmas and contributions were dropped into it. The box was opened when the ship returned and the money generally used as a contribution to some needy person who had Mass said for the mariners. A boxing-day cake was served on this day.

BOY BISHOP

A medieval custom in which a young boy was selected to act as bishop for a specific period of time fulfilling some episcopal duties but never "saying Mass."

The tradition was more common in England and in rural parishes and monasteries. It was intended to illustrate the reverence shown to children in the Gospels. Typically, the boy was elected on December 6, the Feast of St. Nicholas, patron of children, and stayed in office until December 28, the Feast of the Holy Innocents. A number of Church councils condemned the practice, but it remained popular in England until ended by Queen Elizabeth I. A similar custom in Germany had a boy elected to honor St. Gregory the Great on his March 12 feast. By the eleventh century, the feast was transferred in most countries to December 28, when Holy Innocents became the official feast of students and choirboys. The German custom continued into the nineteenth century.

In a number of countries, the impersonation transferred to St. Nicholas day and the role was played by an adult who visited children on the eve of the feast. Holy Innocents remained the feast of the young ones in many religious communities. On that day, novices had first place at meals and meetings; the community member who had most recently made vows acted as superior for the day.

(See also **FEAST OF FOOLS**.)

BRANDEA

A paper or cloth that has been touched to the bodies of saints or persons with a reputation for holiness and is then kept as a relic.

The term is also used for a piece of the tomb or dust from it or other objects that have come in contact with the body of a saint.

(See also **RELICS**.)

BREAD

Principally used as one of the elements of the Mass.

As a sacramental, bread has been used in a number of pious customs that involve blessing it and then eating it for a specific purpose or keeping it in honor of a saint. For example, the legend of St. Nicholas of Tolentino (1245-1305) includes his healing by giving people pieces of bread over which he had invoked the blessing of the Virgin Mary. The custom developed that bread blessed on his September 10 feast was given to the sick, to pregnant women, and even to animals. In central European and the Latin countries, *pan benito* (blessed bread), known as St. Blaise sticks, is given to the people on that saint's February 3 feast as a cure for a sore throat. It is an Italian custom to save bread blessed on the Feast of St. Joseph as a sacramental to be used to avoid storms and sudden death.

(See also **BLESSING OF THROATS; MASS; SACRAMENTALS; ST. BLAISE.**)

BREAD OF THE DEAD

Special breads used in many parts of the world to celebrate All Souls' Day, November 2.

Called *Pan de los Muertos* (Bread of the Dead) in Mexico, *Ossi Dei Morti* (Bones

Bread of the Dead

of the Dead) in Italy, *Seelen Brot* (Soul Bread) in Germany, and "dirge cakes" in central Europe, all are made and eaten in honor of the souls of the faithful departed.

BREAD, SIGNING OF

A reference to a custom in many Catholic countries in which new loaves of bread are

St. Joseph with Blessed Bread
and Fava Beans

served on Sunday morning, and the sign of the cross is made three times over each.

In Germany and central Europe, a new loaf of bread is not cut until the sign of the cross is made over it. If a piece falls from the table, the sign of the cross is made over it again before it is eaten.

BREAD, ST. ANTHONY'S — See ST. ANTHONY'S BREAD.

BREAD, ST. JOSEPH'S — See ST. JOSEPH'S ALTAR.

BREAD, ST. NICHOLAS'S — See BREAD.

BREVIARY — See LITURGY OF THE HOURS.

BRIDAL CINCTURE

A cincture similar to the ropelike belt sometimes worn by a priest at Mass. Also called *El Lazo* (from the Spanish for "the Lasso" and similar appellations).

The sponsors (*padrino* and *madrino*) of the cincture at a Hispanic wedding are responsible for placing it over the bridal couple after the Gospel and removing it after communion. It symbolizes the binding tie of marriage.

BRIGITTINE ROSARY

A chaplet instituted and promoted by St. Bridget of Sweden (1304-1373).

It features six decades rather than five. Each is preceded by an Our Father and is ended by a Credo. After the six decades an Our Father and three Hail Marys are added.

The chaplet therefore includes seven Our Fathers, three Hail Marys, and six Credos. The recitation of it is intended to honor, by the seven Our Fathers, the seven sorrows and the seven joys of the Most Blessed Virgin; by the sixty-three Aves the sixty-three years which according to common custom the divine Mother lived on earth.

Fifteen of the mysteries of this chaplet are the same as the Dominican rosary. In each of the three divisions, there is a sixth mystery in the Brigittine chaplet. The first of the joyful mysteries is the Immaculate Conception. The sixth of the Sorrowful mysteries is the dead Jesus in the arms of his Mother. The sixth of the Glorious mysteries is the patronage of Mary. This chaplet was a favorite devotion of a number of religious orders, among them the Brothers of the Christian Schools.

BROWN SCAPULAR — See SCAPULAR OF OUR LADY OF MOUNT CARMEL.

BRUGES

A Belgian town famous in the Middle Ages for a relic of the Precious Blood.

Tradition says Duke Thierry of Alsace brought the relic in 1150, and a procession in which it is carried began in 1303 to celebrate the city's deliverance from the French. The procession is held annually on the Monday after the first Sunday in May.

(See also **RELICS**.)

BUGA, MIRACULOUS CHRIST OF

A crucifix in Buga, Colombia, said to date back four hundred years.

Miraculous Christ of Buga

Pious legend holds that it was found in the local river by a woman who had put aside money to buy a cross but instead gave her savings to a friend in need.

A number of miracles have been attributed to the Christ of Buga, also known as the "Lord of Miracles." About four feet in length, the crucifix is on display at San Pedro Cathedral, a minor basilica and popular pilgrim destination.

BULTO

A three-dimensional sculpture of Christ, Mary, or a saint, usually carved from wood.

The term is used most often when describing the carved figures made by the *santeros* of New Mexico, Colorado, and other parts of the American Southwest, although in art it refers to carved religious sculptures from South and Central America and Mexico.

(See also **SANTERO.**)

BYZANTINE RITE

One of several divisions or categories of churches within the universal Church, specific to the East.

Example of a Bulto

The Byzantine Rite traces its origin to the ancient capital city of the eastern half of the Roman Empire, Istanbul or Constantinople, formerly Byzantium. It shares its tradition with the churches of Antioch, Alexandria, and Jerusalem. It is the second most used rite and is shared by Eastern Catholics, both Catholic and Orthodox (since 1054, the time of the Great Schism between East and West).

C

CALENDAR

An arrangement throughout the year of a series of liturgical seasons, commemorations of divine mysteries, and commemorations of saints for purposes of worship.

The Church calendar (liturgical calendar) begins with the first Sunday of Advent. The key to the calendar is the central celebration of the Easter Triduum (Holy Thursday, Good Friday, and Easter), commemorating the supreme saving act of Jesus in his death and Resurrection to which all other observances and acts of worship are related.

As explained in the Second Vatican Council's Constitution on the Sacred Liturgy, "Within the cycle of a year ... [the Church] unfolds the whole mystery of Christ, not only from his Incarnation and birth until his Ascension, but also as reflected in the days of Pentecost, and the expectation of a blessed, hoped-for return of the Lord.

"Recalling thus the mysteries of the redemption, the Church opens to the faithful the riches of her Lord's powers and merits, so that these are in some way made present at all times, and the faithful are enabled to lay hold of them and become filled with saving grace" (n. 102).

Norms for a revised calendar for the Western Church as decreed by Vatican II were approved by Pope Paul VI in 1969 and went into effect on January 1, 1970.

Historically, the calendar was originally based on the annual observance of Christ's Resurrection — Easter Sunday — and its weekly memorial, Sunday Mass. Christmas was being observed in Rome by 354. The date for this feast was possibly determined by an earlier belief that Christ had died on March 25. The Feast of the Annunciation was set for March 25 through a belief that Christ had been conceived and died on the same day of the year.

Commemorations for the death of the martyrs began to be held from the middle of the second century. These were known as their *dies natalis*, or "birthday," into heaven. Initially the memorials were celebrated in the area where the saint had died, but as relics became more widely distributed, the celebration of the feasts also spread to other areas. Soon feasts began to be celebrated in honor of some eminent bishops and those who had suffered, but not died, for the faith. These came to be known as feasts of "confessors." Today's calendar is the chronological list of the fixed feasts of those commemorated in a particular church.

In the Middle Ages, the number of saints' days increased dramatically. When canonization became a formal procedure, the differences in local calendars began to decrease. The Council of Trent (1545-1563) attempted to impose a new and uniform calendar on the Church while allowing for some local variation and for the feasts particular to certain religious orders. The calendar was still very crowded with the feasts of the saints and the addition of other feasts of Mary and of Christ himself. When two feasts fell on the same day, the computation of which should take precedence led to a system of ranking. The major reform of the calendar made in 1969 restored to prominence the seasons of the Church year and reduced the number of saints listed in the calendar. Most of the saints who remained in the Roman calendar were given only "optional memorials," and the complicated arrangement of ranking was dropped. The current arrangement allows for a greater freedom to celebrate the memory of saints to whom there may be a local devotion.

CALIX SOCIETY

An organization of Catholic alcoholics.

Members of this group belong to Alcoholics Anonymous and want to develop and deepen their Catholic spirituality.

CANDLEMAS — See PRESENTATION IN THE TEMPLE.

CANDLES

A sacramental used since the early Church when a multitude of candles and lamps was a prominent feature of the celebration of the Easter vigil.

Candles have been used from classical times in worship and in the rites paid to the dead. Just as other items which became sacramentals for the Christians, candles have a history which is secular or pagan in origin. Carrying tapers was one sign of respect for the high dignitaries of the Roman Empire. The Church, from a very early period, took them into her service to enhance the splendor of religious ceremonials. These early candles were any kind of taper in which a wick, often made of a strip of papyrus, was encased in animal fat or wax.

Today the Paschal candle continues to represent Christ as the true light, and the smaller candles held by members of the congregation symbolize their striving to be "the light of the world" (Matthew 5:14).

Candles have been in use continually in liturgies and ceremonies since at least the seventh century. Initially, they were placed on the floor of the sanctuary. When candles were moved to the altar is unknown, but the practice was well established by the twelfth century.

Traditionally, the candles used for liturgical purposes are primarily made of beeswax. At one time the idea of the supposed virginity of bees made the choice of using their wax a symbol of Christ born of a virgin mother.

While it is fitting that candles used for liturgy and worship should be blessed, that is not a regulation. Historically, an elaborate blessing was performed on the Feast of the Purification, Candlemas Day, which was followed by a distribution of candles and a procession (February 2). The first description of the Feast of the Purification tells of the celebration in late fourth-century Jerusalem. When the pope was resident and performed the blessing, a number of the candles were thrown to the crowd and some were sent as special presents to persons of note.

Candles were and are commonly used before shrines toward which the faithful wish to show a special devotion. The candles burning their life out in front of a statue are symbolic of prayer and sacrifice. The custom may have begun with the

Distribution of Candles by the Pope

custom of burning lights at the tombs of the martyrs in the catacombs. There, lights were kept burning for periods of time as a sign of unity with the Christians who remained on earth.

Candles are required on the altar for the solemn recitation of the Divine Office, for the celebration of Mass, and for other services. Candles are lighted beginning with the candles nearest the crucifix on the Epistle side of the altar and working out, from left to right. Next they are lighted on the Gospel side, from right to left. They are extinguished in reverse order to show reverence for the crucifix or tabernacle. At Benediction, twelve candles are lighted. During ordination to the priesthood, the candidate presents a candle to the bishop. Candles are also used during the dedication of a church, at the blessing of a baptismal font, at the churching of a new mother, at the singing of the Gospel, and during liturgical processions, among others. During medieval times, after a sentence of excommunication was read, a bell tolled while the ritual book was closed, and a lighted candle was thrown to the ground to indicate the person's fall from Grace.

On the Feast of St. Blaise, the throat of the person to be blessed is centered between two crossed white candles while the person kneels before the altar rail. The priest prays, "May God deliver you from trouble of the throat and from every other evil through the intercession of St. Blaise, bishop and martyr."

CANONICAL HOURS

Certain hours during the day appointed from ancient times for prayer and devotion.

They are: Lauds (after midnight), Prime (6:00 A.M.), Terce (9:00 A.M.), Sext (noon), None (3:00 P.M.), and Compline (bedtime). Matins, or morning prayer, today is a service made up from Lauds, Prime, and Terce; Vespers, or evening prayer, comes from Sext, None, and Compline.

(See also LITURGY OF THE HOURS.)

CANONIZATION

An infallible declaration by the pope that a person, who died as a martyr and/or practiced Christian virtue to a heroic degree, is now in heaven and is worthy of honor and imitation by all the faithful.

Such a declaration is preceded by the process of beatification and another detailed investigation concerning the person's reputation for holiness, writings, and (except in the case of martyrs) a miracle ascribed to his or her intercession after death. The pope can dispense from some of the formalities ordinarily required in canonization procedures (equivalent canonization), as Pope John XXIII did in the canonization of St. Gregory Barbarigo on May 26, 1960. A saint is worthy of honor in liturgical worship throughout the universal Church.

From its earliest years the Church has venerated saints. Public official honor always required the approval of the bishop of the place. Martyrs were the first to be honored. St. Martin of Tours, who died in 397, was an early non-martyr venerated as a saint. The earliest documented canonization by a pope was St. Ulrich (Uldaric) of Augsburg by Pope John XV in 993. Alexander III reserved the process of canonization to the Holy See in 1171.

In 1588, Pope Sixtus V established the Sacred Congregation of Rites for the principal purpose of handling causes for beatification and canonization: this function is now the work of the Congregation for the Causes of Saints. The official listing of saints and blessed is contained in the Roman Martyrology and related decrees issued after its last publication. Butler's unofficial *Lives of the Saints* (1956) contains 2,565 entries. The Church regards all persons in heaven as saints, not just those who have been officially canonized.

CANTERBURY

A cathedral city in southeast England and the site where in 597 A.D. St. Augustine began the work of converting the Anglo-Saxons to Christianity.

Exterior View of Canterbury Cathedral

Old Photo Showing Interior View of Canterbury Cathedral

The first church there was probably a Roman Empire basilica that was converted into a Christian church. After being destroyed by the Danes in 1067, it was rebuilt and consecrated in 1130. There, St. Thomas à Becket was murdered in 1170. His death made Canterbury into one of Europe's major places of pilgrimage. After a disastrous fire in 1174, the saint's relics were moved, and in 1220 they were placed in a shrine behind the high altar. Today, the cathedral is the premier see in England of the Church of England.

CANTICLE

A scriptural chant or prayer differing from the Psalms.

Three of the canticles prescribed for use in the Liturgy of the Hours are the *Magnificat* (the Canticle of Mary), Luke 1:46-55; the *Benedictus* (the Canticle of Zechariah), Luke 1:68-79; and the *Nunc Dimittis* (the Canticle of Simeon), Luke 2:29-32.

CARMEL — See MOUNT CARMEL, OUR LADY OF.

CARMELITE WATER

A popular medieval remedy for headaches and other afflictions.

It consisted of spirit of balm combined with lemon peel, nutmeg, and angelica root. The name probably comes from the convent at which it was first used extensively.

CARNIVAL — See MARDI GRAS.

CARRYING THE VIRGIN

An Alpine Advent custom.

On each of the nine nights before Christmas, an image of Mary is taken from house to house while the occupants join in prayer.

CARTAGO, OUR LADY OF

A Marian image and devotion dating back to the seventeenth century; the patroness of Costa Rica.

The stone statue, around which has been built one of the biggest Catholic shrines in Central America, is only three inches tall.

The history of the devotion and the Basilica of Our Lady of the Angels in Cartago date to 1635. A tradition says that a poor Cartago woman, Juana Periera, was out gathering wood when she found a small gray stone with the image of the Virgin and the baby Jesus. She took it home, but found another image on a rock the following day. Returning home, she saw the image from the previous day had disappeared from her home.

This happened several times, until Periera brought the image to her parish priest. When the image mysteriously disappeared from the church tabernacle and found its way back to the rock in the woods, the message to Costa Ricans seemed clear: Our Lady wanted to stay there and be venerated in that precise place.

CASCARONES

One of the best loved Latin traditions of fiestas and carnivals are the *cascarones* — eggshells filled with confetti. Laughing party-goers crack the shells over each other's heads for good luck. In the southwestern United States, *cascarones* have become a traditional feature not only of the pre-Lent carnivals but also at Easter and fall celebrations.

CATACOMB, VISITING

A partial indulgence is granted the Christian faithful who devoutly visit a catacomb, a cemetery of the early Christians.

CATACOMBS

Underground Christian cemeteries.

These were found in various cities of the Roman Empire and Italy, especially in the vicinity of Rome. They were also the burial sites of many martyrs and other Christians.

The Church has always prescribed the designation of special places suitable for the burial of her dead. The ground containing the relics of saints and martyrs was considered sacred and, according to the customs of the times, was given a special religious significance and blessed by suitable religious rites.

Since it was not possible for the early, persecuted Church to maintain cemeteries as we know them today, the earliest Christian burials — from apostolic times to the persecution of Domitian — were in family vaults outside the walls and along the roads leading from great cities. St. Peter, St. Paul, and many other early martyrs and saints were originally given burial outside the city walls. The bodies of Sts. Peter and Paul were transferred about the year 258 into the catacombs, to avoid their profanation during the persecutions. For the first three centuries, this tomb burial was the norm for Christianity. The catacombs grew out of this type of burial.

Catacombs with Christian Epitaphs

Catacombs were originally galleries, chambers, and passages openly hewn out of soft rock with public entrances. Later, they were extended enormously due to crypt enlargement for burial purposes. *Fossores* (gravediggers) hewed out large labyrinths of connected burial chambers in the soft volcanic rock under the Roman hills. Catacombs originated in the tombs of the wealthy Christians who had them constructed in their gardens or villas and permitted their use by fellow Christians. The body, wrapped in cloth, was laid in a niche (*loculi*) excavated along the walls of the tunnels. Roman executioners sometimes allowed Christians to take, or buy, the mutilated remains of the martyrs; other bodies were spirited away from the place of execution. The bodies of the martyrs were venerated, and confidence in their intercession spread. Memorial Masses were held at their graves, especially on the anniversaries of their deaths.

At first the Roman government approved the construction of these excavated cemeteries and protected them against vandalism. The catacombs' secondary use as shelter and as a place of assembly for persecuted Christians to hold secret performances of their religious rites resulted in a later spoilation of the vast shelters, culminating in 253 A.D., when a decree by the Emperor Valerian forbade Christians to hold assemblies or to enter their cemeteries. The catacomb type of burial was practiced not only at Rome but also in Naples, Palermo, Syracuse, Greece, Persia, Egypt, Syria and in other places. The catacombs at Paris are a series of charnel houses where the contents of cemeteries thought to contain pestilence were dumped.

In the Roman catacombs, the walls near places where martyrs' bodies rest are usually covered with inscriptions. All these writings belong to the faithful who, close to the martyrs' remains, wished to leave a memorial of themselves or, more often, of their deceased friends and relatives. Usually these inscriptions consist of the names of the faithful and a wish for salvation in the next world. The graffiti soon took on the form of cryptographic writing, whereby the early Christians could secretly express their feelings during times of persecution and could express the highest ideas of the faith in a brief and effective form. Many of the Christian symbols we are so familiar with today had extreme meaning for these early and persecuted members of the Church.

When the great persecutions of the Christian Church came to an end at the close of the fourth century, one sign of the Church's new freedom was the establishment of open-air cemeteries.

In 410, the Goths laid siege to Rome. Later, when invasions, plagues, and pestilence depopulated the region, the catacombs went into decay. Pope Paul I (r. 757-767) began to transfer the remains

Catacombs

St. Thecla's Catacomb

Catacombs

of the martyrs to the churches of the city. Two of his successors continued the removals, and by the twelfth century, the catacombs were all but forgotten.

In 1578, the catacombs on the Via Solaria were accidentally discovered, causing a wave of public interest. Antonio Bosio (1575-1629) made the first serious study of the underground sites. In the late 1800s, Giovanni Battista de Rossi (1822-1894), known as the "Father and Founder of Christian Archaeology," systematically began to explore the catacombs of St. Callixtus. These, as well as excavations in other major catacombs near Rome, turned up tens of thousands of tombs. A wealth of early Christian inscriptions, epitaphs, and paintings provides much information about the Christians of the first centuries. In a large number of cases, the graves of the martyrs mentioned in the old authorities — the martyrologies, itineraries, the *Liber Pontificalis* and the legendary accounts of the martyrs — were rediscovered.

Today, the Pontifical Commission of Sacred Archeology has custody of the catacombs, and visitors are invited to tour certain sections. Catholics are reminded that this is not just an archaeological tour, but a holy place of pilgrimage as well.

CATCHING THE HOLY GHOST

A European custom of climbing hills during early dawn on Pentecost to pray.

CATHOLIC ACTION

A term used to describe the participation of Catholic laity in the apostolic mission of the hierarchy.

Pope Pius XI defined Catholic Action as "the participation of Catholic laity in the apostolic mission of the hierarchy," implying that he understood it to be the activity of the laity in a social sense, under the authority of and in close cooperation with the bishop on a local level or the Holy See on an international level. Pope Pius XII, in 1948, proclaimed that the chief aim of Catholic Action was "to spread the Kingdom of Christ in private and public life."

Catholic Action sought to promote or achieve a spiritual or cultural result, particularly the salvation of souls and the sanctification of society at large. The cooperation of the lay people with the direction and the approval of the hierarchy was what defined Catholic Action and set it apart from the many forms of independent activity undertaken by lay people. Further, Catholic Action was distinguished within the broader lay apostolate by the stress that was placed on the social rather than individual objectives of its labor. Thus, it could be separated from individual efforts at the sanctification of many souls or collective efforts at the salvation of the individual.

The rise of Catholic Action can be traced to the hopes of Pope Leo XIII (r.

1878-1903) of encouraging lay Catholic groups to take part in bridging the gap between the Church hierarchy and the many social and political institutions of the time. There had always been cooperation between the clergy and the laity for the spread of the Gospel — what has been called Catholic action — but Catholic Action was first given official recognition about 1905 by Pope St. Pius X (r. 1903-1914), with the creation of new lay organizations which would begin and remain under the direction of the hierarchy.

In 1922, Pope Pius XI published the encyclical *Ubi Arcano,* which gave sharper definition to the formation of various lay groups that could function under the authority of the clergy. In 1947, Pope Pius XII (r. 1939-1958) proclaimed five tasks for Catholic Action in his address, "The Time for Action is Here": spread the Gospel "in every village and in the most remote corners"; sanctify the feast days of obligation; bring salvation to the Christian family; strive for social justice; and revive loyalty and honesty in economic and social life. Among a few of the more notable movements which were mandated in many dioceses as belonging to Catholic Action were the Christian Family Movement, the Holy Name Society, and the Legion of Mary.

Catholic Action continued to develop under Pope Pius XII, but during the pontificate of Pope John XXIII (r. 1958-1963) there was a movement away from formally declared bodies to a wider concept of the lay apostolate dedicated to working on behalf of the Church. This broader vision of the laity was embraced by Vatican Council II, and the term Catholic Action ceased to be used in a sanctioned manner. The Council's "Decree on the Apostolate of the Laity" (*Apostolicam Actuositatem*), declared that "All associations of the apostolate must be given due appreciation. Those, however, which the hierarchy has praised or recommended as responsive to the needs of time and place, or has directed to be established as particularly urgent, must be held in the highest esteem by priests, religious, and laity and promoted according to each one's ability" (n. 21).

Catholic Action nevertheless served a useful purpose in the decades prior to Vatican Council II. First, it fostered an authentic and organized response to the needs and challenges of modern culture in the days before mass communications. Second, it reached many Catholics — in factories, homes, offices, and schools — who might otherwise have remained without clear direction and authentic participation in the life of the Church. Finally, it nurtured and handed on the rich traditions of Catholic devotions and prayer life at a time when World War II and then the Cold War threatened every aspect of a genuine Christian culture.

CATHOLIC LEAGUE FOR RELIGIOUS AND CIVIL RIGHTS — See **LEAGUE FOR RELIGIOUS AND CIVIL RIGHTS, CATHOLIC**.

CATHOLIC WORKER MOVEMENT

A lay movement begun in the United States by Dorothy Day (1897-1980) and Peter Maurin (1877-1949).

Dorothy Day and Peter Maurin met on December 8, 1932. Shortly thereafter, they began to publish a newspaper called *The Catholic Worker* in New York City and to provide hospitality for the homeless, living out what had been called for in the Gospel and described in the first issues of *The Catholic Worker.* The paper was called *The Catholic Worker* to distinguish it from the communist *Daily Worker* and provide an alternative to it.

Dorothy Day, a journalist, lived a bohemian lifestyle until her conversion to Catholicism in 1927; however, since childhood she had engaged in a search for a synthesis of spirituality and her concern for the poor. She sought a solution through socialism and wrote for socialist papers, but became disillusioned with socialism and politics. As she walked home after nights spent drinking and talking with literary figures in Greenwich Village, Dorothy noticed the immigrant women attending early morning Mass and she began to visit Catholic churches. It was the joy of the birth of her child which brought her to the Church, even though her common-law husband, Forster Batterham, rejected the idea of marriage, children, and religion. Joining the Church meant the end of her marriage, but she was very grateful to God that she could have a child, because she had aborted a previous child.

After becoming Catholic, Dorothy searched for a role in which she could unify her faith with action and respond to injustice in the world. She was not successful until she met Peter Maurin, who presented to her a vision of what he called "blowing the dynamite" of the Catholic Church.

Peter, a French immigrant, had studied and taught with the Christian Brothers in France, although he left the Brothers before he took final vows. He was involved in a lay movement called Le Sillon, which attempted to bring together scholars and workers through study groups and action. Peter immigrated to Canada and later to the United States, where he began his life of voluntary poverty. He began to write his "Easy Essays" and to formulate his program, which included "clarification of thought" through a newspaper and round-table discussions, the practice of the Works of Mercy, including Houses of Hospitality, and farming communes. He also described his program as "Cult, Culture and Cultivation."

Peter had been looking for someone who could implement his program; George Shuster, the editor of *Commonweal*, suggested Dorothy Day.

As soon as they met, Peter began to give Dorothy a Catholic education, to complement her basic instruction in the faith, which included a Catholic outline of history and the social teachings of the Church (he wanted to make the encyclicals "click" for the average person), as well as Christian personalism, liturgy, and hospitality.

When Dorothy asked Peter where they were going to get the money to start the newspaper, he told her, "In the history of the saints, capital was raised by prayer. God sends you what you need when you need it. You will be able to pay the printer. Just read the lives of the saints." Dorothy had been reading about the life of Rose Hawthorne, Nathaniel's daughter, who had started a hospice in New York for the poor who had cancer. Rose's method of raising money simply by telling people what she was going to do appealed to Dorothy.

She began the paper with two small checks she had received for articles written for Catholic magazines. The first issue of *The Catholic Worker* appeared in May 1933 with a printing of 2,500 copies. Within three years the circulation rose to one hundred thousand. Soon after came the first House of Hospitality and bread and soup lines for the hungry. Peter Maurin began his lecture series for the clarification of thought, and Jesuit and Benedictine priests and professors from Columbia University came to speak at the Catholic Worker at his invitation, a tradition that continues to this day. The professors and priests brought their students to help out in the House of Hospitality and to learn about the idea of scholars and workers sharing and working together. In 1936, a twenty-eight-acre farm was found, and the first farming commune began. Young people flocked to the movement.

The movement has its roots in Christian personalism, the theology of the Mystical Body of Christ, and the models of the saints and the founders of religious communities, especially St. Francis and St. Benedict. Dorothy Day presented three women saints as models, all of whom later became Doctors of the Church: St. Catherine of Siena, St. Teresa of Ávila and St. Thérèse of Lisieux. Dorothy also encouraged the retreat movement, provided by Father John Hugo. The hallmarks of the Catholic Worker Movement are personalism, voluntary poverty, pacifism, hospitality, and the Works of Mercy.

The personalist character of the movement demanded the bringing of one's faith to reflect on contemporary and historical currents of thought and engagement with the world in economics, war and peace, and the construction of a more just social order. Because Peter Maurin spoke and read French, he was able to bring to the Catholic Worker the ideas of personalism developed in France. Emmanuel Mounier and Nicholas Berdyaev were among those who gathered on Sunday afternoons at the home of Jacques and Raissa Maritain to share these ideas. The Maritains themselves visited the Catholic Worker in New York a number of times, and Peter and Dorothy quoted Mounier and Berdyaev in their newspaper. These writers emphasized, as did Peter Maurin, the tremendous freedom of the Christian to do good through personalist action in the world, to wash the feet of others, taking personal responsibility, not waiting for governments or bureaucracies to do what needs to be done. Personalism was defined by Mounier and by the Catholic Workers as the opposite of individualism and quite different from collectivism. As Peter Maurin said: "A personalist is a go-giver, not a go-getter."

Peter Maurin saw personalism as part of a long tradition which included St. Francis of Assisi. The emphasis on voluntary poverty in the Catholic Worker comes from St. Francis.

The spirituality of the movement is prophetic, an alternative and challenge to the dominant consumer culture. The movement is based on the Works of Mercy as opposed to the works of war, on a profound understanding of human freedom and personal responsibility, and on a unity of faith and action. The Works of Mercy, based on Matthew 25:31ff. from the New Testament and the earliest tradition of the Church, and lived out in the lives of the saints, are at the heart of the Catholic Worker movement.

Peter and Dorothy understood the tremendous implications of the Church's teaching on the Works of Mercy and found that it was the person who received the poor as the ambassadors of God who was transformed. Dorothy and Peter reflected that the spiritual works of instructing the ignorant and admonishing the sinner could also include publishing a newspaper and picketing to call attention to injustice, or even being arrested. As Pope John Paul II later said many times, hearts and minds must be changed, Christians must respond to Christ in the poor, but unjust social structures must also be changed. Peter and Dorothy emphasized Church teaching on the common good, that one must not simply be concerned about oneself and one's family, but about the good of all. They recommended an economics called distributism, which flowed out of the encyclicals on Catholic social teaching.

Houses of Hospitality were and are the most visible expression of the Works of Mercy in *The Catholic Worker*. St. Benedict's insistence on hospitality to strangers in his monasteries was a great influence on how this was lived out in the Catholic Worker Movement. Benedict's Rule emphasized that the guest who is received by the monks is Christ (see Matthew 25:31ff). Catholic Workers carry on this tradition, receiving guests, not "clients," as the Lord himself, although hospitality is the most difficult thing in the Catholic Worker Movement. The ideal of Hospitality, guest houses, farming communes, and liturgical prayer came from the Benedictine tradition.

For the Catholic Worker, closely allied to the Liturgical Movement, the liturgy — including the Mass and the Liturgy of the Hours — was the school of formation. Their work for a more just social order was closely linked with prayer; both Dorothy and Peter made a Holy Hour each day.

One of Dorothy Day's great gifts to the Catholic Church and to the United States was her drawing together of biblical and theological resources to establish pacifism and conscientious objection as a legitimate stance for Catholics and Americans. She not only articulated Catholic pacifism in the pages of *The Catholic Worker*, but the movement opposed violence in all its forms, embracing the way of nonviolence and what has come to be called the consistent ethic of life. There were times, especially during World War II, when this stance was very controversial; refusal to participate in preparations for war such as air raid drills brought arrests. However, Dorothy stood firm in her commitment. The U.S. Catholic Bishops affirmed pacifism and conscientious objection as an expression of Catholic faith in their 1983 pastoral, "The Challenge of Peace," giving Dorothy Day credit.

Dorothy's cause for canonization was opened in Rome in 2000, giving her the title Servant of God. More than a hundred Houses of Hospitality continue today in different cities in the United States and a few in other countries.

CEBU, SANTO NIÑO OF

A devotion and image of the Christ Child; a patron of the Philippines.

A small wooden image of the Holy Child known as Santo Niño of Cebu is the beloved patron of the Filipino people. The Legazpi-Urdaneta expedition arrived in the Philipines at Cebu on April 27, 1565. On landing, Legazpi's soldiers made a house-to-house inspection, and in the home of Juan Camus, found a box that held a painted wooden image of the Holy Child Jesus. Two of the right-hand fingers of the image are raised in blessing; the left hand holds a globe symbolizing the world. The image was taken to a provisional chapel where the Augustinian Fray Andres de Urdaneta said a thanksgiving Mass for the success of the expedition, a mission to Christianize the islands. Fray Urdaneta observed that the image was like those made in Flanders (Belgium) during the sixteenth century. It is believed to be the image that Magellan gave to Rajah Humabon's wife on her conversion to Christianity.

So many miracles became associated with the little image that, in the seventeenth century, King Charles III awarded it the Toison de Oro or the Golden Fleece. During the rites held to commemorate the fourth centennial of the Christianization of the Philippines, then Prince Juan Carlos, later Spain's king, gifted it with a golden crown.

The convent of the Santo Niño was built by Fray Urdaneta himself in 1565, close to the place where Magellan had planted his cross. It was the first convent in the Philippines. In the same year an urbanization plan for the city was set and a place for the church and convent of San Agustin was allocated. The spot is believed to be the same spot where the image of the Santo Niño was found. Historians believe that at least three churches have been built there before the present one. The church that stands today was constructed in 1735.

Sometime in 1567, the first European-Asia marriage took place inside a makeshift chapel during the fiesta of the Santo Niño of Cebu. The bride was a young, beautiful niece of Rajah Tupas. The bridegroom was the Greek master carpenter of Legazpi's expedition, Andres Calafata.

Religious Dance in Honor of Santo Niño of Cebu

The Adelantado Legazpi acted as *ninong*. The love affair started when Tupas's niece was sent to the convent to receive Christian instructions. While she was being taught, she met the Greek carpenter and they fell in love. The niece was baptized Isabel.

This wedding ushered in mutual friendship between the two races, and peace and understanding were achieved with these first two ambassadors of goodwill. Their wedding ceremony is reenacted every year during the Feast of Santo Niño, and jubilantly celebrated with dances and fireworks to recall the happiness and good omen brought about to the Cebuanos when Princess Isabella married Maestro Andres.

The *sinulog* is a dance ritual of pre-Spanish origin. The dancer moves two steps forward and one step backward to the rhythmic sound of drums. This movement resembles somewhat the current (*sulog*) of the river. Thus, the Cebuanos called it *sinulog*. The dance was meant to honor the *anitos*. In time, the Cebuanos began to honor the Santo Niño with the *sinulog*.

Because the Augustinian missionaries appreciated native culture, the *sinulog* was preserved but limited to honoring the Santo Niño. Once the church was built, the faithful started performing the *sinulog* in front of the church, the devotees offering candles and the dancers shouting "Pit Señor." During the annual feast, the basilica turns into a dancing hall after the solemn Mass, with all the devotees executing the *sinulog*. The dance continues during the procession in front of the carroza which bears the statue along the streets of Cebu until late in the evening.

In 1980, the city authorities of Cebu made the *sinulog* part and parcel of the religious Feast of the Santo Niño. A Mardi Gras atmosphere was added, the innovation becoming more colorful each year. The religious and the earthy sometimes overlap each other, but as a whole, there is much fun for Cebuanos and tourists alike, who find in the Santo Niño festival that part of everyone's childhood that must stay like Santa Claus and Halloween. In a number of cities in the United States where there is a large Filipino population, it has become popular to celebrate the Feast of Santo Niño with the traditional procession and dances.

During World War II, the church where the image was kept was damaged by American bombing. The image, however, was found hanging by its clothes, intact and unharmed. Enshrined at the Basilica Minore side chapel, the Santo Niño image has counterparts and replicas all over the Islands. It has played an important part in the conversion of the Filipinos to the Christian faith.

A perpetual novena to the Holy Child of Cebu was begun at this shrine by the Augustinian fathers in 1958.

CELTIC CROSS — See CROSS.

CELTIC RITE

Liturgical calendar and usages of the ancient churches of Ireland, England, and Wales, superseded over the centuries by the Roman Rite.

CEMETERY, SOCIAL FUNCTIONS OF

A medieval custom of using a church cemetery as a public square, a marketplace, or fairgrounds.

Until the middle of the seventeenth century, it took the place of the Roman forum and corresponded to the idea of a public square and mall. Cemeteries were protected by the privilege of sanctuary or asylum, and were protected by the patron saint from abuses by civil authorities. Here the people conducted their spiritual and temporal business, played their games, and carried on their love affairs.

Medieval writers remarked on the difference between the Christian public cemeteries and the solitary pagan tombs. Some people even lived in the cemetery. Pious female hermits, dedicated to a life of

Cemetery of the Capuchins in Rome

prayer, sometimes confined themselves there while civil authorities sometimes sentenced prostitutes or female criminals to imprisonment there in perpetuity. In the Carolingian period, judicial assemblies of both Church and civil authorities were held in the cemetery, and as late as the fifteenth century, Joan of Arc was tried by a Church court in the cemetery in Rouen. In the twelfth and thirteenth centuries, the cemetery was the scene of a ceremony inspired by the funeral service which celebrated the civil death of lepers. Widows could free themselves from debt by a ceremony in the course of which they laid their belts, keys, and purses on the graves of their husbands. Communal equipment such as ovens were sometimes set up in cemeteries.

The right of sanctuary caused the cemeteries to become not only public forums and meeting places but also marketplaces and fairgrounds. The synods of the time — at Nantes in 1405 and Angers in 1423 — established prohibitions to curb the secular activities at the cemeteries and the council of Rouen forbade "dancing in the cemetery or in the church under pain of excommunication." The disapproval of the synods was reiterated for centuries as the people continued to use the cemeteries as town meeting places. Gradually, the commerce moved just outside the cemetery walls, but remained close, as if it had been separated from it against its will.

CEMETERY, VISITING

An indulgence is granted the Christian faithful who devoutly visit a cemetery and pray, if only mentally, for the dead. This indulgence is applicable only to the souls in purgatory. This indulgence is a plenary one from November 1 through November 8 and can be gained on each one of these days. On the other days of the year this indulgence is a partial one.

CENACLE, OUR LADY OF THE

A Marian image and devotion.

The cenacle was the room chosen by Jesus for the Last Supper. It was where Mary and the Apostles waited for the coming of the Holy Spirit on Pentecost, which can be considered the first Christian "retreat." Images of Our Lady in the

Our Lady of the Cenacle

Cenacle typically portray Mary with up-raised hands, praying for the coming of the Holy Spirit. Devotion to her under this title is promoted by the Religious of the Cenacle.

CHAINS OF ST. PETER

Chains preserved in Rome at San Pietro ai Vincoli.

They are said to be those that bound St. Peter prisoner, as recorded in Acts 12. As a feast, it was formerly celebrated on August 1.

CHALDEAN RITE

Also called the East Syrian Rite.

Liturgical calendar and usages originating in the primitive liturgies of Jerusalem and Antioch, used by Catholics chiefly in and from Iraq.

CHANT

A type of sacred singing.

Rooted in ancient Jewish synagogue music and retaining intonation practices from there, Christian chants moved in various directions. Being plainsong or plainchant, it is always unaccompanied. Texts for the chants are taken largely from the Book of Psalms. Various versions of chants — such as Ambrosian, Gallican, Gregorian, and Mozarabic — have been used throughout the Christian world over the centuries.

CHANTRY

An endowment left for Masses for the dead.

It is also used as a term for the chapel where such Masses were said or chanted for the repose of the benefactor whose bequest built it and supported its clergy.

CHAPI, OUR LADY OF

A Marian image and devotion popular in southern Peru.

The history of the Virgen de Chapi, the most popular Marian devotion in southern Peru, has the traditional elements common to many other Marian devotions in Latin America: an image suddenly found by a group of people, a fountain of water appearing miraculously, and clear signs of where the Virgin wants a shrine built.

The Virgen de Chapi Shrine is located in the heart of a very narrow, barren valley, in the Andean Peruvian region of Arequipa.

The shrine, made of sillar, a shining white material of volcanic origin, hosts a two-foot-tall Spanish image of the Virgin Mary. The statue is a *Candelaria*, an image of the Virgin holding a candle in her right arm, as a symbol of purity.

The devotion of the Candelaria, also

Our Lady of Chapi

known as the *Purísima*, the Most Pure, was very popular among the Spanish missionaries working in the southern Andean region. The Virgen de Cocharcas in Peru and the Virgen de Copacabana in Bolivia are also Candelarias.

According to tradition, the image of the Virgen de Chapi was found at the foot of a mountain in the late sixteenth century by a group of pilgrims traveling by horse from the city of Moquegua to Arequipa. The image was originally brought to the town of Churajon, but in 1600, the whole area was swept by the eruption of the

Huayana Putina volcano, forcing all surviving villagers to relocate.

The inhabitants of Churajon brought the image with them to a valley called Cheipi, which Spaniards re-christened with the simpler name of Chapi.

Since the original small Chapel of the Virgin was located in the road connecting the two most important Spanish cities in the region, the devotion to the Candelaria became popular among travelers. The discovery of precious minerals in the area in 1760 brought a large number of miners who also became devout clients of the Virgen de Chapi.

In 1798, the decision was made to move the image to another town. However, each time an attempt was made to move it, a natural occurrence such as a sandstorm, earthquake, or storm would prevent them from moving her. In 1868, the shrine was destroyed by an earthquake, but the image was unharmed.

In 1876, May 1 was established as the Feast of Our Lady of Chapi, and work on a new shrine was begun in 1893. A lack of water in the area made the construction difficult. According to tradition, one of the masons invoked the aid of the Virgin and was guided to a spot where he found a fountain of crystal-clear water. The fountain remains today as a key place for shrine pilgrims.

The number of pilgrims kept growing, and in 1907, after the inauguration of the new shrine, September 8, the Feast of the Nativity of Mary, was set as a second date to celebrate the Virgen de Chapi. This date has become the most popular, and annually thousand of inhabitants of Arequipa, the largest city in southern Peru, leave their homes and walk through the freezing Andean temperatures for sixty miles, many of them carrying heavy stones as sign of penance, to reach the shrine by noon on September 8. Before attending one of the many Masses, pilgrims pile their penance rocks outside the shrine. After Mass they go under the image of Our Lady, covering themselves with her cape as a sign of her protection. Then they take one of the many buses back to Arequipa.

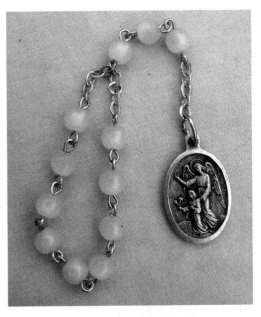

Chaplet of St. Raphael

CHAPLET

A term, meaning "little crown," applied to a rosary or, more commonly, to a small string of beads used for devotional purposes.

Chaplets are intended to honor and ask the help of God, Mary, the angels, or saints. New chaplets are written also to spread devotion to a particular saint or to reinforce devotion to a mystery or aspect of the faith. Some chaplets trace their history to reported private revelations and the origins of many older chaplets are unknown. The recitation of a chaplet could typically include the repetition of basic prayers (the Our Father, Hail Mary,

Chaplet of the Holy Family

Glory Be), prayers addressed to a particular divine image (Christ the King, for example), a Marian image, angel, or saint, and a litany.

CHAPLET OF BLESSED MIGUEL PRO, S.J.

This chaplet honors the well-known of the persecution of the Catholic Church in Mexico in the 1920s and 1930s, Blessed Miguel Agustin Pro, S.J. It was given the imprimatur by Joseph Fiorenza, Bishop of Galveston-Houston, August 13, 1995. The chaplet consists of a crucifix or medal of Blessed Miguel, followed by six white beads to symbolize his purity and eleven red beads that symbolize his martyrdom.

CHAPLET OF DIVINE MERCY

Part of the devotion to Divine Mercy, based on private revelations of Sister Faustina Kowalski.

This chaplet is said on an ordinary set of rosary beads of five decades. It begins with the Our Father, the Hail Mary, and the Creed. Then, on the large beads, pray: "Eternal Father, I offer you the Body and Blood, Soul and Divinity of Your Dearly Beloved Son, Our Lord, Jesus Christ, in atonement for our sins and those of the whole world." On the small beads, pray: "For the sake of his sorrowful Passion, have mercy on us and on the whole world." At

the end, pray three times: "Holy God, Holy Mighty One, Holy Immortal One, have mercy on us and on the whole world."

CHAPLET OF MARY, MODEL FOR MOTHERS

A chaplet to honor Mary as model for mothers, and to thank her for her daily assistance in the most difficult, important, and rewarding job any woman can have. No special beads are needed for the chaplet — ten fingers can serve as a reminder if needed. Each mystery is followed by a single Hail Mary, and the entire chaplet is concluded with the Memorare of St. Bernard. The meditations are: l) Annunciation 2) Visitation 3) Presentation 4) Finding in the Temple 5) The Wedding at Cana 6) The Scourging 7) The Road to Calvary 8) The Crucifixion 9) The Resurrection 10) The Crowning as Queen of Heaven.

CHAPLET OF MERCY OF THE HOLY WOUNDS OF JESUS

Part of the devotion to the Holy Wounds, based on the private revelations of Sister Mary Martha Chambon, a Visitation sister of Chambery, France. This chaplet was approved in favor of the Institute of the Visitation in 1912, and by indult of the Sacred Penitentiary it was extended to all the faithful in 1924.

The Chaplet of Mercy in honor of the Holy Wounds uses the beads of a standard rosary.

On the cross and the first three beads: "O Jesus, divine Redeemer, be merciful to us and to the whole world. Amen. Strong God, Holy God, immortal God, have mercy on us and on the whole world. Amen. Grace and mercy, oh my Jesus, during present dangers; cover us with Thy precious Blood. Amen. Eternal Father, grant us mercy through the Blood of Jesus Christ, Thy only Son; grant us mercy, we beseech Thee. Amen. Amen. Amen." On the small beads: "My Jesus, pardon and mercy, by the merits of Thy Holy Wounds." On the large beads: "Eternal Father, I offer Thee the Wounds of our Lord Jesus Christ to heal those of our souls."

CHAPLET OF ST. ANNE

A nineteenth-century devotion in honor of the saint.

The chaplet consists of three Our Fathers and fifteen Hail Marys. The chaplet is begun by making the sign of the cross and devoutly kissing the medal of St. Anne, praying "Jesus, Mary, Anne." The first section is recited to thank Jesus for his favors, to ask his pardon for sins, and to implore his future favor.

The second part is recited in praise of Mary with a request that she present the current petition to St. Anne. The final set of prayers presents the petition to the good St. Anne. After each Hail Mary, the petitioner prays: "Jesus, Mary, Anne, grant me the favor I ask." At the end of each section, a Glory Be is recited as an act of praise to the Blessed Trinity.

CHAPLET OF ST. ANTHONY

The chaplet to St. Anthony the Wonderworker practiced is based on the thirteen miracles listed in the Miraculous Responsory.

The chaplet is comprised of thirteen groups of three beads each, commemorating Anthony's thirty-six years of life on

Chaplet of St. Anthony

earth. On the beads are said one Our Father, one Hail Mary, and one Glory Be to the Father. The Miraculous Responsory is recited at the end of the chaplet.

CHAPLET OF ST. MICHAEL

A chaplet in honor of the Archangel Michael and the angels based on private revelations to Antonia d'Astonac, a Portuguese Carmelite, in 1751.

The chaplet consists of nine salutations, one to each of the nine choirs of angels. An Our Father and Three Hail Marys are said on each decade. The chaplet concludes with four Our Fathers honoring Sts. Michael, Gabriel, Raphael, and the Guardian Angel. The chaplet was approved and indulgenced by Pope Pius IX in 1851. The chaplet is begun with an act of contrition and the recitation of the following invocation: "O God, come to my assistance. O Lord, make haste to help me. Glory be to the Father, etc." The chaplet is concluded with a prayer to St. Michael.

CHAPLET OF ST. PAUL

A chaplet in honor of the saint composed by Father James Alberione.

The chaplet is prayed by the member congregations of the Pauline family especially for an increase of religious vocations. The chaplet has five petitions, each followed by a prayerful refrain.

CHAPLET OF ST. THERESE

A chaplet in honor of St. Thérèse of Lisieux.

This chaplet was composed by Father Albert Dolan, founder of the Society of the Little Flower in 1923. There are twenty-four beads on the chaplet in honor of the twenty-four years of her life. One additional bead and a medal of the saint complete the chaplet. On the single bead, an invocation to St. Thérèse as Patroness of the Missions is said: "St. Therese of the Child Jesus, Patroness of Missions, pray for us." A Glory Be is recited on each of the twenty-four beads in thanksgiving to the Holy Trinity for having given us the young saint and her "Little Way." It is often customary to recite the chaplet for a period of nine days, or for a period of twenty four days.

CHAPLET OF THE FIVE WOUNDS (PASSIONIST)

A Passionist devotion.

The Passionist chaplet of the Five Wounds was originated by the Most Reverend Father Paul Aloysius, C.P., the sixth Superior General of the Congregation, in order to stimulate devotion to the Passion of Christ through remembrance of the Five Holy Wounds of Jesus in a simple way. This devotion also honors the mystery of the risen Christ, who kept the marks of the Five Wounds in his glorified body. Father

Paul Aloysius presented the idea for the chaplet to Pope Leo XII, who approved it in 1823. Additionally, he transferred to the Passionist format the indulgences previously attached to an older chaplet which was introduced in Rome by the Jesuits at the beginning of the seventeenth century. From its inception, this chaplet has been one of the special devotional exercises of the Confraternity of the Passion.

The chaplet consists of five divisions of five beads each on which are said the Glory Be to the Father. Customarily, the sections are divided by medallions which represent the five wounds of Jesus in order — the wound in the left foot, the wound in the right foot, the wound in the left hand, the wound in the right hand, and finally the wound in the sacred side. At the end of each section of beads, a Hail Mary in honor of the sorrows of Mary is said. At the end of the chaplet, three additional Hail Marys are said in honor of Our Lady's tears. The medallion at the end of the final three beads shows an image of Our Mother of Sorrows.

CHAPLET OF THE HOLY SPIRIT 1

A Franciscan devotion.

This chaplet was composed and promoted by John Mary Finigan of King's Lynn (1857-1931), a Franciscan Capuchin of the Great Britain province. The chaplet was approved by the Vatican in 1900.

There are five mysteries of this chaplet. Each mystery is outlined with a scriptural meditation and a suggested practice for drawing grace into our own life. The chaplet begins with the sign of the cross, an act of contrition and the reciting of the prayer-hymn, "Come Holy Ghost, Creator Blest." On the first two beads of the mystery, the Our Father and the Hail Mary are recited. Then, seven Glory Be to the Fathers are recited. These prayers should be recited after reading the Scripture extract and meditating prayerfully on the suggested practice. The mysteries are as follows: 1) Jesus is conceived by the Holy Spirit of the Virgin Mary 2) The Spirit of the Lord rests upon Jesus 3) Jesus is led by the Spirit into the desert 4) The Holy Spirit in the Church 5) The Holy Spirit in the souls of the just. The chaplet concludes with the Apostles' Creed followed by one Our Father and Hail Mary for the intentions of the Holy Father.

CHAPLET OF THE HOLY SPIRIT 2

A prayer of adoration to the Paraclete in honor of the Seven Gifts of the Holy Spirit.

The chaplet was composed by Father Mateo Crawley-Boevey, SS.CC. The chaplet is said using a set of regular rosary beads. Begin by saying the Apostles' Creed, the Glory Be to the Father, and an

Our Father. Then, the prayer is said: "Father, Father, send us the promised Paraclete, through Jesus Christ Our Lord, Amen." On the ten small beads, say: "Come, Holy Spirit, fill the hearts of your faithful and kindle in them the fire of Your love." After the tenth bead say: "Send forth Thy Spirit and they shall be created, and Thou shalt renew the face of the earth." The other decades follow in the same manner, beginning with the Our Father. After the seventh and last decade, recite the Hail Holy Queen in honor of the Blessed Virgin, our Heavenly Queen, who presided in the Cenacle on the great Sunday of Pentecost. Meditations are made briefly between all decades.

CHAPLET OF THE PRECIOUS BLOOD

A chaplet honoring the Precious Blood.

The Chaplet of the Precious Blood is divided into seven groups containing thirty-three "Our Fathers" in honor of the thirty-three years of Christ's life. After each group, the "Glory be to the Father" is said in thanksgiving for the gift of the Precious Blood. The seven mysteries commemorate when Jesus shed his Blood in 1) the circumcision 2) the agony in the garden 3) the scourging 4) the crowning with thorns 5) the carrying of the cross 6) the crucifixion and 7) when his side was pierced.

Canon Francesco Albertini (1770-1819) is the author of the chaplet of the Precious Blood. The chaplet was approved in 1809 by Pope Pius VII and in a shortened form in 1843 by Pope Gregory XVI. Today, the Precious Blood fathers use a shorter form, reciting only one Our Father for each mystery.

CHAPLET OF THE SACRED HEART

A devotion promoted by the Sacred Heart Society in preparation for the third millennium.

It is composed of thirty-three beads in honor of Christ's earthly life, and a Sacred Heart medal or emblem. On each bead, one prayerfully recites "Sacred Heart of Jesus, I trust in Your love."

Chaplet of the Sacred Heart

CHARITY, WORKS OF

Good actions such as the corporal works of mercy and other social deeds.

They are performed to assist others in need and not for profit or recognition. Works of charity illustrate the love of Christ, give glory to God, and represent the highest form of "active" work in the world.

CHARITY OF EL COBRE, OUR LADY OF

A Marian image and devotion dating back to the early sixteenth century; the patroness of Cuba.

The statue is about sixteen inches tall and features Mary holding the Christ Child in her left hand and a small jeweled cross in her right. The Feast of Our Lady of Charity of El Cobre is held on the Nativity of the Blessed Virgin Mary, September 8.

There are two traditions to explain the origin of this image. According to one, a Spaniard, Alonso de Ojeda, was shipwrecked on the island in 1508, and made a vow that if saved he would give the image of the Virgin which he was carrying to the first village he came to. He survived and presented the statue to the town of El Cobre, an area a few miles west of Santiago which was famous for its copper mines. Another tradition holds that the statue was hidden in a cave during a conflict between

Our Lady of Charity of El Cobre

pagan natives and Spanish settlers. Reportedly, floodwaters dislodged it from its hiding place and washed it out to the Bay of Nipe. In 1600, two Indians and a black slave, all named John, were in a small skiff in the bay when a storm arose. After they prayed fervently to the Virgin, the storm calmed and Our Lady appeared to them in a vision, promising her maternal protection. They then saw a small statue, standing on a plank, floating in the water. When they pulled it into the boat, the plank was carved with the words, "I am the Virgin of Charity." The three docked and presented the statue to a Spanish officer, telling him of their miraculous escape and the odd circumstances of finding the statue. The miracle excited the devotion of the people, and after some time the statue was enshrined at Cobre.

Cuban exiles in the United States built a church in Miami to honor the Virgin of Charity. One group of Poor Clare nuns, whose 300-year-old convent was taken over by Castro's forces, fled to the United States on a cattle boat. With them, they carried a beautiful replica of Our Lady of Charity which now resides in their convent in Brenham, Texas.

CHARTRES, OUR LADY OF

Three shrines within the cathedral named for the Virgin Mary at Chartres, France.

One, Our Lady Underground, claims to be the world's oldest Marian shrine as the location was used as a shrine by Druids in pre-Christian times. The druids had an altar here to the Virgo Paritura, "the virgin who would conceive." Thus, when Sts. Potentianus and Savinianus reached the area with the Gospel, they found a shrine already built to the Mother of God.

CHASTITY RING

A popular sacramental in the form of a ring worn by youth pledged to abstain from sex until marriage.

CHATKY

A Byzantine sacramental.

The *chatky* is one of the major sacramentals of the Byzantine Rite. In Greek, it is also known as the *konboskienon* or the *konbologion*. Its use began with the desert fathers in Egypt about the fourth century, and it became a part of the monastic habit. The *chatky* was likened to the "sword of the spirit," and it was blessed and presented to a monk when tonsured.

From the beginning, the *chatky* was adopted by the devout laity. It found its way to the West through the Russian emigrees who fled the communist revolution. The sacramental is worn about the neck among the Byzantines, and the Orthodox generally wear it on their belt.

Chatkys are generally made of wool, although some are made of wood beads. The *chatky* consists of a varying number of

Chatky

knots, with the shorter and more common having one hundred and some of the longer ones having three hundred. The knots are hand-tied, each made up of seven crosses, one tied atop the other. A cross tied with similar knots ends the chatky. On a new *chatky*, the bead-shaped knots are tight and close together. With use, the *chatky* lengthens considerably.

A single prayer is recited on the *chatky* — the Jesus Prayer: "Lord Jesus Christ, Son of God, be merciful to me, a sinner." Prayers on the *chatky* are the most common penance in the Byzantine Rite, and it is customary to recite it and accompany the prayers with prostration.

CHI RHO

A monogram and symbol formed of the Greek letters X and P, which are an abbreviation of the Greek for Christ.

Chi Rho

Resembling the Latin, or Roman, letters (which evolved from the Greek, which in turn came from the Phoenician alphabet), they are usually represented as one imposed on the other.

CHILD OF MARY

A person who belongs to a specific confraternity of the Blessed Virgin Mary.

Blessed Peter de Honestis founded the oldest known Children of Mary sodality in Italy in the thirteenth century. The most famous of all Children of Mary sodalities is the one begun in 1847 by the Vincentian Fathers and the Daughters of Charity in order to promote the Miraculous Medal.

CHILDERMAS

Medieval English name for the Feast of Holy Innocents observed on December 28.

This feast is often now celebrated in reparation for the crime of abortion against today's innocents.

(See also **HOLY INNOCENTS, THE.**)

CHINA, OUR LADY OF

A Marian image and devotion.

There are a number of popular titles for Mary in China including Our Mother of Mercy, Holy Mother of Tonglu,

Queen of Peace, and Help of Christians. A common representation of Our Lady of China shows her seated on a throne-like chair, dressed in ornate robes. In her right hand she holds a scepter. The Christ Child stands to her left, and her left arm is protectively about his waist. The child is depicted with a symbol of the Holy Ghost on his chest, and both Jesus and Mary wear crowns.

CHING MING AND CHUNG YEUNG

A Chinese remembrance of the dead.

In China, people follow the ancient custom of visiting the tombs of their relatives twice a year at Ching Ming, April 5, and on Double Nine Day, September 9, the festival of Chung Yeung. The families sweep and clean around the tombs and place flowers and food. They burn incense called joss sticks, and then the family has a picnic at the cemetery, or takes the food home for a feast. The days are traditional for those who practice ancestor worship. Chinese Catholics have enculturated the ancient ceremony by adding prayers for the repose of the souls of their beloved departed.

CHIQUINQUIRA, OUR LADY OF

A Marian image and devotion dating back to the sixteenth century; patroness of Colombia.

Painted on a native cotton blanket, Our Lady is depicted with her head slightly tilted toward Jesus, who sits on her left arm. St. Anthony of Padua is to her right, while St. Andrew is situated to her left.

According to the chronicles of New Spain, in 1563 Don Antonio de Santana, the Spanish chief of Sutamarchan, had a beautiful painting of Our Lady of the Rosary in his chapel. The picture was painted by the artist Alonso de Narvaez. By 1578, the picture had become damaged and dirty and was sent to a rancho at Chiquinquira. Here, it was eventually used to carry and sort seed.

Our Lady of Chiquinquira

129

In 1585, Maria Ramos, a relative of the rancho owner, went to work there as a domestic servant. She discovered the painting and cleaned it, although the images were almost too faded to see. She hung it in a little chapel she made from a hut once used by the farm's pigs. Maria, homesick for Spain, prayed in front of the picture daily. She often implored Our Lady to make herself more visible.

The chronicles of this time tell that on the morning of December 26, 1586, a Christian Indian named Isabel was passing the door of the little hut-chapel, carrying her four-year-old son when the child cried out, "Mama, mama, look at the Mother of God who is on the floor!" Isabel saw the picture completely surrounded by a bright light. She called Maria Ramos who, on seeing the prodigy, fell to her knees and began to pray. The picture had ignited itself, and restored itself with beautiful colors. News of the miracle spread rapidly, and a commission was established to study the miracle. January 10, 1587, the Archbishop of Bogota pronounced the restoration as a supernatural occurrence. Twice, the picture was carried out in procession to end epidemics. Through the years, there have been many miracles attributed to the intercession of Our Lady of Chiquinquira, but the one favor most granted is that of conversions.

Since 1636, the image has been in the custody of the Dominican Fathers. Pope Pius VII declared her patron of Colombia in 1829, and she was canonically crowned in 1919. Pope John Paul II paid homage to Our Lady of Chiquinquira when he visited Colombia in July of 1986.

CHRISMONS

A Lutheran custom begun in the 1950s in an effort to "put Christ back in Christmas."

First created by Mrs. Harry W. Spencer of Danville, Virginia, the term *Chrismon* comes from "Christ monograms." Used as ornaments on a Christmas tree, the designs are copies of early Christian symbols. They are made in gold, silver, or white and many churches, Protestant and Catholic alike, now display a Chrismon tree during Advent.

CHRIST BUNDLE

A German term for packages of Christmas gifts for the children. A rod attached to the bundle was a reminder for good behavior.

CHRIST OF ST. JOHN OF THE CROSS

One of the most moving and beautiful modern religious paintings is Salvador Dali's "Christ of St. John of the Cross." Replicas of the painting are found worldwide, although people often do not connect the artist of this deeply religious picture to the flamboyant, often outrageous, master of surrealism Salvador Dali. Painted in 1951, the monumental oil, 80 3/4" x 45 5/8", is Dali's challenge to the Renaissance masters of anatomy and perspective. The figure is strongly foreshortened like a crucifix inclined toward a worshiper as he kisses it. Christ on the cross is suspended over a port landscape with fishermen and boats. Considered one of Dali's most dramatic and popular pictures, it is in the Glasgow Art Gallery and Museum.

Christ of the Andes

CHRIST OF THE ANDES

A statue of Christ in the Uspallata Pass, on the border between Argentina and Chile.

Located atop a mountain twelve thousand feet above sea level, it commemorates the peaceful resolution of a conflict between these countries in the nineteenth century. The figure is made of the melted cannons of the two countries. Thousands of soldiers and sailors of the two countries hitched themselves to the ropes and dragged the statue to the place where it now stands.

CHRIST OF THE SHADOW OF THE CROSS

A mysterious painting in the parish church of San Francisco de Asis in Ranchos de Taos, New Mexico.

"The Shadow of the Cross" was painted by a Canadian artist, Henri Ault, in 1896. In daylight, the picture portrays a figure of Christ standing barefoot by the Sea of Galilee. In the dark, the figure appears to change position, and a cross which is not visible in the light, appears over the left shoulder of Christ. The sea and sky behind the figure glow with a luminescence which outlines the figure, and shades from light blue to green. The quality of light suggests moonlight. The light does not remain constant, but varies in brightness, appearing to be brightest at midnight. The artist himself stated that he could not explain the changes in the picture. He said he thought he was demented when he went in his studio at night and discovered the luminosity. He was commissioned to reproduce the effect, but could not do so. The painting was first exhibited at the St. Louis World's Fair in 1904. Later it was exhibited in Europe. It was donated to the church by Mrs. Herbert Sydney Griffin in 1948.

CHRIST SEATED ON CALVARY

A popular fifteenth-century image of a weary, beaten, and bound Christ awaiting crucifixion.

CHRIST THE KING

A movable feast celebrated on the last Sunday of the liturgical year instituted by Pope Pius XI in 1925.

Devotion to Christ the King was particularly strong in Mexico during the time of the persecutions of the Catholic Church from about 1918 to 1940. The battle cry of the Cristeros and of many of the Catholic martyrs there was *"Viva Cristo Rey"* (Long live Christ the King!) The same battle cry was also on the lips of many of the martyrs of the Spanish Civil War in the 1930s. During this war, the Reds symbolically executed a statue of Christ the King.

CHRIST, RELICS OF

Any of a number of relics associated with Jesus, according to medieval pious legends.

They included, for example, bits of wood said to be from his manger and pieces of cloth said to have been part of the Infant's swaddling clothes.

(See also **RELICS**.)

CHRISTIAN UNITY, WEEK OF PRAYER FOR

Eight days of prayer, from January 18 to 25, for the union of all persons in the Church established by Christ.

On the initiative of Father Paul James Francis Wattson, S.A., of Graymoor, New York, it originated in 1908 as the Chair of Unity Octave. In recent years, its observance on an interfaith basis has increased greatly.

CHRISTMAS

A December 25 solemnity; a holy day of obligation commemorating the birth of Christ (see Luke 2:1-21).

There are texts for three Christmas Masses at midnight, dawn, and during the day. The celebration of Christ's nativity as a special feast on December 25 was introduced in Rome about the middle of the fourth century. Soon after the end of the last great persecution about the year 330, the Church in Rome definitely assigned December 25 for the celebration of the birth of Christ. The date varied in the Eastern Churches, but by the end of the fourth century the Roman custom became universal. The most probable reason for the choice of the date is that the Romans from the time of Emperor Aurelian in 275 had celebrated the feast of the sun god on that day, and it was called the "Birthday of the Sun." Thus, it was natural for the Christians to celebrate the birth of Him who was "The Light of the World" and the "Son of Justice."

By the fifth century, Christmas had become a feast of such importance that it marked the beginning of the ecclesiastical year. After the tenth century, the season of Advent had become an integral part of the Christmas cycle and the ecclesiastical year began on the first Sunday of Advent. In 529, Emperor Justinian prohibited work and public business and declared Christmas a civic holiday. The Council of Agde (506) urged the Christians to receive Holy Communion on the feast. The Council of Tours (567) established a sacred and festive season over the twelve days from Christmas to Epiphany.

As the great missionaries brought Christianity to the pagan tribes of Europe, they brought the celebration of Christmas with them. By 1100, all the nations of Europe had accepted Christianity, and Christmas was celebrated across the continent. This was a time of colorful and inspiring reli-

gious services, Christmas music and plays were written, and this was the time that most of the delightful Christmas customs of each country began. Some of these customs have died out; some, because of improper and scandalous actions were suppressed, and many have survived to our day. During the Reformation in the sixteenth century, there was a sharp change. Often, the Mass was suppressed, and in many countries all that remained was a sermon and a prayer service on Christmas Day. In Scotland, the celebration of Christmas was forbidden in 1583, and persons observing it were punished. In England, the Puritans condemned even the reduced religious celebration held in the Anglican Church, and when they came to political power in England, they promptly proceeded to outlaw Christmas. In 1647, Parliament set punishments for observing Christmas and other religious holidays. Each year, town criers went through the streets a few days before Christmas reminding the citizens that "Christmas day and all other superstitious festivals should not be observed." That year, popular riots broke out in various places against the suppression laws, and the government had to break up Christmas celebrations by force of arms. With the restoration of the monarchy in 1660, Christmas celebrations were restored, but the religious aspect of the feast was left mostly to the ministers in the church service on Christmas day, and the celebrations at home were mere nonreligious amusements and general reveling, although a spirit of good will to all and of charity to the poor remained.

Christmas came to America with the missionaries and settlers from the various European countries. Thus, where the Spanish and French settled, the feast was celebrated with liturgical solemnity and traditional customs. In the New England colonies, however, the Puritans' zeal against Christmas persisted into the middle of the nineteenth century. It did not flourish until large numbers of immigrants from Ireland and continental Europe arrived in the mid-1800s.

CHRISTMAS ANGEL
A medieval legend.

It was believed that every year Mary sent a number of angels each night to awaken little children on Christmas and carry the youngsters to heaven, where each could sing a carol to the Christ Child before being safely returned home to bed.

CHRISTMAS BELLS
A famous American carol based on Henry Wadsworth Longfellow's poem entitled "Christmas Bells." He wrote it for Christmas in 1863. The tune is called "Waltham" and was composed by the English organist

John Baptist Calkin. The song begins: "I heard the bells on Christmas day, their old familiar carols play…."

CHRISTMAS CANDLE
A holiday symbol of Christ as the Light of the World.

In the Slavic nations, a Christmas candle, blessed in church, is displayed on the family table. The Ukrainians place their Christmas candle in a loaf of bread. In parts of South America, the candle is found in a paper lantern with symbols and pictures of the Nativity. In France and England, the candle was often made of three candles twisted together in honor of the Holy Trinity. In Germany, the candle was put on top of a wooden pole decorated with evergreens (*Lichtstock*), or many small candles were distributed on the shelves of a wooden structure made in the form of a pyramid and adorned with evergreens and draped with tinsel. In Ireland, a large holly-bedecked candle is lighted on Christmas Eve and the entire family prays for all its dear ones, living and dead. The Irish also placed candles in the windows during Christmas.

CHRISTMAS CAROLS
Songs and hymns written for Christmas.

This is a popular practice that dates back to the fifth century. The word carol comes from the Greek word *choraulein*, and originally referred to a circle dance accompanied by the playing of flutes. The Romans took the custom and the name to Britain where the dance was accompanied by singing. Gradually the word became applied to the song.

The earliest Latin carols, written from about 400 A.D. to about 1200 were profound and solemn. In Italy, St. Francis and the early Franciscans introduced the joyful spirit which soon spread throughout Europe. St. Francis himself wrote a beautiful Christmas hymn, "*Psalmus in Nativitate.*" A large number of popular Christmas carols were written in Germany in the fourteenth century under the inspiration of the Dominicans.

The earliest known English Christmas carol was written about the first of the fifteenth century. After the Reformation, most of the old hymns and carols were forgotten until their revival in the nineteenth century. Carols in general were discouraged by the Calvinists and suppressed altogether by the Puritans. After Christmas was restored in England, the new songs were festive but not religious. The Methodist revival in the eighteenth century inspired a number of modern hymns first used only in Methodist churches but which were gradually welcomed by all English speaking people. The best known of these is "Hark, the Herald Angels Sing" written by Charles Wesley. The Lutherans wrote new hymns for their own use

and some written by Martin Luther are treasured in many churches today.

The first American carol was written by the Jesuit missionary to the Huron Indians, St. John de Brebeuf. He adapted a sixteenth-century French folk song and wrote the Christmas hymn "*Jesous Ahatonnia*" (Jesus is Born) in the Huron language.

CHRISTMAS CRIB

Various representations of the Christmas story; also called "crèche."

The oldest known image is a Nativity scene dating from about 380 that served as a wall decoration in the burial chamber of a Christian family in the catacombs of St. Sebastian in Rome. The use of the manger in its present form and its use outside a church is credited to St. Francis of Assisi. The word "crèche" is a French corruption of the name of the Italian town Greccio, where St. Francis set up the manger scene.

In central Europe, the beautiful family cribs are sometimes made up of hundreds of figures and fill an entire room of the house. The Moravian Germans were among the sects that kept the tradition of the Christmas crib even after the Reformation, and they brought the custom to the United States. They called it *putz*, from the German word for decorate, and their scenes include not only the figures of the nativity but dozens of figures, fanciful landscaping, waterfalls, houses, villages, etc.

As a devotion, the crèche works by giving the impression of "being there" with Jesus, Mary, and Joseph. The imaginative intimacy provoked is like a three-dimensional meditation. This is particularly illustrated in the large *mistgerion* or *nacimientos* that are customary in Latin American countries. Here, the manger is part of a larger scene in which contemporary figures often play a part. Putting contemporary figures into the Nativity scene is part of the heritage of the Italian crèches.

CHRISTMAS EVE (STEDRY VECER)

Considered a special night in every Catholic country, the Slovaks call it *Stedry Vecer* or "Generous Eve." Slovak Catholics keep a rigid fast until late in the evening the traditional "generous supper" is served. A special grace, traditional foods, carols, and a remembrance of the souls of the faithful departed are all part of the evening's customs.

CHRISTMAS LETTER

A German custom of children writing letters to the Christ Child on the first Sunday of Advent.

CHRISTMAS MASSES

A tradition of three Masses celebrated on Christmas: midnight, dawn, and in the morning.

Prior to the sixth century, only one Mass was celebrated at St. Peter's in Rome. In the sixth century, a midnight Mass began to be said at St. Mary Major, imitating the custom practiced in Bethlehem. A dawn Mass was said to commemorate the martyr St. Anastasia in the church bearing her name. In time, her feast was replaced by Christmas, and it became customary for a church to have Masses at all three times.

CHRISTMAS SHIP

A German custom of presenting gifts to children in a container shaped like a ship.

CHRISTMAS TREE

A German custom, now worldwide.

The Christmas tree was a combination of two medieval symbols: the paradise tree (from the Garden of Eden) and the Christmas light or candle. The paradise tree was a common prop used in mystery plays that told the story of Adam and Eve. The Christmas tree arrived in America with the first wave of German immigrants about 1700. The custom of setting up lighted Christmas trees in public places began in Boston in 1912.

CHRISTMAS YODELING

A Tyrolian custom of yodeling to honor the Christ Child.

It was done before the crèche or in the open on mountain peaks during the Christmas season. In past centuries, it was performed in churches. Some yodels were based on traditional tunes; others were improvised.

CHRISTMASTIDE

A traditional name for the twelve days from Christmas to Epiphany.

CHURCHES, VISITING

A traditional devotion; an indulgenced practice of visiting churches at specified times.

CHURCHING OF WOMEN

The name for the rite that invokes God's blessing on a woman after childbirth, probably having its origin in Jewish puri-

Cockleshell

fication rites (see Leviticus 12 and Luke 2:22-24).

While Christians adopted this custom, it was not seen in the same way. Pope St. Gregory the Great (r. 590-604) protested the notion that any kind of defilement was incurred by childbirth. In the new rite found in the *Book of Blessings* (Latin edition, 1984), the emphasis is on the dignity of woman, who, like Our Lady, gives new life, so great a gift, to the world.

CIRCUMCISION, FEAST OF

A January 1 feast dating back to seventh-century Spain and France.

In the 1969 revision of the liturgical calendar, it reverted to its original Roman title: the Solemnity of Mary.

(See also **CALENDAR; SOLEMNITY OF MARY, MOTHER OF GOD**.)

COCKLESHELL

A symbol of a successful pilgrimage to St. James's shrine in Compostela, Spain.

Traditionally, pilgrims walk to the nearby coast and pick up a shell as a memento. Some wear the shell on their coat or hat.

COLLOP MONDAY

A name used in northern England to refer to the Monday before Ash Wednesday

137

when collops — small portions or slices of meats — mixed with eggs and fried in butter are served. On the following day, Shrove Tuesday, rich pancakes are the common fare.

(See also **MARDI GRAS; SHROVE TUESDAY.**)

COLOR, LITURGICAL

The color of outer liturgical vestments based on the season of the Church year, feast, and other circumstances.

Green: Ordinary Time; symbolic of hope and the vitality of the life of faith.

Violet (purple): Advent and Lent; may also be used in Masses for the dead; symbolic of penance.

Red: Sunday of the Passion, Good Friday, Pentecost, feasts of the Passion of Our Lord, the Apostles, evangelists, and martyrs; symbolic of the supreme sacrifice of life for the love of God.

Rose: May be used in place of violet on the third Sunday of Advent (formerly called Gaudete Sunday) and the fourth Sunday of Lent (formerly called Laetare Sunday); symbolic of anticipatory joy during time of penance.

White: Christmas and Easter seasons; feasts and commemorations of Our Lord, except those of the Passion; feasts and commemorations of the Blessed Virgin Mary, angels, saints who are not martyrs, All Saints (November 1), St. John the Baptist (June 24), St. John the Evangelist (December 27), the Chair of St. Peter (February 22), the Conversion of St. Paul (January 25); symbolic of purity and integrity of the life of faith and may generally be substituted for other colors. White can be used for funeral Masses and other Masses for the dead. (In dioceses in the United States, violet and black may also be used in Masses for the dead.)

COLUMBARIUM

Structure built to hold cinerary urns of cremains.

Columbariums are found in ancient Rome as subterranean sepulchers with niches in the walls for the urns. Today's columbaria are generally chapels or outdoor garden walls with box-like private lockers for the cremated remains. This is the most popular form of burial for Japanese Catholics where the columbaria are called *Nokotsudos*.

COLUMN OF THE SCOURGING

A small stone column (about two-and-one-half feet and made of oriental jasper) in the Church of St. Praxedes in Rome, considered to be a relic of the column at which Christ was scourged.

On its top are indications that an iron ring had been attached to it. An inscription above the entrance to the small chapel housing the column indicates that Cardinal John Colonna brought it from Constantinople to Rome in 1223. It is believed that the column's socle, or base, is in St. Mark's Cathedral in Venice. The Roman column bears a striking similarity to the stone column in the *Ecce Homo* (Behold the Man) chapel in Jerusalem.

COMFORTER OF THE AFFLICTED — See CONSOLATION, OUR LADY OF.

COMMEMORATION OF THE LIVING AND THE DEAD

In Eucharistic Prayer I (Roman Canon), the brief pauses for intercessory prayer during which priest and people silently remember those for whom they wish to pray.

It also refers to similar intercessions, though without the formal pauses, found in all of the Church's Eucharistic prayers.

COMPLINE

From the Latin *completorium*, "completion of the day."

Compline is the night prayer that completes the course of the Liturgy of the Hours that is prayed during the day. Now usually called "Night Prayer," it is said at the end of the day, not long before retiring for the night. In it the Church thanks God for the blessings received that day and begs his protection for her children during the night.

COMPOSTELA, PILGRIMAGE OF

Medieval shrine of St. James the Greater in Compostela, Spain, to which pilgrims have traveled from as early as the eighth century.

Typically, the pilgrims identify themselves with a seashell or some portrayal of one. Often the shell may hang from their pilgrim's staffs or it may be worn on their clothing, especially on the front of their hats, as in the typical portrayal of the saint himself.

COMMUNIONE E LIBERAZIONE

From the Italian for "communion and liberation."

A movement of laypeople, particularly the young, founded in 1958 by Monsignor Luigi Giussani, a professor of philosophy at the Catholic University of Milan, in order to help its members restore Catholic values to secular society.

Its followers are encouraged to bring their Christian convictions to the workplace, school, home, and politics, thus functioning as the leaven of the Gospel. Some members live together in community, while others are free to continue a life of work, home, and family.

CONFESSION

Admission by telling something that was not known to another.

In the Catholic context, confession occurs in the sacrament of penance, in which one reveals one's sins to a priest who grants absolution when there is true repentance. Catholics are to confess once a year when in serious sin. Mortal sins are to be confessed in kind and number. One is to receive the sacrament of penance, if baptized in infancy, before receiving Holy Communion for the first time. The Church strongly urges that Catholics go to confession often in order to grow in sanctity. Venial sins, while not, strictly speaking, necessary to confess, should be confessed in order to receive the grace of the sacrament and the pardon of God.

CONFIRMATION

One of the seven sacraments.

It was instituted by Christ in promising to send the Holy Spirit (see John 14:15-21) and attested to in the early Church (see Acts 8, 19), in which the celebrant (in the Latin Rite, a bishop or priest delegated by him) invokes the gift of the Holy Spirit upon a baptized person and anoints the candidate with holy chrism.

CONFIRMATION NAME

A name chosen by one to be confirmed.

It is properly that of a patron saint on which to model one's life.

CONFITEOR

The name for the prayer said by the celebrant and congregation at the beginning of Mass.

The practice dates back to the twelfth century in the Roman Catholic Church when a public confession was made during the Eucharist. (*Confiteor* is Latin for "I confess.")

Originally, the list of saints included in the prayer varied depending on local tradition and the custom of religious orders. In the Tridentine Mass, the recitation included gently striking one's chest three times when saying *"Mea culpa, mea culpa, mea maxima culpa"* ("Through my fault, through my fault, through my most grievous fault"). The prayer now reads:

I confess to almighty God, and to you, my brothers and sisters, that I have sinned through my own fault [the chest may be tapped] in my thoughts and in my words, in what I have done, and in what I have failed to do; and I ask the blessed Mary, ever virgin, all the angels and saints, and you, my brothers and sisters, to pray for me to the Lord our God.

The celebrant then says: "May almighty God have mercy on us, forgive us our sins, and bring us to everlasting life" and the congregation answers "Amen."

CONFRATERNITY

A voluntary association of clergy or laity established under Church authority.

The Code of Canon Law uses the term "associations of the faithful" to include confraternities, sodalities, pious unions, leagues, third orders, secular orders, and guilds, but "confraternity" is still a popular term used by many groups.

In the early centuries of the Church, societies were formed to promote devotion, care for the sick, and give Christian burial. During the Middle Ages, both societies and guilds were dedicated to works of charity and to the construction and embellishment of churches, bridges, and other public buildings. Some are considered the forerunners of the trade guilds. In the fifteenth and sixteenth centuries, numerous sodalities and pious associations began in Rome to assist pilgrims from other countries. Confraternities of all kinds enjoyed great popularity in the late Middle Ages.

The so-called "third orders" began with the Franciscans. The first order was made up of the priests and brothers and the second order were the nuns; thus, the third order was made up of lay people who followed in a modified manner the spiritual practices, and shared in the special spiritual privileges of the order to which they were attached.

A number of third orders, also commonly called secular orders, are active in the United States today. They are: Third Order Augustians, founded in the thirteenth century and approved in 1400; Third Order Carmelites (Third Order of Our Lady of Mt. Carmel), usually called "lay Carmelites," their rule was approved by Pope Nicholas V in 1452 and revised in 1991; Carmelites, The Secular Order of Discalced (formerly the Third Order Secular of the Blessed Virgin Mary of Mt. Carmel and of St. Teresa of Jesus), approved in 1594 and revised in 1979, with a rule based on the Carmelite reform established by St. Teresa and St. John of the Cross in the sixteenth century; Third Order Dominicans, generally called the Dominican Laity, founded in the thirteenth century; Third Order Franciscans, called the Franciscan Order Secular (SFO), founded in 1209 by St. Francis of Assisi and approved in 1221; Mary, Third Order of, founded in 1850 and approved in 1857; Mary, Secular Order of Servants of, called the Servites, founded in 1233, approved in 1304, and revised in 1995; and Mary, Secular Third Order of Our Lady of (Mercedarian) founded and approved in 1219 by St. Peter Nolasco.

CONFRATERNITY OF BLESSED JUNIPERO SERRA

A lay association founded in 1989 in Monterrey, California, to help promote the process of canonization of Blessed Junipero Serra and to increase the spiritual development of its members.

CONFRATERNITY OF CATHOLIC CLERGY

An association of priests founded in 1976 and pledged to the pursuit of personal holiness, loyalty to the pope, theological study, and adherence to the authentic teachings of the Catholic faith.

CONFRATERNITY OF CHRISTIAN DOCTRINE

One of several societies created around the time of the Council of Trent (1545-1563).

Originally designed to offer religious education to children and adults in Milan, Italy, who had never received formal teaching in a Church-sponsored program, it was promoted by a number of saints (including Charles Borromeo, Robert Bellarmine, and Francis de Sales) and many popes. In 1905, Pope Pius X (r. 1903-1914) said it was to be established in every parish worldwide, and later his decree was incorporated into Canon Law. The Confraternity of Christian Doctrine, referred to as CCD, grew rapidly in the United States, where

there was no provision for teaching religion in other than church schools. In the U.S., it is directed by a board of trustees from the United States Conference of Catholic Bishops but separately incorporated.

CONFRATERNITY OF THE IMMACULATE CONCEPTION OF OUR LADY OF LOURDES

A lay association formed in 1874, headquartered in Notre Dame, Indiana, which distributes Lourdes water.

CONFRATERNITY OF THE MOST HOLY ROSARY

An international lay association. Members strive to pray the fifteen mysteries of the Rosary during the course of each week. The confraternity is under the spiritual guidance of the Dominican friars.

CONGRESSES, EUCHARISTIC

Assemblies of the Catholic faithful intended to show and foster greater devotion to the Lord in the Eucharist.

Devotion is shown by the public celebration of the Mass, reception of Holy Communion by properly disposed Catholics in attendance, and periods of exposition with Benediction of the Blessed Sacrament. Devotion is promoted by way of lectures and discussions conducted during the congress. Since the first formal Eucharistic congress held at Lille, France, in 1881, there have been more than forty international congresses, including two in the United States, at Chicago in 1926 and at Philadelphia in 1976.

CONSCIENCE, EXAMINATION OF

A self-examination to determine one's spiritual state before God, especially regarding one's sins and faults.

Self-examination is recommended as a regular practice to assist in overcoming specific faults and imperfections, and is necessary in preparing for the sacrament of reconciliation.

Usually, the examination is performed during the day (e.g., "particular examen," which focuses on a predominant fault, a virtue that should be obtained, or a duty connected with one's vocation), or before retiring at night (e.g., "general examen," which considers the entire day and how one failed against God, self, and others).

CONSECRATION TO JESUS THROUGH MARY

A pledge promoted by St. Louis de Montfort (1673-1716), who was noted for fostering devotion to Mary and the Rosary. Among the forms in use is:

I, a faithless sinner, renew and ratify today into your hands, O Immac-

ulate Mary, the vows of my baptism. I renounce forever Satan, his pomps and works, and I give myself entirely to Jesus Christ, the Incarnate Wisdom, to carry my cross after him all the days of my life and to be more faithful to him than I have ever been before. In the presence of all the heavenly court, I choose you today for my Mother and Mistress. I deliver and consecrate to you, as your loving slave, my body and soul, my good, both interior and exterior and even the value of all my good actions, past, present and future, leaving to you the entire and full right of disposing of me and of all that belongs to me, without exception, according to your good pleasure, for the greater glory of God, in time and in eternity. Amen.

CONSOLATION, OUR LADY OF

An early Marian title referring to Mary as "comforter of the afflicted."

Devotion to Mary as Consoler of the Afflicted was first expressed by St. Ignatius of Antioch in the second century when he wrote, "Mary, knowing what it is to suffer, is ever ready to administer consolation."

Tradition holds that in the fourth century, St. Monica — distraught with grief and anxiety for her then-wayward son, St. Augustine — confided her distress to the Mother of God, who appeared to her dressed in mourning clothes and wearing a shining cincture. Our Lady gave the cincture to St. Monica as a sign of her support and compassion, directing St. Monica to encourage others to wear it. St. Monica gave it to her son, who later handed it on to his community, which is why, as a token of fidelity to Our Lady of Consolation, members of the Order of St. Augustine wore a cincture.

A second tradition, seemingly separate and dating to the fourteenth century, tells of a Roman nobleman in the Capitoline prison awaiting death. Reflecting on his approaching last moments, he dictated in

Our Lady of Consolation

his will that his son was to have a Madonna and Child painted and placed near the gallows for the consolation of all who would die in that place in the future. The son followed his father's wishes, and when in 1470 a youth who had been unjustly convicted was miraculously saved from the hangman's noose as his mother prayed before the picture, the place became a popular shrine. More miracles followed, and a church was built. The painting was given the title "Mother of Consolation." Visiting pilgrims returned home and spread the devotion throughout Europe.

Shrines dedicated to Our Lady of Consolation have also been established in Luxembourg; Kevalaer, Germany; Turin, Italy; and Carey, Ohio.

At the Carey shrine, administered by the Conventual Franciscan Friars, relics from the original image hang around the neck of the shrine image.

At Kevalaer there is a miraculous image, a small, faded paper print, of the miraculous statue revered in Luxembourg. A miraculous fifth century icon of the Madonna of Consolation is enshrined and honored at the Sanctuary of Consolation in Turin. Here, a religious order is dedicated to her. The Consolata Missionaries, was founded in 1901; the order has spread worldwide.

CONSTANTINOPLE, RITE OF

The largest of the four main patriarchal liturgical branches of the Eastern Churches.

Also known as the Byzantine Rite, it is derived from that ancient empire's capital city and has its roots in ancient Antioch. It is now shared by Catholic and Orthodox Christians.

CONTEMPLATIVE LIFE

A term meaning the "way of life that seeks God by prayers and mortification."

Traditionally, two dimensions of the Christian vocation are delineated by the Church and the spiritual writers: the "active" life (e.g., performing the corporal works of mercy) and the "contemplative" (e.g., praying and sacrificing for oneself and for the world). The "vowed" religious life — a kind of contemplative life — offers a higher degree of perfection than the active life.

COPTIC RITE

An Alexandrian Rite employing the liturgies of St. Basil, St. Mark, St. Cyril, and St. Gregory Nazianzen in Coptic translation.

This rite is used both by Orthodox and Catholic Copts.

COR UNUM

Latin expression meaning "one heart."

It's the name given to an organization set up by Pope Paul VI in 1971 for the purpose of disseminating information and coordinating the various relief efforts under Catholic auspices all over the world.

CORD

A long rope of linen or hemp, tasseled at the ends, used to confine the alb at the waist.

Also known as a cincture or girdle, it is a symbol of purity. The cincture has been recognized as a part of the liturgical attire since the ninth century, but may date back as early as the seventh century. A cord is used by some religious orders and institutes. In the early Church, virgins wore a cincture as a sign of purity. Wearing a cord or cincture in honor of a saint is of ancient origin, and an early mention of this practice is found in the life of St. Monica.

During the Middle Ages, cinctures were often worn by the faithful in honor of saints, and a cincture in honor of

Cord of St. Joseph

St. Michael was common throughout France. Later ecclesiastical authority established special blessings for cinctures in honor of Our Lady, the Most Precious Blood, St. Francis of Paola, St. Francis of Assisi, St. Thomas Aquinas, St. Joseph, and others.

Approved in 1858, the cord of St. Joseph is made from simple cotton twine with seven knots at one end to remind the wearer of the seven joys and seven sorrows of the saint. Today, the devotion is under the care of the St. Joseph's Union, founded by Father John Drumgoole in New York.

The cord of St. Thomas Acquinas was connected with the devotion known as the Angelic Warfare. Based on a mystical experience of the saint, the cord is worn as a reminder of purity. An Angelic Warfare Confraternity was founded in 1649, under the auspices of the Dominicans. Since the mid 1960s, a medal generally replaces the cord.

COROMOTO, OUR LADY OF

A Marian title; patroness of Venezuela, whose feast is celebrated on September 15.

According to tradition, Our Lady appeared to the leader of the Cospes tribe several times in 1652. During the last apparition, fearing Mary was going to scold him for putting off his baptism and continuing his sinful ways, the leader jumped up to strangle her but found himself holding an image of the Virgin on a small piece of paper. The drawing is still venerated at a shrine in Coromoto.

CORONA, CRUCITA

Crowns and crosses made of paper flowers.

Both are used as cemetery decorations in Mexico.

CORONA OF OUR MOTHER OF CONSOLATION

A chaplet also known as the Augustinian rosary.

This chaplet consists of thirteen pairs of beads on which are said an Our Father and a Hail Mary. Two additional beads and a medal of Our Lady of Consolation are attached to the body of the corona; the final prayers are said for the intention of the pope, and the chaplet is ended with the Hail, Holy Queen.

(See also **CHAPLET.**)

CORPORAL WORKS OF MERCY

Seven Christian duties traditionally associated with the body.

Based on Matthew's account of the Last Judgment (see Matthew 25:34-40), they are: feed the hungry, give drink to the thirsty, clothe the naked, shelter the homeless, visit the sick, visit the imprisoned, and bury the dead.

Corona of Our Mother of Consolation

(See also **SPIRITUAL WORKS OF MERCY**.)

CORPUS CHRISTI

Latin for "the body of Christ."

This feast commemorates the institution of the Eucharist and is celebrated on the Thursday after Trinity Sunday. The feast began in Liège in 1246 and was extended throughout the Church in the West by Pope Urban IV in 1264. St. Thomas Aquinas wrote the Liturgy of the Hours for the feast.

(See also **LITURGY OF THE HOURS**.)

CORPUS CHRISTI PROCESSION

A custom dating back to the fourteenth century.

The faithful carry the Blessed Sacrament in a procession through town after the Mass on the Feast of Corpus Christi. The practice was encouraged by many popes, some of whom granted special indulgences for those who took part. The Council of Trent approved and recommended it as a public profession of faith in the Real Presence of Christ in the Eucharist. During the later Middle Ages, processions had developed into splendid pageants of devotion and honor. In many European countries, mystery plays were performed after the procession. Some are still performed today on special occasions. Corpus Christi processions are still held in some areas in Europe and in South America.

(See also **DAY OF WREATHS**.)

COUNSELS, EVANGELICAL

Attributes consisting of poverty, chastity, and obedience.

While religious, clergy, and laypersons are all able to profess the evangelical counsels, members of each group live out that commitment according to their state in life.

CRADLE HERB

A plant also known as Our Lady's bed-straw or cheese rennet.

According to tradition, it was one of the plants in the hay in the manger in Bethlehem. In Europe, it was used to stuff beds and mattresses.

CRADLE ROCKING

A custom that originated in Germany and Austria in the fourteenth century.

Kindelwiegen became a widespread substitute for Nativity plays. A priest would carry a cradle with a figure of the Christ Child to the altar. There, the cradle was rocked while the congregation sang and prayed. The service ended with the devotional kissing of the Christ Child's image. In the sixteenth century, the practice was forbidden in churches, but it continued in convents and private homes.

CRÈCHE — See CHRISTMAS CRIB.

CREED

A formal and official statement of Christian doctrine.

As summaries of the principal truths of faith, creeds are standards of orthodoxy and are used for instructional purposes as well as professions of faith and expressions of faith in the liturgy.

The Apostles' Creed reflects the teaching of the Apostles but was not written by them. A version of it probably began in the second century as a basic formula of faith professed by catechumens before baptism. The prayer as it is known today dates back to the eighth century.

The Nicene Creed (the Creed of Nicaea-Constantinople) dates back to the councils held in those two cities in the fourth century. Since the fifth century, it has been the one creed in liturgical use in the Eastern Churches. The Western Church adopted it for liturgical use by the end of the eighth century. In the sixth century, the phrase that said the Holy Spirit proceeds from the Father "and the Son" (or *filioque* in Latin) was added as an interpolation. Eastern Church theologians objected to the insertion, and it became a key doctrinal point of discussion leading up to and beyond the Western-Orthodox schism of 1054.

Two other prominent creeds are generally less well known today. The Athanasian Creed was written in the late fourth or early fifth century. The Creed of Pius IV was promulgated in 1564.

(See also CREED, APOSTLES'; CREED, NICENE.)

CREED, APOSTLES'

A prayer and profession of faith.

It reads:

I believe in God, the Father almighty,
Creator of heaven and earth.

And in Jesus Christ, his only Son,
    our Lord;
who was conceived by the Holy
    Spirit,
born of the Virgin Mary,
suffered under Pontius Pilate,
was crucified, died, and was buried.
He descended into hell;
the third day he rose again from the
    dead;
he ascended into heaven,
sits at the right hand of God, the
    Father Almighty;
from thence he shall come to judge
    the living and the dead.

I believe in the Holy Spirit,
the holy Catholic Church,
the communion of saints,
the forgiveness of sins,
the resurrection of the body,
and the life everlasting. Amen

(See also **CREED**.)

CREED, ATHANASIAN

Attributed to St. Athanasius, bishop of
Alexandria, who championed orthodox
belief against Arian attacks on the doctrine of the Trinity. In fact, it probably
originated in southern France and dates
from the fifth century, long after the death
of Athanasius in 373. More a hymn than

a creed, it falls into two parts, the first setting out the orthodox doctrine of the Trinity and the second dealing chiefly with the
Incarnation and the two natures of Christ.
    (See also **CREED**.)

CREED, NICENE

The formal presentation of the chief doctrines of the Catholic faith used as the Profession of Faith in the Mass.

Its recitation is prescribed as part of the
Sunday liturgy. It was first formulated by the
First Council of Nicaea in 325, in response
to the Arian heresy. Its present form is the
product of the First Council of Constantinople, held in 381, and is more accurately
called the Nicene-Constantinopolitan
Creed.

It reads:

We believe in one God,
the Father, the Almighty,
maker of heaven and earth,
of all that is seen and unseen.

We believe in one Lord, Jesus Christ,
the only Son of God,
eternally begotten of the Father,
God from God, Light from Light,
true God from true God,
begotten, not made, one in Being
    with the Father.
Through him all things were made.
For us men and for our salvation
he came down from heaven:

by the power of the Holy Spirit
he was born of the Virgin Mary, and
    became man.
For our sake he was crucified under
    Pontius Pilate;
he suffered, died, and was buried.
On the third day he rose again in
    fulfillment of the Scriptures;
he ascended into heaven
and is seated at the right hand of the
    Father.
He will come again in glory
to judge the living and the dead,
and his kingdom will have no end.

We believe in the Holy Spirit, the
    Lord, the giver of life,
who proceeds from the Father and the
    Son.
With the Father and the Son he is
    worshiped and glorified.
He has spoken through the prophets.

We believe in one holy catholic and
    apostolic Church.
We acknowledge one baptism for the
    forgiveness of sins.
We look for the resurrection of the
    dead,
and the life of the world to come.
    Amen.
(See also **CREED**.)

CREMATION

The act of rendering a dead body to ashes
by fire.

The funeral rites of Christianity have always followed the Jewish custom of burial. With the spread of Christianity, cremation became uncommon in the West, although the Church never declared that the practice was intrinsically wrong. There was a movement to reintroduce cremation in late nineteenth-century Europe. Because the Church suspected its promotion by the secularist and materialistic movements of that time and the anti-Catholicism that often were a part of those, it forbade the practice. The old Code of Canon Law said cremation was not allowed, and Church burial to those who ordered their bodies be cremated was not permissible. The revised Code of 1983 reversed the position. It reads: "The Church earnestly recommends that the pious custom of burying the bodies of the dead be observed; it does not, however, forbid cremation unless it has been chosen for reasons which are contrary to Christian teaching" (Canon 1176.3).

CRIB — See **CHRISTMAS CRIB**.

CROAGH PATRICK — See **ST. PATRICK**.

CROSS

The principal symbol of the Christian faith; a sacramental.

Father Campion Laly in a Tokyo Cemetery

At the time of Christ, the Roman Empire typically used the cross for executing criminals who were slaves or noncitizens. Historians say the cross on which Christ died was most likely tau-shaped or t-shaped and Our Lord carried only the transverse beam through Jerusalem to Calvary. (*Tau* is the Greek letter "t." The horizontal beam of a tau, or Greek, cross sits directly on top of the vertical beam. A t-shaped cross places the horizontal beam in the middle or upper half of the vertical. The t-shaped, or Latin, cross is the style most often depicted in Western art and used in the Western Church.)

Pious tradition says that in 326 St. Helena searched for and found the true cross in the Holy Land. Evidence points to its being discovered before 350. St. Cyril (c. 315-386), appointed bishop of Jerusalem that year, wrote of its being venerated by pilgrims in Jerusalem. Egeria, a Spanish nun who was a pilgrim and writer, described veneration of the true cross on Good Friday. Although later it was taken by invading Persians, in 628 or 629 the Emperor Heraclius recovered a major portion of it. Many relics from it still exist in churches and shrines throughout the world. Among the better known is the Cross of Caravaca, Spain. In the nineteenth century, Rohault de Fleury catalogued all the known relics and estimated they made up less than one-third of the

Various Kinds of Crosses — *top row from left:* Latin Cross, Greek Cross, Cross of Constantine; *second row:* Cross of St. Andrew, Celtic Cross, Anchor Cross; *third row:* Patriarchal Cross, Papal Cross, Orthodox Cross; *last row:* Jerusalem Cross, Cross of Caravaca, Pectoral Cross

cross thought to have been used in Christ's crucifixion.

Legend also says that before a pivotal battle, St. Helena's son, the Roman Emperor Constantine, had a vision of a cross accompanied by the words "in this [sign] conquer." He had the sign placed on his banner and defeated his foe. The symbol is the Greek *chi* superimposed on the Greek *rho* (the X and P), the first two letters in the Greek for "Christ."

Until the end of the sixth century, crosses were shown without the figure of Christ. The cross with the figure is known as a crucifix. The majority of Protestant denominations use a cross rather than a crucifix. A crucifix is placed on or above all altars where Mass is celebrated except in the Nestorian and Coptic Churches. In the Eastern Churches, because of the prohibition against rounded representations, the crucifix is usually painted, or a cross with a painted figure is used.

The papal cross, which is carried before a pope, has three transverse bars of varying lengths, the smallest at the top. The patriarchal cross, or archepiscopal cross, has two crossbars of which the upper is shorter. A pectoral cross is worn on the breast by a bishop. It is suspended from a cord or chain and worn outside his clothing.

Other well-known types of crosses include: Russian (Orthodox or Byzantine), with three crossbars, the lowest at an angle near the bottom to represent a foot-rest; St. Andrew's, shaped like an X and said to be the type on which the Apostle was martyred; the Greek, with four equal extensions (a plus sign); the Jerusalem (or Crusaders), similar to the Greek but with crossbars at the end of each arm and four smaller crosses in each corner; and the Celtic (or Iona), which uses a Latin-style cross with a circle centered in the beams' intersection.

(See also **CROSS, FEAST OF THE HOLY; SACRAMENTALS; SIGN OF THE CROSS; STATIONS OF THE CROSS**.)

CROSS, ADORATION OR VENERATION OF THE

Honor paid to a relic of the true cross; liturgical action of the Good Friday service.

During the liturgical action, in a practice that dates back to fourth-century Jerusalem, traditionally the celebrant unveils the crucifix in three stages, singing "Behold the wood of the cross, on which hung the Salvation of the world." The congregation responds "Come, let us worship." The crucifix is placed on a pillow in front of the altar and all devoutly kiss the feet of the image.

CROSS, FEAST OF THE HOLY

A September 14 feast.

This feast commemorates the finding of Jesus' cross in 326, the consecration of Jerusalem's Basilica of the Holy Sepulcher some ten years later, and the recovery in 628 or 629 by Emperor Heraclius of a major portion of the cross that had been removed by the Persians from its place of veneration in Jerusalem.

The feast originated in Jerusalem and spread through the East before being adopted by the West. General adoption followed the building at Rome of the Basilica of the Holy Cross "in Jerusalem," so called because it was the place of enshrinement of a major portion of the cross of crucifixion. This feast is also known as the Exaltation of the Cross and the Triumph of the Cross.

(See also **CROSS; SACRAMENTALS; SIGN OF THE CROSS; STATIONS OF THE CROSS.**)

CROSS OF CARAVACA

A relic of the true cross.

Through papal documents, the medieval Church gave special recognition to the Cross of Caravaca, referring to it as the true cross.

According to tradition, the relic arrived in Spain during the time of the Moorish conquest of that country. Pious legend says that in 1232, Muslim leader El sayid Abu-Ceit asked a prisoner-priest to demonstrate the celebration of Mass. The cleric began the liturgy but then halted because, as he explained, there was no symbol of the cross on the altar. At that moment, two angels transported the *lignum crucis* (literally, "wood of the cross") through the window and placed it on the altar so the Mass could continue. After witnessing the miracle, El sayid Abu-Ceit and his court converted. It was later discovered that the relic was from Patriarch Robert of Jerusalem. The tradition is recorded in the oldest historical books of the area that date to the seventeenth century.

In 1241, Ferdinand III of Castile conquered the region, and the relic was placed in the custody of the Knights Templar.

Over the next two hundred fifty years, during the struggles between the Moors and the Christians, many miracles were attributed to the relic, which became known as a symbol of protection. After the dispersion of the Knights Templar, the city and the relic passed into the custody of the Knights of Santiago. The fame of the cross spread throughout Spain. After the disappearance of that military order of knights, custody of the relic passed to the chaplains of the castle. Today, the custodians are a small band of Claretian Fathers.

Through the centuries, a number of reliquaries have been fashioned to hold the precious wood. The one used now is made of gold and was given by the duke of Alba in 1777.

Cross of Caravaca

The Cross of Caravaca is known worldwide. In some instances, its image has attracted superstitious beliefs as a "good luck" amulet. In 1996, Pope John Paul II declared a Jubilee year for the Cross of Caravaca and a new chapel to house the relic was dedicated.

(See also **RELICS; CROSS.**)

CROSS, OF CONSTANTINE —See **CROSS.**

CROSS OF LIFE — See **ESQUIPULAS, BLACK CHRIST OF.**

CROSS, RELICS OF

Constant tradition holds that it was St. Helena, the mother of Constantine, who discovered the relics of the cross about the year 326, although there are a number of traditions that tell how she ascertained which of three crosses was the cross of Christ. To commemorate the finding of the relics, she and Constantine erected a magnificent basilica over the Holy Sepulcher where a portion of the true cross was retained in a silver reliquary. A piece of the relic was enclosed in a statue of Constantine and placed in the forum of Constantinople for the protection of the city. A large part of the relic was brought to Rome by St. Helena where she erected the Holy Cross in Jerusalem Basilica to house it. She transported dirt from Jerusalem and placed it under the floor; early pilgrims broke the flooring in order to claim pieces of the soil.

As early as the second half of the fourth century, pieces of the relic were scattered throughout the empire. In a practice begun by St. Paulinus of Nola (353-431), a number of relics of the cross were encased in reliquary crosses meant to be hung about the neck. St. John Chrysostom recorded that both men and women had, and wore, such relics. A number of these ancient reliquary crosses are to be found today in museums and church treasuries throughout Europe. During the fifth and succeeding centuries, the cult of the cross became enormously popular, leading to the building of a number of ancient churches to hold the precious relics. The relics of the true cross in Jerusalem were captured by the Persian King Chostoes II in 614, but were returned fifteen years later with the seals intact. This recovery of the relics by Emperor Heraclius was liturgically commemorated on September 14 in the feast called the Triumph of the Cross. A September feast in honor of the cross was initiated in 335 at the dedication of Constantine's church built over the Holy Sepulcher, although today the feast seems to commemorate or include the rescue of the Jerusalem relic from the infidels. A feast known as the Finding of the Holy Cross by St. Helena was kept from early times on May 3 until it was suppressed in the 1960s.

(See also **RELICS**.)

CROWN

A symbol used by the Church for victory and sovereignty.

CROWN AND CROSS

An image used as a symbol of Christ's kingly office.

CROWN OF OUR LORD (CAMALDOLESE)

A chaplet instituted by Blessed Michael Pini (c. 1445-1522).

Also known as the Rosary of Our Lord, it commemorates the thirty-three years of Jesus' life on earth. It has three decades of ten beads and three additional beads. The main prayer of the chaplet is the Our Father.

(See also **CHAPLET**.)

CROWN OF THORNS, THE

A form of torture and humiliation that was part of Christ's Passion (see Matthew 27:29; Mark 15:17; John 19:2).

Made of briars, the crown may have been a ringlet placed around Jesus' head or, more probably, a helmet placed on top. Its alleged survival as a relic is noted first

Crown and Cross

in the fifth century. Other traditions say it was broken into smaller pieces and later distributed as relics. One is kept at Notre Dame Cathedral in Paris.

Studies of this relic have shown that it is from the bush Zizyphus Spire Christi, a plant found along the waysides near Jerusalem which grows 15 to 20 feet in height and consists of crooked branches armed with thorns that grow in pairs.

CROWN OF TWELVE STARS

A chaplet that dates back to the ancient devotion of the Order of Our Lady of Mercy.

It is based on the Book of Revelation: "And a great portent appeared in heaven, a woman clothed with the sun, with the moon under her feet, and on her head a crown of twelve stars" (12:1). The chaplet has three decades of four beads each and an introductory bead and medal of Our Lady of Mercy.

(See also **CHAPLET**.)

CROWNED IMAGE

An image which has been recognized with a papal crowning. The wealthy Italian nobleman Alexander Sfirzo had left in his will a large sum of money for the purpose of crowning certain images as directed by the pope. Images crowned must meet three conditions: l) the devotion to the image

must be approved by the bishop of the area 2) the devotion must have a long history and 3) the picture or statue must have a reputation for being divinely chosen and with a reputation as an instrument of miracles.

CRUCIFIX — See **CROSS**.

CRUCIFIX, PRAYER BEFORE A

A traditional prayer.

One version reads:

Good and gentle Jesus, I kneel before you. I see and I ponder your five

Crucifixion of Our Lord

wounds. My eyes behold what David prophesied about you: "They have pierced my hands and feet; they have counted all my bones." Engrave on me this image of yourself. Fulfill the yearnings of my heart; give me faith, hope, and love, repentance for my sins, and true conversion of life. Amen.

CRUCIFIX OF ST. FRANCIS OF ASSISI

A Byzantine cross with a painted image of the crucifix associated with the call of St. Francis of Assisi (1181 or 1182-1226).

After praying before the image and the figure of Christ speaking to him, Francis went on to begin a life of voluntary poverty and service to the poor that led to his

Crucifix of St. Francis of Assisi

founding of the Franciscan Order. The crucifix, an Umbrian twelfth-century egg tempera work, is preserved in the Church of St. Clare in Assisi.

CULT OF THE SAINTS — See SAINTS, CULT OF THE.

CUP (HOLY GRAIL)

A cup or chalice from which Christ and the Apostles drank at the Last Supper.

The cup has been the subject of many works of poetry, prose, and music, all of which have contributed to the endurance of a number of legends. Early traditions say the cup was in the possession of Joseph of Arimathea, but other legends are so numerous it's not possible to determine the veracity of any. A cup some believe may be the grail is at the New York Metropolitan Museum of Art. Made of silver, it was discovered in a dry well near Antioch in 1910 and is said to date back to the first century. Another cup some say is the grail is housed at the Cathedral of Valencia, Spain. Made of a dark red oriental carnelian stone, it also is said to date back to the time of the Roman Empire.

CURANDERO

A *curandero* (or, feminine *curandera*) is a type of faith healer, a practitioner of *curanderis-*

mo, an elaborate system of faith healing. Herbal cures, sometimes called green medicine, are part of this system. The word derives from the Spanish verb *curar*, "to cure."

Although often mixed with elements of magic, some *curanderos* have attained the status of folk saints. Although he used water, herbs and other natural remedies, Don Pedrito Jaramillo (1829-1907) never claimed cures from these, telling his patients that only God could cure them. Because of some of the elements which became mixed in his popular cult, no process for his beatification is likely, although there are many Catholics in Mexico and the American Southwest who feel he was a holy man and a saint.

CURSILLO MOVEMENT

From the Spanish for "little course."

A spiritual renewal movement that began with a group of laymen in Spain in 1949, this program is divided into three sections of three days each: preparation (pre-cursillo); the course itself (cursillo); and the follow-up (post-cursillo). Cursillistas, those who have attended a cursillo, meet in small groups called ultreyas.

The movement aims to change a person's mind according to the mind of Christ and then to gather with and support others who have committed themselves to Jesus. Their purpose is to transform the world. Today the worldwide movement is a member of the International Catholic Organizations of the Pontifical Council for the Laity in Rome. The first cursillo in the United States was held in Waco, Texas, in 1957.

CURSING PSALMS — See IMPRECATORY PSALMS.

D

DARK NIGHT OF THE SENSES

The spiritual period in which God draws one from meditation to contemplation in order that one may grow in Christian perfection.

During this initial stage of perfection, one cannot rely on one's senses for contact with God and may feel repulsed by prayer and experience temptations against faith and even illness. St. John of the Cross (1542-1591) deals with this stage in his work *Dark Night,* and stresses that, through this period, God is inviting one to the deeper prayer of contemplation.

DARK NIGHT OF THE SOUL

The purification by which God draws one to himself and to a deeper sanctity.

This period is marked by a purging of self-love and a feeling of abandonment by God. One cannot "see" God as before. The "dark night" is a transitory prelude to "mystical marriage" and occurs only for those who have attained contemplation. St. John of the Cross (1542-1591), in his *Dark Night*, writes extensively about this spiritual cleansing.

DAY HOURS

A liturgical term.

In liturgical usage, the word *hour* refers to any section of the daily cycle of prayer, known in its totality — officially since Vatican II — as "the Liturgy of the Hours," formerly as "the Divine Office." Technically, the term "day hours" is best suited to what is now called "Daytime Prayer," which may (but need not) be celebrated in three sections: midmorning (officially, Terce, or the third hour, about 9:00 A.M.); midday (Sext, the sixth hour, noon); and mid-afternoon (None, the ninth hour, about 3:00 P.M.). Only one of these "hours" is obligatory for priests and religious working in an active apostolate. Contemplatives are expected to keep the traditional observance.

(See also **ACOLOUTHIA**.)

DAY OF INDICTION

In the Byzantine Rite, September 1, the beginning of the liturgical year.

The beginning of Advent is December 10.

DAY OF THE LORD — See **SUNDAY**.

DAY OF WREATHS

A former popular name in France and many sections of central Europe for the Feast of Corpus Christi.

Huge bouquets of flowers were carried on the top of wooden poles, and wreaths and bouquets were attached to flags, banners, and houses. Green arches spanned streets. In processions, men wore small wreaths on their left arms and the girls wore them on their heads. The monstrance containing the Blessed Sacrament was adorned with a wreath of choice flowers. In Poland, the wreaths were blessed on the eve of the feast and later the people decorated their homes with them. The wreaths were hung on the walls, windows, and doors of the houses and were on poles in gardens, fields, and pastures with a prayer for protection and blessing upon the growing harvest.

(See also **CORPUS CHRISTI**; **MONSTRANCE**.)

DAYS OF PRAYER

Formerly called "rogation days" and "ember days."

Today, the Church continues the custom of publicly thanking the Lord and prays to him for the needs of all, especially for the productivity of the earth and for human labor. The general norms for the calendar of the Liturgical Year promulgated in 1969 leave the time and manner of the celebration of these days to national conferences. The American Conference of Bishops in 1971 left the determination of such days to the local bishops, and since then they seem to have fallen into disuse.

DE PROFUNDIS (PSALM 130)

A penitential Psalm; Latin for "out of the depths."

The *De Profundis* was included in the Office for the Dead from the tenth century. By the thirteenth, it had become familiar to the laity as a prayer for the repose of the souls of the dead. It reads:

Out of the depths I cry to thee, O
Lord! Lord, hear my voice!
Let thy ears be attentive to the voice
of my supplications!
If thou, O Lord, shouldst mark
iniquities, Lord, who could stand?
But there is forgiveness with thee,
that thou mayest be feared.
I wait for the Lord, my soul waits,
and in his word I hope;
My soul waits for the Lord more than
watchmen for the morning, more
than watchmen for the morning.
O Israel, hope in the Lord! For with
the Lord there is steadfast love,
and with him is plenteous redemption;
And he will redeem Israel from all his
iniquities.
(See also **OFFICE FOR THE DEAD, RECITING THE**.)

DEATH CART — See ANGELS OF DEATH.

DEATH MASK

A plaster, metal, or wax cast of a mold made from a dead person's face.

While the practice began in ancient times and is rare today, it was not uncommon in Europe during the Middle Ages among royalty, the wealthy, and the well-known. During that era, when bodies were not embalmed and funeral services could last up to a week, a death mask or entire effigy might be used in place of a corpse during state and Church ceremonies.

DEATH WATCH

A town crier in medieval England who dressed in black with a skull and crossbones painted on the front and back of his gown.

Also known as the "death crier," he went about the city ringing a bell and announcing the name and time of death of a citizen and calling for prayers for him or her. The custom was that, on hearing his announcement, people opened their doors or windows and said an Our Father and a Hail Mary.

DEDICATION OF A CHURCH

A service by which a building is blessed or consecrated for use as a place of worship.

The earliest known dedication of a Christian church was with the cathedral of Tyre in 314. Over time the term "dedication" came to mean a simple blessing rather than a solemn "consecration," but the revised rite following Vatican II makes no such distinction.

DEDICATION TO CHRIST THE KING, ACT OF

A prayer dedicated to Our Lord.
It reads:

Loving Jesus, Redeemer of the world,
We are yours, and yours we wish to be.
To bind ourselves to you even more closely
We kneel before you today
And offer ourselves to your most Sacred Heart.

R. Praise to you, our Savior and our King.

Have mercy on all who have never known you
And on all who reject you and refuse to obey you;
Gentle Lord, draw them to yourself.

R. Praise to you, our Savior and our King.

Reign over the faithful who have never left you,
Reign over those who have squandered their inheritance,
The prodigal children who now are starving;
Bring them back to their Father's house.

R. Praise to you, our Savior and our King.

Reign over those who are misled by
error or divided by discord.
Hasten the day when we shall be one
in faith and truth,
One flock with you, the one
Shepherd.
Give to your Church freedom and
peace,
And to all nations justice and order.
Make the earth resound from pole to
pole with a single cry:
Praise to the Divine Heart that gained
our salvation;
Glory and honor be his for ever and
ever. Amen.

R. Praise to you, our Savior and our
King.
(See also **CHRIST THE KING.**)

DEISIS

From the Greek for "prayer" or "entreaty."

The term describes the prayers of petition in the liturgy of the Byzantine Rite. Also, in Byzantine art, it is the depiction of Christ as Judge, together with Mary, his Mother, and St. John the Baptist.

DESATANUDOS, MARÍA — See KNOTS, THE VIRGIN WHO UNTIES.

DESCANSOS

Single crosses or small shrines along the wayside in Mexico and the American Southwest.

Descansos (resting places) are a death-related aspect of folk art. In former times, the distance between a church and cemetery meant the pallbearers had to stop and rest. As the procession entered the *camposanto* (graveyard or cemetery), there was also a ritual stop at the entrance and at each of the four corners of the cemetery where prayers were recited. Many cemeteries were built with special shelters to mark these stops, and shelters were also sometimes built at the stopping points on the way from the church to the cemetery. Later the custom extended to marking the place of death; hence the markers along the wayside.

Example of a Descanso

Generally, the families who choose to erect a *descanso* in memory of a lost loved one, place a temporary wooden cross at the site soon after the accident. This cross remains until the permanent memorial is built.

Sometimes the wooden cross is left after the memorial is built, or incorporated into it in some way. The markers are made of many materials. Some incorporate parts of the automobiles involved in a fatal accident, usually reflectors to warn other travelers of a dangerous part in the road. Some of the shrines have a *boveda*, or small replica of a tomb, complete with a glass door at the front. Photographs and votive candles as well as flowers are placed inside.

Many of the *descansos* are lovingly cared for by the families of the deceased and decorations are refreshed seasonally.

DESOLATA

From the Italian for "desolate"; Good Friday service in honor of the Sorrowful Mother held in many countries. It may include prayers, songs, and processions.

In Colombia, this is called the *Descendimiento* and the Procesion de la Soledad de Maria. An immense image of Christ is taken down from the cross in the presence of the Virgin of Soledad. A long procession begins through the barrios, finally arriving at the tomb where the figure of Christ is enshrined. The image of Mary is enthroned and accompanied by the people in her mourning for several hours. In other areas of Colombia, the procession is held on Holy Saturday, and in some parishes a *Homenaje a María*, an hour of prayer before the image of Mary, recalls all the mothers who have lost their husbands or sons because of violence.

In Mexico, the service is known as *Peseme* and is celebrated on Good Friday. The last act on Good Friday consists of a wake service for the dead Lord. The object is to "accompany" the Virgin in her sorrow. Images of the Lord in a coffin, and the Virgin dressed in black, are placed in the sanctuary. What follows depends on the creativity of the person leading the service. The last act of the service is always the "procession in silence." The coffin with the dead Lord, the image of the Virgin, and at times the image of the Apostle St. John, are carried in a silent procession through the pueblo.

In the province of Teramo, Italy, a procession of the Desolata is held at dawn on Good Friday.

DEVIL'S FUNERAL

A medieval British custom.

It consisted of tolling church bells from 11:00 P.M. to midnight on Christmas Eve and then switching to joyful ringing. The practice reflected a popular legend that the devil died when Christ was born.

DEVOTION

A readiness and willingness to dedicate oneself to the service of God; a prayer or a formula of pious acts in adoration to God or veneration to Mary or the saints.

Devotion is an aspect of the virtue of religion, the fundamental interior act by which an individual turns toward God. Promoting devotion is the goal of liturgy, morality, preaching, and prayer.

DEVOTION TO THE SOULS IN PURGATORY

Particular prayers or actions on behalf of the souls in purgatory.

In the early Middle Ages, it was commonly — and erroneously — believed that the souls in purgatory were given a respite each Sunday, and so additional prayers were said for them on Monday. Later it became customary for European churches to have a side chapel consecrated to these souls. The practice of performing spiritual and temporal works of charity and mercy on ember days became associated with special prayers and Masses for the souls in purgatory.

Graphic evidence of the depth and breadth of the devotion to the poor souls in the New World is found in Mexican tin paining. In *retablo* art, four main representations of Mary show her in her role as intercessor for the Poor Souls. These are Our Lady of Mount Carmel, Our Lady of the Rosary, Our Lady of Light, and Our Lady, Refuge of Sinners.

Early Franciscan missionaries brought their devotion to the *Arma Christi*, a depiction of Christ Crucified surrounded by the instruments of the Passion. In Mexico, this takes on the name of *Cruz de Animas* (Cross of Souls), because half figures of young females and bearded males with naked torsos have been lined up at the foot of the cross to represent souls amidst the flames of purgatory.

St. Nicholas of Tolentino, patron of the dead and dying, and the *Anima Sola* are also popular figures in *retablo* art. Sometimes the tin paintings commissioned by a family will contain the names of the family dead.

(See also **ALL SOULS' DAY; ANIMA SOLA; EMBER DAYS.**)

DÍA DE LOS MUERTOS

Spanish for "day of the dead"; Mexican celebration of All Souls.

The Mexican celebration of All Souls is one of the most sacred and revered days in the Mexican cycle of feasts. The celebration includes the cleaning up of family burial plots as well as prayers, processions, special foods, and meals in the cemetery.

Dia de Muertos is an enrichment of the doctrine of the communion of saints. In Mexico, the celebration begins on November 1 when the souls of the *angelitos* —

Day of the Dead Home Altar

Día de los Muertos
(Calavera cartoon by Guadalupe Posada)

children — are remembered. On November 2, deceased adults are honored. Folklore tells that the spirits return to earth to visit, so elaborate preparations are made to welcome them. In some parts of Mexico, offerings of bread and water are hung outside the houses or placed in a corner of the church on October 27 for the spirits which have no one to greet them and no home to visit. Cemeteries are cleaned and decorated and in southern Mexico, the streets are paved with flowers.

The *ofrenda*, or home altar, commemorates the dead of individual families. The altars are covered with black cloth and decorated with papel picado, flowers, candles, food, religious images and reminders of the family dead. Images of skeletons abound. *Calaveras*, or skulls, made of sugar, are exchanged as gifts.

The word *calaveras* has the double meaning of skulls and scatterbrain. It is also the word for satirical poems which are exchanged much as we exchange Valentine cards.

Jose Guadalupe Posada (1852-1913) was a Mexican artist who is particularly known for his illustrations of the calaveras filled with grinning, dancing cadavers miming every conceivable activity in human existence. Today, copies of his work are often seen at the *Dia de Muertos* celebrations.

In recent years, a number of American parishes have adapted this custom to cel-

ebrate the lives of the deceased members of the parish.

DIDUKH

A decorated sheaf of wheat or grain used as a Christmas symbol in Russia and other Eastern European countries. It also symbolizes Christian belief in an afterlife, as well as hope for a bountiful harvest.

Didukh

DIES IRAE

Latin for "day of wrath"; the title of a poem by a thirteenth-century Franciscan.

While it is often attributed to Thomas of Celano (friend and biographer of St. Francis of Assisi), its author is unknown. Formerly used as the sequence of the Re-

quiem Mass, the *Dies Irae* has been translated into many languages and set to music by some of the greatest composers of
all times. Its theme is the final judgment.

One translation reads:

That day of wrath, that dreadful day,
Shall heaven and earth in ashes lay,
As David and the Sybil say.

What horror must invade the mind
When the approaching judge shall
    find
And sift the deeds of all mankind!

The mighty trumpet's wondrous tone
Shall rend each tomb's sepulchral
    stone
And summon all before the throne.

Now death and nature with surprise
Behold the trembling sinners rise
To meet the judge's searching eyes.

Then shall with universal dread
The Book of Consciences be read
To judge the lives of all the dead.

For now before the Judge severe
All hidden things must plain appear;
No crime can pass unpunished here.

Oh, what shall I, so guilty, plead?
And who for me will intercede?
When even saints shall comfort need?

O King of dreadful majesty!

Grace and mercy you grant free;
As fount of kindness, save me!

Recall, dear Jesus, for my sake
You did our suffering nature take.
Then do not now my soul forsake!

In weariness you sought for me,
And suffering upon the tree!
Let not in vain such labor be.

O Judge of justice, hear, I pray,
For pity take my sins away
Before the dreadful reckoning day.

Your gracious face, O Lord, I seek;
Deep shame and grief are on my
    cheek;
In sighs and tears my sorrows speak.

You who did Mary's guilt unbind,
And mercy for the robber find,
Have filled with hope my anxious
    mind.

How worthless are my prayers, I know.
Yet, Lord, forbid that I should go
Into the fires of endless woe.

Divorced from the accursed band,
Oh, make me with your sheep to
    stand,
A child of grace, at your right hand.

When the doomed no more can flee
From the flames of misery
With the chosen call me.

Before you, humbled, Lord, I lie,
My heart like ashes, crushed and dry,
Assist me when I die.
Full of tears and full of dread
Is that day that wakes the dead.
Calling all, with solemn blast
To be judged for all their past.
Lord, have mercy, Jesus blest,
Grant them all your light and rest.
Amen.

DIPTYCHS

A set of tablets, hinged in the center, containing the names of the living and the dead.

It is read by the deacon during the canon of the Divine Liturgy. At the present time, any memorial listing can be used.

DIRGE CAKES — See **BREAD OF THE DEAD**.

DISCIPLINA ARCANI

Latin for "discipline of the secret"; term referring to two practices in the early Church.

The first practice refers to the concealing of Church dogma and liturgical practice, particularly related to Christian initiation and the Eucharistic mysteries from those who might misinterpret and ridicule them or persecute Christians for their beliefs. The second practice was the instructing of catechumens in stages, making certain they had proven themselves worthy before each succeeding step.

DIVINA INFANTITA

A Marian devotion.

While this image of Mary as an infant was originally called *Divina Infantita* (Divine Infant), the name was theologically incorrect and was changed to *María Niña* or *María Niña Immaculata* (The

Maria Niña

Child Mary or the Immaculate Child Mary). It traces its origins to a mid-nineteenth-century Mexico City Conceptionist nun, Sister Magdalena (d. 1859), who had a vision of Our Lady as an infant. The original image was made from the head of an angel which had broken off of a monstrance. Its reputation for favors spread the cult. As with many Marian cults, the devotion to Maria Niña was prohibited by ecclesiastical authorities for a time but was eventually approved and indulgenced by Pope Gregory XVI. Later, during the Laws of the Reform in Mexico, the devotion nearly died out. In 1879, the nineteen-year-old Rosario Arrevillaga, a mystic, was introduced to the devotion. She spread the cult, raised a beautiful temple in the Virgin Child's honor, and founded a congregation of sisters (Slaves of the Immaculate Child) and a refuge for children. The church was completed and dedicated in 1903, but it was later confiscated by the government during the Mexican Revolution.

In 1944, a young Spanish missionary, Father Vicente Echarri, founded an order of priests, the Missionaries of the Nativity of Mary, in Tlalpon, a suburb of Mexico City. Through the work of this order, the Immaculate Little Mary is becoming even better known.

The Feast of Maria Niña is celebrated on September 8, the Feast of the Nativity of Mary.

In Italy, devotion to the infant Mary is popular and the customary image is known as *Maria Bambina* (Little Baby Mary).

(See also **MARIA BAMBINA**.)

DIVINE COMPASSION

A hallmark of God's relationship with his people.

Throughout salvation history, Divine Compassion proceeded from Divine Love. To his "intimate friend" Moses, Yahweh revealed himself as Divine Compassion. "The Lord, the Lord, a God merciful and gracious," he said, "slow to anger, and abounding in steadfast love and faithfulness" (see Exodus 34:6). The more God loved, the more he poured out Divine Compassion on sinful man, out of his infinite mercy. At last, God sent his Son to save and redeem mankind. The Second Person of the Trinity, through the Incarnation, took on all our human nature except our sin.

Compassion was a deep, central, and powerful emotion in Jesus. Its threads bind together all of his earthly life. Through his kenosis, or emptying-out, Jesus came to identify with all of the needs of God's people.

"Be merciful, even as your Father is merciful," Luke tells us. "Judge not," he continues, "and you will not be judged; condemn not, and you will not be condemned; forgive, and you will be forgiven; give, and it will be given to you; good measure, pressed down, shaken together, running over, will be put into your lap. For the measure you give will be the measure you get back" (Luke 6:36-38).

Jesus was asked which was the greatest, or most important, of the commandments. Jesus replied, "The first is, 'Hear, O Israel: The Lord our God, the Lord is one; and you shall love the Lord your God with all your heart, and with all your soul, and with all your mind, and with all your strength.' The second is this: 'You shall love your neighbor as yourself.' There is no other commandment greater than these" (Mark 12:29-31; see also Matthew 22:37-39 and Luke 10:27).

Christ, the Divine Compassion himself, became the supreme sacrifice of atonement; he shed his Precious Blood, the blood of the New Covenant, as the purchase price of man's redemption from the slavery of sin.

DIVINE MERCY

A central biblical theme of God's benevolent, compassionate love.

The modern devotion to Christ as Divine Mercy is based on the private revelations of a Polish nun, St. Faustina Kowalska (1905-1938). St. Augustine, St. Thomas Aquinas, and St. Catherine of Siena also spoke, wrote, and taught about Divine Mercy. Their teachings are echoed in the teachings of Pope John Paul II.

In the convent of the Sisters of Our Lady of Mercy in Warsaw, Sister Maria Faustina of the Most Blessed Sacrament (Helena Kowalska) immersed herself in prayer and the practice of the virtues. Christ gradually led her into a special intimacy with his merciful heart, and she began to receive mystical revelations centered on the theme of God's mercy for those lost in sin or broken by anxiety and suffering. At the command of her spiritual director, Father Michael Sopocko, she wrote a diary, which is now regarded as a spiritual classic of the twentieth century.

In a revelation in 1931, Jesus requested that an image of himself as he had

Jesus as Divine Mercy

174

appeared to her, with the words "Jesus, I trust in you," be made and venerated, first in her convent and later throughout the world. Christ also gave her the Divine Mercy chaplet and requested that she and her confessor labor to establish a Feast of the Divine Mercy for the universal Church.

Unable to paint the Image of Mercy herself, or to propagate the feast, St. Faustina recorded all of the Lord's requests to her in her diary, and trusted that her mission would be completed through Father Sopocko. She died of tuberculosis at the age of thirty-three.

The devotion to the Divine Mercy does not consist primarily in the adoption of a set of pious practices but in a centering of faith and hope in the merciful love of God, and the desire to let his mercy flow through one's heart toward those in need.

"Divine Mercy Sunday" is the title of the second Sunday after Easter.

DIVINE OFFICE — See LITURGY OF THE HOURS.

DIVINE PRAISES

Fourteen praises traditionally recited or sung to conclude the Benediction of the Blessed Sacrament.

The present rite makes their use optional and they sometimes take the form of a litany. The original form is attributed to the eighteenth-century Jesuit Luigi Felici, who promoted them as a reparation for public blasphemy. Over the years, they have been added to and indulgenced by the Holy See. The present form reads:

Blessed be God.
Blessed be his holy name.
Blessed be Jesus Christ, true God and true man.
Blessed be the name of Jesus.
Blessed be his most Sacred Heart.
Blessed be his most Precious Blood.
Blessed be Jesus in the most holy Sacrament of the Altar.
Blessed be the Holy Spirit, the Paraclete.
Blessed be the great Mother of God, Mary most holy.
Blessed be her holy and Immaculate Conception.
Blessed be her glorious Assumption.
Blessed be the name of Mary, Virgin and Mother.
Blessed be St. Joseph, her most chaste spouse.
Blessed be God in his angels and in his saints.
(See also BENEDICTION; LITANY.)

DOMESTIC CHURCH (HOME CHURCH)

An ancient but still used expression referring to the Christian family and the practice of the faith within the home.

The term is found in the documents of Vatican II and the writings of Pope John Paul II.

DOÑA SEBASTIANA

Carved image of a death angel.

Known as Doña Sebastiana or *Nuestra Comadre Sebastiana* (Our Godmother Sebastiana), images of this angel of death are still commonly seen in the folk art of the American Southwest. Often seen in her

Dormition of Our Lady

death cart, Doña Sebastiana serves as a vivid *memento mori.*

DORMITION OF OUR LADY — See ASSUMPTION.

DOVE

An ancient symbol of the Holy Spirit based on all four Gospel accounts of Christ's baptism (see Matthew 3:16, Mark 1:10, Luke 3:21-22, and John 1:32).

The figure of a dove was widely used in medieval times to enact dramatically the descent of the Holy Spirit on Pentecost Sunday. As the priest sang the first words of the sequence, *Veni Sancte Spiritus,* "Come Holy Ghost," the church was filled with the sound "as of a violent wind blowing" (Acts 2:2). In France the noise was made by the blowing of trumpets; in other countries, choirboys made hissing and humming sounds and rattled the benches. From an opening in the ceiling of the church known as the Holy Ghost Hole there appeared a disc the size of a cart wheel which slowly descended in horizontal position, swinging in ever widening circles. On the underside of

Dove

the disc, on a blue background with bundles of golden rays, there was painted the image of a white dove. Then followed a rain of flowers to symbolize the gifts of the Holy Spirit and of water to symbolize baptism. In some towns in central Europe, people even went so far as to drop pieces of burning wick or straw to symbolize the flaming tongues of Pentecost, although this custom had a short life as it tended to put the people on fire externally rather than internally. In thirteenth century France, real white pigeons were sometimes released during the singing of the sequence and flew around in the church while roses were dropped from the Holy Ghost Hole.

A custom common in medieval times and even today in some parts of central and eastern Europe is the use of artfully carved and painted wooden doves suspended over the dining table. Sometimes it is encased in a glass globe in which it has been assembled with painstaking effort, a constant reminder for the family members to venerate the Holy Spirit.

DOXOLOGY

A short formula of praise at the end of a prayer.

The use of a doxology was a common practice in first-century Judaism. Among the best known doxologies is the "Glory Be." It reads:

> Glory be to the Father and to the Son and to the Holy Spirit. As it was in the beginning, is now and ever shall be, world without end. Amen.

The first half of the Glory Be dates back to the early Eastern Church. The second was added probably during the fourth century. The prayer came into the Western Church during the fifth century and spread rapidly. Since then, it has been in constant use in both liturgical prayer and private devotions.

DULIA

The kind and degree of honor or veneration given to angels and saints.

From the Greek for "slavery" (or, more broadly, "respect"), it is governed by ecclesiastical authority and distinguished from *hyperdulia* and *latria*.

Hyperdulia, or extended praise, is given to Mary alone because of her unique place in humanity and her role in salvation history. *Latria* (from the Greek for "service") is the kind and degree of praise given to God alone.

E

EASTER

The oldest and greatest Christian feast.

It is the annual celebration of Christ's Resurrection from the dead (see Matthew 28:1-15, Mark 16:1-14, Luke 24:1-12, and John 20:1-21).

The etymology of the name *Easter* is uncertain. According to St. Bede the Venerable (d. 735), it was derived from Eastre, a Teutonic goddess of spring. The feast is also called the "Pasch," or *Pascha* (from the Hebrew for "Passover"). Among Christ's titles are "Paschal Lamb" and "Lamb of God."

Since apostolic times, Christians have gathered for "the breaking of the bread," the celebration of the Eucharist, on Sundays because each is seen as a "little Easter." In the early Church, catechumens were baptized, confirmed, and given First Holy Communion during the Easter Vigil, a practice that has been revived in recent times.

Unlike Christmas, which has a set date, Easter is a movable feast. In the Catholic and Protestant churches, it is celebrated on the first Sunday after the vernal equinox. The Orthodox base the date on the Julian or a modified Gregorian calendar rather than the Gregorian calendar. (See also **EASTER CANDLE** ; **TRIDUUM**.)

Blessing of Bread on Holy Thursday

EASTER BELLS

An ancient Slavic custom of ringing church bells intermittently throughout Easter day.

EASTER BREAD (PASKA, BABKA) — See BLESSING OF EASTER BASKETS.

EASTER CANDLE

A tall candle blessed and lighted during the Easter Vigil as a symbol of the risen Christ.

Typically, the candle is highly ornamented and must have, in the form of a cross, five imbedded or mounted grains of incense representing Christ's wounds. The candle is lighted at Masses from Easter to the end of Vespers on Pentecost Sunday.

EASTER CAROLS

Hymns written and sung to celebrate the Resurrection.

A number of them date back to the fourth century and are attributed to St. Jerome, St. Augustine, St. Gregory of Nazianzen, and St. Ambrose.

EASTER DUTY

The obligation, established at the Fourth Lateran Council (1215), that the faithful were obliged to confess their sins and re-

Easter Ceremonies

ceive Holy Communion at least once a year during the Easter season.

This precept is still binding (see Canon 920), with the common understanding that the period in question lasts from the first Sunday of Lent through Trinity Sunday.

EASTER EGGS

A custom developed among the nations of northern Europe and Christian Asia, soon after their conversion to Christianity.

Making Easter Eggs

An ancient symbol of spring and fertility, the egg came to represent the stone tomb from which Christ emerged to new life. Because at one time eggs were forbidden during the Lenten fast, they became a special sign of Easter joy and were painted or dyed in festive colors, blessed, and given as gifts.

In medieval times, eggs were traditionally given at Easter to servants and to children, along with other gifts. In most countries the eggs are stained in plain vegetable-dye colors. Among the Chaldeans, Syrians and Greeks, the eggs are dyed crimson in honor of the blood of Christ. In Poland and Ukraine, special eggs known as *krashanky* and *pysanky* are popular. In central Europe,

the Armenians decorate empty eggs with religious pictures as gifts, and in parts of Germany the eggs are decorated and hung from shrubs and trees much like a Christmas tree. The custom of hiding the eggs is universal.

(See also **KRASHANKY, PYSANKY**.)

EASTER KISS

A Russian Easter custom at church services, in homes, and in public.

EASTER LAMB

A symbol of Easter and Christ, the "Lamb of God" and "Paschal Lamb."

A principal item of the Passover meal (the seder), a lamb has become traditional Easter fare. Prayers for the blessing of lambs date back to the seventh century.

EASTER LILY

A traditional symbol of beauty, perfection, and goodness, used universally and in Scripture.

The plant known as the Easter lily acquired religious symbolism after being introduced in Bermuda from Japan in the mid-nineteenth century. The florist W.K. Harris brought it to the United States in 1882, and spread its use here. Because in America it first flowers in mid-spring, it came to be called the "Easter lily." Its flower, known as a trumpet, parallels the jubilant *Alleluia* proclaimed throughout the Church at the Resurrection of Christ from the dead.

(See also **LILY**.)

EASTER MONDAY

The day after Easter.

In medieval times it was a day of rest, relaxation, and special festivities. One custom, the Emmaus walk, was inspired by a passage from Luke 24:13-35. Families and friends went on outings or long walks, taking a picnic lunch and spending the afternoon dancing, singing, and playing games. In parts of Canada, it was customary for children to visit their grandparents. An Armenian tradition consisted of celebrating the memory of all the faithful departed by reciting the Office of the Dead. In Italy this day is called *Lunedi dell' Angelo* (Angel Monday) to commemorate the angel who greeted the women at Christ's empty tomb. Catholic countries and regions continue to observe Easter Monday as a public holiday.

EASTER PARADE

An ancient custom of dressing in fine clothes and walking through fields after Easter Mass.

A decorated crucifix or the Easter candle was carried at the head of the procession as people prayed and sang. After the Reformation, the walk lost its religious character and gradually developed into Easter parades.

EASTER SEASON (EASTERTIDE)

The liturgical year's period from Easter to Pentecost.

(See also **CALENDAR**.)

EASTER VIGIL

A central liturgical celebration of the Church year.

Celebrated on Holy Saturday, the night before Easter, ceremonies all relate to the Resurrection and renewal-in-grace theme of Easter. The vigil includes the blessing of a new fire, a procession with the Easter candle, the singing of the Easter Proclamation (*Exsultet*), the Liturgy of the Word with at least three Old Testament readings, the Litany of the Saints, the blessing of water, the baptism of catechumens and infants, the renewal of baptismal promises, and the Liturgy of the Eucharist. Catechumens and candidates (those who have already been baptized and are making a formal profession of faith) receive the sacraments of confirmation and First Holy Communion.

EASTER WATER

Holy water blessed during the Easter Vigil.

It is used for Christian initiation that night, renewal of baptismal vows at Masses on Easter day, and baptisms throughout the Easter season.

EASTERN RITES, SACRAMENTALS IN

Religious objects and actions used in the Eastern Church.

Prominent sacramentals include the sign of the cross, standing through much of the Eucharist, prostrating and bowing deeply as signs of devotion, kissing sacred objects such as icons, holy water, holy oil (myron), incense, crosses, and medals.

In the Byzantine Rite, the sign of the cross is made by joining the thumb and the next two fingers to represent the Holy Trinity. The last two fingers are folded down on the palm of the right hand to represent the two natures in Christ. Formerly in Russia, and still among the "Old Believers" this order is reversed. The thumb and the next finger are joined while the next three fingers are held down over the palm and the symbolism is reversed. One then touches the forehead, then the upper sternum, then the right shoulder and finally the left. Some believers touch their hearts instead of the left shoulder. The invocation is the same as in the West. The sign of the cross is made continually in the course of Byzantine worship and whenever the Holy Trinity is invoked.

There are blessings by the celebrant often during the liturgy. In blessing the faithful, he disposes the fingers of his right hand in such way as to form I.C.X.C., Our Lord's initials. He also blesses with the Gospel Book and the chalice and paten. If a bishop is celebrating, he makes the sign of the cross with the *Dikeron* and the *Trikerion*, a two and three branched candelabra. One often sees bishops and priests blessing, outside of church, with both hands with their fingers disposed as are the candles on the Dikerion and Trikerion, three fingers on the right hand held erect and two on the left. Among the other Oriental rites, the sign of the cross is made as Latin Catholics make it, except the Syrian Jacobites often make it with the middle finger only to emphasize their belief that in Our Lord there is but one person and one nature.

(See also **ICON; SIGN OF THE CROSS; SACRAMENTALS.**)

ECCE HOMO
Latin for "behold the man."

These were Pilate's words as he presented the beaten Christ to the chief priests (see John 19:5).

ECHTERNACHT
A dancing procession held at the Benedictine shrine of Echternacht near Luxembourg.

The custom honors St. Willibrord, who died there in 739, and whose relics are kept there. Participants line up in rows joined to their neighbor by a handkerchief held between them. The procession dances forward while repeating a litany to the saint in time to the music of bands. The final step of the procession is a leap past the tomb of the saint in the crypt of the basilica.

ECSTASY
A state of mystical experience in which a person is so absorbed in God that the exterior senses are suspended.

Contemporaries of mystic saints have reported that these holy men and women were seen in states of ecstasy.

ECUMENISM
The movement of Christians and their churches toward the unity willed by Christ.

EINSELDELN, OUR LADY OF
A Marian image enshrined in a Benedictine monastery in Switzerland.

Tradition says it dates back to St. Meinrad (d. 861). It was one of the great pilgrimage centers of Medieval Europe.

EJACULATIONS, ASPIRATIONS, PIOUS INVOCATIONS
Short exclamatory prayers.

EKTENE
A litany.

There are two *Ektenes* recited during the celebration of the Divine Liturgy in the Byzantine Rite.

EL DIVINO NIÑO
A twentieth-century Colombian image of the Child Jesus first promoted by Salesian Father Juan del Rizzo.

Miracles have been attributed to *El Divino Niño* (The Divine Child), and it remains a popular devotion in Colombia. Today, the devotion to El Divino Niño is probably the greatest devotion in Colombia; it vies with devotion to El Señor de los Milagros. Masses are attended by the thousands each weekend in the church.

After visiting the shrine in 1995, Mother Angelica, of Eternal Word Television, seemed to hear the image of El Divino Niño speaking to her, asking her to build a temple for him. She set to work and the new shrine at Our Lady of the Angels Monastery in Hanceville, Alabama is dedicated to the Blessed Sacrament and Divino Niño.

EMBER DAYS

Wednesdays, Fridays, and Saturdays of four weeks of the year on which fast and abstinence were required.

Observing ember days was an ancient practice. The origin of the tradition and the derivation of the term are uncertain. Ember days have been associated with Roman agrarian concerns, including sowing and reaping festivals. In the fourth century, Pope Gelasius permitted ordinations on the Saturdays of an ember week. Prior to this, the sacrament was celebrated only at Easter. In the eleventh century, Pope Gregory VII arranged and prescribed

for the entire Church that they would be held on the Wednesday, Friday, and Saturday after the Feast of St. Lucy (December 13), Ash Wednesday, Pentecost, and the Triumph of the Cross (September 14). Since 1969, how and when ember days are celebrated is determined by the local conference of bishops.

EMMAUS WALK — See EASTER MONDAY.

ENTHRONEMENT OF THE SACRED HEART

A devotion promoted by Father Mateo Crawley-Boevy (1875-1960).

The enthronement ritual is a paraliturgical family celebration in which Christ is proclaimed the Lord of the home and an image of the Sacred Heart is installed in a prominent place there.

Father Mateo saw the sanctification of the family as the ultimate goal of the apostolate. He believed the enthronement fulfilled all of the requests of the Sacred Heart made to St. Margaret Mary at Paray-le-Monial. To him, the family as a social cell must be the living throne of the King of Love. In the United States, the devotion is promoted through the Men of the Sacred Hearts, a lay association. Headquarters for the devotion is in Fairhaven, Connecticut.

EPIPHANY

A feast celebrated on January 6 (or in some countries on the Sunday between January 2 and 8); also known as Twelfth Night and Three Kings Day.

The Epiphany (from the Greek for "manifestation") commemorates the manifestations of God to the world symbolized by the three Magi from the East (see Matthew 2:1-12). The feast began in the third century in the Eastern Church where it continues to refer to the "manifestation" of God to the world through the Magi and Jesus' divinity, manifested at his baptism in the Jordan River and the miracle at the wedding feast at Cana. By the fourth century it was ranked in importance with Easter and Pentecost. When introduced in the West at that time, the focus shifted from Jesus' baptism to his birth. The feast is also known as the Twelfth Night because it is the last of the "twelve days of Christmas," and Three Kings Day, because of the Magi. In some countries Epiphany, rather than Christmas, has been the day on which gifts are traditionally exchanged.

(See also **KINGS' CAKE**.)

EPIPHANY CAROLS

Carols and ballad-like songs that tell the story of the Magi.

In many places of Europe, it became a custom for young people to dress up as the Three Kings and go door to door carrying a pole with a star of Bethlehem. They sang along the way and wished the homeowners happiness and blessings. A simplified form of ancient Epiphany plays, the tradition was widespread from the end of the fourteenth century until the Reformation and is still practiced in some parts of Germany and the Slavic countries.

EPIPHANYTIDE

The Epiphany season extends from January 6 to Septuagesima Sunday, and has from one to six Sundays, according to the date of Easter. White is the color for the octave; green is the liturgical color for the season.

ESCHATOLOGY

Theology concerning the last things.

The last things are: death, judgment, heaven and hell, and the final state of perfection of the people and kingdom of God all gathered from the corners of the earth at the end of time.

ESQUIPULAS, BLACK CHRIST OF

A crucifix venerated in Guatemala since the late sixteenth century.

Miracles have been attributed to "The Black Christ of Esquipulas," and devotion to it is widespread in Central America. The cross sculptor, Quirio Catano, was a mystic and artist, originally from Portugal, who emigrated to Guatemala. Through his art, he was able to project the pain and the compassion of Our Lord dying on the cross. The expression on the face of the corpus, along with the dark color of the skin, appealed greatly to the native *Chortis* of the area. The crucifix is carved of orange wood. An unusual feature is the leaves with which the cross is covered.

From its delivery in 1595, pilgrimages to Esquipulas began which still occur. Today, Esquipulas is considered one of the most holy places of Central America.

When the Central American presidents met to work out a peace plan, they were lodged at the Benedictine convent that is charged with the pastoral care of the basilica. A copy of the crucifix was blessed in front of the original and is in the cathedral in the capitol, Guatemala City. In l988, another replica of the Black Christ of Esquipulas was brought to San Antonio, Texas to San Fernando Cathedral.

Black Christ of Esquipulas

EUCHARIST

The principal Christian liturgical celebration of, and communion in, the Paschal mystery of Christ.

The Eucharist is a ritual, sacramental action of thanksgiving to God, which is traditionally known as the Holy Sacrifice of the Mass. It is one of the seven sacraments of the Church. (The others are baptism, penance or reconciliation, confirmation, matrimony, holy orders, and anointing of the sick.) The Sunday celebration of the Eucharist is at the heart of the Church's life.

(See also **MASS**.)

EUCHARISTIC CONGRESS

National and international gatherings held periodically to give glory to God in the Eucharist and to promote devotion to the Blessed Sacrament.

The first Eucharistic congress was held in Lille, France, in 1873.

EUCHARISTIC CONGRESSES — See CONGRESSES, EUCHARISTIC.

EUCHARISTIC DEVOTIONS

The postconciliar ritual and instruction regarding *Holy Communion and Worship of the Eucharist Outside Mass* (1973).

It appropriately places Eucharistic devotions in the context of instructions about the relationship between Eucharistic worship outside Mass and the celebration of the Eucharist, the purposes of Eucharistic reservation (the administration of Viaticum and adoration), and the forms of worship of the Eucharist. It asserts that "the Eucharistic sacrifice is the source and culmination of the whole Christian life" and that the cult of Eucharistic devotion "should be in harmony with the sacred liturgy in some sense, take their origin from the liturgy, and lead people back to the liturgy" (n. 79). Four forms of Eucharistic devotions derive from reserving the sacrament: exposition, benediction, processions, and congresses.

EUCHARISTIC FAST — See FAST, EUCHARISTIC.

EUCHARISTIC PROCESSION

A custom, begun in the Middle Ages, of carrying the Blessed Sacrament along a public route.

After the establishment of the Feast of Corpus Christi in the thirteenth century, the tradition of a Eucharist procession became known throughout Europe. Typically, the Blessed Sacrament was carried in a splendid procession through town after the Mass. In the late Middle Ages, the custom developed into splendid pageants of devotion and honor to Christ in the Eucharist. The tradition continued in some areas into the twentieth century.

(See also **CORPUS CHRISTI PROCESSION**.)

EUCHARISTIC MIRACLES — See BLOOD MIRACLES.

EUCHOLOGY

A liturgical book of the Byzantine Rite.

The book contains the prayers of the Eucharistic liturgies and Liturgy of the Hours as well as ceremonies and blessings. Also called the *Euchologion*, it is a combination of the missal, ritual, and breviary of the Roman Rite.

EVANGELICAL COUNSELS — See COUNSELS, EVANGELICAL.

EVANGELIZATION

From the Greek for "good news" or "gospel."

All those activities by which every member of the Church proclaims and presents to the world the saving message of the Gospel of Jesus Christ.

EVERGREENS

Boughs traditionally used in the ancient and widespread custom of decorating homes for festivals.

After the end of the Roman persecutions, the Church approved the practice of decorating homes and churches with boughs and plants, especially for Christmas. Pope St. Gregory I (r. 590-604) wrote to St. Augustine of Canterbury advising him to permit and even encourage harmless popular customs which in themselves were not pagan, but were natural, and could be given a Christian interpretation.

The plants traditionally used in the Christmas season are mainly evergreens because they were available in the winter season and also because from ancient times evergreens symbolized eternal life. Mistletoe was called by the Druids, to whom it was sacred, "all heal." To the Christians it was used as a symbol of Christ the Divine Healer. Holly was, for the early Christians in northern Europe, the symbol of the burning thorn bush of Moses and the flaming love for God that filled Mary's heart. Its red berries resembling drops of blood and its prickly leaves reminded the faithful of the crown of thorns. At first, ivy was shunned by the Christians because of its association with the pagan wine god Bacchus. Some old English poets defended its use by attributing to it a symbolism of human weakness clinging to divine strength. Laurel, an ancient symbol of triumph, was the first plant to be used as a Christmas decoration; the early Christians at Rome adorned their homes with it. The legend of the rosemary says that on the way to Egypt Our Lady washed the infant's clothes and hung them on rosemary to dry. In other medieval legends the plant is pictured as a great protection against evil spirits.

EX VOTO

Latin for "out of a promise"; an offering made because of a vow or as a show of gratitude.

An *ex voto* can be a work of art, an action or donation, a reminder of a favor granted (such as crutches seen at Marian shrines), or a votive candle.

The candles lighted by the faithful in churches or shrines are *ex votos*. Their origin is obscure, but from earliest times there was a symbolism attached to their use: the candle consuming itself was a type of sacrifice. Grateful clients in the Middle Ages "measured themselves" to a particular saint by setting up a candle the same height or weight as the person who had received or desired some favor.

Some shrines, churches, or saints become known for the particular type of *ex voto* given by their grateful clients. The crutches and medical instruments at Lourdes, the silver hearts of the Church of the Assumption in London, the wedding rings on the tabernacle-veil of Westminster Cathedral, and the model ships at Notre Dame de Boulogne are examples. Other examples are the money pinned to the trees at the hillside shrine of St. Michael in Albania, handmade crosses at Siauliai Lithuania, baby shoes at the shrine of Chimayo, New Mexico, and the watches and jewelry presented to Maria Niña in Mexico City. The Madonna della Guardia in the church on Monte Figogna near Genoa also receives jeweled tokens. The miraculous image of the Blessed Virgin known as "Comforter of the Afflicted" in Kevalaer Germany is surrounded by *ex votos* of gold: roses, angels, medals, and jeweled ornaments.

Photographs and locks of hair are found in many places, as are the needles of silver and gold in some Italian shrines, and the Hispanic *milagros* — small figures of wax, gold, silver or tin. Also called *promesas*, the most common are arms, legs, eyes, cattle, horses, praying children, and hearts, both plain and pierced by a sword.

A rose — real, jeweled, gold, paper or made of other material — is a common gift to Our Lady. Coins or paper money are sometimes placed near depictions of the child Jesus, manger scenes, or images of the three kings.

Perhaps one of the more unusual *ex voto* customs is found at the Mexican pilgrimage centers of Chalma, which has a crucifix venerated as miraculous, and at Sacromonte, where there is a famous representation of Christ in the Sepulchre. Here, parents traditionally bring the umbilical cords of their newborns, contained in cloth bags.

Paintings on wood, metal, or paper are known as pictorial *ex votos* or *retablos*. The basic scheme of the pictorial *ex voto* has these elements: the event in the course of which the blessing was sought, the image of Jesus, Mary, or the saint which was petitioned, the figure of the devotee, and the inscription which clarifies the details of the event or adds the formulas of thanks.

The inscriptions may be standard words or initials. The Latin inscription VFGA or *Votum Fecit Gratiam Accepit* stands for "Vow made, blessing received." In Italian, the initials PGR stand for *Per Grazia Ricevuta* or "for blessing received." Phrases such as *Por un favor*, meaning "for a favor" in Spanish, or "given in gratitude by ..." in English are common.

EXALTATION OF THE CROSS — See **CROSS, FEAST OF THE HOLY**.

EXAMEN

The daily examination of conscience done to root out sin and to "put on the Lord Jesus Christ."

This discipline is crucial for one who desires sanctity.

EXAMINATION OF CONSCIENCE — See **CONSCIENCE, EXAMINATION OF**.

EXPOSITION OF THE BLESSED SACRAMENT

A form of devotion to the Blessed Sacrament in which the host is displayed in a monstrance.

(See also **BENEDICTION**.)

EXTREME UNCTION — See **ANOINTING OF THE SICK**.

EYE OF GOD

An image used as a symbol of God's omniscience.

Eye of God

F

FAMILY GUILD MOVEMENT

A ministry for, and by, Christian families begun in Texas in 1946.

The Association of Holy Family Guilds, which flourished in the 1960s, was an outgrowth of a small social club organized in 1938 in San Antonio. Wanting to share the benefits from their time spent with other Catholic couples, the members of the original group began to form guilds. Each was made up of five to twelve couples in a parish with a priest or deacon moderator. Members studied, played, prayed, and did volunteer work together.

(See also **CONFRATERNITY**.)

FAMILY ICONS

A tradition in Byzantine Catholic homes of setting aside a place for icons at which the family prays.

Also known as an icon corner, it may include other sacramentals such as a censer, holy water, prayer book, and Bible. The backs of icons given as wedding presents are used to record births and baptisms. Blessings are given with the family icon: children on their first day of school, brides on their wedding day, young adults on entering military service, and other similar occasions. A custom when entering a Byzantine home is first to acknowledge the icons before greeting the hosts.

(See also **ICON**.)

FAMILY ROSARY CRUSADE

An international promotion of the family praying the Rosary together.

Holy Cross Father Patrick Peyton, who came to be known as "The Rosary Priest," began The Family Rosary, Inc., in 1942, and coined the phrase, "The family that prays together stays together." Father Peyton used the media — films, radio, and television — to promote the family Rosary. The crusade has distributed more than three million rosaries worldwide.

FAST, EUCHARISTIC

Abstaining from food and drink (except water and medicine) for one hour prior to receiving Holy Communion.

Although in the earliest days of Christianity the Eucharist was probably received during the course of a meal, fasting has been the custom since the fourth century and regulations have varied. The usual one-hour fast is mitigated in certain circumstances. The elderly, infirm, and ill — as well as their caregivers — are generally required to fast at least fifteen minutes before receiving communion; but if the minister of communion arrives early or without advance notice, such recipients are dispensed from even this mitigated fast.

FASTING

The practice of abstaining from food for

a period of time for devotional purposes.

The concept was acquired from Judaism; the Jews fasted before the Passover meal and, among the devout, on Mondays and Thursdays. According to the *Didache*, a second-century text, the early Christian practice was to fast before Easter and on Wednesdays and Fridays. Preparation for the sacraments of baptism, Eucharist, and orders likewise involved fasting. Through the centuries and in various cultures, fasting marked a spirit of penance before a number of feasts of the Church, including Christmas, Easter, and Pentecost.

(See also **ABSTINENCE**; **LENT**.)

FÁTIMA, OUR LADY OF

A Marian title and image based on six apparitions seen by three children in Fátima, Portugal, between May 13 and October 13, 1917.

During her final visit to Lucia dos Santos and her cousins Francisco and Jacinta Marto, "the Lady" revealed she was Our Lady of the Rosary.

The children reported that Mary requested frequent recitation of the Rosary, penance, increased devotion to her Immaculate Heart, prayers for the conversion of Russia, and the building of a church in her honor. Her promised miracle — the appearance of the sun "spinning" — was witnessed by fifty thousand

people, including skeptics, agnostics, and atheists. Francisco died in 1919, followed by Jacinta in 1920. Lucia, who became first a Sister of St. Dorothy, then afterward a Carmelite nun, received a seventh apparition in 1921.

In 1930, Pope Pius XI authorized devotion to Our Lady of Fátima. The Marian shrine in Fátima is among the most famous in the world.

Fátima became especially prominent in the papacy of John Paul II. The 1981 attempt on his life took place on May 13, the anniversary of the first apparition. The

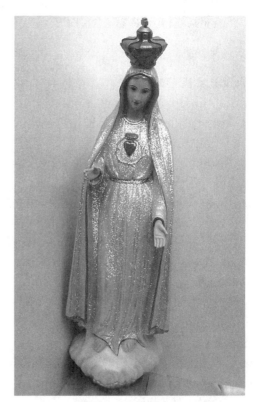

Our Lady of Fátima

pontiff attributed his survival to a direct intervention of Our Lady of Fátima, and in 1984 he formally consecrated Russia to the Immaculate Heart. In 2000, Pope John Paul II beatified Francisco and Jacinta and revealed the third prophecy (or secret) given to the children by Mary. Known until then only to the visionaries and a select few within the Church, it had been the subject of much speculation. The third secret spoke of an assassination attempt on the pope and the collapse of the Soviet Union.

(See also **APPARITION**.)

FÁTIMA WATER

Water from a spring discovered at the Fátima site in 1921.

(See also **SACRAMENTALS**.)

FEAST OF THE CIRCUMCISION — See **CIRCUMCISION, FEAST OF**.

FEAST OF FOOLS

A day set aside annually in the Middle Ages for jokes and pranks among clerics enrolled in the schools and universities.

The custom began in the eleventh century (to curb the clergy from taking part in pre-Christmas reveling) and continued through the eighteenth.

(See also **BOY BISHOP**.)

FEAST OF THE HOLY CROSS — See **CROSS, FEAST OF THE HOLY**.

FEASTS

Technically, one category of liturgical day, namely, of lesser rank than a "solemnity" and of a higher rank than a "memorial."

In popular usage, however, "feast" is applied indiscriminately by the faithful to all liturgical days on which the Church commemorates a mystery of the Lord or Our Lady, or keeps the memory of a saint.

FEASTS OF MARY — See **MARY, FEASTS OF**.

FEAST OF THE SEVEN SORROWS

In the Latin countries, especially in Spain and South America, the Feast of the Seven Sorrows is a great day of popular devotion. The people thronged the churches to visit the shrine of the Sorrowful Mother. This shrine is radiant with many lights and is richly decorated with flowers, palms, and with shade-grown clusters of pale young wheat. In central Europe, the feast is called *Schmerzenfreitag*, Friday of Sorrows, and after the popular devotions in the churches a soup consisting of seven bitter herbs is served in the homes for supper.

FELLOWSHIP OF MERRY CHRISTIANS

An ecumenical group formed in 1986 to promote joy and humor.

Its motto is: "A cheerful heart is a good medicine, but a downcast spirit dries up the bones" (see Proverbs 17:22).

FESTIVAL OF WREATHS

European celebration on the Feast of Corpus Christi.

In parts of central Europe and in France, Corpus Christi Day is the Day of Wreaths. Wreaths and bouquets of flowers in various colors are attached to flags, banners, houses, and arches of greenery that span the streets. The clergy and altar boys wear little wreaths on their arms in the procession, and girls wear wreaths on their heads. In Poland the wreaths are blessed by the priest on the eve of the feast. Later the wreaths are hung in the homes or in the fields with a prayer for blessing on the growing harvests.

FIFTEEN SATURDAYS

A devotion promoted by Dominicans.

It consists of the saying of five decades of the Rosary over the fifteen Saturdays preceding the Feast of Our Lady of the Rosary, going to confession, and receiving Holy Communion.

(See also POMPEII, OUR LADY OF THE ROSARY.)

FIFTEEN TORTURES OF OUR LORD

A devotion to the fifteen tortures based on private revelations of Blessed Mary Magdalen Martinengo (1687-1737), a Poor Clare nun of Rome. The devotion was approved by Pope Clement II.

FINDER OF LOST ITEMS — See ST. ANTHONY OF PADUA.

FIRST FRIDAY

The practice of devoting the first Friday of each month for nine months to the Sacred Heart of Jesus.

Observing the "First Fridays" is based on the private revelations of St. Margaret Mary Alacoque (1647-1690).

(See also SACRED HEART OF JESUS; ST. MARGARET MARY ALACOQUE.)

FIRST HOLY COMMUNION

The reception of the Eucharist for the first time.

Since the pontificate of Pope St. Pius X (r. 1903-1914), the age for receiving First Holy Communion was lowered to seven years. In the Eastern Church, infants receive their First Holy Communion at their baptism and chrismation.

A plenary indulgence is granted to the Christian faithful when they receive their First Holy Communion and also when they devoutly assist at a first communion ceremony.

(See also **EUCHARIST**.)

FIRST MASS OF NEWLY OR-DAINED PRIESTS

A plenary indulgence is granted a priest celebrating his first Mass with a congregation on a scheduled day. The same indulgence is also granted to the faithful who devoutly participate in that Mass.

FIRST SATURDAY

Attendance at Mass and reception of Holy Communion on the first Saturday of the month in reparation for the sins of the world.

The practice is based on messages given to the seers at the apparitions of Our Lady of Fátima.

(See also **FÁTIMA, OUR LADY OF**.)

FIRSTFRUITS

Sacred to Yahweh, the first products of man.

These include animals, fleece, trees, grain, wine, oil, and "whatsoever was sown in the field," by the law of Moses to be offered to the Lord.

FISH

An image used as a symbol for Christ.

The letters from the Greek word for fish, *ichthus,* were used as an abbreviation for "Jesus Christ, Son of God, Savior."

Ichthus

FIVE WOUNDS

The marks on the hands, feet, and side of Christ's body.

These were inflicted during his crucifixion and have been the focus of a special devotion by the faithful since the Middle Ages.

FLAGELLATION

An archaic practice of flailing one's body with rods or a small whip as a form of penance.

The custom flourished in the Middle Ages among religious and the laity, and was not uncommon in religious orders until the 1960s.

FLOS CARMELI

Latin for "Flower of Carmel"; the title of a prayer.

The prayer was written by St. Simon Stock (c. 1165-1265), and in response, tradition holds, he received the scapular from Mary. It reads:

> O Beautiful Flower of Carmel, most fruitful vine, splendor of heaven, holy and singular, who brought forth the Son of God, still ever remaining a pure virgin, assist us in our necessity! O Star of the Sea, help and protect us. Show us that you are our Mother.

(See also **SCAPULAR**.)

FLOWERS

Universal symbols and decorations, used as such within the Church since the early Middle Ages.

There are restrictions on flowers in churches during Lent, except for Laetare Sunday.

Flowers began to be important for their own sake about the sixth or seventh century when the Church ceased condemning them as heathenish and took over their use in ritual and symbolism. At first, the Christian laymen considered flowers in church to be pagan, associating them with the wreathed Romans and their orgies. The monks, however, sought their beauty to decorate the altars, and on feast days flowers were woven into chaplets or wreaths for the priest to wear. Slowly, the monks began to christianize and convert the meanings of flowers, giving them associations with Christ, Our Lady, and the saints. For example, the white of the Madonna lily symbolized the Virgin's purity; the deep red of the rose with its thorny branches signified the blood of Christ.

Monasteries were the pioneers of garden-making. The founders of the monasteries took over from the Romans the idea of schools-in-gardens, yet the oldest Byzantine basilicas had adjoining porticoes called "paradises" that were planted as gardens. These cloister gardens were the first real gardens of the European Middle Ages and were being planted at least as early as the eighth century. Flowers were grown as decorations for the church, and monks improved gardening techniques throughout the Middle Ages. Secular lords soon learned the worth of the garden from the Church, and traveling soldier-noblemen and priests brought ideas from their travels. The ladies became the castle gardeners, and like the monks they included flowers in their plantings. After Charles VII of France invaded Italy in 1495, he

Flowers from Jerusalem

brought home a gardener among his spoils of war; the priest Pasello da Mercogliano began the work of bringing the Italian influence to France. After the reign of Henry VIII, the great men of England patronized the arts, including garden artists. St. Thomas More was an avid gardener. By the mid-sixteenth century, Germany had copied the Italian practice of urban gardens.

The illustrated manuscripts crafted in the monasteries often included flowers in the borders. Tapestries, miniatures, and paintings often were based on floral themes.

As plants became associated with Christian saints and martyrs, they lost their pagan connotations. The rose is a good example. Long associated with Greek and Egyptian gods, the rose was rededicated to the Virgin Mary by the Church Fathers. Holly, sacred to the druids, became a symbol of Christ's sacrifice. As missionaries spread across Europe, they converted plants as well as people, using them as teaching tools. The largely uneducated population could not read, but as farmers they were familiar with the native plants. Those who could not read a calendar could remember that Michaelmas daisies flowered near the time for the Feast of St. Michael. The wood sorrel was nicknamed "alleluia" because it bloomed when the Gospel response was "alleluia" between Easter and Whitsuntide.

Hundreds of Catholic customs worldwide are connected in some way with flowers. From the golden rose of the pope to the humble marigold dedicated to Our Lady, flowers enrich Catholic life in many ways.

FOCOLARE MOVEMENT

An international association of men and women founded in 1943 in Trent, Italy, by Chiara Lubich.

Its purposes include the enhancing of members' spirituality and promoting spiritual good through work and service. *Focolare* is Italian for "hearth."

FORTY HOURS DEVOTION

A period of continuous or semi-continuous adoration before the Eucharist on display in a monstrance.

While the origins of the devotion are uncertain, from the second century it was a widespread custom for people to fast and pray for forty hours from Good Friday afternoon until Easter morning. As practiced today, Forty Hours probably dates back to sixteenth-century Milan, where it was advocated by St. Anthony Zaccaria, St. Philip Neri, and St. Charles Borromeo.

(See also **BENEDICTION**.)

FOUNDATION MASSES

Masses celebrated for the intentions of donors who bequeath an amount of money to an ecclesiastical institution.

FOURTEEN HOLY HELPERS — AUXILIARY SAINTS

A grouping of saints that began in medieval Germany and gained popularity throughout Europe.

Called "Holy Helpers" because they were regarded as being particularly effective against various common diseases and at the hour of death, they each had their own separate feast day as well as sharing a common feast (July 25) until the reform of the liturgical calendar in 1969. Although, at times, the roster varied from place to place, the most common listing was: Sts. Acacius, Barbara, Blaise, Catherine of Alexandria, Christopher, Cyriacus, Denis, Erasmus (or Elmo), Eustace, George, Giles, Margaret, Pantaleon, and Vitus.

FRANCISCAN APOSTOLATE OF THE WAY OF THE CROSS

A ministry established in 1949 for the distribution of religious materials to the sick and homebound.

Its headquarters is in Boston, Massachusetts.

FRANCISCAN CROWN ROSARY

A chaplet.

It is also known as the Rosary of the Seven Joys of the Blessed Virgin Mary and has been associated with the Franciscan Order since the fifteenth century.

Father Luke Wadding, a well-known Franciscan historian, dates the inception of this chaplet to 1422, and a vision of a pious novice. The boy had been accustomed to decorate a statue of the Virgin with crowns of fresh flowers, a practice forbidden to him in the novitiate. In his

Franciscan Crown Rosary

vision, the Virgin taught him a chaplet of prayers. Our Lady requested the young friar to say one Our Father and ten Hail Marys in honor of seven joyous occasions in her life: 1) the annunciation 2) the visitation 3) the birth of Christ 4) the adoration of the Magi 5) the finding of Jesus in the temple 6) the Resurrection of Our Lord and 7) the Assumption of the Virgin into heaven.

While the young friar was devoutly praying, the novice master passed by and saw an angel weaving a wreath of roses. After every tenth rose, he inserted a golden lily. When the wreath was finished, the angel placed it on the head of the praying novice.

Under obedience, the novice explained the vision, and the chaplet spread to the entire order.

Later, two Hail Marys were added to make the total of the Hail Marys equal to seventy-two, the traditional age of Our Lady at her Assumption. A final Hail Mary and Our Father were added for the intention of the pope. In the twentieth century, it became customary to add a profession of faith. Since 1968 the third and fourth mysteries were combined, and the presentation of Jesus in the temple and the purification of the Blessed Virgin are now the meditation for the fourth decade.

(See also **CHAPLET**.)

FRUITS OF THE HOLY SPIRIT

The perfections the Holy Spirit forms in a person as the "first fruits" of eternal glory.

Based on Galatians 5:22-23, they traditionally are: charity, joy, peace, patience, kindness, goodness, generosity, gentleness, faithfulness, modesty, self-control, and chastity.

(See also **GIFTS OF THE HOLY SPIRIT**.)

FUNERAL FEAST

A shared meal following a funeral.

While the custom did not originate within the Church, it has been a common practice among Christians since early times.

As early as the time of St. John Chrysostom, doles of food were made to the poor for thirty days after a funeral.

In the Middle Ages, a feast was always given to the chief mourners to welcome the principal heir. The old name for the funeral feast was *averil*, or *arvel*, which meant "heir ale." In Medieval England, a cup of wine was placed in the coffin next to the corpse. By drinking a taste from this cup, the living felt that they had established a type of communion with the dead.

By the mid-eighteenth century, after the body was committed to the ground, all those who had traveled some distance to attend were feted with a funeral feast. These feasts mixed festivity with gloom. A great deal of strong liquor and copious quantities of food were served. The cost of one funeral feast in 1797 was equivalent to between five and ten thousand dollars in today's purchasing power.

(See also **AGAPE**.)

FUNERAL FLOWERS

An ancient and widespread custom of presenting floral tributes at funerals.

Originally pagan, the custom was adopted by Christians. Through the years, floral tributes of various kinds have been popular in many places. In nineteenth-century America, evergreens were used to cover the exposed dirt at the cemetery before the mourners arrive; fresh flowers were used for a child's burial. In El Salvador, the people *Enflorar a los Ninos* — literally, flower the children — by covering the graves of the children with flowers on November 1.

FUNERAL HERBS

Plants particularly used in funeral ceremonies.

Parsley was known as a funeral plant to the Greeks. It was later consecrated to St. Peter in his role as heavenly gatekeeper. St. Thomas More pointed out that rosemary was the chosen emblem of English funeral wakes and burial grounds. In France, rosemary was carried by mourners at funerals and thrown into the open grave. In England, an elder bush trimmed in the shape of a cross was planted on a new grave. If the bush bloomed, the common folk said the spirit of the deceased was happy. Green branches of the plant were also buried in the grave to protect the occupant from demons. Funeral hearse drivers often carried a whip of elder. Thyme is one of the fragrant flowers planted on graves in Wales. The Order of Oddfellows carried sprigs of thyme at funerals and threw them into the grave of a dead lodge member.

G

GAUDETE SUNDAY

A term formerly referring to the third Sunday of Advent.

It was set apart by the wearing of rose-colored vestments to symbolize particular joy, since Advent was half over and Christmas was near. Under the new norms, it is simply known as the third Sunday in Advent, and rose vestments may now also be worn on the fourth Sunday as well. The rose-colored candle in Advent wreaths is lit on Gaudete Sunday.

GENERAL JUDGMENT — See JUDGMENT, GENERAL.

GENUFLECTION

The act of bending the right knee to the floor and rising back up as an act of reverence before the Blessed Sacrament.

During the Mass, the celebrant genuflects three times: after elevating the host, after elevating the chalice, and before receiving Holy Communion.

GIFT OF TONGUES

One of the many gifts of the Holy Spirit described by St. Luke (see Acts 2:4 and 19:6) and referred to thirty-five times in the New Testament.

This gift (*glossolalia*) enables one to speak so as to be understood (as at Pente-

cost) and also in a manner incomprehensible to the hearers. It is meant to praise God and to communicate the "mind of God" to the listeners.

GIFTS OF THE HOLY SPIRIT

Permanent dispositions that make a person docile to follow the promptings of the Holy Spirit.

The traditional list is derived from Isaiah 11:1-3: wisdom, understanding, counsel, fortitude, knowledge, piety, and fear of the Lord.

(See also FRUITS OF THE HOLY SPIRIT.)

GOD THE FATHER OF MANKIND, DEVOTION TO

Devotion to the First Person of the Trinity based on private revelations to Sister Eugenia Elizabetta Ravasio (1907-1990).

GOLDEN ARROW, THE

A prayer based on private revelations of Carmelite Sister Marie de Saint-Pierre (Perrine Eluere) in Tours, France, in 1843.

She said she called it "The Golden Arrow" because it will "wound" Christ's heart "delightfully." It reads:

May the most holy, most sacred,

most adorable, most mysterious
and unutterable Name of God
be always praised, blessed,
loved, adored, and glorified,
in heaven, on earth, and under the
    earth,
by all the creatures of God,
and by the Sacred Heart of Our Lord
    Jesus Christ
in the most Holy Sacrament of the
    altar.

GOLDEN COUNSELS OF ST. FRANCIS DE SALES

A popular pamphlet based on the writing of St. Francis de Sales (1567-1593).

GOLDEN LEGEND

A highly popular collection of saints' lives compiled by Dominican Bishop James of Voragine (1228-1298).

Originally titled *The Legends of the Saints*, this best-seller of the Middle Ages made a long-standing contribution to the devotional writings on saints.

GOLDEN NIGHTS

A nine-day, pre-Christmas festive season celebrated in central Europe.

Since most of the devotions were held after dark, the faithful began to call this season the "Golden Nights." Carrying the Virgin and *Josephstragen* are popular de-

votions in the Alpine regions. In a number of areas of central Europe a special Rorate Mass was held long before sunrise. The name comes from the first words of its text: *Rorate coeli desuper* — "Dew of Heaven, shed [the Just One]." The faithful carried lanterns through the darkness of the early winter morning. The last of the Golden Nights, December 24, is the feast day of our first parents, Adam and Eve. They are commemorated as saints in the calendars of some of the Eastern Churches. The Latin Church never officially introduced their feast, although it did not prohibit popular veneration of them. In Germany, in the sixteenth century, the custom was begun of putting up a paradise tree in honor of Adam and Eve. This was a fir tree covered with apples which was a forerunner of our modern Christmas tree.

GOLDEN ROSE

A medieval symbol of joy once carried by the pope after Mass on the fourth Sunday of Lent.

The day is known as Laetare Sunday or "Rose" Sunday because rose-colored vestments could be worn on that day.

Originally a natural rose, in the eleventh century it became customary to use one made of gold. Since the fifteenth century, this golden rose consists of a cluster or branch of roses made of pure gold and set with precious stones. The pope sometimes confers it on churches, shrines, cities, or distinguished persons as a token of esteem and paternal affection. If the rose is given away, a new one is made during the next year. The prayer of blessing expresses the symbolism: Christ in the shining splendor of his majesty is the flower sprung from the "stump of Jesse" (see Isaiah 11:1).

(See also **LENT.**)

GOOD COUNSEL, OUR LADY OF

A Marian image and devotion centered in Albania and Italy.

In Albania, the medieval icon is known as Our Lady of Shkodra. Tradition holds that the painting was taken to Italy after an invasion of Albania by Ottoman Turks and later placed in a shrine in Genazzano, Italy. Miracles and favors have been attributed to Our Lady of Good Counsel, the patroness of Albania.

According to pious tradition in Italy, in pre-Christian times a small town thirty miles from Rome was noted as a center for the cult of Venus, the goddess of spring, bloom, and beauty, then later as the goddess of love. After the conversion of Rome, Genazzano became a center for devotion to Our Lady, and about the fourth century a church was built there under the name of St. Mary, Mother of Good Counsel.

In 1356, the church was placed under the care of the Order of St. Augustine. By then the building was in ruins, and it took another century to restore it. These early Augustinian friars lived in near destitution, and a devout widow, Petruccia, sold all her property to begin the restoration on the church. Since there was not enough money to complete the restoration, she began to pray for the rest.

On April 25, 1467, the town was celebrating the feast of its patron, St. Mark, when people noticed a strange cloud slowly moving toward the village. It came to rest on the walls of the half-finished church, and then the people found a striking picture of the Madonna and Child there. They immediately banded together to complete the restoration of the building.

As the residents continued to wonder where the image had come from, two pilgrims from Albania arrived and declared they had been searching for this very picture, which was missing from its customary place in the Albanian town of Scutari. The picture had been a great object of devotion there until the city came under siege by the Ottoman Turks, and thus, the visitors declared, Mary had come to Genazzano.

Careful investigations made between 1957 and 1959 during restoration of the fresco have revealed something of the true origin of the fresco. The image of the Madonna is about a foot wide and seventeen inches high and is now encased in an elaborate glass, metal, and marble framework. It is part of a larger fresco that once covered part of the wall but was later hidden by the baroque shrine altar. Art experts postulate that the fresco may be the work of the early fifteenth-century artist Gentile da Fabriano. It was probably painted about the time of Martin V (r. 1417-1431). At some later date before 1467, the fresco was probably covered over with plaster, and a terra-cotta image of the Madonna was hung on the wall. During the restoration by the friars and the pious widow Petruccia, the image of the Madonna appeared and was seen as a token of divine favor. Possibly when a stone ledge was being inserted into the wall, the plaster covering the image cracked and separated from the wall, revealing the fresco beneath.

One striking aspect of the fresco is that the upper portion of the image is separated from the wall so that much of it is only a thin sheet of plaster. Even so, the image has survived for centuries in such a precarious and fragile state through a number of earthquakes and the bombing of the town during World War II.

The initial approval of devotion to Our Lady under the title of Our Mother of Good Counsel was given by Pope Paul II. Later, other popes ratified this approval, and in 1682 the image was crowned with the approval of Pope Innocent XI.

(See also **SCAPULAR OF OUR LADY OF GOOD COUNSEL**.)

GOOD FRIDAY

The Friday before Easter, second day of the Easter Triduum.

The liturgical elements of Good Friday are the commemoration of the Passion and death of Jesus in the reading of the Passion according to John; special prayers for the Church and people of all ranks; the veneration of the cross; and a Communion service. The celebration takes place in the afternoon, preferably at three o'clock.

Good Friday has been a part of the liturgical observance of the Easter Triduum since the fourth century, and a form of fasting on Good Friday has been observed since that time. Particular ethnic and regional traditions relating to fasting and mourning have developed over the centuries.

Since the liturgical revival after Vatican II, the emphasis of Good Friday is now on Christ's love for the Church, signified by the red vestments of the celebrants, and his triumph over sin and death, rather than on any maudlin expressions of grief and mourning.

In addition to the liturgical services, a number of popular devotions on that day have sprung up in various places. In Spanish-speaking countries, this is the time for the Desolata, when the Christ figure is removed from the crucifix and the people accompany Our Lady in her desolation. In the Latin nations, women dress in black mourning clothes on this day; in Malta the men dress in mourning as well. In the Greek Church, a night vigil is held from the night of Holy Thursday to the morning of Good Friday. This was called the Royal Hours, because the East Roman emperors used to attend the service in the cathedral of Constantinople. The Ukrainians celebrated the Royal Hours on Good Friday morning. The moving Adoration of the Cross is held on this day. One of the most ancient and impressive of the extra-liturgical rites is held at the shrine of the Holy Sepulcher. The tradition was brought from Jerusalem to Europe and spread through many countries. The crucifix, or in some cases the Blessed Sacrament, was borne in solemn procession to a shrine called the Sepulcher and the faith-

Preparing for a Good Friday Procession

ful visited the shrine all through Good Friday and Holy Saturday. This is actually a form of spiritual "wake" of devotion and adoration. In Austria it was the custom for soldiers in full uniform to man a guard of honor at the shrine in atonement for the irreverent guard of Roman soldiers at the tomb of Christ. In the Byzantine Church, the elders of the parish carried a cloth containing a pic-

Carrying a Statue of Mary During a Good Friday Procession

ture of Our Lord resting in death. Followed by the priest, they processed to the shrine of the Sepulcher where the cloth was placed on a table to be venerated by the people. In Russia, a silver coffin bearing a cross was placed in the center of the church and the faithful crept on their knees to kiss the cross and to venerate the image of Christ's body painted on the "winding sheet." Another popular Good Friday service is the Devotion of the Three Hours, a Jesuit devotion from Peru which consists of sermons on the seven last words of Christ and which has spread to many Protestant churches in recent years. In the Latin countries public processions were held as they were in many countries of Europe up until the nineteenth century. In many regions, especially in Spain, the confraternities of lay people wear hoods and carry lighted candles as they walk through the streets in these religious parades. Images of the suffering Christ and the Blessed Virgin are carried in pageants of great splendor. In Malta, the bearers wear oriental robes and go barefoot. The annual *Semana Santa* observance in Mexico City takes the form of a funeral procession where there is a touching scene in which the Mother of the Lord meets the lifeless body of her Son. In India, the Catholics accompany the funeral of Christ which is met outside the church by a statue of the Sorrowful Virgin. Inside the church the people perform the *purana*, a service of wailing and hymns sung to the ancient plaintive tunes. In most countries this day is kept as a day of strict fast, and in many places the people go beyond the liturgical regulations. The Irish held a "black fast" which usually meant that they took only water or tea on that day. In central Europe the people ate only vegetable soup and bread at noon and cheese and bread in the evening, taking both meals standing and in silence. In England, plain rice cooked in milk was once the traditional Good Friday meal, although, of course, the popular hot cross buns were also a feature of the day.

(See also **ABSTINENCE; CROSS; FASTING; HOLY WEEK; TRIDUUM.**)

GOOD REMEDY, OUR LADY OF

A Marian title promoted by St. John of Matha (1160-1213), founder of the Order of the Most Holy Trinity.

The Trinitarians raised large amounts of money to buy Christian slaves being sold by Muslims, and the order credited its success to Mary's intervention. Images of Our Lady of Good Remedy sometimes show Mary handing a bag of money to St. John. The order has recently revived its original charism in light of the widespread practice of enslaving Christians in some Muslim countries.

The Good Shepherd

GOOD SHEPHERD, THE

A title of Christ dating back to the early Church based on John 10:11: "I am the good shepherd. The good shepherd lays down his life for the sheep."

The figure of Jesus as Good Shepherd was one of the favorites from the earliest Christian centuries. Some of the earliest artistic representations of him in the catacombs show him with his sheep.

GOOD THIEF, THE — See ST. DIS-MAS.

GORZKIE ZALE

A traditional Polish Lenten devotion.

Meaning "bitter sorrows," it consists of hymns, chanted lamentations, and meditations on Our Lord's Passion.

GRACE AT MEALS

A custom of praying before eating.

The term *grace* comes from the Latin word for "thanks." The tradition goes back to apostolic times. A commonly used grace before meals reads:

> Bless us, O Lord, and these your gifts which we are about to receive from your bounty through Christ Our Lord. Amen.

An equally common grace after meals is:

We give you thanks, Almighty God, for these and all your benefits, who live and reign forever. And may the souls of all the faithful departed rest in peace. Amen.

GRACE, OUR LADY OF

A Marian title based on the picture found in 1610 by Venerable Dominic of Jesus and Mary, a Spanish Discalced Carmelite.

Our Lady of Grace

The portrait shows the Madonna wearing a full veil, a blue mantle decorated on the right shoulder with a rosette-backed star, and a red gown. A jeweled crown and a necklace were added later. Because the head tilts slightly to the left, the image is sometimes called "Our Lady of the Bowed Head." It has been enshrined in Vienna ever since the seventeenth century and is now in the Carmelites' Church of the Holy Family. Miracles have been attributed to the intercession of Our Lady of Grace.

GRAFFITI

Writing on the walls of the Roman catacombs dating back to the first centuries of the Church.

The inscriptions were written as memorials to, and prayers for, the martyrs and other Christians buried there.

Usually, the graffiti consist of the names of persons, accompanied by a wish for salvation in the next world. The graffiti soon took on the form of cryptographic writing, where the early Christians could secretly express their feelings and the highest ideas of the faith in a brief and effective form during times of persecution. Many of the Christian symbols we are so familiar with today had special meaning for these early, persecuted members of the Church.

Front and Back Views of the Green Scapular

GREEN SCAPULAR (IMMACULATE HEART)

A sacramental.

The green scapular is not the habit of any confraternity and is not properly a scapular because it does not have a front and back part but only two pious images attached to a single piece of green cloth that hangs on a single string of the same color. One side features an image of Mary, the other her Immaculate Heart. Its use is based on the private revelations of Daughter of Charity Sister Justine Bisqueyburu in the nineteenth century.

(See also **REVELATION; SACRA-MENTALS; SCAPULAR.**)

GREEN THURSDAY

A term used in central Europe for Holy Thursday.

It is based on the tradition of people eating green-colored (i.e., meatless) food that day.

GREGORIAN CHANT

An ancient form of sung prayer.

Also known as Gregorian music, plain-chant, or plainsong, it has more individuality and characteristic expression than other early chants such as the Ambrosian.

Its name refers incorrectly to Pope St. Gregory the Great (r. 590-604), who, at one time, was thought to have created it. Gregorian chant uses the conventional diatonic scale of eight tones, or notes, to an octave.

GREGORIAN MASSES (TRENTAL OF ST. GREGORY)

The custom of saying thirty Masses in the course of a year for a recently deceased person.

The practice was particularly popular during the Middle Ages and was attributed to a legend associated with Pope St. Gregory the Great (r. 590-604), who celebrated that number of Masses for his mother after he had a vision.

GREGORIAN WATER

A mixture of water, ash, salt, and wine.

Based on a prescription of Pope St. Gregory the Great (r. 590-604), it is blessed by the bishop at the consecration of a church and is used for sprinkling parts of the building.

(See also DEDICATION OF A CHURCH; WATER, HOLY.)

GROTTOES OF ST. JAMES

Small grottoes (man-made representations of caves) constructed of scallop shells used to raise money for pilgrimages to St. James's shrine in Compostela, Spain.

Patrons would make a small donation, light a candle in the grotto, and say a prayer for the pilgrim.

GRUTA (GROTTO)

A small yard or roadside shrine in northern Mexico and the southwestern United States.

In Mexico, these shrines are known as *traileros*, and across the border to the north they are called *grutas*. They are usually erected in the yards of family homes. Unlike the *descanos*, which mark the site of a death, the *traileros* and *grutas* are usually erected to fulfill a *manda* (vow) or a

Grotto

promesa (promise) of the maker, made to repay a favor done through the intercession of a favorite saint. Worldwide, outdoor religious shrines that use a rocky or cave-like background are known as grottoes.

GUADALUPE, OUR LADY OF

A Marian image and devotion based on the apparitions seen by St. Juan Diego at Tepeyac, near Mexico City, in 1531.

The Indian narrative is simple. Juan Diego, about fifty-seven years old, a humble peasant, and a recent convert to the Catholic faith, was on his way to Saturday Mass, "very early in the morning," and to catechism lessons. It was December 9, 1531, at that time the Feast of the Immaculate Conception. Lovely music attracted his attention to the foot of the rocky and barren hill of Tepeyac. A woman's voice called to him affectionately by name. "Juanito, Juan Dieguito." The Lady told him she was the "ever Virgin Mary, Mother of the true God." Then she designated the spot for a church built for the people, where "I will hear their weeping, their complaints, and heal all their sorrows, hardships, and sufferings." She told Juan Diego to be her messenger to the recently arrived bishop-elect from Spain, Fray Juan de Zumarraga, a holy and zealous Franciscan. Zumarraga had a great de-

Our Lady of Guadalupe

votion to Mary and had entrusted the New Spain to her.

Juan Diego set out at once for the bishop's house. After much delay, he was allowed to see the bishop who feared the story was just a dream of the new convert. After a second appearance, Juan again approached the bishop who asked for a special sign to prove the story. For a third time the Lady appeared and promised to give him the sign for the bishop the next day. But that day Juan spent looking for a doctor to attend to his very sick uncle, Juan Bernardino, also a recent convert, and Juan Diego did not keep his appointment with the Lady.

The doctor's efforts did not help his uncle, so very early the next day Juan Diego left to call a priest for his dying uncle. He tried to avoid running into the Lady by taking another route, but she appeared anyway. In this fourth apparition, she assured him he must have no fear for his uncle's health, for she was the merciful Mother of all. "Am I not here, I who am your Mother? Are you not under my care? Do I not hold you as a dear child in the folds of my garments? Am I not your hope and salvation? Is there anything more you need?"

The Lady directed Juan to go to the top of the barren hill of Tepeyac where he found and gathered fresh Castilian roses which he carried to her in his *tilma*, or cloak. She arranged the roses and tied his cloak at the shoulders, instructing him to open it only in the presence of the bishop. Roses were out of season in December, and nothing else grew on the barren hill, so Juan believed this would be the sign the bishop had requested.

Again, after more delays and difficulties, Juan was allowed to see the bishop. He told the bishop he had the requested sign and opened his *tilma*. As the roses spilled to the floor, the bishop fell to his knees, praying with tear-filled eyes. The others in the room also fell to their knees. An image of Mary had appeared miraculously on the humble mestizo's *tilma*.

Immediately, the image was enthroned in the bishop's chapel until a church could be built. To the end of his life, at age seventy-four in 1548, Juan Diego was the guardian of the *tilma*, explaining the story over and over again of the merciful Mother who wished to lead all peoples to her Divine Son.

Although made of natural fibers that normally would have rotted in about twenty years, the *tilma* is still in a remarkable state of preservation after more than four hundred years and is enshrined at the basilica in her honor near Mexico City. Various scientific studies have been done on the *tilma*, and modern science continues to reveal much about the picture.

Her present sanctuary in Mexico, the new basilica blessed on October 12, 1976, is ranked second only to St. John Lateran in Rome, the pope's cathedral.

At the time of the apparitions, Our Lady also appeared to Juan Diego's uncle, Juan Bernardino, curing him and giving her name as "Holy Mary, ever Virgin of Guadalupe." She spoke in the native Indian language, and the name means "She who crushes the stone serpent." To Spanish ears, the name sounded like Guadalupe, the name of one of the favorite images of Our Lady in Spain. The primary god of the pagan religion of the area was a stone serpent; the religion practiced human sacrifice. At the time of the apparition, the Indian people were on the verge of revolt. The Mother of the true God reconciled and united peoples and cultures, and through this miraculous image the Catholic faith took hold. Mary of Guadalupe is the greatest evangelizer of all time. No one else has ever brought so many millions to the Catholic faith in so short a time.

In the image, Mary is depicted as a young *mestiza* maiden, one who is of both Native American and European background. Thus, she is often called *La Morenita*, "The Little Brown One." She is pictured as a pregnant woman, about age fifteen. The image is recognized as a version of the Immaculate Conception. Under this title she is also invoked as Help of the Sick.

At Tepeyac, there are no new devotions, no special instructions, no warnings. Here there is only the pure and simple love of a mother; she appeals to those who have a simple faith in God and a strong love for his mother. Pope Pius XII declared Our Lady of Guadalupe patroness of all the Americas, and her celebration on December 12 was raised to the rank of feast for all countries of the Americas in 1999.

GUARD OF HONOR OF THE IMMACULATE HEART OF MARY

A worldwide confraternity.

It was begun by Franciscan Father Bonaventure Blattmann in Germany, in 1932, to promote devotion to Mary, particularly through the daily prayers of members.

(See also **CONFRATERNITY**.)

GUARDIAN ANGELS — See ANGELS.

GUILD — See **CONFRATERNITY**.

Guardian Angel

H

HABIT

The traditional, distinctive garb worn by some religious orders.

The majority of habits stem from the type and style of the clothing worn by common people at the time of the founding of the order. Colors vary; most habits are black, brown, blue, gray, white or a combination. A few orders use red, purple, light blue, or rose. In many cases, the habit consists of a tunic with a girdle or belt and a scapular. Cloaks may be worn outdoors. Male religious often have a hood; traditionally, women religious had a variety of headdresses. Since Vatican Council II, many of the orders have chosen to modify or discard their traditional habits.

During the Middle Ages, it was a common devotional practice for laypeople to request to be buried in the habit of whichever religious order they felt spiritually drawn to. They first took religious vows in that order on their deathbed.

HAGIA

The name of the Consecrated Species in the Byzantine liturgy, from the Greek for "holy things."

HAHILKY AND VESNYANKY

Ukrainian customs of the blessing of Easter baskets and the performance of children's circle dances outside the church.

At one time it was believed that ritual spring dances and games served a magical function by enticing the spring and chasing the winter away. The day is also enhanced by the singing of the *Vesnyanky,* songs dedicated to spring.

HAIL HOLY QUEEN

A Marian hymn dating back to the eleventh century and attributed to Notker Balbulus.

The *Hail Holy Queen* is often recited during the Liturgy of the Hours at the end of Compline (night prayer) and in public celebrations of Vespers (evening prayer) and at the end of the Rosary. In Latin, its title is *Salve Regina*.

It reads:

Hail, Holy Queen, Mother of mercy, our life, our sweetness, and our hope. To you do we cry, poor banished children of Eve. To you do we send up our sighs, mourning and weeping in this valley of tears. Turn then, most gracious advocate, your eyes of mercy toward us, and after this our exile show unto us the blessed fruit of your womb, Jesus. O clement, O loving, O sweet Virgin Mary.

Pray for us, O Holy Mother of God.

That we may be made worthy of the promises of Christ. Amen.

HAIL MARY — See AVE MARIA.

HAIL MARY OF OUR SORROWFUL MOTHER

A prayer attributed to St. Bonaventure (d. 1274) used in the novena to Our Sorrowful Mother, a Servite devotion.

It reads:

> Hail! Mary, full of sorrows, the Crucified is with you; tearful are you among women, and tearful is the fruit of your womb, Jesus. Holy Mary, mother of the Crucified, give tears to us, crucifiers of your Son, now, and at the hour of our death. Amen.

HAIR SHIRT

A shirt or girdle of rough cloth, often made from goat's hair, worn by early Christians as a form of penance.

In the Middle Ages, the practice was common among members of religious orders and not unusual among the laity.

HAL, OUR LADY OF

A Marian statue originally owned by St. Elizabeth of Hungary (1207-1231).

The statue was passed down to several members of the royal family until Princess Alice of Holland gave it to the church in Hal, Belgium, in 1267. Made of dark wood, the statue is dressed in queenly robes, and she and her infant Son have been given papal crowns. The shrine that houses the statue became a favorite place of pilgrimage in the late thirteenth century. Miracles have been attributed to the intercession of Our Lady of Hal.

HALLOWEEN

A traditional secular celebration dating back to pre-Christian Celtic autumn observances, customs, and superstitions.

Its name is derived from the day on which it is celebrated: October 31 or All Hallows' Eve (Vigil of All Saints' Day).

HALO

A device in Christian iconography of a circle of gold or light around the head of Christ, a saint, or an angel.

It represents the holiness or light of grace in a saint. The halo is distinct from the aureole and the nimbus.

HAND OF GOD

An image used as a symbol of God's creative power, protection, and possession.

It is usually pictured emerging from a cloud.

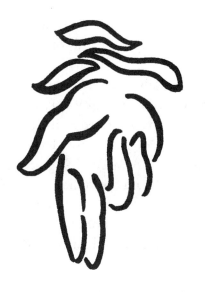

Hand of God

HARMONY, BIBLICAL

An attempt at integrating the four Gospels in such a way that a single narrative is produced, with the verses of all four Gospels arranged in chronological order.

In recognition of the distinctive theological perspectives and characteristics peculiar to each of the evangelists, most biblicists today reject the attempt at a biblical harmony, which otherwise imposes an artificial reordering of the biblical texts at odds with the original intentions of the inspired writers.

HARROWING OF HELL

An archaic phrase that referred to Christ's "descent into hell" following his death.

A popular medieval theme, it stressed his releasing the souls of the just who had waited for their salvation.

HEARING OF THE CHILDREN

A popular Sunday custom in many European countries.

At a Sunday meal following Mass, parents listened as the children repeated what the priest had said during his homily and announcements. The mother usually provided any corrections or explanations, ensuring that the children had both paid attention and understood the message.

HEARSE

A metal or wooden framework placed over the bier or coffin at funeral services. Also, a hearse is any receptacle in which the coffin is placed for transportation.

In addition, it is a type of candelabrum used since the seventh century for the Holy Week service of Tenebrae during which the candles are extinguished ceremonially, one by one. This hearse is a triangular candlestick on which, historically, there have been from seven to twenty-four candles of unbleached wax. The usual number now, where Tenebrae has been revived (as it fell into disuse after Vatican Council II), is fifteen. The triangle itself represents the Blessed Trinity. The highest candle represents Christ, and the rest of the candles represent the twelve Apostles.

227

HEART OF JESUS — See **SACRED HEART OF JESUS**.

HEART OF MARY — See **IMMACULATE HEART OF MARY**.

HELP OF CHRISTIANS, OUR LADY

An ancient Marian devotion.

More than a thousand Byzantine texts of early times refer to Mary as "Empress Helper." An inscription found among the ruins of basilicas in fifth-century Africa reads: "Holy Mary, help us." By the tenth century, the Greek liturgy had a special patronage of Mary asking for her help as God gave to Mary "the office of protecting the Christian people." The title "Mary Help of Christians" has been found in the various forms of the Litany of Loreto from the sixteenth century. Victories attributed to the intercession of Our Lady at the Battle of Lepanto in 1571 and again at the Battle of Vienna in 1683 popularized the title "Help of Christians."

A picture of Our Lady painted in the mid-1500s was enshrined in a public shrine built in 1624 in honor of Mary Help of Christians in Passau, Bavaria. Pilgrims to this shrine prayed the short prayer, "Maria, hilf." In 1627, Pope Urban VIII approved a confraternity of Mary Help of Christians of Passau.

This title became historically entwined with the titles "Our Lady of Victory" and "Our Lady of the Rosary."

In the early 1800s, Napoleon Bonaparte imprisoned Pope Pius VII. From his prison, the pope organized an intense Rosary campaign of prayer to Mary, Help of Christians. As a sign of gratitude for Mary's help, on the abdication of Napoleon and the release of the pope, Pius VII instituted the Feast of Our Lady, Help of Christians to be celebrated on May 24 of every year.

Our Lady Help of Christians

The Salesians, since the time of St. John Bosco (d. 1888), have invoked Our Lady under this particular title as the patroness of their congregation. Our Lady Help of Christians is the patroness of Australia.

(See also **POMPEII, OUR LADY OF THE ROSARY OF.**)

HEORTOLOGY

The study of the origin, significance, and development of the Church's feasts.

HERBAL LORE IN CHRISTIAN TRADITION

Medieval traditions about plants and herbs.

During the chaotic Dark Ages, the Christian Church grew steadily. By the fourth century, monasteries were founded and became storehouses of learning. Throughout the Middle Ages, the monks preserved the knowledge of plants and herbal lore. Each monastery had several gardens. Vegetables, fruits, herbs, and flowers were grown. At first, Christian laymen considered flowers to be pagan, associating them with the wreathed Romans and their orgies. The monks, however, used them to decorate the altars and to make wreaths which priests wore on feast days. The monks "Christianized" the flowers and herbs, associating them with Christ, Our Lady, and the saints. Many popular legends became associated with plants familiar to today's gardeners. Legend tells that St. Helen found the true cross in a patch of basil. The ancient plant flax was used to make the linen of the shroud of Our Lord. Garlic was a protection against plague, and legend holds that it grew at Calvary. Lavender represented the Virgin's purity and virtue and was burned on St. John's Eve to drive away evil spirits. On St. Luke's Day, single women anointed themselves with a marjoram mixture and prayed to St. Luke to dream of their future husband. A good growth of parsley on a grave meant the soul of the person there was at rest. The legend of rosemary says it sheltered the Virgin on her flight to Egypt. She dried her cloak on the plant, imparting the blue color to the flowers. Spearmint was dedicated to the Virgin and was called *Erba Santa Maria* or "Menthe de Notre Dame." Legend holds that the Virgin accompanies children when they pick strawberries on St. John's Day. Thyme, by ancient tradition, was one of the herbs that formed the bed of the Virgin. It was a symbol of courage and energy to the knights of the Crusades. Roses and lilies are associated with the Virgin. The red rose with its thorns symbolized the crucifixion. Wood sorrel (oxalis) was nicknamed "alleluia" because it bloomed after Easter when the Gospel response was alleluia. Hundreds of other legends were associated with plants and herbs during this time.

HERBERGSUCHEN

A German Advent play titled "Search for an Inn."

The entire performance is generally sung and is often followed by a tableau at the end showing the cave with the Nativity scene. There are many different versions of the play that is similar to the Spanish custom of the *Posadas*.

HERBS, HOLY

A Christian use and orientation of the ancient practice of using herbs for medicinal purposes.

The custom was enhanced by medieval monastic communities that both preserved and applied early Greek and Roman knowledge of the medicinal use of plants. Common recommended practices (prescriptions) were written in books called "herbals." In the twelfth century, the German abbess Hildegard of Bingen wrote the *Book of Healing Herbs*, which described a wide range of plants and their uses. Called the "Sybil of the Rhine" for her powers as seeress and prophetess, this flamboyant Benedictine was one of the most remarkable women of the middle ages. A book on ailments of the human body was also among her prolific writings. As many plants became associated with Christian saints and martyrs, and so lost previous pagan symbolism, Christian missionaries used them as teaching aids.

Although many of today's botanicals were known and used by our pre-Christian ancestors, it was the Church that preserved much Greek and Latin herbal knowledge when scholars in monasteries transcribed ancient documents. In the gardens of these same monasteries, this knowledge was used and given a Christian orientation. The treatment of human illness became an extension of Church teaching, and Christian healers followed the example of St. Basil, Bishop of Caesarea, in proving care and shelter for the sick, for lepers, and for travelers.

In the eighth century, Charlemagne, King of the Franks and the First Holy Roman Emperor, designated a group of useful plants to be grown in his domain. In the ninth century, the patriarch of Jerusalem sent prescriptions from the East to Alfred the Great, King of the West Saxons. These cures were written in books called herbals.

During the middle ages, many plants became associated with Christian saints and martyrs, thus losing their pagan connotations. The rose is a good example of this. Long associated with Greek and Egyptian divinities, it was rededicated by the Church fathers to the Virgin Mary. Holly, sacred to the druids, became a symbol of Christ's sacrifice. The spiny leaves recalled the crown of thorns and the red berries became symbolic of his blood.

As Christian missionaries spread across

Europe, they converted plants as well as people, often using the plants as teaching tools. The largely uneducated population could not read, but, as farmers, were familiar with the native plants which missionaries used to teach Christian lessons. One famous example of this practice was St. Patrick's use of the shamrock as a symbol of the Holy Trinity. Plants were sometimes even used as calendars. Those who could not read a calendar could remember that Michaelmas daisies flowered near time for the Feast of St. Michael. The wood sorrel was nicknamed "alleluia" because it bloomed when the Gospel response was alleluia, between Easter and Whitsuntide. St. John's wort received its name because it bloomed near the Feast of St. John the Baptist. Dedicated to the saint, the Christians continued to hang the plant in doorways to repel evil spirits, just as they did in previous, pagan times. The priests and monks collected the newly "holy" herb to use in casting out devils. Even after the advent of modern, laboratory-manufactured pharmaceuticals, botanical medicines and folk healers remained popular among the common people and in recent years have resurged in popularity.

European immigrants took their folk medicine to America, where it blended with that practiced by native Americans for centuries. In rural areas of the Ozark and Appalachian mountains, many people traditionally use botanicals as home remedies. The *curanderos* and native American medicine men of the American Southwest do a brisk business in herbal remedies even today. Some famous *curanderos*, notably Don Pedrito Jaramillo and Nino Fidencia, have been acclaimed as folk saints by the people who believe it is only a matter of time before the Church canonizes them. Medical science has proved that there is some truth to many "old wives' tales" of herbal folk medicine. The useful properties of plants such as aloe vera, garlic, mint, and peppers, for example, have been known and used for centuries. Today's scientists have analyzed the chemicals in these plants to explain how and why they work.

HERMIT

A person who lives alone apart from society in order to devote himself or herself to prayer and the interior life.

After martyrdom ceased to be the usual way to manifest holiness, following the persecutions of the third and fourth centuries, the practice of eremitical life became the new way of expressing total commitment to God and the spiritual life.

HEROIC ACT OF CHARITY

The complete and unselfish offering to God of one's good works and merits for the benefit of the souls in purgatory rather than for oneself.

Through a heroic act of charity, a person may offer to God for the souls in purgatory all the good works he performs during his life, all the indulgences he gains, and all the prayers and indulgences that will be offered for him after his death. The act is revocable at will and is not a vow. Its actual ratification depends on the will of God.

HEROIC VIRTUE

The exemplary practice of the four cardinal virtues (prudence, justice, temperance, and fortitude) and the three theological virtues (faith, hope, and charity) over an extended period of time out of just and worthy service.

Proof of the practice of heroic virtue on the part of a Servant of God is considered a crucial part of the canonization process.

HESPERINOS

The evening prayer in the Byzantine Rite.

HESYCHASM

A form of Eastern spirituality that emphasizes prayer and contemplation as a means to interior peace.

In part, the interior peace was to be achieved by renouncing the world and its distractions, so the life of a solitary is an ideal. The hesychast also renounces his own will and pledges obedience to a spiritual teacher, achieving union with God both through his tranquillity and through the constant repetition of a simple prayer that enables him to drive other thoughts away and turn his mind solely to God. In the Christian tradition, one such prayer became known as the "Jesus Prayer." In its earliest appearance, *hesychast* is synonymous with "hermit" or "anchorite."

(See also **JESUS PRAYER**.)

HESYCHASTS

Name often applied to Orthodox monks who dedicate themselves to contemplation.

HILL OF CROSSES

A site in Siauliai, Lithuania, on which pilgrims place handmade crosses symbolic of the tribulations that country has faced and the hope for an end to them.

Pope John Paul II visited the hill in 1993 and placed a cross there.

HOLINESS

The state of being spiritually in conformity with God's will.

Regarding material things, holiness means their consecration or dedication to the service of God. In terms of persons, holiness refers to a degree of union with God through sanctifying grace and the performance of morally good acts.

HOLLY

A plant given Christian symbolic interpretation.

The red berries are said to be reminders of Moses' burning bush and the flaming love for God in Mary's heart. The berries and prickly points on the leaves call to mind Jesus' crown of thorns and drops of the Precious Blood. In former times in England, the appearance of holly in the home signaled the beginning of the festive season; today, it has become a universal symbol for Christmas. In medieval times, superstition endowed the holly with a special power against witchcraft. Unmarried women fastened a sprig to their beds at Christmas to guard them from being turned into witches by the Evil One. In Germany, to guard against lightning, the people brought home the branches of holly that had been used in church. Other superstitions held that the holly brought good luck to men (as the ivy did to women), hence holly was referred to as "he" and ivy as "she."

HOLY CARDS

Hand-size printed religious images, typically of Christ, Mary, an angel, or a saint.

The cards are used as a devotion, usually slipped in a prayer book and often distributed to children during catechism or given on the occasion of certain religious ceremonies.

The history of holy cards is linked with the history of paper and printing itself. The very first holy cards were made by hand, in imitation of miniatures, illuminated manuscripts, book illustrations, stained-glass windows, and paintings. The

Various Holy Cards

prints or cards served as religious texts for the almost illiterate public. The first holy cards were xylographs, or woodcuts, created initially in monasteries, on paper or parchment. The earliest dated European wood-block print is a picture of St. Christopher, printed in 1423. By 1550, production from the monasteries decreased and holy picture making passed progressively to engravers and print-sellers. Antwerp became the world center for picture-engravers. The Jesuits encouraged their distribution as a means to counteract Protestantism. Jesuit missionaries also used the holy cards to catechize the people in mission lands.

As print technology developed, the pious activity of creating handmade devotional cards — in France known as *dévotes dentelles*, and in German lands, *Andachtsbilden* — was exceptionally popular from the fourteenth to eighteenth century. The cards were carefully hand-cut with a pen-knife from parchment paper and decorated in the center with a miniature of a male or female saint. Only a few well-preserved specimens of cutouts are found today. These cards were the likely forerunners of greeting cards and present-day holy cards, and they became popular as gifts and remembrances of special events.

By the seventeenth century, Augsburg, Munich, Lyons, Nuremberg, Vienna, and Prague had joined Antwerp to become centers of religious engravers, publishers, and sellers of religious holy cards, and continued to be so up to the nineteenth century. Holy cards from the seventeenth and eighteenth centuries are works of art comparable to the engravings of the great artists of that period; many are currently found in European museums.

The history of modern religious cards dates back to the work of a German map inspector named Aloys Senefelder (1771-1834), the inventor of the printing process known as lithography. In 1796, he discovered a method of marking with wax on stone that he called chemical printing. The German's process, a versatile and inexpensive means of multiplying drawings, rapidly gained popularity in Europe. Within twenty-five years, European printers were producing floods of lithographed devotional prints, and industrialization brought a radical increase in the quality of prints available to worldwide markets. By 1825, the new technology was being used successfully in the United States. By the 1840s, the reproductive color process known as "chromolithography," also a Senefelder invention, was in wide use.

With the invention of lithography, the art of the cutout holy card disappeared in 1820. Instead, they were made by industrial processes. Whole picture were made of die-cut lace; they were found in Prague and in Paris in the first third of the nineteenth century. Later, just the edging would be perforated and, in the nineteenth century some of the finest lace cards had swirling cuts reaching deep into the card and surrounding the image. Notable publishers of the finer die-cut lace cards are Bouassee Lebel and L. Turgis of Paris, France; Benziger of Einsiedeln, Switzerland, and Verlag von Carl Mayer and Verlag von Serz both of Nurnberg, Germany.

As early as the 1840s, a good deal of Catholic religious material was generated by French companies in Paris in the area of rue Saint-Jaques and the Church of St. Sulpice. In 1862 there were at least 120 firms that made and marketed mass-produced religious goods, including holy cards, much of which was sold in America. The design style of this time, characterized by soft, feminine-looking images, came to be known as l'art St. Sulpice.

Catholics commonly exchanged holy cards as gestures of affection. Some bought fancy lace cards and tied medals on them; other cards were hand-decorated with flowers and designs. Small pictures of Christ and the saints were assembled on velvet. These intimate gifts were exchanged between Catholic women, nuns, and children as signs of mutual friendship.

To increase sales in America, some European printers set up branches in the United States. Carl Benziger and Sons, in operation since 1792 in Switzerland, opened in Cincinnati as early as 1838. Later known as Benziger Brothers, the company became the most important

Catholic publishing house in the United States, with branches in a number of cities. Local competitors exploited the lucrative print market by setting up their own shops where European compositions were often pirated or adapted.

Records exist of how and when holy cards were used in the lives of some famous saints of the nineteenth century. St. John Neumann (1811-1860) distributed holy cards to children who, in their old age, cherished their cards as relics. St. Anthony Maria Claret distributed more than 83,500 holy cards as he evangelized the Caribbean. Mementos of St. Thérèse of Lisieux's life from 1873 to 1897 include numerous holy cards that she received from family members.

Early Catholic holy cards were most commonly used to commemorate funerals. The cards with somber black borders and black-and-white lithographs of crucifixion, crosses, and other images were common at the turn of the century. Funerals are still the prime occasion for the distribution of holy cards.

Religious subjects were represented as well in the "scrap" and die-cut lace style in the Victorian era. Pasting commercially-printed die-cut scrap into scrapbooks was a popular pastime of the late 1800s. Another Victorian innovation was the mechanical folding and stand-up holy card.

In the steps toward sainthood, holy men and women are first declared venerable, then blessed, before they are canonized. Holy cards with an image and biography of the saint-to-be are usually published by those advancing a canonization cause, in efforts to solicit reports of favors and miracles achieved through the intercession of the potential saint. These are often produced with small cloth relics mounted onto the cards.

In 1935, the influential religious art journal *L'Art Sacre* was founded by Dominican Marie-Alain Couturier. Modern liturgical art or *l'art sacre* was represented by simpler, often abstract and masculine-looking images in contrast to the much more ornamented, stereotyped images of the *l'art St. Sulpice*. This trend in Catholic art was reflected in the images of holy cards as well. One example of the *l'art sacre* style is the work of Ade Bethune, whose woodcut-looking art was popularized in the *Catholic Worker Magazine*. Bethune's series of saints illustrations are still popular today.

From the 1930s through 1950s, devotions to Mary and the saints swelled in popularity, and there was an increased production and distribution of holy cards which became a staple presentation token in parochial schools.

A German nun, Sister Mary Innocentia Hummel, produced more than 600 drawings of cherub-like figures of children while living at the Seissen Convent before and during World War II. Some of these were published as holy cards in the Netherlands in the 1940s and 1950s.

Publishers began to trim cards with gold borders during the 1950s and '60s. In the years after the Second Vatican Council (1962-65), calligraphic quotations from Scripture and symbols such as the fish and *chi rho* were offered in place of the more old-fashioned images.

Though holy cards have been collected in Europe for centuries, paper collectibles, known as ephemera, only became popular in America in the 1970s and '80s. Possibly the largest collection of holy cards worldwide is contained in the Liturgy and Life Collection at the Burns Library of Rare Books and Special Collections at Boston College. The collection includes some 100,000 Mass cards, posters, programs, leaflets, and holy pictures.

Catholic archivists and genealogists view religious paper, such as holy cards, as a very under-explored genre of heritage material. Today, holy cards are experiencing a revival. The new cards are often encased in or printed on plastic, although paper versions are still available. In order to appeal to today's children, publishers have begun to print holy cards in a collectible trading-card format. "Superhero art" might be used to characterize artistic styles for much of the recent religious trading-card art of the 1990s.

Card collectors are making use of modern technology, and using the Internet to locate and purchase items for their collections. Various Catholic Internet web sites allow computer users to send electronic holy cards. An image is selected along with a verse and then sent via e-mail to a friend anywhere in the world.

HOLY CHILD JESUS

The devotion to Christ as a child.

The Holy Child is seen as a model from which the Christian can learn greater childlike love of God the Father.

HOLY CHILD OF ARACOELI — See ARACOELI, HOLY CHILD OF.

HOLY CHILD OF THE DOVES

The title of a statue and devotion in Mexico, begun and promoted by Carmelite Father Clemente of St. Joseph (1879-1974).

The statue was a gift to the priest and features the Child Jesus holding two doves. The devotion was approved by the Archbishop of Mexico in 1944, and in 1945 the image was placed on a special altar in the Church of Our Lady of Carmel, where the Carmelites began their apostolic labors on the American continent in 1585.

In gratitude for a cure, a replica of the original was made for a private family in Zacatecas. This image has a third dove near

Holy Child of the Doves

his left foot. A beautiful work of art, the little image of Jesus seems to radiate peace and faith.

From the small family oratory, the devotion began to spread, and many favors were reported. The image gained the reputation as a miracle worker, a thaumaturge. By 1976, so many people were coming to the little family oratory that the Archbishop of Zacatecas authorized the construction of a new chapel. In 1989, the archbishop closed the chapel and ordered the image translated to a temporary shrine closer to the highway. The shrine is in a hanger of an old airport near the town of Palomitas.

Today, the shrine is a popular place of pilgrimage, especially from the states of central Mexico, although the devotion has crossed the border to the United States with the wave of Mexican Catholic immigrants.

HOLY CHILD OF GOOD LUCK

The title of a statue and devotion centered in the Mexico City suburb of Tacubaya.

The first sight of this image of the Christ Child is shocking. His small head rests on a human skull for a pillow. A second glance confirms the peaceful expression of the sleeping infant. Pious tradition holds that in the early twentieth century, two missionary priests were crossing a large field when they heard a baby crying but found the statue "sleeping peacefully" on a skull. As they picked it up, a spring gushed forth which still flows today. They gave it to Archbishop Francisco de Lizana Beaumont, who saw in the image a reminder of the Resurrection. The archbishop entrusted the image to the Bernardine Sisters at the Immaculate Conception convent where it is housed today.

HOLY CHILDHOOD SOCIETY

A missionary organization of school children who raise funds for children in mission lands.

HOLY COMMUNION — See EUCHARIST.

Holy Child of Good Luck

HOLY DAYS OF OBLIGATION

Also called days of precept.

These feasts are of such importance in the liturgical calendar that attendance at Mass is required. The Code of Canon Law (Canons 1246-1248) discusses these, rightly beginning with Sunday, describing it as "the day on which the paschal mystery is celebrated in light of the apostolic tradition" and which "is to be observed as the foremost day of obligation in the universal Church" (Canon 1246).

The code then lists the following to be observed: Christmas; Epiphany; Ascension; Corpus Christi; Mary, Mother of God; Immaculate Conception; Assumption; St. Joseph; Sts. Peter and Paul; and All Saints.

The present code states that "the conference of bishops can abolish certain holy days of obligation or transfer them to a Sunday with the prior approval of the Holy See" (Canon 1246). The United States bishops decided not to make the feasts of St. Joseph and Sts. Peter and Paul days of precept and transferred the Solemnities of the Epiphany and Corpus Christi to a Sunday.

HOLY FACE MEDAL

A devotion based on private revelations to Sister Maria Pierina of the Daughters of the Immaculate Conception in Milan, Italy.

In 1940, under Sister Pierina's direction, a medal of the Holy Face was cast and approved by the Curia of Milan. The front of the medal has the Latin words for "May God be gracious to us and bless us and make his face to shine upon us, [Selah]. (Psalms 67:1). The words encircle a picture of the face of Christ. On the reverse of the medal is a radiant host with the words "Stay with us, O Lord." This medal is to be worn in a spirit of reparation. If possible, the wearer should make a visit to the Blessed Sacrament each Tuesday.

HOLY FAMILY

A movable observance on the Sunday after Christmas that commemorates the Holy Family of Jesus, Mary, and Joseph as the model of domestic society, holiness, and virtue.

The Holy Family

The devotional background of the feast was strong in the seventeenth century, particularly in France and Spain. In the eighteenth century, in prayers composed for a special Mass, Blessed François Laval, the first Canadian bishop, likened the Christian family to the Holy Family. Pope Leo XIII consecrated families to the Holy Family and composed his own Office of the Holy Family. In 1921, Pope Benedict XV extended the office and Mass of the feast to the whole Church.

HOLY FOOLS

Individuals who humbled themselves by feigning madness.

The holy fools played a major role in the history of Russian spiritual life. During the sixteenth century, they fulfilled social and political roles as well, using their position at the margins of society to denounce the injustice of those in positions of civil authority. Western parallels of this unusual phenomenon of sanctity were demonstrated in the persons of St. Philip Neri and St. Benedict Joseph Labré.

HOLY GHOST HOLE

In medieval times an opening in the top of some churches that allowed for a theatrical presentation of the descent of the Holy Spirit.

In some churches, a figure of a dove on a disk as large as a cartwheel was lowered through this opening at the appropriate part of the sequence during the Mass on Pentecost Sunday. During the thirteenth century in many cathedrals in France, white pigeons — which were released during the singing of the sequence — flew around the church while roses were dropped from the Holy Ghost Hole. In Germany on the Feast of the Assumption, a boy dressed as an angel would be lowered on ropes from this opening while he addressed a figure of Mary with the words of Gabriel. While the children stared up at the approaching angel, their mothers put cookies and candy on the pews, making their little ones suspect that Gabriel's invisible angel companions had brought them treats from heaven.

HOLY HERBS — See HERBS, HOLY.

HOLY HOUR

An hour of meditation before the Blessed Sacrament.

In 1673, St. Margaret Mary Alacoque reported that she had received instructions in a vision of Christ, who told her to spend an hour in meditation every Thursday night. The meditation was to focus on the sufferings of Christ in the Garden of Gethsemane. This practice spread to many countries.

(See also **ST. MARGARET MARY ALACOQUE.**)

HOLY HOUSE OF LORETO — See LORETO: HOLY HOUSE OF NAZARETH.

HOLY INNOCENTS, THE

The feast celebrated on December 28 to commemorate the male infants who suffered death at the hands of Herod's soldiers seeking to kill the Child Jesus (see Matthew 2:13-18).

The Holy Innocents have been venerated as martyrs since the early Church, and a feast in their honor has been observed since the fifth century. Among the traditions associated with "Childermas," as it has sometimes been called, is children gathering in Bethlehem's Church of the Nativity on the afternoon of the feast to sing a hymn in their memory. The Christian poet Prudentius composed a short poem in their honor titled *Salvete, flores martyres!*, "Hail, O flowers of martyrs!"

HOLY NAME OF JESUS

A devotion apparently begun in the eleventh century, although invoking the name as a means of dispelling demons had been popular since early Christian times.

A meditation of St. Anselm (1033-

1109) in which he dwells upon the name itself was important in the development of this devotion. The custom of bowing the head on hearing the name was established before the thirteenth century and was commanded by a decree of the Second Council of Lyons in 1274. The Franciscan Guibert of Tournai (c. 1200-1284) wrote a treatise on the Holy Name, and the Franciscans and Dominicans were active in spreading the devotion. Confraternities were established from the thirteenth century onward.

During his popular preaching, St. Bernardine of Siena (1380-1444) was known to hold up a plaque or banner with the monogram I.H.S. (derived from the first three letters of the Greek for Jesus: *Iota, Eta, Sigma*; a more ancient form is I.H.C.). The symbol became very popular and is used in many places.

I.H.S.

Masses were composed for the Holy Name, and an office was approved for limited use in the fifteenth century. Litanies began to appear from the sixteenth century. Pope Innocent XIII extended the feast to the whole Church in 1721. Although it was dropped from the revised calendar in 1969, the feast was restored by John Paul II in 2002 and assigned as an optional memorial to January 3.

HOLY NAME OF MARY

The Feast of the Most Holy Name of Mary.

It was introduced by Pope Innocent XI after the Christian victory over the Turks at the city walls of Vienna on September 12, 1683. The deliverance of Vienna proved of pivotal importance for the future of Christian Europe. The feast, therefore, was votive in nature and devotional, an act of thanksgiving for the intercession of the Blessed Virgin Mary. Although expunged from the calendar in 1969, it was restored as an optional memorial by Pope John Paul II in 2002.

HOLY NAME SOCIETY

A confraternity founded in 1274 by Blessed John Vercelli, master general of the Dominicans, to promote reverence for the Holy Name of Jesus.

While that remains the principal purpose of the society, it also develops lay apostolic programs in line with directives from the Second Vatican Council.

The Holy Name Society was introduced in the United States in 1870-1871 by Dominican Father Charles H. McKenna. There are some five million members on diocesan and parochial levels. With approval of the local bishop and pastor, women as well as men may be members.

HOLY OILS — See OILS, HOLY.

HOLY PLACES

Those sites in the Holy Land, Palestine, or modern Israel associated with the life and ministry of Our Lord.

HOLY SATURDAY

The Saturday of Holy Week.

Originally, it was kept as a quiet day of fasting and meditation. By the late fourth century in some places, converts made public profession of their faith on that day before being received into the Church at the Easter Vigil.

(See also HOLY WEEK; TRIDUUM.)

HOLY SOULS, DEVOTION TO THE — See ALL SOULS' DAY.

HOLY WATER — See **WATER, HOLY**.

HOLY WEEK

Passion (Palm) Sunday through Holy Saturday.

Passion Sunday, formerly called Palm Sunday, marks the start of Holy Week by recalling Christ's triumphal entry into Jerusalem at the beginning of the last week of his life (see Matthew 21:1-11). A procession and other ceremonies commemorating the event were held in Jerusalem from the fourth century and were adopted by Rome by the ninth century. At that time, the blessing of palms for the occasion was introduced. Later, in the Middle Ages, a wooden statue of Christ sitting on a donkey, the whole image on wheels, was drawn in the center of the procession. These statues, known as *Palmesel* or "Palm Donkey," may still be seen in a number of museums in European cities. Full liturgical observance includes the blessing of palms and a procession before the principal Mass of the day. The Passion — by Matthew, Mark, or Luke, depending on the year — is read during the Mass of this Sunday.

Holy Thursday, or Maundy Thursday, commemorates the institution of the sacraments of Eucharist and holy orders, and features a foot-washing rite that commemorates Christ's washing of the feet of the Apostles at the Last Supper. The Mass of the Lord's Supper in the evening marks

Palms Blessed During Holy Week

the beginning of the Easter Triduum. The term "Maundy" is derived from the Latin *mandatum*, the first words for the rite of foot-washing: "My commandment is: love one another as I have loved you."

From the Latin for "three days," the Triduum continues until Vespers (evening prayer) on Easter Sunday. The period recalls Christ's institution of the sacraments of Eucharist and holy orders, his Passion and death, and his triumphant Resurrection from the dead.

Following the Mass on Holy Thursday, there is a procession of the Blessed Sacrament to a place of repose for adoration by the faithful. Usually at an earlier Mass of Chrism, bishops bless oils (of catechumens, of the sick, and sacred chrism) for use during the year.

Good Friday commemorates the Passion and death of Christ. The liturgy includes the reading of the Passion according to John, special prayers for the Church, civil rulers, and people of all ranks, the veneration of the cross, and a Communion service. The celebration takes place in the afternoon, usually at three o'clock, the hour that Christ is believed to have died on the cross. The Communion service, held in lieu of the sacrifice of the Mass, is known as the "Mass of the Presanctified."

On Holy Saturday, the Sacrifice of the Mass is not celebrated and Holy Communion may be given only as Viaticum.

Since at least the fourth century, Christianity has marked Holy Week. After the time of the persecutions, Christian emperors of both the East and West issued various decrees forbidding amusements and games and directed that these days were to be spent free from worldly occupations and entirely devoted to religious exercises. Pardons were granted to those in prison, and many charges in court were dropped in honor of Christ's Passion.

In the Middle Ages, all secular business was prohibited, and the time was spent in recollection and prayer. Often, kings and rulers secluded themselves in monasteries. During some eras, no servile work was allowed during the Triduum, and the faithful were to be present at all liturgies. In 1642, Pope Urban VIII, because of the changing conditions of social life, rescinded this obligation.

In most countries, real palms are unattainable for Passion Sunday, so a variety of other branches are used. Centuries ago, not only branches but flowers were blessed, and in some countries the day is called "Flower Sunday." (The term *Pascua Florida*, which in Spain originally meant just Palm Sunday, was later applied to the entire festive season of Easter Week or Octave. The state of Florida received its name when Ponce de León first sighted the land on Easter Sunday of 1513 and named it in honor of the great feast.)

In central Europe, large clusters of plants interwoven with ribbons and flowers are fastened to a top of a wooden stick and are called palm bouquets. The main plant used, however, is the pussy willow bearing its catkin blossoms. In Latin countries and in the United States, palm leaves are often shaped into little crosses or other symbolic designs. The faithful reverently keep these in their homes during the year. This custom was originated by a suggestion in the ceremonial book for bishops that "little crosses of palm be attached to the boughs wherever true palms are not available in sufficient quantity."

In the early Christian centuries, the bishop celebrated three Masses on Holy Thursday. The first, the Mass of the Penitents, was for the reconciliation of public sinners. The second, the Mass of Chrism, featured the blessing of holy oils and consecration of sacred chrism. The third commemorated the Last Supper of Christ and the institution of the Eucharist.

Today, after the Mass of the Lord's Supper on Holy Thursday, the altar is stripped, and all decorations except those at the repository shrine are removed in symbolic representation of the body of Christ, which was stripped of its garments.

Good Friday has been celebrated from the earliest centuries as a day of mourning, fasting, and prayer. After the solemn ceremonies of Good Friday are concluded, the altar is stripped again, the tabernacle is left open, no lights are left burning in the sanctuary, and only the crucifix takes the place

of honor in front of the empty tabernacle. On this day the cross is venerated by genuflection rather than a bow.

Traditionally, Holy Saturday has been a time of preparing at home for the Easter celebration.

HOLY WOUNDS (FIVE WOUNDS)

Popular medieval devotion focusing on the tortures of Christ's Passion.

The five wounds refer to the nailing of Jesus' hands and feet to the cross and the piercing of his side with a lance.

A number of mystics of the Church, including St. Francis of Assisi, have received private revelations which encouraged the devotion to the Sacred Wounds. In modern times, Sister Mary Martha Chambon, a humble lay sister of the Visitation Order of Chambery, France, who died in the odor of sanctity in 1907, received a mission to adore the Sacred Wounds and to revive this devotion in the Church. The essential acts of the cult of the Holy Wounds and of the devotion to them are acts of worship and love; it does not consist of a set of pious practices or exercises. Instead, any act of worship, of praise or of love to Jesus Crucified, is an act of true devotion to the Holy Wounds. Christians are encouraged to offer the Holy Wounds to the Eternal Father in the offering of Mass, and in Adoration of the Blessed Sacrament. Exhibition of the crucifix as a reminder of Christ's suffering and dying for us is another part of this devotion. There is, however, a chaplet known as the chaplet of Mercy of the Holy Wounds of Jesus which may be prayed as part of the devotion.

(See also **CHAPLET OF MERCY OF THE HOLY WOUNDS OF JESUS; FIVE WOUNDS.**)

HOLY YEAR

A year during which the pope grants the plenary Jubilee Indulgence to the faithful who fulfill certain conditions.

Pope Boniface VIII formally proclaimed the first Holy Year in 1300, and the first three were observed in 1300, 1350, and 1390. Holy Years, beginning in 1475, were celebrated at twenty-five-year intervals except in 1800 and 1850 when, respectively, the French invasion of Italy and political turmoil made observance impossible. The Holy Year of 1900 was delayed one year and celebrated in 1901.

Pope Paul II set the twenty-five-year timetable. In 1500, Pope Alexander VI prescribed the start and finish ceremonies — the opening and closing of the Holy Doors in the major basilicas on successive Christmas Eves. All but a few of the earlier Holy Years were classified as ordinary. Several — like those of 1933 and 1983 to commemorate the 1900th and 1950th an-

niversaries of the death and Resurrection of Christ — were in the extraordinary category. Pope John Paul II designated Jubilee Year 2000 to be a Holy Year ending the second and beginning the third millennium of Christianity.

For those who made a pilgrimage to Rome during the year, the conditions to receive the plenary indulgence were reception of the sacraments of penance and the Eucharist, and visits and prayer for the intention of the pope in the basilicas of St. Peter, St. John Lateran, St. Paul-Outside-the-Walls, and St. Mary Major. For those who did not make a pilgrimage to Rome, the conditions were reception of the sacraments and prayer for the pope during a visit or community celebration in a church designated by the local bishop.

(See also **INDULGENCE.**)

HOME ALTARS

Also called *altarcitos* (little altars); the custom of setting aside a shelf or small table for sacramentals, which is used as a focal point for family prayer.

The traditions of such domestic shrines vary. For example, in Slovak homes, there may be an elaborately carved and painted wooden altar that contains images of favorite saints and pictures of loved ones who have died. A Hispanic home altar would typically include candles and a number of statues.

The Child Jesus Home Altar

The Blessed Mother Home Altar

HOPE, OUR LADY OF

An ancient Marian devotion.

One of the first shrines with that title was built in Mezières, France, in 930. It was reported that in 1871 Our Lady of Hope appeared in the French village of Pontmain, revealing herself as the "Madonna of the Crucifix," and gave the world a message of hope through prayer and the cross.

(See also **PONTMAIN, OUR LADY OF**.)

HORARIA

Medieval prayer books.

Designed for people who wanted to pray the Liturgy of the Hours on their own, *horaria* contained Psalms, selections from liturgical texts, and many other

Our Lady of Hope

247

prayers of private origin. Those who could not read, especially the lay brothers or sisters in monasteries, substituted a certain number of familiar prayer formulas that they knew by heart; in this way the Rosary gradually developed during the High Middle Ages. At various times and in various centuries, many Psalters have been popular among the pious laity. During the seventeenth and eighteenth centuries, however, a new kind of prayer book with an emphasis on personal piety and individualistic devotion gradually supplanted the Psalters and books of hours, causing the ancient devotion of daily hours to be prayed less frequently by the laity.

(See also **LITURGY OF THE HOURS; BOOKS OF HOURS.**)

HOSANNA

An exclamation of praise and adoration to God.

It is from the Hebrew for "Save us now, we pray."

HOST

Originally referring to any victim used in sacrifice to a divinity (in pagan lands, to their gods) but more specifically to God.

As such, Christ the perfect Sacrifice is also the perfect and spotless Victim, or Host. By extension and intrinsic association — as designated by Christ himself — the bread that is used at the Eucharistic Sacrifice of the Mass, the unbloody re-enactment of the bloody Sacrifice of the Cross on Calvary, is also signified by this term. Strictly speaking, then, this bread, which will receive consecration, is not yet a "host" and becomes this only after the consecration and in view of its consummation at Holy Communion.

HOT CROSS BUNS

Bread rolls with a cross sliced into or frosted on the top.

Hot cross buns were a Good Friday tradition in medieval England and Ireland. The custom is said to have originated in St. Alban's Abbey in the mid-fourteenth century when monks began distributing the marked buns to the poor on Good Friday in place of the ordinary ones. Pious legend held the buns did not mold as regular bread did, and that eating them on Good Friday would protect the home from fire. They were kept through the year to be used as medicine or to ward off disease, lightning, and shipwreck.

HOURS, BOOKS OF — See BOOKS OF HOURS.

HOURS, LITTLE

The four lesser sections of the Divine

Office that took their names from the times of the day at which they are recited.

Originally Prime, Terce, Sext, and None, they have been replaced by one "hour" called "daytime prayer" in the revised Liturgy of the Hours.

HUMILIATION OF RELICS

Ritual of Clamour: a medieval ritual condemned by the Council of Lyon.

Monastic communities performed two religious functions vital to medieval society. First, the religious prayed for the salvation and well-being of the local population both living and dead. This was a vital concern to a population obsessed with the insecurity of this life and the uncertainty of the next. Second, through the Divine Office, the Mass, and the cult of the saints whose relics were honored in the community's church, they fulfilled the ritual actions necessary to keep the spiritual powers benevolently disposed towards human society. The relationship between the saint and the community who venerated his relics or body was reciprocal; the saint was a powerful protector for the community. In order to force cooperation or fair dealing, the monks manipulated their "salvific" function by ceasing to pray for or by cursing their opponents. Through the ritual of the clamor (clamour) and the accompanying humiliation of relics and images, they mistreated cult objects and prevented popular access to them, thus disturbing the proper relationships between the human and the supernatural orders and involving not only the alleged opponent but all of society which depended on these powers. The clamour and the humiliation are closely related, and they appear in a variety of combinations in liturgical manuscripts from the tenth until the thirteenth century. The history of one ritual of humiliation that has been preserved is that of the liturgy as practiced at St. Martin of Tours.

After Prime, when all the bells of the tower had been rung, the canons entered the choir. They sang seven Psalms and a litany. The most important members of the community and the ministers then placed on the ground a silver crucifix and all of the reliquaries of the saints, and put thorns on top of and around the tomb of St. Martin. In the center of the nave, they placed a wooden crucifix, likewise covered with thorns, and they blocked all but one of the church doors with thorns. At dawn, the office of the day began in a subdued tone. Everything was muted, and the Mass of the day was celebrated as though it were a private Mass. The canons joined the relics on the floor before the Eucharist. The prayers and Psalms sung during the rite explained the situation, the nature of the injustice, and articulated the necessary conclusion of the affair. The main prayers were drawn from the rich Psalm literature of cries to the Lord in times of oppression. A few members of the laity were admitted to the church to observe the humiliation. The relics remained humiliated until a successful conclusion to the affair was reached.

In late 996 or early 997, Count Fulk Nerra of Anjou and Touraine entered the cloister of St. Martin of Tours with armed soldiers and damaged the house of the treasurer. The canons saw this as an atrocity, as the monastery was supposed to be immune from the count's jurisdiction. Therefore, they humiliated the relics of their saints. In addition to covering the relics with thorns, they kept the doors of the church closed day and night, refusing admission to the count or any of the members of his castle. At least five of the count's ancestors were buried in the monastery, so he thus had no access to their tombs either.

Finally, the count, regretting his actions and seeking forgiveness, entered the cloister. He walked barefoot into the church with some of his followers. Stopping first before the sepulcher of Blessed Martin, he promised to God and to the saint never to do such a thing again. In turn, he went to each humbled, sacred object, asking forgiveness and humbling himself. Subsequently, the relics were returned to their place of honor and good relations were re-established between the count and the monastery.

The humiliation of relics was often effective, although sometimes the crimes of the "oppressors" of the monastery were not grave ones. By the end of the thirteenth century, the Episcopal and papal hierarchy was becoming increasingly unhappy with the tendency of communities to humiliate their relics and to discontinue services without canonical grounds. The Second Council of Lyon, in 1274, condemned humiliation as an arbitrary cessation of the liturgy, terming it a "detestable abuse of horrendous indevotion."

HYMN

A song of praise or petition to God, Mary, or the saints.

Age-old discussions continue as to the thin line separating sacred and secular hymns and, within the sacred realm, those in the liturgical group as opposed to those in the non-liturgical group. The document *Music in Catholic Worship* (1972) by the United States Bishops' Committee on the Liturgy aids in the clarification of music suitable for liturgical use by its threefold judgment: pastoral, musical, and liturgical. Hymns constitute a distinct genre of musical poetry. One of the rules for the composition of hymns is that they always end with a doxology made to fit the rhyming scheme of the verses.

HYPERDULIA — See DULIA.

I

I.H.C., I.H.S. — See **HOLY NAME OF JESUS**.

I.N.R.I.

The monogram for *Iesus Nazarenus Rex Iudaeorum*, Latin for "Jesus of Nazareth, King of the Jews" (see John 19:19-22).

Pilate ordered the inscription written in Latin (the language of the Romans), Aramaic (the spoken language of the Jewish people), and Greek (the third most common language in early first-century Palestine), and placed on Christ's cross. Under Roman law, claiming kingship was considered treason; the plaque told the public the alleged crime for which Jesus was being executed. When Jewish leaders complained that Jesus only claimed to be king of the Jews but was not, in fact, a king, Pilate refused to change it; hence it remained a testimony to Jesus' true kingship. It has become customary that crucifixes used as sacramentals bear the monogram.

ICON

A form of religious art, coming from the Greek *eikon* for "image."

It is also a theological term central to the Eastern understanding of the world: visible things are revealed images (*eikones*) of the invisible. St. Paul wrote that Christ "is the image [or *eikon*] of the invisible God" (see Colossians 1:15).

Icons do not depict God in the mythological or allegorical manner of pagan antiquity. Instead, they display a realism based on the Gospel of John: "No one has ever seen God; the only Son, who is in the bosom of the Father, he has made him

Icon

known" (1:18). Canonical icons always avoided representing God the Father as a venerable old man. This type of imagery only appeared in the period of decline and provoked strong objections. The subject matter of an icon is not the natural flesh and blood of the subject. It lies rather on the border between the visible and the invisible and is focused on the point where the boundary between these two worlds is transcended through the Incarnation.

In art, the symbol of light is gold, and the golden background of an icon signifies the unapproachable light that existed before creation and in which St. Paul says God dwells (see 1 Timothy 6:16). The faces of the saints depicted in icons are not left to the artist's imagination, as in Western art, but are fixed by tradition. The proportions of the face represent qualities of sanctity rather than realistic portraiture

of the person: the eyes are large, the forehead broad, the nose finely elongated, and the lips devoid of sensuality. The spiritual nature of the entire icon is expressed through stylization.

Iconoclasm, from the Greek for "image-breaking," was a prominent heresy in the Eastern Church in the eighth and ninth centuries. Its proponents claimed that veneration of pictures and images was against the commandment to worship God alone. At an ecumenical council in Nicaea in 787, the Church defined the distinction between adoration given to God (*latria*) and veneration (*dulia*) given to the saints. The Council Fathers said veneration is an act of homage to the person depicted in an image, not to the image itself.

(See also **DULIA.**)

Portable Icon

ICON CORNER — See **FAMILY ICONS**.

ICONOSTASIS

A screen separating a church's sanctuary from the nave.

In the early centuries in both the East and West, the sanctuary was separated from the nave by some form of open or low barrier. Over time, an array of images was established on the sanctuary screen. Originally only about waist high, the screen rose through the centuries until in Russia during the fifteenth century it was a solid wall of icons. A parallel phenomenon in the West was the Rood Screen.

The screen serves much as a "history of salvation," displaying the working of God's plan for the redemption of the world through tiers of icons depicting the patriarchs and prophets, followed by the great events of the Incarnation that are described in the New Testament and commemorated in the cycle of festivals throughout the Church year. The local tier contains, for the most part, whatever icons held special significance for the local community.

By the end of the Middle Ages, the iconostasis had become a compact wall hiding the sanctuary, which contained no images. The central or royal door of the iconostasis, through which Holy Communion is brought out and offered to the faithful in the Orthodox and Byzantine churches, is always flanked by an image of the Mother of God on the left and Christ on the right.

IDOLATRY

The giving to a creature the worship that is due to God alone (*latria*).

A Russian Cathedral Iconostasis

IESUS NAZARENUS REX IUDAE- ORUM — See I.N.R.I.

IGNATIUS WATER

A sacramental made by dipping a relic or a medal of St. Ignatius of Loyola in water and reciting a specified blessing.

The custom is centuries-old and was used as a safeguard against sickness, particularly in countries where the Jesuits were active as missionaries.

ILLUMINATIVE WAY

The intermediate stage of the mystical life.

This particular stage is between the purgative way, in which one gains a facility for virtue by the practice of mortification and meditation, and the unitive way, in which one achieves union with God, passive contemplation, and habitual practice of the virtues, often to a heroic degree.

In the illuminative way, one aims at perceiving Christ through the infused gifts of the Holy Spirit and following him. Achievement of this level of mystical union comes about through the ordinary movements of grace, and most mystics have been able to express their experience in rather ordinary terms.

IL PROCESSIONE IN TRAPANI, SICILY

The Sicilian Good Friday tradition of carrying statues representing Christ's Passion through the city.

The procession moves with short steps, left to right and forward and backward, which produces a rocking known as the *annacata*. Music is provided by local bands, and hooded men with colored tunics represent the different confraternities, religious orders, and workers' guilds.

IMAGES

Artistic representations of God, Mary, saints, and angels used as sacramentals to promote meditation and prayer. The tradition of using images dates back to the early Church.

One of the major criticisms of the Catholic Church by the uninformed deals with the Catholic veneration of images. Catholics, according to the critics, are idolators. Catholic doctrine is quite clear on this point. Catholics are not guilty of idolatry because the pictures and statues in the Church are honored, not adored. Just as people cherish photographs of their family and friends as reminders of them, so, too, Catholics cherish sacred images as reminders of Our Lord, the Blessed Virgin, and the saints. A nation's flag is honored not because of the cloth out of which it is made, but because of what it represents. It is this type of honor and respect that belongs to sacred images. By the veneration of sacred images, effective and sometimes supernatural graces are obtained. There have been instances of miraculous pictures, statues, and crucifixes.

Sacred images help the faithful avoid distractions while praying by fixing their attention. They serve as a silent admonition which encourages imitation, and they are a good means for instructing the faithful in religion — even an illiterate can understand a picture.

Catholics honor Christ and the saints when they pray before crucifixes, relics, and sacred images. They honor them because it is the persons they represent that are honored; the faithful adore Christ and venerate the saints. Holy images have a holy purpose. Catholics venerate the saints for God's sake and to increase in themselves the wish to imitate their virtues. They venerate images by praying before them, adorning them with flowers or precious objects, by burning lights before them and by kissing them with reverence. Catholics visit the tombs and shrines of the saints just as Catholics and non-Catholics alike honor their nation's heroes by placing wreaths on their graves on civil holidays.

Of all sacred representations, the crucifix deserves the highest veneration because it is the sign of our redemption. It was on the cross that Our Lord died to save sinners from the consequences of sin. The Church pays such honor to the crucifix that sacraments are administered,

Mass is celebrated, and all acts of worship are performed in the presence of a crucifix. The crucifix is placed in the hands of the dying.

Catholics do not pray to the crucifix or to the sacred images, but to the persons they represent. Disrespect to a sacred image is disrespect to the one represented. Catholics do not believe that any divine power resides in any sacred image, and it is not the image that works any miracles. The numerous miracles worked through the use of relics and images are a result of God acting through them. Even today, relics and images continue to play a part in the working of miracles and the suspension of the natural law, but always and only as mere instruments of Almighty God.

There are literally hundreds of thousands of famous or well known sacred images. Although paintings and statues are more common in the Western Church, and icons are more prevalent in the Eastern Churches, there is no form of artistic expression which has not been used in the creation of sacred images. Many great artists have been Catholics, and their greatest masterpieces include religious subjects. The history of art itself cannot be separated from religion, for man has always given of his best artistic talents to his god. Just as with the case of relics, Christianity is not alone the custodian of sacred images.

(See also **CROSS; DULIA; ICON; SACRAMENTALS.**)

IMITATION OF CHRIST

The famous spiritual work traditionally ascribed to Thomas à Kempis (d. 1471).

Teaching Christians how to attain perfection by imitating Jesus, the volume has four parts: the first two are devoted to general comments about the spiritual life, the third about the splendor of Christ, and the fourth about the Holy Eucharist.

IMMACULATE CONCEPTION OF THE BLESSED VIRGIN MARY

A Marian dogma.

It teaches that Mary, in view of her calling to be the Mother of Christ and in virtue of his merits, was preserved from the first moment of her conception from original sin and was filled with grace from the very beginning of her life.

It is a solemnity and holy day of obligation, which falls on December 8. The present form of the feast dates from 1854 when Pope Pius IX defined the dogma. An earlier feast of her conception, which testified to the long-existing belief in this truth, was observed in the East by the eighth century, in Ireland by the ninth, and later in other European countries. In 1846, Mary was proclaimed the patroness of the United States under this title.

(See also **LOURDES, OUR LADY OF.**)

IMMACULATE HEART OF MARY

A Marian devotion that began in the Middle Ages and was popularized by the preaching of St. John Eudes (1601-1680), who was the first to celebrate a Mass and Divine Office of Mary under this title.

A feast, which was celebrated in various places on different dates, was authorized in 1799. Now it is a memorial on the Saturday following the second Sunday after Pentecost, the day following the

Immaculate Heart of Mary

Feast of the Sacred Heart of Jesus. In 1944, Pope Pius XII ordered it be observed throughout the Church in order to obtain Mary's intercession for "peace among nations, freedom for the Church, the conversion of sinners, the love of purity and the practice of virtue." In 1942, he had consecrated the entire human race to Mary under this title.

IMMANENCE

The philosophic use of the word referring to a) an activity when it produces its effect from within or b) an entity when its being within something else contributes to the existence of that thing.

In theology, the absolute immanence of God in the universe would be pantheism, and the absolute independence of God from the universe would be deism. The Christian doctrine of immanence teaches that God is present in his creation but is not part of it.

IMMUTABILITY

A term meaning "unchangeableness."

Referring to God, it means that he can never experience any alteration because he is immaterial and perfect.

IMPOSITION OF HANDS

An ancient symbol adopted by the Catholic Church from apostolic days to convey power, blessing, or consecration.

In the Old Testament, the laying on of hands carried with it a sacrificial connotation. It also imparted blessing. In the New Testament, Our Lord imposed hands to cure the sick. The Apostles imposed hands to confer authority and powers, and this gesture was soon acknowledged as the means of ordaining and conferring office. There is also a laying on of hands by the priest in the sacrament of the anointing of the sick. At the epiclesis in the Canon of the Mass, the priest places his hands over the Eucharistic gifts. In the sacrament of penance, the priest extends his right hand forward when imparting absolution.

IMPRECATORY PSALMS

Psalms that give expression to an extreme vindictiveness, also called the cursing Psalms.

These Psalms speak vividly of the retribution that is exacted for evil that is done. Such Psalms should be read as the ardent statement of the human writer seeking God's punishment of evildoers while still faithful to the inspired intention of God to thwart those who oppose his will (see Psalms 7, 35, 69, 109, 140).

IMPRIMATUR

Latin for "let it be printed."

It is a canonical term for the permission needed to publish certain kinds of religious books.

IMPROPERIA

A series of reproofs imagined to be addressed by Our Savior from the cross to an ungrateful people.

Beginning in the seventh century, the reproaches have been chanted on Good Friday during the Veneration of the Cross. They are retained in the current rite but are optional. Correctly understood, these are not anti-Semitic but are reminders to all of the need for repentance and conversion.

IN ARTICULO MORTIS

Latin term for "at the approach of death."

It is used most often when discussing reception of the sacraments by someone in danger of death.

INCARNATE WORD, THE

A popular title and image of Our Lord based on the Incarnation.

INCARNATION

One of the central mysteries of Christianity.

It is the doctrine that in the union of the divine nature of the Second Person of the Holy Trinity with human nature, the Son of God assumed our humanity, body and soul, and was born of the Virgin Mary, to dwell in our midst in order to accomplish the work of our redemption.

INCENSE

A granulated or powdered aromatic resin obtained from various plants and trees.

When sprinkled on glowing coals in a vessel called a censer (or thurible), incense becomes a fragrant cloud of smoke and so is used to symbolize prayer rising to God (see Revelation 8:3-4). The use of incense in the Church came from both pagan worship and Judaism. It is used liturgically in both the East and West. The primary component of liturgical incense is frankincense.

The earliest recorded use of incense is found in Egyptian hieroglyphics. About 1500 B.C., Queen Hatshepsut sent a fleet to what is now part of northern Somalia to acquire frankincense and myrrh tree seedlings, the two "perfumes of the gods." When the tomb of Tutankhamen (c.1340 B.C.) was opened in the early twentieth century, the air inside still smelled of myrrh. In addition to the Ten Commandments and other instructions, Moses brought two recipes down from Mount Sinai. These were for sacred incense made with frankincense and sacred anointing oils with a myrrh base (see Exodus 30:22-

38). The Magi brought gifts of gold, frankincense, and myrrh to the Messiah. Both frankincense and myrrh are aromatic gum resins, or dried tree sap. Because the trees were scarce and difficult to transplant, and harvesting was a laborious process, the resins were very valuable. Around the time of Christ, a pound of frankincense cost more than the equivalent of $500 in today's currency; a pound of the choicest myrrh was as much as eight to ten times that amount.

Incense

Modern scholars believe that the use of incense was not a part of the earliest Christian worship for two reasons. First, its pagan connotations left a bad taste in Christian mouths — during the Roman persecution, Christians were ordered to offer incense before an image of the emperor or other pagan deities. Those who capitulated were called *thurificati*, after the thurible or censer in which incense was burned. Second, much of the early Christian worship was held in secret, and the strong odor of incense could have brought danger, persecution, or death to the worshipers. After the time of the persecutions, incense began to be used in Christian celebrations and its use continues today. The rising smoke suggests the ascent of the prayers of the faithful gathered there. The ritual censing of church objects symbolizes sanctification — to sanctify is to make holy. The incensing of the worshipers not only implies sanctification, but also celebrates participation in the liturgical ceremony.

In the orient, a particular type of incense known as *Joss* is used in many religious ceremonies. The name is a corruption of the Portuguese word *Deos,* meaning "god," and these incense sticks have been burned before the Chinese idols for centuries. In Japan, the incense is known as *senko*. The use of this type of incense has become common in Catholic ceremonies in the orient. Often, the incense is lighted as a prayer for the dead much as Europeans use votive candles.

INDIFFERENTISM
The refusal to give God the worship and glory that he deserves because of sloth or neglect.

Also, the notion that all religions are

the same and that one is as good as another. This theory contradicts the Church's teaching that it alone possesses the "fullness of truth" and was the only Church to be founded by Jesus Christ. One has an obligation to follow one's correctly formed conscience concerning which religion to adopt.

INDULGENCE

The remission before God of the temporal punishment due to sin whose guilt has already been forgiven.

A properly disposed member of the Christian faithful can obtain an indulgence under prescribed conditions through the help of the Church. As the minister of redemption, the Church dispenses and applies with authority the treasury of satisfaction of Christ and the saints. A partial indulgence removes part of the temporal punishment due to sin; a plenary indulgence removes all punishment.

In 2000, the Holy See published a revised edition of the *Enchiridion Indulgentiarum*, a manual on indulgences.

INDULGENCES OF THE HOLY LAND

Special indulgences.

They are granted to the faithful who either carry or reverently keep at home sacramentals that have been touched to places in the Holy Land or to the sacred relics preserved there.

(See also **INDULGENCE**; **RELICS**; **SACRAMENTALS**.)

INDWELLING OF THE HOLY SPIRIT

The presence of the Holy Spirit, which implies the residence of the Holy Spirit within a person, as a manifestation of the love of God.

INFANT JESUS

A particular devotion to the Infant Jesus.

It is seen also as devotion to a merciful God, who gave his Son for the redemption of all who believe in him (see John 3:16). The devotion was promoted by St. Vincent Pallotti (d. 1850), founder of the Society of the Catholic Apostolate, the Pallottines.

In order to encourage devotion to the Infant Jesus, St. Vincent commissioned a Roman sculptor to make a statue of the babe. This beautiful statue is revered in the Church of San Salvatore in Onda in Rome. A copy of this statue is enshrined at the Infant Jesus Shrine in North Tonawanda, New York. The statue depicts the Christ Child in a natural and simple pose, seated on a small pillowed chair. The babe is dressed in simple swaddling, and his chubby, baby arms are held out in a pose suggesting that he is waiting to hug

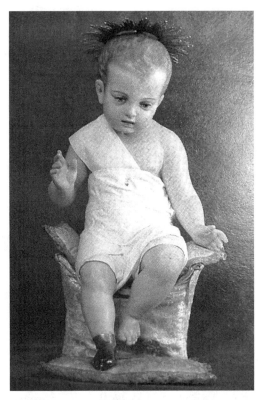

Infant Jesus

with love those who are devoted to him. The right foot of the original statue is covered with a protective plate. This is due to the Roman custom of kissing the foot of the statue, and is for its protection.

INFANT JESUS OF PRAGUE

A devotion and image of the Child Jesus depicted in royal and priestly vestments.

Of uncertain origin, the statue of the Infant Jesus of Prague was presented by Princess Polixena to the Carmelites of Our Lady of Victory Church, Prague, in 1628.

In 1556, Maria Manriquez de Lara of Spain brought a precious family heirloom, a statue of the Child Jesus, with her to Bohemia when she married the Czech nobleman Vratislav of Pernstyn. The statue of the child is eighteen inches tall, carved of wood and thinly coated with wax. The left hand holds a miniature globe surmounted by a cross. The right hand is extended in the form of the papal blessing. The head of the image has a wig of blonde human hair. In 1655, the statue was solemnly crowned in a special coronation ceremony. With a crown, it was presented by the supreme burgrave of the Czech kingdom. The original garments worn by the statue when it arrived in Bohemia are still preserved, but since 1713, the garments of the statue have been changed with the liturgical season. The wardrobe of the Infant of Prague resembles liturgical vestments. At the time the change of vestments is made, numerous devotional objects such as medals, pictures, and rosaries are touched to the statue to be distributed to all parts of the world.

Princess Polyxena Lobkowitz inherited the statue of the infant from her mother, and in 1628 she presented the statue to the discalced Carmelites of Prague, telling them, prophetically, that as long as they honored the Child Jesus as King, and venerated his image, they would not want. Her prediction was verified, and as long as the Divine Infant's image was honored, the community prospered, spiritually and temporally.

The statue was set up in the oratory of the monastery, and twice daily special devotions were performed before it. One of the novices, Cyrillus of the Mother of God, became the greatest apostle of the Holy image.

In 1631, King Gustavus Adolphus of Sweden, an inveterate foe of Catholicism, invaded, and many inhabitants of Prague

Infant Jesus of Prague

fled, including all but two of the Carmelites who remained to protect the monastery. The monastery was plundered, and the image was thrown in a heap of rubbish behind the high altar where it remained for seven years.

In 1637, Father Cyrillus returned to Prague, searched for and found the little image, repaired it, and renewed the devotions. The devotion spread, and miracles and favors multiplied. The Carmelites of the Austrian Province, in 1739, made the spread of the devotion a part of their apostolate. In 1741, the statue was moved to a magnificent shrine on the epistle side of the Church of Our Lady of Victory, and the popularity of the Little King of Prague spread to other countries in the eighteenth century. Pope Leo XIII indulgenced the devotion, and Pope Pius X approved a confraternity under the guidance of the Carmelites, which increased the spread of the devotion in the twentieth century. The shrine in Prague has become one of the most famous and popular shrines in the world. There is a canonically-established national shrine to the Infant Jesus of Prague at Prague, Oklahoma.

INFANT OF GOOD HEALTH

A devotion associated with an image of the Child Jesus.

First venerated in a private home in Morelia, Mexico, in the mid-twentieth century, the image is now located in a shrine built in his honor and dedicated in 1963. A replica of the statue is taken on pilgrimages throughout Mexico and the southwestern United States to promote the devotion.

The statue of the Infant of Good Health is an image of the Child Jesus, carved from wood, approximately eleven inches tall. The coloring of the statue is natural, and the glass eyes are shadowed by thick eyelashes. The image is dressed with the symbols of the power of Christ and wears a royal mantle trimmed with ermine and holds a gold scepter in the left hand. The

Infant of Good Health

right hand is lifted in blessing. The crown is of gold and precious stones. Although the image is dressed with the attributes of royalty and power, it has a childish countenance which inspires the viewer with thoughts of love and protection. In the prayers of the novena, Jesus is called on as the "Health of Our Souls, Divine Healer."

The last Sunday of April is the feast day of the Infant of Good Health. On that Sunday, thousands of pilgrims from Mexico and the United States travel to Morelia to celebrate. Nine days previous to the celebration, a novena is held in the Morelia cathedral. On the last day of the novena, in the evening, there is a three mile parade from the cathedral to the Holy Infant Church with the statue carried on a decorated float.

INTENTION

An act of the human will for the achievement of some purpose or objective, for example, in prayer.

In sacramental theology, the necessary disposition and purpose required for both the administration and reception of a sacrament. It may also refer to the special object for which a prayer or sacrifice is made; thus, the intention of a Mass is the particular end for which the celebrant prays that the fruits of the sacrifice might be applied by God — for example, for the repose of one departed.

265

INTERCESSION

A form of the prayer of petition made to God on behalf of others, whether living or departed.

INTERNAL FORUM

The place of judging or dispensing that remains totally confidential and not recorded in public records of the Church (e.g., sacramental confession).

INTERNATIONAL INSTITUTE OF THE HEART OF JESUS

A secular institute of pontifical right which originated in France. The institute is for diocesan priests and laity. The U.S. headquarters are in Chelsea, Massachusetts.

INTERPRETATION, BIBLICAL

Also called "hermeneutics," from the Greek word meaning "to interpret."

It is the theological science that attempts to give a clear explanation of biblical texts, taking into account the historical background of the human writer and the literary genre of the text, read in the context of the whole of Sacred Scripture, while remaining faithful to the Magisterium of the Church in determining the divine truth intended by God as the divine author of Scripture.

Whether one examines the spiritual sense of the passage or the more straightforward meaning derived from the literary-historical methods of criticism, the meaning or interpretation must further be faithful to the use of the passage in the Sacred Liturgy and by the Fathers and Doctors of the Church, who enjoy an especially significant place in biblical interpretation. The Fathers taught four basic ways of interpreting Scripture: *littera*, which corresponds to modern literary criticism; *tropologica*, the moral or homiletic interpretation; *allegoria*, the symbolic, figurative interpretation; and *anagogia*, the mystical, which often attempts to draw a spiritual, rather than literal, interpretation from the text.

INTINCTION

A way of distributing the Holy Eucharist under both species.

The one distributing Holy Communion dips a particle of Eucharistic Bread (or a small Host) "into the chalice, and showing it, says: The Body and Blood of Christ. The communicant responds: Amen, and receives the Sacrament in the mouth from the priest ...and returns to his or her place" (*General Instruction of the Roman Missal*, n. 287).

INVITATORY

The verse or Psalm that begins the Liturgy of the Hours for a given day, the *invitatorium*.

The *General Instruction on the Liturgy of the Hours* stipulates that the Office begin with the invitatory (n. 34). The verse reads, "Lord, open my lips: And my mouth shall proclaim your praise," followed by Psalm 95. Sometimes another verse is added as a response to Psalm 95. Other Psalms that may be used are Psalms 100, 66, or 24.

INVOCATION OF SAINTS

The appeal made by the faithful to the saints, or to a particular saint, for their intercession.

The invocation of saints is an important aspect of the tradition and doctrine of the communion of saints (the intimate union that exists among the saints in heaven, the souls in purgatory, and the living on earth) and has been proposed for the faithful by a number of Church councils, most notably the councils of Nicaea II (787), Trent (1545-1563), and Vatican II (1962-1965). Central to the understanding of saintly invocation — and its true purpose — is the reality that a supplicant is neither worshiping the saints nor asking them directly for some action or miracle. Rather, the faithful pray to the saint in the sincere hope that the Servant of God will use his or her special place among the select in heaven to petition or intercede on the behalf of the petitioner in some special intention. The saint will add his or her own meritorious prayers to those of the living.

IRISH PENAL ROSARY

A single-decade rosary used in Ireland when it was against the law for Catholics to own religious objects.

Also known as the *An Paidrin Beag*, the crucifix typically features symbols of the Passion.

Religious persecution in Ireland began under Henry VIII. The local parliament adopted acts establishing the king's ecclesiastical supremacy, abolishing the pope's jurisdiction, and suppressing religious houses. In 1691, King James II signed the Treaty of Limerick, which guaranteed freedom of religion for the Catholics; but the treaty was soon broken and a penalty of death was not unknown for celebrating or even attending Mass. The era became known as the "Penal Times," and the one-decade rosary was popular because it could easily be hidden.

ITINERARIUM

Prayers for a spiritually profitable journey.

IVY

A common house plant initially banned by the Church.

In pagan Rome, Ivy was the badge of the wine god Bacchus, displayed to symbolize drinking and feasting. Later, for this reason, it was banished from Christian homes. In England, it was banned from the inside of homes and only allowed to grow on the outside. Thus, its use as a Christmas decoration was not common during medieval times. The symbolism of human weakness clinging to divine strength was frequently ascribed to ivy, and some poets in old England defended its use as a decoration. Later, the delicate ground ivy became a favorite plant of the English home and it traveled to the New World with the pioneer settlers.

J

JAMES, LITURGY OF ST.

The liturgy belonging to the city of Jerusalem, where St. James the Apostle was bishop.

The texts of the Mass are strikingly similar to the *Catecheses*, probably written by St. Cyril of Jerusalem. The Liturgy of St. James spread outside Jerusalem but was suppressed in the twelfth century.

JANUARIUS, MIRACLE OF ST.

A vial of dried blood that liquefies.

Said to be that of the martyr St. Januarius, the blood is kept in the Cathedral of Naples. On several feast days during the year, this blood liquefies during the public exposition of the relic. If the liquefaction does not take place, it is considered to portend ominous events. The liquefaction has been the subject of investigation, and there is photographic evidence of the event. The Church has never given official confirmation of the "miracle."

JASLICKARE

A Slovakian Christmas tradition.

Young men dressed as shepherds and angels carry "Bethlehem," a representation of the stable, from house to house in their area. After requesting permission to enter the home, they recall in music and verse the events of the first Christmas night.

YHWH or Jehovah

JEHOVAH (J-H-V-H)

English equivalent of the Hebrew *Adonai* (my Lord), which is used out of fear and reverence for the Holy Name of Yahweh.

"Jehovah" uses the consonants YHWH and the vowels of *Adonai* (a, o, a). Scholars maintain that "Jehovah" is a false derivation.

JERUSALEM

The "Holy City."

It is located on the crest of some Palestinian mountains, which served as the religious and political center of Judaism, the site of the Temple, and the home of the Benjaminite tribe. Its inhabitants were known as Jebusites. Symbolically, Jerusalem became the capital of belief in and fidelity to Yahweh.

JESSE TREE

Originally a representation of the genealogy of Jesus Christ.

It features a reclining figure of Jesse

from whose loins emerge a great trunk with branches holding figures of his royal descendants. The tree culminates with the figures of Mary and Jesus frequently represented in a flower or bud. More recently, it is a family Advent custom of decorating a Christmas tree with ornaments or objects representing Old Testament events from creation to the birth of Jesus. The Jesse Tree gets its name from the Book of Isaiah: "There shall come forth a shoot from the stump of Jesse, / and a branch shall grow out of his roots" (11:1).

JESSE WINDOW

A stained-glass depiction of the genealogy of Christ in the form of a multi-branched tree growing from the loins of Jesse reclining.

JESUIT RINGS

Rings made of brass or bronze showing religious representations.

In the second half of the seventeenth century, Jesuit missionaries used to award rings to converts in the area of present-day New York state.

JESUS BEADS

A string of one hundred beads connected at the ends by a crucifix.

Jesus Beads

No prayer is said on the crucifix, although the beads may be begun by making the sign of the cross. The person then slowly and thoughtfully repeats the Jesus prayer on each bead.

(See also **JESUS PRAYER**.)

JESUS DOCTOR

A devotion and title of a small statue of the Christ Child that began in Mexico in the mid-twentieth century.

Sister Josephine Carmen Barrios Baez brought this beautiful image of the Child Jesus to a new hospital in Tepeaca. Devotion to the Holy Little Doctor grew, and his devotees began to bring him new

Jesus, Doctor of the Sick

is taken down from the cross and "interred" or "buried" in the *monumento*.

In some churches, this life-size figure is kept as a devotional image in a glass casket on a side altar during the year, and only removed for the Holy Week processions. In Mexico, a number of these figures date back to the sixteenth century. The images are made with jointed arms and legs so the limbs may be stretched out to hang on the cross and folded to the sides when placed in the tomb. They are generally made of gesso-covered wood and ornamented with human hair and a crown of thorns. During the procession, they are dressed in purple robes.

clothes. He is often dressed as a little doctor, complete with medical bag. In 1991, a small chapel dedicated to the Holy Child was added to the parish of St. Francis of Assisi Church, Tapeaca. After Sister Carmen's death, the statue was carried in procession there, where it still remains. His feast is celebrated annually on April 30.

JESÚS ENTIERRO

A name used in Spain, Mexico, and other Spanish-speaking countries for the image of Christ on Good Friday when the body

JESUS KING OF ALL NATIONS

A recent devotion and image of Christ that includes medals, prayers, and a chaplet that emphasize Jesus' kingship, based on private revelations to two American women.

"Jesus King of All Nations" is a title derived from Sacred Scripture. In the Book of Revelation Jesus is referred to as the "ruler of the kings on earth" (1:5), as "the King of kings and Lord of lords" (19:16) to whom "all nations shall come and worship" in [his] presence (15:4), and as he who shall judge all nations which will be assembled before him where "he will sit on his glorious throne" (see Matthew 25:31). His kingship is taught in the

Encyclical Letter *Quas Primas* by Pope Pius XI. The devotion has been granted the *Nihil Obstat* by Bishop Enrique Hernandez Rivera D.D., Bishop of Caguas, Puerto Rico. Some of the revelations of the devotion occurred in Puerto Rico.

Large 4' x 6' images have journeyed throughout the world and have been displayed before millions of people for veneration.

Christ the King (Cubilete, Mexico)

JESUS' NAME — See **HOLY NAME OF JESUS**.

JESUS PRAYER

Prayer of Eastern origin, dating back to the fifth century: "Lord Jesus Christ, Son of God, have mercy upon me, a sinner."

Tradition holds that from about the sixth century, the Jesus prayer was used in the Monastery of St. Catherine on Mount Sinai. In the fourteenth century, Gregory of Sinai took the prayer to Mount Athos in Macedonia, which became a center for the praying of it. Gradually, a considerable literature on the use of this prayer developed, and in the eighteenth century, many of these writings were collected and published in Venice under the title *Philokalia: The Love of the Beautiful.* Sometimes the prayer is known as the "Prayer of the Heart." It was not until the middle of the twentieth century that the prayer gained popularity in the Western Church.

(See also **JESUS BEADS**.)

JOCISTS

A popular name of the Catholic association of factory workers known as the *Jeunesse Ouvrière Chrétienne* (J.O.C.), French for "Young Christian Workers."

It was founded by Joseph (later Cardinal) Cardijn in Brussels after World War

I, inspired by the principles enunciated in the encyclical *Rerum Novarum*, issued by Pope Leo XIII. It endeavors to assist in the Christian formation of an active and socially aware laity within the Church.

JOSEPH, RELICS OF ST.

The best know relic of St. Joseph was his girdle or belt, which was brought to France in 1254 by Sire de Joinville on his return from the crusades. The relic was accidentally destroyed in 1668.

JOSEPH, ST. — See ST. JOSEPH.

JOSEPHSTRAGEN

From the German for "the carrying of St. Joseph."

A nine-day pre-Christmas custom in central Europe. Traditionally, boys carry a statue of St. Joseph every night to one of their homes, where they pray to the saint. The number of boys increases by one each night until, on Christmas Eve, all nine, accompanied by girls dressed in white, proceed through the town and place the statue in the manger scene in the parish church.

JOYFUL MYSTERIES — See ROSARY.

JOYS OF THE BLESSED VIRGIN MARY — See SEVEN JOYS OF THE BLESSED VIRGIN MARY.

JUBILATE DEO

Latin for "Be joyful in the Lord."

The opening words of Psalm 100, arranged as a canticle used in the service of morning prayer.

(See also LITURGY OF THE HOURS.)

JUBILATE SUNDAY

The name given to the third Sunday after Easter.

JUBILEE CELEBRATIONS OF PRIESTLY ORDINATION

The jubilee celebrations of priestly ordination can range from a simple personal remembrance to elaborate communal festivities, depending upon prevailing traditions of the area or religious congregation of the priest involved, and on the desire of the individual priest. A plenary indulgence is granted to a priest who on his twenty-fifth, fiftieth, and sixtieth anniversary of priestly ordination renews before God the promise made by him to faithfully fulfill the duties of his vocation. When the Christian faithful participate in the jubilee Mass celebrated by the priest, they also can obtain a plenary indulgence.

JUBILEE CELEBRATIONS OF RELIGIOUS VOWS

Men and women who take religious vows of obedience, poverty, and chastity celebrate the anniversaries of the profession of their vows. The most important milestones are called jubilees and ordinarily occur on the twenty-fifth and fiftieth anniversary.

The most essential aspect of a jubilee celebration for a religious is the Eucharistic Liturgy with Scripture texts specially chosen to highlight God's call of the person. The jubilee celebration can range from a simple personal remembrance, to elaborate community festivities, depending upon prevailing traditions of the specific order or congregation and on the desire of the individual woman or man religious.

Many religious in the active apostolate take a sabbatical from their usual ministries using the designated free time for special studies, renewal programs, or going on pilgrimage. They may become involved in a different ministry. Religious in monastic or contemplative communities often prefer a simple Eucharistic celebration and extra days of retreat for prayer and reading. Special meals and a program about the person's patron saint or a spe-

cial interest may mark the day of the monastic celebration. Jubilee songs and gifts are often added, increasing the joy of the occasion.

JUBILEE YEAR

Derived from a reference in Leviticus 25:8-55 to a "jubilee" year.

Leviticus says it is every "fiftieth year" (25:10). The jubilee was a special year of remission from guilt and sin and the return of lands to their original owners. The year began on the Day of Atonement, the tenth day of Tishri. The Catholic Church uses this term to refer to a "holy year" every twenty-fifth year. It is also used in reference to an extraordinary year of jubilee declared by the Holy Father. When a

Jubilee Year 2000

jubilee year is called, the bishop and his cathedral are the major focal points for celebration. When it is centered in Rome, the right inside door of St. Peter's, which is usually bricked closed, lies open, allowing for pilgrims to walk through and be the recipients of the graces of the jubilee year.

JUDGMENT, GENERAL

The judgment given by God at the end of the world, occurring after Christ's Second Coming.

Each human body will rise. Those who have merited eternal life will possess a glorified body, while those condemned to hell will have bodies that are corrupt.

JUDGMENT OF GOD

A superstitious practice that was used to determine guilt or innocence before legal procedures were established.

Direct, even miraculous, intervention of God was sought to prove innocence.

JUDGMENT, PARTICULAR

The judgment rendered by God at one's death.

The deceased will then go to heaven, purgatory, or hell. When the general judgment occurs, body and soul will be reunited.

JUSTICE

Giving another what is one's due.

Justice is extolled in the Scriptures and by the Magisterium. Commutative justice regards actions between individuals. Distributive justice regulates actions between groups and persons. Social justice concerns the rights and duties that society and individuals have toward each other. Original justice was the state that Adam and Eve enjoyed before the fall. The term is used in some Bible translations as a synonym for "holiness" or "righteousness."

JUSTIFICATION

The process by which a sinner is made "righteous" in the sight of God.

This occurs when one accepts the free and unearned gift of faith and responds to it by acts of charity (i.e., good works performed out of love of God and neighbor).

JUST JUDGE, JESUS THE

An image of Christ based on Matthew 25:31, 26:64; John 5:22; and Acts 10:42. The Just Judge (or, in Spanish, *Justo Juez*) was an early symbol in the Church.

There is a picture often seen in Mexico and other Spanish-speaking countries which is called *Justo Juez* or Just Judge. Jesus is invoked under this title when facing trials in daily living and in particular when fac-

Jesus the Just Judge

ing court battles. The picture is a symbolic reminder of the Passion of Christ.

Jesus crucified and crowned with thorns is at the center of the picture. The artist has painted in many items of the Passion. The post from the scourging, the whip and flagellum, the ropes which bound Christ, the spear which pierced his side, the hammer and other items are shown. A rooster and sun represent Peter's denial. (Veronica's veil showing the face of Christ hangs on the pillar. Even the dice that the soldiers cast to divide Jesus' clothes are shown. A careful inspection of this pic-

ture can lead the viewer to contemplate the entire Passion of Our Lord. Prayers to Jesus under the title of the Just Judge call on him to obtain justice and mercy for the petitioner through the grace of his precious blood.

Unfortunately, like many other true Catholic devotions, devotion to the *Justo Juez* has been corrupted and transferred to an almost magical symbol in some places. Botanicas which sell items for Santeria and the spiritualists sell "magical" candles and "lucky mojo charms" of *Justo Juez* which are practically guaranteed to keep the owner safe from judicial persecution; no mention is made as to whether the petitioner is guilty or not.

One prayer to the Divine and Just Judge claims to date back to the 1500s; it was supposedly approved by the Inquisition and spread by Pope Leo XI. It is also said that Pope Pius IX prayed this prayer to be delivered from assassination, and he was "made invisible to his enemies." It is true that in 1848 Pope Pius IX had to flee Rome during the Italian Revolution and he dressed in disguise to escape. Another claim is that Pope Leo XIII prayed the invocation to be delivered from his enemies and became invisible. What is true is that Pope Leo XIII also lived in an anti-clerical age and was often beset by enemies.

The prayer, written in flowery language, calls upon Jesus as a divine and just judge and implores his aid against all enemies.

It requests that the petitioner be hidden in Christ's sacred wounds and the Holy Sacrament. It calls the cross a strong shield, and prays that the supplicant be given a good death through the merits of the Precious Blood and the Passion of the Redeemer. The prayer closes with the petition: "May the Father deliver me, the Son guard me, and the Holy Spirit accompany me and speak for me."

There is a feast in honor of *Justo Juez* celebrated in Peru.

K

KATERI INDIAN ROSARY

A chaplet associated with Blessed Kateri Tekakwitha, the "Lily of the Mohawks" (1656-1680), and promoted by the Tekakwitha League.

The chaplet is used as a private devotion. The chaplet is made in two basic patterns; one begins with a cross and the other starts with a medal of Blessed Kateri and three beads. The cross is made of sturolite, a mineral which is naturally formed in the shape of a cross. There is an Indian legend that on the day that Christ died, the woodland animals wept, and their tiny tears falling upon the earth crystallized into these small crosses.

There are twenty-four beads of the main rosary representing the twenty-four years Kateri lived on earth. The chaplet has three colors — crystal clear, red, and brownish gold. Many Indians believe that the crystal clear lakes and rivers are the tears of the Great Spirit. The Glory Be is recited on each of the crystal beads. An Our Father is said on each of the brown or gold beads. Earth colors were popular with the Indians, and golden brown is the predominant color of the earth. A Hail Mary is said on the red beads. Red, the traditional color of love, is also the color of the blood that flows in all mankind, transcending race and color.

(See also **CHAPLET**.)

Kateri Indian Rosary

Chaplet of Blessed Kateri Tekakwitha

KATHISMA

From the Greek for "seat" or "stall."

When the Book of Psalms is divided into twenty sections, as it is in the Byzantine Rite, each section is called a *kathisma*. Each *kathisma* is further separated into three segments, concluding with the Glory Be. Psalm 119 is its own *kathisma* because of its length (one hundred seventy-six verses). The other nineteen range in length from six to fifteen Psalms, all depending on the length of the Psalms.

KENOSIS

From the Greek for "an emptying."

In theology, it is Christ's emptying of himself in his free renunciation of his right to divine status, "the form of God," by reason of the Incarnation, particularly as celebrated in the kenotic hymn of Philippians 2:6-11, where it is said that Christ "emptied himself, taking the form of a servant, being born in the likeness of men" — that is, a full and real humanity, totally integrated with his divinity.

In Gnostic circles, it was popular to depict the crucified Christ in the position of *kenosis*, namely, with his hands raised above his head to bespeak total and utter dependence upon the Father from whom he had descended to earth.

KERYGMA

Proclaiming the Word of God, in the manner of the Apostles, as here and now effective for salvation.

This method of preaching or instruction, centered on Christ and geared to the facts and themes of salvation history, is designed to dispose people to faith in Christ and to intensify the experience and practice of the faith in those who have it.

KEVALAER

A center of devotion to Mary as Comforter of the Afflicted located in Kevalaer, Germany.

(See also **CONSOLATION, OUR LADY OF**.)

KEYS, POWER OF THE — See **POWER OF THE KEYS**.

KIBEHO, OUR LADY OF

A Marian devotion and image.

It is based on a claim by seven children that Mary appeared to them in Kibeho, Rwanda, in the early 1980s.

KINGS' CAKE

A food associated with the Feast of the Epiphany and the visit of the three Magi.

In some traditions, a tiny doll representing the Infant Jesus is baked in a cake. The guest who receives the piece containing the doll hosts a party later in the year or the following year.

(See also EPIPHANY; MAGI.)

KINGSHIP OF CHRIST

A Christological doctrine.

It was formally declared by Pope Pius XI, in 1925, in his encyclical *Quas Primas*, that Jesus Christ is King (see Matthew 21:9; Mark 11:10; Luke 1:33), both by birthright as the Son of God and by right as Redeemer. As early as the Annunciation, God's plan of salvation is revealed to Mary that she is to give birth to God's divine Son (see Luke 1:26-38), and is thus linked to God's promise to give the Child the throne of David, his royal ancestor. For the individual believer, Christ's kingship will be realized as the fulfillment of his pledge of everlasting life and peace at the end of history. The kingship of Christ signifies his rule, reign, and dominion, whereby he grants salvation, justice, and mercy to the righteous and judges the unrighteous with the same justice and mercy.

KISS OF PEACE

A term sometimes used for the sign of peace exchanged at Mass; in early funeral rites, the kissing of the body.

While the funeral custom continues to-day among some laity, the practice has long since been discontinued by the clergy.

KISSING — See EASTERN RITES, SACRAMENTALS IN.

KISSING THE FOOT OF ST. PETER'S STATUE

An ancient custom of pilgrims to Rome.

Visitors kiss or touch the foot of the bronze statue of St. Peter in the basilica named for him while praying for the intentions of the pope.

KISSING THE HANDS OF A NEWLY ORDAINED PRIEST

A pious custom.

Traditionally, the palms are kissed on the day of ordination and on the day of the new priest's first Mass.

KISSING THE RING

A traditional sign of respect.

The kissing of the pope's ring (or that of a cardinal or bishop) has fallen out of use in recent times.

KNIGHTS OF COLUMBUS

A Catholic layman's fraternal organization begun in 1882 by Father Michael McGivney in New Haven, Connecticut.

Knights of Columbus Emblem

This organization serves the Church by promoting unity among Catholic laymen, resulting in the performing of charitable works such as contributing to causes to assist the mentally handicapped and financially supporting the Holy See.

KNIGHTS OF MALTA
The common name of the sovereign Military Hospitaler Order of St. John of Jerusalem, of Rhodes and of Malta, also referred to as the "Hospitalers." The oldest religious order of chivalry.

Begun during the First Crusade in 1070, the group had as its purpose the protection and care of pilgrims in the Holy Land. The order received papal approval in 1113, and when it was expelled by the Muslims, its members retreated finally to Malta, where they were the temporal rulers until the Napoleonic invasion in 1798. The Knights of Malta is a religious order recognized not only by the Holy See but also under international law as a sovereign entity. At one time its membership was restricted to members of the nobility, but there is a more recent category of knights and dames for persons not of the noble classes.

KNIGHTS, ORDERS OF
Special organizations of laymen.

Originating in the Middle Ages, a knight was a man who was raised to an honorable military rank by the monarch or other qualified person after serving an apprenticeship as a page or squire and pledging himself to the principles of chivalry. The most worthy of these knights were sometimes organized into orders, and some even made religious vows.

KNIGHTS, PAPAL
Pontifical orders of knighthood.

They include: the Supreme Order of Christ (Militia of Our Lord Jesus Christ); the Order of the Golden Spur (Golden Militia); the Order of Pius IX; the Order of St. Gregory the Great; and the Order of Pope St. Sylvester. Membership in these orders is granted by the pope to honor certain individuals, most often those who have rendered some meritorious service to the Church or society.

KNOCK, OUR LADY OF
A Marian devotion and image.

It is based on reported apparitions in Knock, Ireland, in 1879. Eighteen witnesses, ages six to seventy-five, reported seeing Mary, St. Joseph, and St. John the Evangelist. None of the three spoke. The scene lasted for a little over an hour and a half. Cures have been attributed to Our Lady of Knock, and a shrine has been established in the town.

The image is also sometimes called Our Lady of Silence.

KNOTS, THE VIRGIN WHO UNTIES
A traditional German Marian devotion.

Particularly popular in Argentina under its Spanish equivalent, *La Virgen Desatanudos*, the devotion was brought to that country in the early 1980s by Archbishop Jorge Mario Bergoglio, S.J., who at that time was rector at the Jesuit University of El Salvador in Buenos Aires. The archbishop had come upon the image at the Church of St. Peter am Perlach, during a visit to

Our Lady of Knock

Augsburg where it is known as *Knotenlöserin* (the one who unties the knots).

The painting, attributed to Baroque German artist Johann Melchior Georg Schmittdner, dates to the early seventeenth century. Mary is represented with an angel on her left side handing her a white ribbon full of knots; as the ribbon continues through Mary's hands, it falls to her right side, with the knots untied, into the hands of a second angel.

Some historians claim that the original devotion was painted to symbolize Mary as the one who unties the knots, the troubles, of married life. Others claim the theme is an ancient one, going back to St. Irenaeus, with Mary, "the New Eve," untying the knots of sin and the consequences of sin first caused by Adam and Eve.

The prayer to Our Lady of Desatanudos, composed by Archbishop Mario Bergoglio, reads:

Holy Mary, full of God's presence, during the days of your life you accepted with full humility the Father's will, and the Devil was never capable to tie you around with his confusion. Once with your Son, you interceded for our difficulties and, full of kindness and patience, you gave us example of how to untie the knots of our life. And by remaining forever Our Mother, you put in order and make more clear the ties that link us to the Lord. Holy Mary, Mother of God and Our Mother, to you, who untie with motherly heart the knots of our life, we pray you to receive in your hands (the name of the person) and to free him/her of the knots and confusions with which our enemy attacks. For your grace, your intercession, and your example, deliver us from all evil, Our Lady, and untie the knots that prevent us from being united with God, so that we, free from sin and error, may find Him in all things, may have our hearts placed in Him, and may serve Him always in our brothers and sisters. Amen.

KOIMESIS

A Greek term meaning "a falling-asleep."

In the Byzantine Church this is applied to death in general. In particular, *koimesis* refers to the holy dormition (assumption) of the Mother of God, observed on August 15. July 25 marks the *koimesis* of St. Anne, the mother of Mary.

KOINONIA

From the Greek *koinos* (to have or share in common partnership).

Generally, it means anything from an association, communion (social), fellowship, and sometimes close relationships, to solidarity or generosity, to the more abstract notion of a verbal sign of fellow-ship or proof of brotherly unity, to the explicit concept of participation and sharing in or of something.

It was a term favored by St. Luke for the fellowship of believers who worshiped together and held all their possessions in common.

KONTAKION

A Byzantine Rite hymn.

It recalls in an abbreviated form the subject of the day's feast; it is sung after the sixth ode of the canon at the Little Hours and the Liturgy. For example, the *kontakion* for a funeral is: "With the saints, O Christ, give rest to your servant(s) where there is no pain, sorrow, nor mourning, but life everlasting."

KRASHANKY, PYSANKY

A Ukrainian Easter tradition.

It consists of using decorated eggs as symbols of the tomb from which Christ arose and of hope. *Pysanky* are highly decorated and are exchanged with friends and relatives to show the good wishes given to them. *Krashanky* are plain-colored and are used at Easter breakfast at which a family shares one as a symbol of unity.

(See also EASTER BREAD (PASKA, BABKA); EASTER EGGS.)

KUCIOS

The Twelve Apostles' Dinner; a Christmas Eve tradition in many areas of Europe.

A sumptuous, and often meatless, family dinner that ends the Advent fast, the *kucios* has a number of customary dishes particular to certain regions. For example: a bowl of porridge with fruit and honey to represent the Holy Crib or apples as a reminder of Adam and Eve. In some homes, the head of the household breaks a traditional Christmas wafer and all who are there share it. Another custom is setting a place at the table for a family member unable to attend or for one who has died during the previous year.

(See also OPLATKI.)

KYRIALE

A book of Gregorian chants.

It predates Vatican II and is no longer used today. Some of these chants can now be found in *Jubilate Deo.*

KYRIE ELEISON — CHRISTE ELEISON

Greek for "Lord, have mercy" and "Christ, have mercy."

An ancient Greek petition that is said or sung in services or worship of both the Eastern and the Western Churches.

L

LA CHAPELLE, OUR LADY OF

A shrine in the Church of La Chapelle in Brussels, Belgium.

It contains an ancient Marian image.

LA CONQUISTADORA

A Marian devotion and small wooden statue.

Near Christmas of 1625, Father Alonso Benavides, Franciscan superior of the New Mexico missions, brought the statue to the Church of the Assumption in Santa Fe. Decorated with bright arabesques over gold leaf, it was a representation of the Assumption of Our Lady. The image became the focus of a Marian confraternity, and her devotees dressed her to look like a Spanish queen in the style of those days. The image was given the official title "Our Lady of the Rosary," but came to be known as *La Conquistadora* because it had arrived in the days of the conquistadors. 1694, the colonists began an annual thanksgiving observance, carrying the image in procession to a shrine of boughs and singing a novena of Masses. *La Conquistadora* has been venerated and feted continuously to this day, not

Two Versions of Our Lady, La Conquistadora

as a miraculous statue but simply as a long-enduring symbol of a people's unfailing love for the Mother of God. The image was crowned in 1954 with an Episcopal Coronation and with a Papal Coronation in 1960.

LA NAVAL

A Marian devotion and image; also known as Our Lady of the Rosary of the Philippines.

The statue, depicting Mary as a Filipina in royal clothes typical of seventeenth-century Spain, was commissioned 1593 by the Spanish governor-general of the Philippines on the death of his father. Because victories at sea became associated with the October 7 Feast of Our Lady of the Rosary, the title *La Naval* came to be used for Mary in her role as helper of navies. Miracles have been attributed to her intercession.

Almost five feet in height, the statue — which is made of hardwood but with Jesus' and Mary's faces carved from ivory — was presented to the Manila Dominicans and enshrined in the old Santo Domingo Church. During World War II, the shrine was bombed and, after being hidden in the church's vault, the statue was moved to the chapel at the University of St. Thomas. In l952, the cornerstone was laid for a new shrine at the Santo Domingo Church in Quezon City.

LA SALETTE, OUR LADY OF

A Marian devotion.

It is based on an apparition of the Blessed Mother reported by two children, Maximin Giraud and Mélanie Calvat Matthieu, outside the French village of La Salette in 1846. The basilica that was later built there has become a major pilgrimage destination.

September 19, l846 was the eve of the Feast of Our Lady of Sorrows. Maximin, age eleven, and Melanie, age fourteen, were tending cows in a field in the French alps in the parish of LaSalette. The children had met only the day before, so there was no chance of their making up the incredible story that they told of the events of that day.

The children were typical of many of the inhabitants of the area. After the French Revolution, this part of France had never returned to the Catholic faith. Only a few old people attended Mass. Sunday was seen by most of the people as only another working day. Days of fast and abstinence were ignored. Blasphemy was common. Neither of the children had attended school, neither attended church regularly, and each knew only a few prayers.

At the ringing of the angelus, Maximin and Melanie took their small herd to water them in a small ravine, after which they ate their rude lunch of cheese and bread and stretched out in the sun for a short nap. Awakening, Melanie realized they had overslept, and the children rushed to find the cows. Fortunately, they were all grazing peacefully together. With a sigh of relief, Melanie returned to the ravine to retrieve their knapsacks. There in the ravine, only a few steps away, blazed a great circle of light. Quickly she called Maximin, who saw it too. Both children were frightened, although Maximin told her that if it attempted to hurt them he would hit it with his staff.

Before their eyes, the globe of light grew in intensity and brilliance, then opened up to reveal the figure of a woman, seated, with her face bowed in her hands. Her elbows rested on her knees and she was weeping.

The luminous figure then arose, her head inclined a little to one side, her arms crossed on her breast. The beauty of her face was extraordinary, despite the tears. A white headdress covered her hair, clung to her cheeks and hid her neck. A towering crown rested on her brow, edged below with roses of many colors which gave off shimmering rays of light. She wore a long white dress with full sleeves which was sprinkled with bursts of light. She wore a small shawl trimmed with roses which seemed to form golden lace. Along the hem of the shawl were metal links, not joined in a chain but distinctly separated one from the next. Tied about her waist was a large apron, yellow and glittering as

gold. She wore white slippers decorated with clusters of pearls, gold buckles, and the same sort of roses as those on the crown and shawl. She wore a crucifix depended from a chain, and the children later described the figure on the cross as of fire. To the left of the crucifix was a hammer; to the right a pair of pliers, half open.

Then the woman spoke gently, "Come to me my children, do not be afraid. I am here to tell you something of the greatest importance."

Their fright disappeared, and the children stepped forward, descending into the ravine and crossing the bed of the stream. The beautiful lady moved toward them, until they, too, were enveloped in the globe of light.

Our Lady told the children that prayer, penance, and humility were needed and that a terrible disaster would strike if the people did not repent of their sins. She also complained that Sundays were not being observed and that blasphemy was prevalent.

Initially speaking in French, the lady changed to the local dialect which the children understood. After telling the children to make her message known, the apparition disappeared.

The children told their story at home that night and word spread. The adults instructed them to report to the parish priest the following day.

The bishop began a lengthy, exacting, and proper investigation. A number of miraculous healings occurred, and the people of the area began to heed the warning and return to the practice of their religion. Eventually, the bishop drew up the doctrinal pronouncement on LaSalette, which he signed on the fifth anniversary of the apparition, September 19, 1851. It was examined by Rome and then printed and distributed in all of the churches under Bishop de Bruillard's authority. In it, he declared that the apparition had all the marks of truth, and authorized the cult of Our Lady of LaSalette. A basilica was built in her honor at the site, and successive popes have given statements of credence to the cult. Both St. John Bosco and St. Peter Julian Eymard found inspiration in LaSalette. An order of priests dedicated to Our Lady under this title was begun with a specific mission to work for reconciliation. These priests have spread throughout the world, carrying Our Lady's message to the millions.

The children of LaSalette did not go on to become great saints. They did, however, fulfill their mission, to make known Our Lady's words. With the exception of the beautiful thirty minutes when they were privileged to behold the wonderful visitor from heaven, and the joy of being chosen to communicate her message to the world, the entire lives of Melanie Calvat Matthieu and Maximin Giraud are to be pitied. Both began in poverty and ignorance, and both ended in mental instability. It is to their credit that they never deviated from the facts of their initial story of the apparition.

LADY CHAPEL

A chapel dedicated to the Virgin Mary.

Traditionally, it was behind or near the main altar.

LADY DAY

Another name for the Feast of the Annunciation.

(See also **ANNUNCIATION**.)

LADY IN BLUE

Mysterious appearances of a Spanish nun in the New World.

Sister Marie de Jesus Agreda was born April 2, 1602, in Agreda, Spain, and was christened Maria Fernandez Coronel. Eventually, she became a nun of the Franciscan order, at the Agreda monastery. In 1627 she became abbess, an office she held until her death in 1665. These nuns, known as the Conceptionists, wore a brown Franciscan habit with a rough blue cloak over it.

Her best known work is *The Mystical City of God* (1670), a life of the Virgin Mary ostensibly based on divine revelations granted to Maria. It was placed on the list of forbidden books in 1681, but the ban was lifted in 1747. Her virtues and holy life were universally acknowledged, but controversy arose over her mystical writings, her political influence, and her bilocation.

In 1620, when the young nun was only eighteen, she began having visions, or raptures. After long meditation, she would sometimes tell the other nuns that she had spiritually traveled to a faraway land, meeting dark-skinned people to whom she told the story of Christ. Convinced of the reality of her experiences, she wrote a book in which she described, in great detail, her missionary work in the New World. Word spread and people began to talk about the strange young nun. Before long the Inquisition heard of her controversial claims. Although she insisted that she was bilocating and doing God's work, a public trial ensued in 1635.

During the trial, a newly-returned expedition of conquistadors and friars arrived in Spain with an amazing story. These explorers had entered the unexplored region north of Mexico and had encountered numerous Native American tribes in what is now New Mexico, Arizona, and Texas who already knew of Jesus Christ the Savior, and who requested to be baptized. The Indians claimed to have been visited by a light-skinned woman dressed in blue who appeared drifting in a haze while she spoke of the Lord in their own language. They, naturally, assumed that the Indians had seen the Blessed Mother, until they heard of the claims of Maria Agreda. She was acquitted by the Inquisition.

Sister Maria is buried in a secluded crypt on the grounds of the Conceptionist Convent, the same monastery where she had lived. Her body is incorrupt. Her casket was opened in 1909 and the body seemed in peaceful repose. It was exhumed again in 1989, and respectfully re-buried in a glass-fronted casket. She has been declared Venerable by the Catholic Church.

LAETARE SUNDAY — See GAUDETE SUNDAY.

LAICISM

An idea that gained prominence in the nineteenth century.

It called for a minimizing of the role of the clergy in both ecclesiastical and civil affairs, and making all temporal and almost all spiritual matters the responsibility of the laity. It was a form of anticlericalism and secularism, opposed to any influence by the Church upon political or cultural matters. For these reasons, it was condemned in 1864 by Pope Pius IX in the *Syllabus of Errors*.

LAMB (EUCHARIST)

In the Byzantine Rite, the name given to

the larger portion of the Bread of Offering detached by the priest for Consecration.

The Lamb is inscribed with Greek letters that stand for "Jesus Christ conquers."

LAMB OF GOD

A liturgical title for Christ recited three times before the distribution of the Eucharist at Mass.

The priest then elevates the consecrated Host before the people and says: "This is the Lamb of God who takes away the sins of the world" (see John 1:29).

(See also **EASTER; AGNUS DEI.**)

LAMBS OF ST. AGNES — See **PALLIUM**.

LAMENTATIONS, BOOK OF

Five poems, written in the style of a dirge or elegy, that tradition ascribes to Jeremiah, to whose prophecy the Septuagint and Vulgate attach them, though they are likely the work of his disciples.

They provide an answer for the believing Jews to all the complaints of those whose faith had weakened with the fall of Jerusalem (586 B.C.). The Catholic liturgy appropriates these poems in the Office of Tenebrae, celebrated during Holy Week to express the mourning of Christians over

the suffering and death of the Messiah.

LAMMAS-DAY

The name applied in the early days of the Church to the Feast of the Chains of St. Peter, celebrated on August 1.

LAMP

The symbol representing God's Word.

It portrays knowledge, one of the seven gifts of the Holy Spirit. Also, it is an object, mandated by Canon Law, that reminds believers of the Real Presence of Christ in the Blessed Sacrament. Used in the sanctuary since the thirteenth century, the lamp also provided light during the liturgy in the early Church.

LAMP-LIGHTING

An ancient ritual.

The practice of lamp-lighting at Vespers, or evening prayer, harks back to the Jewish ritual of lighting lamps at the beginning of the Sabbath. In her fourth-century diary reflecting liturgical practice in Jerusalem, the Spanish nun Egeria observes that Vespers was celebrated in the late afternoon and that lights were kindled from the lamp that always burned in the grotto of the Anastasis (the Sanctuary of the Resurrection). The revival of such a practice today seems appropriate. The theme of light is present in many Vespers antiphons, Psalms, and prayers.

LANCE, HOLY

A relic reputed to be the weapon with which Jesus' side was pierced during the crucifixion.

Its existence is not recorded before the middle of the sixth century. In 629, it was placed in the Church of the Holy Sepulcher in Jerusalem. Before this, the tip had been broken off and taken to Constantinople to the Church of Hagia Sophia. In 1241, the tip was used in payment of a debt to the French king St. Louis IX, and the relic was eventually enshrined in Paris's Sainte-Chapelle. It disappeared during the French Revolution. The main body of the lance seems also to have been taken to Constantinople at an unknown date, and in 1492 it was sent as a gift to Pope Innocent VIII and has since remained at the Vatican. There are other relics that claim to be the remnants of the spear.

(See also **RELICS**.)

LAPSED

A term used as early as the time of Cyprian of Carthage (d. 258) to refer to those Christian converts who had abandoned the Christian faith and practice and returned to their pagan beliefs.

In modern usage, a lapsed Catholic is understood to be one who has consciously abandoned the Catholic faith, specifically by absenting oneself from the sacramental life of the Church, which is most clearly observable in the failure to make the Easter duty.

LAS MANANITAS

A Mexican folk song traditionally sung early in the morning on birthdays and anniversaries, and to the dying who are "being born into eternal life."

It has become the custom in some parishes on the Feast of Our Lady of Guadalupe to spend part of the night in prayer and to form a very early morning procession carrying an image of the Virgin and saluting her in song. The first verse and refrain are:

How beautiful is this morning,
And our hearts are light and gay,
As we sing this song of blessing,
To awaken you today.

The sun is now appearing,
As the day begins anew.
Arise now and greet the morning
That dawns with joy for you.

LAST SACRAMENTS

Usually refers to the sacraments of penance, anointing of the sick, and Viaticum.

It may also refer to confirmation, when it is known that this sacrament had not been received already. These may be administered to those who are dying or are in imminent danger of death.

LAST SUPPER

The traditional name given to the Passover meal that Christ ate in the upper room in Jerusalem with his Apostles the night that began his Passion.

The site of this meal is also called the Cenacle, from the Latin *cena* (meal), in recognition of the Last Supper that was eaten there. During this meal, Christ instituted the sacraments of the Eucharist and the priesthood. While the Eucharist does repeat the historical event of the Last Supper, it also brings the participants into a present relationship with Christ and anticipates their future glory, with all three dimensions necessarily present at once in the sacrament.

LAST THINGS — See ESCHATOLOGY.

LATERAN BASILICA

The Church of the Most Holy Savior, in Rome.

It is the cathedral of the bishop of Rome, the pope. It was presented to the Church in 311 as part of a donation from the Laterani family and is considered the mother church of the Christian world. It is the oldest Christian basilica. Its alternate name, St. John Lateran, derives from the great baptistery built beside it. Because it was Rome's earliest baptismal church, it soon acquired the secondary title of St. John the Baptist.

(See also **BASILICA**.)

LATIN

In ancient times the language of the inhabitants of the Italian province of Latium, whose capital is Rome.

With the increased influence and power achieved by the Romans and their subsequent colonization of most of the then-known world, the Latin language also spread along with Roman customs and laws. The Latin language was gradually adopted by Christians in the early Church as more and more Latin-speaking peoples were converted to the faith. By the middle of the fourth century, the liturgy was also celebrated in Latin. Since then, up to our own day, Latin has been the official language of the Latin Rite of the Church. Even though today the vernacular may be used regularly in the liturgy, the Second Vatican Council, responsible in part for the introduction of native tongues into official worship, nevertheless refers to Latin as the official language of the Latin (i.e., the Roman) Church and the liturgy of the Latin Rite.

LATIN MASS

The Eucharistic Sacrifice celebrated in the official language of the Roman Catholic Church.

The vernacular is used predominantly in most places where Mass is offered in the Latin Rite; however, Vatican II did not abolish Latin and use of Latin is permissible at any time, in accord with the pastoral judgment of the celebrant.

LATIN RITE

The portion of the Catholic Church that follows the disciplines and teachings of the diocese of Rome, especially regarding the liturgy.

This rite is called "Latin" because that has been its official language since the fourth century. Most of the world's Catholics belong to the Latin Rite, which is headed by the pope, the bishop of Rome.

LATRIA

The highest form of worship, which can be offered to God alone.

(See also **DULIA**.)

LAUDS

The traditional name for the office of morning prayer of the Liturgy of the Hours.

LAURA

A group of individual cells or rooms occupied by monks.

It was centered around the church. While living in the *laura* the monks maintained a community life. The name is still applied to any large monastery of the Byzantine Rite.

LAUREL

Bay laurel, a small evergreen with a long historical and mythological tradition.

In Psalm 37, David mentions the bay tree. In ancient Greece and Rome, laurel leaves were awarded to the victors in games and heroes returning from war. From the Greek word for laurel berry (*bacca lauri*) comes the English "baccalaureate." Used as a Christmas decoration, the laurel proclaims the victory over sin and death that Christ's birth signifies. Laurel was the first plant used as a Christmas decoration; the

Bay Laurel

early Christians in Rome adorned their homes with it in celebration of the Nativity of Christ.

LAVABO

From the Latin for "I will wash."

This the part of the Mass after the Offertory at which the server pours water on the thumbs and index fingers of the priest, the parts of his hands that will touch the Host. It symbolizes the need for the priest to be purified before offering the sacred mysteries in *persona Christi*. Also, it is the name of the dish into which the poured water drops or the name of the sink in the sacristy.

LAVANG, OUR LADY OF

A Marian devotion based on apparitions reported by the Catholic community in Hué, Vietnam, in 1800; also known as Duc Me La Vang.

The first Catholic missionaries arrived in Vietnam in 1533. A scant hundred years later, there were more than 100,000 Catholics. Seminaries were established, and by 1668, two native priests were ordained. A group of women religious was formed in 1670 which is still active today.

Throughout history, Catholics have been persecuted for their faith, and Vietnam was no exception. Severe persecutions broke out in 1698. In the eighteenth century, there were three more persecutions, and again in the nineteenth century, Vietnamese Catholics were persecuted, but stood firm, in spite of the danger. More than one-hundred-thousand Catholics were martyred in the mid-1800s alone. Today, under the communist regime, the bishops and priests are still harassed. Still, pilgrims flock annually to the site of the former shrine of Our Lady of Lavang which was established in 1800 near Hué.

At the end of the eighteenth century, the persecution of Catholics in central

Our Lady of Lavang

Vietnam was so severe that a large group of Catholics fled to a remote jungle area in the mountains near Lavang. This is in a forested area in the central part of the country where there are numerous trees named La' Vang. The Vietnamese meaning of the word is "Crying Out" and denotes the cries for help of the people. They wished to be free to practice their religion, as well as to save their lives.

One evening in 1798, as the community was reciting the Rosary together, there was an apparition of a beautiful lady holding a little child in her arms, and with angels surrounding her. The lady was dressed simply, but wearing a crown. The people recognized the beautiful Lady as the Queen of heaven. She spoke to the people in the loving tones of a mother. She encouraged and comforted them. Displaying a tender concern for her children, she taught the people how to make medicines from the plants and herbs that grew in the area.

She also promised her protection to any who would come to that particular site to pray. As at Guadalupe, Our Lady came as a mother, bringing only messages of comfort. The apparition appeared again a number of times in the grassy area where the people were praying near an ancient banyon tree.

The people of Lavang built a simple church of leaves and rice straw, and dedicated it to Mary. Devotion to her grew,

and a number of miraculous cures and favors were reported. Through other persecutions, the Lavang area continued to be a sanctuary for oppressed Catholics.

In 1805, officers of the Vietnamese emperor began an anti-colonial movement. They were determined to rid the country of all Catholics, and Lavang was no longer safe. Thirty Catholics were put to death by the emperor's soldiers right at the door to their little church. The church was burned, although not by one of the soldiers. The soldiers had heard of the miraculous deeds at Lavang and were frightened to destroy the chapel. Amazingly, the altar and the chandeliers, both made of wood, survived the fire. The people then rebuilt their beloved shrine. On the site where the original apparitions took place, a new brick church was begun in 1885. It was completed in 1900, and in 1901 the first annual celebration of the Shrine of Our Lady of Lavang took place. More than 130,000 Catholics from all over the country participated. Devotion to Our Lady of Lavang grew rapidly, and by 1925 it was necessary to enlarge the complex because of the throngs of worshipers. This church was completed in 1928. Many non-Christians acknowledged that there was something special about this place. In the early 1920s, the emperor of Vietnam fell ill. A non-Christian, he sent one of his Christian ministers to pray for him at the shrine. He recovered speedily.

During World War II, Vietnam was a battleground for the Japanese and the French. After this, the French and the communists, known as the Vietcong, battled until 1954 when they split the country into two governments. Almost a million people fled from the communists in the north. At that time, Lavang became a center of pilgrimage. In 1961, the conference of the Vietnamese bishops made the church the national shrine of the country. In August of 1961, Pope Paul VI conferred on the church the title of Basilica of Our Lady of Lavang.

By April 1975, when South Vietnam fell under the control of the communists, the Lavang complex had enlarged to include a retreat center, a hospitality center, an outdoor amphitheatre, and a beautiful statue of Mary commemorating her apparitions. The shrine was destroyed during the war, but the outside altar remains a place of pilgrimage.

LAXISM

A system, arising in the seventeenth century within moral theology, which taught that if any doubt could be raised concerning the morality of some action, one would be free to ignore the law without sinning.

Laxism was condemned by Pope Alexander VII in 1665 and again in 1666. In 1679, Pope Innocent XI condemned sixty-five propositions drawn from the Laxist system.

LAY BAPTISM

The administration of the sacrament of baptism by a layperson when a sacred minister is not available or is impeded.

LAY BROTHERS AND SISTERS

Those who enter religious life, receiving habits and taking vows, but who engage themselves chiefly in manual labor and do not assume the choir duties, study, or other functions of the religious, and who do not receive holy orders.

LAYMEN AND LAYWOMEN

Members of the faithful.

Laypersons are those who have not been admitted to the ranks of the clergy and those who have no ecclesiastical title.

LAY ORGANIZATIONS

Groups of laypeople.

Like all the faithful, laymen and laywomen are called by God to the apostolate in virtue of their baptism and confirmation. They have the obligation and right, individually or together in associations, to work for the spread and acceptance of the divine message of salvation everywhere. This obligation is more urgent in those circumstances in which people can hear the Gospel and get to know Christ only through them (laypersons). They are bound to bring an evangelical spirit to bear on the order of temporal things and to give Christian witness in carrying out their secular pursuits.

Some apostolates and groups include: Apostleship of the Sea; Auxiliaries of Our Lady of the Cenacle; Catholic Central Union of America; Catholic Medical Mission Board; Catholic Movement for Intellectual and Cultural Affairs; Catholic Network of Volunteer Service; Center for Applied Research in the Apostolate (CARA); Christian Family Movement (CFM); Christian Life Communities; Cursillo Movement; Franciscan Mission Service of North America (an Overseas Lay Ministry Program); The Grail; Jesuit Volunteer Corps; LAMP Ministries; Lay Mission-Helpers Association; The Mission Doctors Association; Legion of Mary; Movimiento Familiar Cristiano — USA (MFC); National Catholic Conference for Seafarers; Pax Christi USA; Schoenstatt Lay Movement; Volunteer Missionary Movement; and Volunteers for Educational and Social Services (VESS).

LEAGUE FOR RELIGIOUS AND CIVIL RIGHTS, CATHOLIC

An organization founded in 1973 by Jesuit Father Virgil Blum.

Numbering about thirty thousand members, the Catholic League works to defend the civil and religious rights of Catholics in the United States. Through educational programs, the League provides a forum for discussion of Catholic participation in the public life of the nation. The League also seeks to counter anti-Catholic propaganda and prejudice.

LEAGUE OF THE CROSS

An organization founded in 1873 by Cardinal Manning (d. 1892).

Its full name is The Catholic Total Abstinence League of the Cross, and its goal is to foster abstinence from intemperance among English Catholics.

LECTOR (LAY READER)

A layperson (whether male or female) who has been trained and is competent to proclaim the Word of God (Sacred Scripture, except the Gospel) during liturgical celebrations.

He or she may read the Psalm and announce the intentions of the Prayer of the Faithful.

LEGION OF MARY

An international apostolate begun in Dublin, Ireland, in 1921 by Frank Duff.

Its purpose is for members to give glory

Legion of Mary

to God through prayer and service. The Legion of Mary is the largest apostolic organization of laypeople in the world with some three million members. Among its works are door-to-door evangelization, parishioner visitation, prison ministry, and visitation of the sick or aged. Legionaries are under the guidance of a spiritual director named by the pastor.

LEGEND, GOLDEN — See **GOLDEN LEGEND**.

LENT

The Church's primary penitential season in the liturgical year.

Lent begins on Ash Wednesday and lasts until the Mass of the Lord's Supper on Holy Thursday. The season has six Sundays; the final one, known as Passion (or Palm) Sunday, begins Holy Week. The origin of Lenten observances dates back to the fourth century or earlier. The length of the season reflects the forty days Christ spent praying and fasting in the desert (see Matthew 4:1-11) and is a time of preparation for the great feast of Easter.

(See also **EASTER**; **HOLY WEEK**.)

LENTEN MOURNING

A medieval tradition of both Church and state forbidding public entertainment and festivities.

Among some royal courts the season was seen as an official period of mourning, and the monarchs and their households dressed in black. Many of the nobility and even the commoners often followed the custom.

LEOPOLDINE ASSOCIATION

A missionary aid association founded in Austria in 1829 to channel resources to the developing Church in the United States.

LEPANTO, BATTLE OF

A naval battle that took place in 1571 between Christian and Turkish forces, marking the decline of the Muslim military forces in Europe.

Pope St. Pius V, who had urged devotion to the Rosary as spiritual preparation for the battle to come, declared October 7 as the Feast of Our Lady of the Rosary, in honor of the victory.

LEPER WINDOW

A low window in the chancel wall of a church that enabled lepers, who had to stay outside the church, to attend Mass and receive alms.

Covered with bars or shutters, this window was found in medieval churches and is not presently used.

LIBER PONTIFICALIS

Latin for "the papal book."

It contained biographies of the popes through Martin V (1431). For the first four centuries, these biographies are very sketchy. In later centuries, though, especially the eighth and ninth, the biographies of some popes were so extensive that each could constitute a volume in itself.

LIBER USUALIS

A book containing chants for the Ordinary and Propers of the Mass, along with those used in the Liturgy of the Hours.

Even though the chants were used before the Second Vatican Council, those chants for the Ordinary of the Mass are still usable today. The book is edited by the Benedictine monks of Solesmes.

LILY

A flower that has come to be symbolically associated with the purity of Mary, St. Joseph, and other saints.

The white of the *Lilium candidum* (Madonna lily) came to symbolize the Virgin's purity. Even today, this flower is traditionally used in Europe in the celebrations of the Visitation. In early paintings of the Annunciation, St. Gabriel originally carried a scepter or a spray of olive leaves; later, the lily replaced these in artistic representations of the occasion. Native to warmer regions, lilies began to appear in the gardens of Europe by the fourteenth century. Lilies are blessed on the Feast of St. Anthony of Padua. As part of the ritual blessing, the priest prays:

> You [God] in your great kindness have given them to man, and endowed them with a sweet fragrance to lighten the burden of the sick. Therefore, let them be filled with

such power that whether they are used by the sick, or kept in homes or other places, or devoutly carried on one's person, they may serve to drive out evil spirits, safeguard holy chastity, and turn away illness ... all this through the prayers of St. Anthony ... and finally impart to your servants grace and peace through Christ our Lord.

St. Joseph is usually represented in art holding lilies to symbolize the blooming branch he took to the temple and also to symbolize his purity, virginity, and virtue. (See also **EASTER LILY**.)

LILY OF THE VALLEY

A flower and one of the titles for Christ.

Anna Maria Taigi, a housewife, mother, and mystic who is now counted among the beati of the Church was one day in church when Our Lord appeared to her in the Eucharist. She saw within the Host a beautiful lily in full bloom. Upon this flower, as though it were a throne, appeared the Lord in supernatural beauty. While admiring this vision, she heard a voice saying: "I am the flower of the field, the lily of the valley." St. Francis of Assisi gave orders to the brother gardener not to plant the entire garden in pot herbs (useful herbs and food) but to leave part to produce flowers "for the love of Him Who is called the flower of the field and the lily of the valley."

Another name for the Lily of the Valley is "Mary's tears." It was a popular flower for the garlands used on Whitsunday in England.

LIMPIAS, CRUCIFIX OF

The Crucifix of Christ of the Agony of Limpias.

In Limpias, a suburb of the capital city of Spain, the parish church contains a life size wooden crucifix known as the "Christ of the Agony." The crucifix is the work of a seventeenth century artist, Pedro de Mena. It was brought from southern Spain and donated to the church by a parishioner about the year 1776.

March 30, 1919, the crucifix began a number of supernatural manifestations that lasted for about a year, and fifteen hundred people gave sworn testimonies in the years 1919 and 1920. Different witnesses testified to seeing different things; for some, the eyes appeared to move, for others the expression on the face of the Christ changed. For some, the crucifix appeared to be alive, and suffering in agony.

The crucifix of Limpias is only one of many representations of Christ which have, throughout the years, been surrounded by supernatural phenomenon. In January and February of 1986, a copy of the head of the Limpias crucifix belonging to Mrs. M. Linden of Maasmechelen, Belgium, was seen to shed tears of blood.

LISTENING TO PREACHING

A partial indulgence is granted the Christian faithful who attentively and devoutly assist at the preaching of the Word of God. A plenary indulgence is granted the Christian faithful who on the occasion of a mission have heard some of the sermons and are present for its solemn conclusion. (*The Handbook of Indulgences*, n. 41.)

LITANY

A prayer in the form of responsive petition.

In Old Testament times, the Jews had a form of public prayer in which one or more persons would pronounce an invocation and those present would answer by repeating a certain prayer. The early Church retained this practice, calling these alternating prayers a litany, from the Greek *litaneia*, meaning "a humble and fervent appeal."

In the Latin Church, a typical structure developed gradually. In later centuries, many invocations of individual saints and special petitions were added. So many additions were made that in 1601 Pope Clement VIII determined an official text of the Litany of All Saints and prohibited public use of any other litanies unless approved by Rome. Succeeding popes approved other litanies for public use; among them are those of the Most Holy Name of Jesus, the Sacred Heart, the Blessed Virgin Mary, and St. Joseph.

LITANY OF THE BLESSED VIRGIN MARY

Popular Marian devotion; also known as the Litany of Loreto.

This is the most popular of the litanies. In its present form it seems to have been included in a book of prayers published, possibly under the influence of St. Peter Canisius, in 1551. An earlier and much longer version seems to have been printed in a missal of the mid-fourteenth century.

The prayer goes:

Lord, have mercy on us. *Christ, have mercy on us.*
Lord, have mercy on us. Christ, hear us. *Christ, graciously hear us.*

God the Father of heaven, *Have mercy on us.*
God the Son, Redeemer of the world,
God the Holy Spirit,
Holy Trinity, one God,
Holy Mary, *Pray for us.*
Holy Mother of God,
Holy Virgin of virgins,
Mother of Christ,

Mother of the Church,
Mother of divine grace,
Mother most pure,
Mother most chaste,
Mother inviolate,
Mother undefiled,
Mother immaculate,
Mother most amiable,
Mother most admirable,
Mother of good counsel,
Mother of our Creator,
Mother of our Savior,
Virgin most prudent,
Virgin most venerable,
Virgin most renowned,
Virgin most powerful,
Virgin most merciful,
Virgin most faithful,
Mirror of justice,
Seat of wisdom,
Cause of our joy,
Spiritual vessel,
Vessel of honor,
Singular vessel of devotion,
Mystical rose,
Tower of David,
Tower of ivory,
House of gold,
Ark of the covenant,
Gate of heaven,
Morning star,
Health of the sick,
Refuge of sinners,
Comforter of the afflicted,
Help of Christians,
Queen of angels,
Queen of patriarchs,

Queen of prophets,
Queen of apostles,
Queen of martyrs,
Queen of confessors,
Queen of virgins,
Queen of all saints,
Queen conceived without original
    sin,
Queen assumed into heaven,
Queen of the most holy Rosary,
Queen of the family,
Queen of peace,

Lamb of God, who take away the sins
    of the world. *Spare us, O Lord.*
Lamb of God, who take away the sins
    of the world. *Graciously hear us, O
    Lord.*
Lamb of God, who take away the sins
    of the world. *Have mercy on us.*

V. Pray for us, O holy Mother of
    God.
R. That we may be made worthy of
    the promises of Christ.

Let us pray:
 O God, whose only-begotten Son, by
his life, death, and Resurrection, has
purchased for us the rewards of
everlasting life; grant, we beseech you,
that we who meditate on these
mysteries of the most holy Rosary of
the Blessed Virgin Mary, may both
imitate what they contain and obtain
what they promise. Through the same
Christ our Lord. Amen.

(A pious custom suggests adding the following prayers after the litany.)

For the needs of the Church and of
   the nation:
Our Father, Hail Mary, Glory Be.

For the (arch)bishop of this diocese
   and his intentions:
Our Father, Hail Mary, Glory Be.

For the holy souls in purgatory:
Our Father, Hail Mary, Glory Be.
May they rest in peace. Amen.

LITANY OF THE HOLY NAME

A popular prayer devoted to Jesus' name.

   Litanies of the Holy Name began to appear in the sixteenth century. The litany as we know it today was approved and indulgenced in 1886.

It reads:

Lord, have mercy. *Lord, have mercy.*
Christ, have mercy. *Christ, have mercy.*
Lord, have mercy. *Lord, have mercy.*

God the Father of heaven, *Have mercy*
   on us.
God the Son, Redeemer of the world,
God, the Holy Spirit,
Holy Trinity, one God,
Jesus, Son of the living God,
Jesus, splendor of the Father,
Jesus, brightness of everlasting light,

Jesus, king of glory,
Jesus, dawn of justice,
Jesus, Son of the Virgin Mary,
Jesus, worthy of our wonder,
Jesus, mighty God,
Jesus, father of the world to come,
Jesus, prince of peace,
Jesus, all-powerful,
Jesus, pattern of patience,
Jesus, model of obedience,
Jesus, gentle and humble of heart,
Jesus, lover of chastity,
Jesus, lover of us all,
Jesus, God of peace,
Jesus, author of life,
Jesus, model of goodness,
Jesus, seeker of souls,
Jesus, our God,
Jesus, our refuge,
Jesus, father of the poor,
Jesus, treasure of the faithful,
Jesus, good shepherd,
Jesus, the true light,
Jesus, eternal wisdom,
Jesus, infinite goodness,
Jesus, our way and our life,
Jesus, joy of angels,
Jesus, king of patriarchs,
Jesus, teacher of apostles,
Jesus, master of evangelists,
Jesus, courage of martyrs,
Jesus, light of confessors,
Jesus, purity of virgins,
Jesus, crown of all saints,
Lord, be merciful, *Jesus, save your*
   people.
From all evil,

From every sin,
From the snares of the devil,
From your anger,
From the spirit of infidelity,
From everlasting death,
From neglect of your Holy Spirit,
By the mystery of your incarnation,
By your birth,
By your childhood,
By your hidden life,
By your public ministry,
By your agony and crucifixion,
By your abandonment,
By your grief and sorrow,
By your death and burial,
By your rising to new life,
By your return in glory to the Father,
By your gift of the Holy Spirit,
By your gift of the holy Eucharist,
By your joy and glory,

Christ, hear us. *Christ, hear us.*
Lord Jesus, hear our prayer. *Lord
Jesus, hear our prayer.*
Lamb of God, who take away the sins
of the world. *Spare us, O Lord.*
Lamb of God, who take away the sins
of the world. *Graciously hear us, O
Lord.*
Lamb of God, who take away the sins
of the world. *Have mercy on us.*

Let us pray:
Lord, may we who honor the holy
name of Jesus enjoy his friendship in
this life and be filled with eternal joy
in the kingdom where he lives and
reigns for ever and ever. Amen.

**LITANY OF LORETO — See LITANY
OF THE BLESSED VIRGIN MARY.**

LITANY OF THE PRECIOUS BLOOD

A litany in honor of the Precious Blood.

In 1960, Pope John XXIII approved the
Litany of the Precious Blood, and through
special indulgences encouraged its public
and private recitation. In his apostolic letter on promoting devotion to the Most
Precious Blood (June 30, 1960), Pope
John remarked that the litany was one he
had learned from his own family at home.
His family recited the litany daily during
the month of July. In the 1991 *Handbook
of Indulgences,* this is one of the litanies
recommended as standing out from all the
others.

Lord, have mercy on us.
Christ have mercy on us.
Lord, have mercy on us.
Christ, hear us
Christ graciously hear us
God, the Father of heaven,
Have mercy on us
God, the Son, Redeemer of the
world,
Have mercy on us
God, the Holy Spirit
Have mercy on us
Holy Trinity, One God,
Have mercy on us
Blood of Christ, only begotten Son of
the Eternal Father,

Save us.

Blood of Christ, Incarnate Word of
God,
Blood of Christ, of the New and
Eternal Testament,
Blood of Christ, falling upon the
earth in the Agony,
Blood of Christ shed profusely in the
Scourging
Blood of Christ, flowing forth in the
Crowning with Thorns
Blood of Christ, poured out on the
Cross,
Blood of Christ, price of our
salvation,
Blood of Christ, without which there
is no forgiveness,
Blood of Christ, Eucharistic drink and
refreshment of souls,
Blood of Christ, stream of mercy,
Blood of Christ, victor over demons,
Blood of Christ, courage of martyrs,
Blood of Christ, strength of
confessors,
Blood of Christ, bringing forth
virgins,
Blood of Christ, help of those in
peril,
Blood of Christ, relief of the
burdened,
Blood of Christ, solace in sorrow,
Blood of Christ, hope of the penitent,
Blood of Christ, consolation of the
dying,
Blood of Christ, peace and tenderness
of hearts,

Blood of Christ, pledge of Eternal
life,
Blood of Christ, freeing souls from
Purgatory,
Blood of Christ, most worthy of all
glory and honor,

Save us.

Lamb of God, You, Who take away
the sins of the world,
Spare us, O Lord.
Lamb of God, You, Who take away
the sins of the world,
Graciously hear us, O Lord.
Lamb of God, You, Who take away
the sins of the world,
Have mercy on us.

V. You have redeemed us, O Lord, in
Your Blood
R. And made us, for our God, a
kingdom.

Let us pray:
Almighty and Eternal God, You
have appointed Your only-begotten
Son the Redeemer of the world,
and willed to be appeased by His
Blood. Grant, we beg of You, that
we may worthily adore this price
of our salvation, and through its
power be safeguarded from the
evils of this present life, so that we
may rejoice in its fruits forever in
heaven. Through the same Christ
our Lord. Amen.

LITANY OF THE SAINTS

A well-known devotion.

When a person is in danger of death, the litany may be prayed for him or her with special mention of the person's patron saint or saints. This litany is also prayed at Easter, baptisms, and ordinations.

Lord, have mercy. *Lord, have mercy.*
Christ, have mercy. *Christ, have mercy.*
Lord, have mercy. *Lord, have mercy.*

Holy Mary, Mother of God, *Pray for us (him/her).*
Holy angels of God,
Abraham, our father in faith,
David, leader of God's people,
All holy patriarchs and prophets,
St. John the Baptist,
St. Joseph,
St. Peter and St. Paul,
St. Andrew,
St. John,
St. Mary Magdalene,
St. Stephen,
St. Ignatius,
St. Lawrence,
St. Perpetua and St. Felicity,
St. Agnes,
St. Gregory,
St. Augustine,
St. Athanasius,
St. Basil,
St. Martin,
St. Benedict,
St. Francis and St. Dominic,
St. Francis Xavier,

St. John Vianney,
St. Catherine,
St. Teresa,
(Other saints may be included here.)
All holy men and women, *Pray for us (him/her).*

Lord, be merciful, *Lord, save your people.*
From all evil,
From every sin,
From Satan's power,
At the moment of death,
From everlasting death,
On the day of judgment,
By your coming as man,
By your suffering and cross,
By your death and rising to new life,
By your return in glory to the Father,
By your gift of the Holy Spirit,
By your coming again in glory,
Be merciful to us sinners, *Lord, hear our prayer.*
Bring N. to eternal life, first promised to him (her) in baptism,
Raise N. on the last day, for he (she) has eaten the Bread of life,
Let N. share in your glory, for he (she) has shared in your suffering and death,
Jesus, Son of the living God,

Christ, hear us. *Christ, hear us.*
Lord Jesus, hear our prayer. *Lord Jesus, hear our prayer.*

LITANY OF ST. JOSEPH

A popular prayer among those devoted to Jesus' foster father.

The litany is:

Lord, have mercy. *Lord, have mercy.*
Christ, have mercy. *Christ, have mercy.*
Holy Trinity, one God. *Have mercy on us.*

Holy Mary, *Pray for us.*
St. Joseph,
Noble son of the House of David,
Light of patriarchs,
Husband of the Mother of God,
Guardian of the Virgin,
Foster father of the Son of God,
Faithful guardian of Christ,
Head of the holy family,
Joseph, chaste and just,
Joseph, prudent and brave,
Joseph, obedient and loyal,
Pattern of patience,
Lover of poverty,
Model of workers,
Example to parents,
Guardian of virgins,
Pillar of family life,
Comfort of the troubled,
Hope of the sick,
Patron of the dying,
Terror of evil spirits,
Protector of the Church,

Lamb of God, who take away the sins of the world. *Have mercy on us.*
Lamb of God, who take away the sins of the world. *Have mercy on us.*
Lamb of God, who take away the sins of the world. *Have mercy on us.*

V. The Lord made him master of his household.
R. And put him in charge of all that he owned.

Let us pray:
Almighty God, in your infinite wisdom and love you chose Joseph to be the husband of Mary, the mother of your Son. As we enjoy his protection on earth, may we have the help of his prayers in heaven. We ask this through Christ our Lord. Amen.

LITANY TO THE SACRED HEART

A litany particularly dear to those who are devoted to the Sacred Heart of Jesus.

The prayer goes:

Lord, have mercy. *Lord, have mercy.*
Christ, have mercy. *Christ, have mercy.*
Lord, have mercy. *Lord, have mercy.*

God the Father in heaven, *Have mercy on us.*
God the Son, Redeemer of the world,
God the Holy Spirit,
Holy Trinity, one God,
Heart of Jesus, Son of the eternal Father,

Heart of Jesus, formed by the Holy Spirit in the womb of the Virgin Mother,

Heart of Jesus, one with the eternal Word,

Heart of Jesus, infinite in majesty,

Heart of Jesus, holy temple of God,

Heart of Jesus, tabernacle of the Most High,

Heart of Jesus, house of God and gate of heaven,

Heart of Jesus, aflame with love for us,

Heart of Jesus, source of justice and love,

Heart of Jesus, full of goodness and love,

Heart of Jesus, wellspring of all virtue,

Heart of Jesus, worthy of all praise,

Heart of Jesus, king and center of all hearts,

Heart of Jesus, treasure house of wisdom and knowledge,

Heart of Jesus, in whom there dwells the fullness of God,

Heart of Jesus, in whom the Father is well pleased,

Heart of Jesus, from whose fullness we have all received,

Heart of Jesus, desire of the eternal hills,

Heart of Jesus, patient and full of mercy,

Heart of Jesus, generous to all who turn to you,

Heart of Jesus, fountain of life and holiness,

Heart of Jesus, atonement for our sins,

Heart of Jesus, overwhelmed with insults,

Heart of Jesus, broken for our sins,

Heart of Jesus, obedient even to death,

Heart of Jesus, pierced by a lance,

Heart of Jesus, source of all consolation,

Heart of Jesus, our life and Resurrection,

Heart of Jesus, our peace and reconciliation,

Heart of Jesus, victim for our sins,

Heart of Jesus, salvation of all who trust in you,

Heart of Jesus, hope of all who die in you,

Heart of Jesus, delight of all the saints,

Lamb of God, who take away the sins of the world. *Have mercy on us.*

Lamb of God, who take away the sins of the world. *Have mercy on us.*

Lamb of God, who take away the sins of the world. *Have mercy on us.*

V. Jesus, gentle and humble of heart.
R. Touch our hearts and make them like your own.

Let us pray:
Father, we rejoice in the gifts of love we have received from the

heart of Jesus, your Son. Open our hearts to share his life and continue to bless us with his love. We ask this in the name of Jesus the Lord. Amen.

LITERAL SENSE OF SCRIPTURE

The sense understood and intended by the human writer of Scripture, as distinct from the moral or allegorical senses.

Mainly this sense is determined by the literary and historical criticism of the biblical texts. The literal sense can be explicit, as in the interpretation of John's Gospel: "The Word became flesh" (1:14), that Jesus Christ became human; or it can be implicit, from this same text, that the Son of God, as human, had a human soul, with intellect and will, and the sexual identity of a male.

LITTLE CROWN OF THE BLESSED VIRGIN

A chaplet based on Revelation: "And a great portent appeared in heaven, a woman clothed with the sun, with the moon under her feet, and on her head a crown of twelve stars" (12:1).

It was a favorite prayer of Sts. John Berchmans (1599-1621) and Louis de Montfort (1673-1716). The beads are arranged in three sets of four with a single bead before each group. The chaplet ends with a medal of Our Lady, Queen of All Hearts. After an introductory prayer and an Our Father, four Hail Marys are recited in honor of Our Lady's crown of excellence. The invocations of this crown honor the divine maternity of the Blessed Virgin, her virginity, her purity, and her innumerable virtues. After the second Our Father is prayed, four Hail Marys are said in honor of the crown of power which honor the royalty of the Blessed Virgin, her magnificence, he universal mediation and the strength of her rule as Queen of Heaven.

Little Crown of the Blessed Virgin

After the third and final Our Father, four Hail Marys are prayed with invocations which honor her crown of goodness: her mercy toward sinners, toward the poor, toward the just and toward the dying. The chaplet ends with a Glory be to the Father and a final prayer.

LITTLE CROWN OF THE INFANT JESUS OF PRAGUE

A chaplet focusing on devotion to the Child Jesus under the title "Infant Jesus of Prague."

Introduced by Venerable Margaret of the Blessed Sacrament (d. 1648), a Carmelite sister, and based on her reported

Little Crown of the Infant Jesus of Prague

private revelation, the chaplet is promoted by the Carmelite Order. The chaplet consists of fifteen beads. Three beads are in honor of the Holy Family, Jesus, Mary, and Joseph. On these are recited the Lord's Prayer. The other twelve beads are in honor of the Holy Childhood of Christ, and on them are recited twelve Hail Marys. Before each of the Lord's Prayers one says, "And the Word was made flesh." Before the first of the Hail Marys, one prays, "And the Word was made Flesh and dwelt among us." On the medal, one prays, "Divine Infant Jesus, I adore Thy Cross, and I accept all the crosses Thou wilt be pleased to send me. Adorable Trinity, I offer Thee for the glory of the Holy Name of God, all the adorations of the Sacred Heart of the Holy Infant Jesus."

(See also **INFANT JESUS OF PRAGUE**.)

LITTLE FLOWER — See **ST. THÉRÈSE OF LISIEUX**.

LITTLE HOURS — See **HOURS, LITTLE**.

LITTLE OFFICE

A form of prayer modeled after the Liturgy of the Hours but with shorter prayers.

Little offices have been written with

particular emphasis on the Passion, the Sacred Heart, the Holy Spirit, Mary, the Immaculate Conception, and St. Joseph.

(See also **LITURGY OF THE HOURS**.)

LITTLE OFFICE OF THE BLESSED VIRGIN MARY

This is a form of prayer to the Virgin Mary modeled on the Divine Office, containing the usual division into hours but considerably shorter. Its first recorded use was in the tenth century in the life of Bishop Ulrich of Augsburg (d.973). In 1095, Pope Urban II requested it to be said for success in the first crusade. From the monasteries, it spread to the laity, particularly to the members of the third orders. It was retained in the reforms of the breviary in 1568 and Pope Pius V enriched it with an indulgence. The office is a simple one and makes use of the Psalms, hymns to the Virgin, and the Hail Mary.

(See also **LITURGY OF THE HOURS**.)

LITTLE ROSARY OF ST. ANNE

A chaplet dating back to the late nineteenth century with particular devotion to St. Anne, the mother of Mary.

It begins with the sign of the cross and is divided into three parts. Each part consists of an Our Father, followed by five Hail Marys and a Glory Be. The first part is recited in honor of Jesus, the second in honor of Mary, and the third in honor of St. Anne.

(See also **ST. ANNE**.)

LITTLE SACHET

A small pouch containing Gospel verses about the naming of Jesus worn as a sign of devotion to the Holy Name.

The practice was introduced in mid-nineteenth-century France by Sister Marie de St. Pierre of the Carmel of Tours. The faithful are encouraged to recite the doxology five times and say the ejaculation, "Blessed be the Most Holy Name of Jesus without end" frequently while wearing the sachet.

Little Sachet

LITTLE WAY

A form of spirituality advocated by St. Thérèse of Lisieux (1873-1897).

It recommends trusting in God in the very ordinary moments of daily life.

(See also ST. THÉRÈSE OF LISIEUX.)

LITURGICAL COLOR — See COLOR, LITURGICAL.

LITURGICAL MOVEMENT

A movement in the Church that seeks to revitalize the liturgy in modern life and to promote a renewal of active participation by Catholics in the Mass, the sacraments, the Liturgy of the Hours, and other forms of worship.

Although some influences can be traced to the nineteenth century, the modern liturgical movement has its true beginning in the pontificate of St. Pius X (1903-14). For many centuries the laity actively participated in the Mass only when they received Holy Communion, which most did rarely. By encouraging frequent reception of the sacrament and by lowering the minimum age, Pius X opened the gates to the reforms which followed.

In 1909 the Catholic organizations of Belgium held a conference to explore means of involving the laity more fully in the life of the Church. In a historic address, Dom Lambert Beauduin, OSB, pointed out that the means already existed in the liturgy, which was the prayer of the whole Church rich in sources of grace for all its members. So began a powerful program to make Catholics more aware of the liturgy and in particular to make them active participants at Mass. Thousands of cheap vernacular missals were printed and made freely available in churches, so that congregations could follow closely what was happening at the altar. Within a few years similar missals were commonplace in countries across the world. Before the advent of the missals, most lay people recited the Rosary or their own prayers during Mass, leaving the priest to get on with his own business in a language which few understood. Naturally change did not happen overnight, but in the years that followed knowledge and love of the liturgy became more widespread than it had been for many centuries, as lay Catholics learned to follow each part of the Mass through the translation and commentary which the missals provided.

Before long, many felt the need to participate more actively. This led to the dialogue Mass, in which the whole congregation made the responses formerly made only by the altar server. This innovation received a somewhat grudging acceptance from the Sacred Congregation of Rites, which in 1922 ruled that while dialogue Masses were lawful they might not always be useful. Among other objections, it was pointed out that the sound of a whole congregation making the responses might disturb Masses being celebrated at other altars elsewhere in the same church. Dialogue Masses nevertheless became increasingly popular, especially among young people. As one might expect, liturgical renewal has continued to draw much of its strength from the enthusiasm of the young. In time, the Sacred Congregation was itself to be converted: in a 1958 instruction, dialogue Masses were not merely approved but highly recommended.

In the United States, as in other English-speaking countries, the liturgical movement initially grew more slowly than in Continental Europe but gained ground steadily through the 1920s and 1930s. By the time the U.S. entered the war in 1941 the Liturgical Conference, the principal American organization for promoting the movement, had thousands of members. The war brought more innovations: Mass could be celebrated during the evening for men and women on active service, who were not required to fast before receiving Holy Communion. The 1950s saw the introduction of evening Masses throughout the Church, together with a substantial relaxation of the fasting laws. No longer was it necessary to fast from midnight in order to receive. The same decade saw the

Holy Week liturgy reformed. The Easter Vigil service, which for centuries had been celebrated on the morning of Holy Saturday, was transferred to midnight. Like many other liturgical changes, this was a return to the practice of the early Church. (Today, for practical reasons, many parishes celebrate both the Easter Vigil and the First Mass of Christmas during the early evening rather than at midnight). The changes which preceded the Second Vatican Council were the result of both pastoral experience and years of intense study by scholars of many countries. New and radical changes were introduced by the Council's *Constitution on the Sacred Liturgy*, enacted on December 4, 1963.

As Pope Paul himself observed with reference to the Vatican II Council: "The liturgy was the first subject to be examined and the first, too, in intrinsic worth and importance for the life of the Church."

The *Constitution's* first requirement was that all the faithful be led to a full and active part in liturgical celebrations and that the clergy be better instructed. In ordering a reform of the liturgy it declared: "The rites should be distinguished by a noble simplicity; they should be short, clear and unencumbered by useless repetition; they should be within the people's comprehension and normally should not require much explanation" (*CSL*, 34).

Latin was obviously the great obstacle to this ideal, but the *Constitution* stopped short of bringing its use to an end. Seeking to reconcile the views of conservatives and reformers, it decreed that while Latin should be preserved in principle, in practice the vernacular might be employed to a greater extent at the discretion of Episcopal conferences and could be used in administering all the sacraments. With the needs of mission lands particularly in mind, variations in ritual were permitted where appropriate.

The *Constitution* placed a new emphasis on the Mass as both a sacrifice and a communal meal. The altar, it ruled, should be placed roughly in the center of the church. The widespread effect of this ruling has been a return to the early practice in which the priest faced the people.

Among other reforms the *Constitution* introduced Holy Communion under both kinds for the laity and concelebration by priests. It restored the catechumenate for adults and recommended that Extreme Unction be renamed Anointing of the Sick. Composers and artists were encouraged to enrich the Church's worship with their talents. Wherever possible, congregations should join in worship by singing. While acknowledging the place of local musical and artistic traditions, the *Constitution* insisted that Gregorian chant be given "pride of place" in liturgical services.

The liturgical changes took immediate effect. Paul VI gave them a powerful im-

petus when he celebrated Mass in the reformed rite at New York's Yankee Stadium during a visit to the U.S. in October 1965. During the years following Vatican II, more liturgical reforms have been introduced. Notable among these are the permanent diaconate, the participation of lay Eucharistic ministers and readers, and the option to receive the Host in the hand.

Today, few would deny that liturgical reform has brought many benefits. Lay participation in the liturgy is certainly greater than in former days and the use of the vernacular has brought wider knowledge of both liturgy and Scripture. Yet there is considerable dissatisfaction with the present state of the Church's worship, and a general feeling that a silent majority of Catholics attend Mass without any real sense of engagement. There have been complaints that liturgical reform is too often imposed arbitrarily and in bureaucratic fashion. On the other hand, the leeway given to local needs and traditions has sometimes led to wayward creativity and liturgical abuse. Much criticism has been directed at the translations issued by the International Commission on English in the Liturgy (ICEL), the body charged with the task of producing texts for the English-speaking world. The language of the translations has frequently been called "banal" and even the theology of some texts has been questioned. In October 1999, the Vatican instructed that the translators and their advisors be brought under the closer supervision of the national Episcopal conferences and of the Holy See itself. ICEL is not, however, the only target of criticism. Many of the newer popular hymns are felt by some to be human-centered and lacking a sense of the sacred.

Despite the primacy conferred on it by the *Constitution on the Sacred Liturgy,* Latin has now disappeared from worship in most Catholic parishes. Gregorian chant is likewise rarely heard.

That the liturgical movement remains vigorous is shown by such organizations as Adoremus and the Society for Catholic Liturgy, and by a number of journals promoting varying points of view. In June 1996, an international conference of liturgists in Oxford, England, called for a revived liturgical movement which would recover the sense of the sacred. Specifically it would promote the sung Liturgy of the Hours in cathedrals, parishes, monasteries, and families. It would also promote Eucharistic adoration, which, it noted, was already spreading. In achieving its aims, the "Oxford Declaration" said the revived movement would be aided by a closer and deeper acquaintance with the traditions of the Christian East. Liturgical change would not be imposed on the faithful from above but would proceed with caution and sensitivity to the *sensus fidelium.*

Addressing a group of American bish-

ops in October 1998, Pope John Paul II blamed the problems besetting the liturgy principally on a lack of explanation and instruction. In what seemed almost an echo of the "Oxford Declaration," he told the bishops: "The challenge now is to move beyond whatever misunderstandings there have been and to reach the proper point of balance, especially by entering more deeply into the contemplative dimension of worship."

LITURGY

The public worship of the Church, including the rites and ceremonies of the Mass and sacraments, by which the faithful express their worship of God.

In addition to the liturgies of the sacraments, the official worship of the Church includes many non-sacramental liturgies such as the Liturgy of the Word, the Liturgy of the Hours, or Divine Office, numerous blessings, and sacramentals.

LITURGY OF THE HOURS

The public prayer of the Church for praising God and sanctifying the day; also referred to as the Divine Office.

The actual book used for the recitation of the Office is often called the *Breviary.* The daily praying of the Liturgy of the Hours is required of priests and religious (both male and female) who have professed solemn vows. The Church highly commends the saying of the Liturgy of the Office by the lay faithful, particularly in public.

The Liturgy of the Hours is rooted in early Church practice; From the earliest times, Christians gathered at various hours of the day to pray, especially in the morning and evening. Following the admonition to pray always, services developed around the important times of the day — morning, noon, and night. The practice was not highly structured at first, since people met as they could during waves of persecution, and there was some difference in the content of the prayer in different countries and regions; However, the recitation of the Psalms was always core to early Christian prayer of the Hours. Historians differ on whether the development of the Hours was related to synagogue practice, although many of the early Christians were Jewish. Christians did base much of the service on readings of the Jewish Scripture (the Old Testament) and the Psalms, the prayers of the Jewish people.

With Constantine (313) came the end of persecution, and as a result, more standardization in the development of the Liturgy of the Hours. The custom was established of celebrating morning and evening prayer in the cathedral churches where the local bishop was the leader, along with priests, deacons, acolytes, lectors, and lay Christians who gathered to participate in the liturgy of singing Psalms and praying. This practice was recommended for priests and "everyone of the laity" in the Apostolic Constitutions, a manual of Church order and liturgy written about 380 A.D.: "Assemble yourselves every day, morning and evening, singing Psalms and praying in the Lord's house."

Morning prayer was and is a service of praise dedicating the day to God and is especially related to the Resurrection. Evening prayer is for the close of the day and a service of thanksgiving for the day, asking pardon for one's faults and prayers for protection during the darkness of the night. Evening (and later night) prayer includes eschatological themes of death and not knowing the hour when the Lord will appear. Both morning and evening prayer praise and thank God for salvation in Christ, for God's mighty deeds.

With the development of monasticism, beginning in the late third century, came a parallel and more extensive development in the Liturgy of the Hours. In a deeply spiritual movement, lay people began to move to the desert, or away from cities, to live their whole lives in prayer. Eventually they formed themselves into communities in which the focus of their communal prayer was the Psalms. The emphasis was on the primacy of the spiritual, and the monks recited or sang the Psalms as a part of their continuous contemplative prayer, often prostrating themselves in prayer after reciting the Psalms. While in the early monasteries this prayer of the Psalms with contemplation was not separated into special hours, it was in the monasteries that the Hours of prayer were eventually defined to include the others besides morning and evening prayer, on a schedule of seven hours of prayer. This practice influenced the cathedral celebrations of morning and evening prayer, with some cathedrals later began to celebrate the seven hours as well, especially as monasteries grew and flourished and laypeople related to monasteries in an urban setting. Sometimes monks led the prayers in the churches. While the lesser Hours were celebrated in the cities at the cathedral churches, the emphasis for lay people continued to be on morning and evening prayer.

As monastic influence grew, the celebration of the Liturgy of the Hours began to be more and more a service of reading from a book in Latin (the *Breviary*), and by the Middle Ages it had became privatized and limited to the prayer of priests and religious. The communal celebration of the Office became limited to the monasteries, where it was sung. This privatization of the Hours continued for centuries.

In the Liturgical Movement of the twentieth century there was much study of the early sources of Church history and liturgy. In addition to renewal in the Eucharistic liturgy and the sacraments, the movement emphasized participation in the Liturgy of the Hours for all of the people. Many laypeople began reciting the Divine Office and drew inspiration from it regarding the sense of the Mystical Body of Christ, being joined to people all over the world in the same communal prayer. It gave people a sense of continuity with the Church to realize that even before the time of St. Benedict, the Church has been offering these beautiful liturgical prayers.

Following decades of liturgical studies which emphasized the practice of the early Church, the Second Vatican Council attempted to recover the traditions of the Liturgy of the Hours in its communal celebrations and inclusion of the laity in the prayer of the Hours, especially morning and evening prayer. The council reminded the Church that the great prayer of the Church, the Liturgy of the Hours was for all of the People of God, not just for clergy and religious.

The Liturgy, revised since 1965, consists of:

- Office of Readings, for reflection on the Word of God. The principal parts consist of three Psalms, biblical and non-biblical readings.
- Morning and evening prayer, called the "hinges" of the Liturgy of the Hours. The principal parts are a hymn, two Psalms, an Old or New Testament canticle, a brief biblical

reading, Zechariah's canticle (the *Benedictus*, morning) or Mary's canticle (the *Magnificat*, evening), responsories, intercessions, and a concluding prayer.

- Daytime prayer. The principal parts are a hymn, three Psalms, a short biblical reading, and one of three concluding prayers corresponding to the time of day.
- Night prayer. The principal parts are one or two Psalms, a brief biblical reading, Simeon's canticle (*Nunc Dimittis*), a concluding prayer, and an antiphon in honor of Mary.

The former traditional names of the particular hours were: Matins, Lauds, Terce, Sext, None, Vespers, and Compline.

LITURGY OF ST. JAMES — See JAMES, LITURGY OF ST.

LIVING ROSARY, ASSOCIATION OF THE

A worldwide confraternity founded in 1826 in France by Pauline Jaricot (who also founded the Society for the Propagation of the Faith).

The association was later placed under the spiritual guidance of the Dominicans. Members say an assigned decade of the Rosary daily.

LIVING WAY OF THE CROSS

A live performance of the Way of the Cross.

Participants enact the events portrayed in each of the stations.

LONGANIMITY

The good habit, related to the virtue of hope, that grants perseverance in the midst of trials.

One with longanimity is blessed with "equanimity" (i.e., a balance and positive attitude in confronting obstacles).

LORD OF THE MIRACLES

A devotion and image dating back to seventeenth-century Peru.

Since 1687, a procession in honor of the Lord of the Miracles has been held each October in Pachacamilla, near Lima, Peru. The icon of the image is escorted through the streets by close to a million Peruvians to recall the city's survival of a seventeenth century earthquake that devastated the town and surrounding area. The shrine, a rather small gray temple called the Shrine of Our Lord of the Miracles, is the most popular shrine in Lima, a city famous for its beautiful temples and shrines.

In the 1600s, Lima was the center of the Spanish Empire in South America. Black slaves gathered in confraternities to celebrate the faith in their own way with songs and dances. One of these confraternities was established in Pachacamilla, where members erected a small, crude chapel of mud and straw. On one of the walls, an unknown slave drew the image of the Crucified Christ. In a 1655 earthquake, all the walls of the chapel collapsed except for the one with the image. The chapel had been abandoned a few years before the quake, and the remaining wall was not discovered for fifteen years. Spaniard Antonio León found the wall and realized the miracle that it alone was left standing. He prayed to be healed of a tumor, and when his healing was granted, he devoted his life and money to build a small temple around the wall and spread the devotion. Although it did not catch on among the Spanish, the devotion immediately spread among the blacks. Because the blacks held what were considered "noisy and annoying celebrations," the viceroy ordered the image to be erased, but the painters sent to do this were paralyzed. The viceroy then rescinded his order and demanded a "proper cult to the image of Our Most Holy Redeemer." A second earthquake in 1687 again left only the wall with the image intact. From then on, the image was known as "The Lord of the Miracles." The viceroy ordered a copy of the image to be made to be carried in procession around Lima. Today, the procession is one of the largest regular religious procession in the world. Another

Spaniard healed at the shrine, Sebastian de Antunano y Rivas, founded the Confraternity of Our Lord of the Miracles, the sodality responsible for organizing the procession. He also secured a community of Spanish Carmelite nuns from Spain to care for the shrine. These nuns wear a nontraditional purple habit symbolizing penance. Devotees also wear purple during the procession.

By far the most popular devotion in Peru, the devotion to the Lord of the Miracles has traveled with Peruvian immigrants to the United States. Annually in October, processions are held in Denver, Miami, Chicago, and New York.

LORD'S PRAYER
A prayer that Christ taught his disciples.

This fundamental prayer of Christianity is recited at morning prayer, evening prayer, and at the beginning of the Communion Rite of Mass in the Roman Rite.

Popularly called the "Our Father" (or, in Latin, *Pater Noster*), the prayer can be found in Matthew 6:9-13, where Jesus responds to the disciples' request that he teach them how to pray. A briefer version is in Luke 11:2-4.

Some documents suggest that in the early Church it was prayed three times daily as a part of private devotional practice. Until the end of Roman persecution of Christians in the early fourth century, as a matter of safety, only those who had been baptized were taught the Lord's Prayer.

The prayer reads:

> Our Father, who art in heaven,
> hallowed be thy name;
> thy kingdom come;
> thy will be done
> on earth as it is in heaven.
> Give us this day our daily bread;
> and forgive us our trespasses
> as we forgive those
> who trespass against us;
> and lead us not into temptation,
> but deliver us from evil.
> Amen.

In Protestant practice, a gloss (an addition to the Scripture that in some manuscripts later became part of the text) is recited before "Amen."

LORD'S SUPPER

Another name for the Last Supper.

It also may refer to Holy Thursday, the day of the Last Supper. In non-Catholic usage, too, it is commonly applied to a ritual reenactment of the Lord's Supper, as in a communion service.

LORETO: HOLY HOUSE OF NAZARETH

A pilgrimage site in Loreto, Italy.

According to pious legend, Mary's house at the time of the Annunciation was transported by angels from Nazareth in 1291 first to a spot on the coast and then in 1294 to Loreto. The earliest recorded pilgrimage to the site occurred in 1313, and from that time the holy house became one of the major pilgrimage sites of Europe. In addition to the house itself, there is an image of the Virgin there that is the object of much veneration. Pope Benedict XV (r. 1914-1922) declared Our Lady of Loreto the patron of all those involved in flying. The house is a small rectangular building encased in marble but was originally constructed from materials not

Our Lady of Loreto

328

found in the vicinity of the domed basilica that now surrounds it. The original statue of the Virgin was destroyed by fire in 1921 and has been replaced by a replica.

LORETO, LITANY OF — See LITANY OF THE BLESSED VIRGIN MARY.

LORICA

The *Book of Armagh* ascribes the authorship of the beautiful prayer called "Breast Plate" or Lorica to St. Patrick, and it may be that he composed it. Millions of faithful have used it through the centuries with devotion. Here are some passages from this famous prayer in a traditional English version:

> I arise today
> Through God's strength to pilot me,
> God's might to uphold me,
> God's wisdom to guide me,
> God's eye to look before me,
> God's ear to hear me,
> God's word to speak for me,
> God's hand to guard me,
> God's way to lie before me,
> God's shield to protect me,
> God's host to save me
> From snares of devils,
> From temptations of vices,
> From every one who shall wish me ill,
> Afar and anear,
> Alone and in a multitude.

LOS ANGELITOS

Mexican customs associated with the death of a child including prayers and family memorial shrines.

In Mexico, there is a traditional set of customs concerned with the death of children. Dead children are known as *angelitos* (little angels), and the customs surrounding their burial rites emphasize true Christian joy that the soul of the little one is secure in eternal happiness. These rituals connected with child death attempt to convert grief into joy, and to celebrate the entrance of a pure soul into a new life. The expression "child death" refers to a Mexican cultural phenomenon, the ritual in which recently deceased children are no longer considered children, but instead are thought of as little angels, and as such their death is celebrated rather than mourned. The ritual of child death is also practiced to some extent in other Latin American countries, most notably Argentina and Guatemala. These children are considered innocent of all eternal misery, and their death is considered a joyful birth into another world. Parents who have lost a child experience the normal grief for their loss, but the grief is tempered with the joy of knowing the child lives forever.

Beginning in the eighteenth century, when the child of a wealthy family died, the parents had a memorial portrait painted of the child. These effigies helped the parents to forget them as children of flesh and blood and to remember them as *angelitos*. The portraits would be placed in the family gallery where a place was kept for the departed.

Around the turn of the century, photography gave the portraiture part of the ritual a great popular appeal, and in a number of towns throughout Mexico the tradition is carried on by local photographers. The rise of photography allowed families of more modest means to be able to afford to preserve the child's image and memory until the time came for the final reunion in the life after death. Until the 1930s, there was an extremely high rate of infant mortality in Mexico; about one of every three children died in infancy. The visual reminder of the *angelito* and the special ritual of his or her funeral helped the parents to overcome their feeling of impotence at their failure to be able to prevent the death of their child.

Although funeral customs are constantly changing, much of the tradition regarding the funerals of children still remains, especially in the rural areas. It is the godparents who dress the child and lay him or her out for burial. A male child is usually dressed to represent St. Joseph or the Sacred Heart of Jesus, and the girls are dressed as the Immaculate Conception. Infants are usually dressed all in white, or in their best clothes. Little gold paper sandals are placed on the child's feet, and a spray of flowers made of palm leaves, orange blossoms, spikenards, or lilies are put in the child's hands. A floral wreath for the child's head is presented by the godmother. The clothing emphasizes the holy and innocent state of the child. Sometimes gilt or silver wings are added. In addition to the clothing and the wreath, the godparents also shoulder the costs for items such as fireworks, mariachis, or other expenses the parents may not be able to afford.

For the wake, the child is laid on a table spread with a white sheet or tablecloth, and the friends and relatives encircle the body with flowers brought from their homes. Pots of flowers surround the table. Prayers sung at the wake are called *Alabanzas*, and they express devotion to the Virgin Mary, comparing her virtues and qualities with those of the *angelito*.

Throughout the night, coffee, bread, and an alcoholic cinnamon drink are served. The following day, the body is carried in a small white coffin adorned with angelic symbols. The child is buried with music, fireworks, and joy in order to return to God the child in the same joy with which the child was received.

LOURDES, OUR LADY OF

A Marian image, shrine, and optional memorial celebrated on February 11.

Between February 11 and July 16 in 1858, fourteen-year-old Bernadette Soubirous reported seeing eighteen visions of

Our Lady of Lourdes

she knelt, an unknown spring began to flow. It still provides water for the healing baths at the shrine at Lourdes today. During the last appearance, Bernadette asked the woman who she was and was told "I am the Immaculate Conception."

A basilica was dedicated at the site in 1901, and it has been estimated as many as six million pilgrims visit Lourdes annually. The shrine has been the site of many reported miracles.

(See also **IMMACULATE CONCEPTION OF THE BLESSED VIRGIN MARY; LOURDES WATER.**)

LOURDES WATER

A sacramental associated with the Marian shrine in Lourdes, France.

The water comes from a spring discovered by St. Bernadette during a vision of

Lourdes Water

a woman dressed in white in a grotto near Lourdes, France. The woman's head and shoulders were covered with a white veil that fell to the full length of her robe. She wore a plain blue sash around her waist and on each foot there was a golden rose. Over her right arm she carried a white rosary with a cross and chain of gold.

During the ninth visit, the woman commanded the adolescent to "drink from the fountain and bathe in it." Bernadette was confused because there had never been a water source at the grotto. As she scraped the gravel away from the ground where

Mary. Miracles have been attributed to its use.

(See also **LOURDES, OUR LADY OF; SACRAMENTALS.**)

LOVE OF ST. JOHN

The name of a medieval tradition of blessing and drinking a cup of wine during the Feast of St. John the Evangelist, December 27.

The practice was based on the pious legend that the saint once drank a cup of poisoned wine without suffering harm.

LUJAN, OUR LADY OF

A Marian image and shrine in Lujan, Argentina, dating to the seventeenth century.

According to pious tradition, a Portuguese landowner in Cordoba wished to build a church in honor of the Immaculate Conception and asked a friend in Buenos Aires to send him an appropriate statue. Uncertain how the landowner wished the Blessed Virgin to be portrayed, the friend sent two terracotta images. The second was left behind near Lujan when the oxen refused to move until the case containing the statue had been removed. A local landowner constructed a shrine for the statue, and the first church was completed in 1685. A second church was built in 1754, and a basilica completed in 1930. Our Lady of Lujan is the patron of Argentina, Uruguay, and Paraguay, and devotion to her is strong throughout South America.

LUMINARIOS

A Mexican Advent and Christmas custom.

Traditionally, *luminarios* (from the Spanish verb *iluminar*, "to light") are made by partially filling a paper sack with sand and lighting a small candle that has been stuck in the sand. *Luminarios* are placed along walkways leading to homes.

M

MACARONIC

A carol written partly in Latin and partly in the vernacular.

There are many, using French, English, and German.

MAGI

In the infancy narrative of St. Matthew's Gospel (2:1-12), wise men from the East whose visit and homage to the Child Jesus at Bethlehem indicated Christ's manifestation of himself to non-Jewish people.

The narrative teaches the universality of salvation. By the sixth century, tradition had named them (Caspar, Melchior, and Balthasar) and assigned a particular gift to each. Pious legend attributes the finding of their relics to St. Helena, who gave them to her son, the Emperor Constantine. There is more than one version of the long route the relics took to arrive in the Cologne cathedral by the early twelfth century.

(See also **EPIPHANY**; **RELICS**.)

The Magi Adoring the Infant Jesus

MAGNIFICAT (ORGANIZATION)

A ministry to Catholic women.

The organization began in 1981 with a group of Catholic women from the Archdiocese of New Orleans. A faith sharing experience in a relaxed social setting born out of the Catholic Charismatic Renewal, the ministry's purpose is to bring women to a deeper commitment to Jesus as their Lord, a deeper knowledge of the release of the power of the Holy Spirit, and an appreciation and love for Mary and the Catholic Church. The charism of Magnificat is the love of God manifested as women share their prayers, tears, and laughter in an environment of unconditional love. The inspiration for Magnificat is the Visitation, the great hymn of praise that Mary prayed while visiting Elizabeth. Both women were deeply touched by God. They came together to help each other, to speak of God's actions in their lives, to sing, pray, share a common table, and to be strengthened and called by the power and presence of the Holy Spirit.

MAGNIFICAT

The canticle or hymn of the Virgin Mary on the occasion of her visitation to her cousin Elizabeth (see Luke 1:46-55).

The *Magnificat*, which gets it name from the first word of the prayer in Latin, is an expression of praise, thanksgiving, and acknowledgment of the great blessing given by God to Mary as the Mother of the second person of the Blessed Trinity made flesh. The canticle is recited in the Liturgy of the Hours as part of the evening prayer. One version (from the *Catholic Edition of the Revised Standard Version Bible*) reads:

> My soul magnifies the Lord,
> and my spirit rejoices in God my
>   savior;
> for he has regarded the low estate of
>   his handmaiden.
> For behold, henceforth all generations
>   will call me blessed;
> for he who is mighty has done great
>   things for me,
> and holy is his name.
> And his mercy is on those who fear
>   him
> from generation to generation.
> He has shown strength with his arm,
> he has scattered the proud in the
>   imagination of their hearts,
> he has put down the mighty from
>   their thrones,
> and exalted those of low degree;
> he has filled the hungry with good
>   things,
> and the rich he has sent empty away.
> He has helped his servant Israel
> in remembrance of his mercy,
> as he spoke to our fathers,
> to Abraham and to his posterity for
>   ever.

MANDATUM

The name of the ceremony of the washing of the feet on Holy Thursday.

Mandatum is the first word in Latin for an antiphon that is used.

MANGER SCENE — See **CHRISTMAS CRIB**.

MANIFESTATION OF CONSCIENCE

The disclosing of one's spiritual condition outside the sacrament of penance, usually done in order to obtain guidance.

This generally takes place within the internal forum of spiritual direction. Religious superiors are forbidden by Canon Law to require a manifestation of conscience from their subjects.

MANNA OF THE SAINTS

An oil reported to appear on relics and sometimes flows from them.

It generally takes the form of a colorless, odorless, and tasteless fluid. The first reported case involved the relics of St. Andrew the Apostle. A Greek text detailing the event was translated by St. Gregory of Tours in the sixth century. The substance presented itself either in the form of a powder or of a perfumed oil and was collected and distributed as relics. The manna has also been called unction, myrrh, medicinal liquor, balm, and oil.

(See also **RELICS**.)

MARDI GRAS

French for "Fat Tuesday."

This is a pre-Lenten nonreligious celebration dating back to the Middle Ages. Mardi Gras typically features carnivals, masquerade balls, and parades with costumed participants. The name reflects the medieval custom of using up meats prior to the abstaining that began with Ash Wednesday. In some regions, it is known as Carnival, Fat Tuesday, Butter Week, or Fat Days.

The name *carnival* comes from the Latin *carnem levare* (*carnelevarium*), which means "withdrawal" or "removal" of meat. The German word for this time of carnival is *Fassnacht*, or *Fasching*, which probably comes from the ancient *vasen*, a word which means "running around crazily."

As a time of feasting, carnival celebrations the world over developed many traditional foods for the celebration. England enjoyed her famous Shrove Tuesday pancakes and collops of sliced meat mixed with eggs and fried in butter. *Fastelavnsboller*, muffins filled with whipped cream and coated with frosting, were traditional in Norway; Russians served rich, unsweetened buckwheat pancakes known as blinni. The Scots ate crowdie, a kind of porridge cooked with butter and milk. Germans baked pastries called *Fassnachstollen*. In New Orleans and Galveston, a special cake known as a kings' cake is baked and served at parties. The guest who receives the slice containing a tiny figure of a baby (perhaps Baby Jesus) is the one who will host the party the following year. Many elements of the Indo-European pre-Christian spring lore have traditionally been included in carnival celebrations. Our pre-Christian ancestors had many rites and celebrations to drive away winter and welcome the fertility of spring. Lent excluded the boisterous practices of mumming and masquerading, so what better time for these than the gay days of carnival? The mummer's parade in Philadelphia stemmed from this tradition. In pre-communist days in the country regions of Russia, a fantastic figure called *Masslianitsa* was gaily decorated and driven about on a sledge while the peasants sang special songs. At the end of the week, this butter goddess was burned and a formal farewell was bidden to pleasure until Easter.

In Latin countries, much of the pre-Christian element of the carnival frolics seem to stem from the celebration of the Roman Saturnalia, a pagan feast in honor of the field god Saturnus which was annually held in December. Our pre-Christian ancestors knew nothing of biology, but through observation knew of the life that sprang from eggs. One of the best loved Latin traditions of fiestas and carnivals are the *cascarones*, eggshells filled with confetti. Laughing party-goers crack the shells over one another's heads for good luck. In the southwestern United States, these *cascarones* have become a traditional feature not only of the pre-Lent carnivals but also at Easter and fall celebrations.

The popes acknowledged the carnival practice in Rome and tried to regulate its observance, correct its abuses, and provide entertainment for the masses. In 1471, Paul II started the famous horse races which gave the name *Corso* to one of Rome's ancient streets. He also introduced carnival pageants for which the Holy City was famous. In the centuries following, other cities developed special features of their carnival celebrations such as the parade of gondolas in Venice, floats and parades in South America, and carnival balls in many cities throughout Europe.

The two best-known celebrations of carnival in the United States today are the Mardi Gras celebrations held in New Orleans and Galveston. The celebration in New Orleans began in 1766; the krewes, social clubs, that stage the elaborate parades and calls began organizing in 1857. The celebrations in both cities are hallmarked by the selection of a king and queen, a parade, and the large Mardi Gras costume balls, both public and private. Some of today's balls are held as fund-raisers for charity; many private parties are just for fun. Krewes, or groups of participants, have special coins minted, and these, along with the traditional strings of brightly colored beads, are thrown to the crowds as the parade passes by. Participants are encouraged to wear fancy dress, and items such as gaily feathered masks and silvery, ribbon-decorated coronas are popular items sold by street vendors along with plenty of food and beer. Bands from throughout both states travel to the cities to play in competition. Thoroughfares are thronged with crowds, all happily celebrating the last fling before the coming somber period of Lent.

In many countries, such great excesses were committed at carnival that the bishops sought to prepare the people for the penitential season by exposing the Blessed Sacrament solemnly in the churches for forty hours in memory of the time during which the Sacred Body of Jesus was in the sepulcher. Pope Benedict XIV, in 1748, instituted this special devotion for the three days preceding Lent, calling it "Forty Hours of Carnival." The devotion was at one time held in many churches of Europe and America in places where the carnival frolics were of general and long-standing tradition, and was a precursor to today's Forty Hours Devotion.

MARIA BAMBINA

A devotion to the Infant Mary.

Maria Bambina dates back at least to the early eleventh century, when Santa Maria Fulcorina Church in Milan, Italy, was dedicated to the mystery of the Nativity of Mary. Later, it was named the cathedral. Today the center of devotion to Mary as an infant is based in the motherhouse chapel of the Sisters of Charity in Milan. The sisters have a wax image of the Infant Mary made in 1735. It was modeled in wax in 1735 by Sister Isabella Chiara Formari, a Sister of the Poor Clares in Todi, Italy (1697-1744). Modeling of and devotion to wax images of both the Infant Jesus and the infant Mary were popular in convents and elsewhere during the Counterreformation. Miracles have been attributed to the intercession of Maria Bambina.

In 1904 the image was solemnly crowned. It became the custom to offer newly married couples as a wedding gift a small wax image of Maria Bambina. The devotion spread from the Milan area to the whole of Italy and traveled to the United States with Italian immigrants in the past century.

MARIA STEIN

A shrine and monastery near Basel, Switzerland.

Tradition holds that in the fourteenth century, after a child fell down a cliff there but was unharmed, grateful residents placed a statue of Mary in a nearby cave. It became a pilgrimage destination. After a similar accident with the same result in 1540, the number of visitors increased and a monastery was established to care for them.

MARIAN MOVEMENT OF PRIESTS

A worldwide movement for priests, religious, and laity begun in Milan, Italy, in 1972 for spiritual renewal through consecration to the Immaculate Heart of Mary.

MARIAN YEAR

A twelve-month period dedicated to encouraging devotion to the Virgin Mary.

The first Marian Year was called by Pope Pius XII in 1954 to mark the centenary of the definition of the dogma of the Immaculate Conception. The second was called by Pope John Paul II and ran from Pentecost 1987 to the Feast of the Assumption 1988.

MARRIAGE ENCOUNTER

A movement founded in Spain in 1958 that assists husbands and wives to deepen their relationship within the context of the sacrament of matrimony.

The movement was brought to the United States in 1968 and continues to develop through its weekend conferences, using counseling, prayer, private reflec-tion, interpersonal dialogue, and the Mass.

MARRIAGE, SACRAMENT OF

The institution of marriage as recognized by the Church to be sacramental if between a baptized male and female.

MARTINMAS

A common medieval harvest and thanksgiving celebration held on the Feast of St. Martin of Tours, November 11.

Martinmas was a holiday in Germany, France, Holland, England, and other areas in central Europe. After Mass, there were games, dances, parades, and a festive dinner with a traditional roast goose. "St. Martin's wine" was the first from the recent harvest. Martinmas is still observed in some rural sections of Europe and is a popular celebration throughout Germany.

(See also ST. MARTIN OF TOURS.)

MARTYR

One who gives up his or her life rather than deny Christ and the Gospel.

MARTYROLOGY

A catalog of martyrs and other saints, arranged according to the calendar.

The Roman Martyrology contains the official list of saints venerated by the

Church. Additions to the list are made in beatification and canonization decrees of the Congregation for the Causes of Saints.

MARY GARDENS

A medieval custom that consists of planting small gardens featuring flowers and herbs associated with Mary by legend.

In the mid-twentieth century the practice was revived in Europe and the United States. Hundreds of plants and herbs are associated with the Virgin in various ways and traditions. Most simply, a Mary Garden is a portion of a larger garden set aside in honor of Mary.

The first Mary Garden in the United States is believed to be that at St. Joseph's Church in Woods Hole, Massachusetts. In 1932, Mrs. Frances Crane Lillie, a summer resident of Woods Hole, researched herbs and plants with old religious names that symbolized the Virgin Mary. She planted a selection of these in a garden at St. Joseph's Church. After the first year of Mrs. Lillie's "Garden of Our Lady," revisions were made and in 1933 it was replanted with forty-eight specimens which were planted around a commissioned statue of the Virgin Mary in a cross-shaped bed.

After twice being destroyed by hurricanes, the garden has been restored to its original planting plan. The restoration was prompted by the rediscovery of the garden's historical uniqueness and signifi-

cance by the parishioners in the course of the research undertaken for the writing of a commemorative history for the centennial of the parish.

The Woods Hole garden was the inspiration for the foundation of an organization called Mary's Gardens which was begun in Philadelphia in 1951 by two young businessmen, Edward A.G. McTague and John S. Stokes, Jr. The aim of the non-profit group is to revive the medieval practice of cultivating gardens of herbs and flowers which have Marian

A Mary Garden

341

names and to research the hundreds of plants symbolic of the life, mysteries, and privileges of the Blessed Virgin Mary. The founders hope that people will plant Mary Gardens as a prayerful, religious work of stewardship for God's flower riches and artistry with devotion, praise, meditation, and commitment. Research by this foundation has resulted in a list of over a thousand herb, flower, shrub, and tree names that are symbolic of Mary. Proposed initially for home gardens, Mary Gardens soon became established also at schools, parishes, burial plots, institutions, and shrines. In 1983, a Mary Garden was even established inside prison walls at the Idaho State Penitentiary. The traditional image of Our Lady of Guadalupe was painted by a prisoner-artist and a shrine was built around it made of rocks dug from the prison yard, flowers and grass.

Some of the better-known Mary Gardens today are those at Our Lady's national shrines at Knock, Ireland, and Akita, Japan; at the Artane Oratory of the Resurrection in Dublin and in the cloister planting of Lincoln Cathedral in England. In the United States, there is a beautiful Mary Garden at St. Mary's Parish in Annapolis, Maryland, adjacent to the historic Carroll House.

Today, the work of Mary's Gardens is continued by an informal association of committed persons in Pennsylvania, Massachusetts, Maryland, Ohio and Dublin,

Ireland. In 1995, the organization opened an internet web site to make their literature available in electronic form.

MARY, FEASTS OF
Special commemorations dedicated to the Blessed Mother.

The most ancient of the Marian feasts are thought to be Byzantine in origin. They demonstrate how the early Christological controversies influenced devotion to Mary. They are: Feast of the Presentation of Our Lord (February 2, sometimes referred to as the "Purification of Mary"), Solemnity of the Annunciation (March 25), Solemnity of the Assumption (August 15), and Feast of the Birth of Mary (September 8).

These celebrations came to the Roman liturgy through the Gelasian Sacramentary. The oldest Marian feast in the West is the Solemnity of Mary, Mother of God (January 1).

Other Marian feasts of later origin include: Immaculate Conception (December 8), Visitation (May 31), Queenship of Mary (August 22), Our Lady of Sorrows (September 15), and Our Lady of the Rosary (October 7).

Optional memorials include: Our Lady of Lourdes (February 11), Our Lady of Mount Carmel (July 16), Dedication of the Basilica of St. Mary Major (August 5), Presentation of Mary (November 21), and

Immaculate Heart of Mary (Saturday after the second Sunday after Pentecost).

MARY, MOTHER OF GOD

Christ's mother.

Devotion to Mary has been constant and profound since apostolic times. Since the earliest days of the Church, she alone has been given a veneration and honor second only to God.

Her unique, central, and pivotal role in Jesus' redemption of the world and the life of the Church continues to be examined through the development of doctrine. She is rightly called the Mother of God (*Theotokos*), "full of grace," "Mother of the Church," and in prayer and devotion "Our Lady," the "Blessed Virgin Mary," and the "New Eve."

The Church's liturgical calendar has Marian feasts throughout the year. The Hail Mary is among the most basic prayers; the Rosary among the most often said. Through the centuries she has been honored in countless prayers, hymns, litanies, songs, and works of literature and art. Many countries have named her their patroness.

(See also **DULIA**.)

MARY, SATURDAY OFFICE OF

A Marian practice.

Tracing its origins to the Middle Ages, this practice went along with the use of the Mass Proper in honor of the Blessed Virgin Mary on Saturday, when no other obligatory commemoration was observed. The present reform of the Liturgy of the Hours makes the Saturday Office of Mary optional under the title of "Memorial of the Blessed Virgin on Saturday."

MARYMAS

Technically, any feast of Mary.

Usually, though, Marymas refers to the Feast of the Annunciation (March 25). It is so named because of its direct relation to December 25, the Feast of Christmas. The two feasts, therefore, are united in the use of *mas* (for "Mass").

MASS

The Eucharist; the Church's principal sacramental celebration.

The Eucharist (from the Greek for "thanksgiving") was established by Christ at the Last Supper. In the Mass, the mystery of the salvation of humanity through participation in the sacrificial death and glorious Resurrection of Jesus is renewed and accomplished. The Mass renews the Paschal sacrifice of Christ as the sacrifice offered by the Church. It is called the Mass (from the Latin *missa*) because of the "mission," or "sending," with which the liturgy concludes: *"Ite, missa est"* (Latin for "Go, you are sent").

(See also **EUCHARIST**.)

MASS FOR THE DEAD — See **REQUIEM MASS**.

MASS OF THE CATECHUMENS

The original name of what is currently called the Liturgy of the Word.

Until Pope Paul VI revised the rites of the Western Church, the first part of the Mass was known as the Mass of the Catechumens and included everything from the entrance antiphon (or Introit) through the sermon. At the conclusion of the sermon, the catechumens (adults preparing for baptism) were dismissed. Now, we refer to the first part of the Mass as the Liturgy of the Word, with the catechumens still being dismissed at this point in the Mass.

MATACHINES

A traditional religious dance drama depicting the struggle between good and evil.

Its roots go back to medieval Spain and the morality plays about the conflict be-

Matachine Dancers

tween the Moors and the Christians, and it was brought to the New World by the Franciscans. Through the years, it incorporated Mexican and Indian religious and social symbols. Versions and meanings of the dance vary, according to the identity and traditions of the performers; but the dancers always wear elaborate headdresses or masks and colorful robes. The dance is usually performed in connection with major feast days and most often dedicated to the Holy Cross or to the Virgin Mary.

MATINS

Originally, the morning hours of Lauds.

Later on, it referred to the preceding hour of vigils, sung around midnight. These vigils eventually were incorporated into monastic practice and evolved into the hour of the Divine Office known as Matins.

MATRIMONY — See MARRIAGE, SACRAMENT OF.

MAUNDY THURSDAY

The traditional name for Holy Thursday.

It comes from *Mandatum*, a part of the Mass of the Lord's Supper.

(See also HOLY WEEK; MANDA-TUM.)

MAY

The month dedicated to Marian devotion, a popular tradition dating back to the sixteenth century.

Although May is a form of "Mary," the name of the month comes from the Latin for the "month of Maia," the Roman goddess of grain. The people of ancient Rome celebrated the first day of May by honoring Flora, the goddess of flowers. She was represented by a small statue wreathed in garlands. A procession of singers and dancers carried the statue past a sacred blossom-decked tree. Later, festivals of this kind spread to other parts of Europe, reaching their height of popularity in England during the Middle Ages. Dances around a flower-bedecked May pole were common. Often a May queen was chosen as part of the festivities.

Devotions to Our Lady on the first days of May date back to St. Philip Neri (1515-1595) who began the custom of decorating the statue of the Virgin with spring flowers. Annibale Dionisi, an Italian Jesuit, proposed devotions to Mary throughout the entire month. Just as happened with other pre-Christian customs and festivals, the Church incorporated the pre-Christian May celebrations and gave them a Christian dimension. May began to be celebrated in honor of Our Lady with much the same type of festivities, including floral tributes and processions and the crowning of a statue of Mary. Those

May Crowning Ceremony

customs continue, as does another: the May altar, a Marian shrine set up in the church or at home. Typically, it features an image of Mary and is decorated with flowers. In some households, it is the focal point for evening prayer during the month.

MEDAL

A sacramental; a flat metal, wood, or plastic disc with a religious image and/or inscription on one or both sides.

The custom of wearing medals is an ancient one, traced back as far as the time of the catacombs. Religious medals are flat, metal disks, usually in the form of a coin, which are struck or cast for a commemorative purpose. Religious medals are enormously varied, and are used to commemorate persons (Christ, the Blessed Mother, the saints) places such as famous shrines, past historical events (dogmatic definitions, miracles, dedications), or personal graces such as First Communion, ordination, etc. Medals are often concerned with ideas, such as the mysteries of our faith, and some serve as badges of pious associations. Medals are worn around the neck or on the person and serve as a reminder, as does a photograph or other relic of a loved one.

Medals should be regarded in the same way as any other image; they are merely signs of the prototype inscribed thereon, and in themselves have no efficacy. To consider them otherwise would be superstition. The medal is to be used as a reminder to honor the subject displayed on the medal, and a reminder of the need to advance in Christian perfection. The benefit of the medal used as a sacramental is the blessing called down from God on the wearer. Indulgences have sometimes been attached to various ones of the innumerable medals struck. The use of amulets in pagan antiquity was widespread. These were talismans worn about the neck. It is possible that the early Church tolerated an analogous practice. Christians sometimes wore phylacteries, containing relics or other devotional objects, and in Africa ancient molds for crosses have been found. The wearing of these phylacteries and encolpia or pectoral crosses soon lent itself to abuses when magical formula began to join the Christian symbols. Thus, we find record of protests from many of the Church Fathers from the fourth century on.

There are some early medals which have been found in the catacombs. Sometimes, regular coins were overprinted with a Christian symbol and holes were drilled

so the medals might be hung around the neck. There is no way of telling, however, how popular the custom was prior to the Middle Ages. By the twelfth century there was a custom at well-known places of pilgrimage of casting tokens of lead and sometimes other medals which served the

Various Medals

Miscellaneous Religious Medals

pilgrim as souvenirs, objects of piety, and a proof that the pilgrim had reached his destination. These *signacula*, or "pilgrim's signs," were cast in a variety of forms and were worn prominently on the hat or on the breast. By the sixteenth century, these began to be replaced by medals cast in bronze or silver with more artistic work on them. Beginning in the thirteenth century, *jetons*, or counters, began to be used for religious purposes. These were flat pieces of metal, generally a form of brass, but later more precious metals which were used as vouchers for attendance at ecclesiastical functions, or given as souvenirs. Commemorative medals began in the last years of the fourteenth century. The first ones were elaborate works of art, and were, therefore, restricted to the wealthy.

Papal Jubilee medals began as early as 1417. During the sixteenth century, the custom began of giving papal blessings to medals. One of the first of these was a medal worn by the Spanish during the revolt of the Gueux in Flanders, in 1566. This medal bore an image of Our Lord on one side, and an image of Our Lady of Hal on the other. Pope Pius V granted an indulgence to those who wore this medal on their hats. This vogue soon spread throughout Catholic Europe, and soon each city had medal craftsmen of its own.

Medals were so popular, and were struck for so many reasons and in so many designs, that it seems almost impossible to even classify them. Plague medals were struck and blessed as a protection against pestilence. Popular subjects for these are St. Sebastian, St. Roch, and shrines of the Virgin, sometimes with a view of a particular city on them. These medals often carried letters as abbreviations for prayers or mottos. Eucharistic miracles were often commemorated with medals, especially on jubilees or centenaries. These were issued in the different places where the miracles were believed to have happened, and some carry picture stories of the miraculous events.

There is a large class of private medals which were struck to commemorate incidents in the life of individuals and were distributed to friends. Baptism medals often contained precise details of the date of birth so that a child's horoscope could be calculated. The cross of St. Ulrich of Augsburg is an example of medals commemorative of special legends. Supposedly an angel brought the cross to St. Ulrich so that he might carry it into battle against the Huns in 955. More than 180 examples of this one commemoration have been found.

Papal medals, especially in conjunction with the opening and closing of the Holy Door during jubilee years, have been struck since 1417. Almost all major events of the reigns of the popes since that time have been commemorated in medals. Other semi-devotional medals have been

Top row: Jubilee Medal of St. Benedict; Medal of Our Lady of Guadalupe
Middle row: Medal of Our Lady of Confidence; The Church War Cross Medal
Bottom row: St. Christopher Medal; St. Dymphna Medal

struck by religious associations such as the Knights of Malta, and by abbeys in commemoration of their abbots.

(See also **SACRAMENTALS; MIRACULOUS MEDAL**.)

MEDAL OF MARIA GORETTI AND OUR MOTHER OF CONFIDENCE

A medal in honor of St. Maria Goretti struck at her canonization (1950).

The obverse of this medal displays a picture of Our Lady of Confidence which is surrounded by the aspiration "My Mother, My Confidence."

MEDAL OF OUR LADY OF FÁTIMA

A medal of Our Lady inspired by Father Joseph Cacella, the apostle of Fátima.

Father Cacella, a young Portuguese priest came to America in 1914. While at Graymoor, Father Cacella received letters from his mother in Portugal telling of the apparitions to the three shepherd children of Fátima. Her letters were intimate and full of details, as she knew and had spoken with the parents of the children and with the children themselves. She was convinced the children were speaking nothing but the truth.

A seminary classmate of Father Cacella, Monsignor Formigao, was the first representative of the Church to visit the young seers, and he began to write inspiring accounts of the apparitions. The radical communist government tracked down the identity of this priest and he was suspended, silenced, and imprisoned for months. Monsignor Formigao appealed to Father Cacella's mother to send information to her son. Father Cacella joyfully took up the task of making Fátima known, world-wide. America, with its freedom of the press, would be the herald of the news of Fátima. A small medal that Father Cacella had received in 1920 from his mother in Portugal became the prototype for the millions of medals commemorating the apparition which have since been struck.

MEDAL OF OUR LADY OF OLIVES

A medal of French origin based on a fourteenth century image of Our Lady.

Traditionally, people wear the medal as a protection against lightening in a storm, and women wear it at the time of childbirth, asking the Virgin to assist them in the hour of delivery. The prayer to Our Lady of Olives refers to her as the "Olive of Peace" and pleads for harmony between all nations.

MEDAL OF ST. BENEDICT

One of the oldest and most highly honored medals used by the Church. Because of the extraordinary number of miraculous occurrences attributed to this medal, it became popularly known as the "devil-chasing medal."

On the face of the medal is an image of St. Benedict standing before an altar. He holds the cross in one hand and the Benedictine rule in the other. On either side of the altar are an eagle and the traditional chalice. Inscribed in small letters beside two columns are the words *Crux E. Patris Benedict* (Cross of our Holy Father Benedict). Written in larger letters in a circular margin of the medal are the words *Ejus in obitu nostro praesentia muniamur* (May we be protected in our death by his presence).

Below the figure of the saint is the year the medal was struck: 1880. This is known as the Jubilee medal as it was struck to commemorate the fourteenth centenary of the birth of the saint. Near this is the Monte Cassino inscription, the abbey where the medal was struck.

The back side of the medal has a Cross of St. Benedict surmounted by the word *Pax* (Peace), the Benedictine motto, and a circular margin which bears the inscription: "VRSNSMVSMQLIVB." This inscription stands for: *Vade Retro Satana* (Get thee behind me Satan), *Nunquam Suade Mihi Vana* (Persuade me not to vanity), *Sunt Mala Quae Libas* (The cup you offer is evil), and (Drink the poison yourself). On the upright bar of the cross are found the letters: C.S.S.M.L., which stand for *Crux Sacra Sit Mihi Lux* (May the sacred cross be my light) and on the hori-

zontal bar of the cross N.D.S.M.D., *Non Draco Sit Mihi Dux* (let not the devil be my guide). The four large letters around the arms of the cross stand for *Crux Sancti Patris Benedicti* (The Cross of the Holy Father Benedict). The older version of the medal-cross carried the letters U.I.O.G.D., which stand for *Ut In Omnes Gloriam Deum* (That in all things God be glorified).

Much of the origin and early history of this medal is hidden in the twilight of antiquity. In its initial format, it appears to have been in the form of a cross. Shortly after the year 1000, a saintly youth named Bruno was miraculously cured of a deadly snakebite by the Cross of St. Benedict. In 1048, this young Benedictine became Pope Leo IX. His reign marked the end of a deplorable period in the history of the papacy. As pope, St. Leo IX carried out vigorous reforms of the clergy and prepared the way for the future popes to be elected by the cardinals of the Roman Church alone. He did much to spread the devotion to the Holy Cross and to St. Benedict. He enriched the medal of St. Benedict, which replaced the Cross of St. Benedict, with many blessings and indulgences. Later, Pope Benedict XIV urgently recommended it to all the faithful.

MEDAL OF ST. DYMPHNA

A devotion in favor of the mentally ill.

The medals are blessed and distributed from the shrine of the saint in Ohio.

MEDAL OF ST. JOSEPH — See **ST. JOSEPH MEDAL**.

MEDIATRIX OF ALL GRACES

A Marian title.

The Second Vatican Council explained that the reference "is to be so understood that it neither takes away anything from nor adds anything to the dignity and efficaciousness of Christ the one Mediator" (*Lumen Gentium*, n. 62).

MEDITATION

Mental, as distinguished from vocal, prayer in which thought, affections, and resolutions of the will predominate.

There is a meditative element to all forms of prayer, which always involves the raising of the heart and mind to God.

MEDJUGORJE, OUR LADY OF

A Marian title and devotion.

It is associated with the Bosnia-Herzegovina site of the alleged apparitions of Mary to eight children beginning in 1981. Many pilgrims have been attracted to the spot.

MEMENTO MORI

Reminders that all die; from the Latin for "reminder of death."

During the Middle Ages, human mortality was a frequent topic of preaching, and the laity became fascinated with the physical properties of death almost to the point of overshadowing the Christian message of the Resurrection. This morbid fascination became enormously popular and resulted in works of art including paintings, statues, plays, dances, and other daily reminders of death.

MEMORARE

A Marian prayer attributed to St. Bernard of Clairvaux (c. 1090-1153).

It reads:

Remember, O most gracious Virgin Mary, that never was it known that anyone who fled to your protection, implored your help, or sought your intercession was left unaided.

Inspired by this confidence, I fly unto you, O Virgin of Virgins, my Mother. To you I come, before you I stand, sinful and sorrowful. O Mother of the Word Incarnate, despise not my petitions, but in your mercy hear and answer me. Amen.

(See also **ST. BERNARD OF CLAIRVAUX**.)

Memoriam Cards

MEMORIAM CARDS

Memorial cards that typically include the deceased's name, dates of birth and death, a short prayer, and sometimes a photograph of the person.

Mortuary or memoriam cards have long been a custom in Ireland and are popular in many other countries today.

MENAION

In the Byzantine Rite, the liturgical book that contains the Proper of Saints and of the fixed feasts for the whole year.

MENOLOY (ALSO MENOLOGION)

In the Eastern Church, a book containing the lives of the saints in accordance with the liturgical year.

It corresponds to the martyrology and the *Acta Sanctorum* of the Western Church.

MENTAL PRAYER — See MEDITATION.

MERCY SUNDAY — See DIVINE MERCY.

MERCY, OUR LADY OF — See MOTHER OF MERCY.

MERCY, WORKS OF — See CORPORAL WORKS OF MERCY; SPIRITUAL WORKS OF MERCY.

MERIENDA DEL CORDERO

Spanish for "repast of the lamb."

It is a traditional meal associated with pilgrimages to the Spanish shrine of St. Joseph on his feast day, March 19.

METANOIA

A New Testament term referring to conversion, entailing repentance of sin and a subsequent turning toward the Lord.

Metanoia is essential to the Christian life and is necessary for spiritual growth. St. Paul speaks of the "new creation," involving a renewal of mind and heart through baptism or sanctifying grace.

METANY

A ritual gesture.

In the East, it consists of an inclination of the head and shoulders (lesser metany) or a prostration to the ground (greater metany).

Both are penitential gestures.

MICHAEL THE ARCHANGEL — See ST. MICHAEL THE ARCHANGEL.

MIDNIGHT MASS ON CHRISTMAS

The traditional time of the first Mass on the Feast of the Nativity based on a pious legend that Christ was born at that hour.

There is no evidence that supports this particular story.

MIDSUMMER'S EVE

Also known as St. John's Eve.

A variety of medieval customs are associated with the Feast of St. John the Baptist, which falls on June 24. Many of the customs were Christianized versions of pagan traditions.

In Sardinia at the end of March of the first of April, the young men of the villages presented themselves to the young ladies and made a pact to be sweethearts. At the end of May, the girls made pots from the bark of the cork tree and filled them with earth, sowing wheat and barley in each pot. By St. John's Eve the plant had a good head on it. On St. John's Day, the couple dressed in their best and went in procession to the local church where they threw the pot against the door of the church, after which they sat and ate eggs and herbs to the music of flutes. Wine was passed around and all partook. In Sicily, couples became sweethearts (gossips) of St. John on his feast. They presented each other with plates of sprouting corn, lentils, and canary seed which had been planted before the festival. Throughout Europe, bunches of blessed herbs were hung over the door to ward off evil spirits. In Rome, St. John's night was and is celebrated with the eating of snails. At Catania, the sweethearts exchanged pots of basil and great cucumbers. In Portugal, basil and garlic were the important plants in his cult. On the eve of the feast, people danced through the streets until all hours, hitting each other with leeks. In New York the many Americans of Puerto Rican descent honor St. John as patron of Puerto Rico and hold colorful fiestas in his name. The fiestas include Mass, processions, piñatas, and picnics.

MILAGROS

Spanish for "miracles."

Milagros are small metal images of hearts, people, animals, and body parts that are used as *ex voto* offerings in Hispanic countries. They are hung on the images of the saints in thanksgiving for favors. Another term for these is *promesa* (promise).

(See also **EX VOTO**.)

Milagros

MINCE PIE

A traditional Christmas dish; originally known as *shrid pye* (shredded pie).

Mince, or mince meat, was finely chopped meat or a combination of apples, spices, suet, and meat. The pies were baked in the form of the manger, and the ingredients represented spices of the East, symbolizing the gifts of the Magi to the Christ Child. A small image of the child made from pastry decorated the top. During the time of the reformation, many writers of religious tracts called the pies "idolatrie in crust." One wrote, "Such pye is an hodgepodge of superstition, Popery, the devil and all its works." When it was forbidden, the English simply changed the shape of the pie to round to remove its religious significance.

MINIMS

The Order of Friars founded in 1435 by St. Francis of Paola.

MINISTRY OF THE WORD

The spreading of the Gospel through evangelization and catechesis.

It is the Liturgy of the Word during the Sacrifice of the Mass, which contains, in part, the Scripture readings and homily. It is also the office of theologians as they plumb the depths of the Church's teaching and explain it to the faithful.

MIRACLE OF ST. JANUARIUS —
See **JANUARIUS, MIRACLE OF ST**.

MIRACLE PLAY

A medieval dramatic representation with a religious theme.

Miracle plays depicted the life of a saint, a religious historical event, a story from the Bible, or some teaching of the faith. Primarily catechetical, a miracle play was performed by a touring troupe of players outdoors, often in the courtyard or square in front of a cathedral. The performance could include songs, prayer, and other devotions. Miracle plays preceded mystery plays, which usually concentrated more on scriptural events.

MIRACLES

Observable events or effects in the physical or moral order of things, with reference to salvation, which cannot be explained by the ordinary operation of laws of nature and which, therefore, are attributed to the direct action of God.

A miracle makes known, in an unusual way, the concern and intervention of God in human affairs for the salvation of humanity.

MIRACULOUS CHRIST OF BUGA —
See **BUGA, MIRACULOUS CHRIST OF**.

Miraculous Medal

MIRACULOUS MEDAL

A Marian devotion and image associated with visions of Our Lady reported by St. Catherine Labouré (1806-1876).

The first Miraculous Medal, struck in 1832, was based on Mary's instructions to the young French Vincentian nun. Because many cures and conversions were soon attributed to Mary's intercession in association with the medal, it soon became popularly known as the Miraculous Medal.

(See also **MEDAL**.)

THE MIRACULOUS RESPONSORY

A responsory in favor of St. Anthony written by St. Bonaventure.

If miracles thou fain wouldst see
Lo, error, death, calamity,
The leprous stain, the demon flies,
From beds of pain the sick arise.

Refrain: The hungry seas forgo their prey,

The prisoner's cruel chains give way;
While palsied limbs and chattels lost,
Both young and old recovered boast.

And perils perish; plenty's hoard
Is heaped on hunger's famished board;
Let those relate who know it well,
Let Padua of his patron tell.

Refrain

To Father, Son let glory be,
And Holy Ghost eternally.

Refrain

Pray for us O blessed Anthony, that
we may be made worthy of
the promises of Christ.

Let Thy Church, O God, be
gladdened by the solemn
commemoration of blessed Anthony
thy Confessor: that she may
evermore be defended by Thy
spiritual assistance, and merit
to possess everlasting joy. Through
Christ Our Lord. Amen.

MISERERE

Psalm 51; A penitential Psalm that, in Latin, begins: *Miserere mei, Deus,* "Have mercy on me, O God."

King David has been credited with

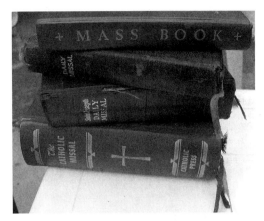
Various Missals

composing the prayer after repenting of his sin of adultery with Bathsheba and having her husband killed. The prayer is said during the Liturgy of the Hours on Fridays to denote the penitential character of that day.

MISSAL

The book containing the introductory documents and prayers of the celebration of Mass according to the Roman Rite.

It is also a small prayer book used by the laity and which contains the prayers and the readings for Mass and other private prayers.

MISSION CROSS

A small cross or crucifix presented ceremonially by some religious orders to their members when they leave for mission territory.

Also, it is a permanent cross erected at the place where a mission has been preached. Various types of the latter are made of durable and appealing material, fastened in a definite place or sustained by a firm base, blessed by the priest who preached the mission, and erected with the permission of the local bishop.

MISTLETOE

A plant and ancient Christmas custom.

As a Christmas custom, kissing under the mistletoe has been an enduring tradition, expressing love for the Messiah and each other during the Christmas season. This mistletoe custom is an ancient one, going back to the Celts both in Ireland and in England on the continent of Europe. "The Golden Bough" is the name given to mistletoe by the Celts. It is a characteristic of mistletoe that when dry it has a golden tinge.

Many species of mistletoe are used in religious ceremonies in many parts of the world. The plant itself is a parasite and often grows from seeds which were dropped by birds on the bark of trees, especially oaks. The mistletoe inserts its woody "sinkers" into the host tree and derives almost its entire sustenance thereby. The most magical and sacred mistletoe is said to grow on oak trees, but the most common growth is found on apple and other deciduous trees. It is occasionally found on evergreens.

According to Pliny, a first century Roman historian, the Druids considered the mistletoe sacred, and many rituals developed around it. The name "all healer" is given to the plant in various Celtic languages, although the berries of the plant are poisonous. American pioneers used it as a remedy for snakebite and toothache. Today, derivatives of the plant are used in treating lung cancer.

It is somewhat uncertain how the Celtic custom of mistletoe survived in Britain or how it came to be associated with Christmas rather than Midsummer as in Scandinavian countries. Some antiquarians reason that a likely association with other evergreens was made because the color of the black and red berries of the holly and ivy was a natural contrast to the white berries of the mistletoe. Also, it might be the constant green of the plant which promised spring in the midst of the winter's darkness.

During the Victorian Era, the English transported many traditions to the U.S. When some churchmen became aware of the pagan background of the plant and its attendant customs, they attempted to ban its use in church. This was an unusual reaction, since there are ancient Christian legends that the mistletoe was the *sancta crucis lignum* (the wood of the holy cross) used in the Crucifixion of Christ. According to the legend, it was once a strong tree but since its unholy use it was degraded to a parasite.

The multitude of Irish immigrants to the U.S. brought the Christmas custom of kissing under the mistletoe with them and, along with the English immigrants, shared it with their American neighbors.

MOLEBEN

In the Byzantine Church, a service of prayer honoring a particular saint, the Blessed Virgin Mary, or Christ himself.

It may include prayers of thanksgiving, petition, and penance.

MONK

One who withdraws from society in order to pursue a life totally dedicated to God in prayer, penance, and solitude.

Monks are commonly distinguished from communities of clerics or friars who engage in some form of active ministry. While the term "monk" can refer both to men and women monastic religious, common English usage restricts it to men and prefers the term "nun" for women.

MONSTRANCE

From the Latin *ostensorium*.

It is a vessel in which the Eucharist is exposed during Benediction and adoration services.

(See also **BENEDICTION**.)

MONTHLY DEVOTIONS

The custom of dedicating a particular month to a specific devotion.

Traditionally they are: January, the Holy Name; February, the Passion of Our Lord; March, St. Joseph; April, the Holy Eucharist; May, Our Lady; June, the Sacred Heart; July, the Most Precious Blood; August, the Immaculate Heart of Mary; September, Our Lady of Sorrows; October, the Most Holy Rosary; November, the Holy Souls; December, the Divine Infancy.

Monstrance

MONTHLY MASS IN HONOR OF THE HOLY SPIRIT

The consecration of the first Monday of each month with Mass and Communion in honor of the Holy Spirit.

The practice was recommended by the Archconfraternity of the Holy Spirit.

(See also **CONFRATERNITY**.)

MONTHLY PERIOD OF RECOLLECTION

A particular time each month for recollection.

It consists of a meditation, an attitude of concentration, or an awareness of spiritual matters and things pertaining to salvation and the accomplishment of God's will. Various parishes and organizations hold monthly periods of recollection.

MONTH'S MIND MASS

The custom of having a Mass offered one month after the death of a family member with the members in attendance.

A similar practice takes place on the anniversary of the death.

MONTSERRAT

A Benedictine monastery and a shrine to Our Lady near Barcelona, Spain.

The image of the Virgin there dates back to the twelfth or thirteenth century. It is made of polychrome wood and has black features and so is called *La Morenita* (the little dark one). The monastery began in the eleventh century and was rebuilt in the nineteenth century. This particular Black Madonna is the patron of Catalonia. Her feast day is April 27.

(See also **BLACK MADONNAS**.)

Our Lady of Montserrat

MONUMENTO

A Hispanic custom of building a special altar in the church for Holy Thursday.

Typically it is decorated with flowers and candles as a tribute to the Eucharist. In some regions, the people walk to as many churches as possible that night to visit the Blessed Sacrament and to offer prayers of adoration. The altar is taken apart on Good Friday and replaced with a representation of Calvary.

MORALITY PLAY

A dramatic work so designated for the moral struggle between virtue and vice that figures at the core of this genre of religious drama.

MORAL VIRTUES

The good habits that develop in one who has performed morally good acts.

Moral virtues incline one to do good with ease, whereas intellectual virtues empower one to know the truth and supernatural virtues order one to seek God explicitly. The four fundamental cardinal virtues are prudence, justice, fortitude, and temperance.

MORNING OFFERING

A prayer recited each morning, offering the day in union with Christ's self-offering.

The most common form in the United States is that used by the Apostleship of Prayer:

O Jesus, through the Immaculate Heart of Mary, I offer you all my prayers, works, joys, and sufferings of this day, for all the intentions of your Sacred Heart, in union with the Holy Sacrifice of the Mass throughout the world, in reparation for my sins, for the intentions of all our associates, and for the general intention recommended this month.

(See also **APOSTLESHIP OF PRAYER**.)

MORNING PRAYER — See **LITURGY OF THE HOURS**.

MORTIFICATION

Acts of self-discipline.

They may include prayer, hardship, austerities, and penances undertaken for the sake of progress in virtue.

MOST BLESSED SACRAMENT, OUR LADY OF THE

A Marian title and devotion.

It is associated with St. Peter Julian Eymard (1811-1868), founder of the

Our Lady of the Most Blessed Sacrament

MOTHERHOOD OF MARY — See **SOLEMNITY OF MARY, MOTHER OF GOD**.

MOTHERING SUNDAY

Formerly a popular name for the fourth Sunday of Lent, which had also been known as Laetare Sunday. It was a day on which mothers were honored.

The Romans honored their goddess of motherhood in the spring with the Feast of Matronalia. Small cakes made of a special extra fine white flour known as simila were baked and offered to her at her

Congregation of the Priests of the Blessed Sacrament.

MOTHER OF MERCY

A Marian image and devotion; also known as "Our Lady of Mercy."

It is based on visions reported by Antonio Botta on a hillside near Savona, Italy, in 1536. Botta said Our Lady told him, "I want mercy and not justice." A shrine was built on the spot and later was replaced by a basilica.

MOTHER THRICE ADMIRABLE — See **SCHÖNSTATT, OUR LADY OF**.

Mother of Mercy

shrine. When the Christian Church started to grow in the different parts of the Roman Empire, the old customs were often incorporated into the new Church's own traditions. Matronalia changed into a day to honor Mother Church. Gradually the custom grew of honoring earthly mothers on this day. By the eighteenth century, the custom was well established, and youth working away from home as servants were allowed to go home for the day. They would usually take a basket of goodies to their mothers, including a simnel cake which in England was made with the inclusion of plums or raisins.

MOUNT CARMEL, OUR LADY OF

A Marian image and early devotion associated with the Carmelites, an order that began in the late twelfth century.

Located near the port city of Haifa, Israel, Carmel had been considered a holy place since ancient times. It was associated with the activities of both Elijah and Elisha (see 1 Kings 18:19-20, 42; 2 Kings 2:25; 4:25).

Twelfth-century pilgrims on their way to Jerusalem reported the presence of the Carmelites at the Fountain of Elijah and said the oratory was dedicated to the Virgin Mary. That devotion has remained a focal point of the order.

As the political and religious situation worsened in the Holy Land, the Car-

melites began to move from Mount Carmel in 1238 to such places as Cyprus, Sicily, France, and England. By 1291, after a century's existence there, all the Carmelites had left the Fountain of Elijah.

The Marian tradition of the Carmelites is united with the Elijah tradition in an ancient book of the order entitled *The Institution of the First Monks*. This book dates back at least to the late fourteenth century, when it was first circulated among the Carmelites.

When Elijah sends his servant to look out to sea during a drought in Israel, the servant tells of seeing a small cloud. To Elijah, God revealed four mysteries about the cloud: 1) the future birth of a girl born without sin; 2) the time of her birth; 3) that she would be the first woman to take the vow of virginity (after Elijah, who was the first man to do so); and 4) that the Son of God would be born of this virgin.

The Carmelites then understood that these mysteries were fulfilled in Mary and devoted themselves to her, choosing her as their patroness. From that point they considered Mary their sister, and they were known as the "Brothers of the Blessed Virgin of Mount Carmel." As early as 1252, papal documents contain that title in reference to the Carmelites.

Other early members of the order, such as the Frenchman Jean de Cheminot in 1337 and the Englishman John Baconthorpe (d. 1348), wrote about the relationship of Mary and Elijah in Carmelite tradition.

The Carmelite habit is the theme of the final section of *The Institution of the First Monks*. The habit is understood as a sign of poverty, humility, separation from the world, dedication to God, and of a common fraternity. The scapular itself is viewed as the yoke of obedience.

It is important, too, to understand that for some one hundred fifty years the scapular was identified not with Mary but with the Christological theme of obedience. The first reference to the scapular is found in the Carmelite Constitutions of 1281: "The Brothers are to sleep in their tunic and scapular under the pain of severe penalty."

Our Lady of Mount Carmel

No mention is made at this point of the scapular vision to St. Simon Stock in any of the documents of the thirteenth century.

An account written in the late fourteenth century tells of an appearance by Mary to Simon Stock who, according to at least one tradition, was elected prior general of the Carmelite Order in 1254 at the general chapter held in London. According to this account, Mary held the scapular in her hand and said that the one who dies in it will be saved. However, it is not possible to verify the historicity of this event that only surfaces in accounts almost one hundred fifty years after the supposed happening. A more contemporary approach to the scapular devotion understands the scapular as an expression of devotion to Mary, a sign of her protection and care, some type of affiliation to the Carmelites, and a willingness to imitate her prayerful submission to God's plan of salvation. "The Brown Scapular of Our Lady of Mount Carmel is best understood in the context of the Catholic Faith," wrote the North American Carmelite superiors in a recent publication. They continue:

It offers us a rich spiritual tradition that honors Mary as the first and foremost of her Son's disciples. This scapular is an outward sign of the protection of the Blessed Virgin Mary our sister, mother and queen. It offers an effective symbol of Mary's protection to the Order of Carmel — its members, associates, and affiliates — as they strive to fulfill their vocation as defined by the Carmelite Rule of St. Albert 'to live in allegiance to Jesus Christ.'

While Christ alone has redeemed us, the Blessed Virgin Mary has always been seen by Catholics as a loving mother and protector. The Blessed Virgin has shown her patronage over the Order of Carmel from its earliest days. This patronage and protection came to be symbolized in the scapular, the essential part of the Carmelite habit.

Stories and legends abound in Carmelite tradition about the many ways in which the Mother of God has interceded for the Order, especially in critical moments of its history. Most enduring and popular of these traditions, blessed by the Church, concerns Mary's promise to an early Carmelite, St. Simon Stock, that anyone who remains faithful to the Carmelite vocation until death will be granted the grace of final perseverance. The Carmelite Order has been anxious to share this patronage and protection with those who are devoted to the Mother of God and so has extended both its habit (the scapular) and affiliation to the larger Church.

The Carmelite superiors then point out that private revelation can neither add to nor detract from the deposit of faith in the Catholic Church:

Therefore, the Brown Scapular of Our Lady of Mount Carmel simply echoes the promise found in Divine Revelation, i.e., 'The one who holds out to the end is the one who will see salvation' (Matt. 24:13).

'Remain faithful until death and I will give you the crown of life' (Rev. 2:10). The Brown Scapular of Our Lady of Mount Carmel must be regarded as a reminder to its wearers of the saving grace that Christ gained upon the cross for all people, and that there is no salvation for anyone other than that won by Christ himself. It is the sacraments that mediate this saving grace to all the faithful. The sacramentals, however, including the scapular, do not mediate this saving grace but prepare the faithful to receive grace and dispose them to cooperate with it.

(See also **SABBATINE PRIVILEGE**.)

MOURNING ANGELS — See ANGELS OF DEATH.

MOVABLE FEASTS

Feasts on the liturgical calendar that are not assigned a specific date because their celebration is based on means of calculating time other than chronological dates.

Easter is the prototypical example. Its date depends on the lunar calendar. Because Easter moves every year, other feasts are subject to movement also. Some of these include: Ash Wednesday, Ascension, and Pentecost, along with the Sundays of Advent, Lent, and Easter.

MY MOTHER, MY CONFIDENCE

A short prayer ("My mother, my confidence") associated with an image of and devotion to Our Lady of Confidence.

The first known painting of Our Lady of Confidence was given to Sister Chiara Isabella Fornari (1697-1744) by the artist Carlos Maratta in Todi, Italy. Venerated in that country for more than two centuries, it shows Mary holding the Child Jesus.

MYRON

The chrism consecrated by a bishop on Holy Thursday at the Mass of Chrism and used throughout a diocese in sacramental ministrations.

It may also be used by a bishop or designated priest in the consecration of churches and altars. It is also the oil that exudes from the bones of certain saints

— for instance, St. Nicholas of Myra, or the oil that appears to stream from a holy icon, frequently bearing a sweet scent.

MYRRH

An aromatic plant gum.

It is used in perfumes and formerly for incense.

(See also **EPIPHANY; INCENSE.**)

MYSTERY PLAY — See **MIRACLE PLAY**.

MYSTERIES OF THE ROSARY — See **ROSARY**.

MYSTIC

A person who enjoys special gifts given through the practice of meditation and contemplation.

MYSTICAL DEATH

The dying to self in order to live for God.

Mystical death was part of the core charism of the great mystic and founder of the Passionist Order, St. Paul of the Cross (1694-1775).

MYSTICAL ROSE

A Marian title.

It is associated with visions reported by Sister Pierina in Italy in the late 1940s.

N

NACIMIENTO (PRECIPIO, POR-TAL) — See **CHRISTMAS CRIB**.

NAILS, HOLY

The nails with which Christ was fixed to his cross.

It is unclear how many there would have been. St. Ambrose, writing several decades after the alleged finding of them, suggests that there were only two found by St. Helena, the mother of Emperor Constantine. Pious legend holds that Constantine made one nail into a bit for his horse, placed another into a statue of himself along with relics of the true cross, and forced a third into the royal diadem.

According to the hagiographer Alban Butler (1710-1763), St. Helena was informed that if she could find the sepulcher she would likewise find the instruments of the Passion. Such instruments were customarily thrown in a hole and buried near the place where the executed criminal was buried. This custom is supported in the writings of St. Ambrose, who was the first author to reveal that St. Helena found the nails together with the cross and the title. Pope St. Gregory the Great (d. 604), who had served as emissary from the bishop of Rome to Constantinople, is reported to have brought a fourth nail back with him when he returned to Rome in 585. It was

A Nacimiento

placed in the Church of the Holy Cross in Jerusalem, which had been built to house the relic of the cross. This nail is still venerated there. More than thirty places claim to have these relics. According to Butler, nails made to resemble the holy nails were forged to include filings from the original nails. Others were simply touched to the original and given as mementos.

(See also **RELICS**.)

NAME

In Catholic practice, there is a tradition of choosing a saint's name for a child.

While this practice is not mandatory, the Church recommends every child be given a name with Christian significance to symbolize newness of life in Christ. It is also customary, but not required, to choose a "confirmation name," a second personal patron saint, for confirmation.

The children learn the stories of their saints, are encouraged to emulate the attributes of the saints, and are told to pray to and request the saint's loving help in their daily life. This close relationship of an individual to his personal patron saints is a beautiful custom highly recommended by the Church.

Names, like all other words, were in existence long before anyone ever wrote them down. Customs regarding the bestowing of names have changed through-

out the centuries. In America today, children enter the world with a family, or surname, attached. Parents give their children one or more names as personal or given names, at baptism. Friends and family often refer to others by a nickname. In American Roman Catholic tradition, another name is given at the time of receiving the sacrament of confirmation.

The first family names came about in a number of ways. A man was often named after the place in which he lived, the work he did, or even from the main physical features of his property. Often, the word *son* was added to the name of the father. Physical features, such as a person's coloring, sometimes contributed family names.

When people emigrated to other countries, often those in the new countries could not pronounce the original names in the various languages of the new immigrants. Thus, many names were changed to better blend with those of the new country. This was especially true in America, a land of immigrants. Persecution, too, left its mark on family names. It was often dangerous for a man to keep his original name and thus he changed it to match his new situation. In America, the family name comes from the father, although immigrants from Spanish speaking countries have brought their custom of adding their mother's family name after their father's surname.

Names are not fixed, but are changeable. Spelling has always been a matter of personal choice, and the pronunciation of names changes greatly even within single countries.

Many given names are derived from Greek and Latin words. Each of these words have meanings, and these same meanings are found in other languages. The Bible has provided a wealth of given names. Names have been taken from nature, from famous people, and new names are constantly being derived from old ones.

Nicknames, familiar names given to us by friends and family, have often devolved into common given names. The word *nickname* is actually a slurred form of "an ekename." "An" shortened into "n" makes "nekename." *Eke* is an old English word meaning "additional." So an ekename, or a nickname, is an extra name.

Although the vast majority of American names have come through the European traditions of the waves of immigrants who came to the United States, many beautiful and meaningful names have come from other languages and traditions. A good case in point are the names often chosen today by African Americans, who have looked to their roots to select meaningful names from the many and varied African languages. Many of these names have the same meanings, if different sounds, as European-based ones.

The exact way a name is written is only a matter of tradition. There are many languages and several alphabets, so the same name may look quite different when it is transliterated from one language to another. The writer we know as Chekhov is known as Tschechow in Germany, Tjechov in Sweden, and Cechov in Italy. He wrote his own name as *lexob* because his native language, Russian, uses the Cyrillic alphabet.

Names from all languages have meanings, and names with Christian meanings can be found in all languages. The names *Chinue, Ibo* for "God's own blessing," *Olufemi, Yoruba* for "God loves me," and *Jamala, Chaldean* for "the beauty of Mary," are only three of many names which have Christian meaning as well as uniqueness.

Unusual names can also be dictated by their spelling. Thus the name *Toby*, from the Hebrew meaning "The Lord is Good," could be spelled T-o-b-i for a name both unusual and meaningful.

The practice of giving children the names of Christian saints dates from the first millennium, and began in France and Germany. The people gave their children the names of Apostles, Biblical saints, early martyrs, or confessors. By the thirteenth century, the custom had spread throughout the European continent.

Originally, the Gaelic population of Ireland did not follow this custom, and there are no Christian names found in the ancient Irish documents. Early Irish parents considered it irreverent to claim such hallowed names for their own. The continental practice came into usage only in the thirteenth century. Some early Gaelic clans did call themselves "servants" (*gil, mal*) of Christ and the saints, but the custom affected their surnames rather than their given names. Gilmartin, for example, designated the servant of St. Martin, as the name *Malone* designated the servant of St. John.

Through a special feeling of reverence, all Christian nations except the Spanish-speaking people have consistently avoided giving their children the given name of Our Lord, Jesus. It is, however, customary and common to bestow this name on Spanish-speaking boys. This same feeling of reverence has kept the popes from using the name of Peter, and the Irish set apart the original name of Mary — *Muire* — never giving it to their daughters in this form.

In Spanish-speaking countries, girls are not only given the name of Mary, but also some of her liturgical titles and attributes. Thus, names such as *Luz* (Our Lady of Light), *Dolores* (Our Lady of Sorrows), *Concepcion* (The Immaculate Conception) or *Stella* (Star of the Sea), are common names for Spanish-speaking girls.

The Chaldeans and Syrians gave girls names that refer to Mary's attributes, such as *Afifa* (her purity), *Farida* (her uniqueness) or *Kamala* (her perfection). Although there are only about a thousand saints that have been officially canonized by the Catholic Church, there are more than four thousand generally recognized by the Church, many of which come from the lists of ancient martyrologies. Pope John Paul II has heeded wisely the call of Vatican II to hold up more saintly examples for the world to imitate and has beatified many new saints.

Many of the new saints were, of course, named after previous saints. This does not preclude the naming of children after the newer saints, and parents might choose to use the new saint's given name in his or her native language, or another derivative. The Native American Kateri Tekakwitha was named for St. Catherine of Siena. Now, Kateri herself is held up for honor, and a new spelling has been added to the roster of saints' names.

Today's saints are canonized with their complete name. Thus, a surname might be used as a given name to reflect the new saint. When he became a Christian, the European missionaries followed the custom of bestowing a saint's name on the courageous African Charles Lwanga. *Lwanga*, his Bugandan surname, could be given to a child in honor of this great martyr. In the same manner, the name *Kim* could be given in honor of the Korean saint Andrew Kim.

Among the saints and blesseds proclaimed in the last few decades, there are a number of beautiful native names, especially among the Ugandan, Korean, Japanese, and Vietnamese martyrs. For example, Kizito, the youngest of the Uganda martyrs, was a martyr for chastity. He incurred the wrath of the king by refusing his unchaste advances, and was willingly executed at the tender age of thirteen. In today's sexually oriented America, what a beautiful example this young saint could be for an African-American Catholic child. Mbaga was another youthful martyr for charity. Mukasa was a dedicated lay catechist. Syeng-im, A-ki, Mai-im, and Yeng-tek were all dedicated lay Catholic women and martyrs. One day soon, you may hear the priest say, "Mukasa Mbaga I baptize you in the name of the Father, the Son, and the Holy Spirit." At confirmation, the bishop may intone "Syeng-im, be sealed with the gift of the Holy Spirit."

NAME DAY

Before the Reformation, and even today in some Catholic countries, it was a general custom to celebrate not so much a child's birthday, but rather the feast of the saint whose name was received in baptism. This practice has never been strong in American usage except in the religious orders. Celebrations generally include Mass, a gathering with relatives and friends, small gifts, and decorations and food carrying out the theme or emphasizing the attributes of the saint. In the celebrations of name days held by religious orders, skits or small plays are sometimes included.

NATIVITY

Literally, "the process of being born."

The Church celebrates three birthdays in the liturgical calendar: that of Our Lord (December 25), Our Lady (September 8), and St. John the Baptist (June 24). Normally, liturgical commemorations of saints correspond to their dates of death that are, in reality, their "birthdays" into the life of heaven.

NATIVITY OF JESUS — See CHRISTMAS.

NATIVITY OF MARY

The feast celebrated on September 8 to mark the birth of Mary.

The feast originated in the East and came to Rome before the middle of the seventh century. Pope St. Sergius I (r. 687-701) instituted a procession for it as he had for the other three major feasts of Mary then observed in Rome, but that custom did not survive long. The Nativity of Mary was observed throughout the Church by the ninth century, and in the

Nativity of Mary

Another feast, on August 29, commemorates his passion and death as ordered by Herod. The precursor and cousin of Christ was commemorated universally in the liturgy by the fourth century. St. John the Baptist is the only saint, except for Mary, whose earthly birthday is observed as a feast. At times, it was considered a holy day of obligation.

The birth of Jesus is celebrated on December 25 to coincide with the winter solstice, whereas the birth of his forerunner, John, is observed six months earlier at the time of the summer solstice. From St. John's birthday the sun will decline and the days begin to be shorter, whereas with Christmas the sun will return and the days lengthen. The analogy is that John is the lamp, but Christ is the true light of the world. Hence, by the arrangement of these two births on the liturgical calendar, the prophetic motto of the Baptist is fulfilled annually: "He must increase, I must decrease."

The Council of Agde in 506 listed it among the highest feasts of the year. Its rank was so great that, just as on Christmas, three Masses were celebrated. In 1022, a synod at Seligenstadt, Germany, prescribed fourteen days of fast and abstinence in preparation for the Feast of St.

eleventh it became a holy day of obligation. There are no historical data to support the celebration of Mary's birth on this particular date, although it is celebrated nine months after the Feast of the Immaculate Conception.

NATIVITY OF ST. JOHN THE BAPTIST

The feast celebrated on June 24 honoring John the Baptist's birth.

John the Baptist. The practice was never accepted universally by Rome.

In folklore, as the first day of summer, St. John's Day was associated with a number of festivals and traditions, including the burning of St. John's fires, a reference to light. The day was considered as one of the great "charmed" festivals of the year. Hidden treasures are said to lie open in lonely places, waiting for the lucky finder. Divining rods should be cut on this day, and herbs are given unusual powers of healing which they retain if they are plucked during the night of the feast. In Germany, these herbs were called *Johanneskraut* and people brought them to church for a special blessing.

(See also **MIDSUMMER'S EVE; ST. JOHN'S FIRES**.)

NEOPHYTE

A newly baptized person.

In the early Church, and to some degree today with the revival of the Rite for the Christian Initiation of Adults, the Easter season was used as a time of "continuing education" in the faith as a necessary follow-up to the pre-baptismal catechesis of Lent.

NESTEIA

The religious fast and abstinence as practiced in the rites of the Eastern Churches.

NICENE CREED — See CREED, NICENE.

NICHO

A Mexican custom involving yard and garden shrines popular throughout the American Southwest.

A *nicho* (Spanish for "niche") is often built as the result of a promise made to a favorite saint, although some simply make a statement that the home is a Catholic one. When the *nicho* or *gruta* (grotto) is made in gratitude, the petitioner asks the saint for some form of intervention during a life crisis such as a debilitating illness or dangerous military service. He or she promises to dedicate a shrine to the saint if prayers are answered. The completion of this vow, or *manda*, is seen as a serious and binding one.

Nichos are made in different sizes using a variety of material and generally have a border. The boundary, often made of bricks, rocks, or plants, sets off the sacred area. *Milagros*, small metal *ex votos* in the shape of people, animals, or hearts, are sometimes attached to the hands of the statue. Other *ex votos* — such as photographs of the loved one who was helped — are sometimes incorporated in the *nicho*.

Although *nichos* feature many favorite saints, in the American Southwest the most popular is Our Lady of Guadalupe. A shrine in her honor may also contain the figure of

St. Juan Diego. While the majority of the images depicted in *nichos* are those canonized by the Catholic Church, so-called "folk saints" (such as the famous *curandero* ["holy one" and faith healer] Don Pedrito Jaramillo) are also honored in this way. Even the process of acquiring an image can be part of the vow, and families often travel together to a famous shrine to acquire a replica of the image there.

Small *nichos* in the form of glass-fronted boxes are often placed near the door of the home. Folk artists also make small *nichos* as decorative holders for religious icons to be hung inside on the walls of the home.

(See also **EX VOTO**.)

NIHIL OBSTAT

The approval of a book or writing by an official Church censor before the issuing of an *Imprimatur*.

NINE FIRST FRIDAYS — See **FIRST FRIDAY; SACRED HEART OF JESUS; ST. MARGARET MARY ALACOQUE**.

NINE TUESDAYS DEVOTION

The pious tradition of visiting a Franciscan church on nine consecutive Tuesdays.

The custom was based on reported visions of St. Anthony of Padua by a wom-

an in seventeenth-century Bologna, Italy. Gradually the number of days increased to thirteen in remembrance of the date of the saint's death.

(See also **ST. ANTHONY OF PADUA**.)

NIÑO CIEGUITO — See **BLIND CHILD JESUS**.

NIÑO PERDIDO

A devotion to and image of the Christ Child lost in the temple (see Luke 2:41-50).

In Mexico, the cult of *Niño Perdido* revolves around a popular image revered in Cuenceme de Ceniceros, Durango. The patron of lost children, the Child is shown with a ruffled cap and a long gown similar to a nightgown. Devotees pin gold coins to his gown in thanksgiving and supplication. In New Mexico, where he became the patron of kidnapped children, *Niño Perdido* is generally depicted in short pants, chest bared, with no cloak or tunic. His hand is raised in blessing.

Niño Perdido is loved and revered in Guam also, and is the subject of one of the many traditional village-wide fiestas held annually by the island's Chamorro people. These celebrations were introduced by the Spanish in 1668. Today, the fiesta typically begins with a Saturday night Mass, followed by a procession carrying a statue of *Niño Perdido* through the streets and back to the church, where the festivities continue until late in the night. On Sunday, village residents invite family and friends to their homes for private celebrations.

NOCTURN

Originally, the whole of the night office (Matins and Lauds).

Later, it became a part of Matins (three nocturns on feasts, one nocturn on ferias). Among the monks, two nocturns were usual (up to twelve Psalms and readings for Matins).

NOCTURNAL ADORATION — See ADORATION, NOCTURNAL.

NOCTURNAL ADORATION SOCIETY

An association begun in the mid-nineteenth century dedicated to prayer before the Eucharist for the praise of God and for the needs of the world.

Its goal is to unite the members in prayer before the exposed Blessed Sacrament during the hours of the night. The society is established in thirty-six countries and has more than one million members. Members are asked to spend one assigned hour per month before the

Blessed Sacrament exposed in a church where the society, in the form of a local chapter, is established.

The Nocturnal Adoration Society developed from the practice of night adoration of the Blessed Sacrament during Forty Hours devotion. In 1595, a time when the Church was threatened by widespread heresy in Europe and by an invading hostile Muslim force in the East, Pope Clement VIII instituted Forty Hours devotion in Rome. The pontiff asked people to offer incessant prayers imploring the Lord's help and grace for their protection.

Some two centuries later, in 1809, another crisis threatened the Church. In the aftermath of the French Revolution and the political and religious upheaval in Europe, Napoleon had risen to power and had made Pope Pius VII his prisoner. A priest in Rome, Father Giacomo Sinibaldi, was inspired to gather groups of men to pray in the presence of the Blessed Sacrament during the night hours in Roman churches when Forty Hours devotion was in progress. The response to his idea was so enthusiastic that in a short time there were groups meeting for prayer every night in the churches where the Blessed Sacrament was exposed.

Ecclesiastical approval was given to the society in 1810. Its center was the Church of Santa Maria in Via Lata in Rome. In 1851, the society was approved as a pious union and in 1858 was raised to the status of an archconfraternity, with authority to establish Nocturnal Adoration Societies elsewhere.

During the civil unrest of 1848, a Carmelite monk, Father Hermann Cohen, obtained approval from the archbishop of Paris to form a Nocturnal Adoration Society there. In 1863, he started a society for nocturnal adoration in London. The cause for his canonization has been introduced in Rome.

The society spread to Madrid in 1877. Its growth in Spain was so extraordinary that in a short time there were five hundred centers with more than a hundred thousand members. From Spain, it traveled to South and Central America and then into Texas and California. At the same time, the society was spreading from Paris to Canada and into the northeast United States. In 1881, through the efforts of Louis Joseph Delorme, a publisher in Montreal, a group formed there after he came in contact with the society during a trip to Paris. Another layperson, Dr. Thomas Dwight, established the society in Boston in 1882. The following year Father William Bartlett began a chapter in Baltimore. New York followed in 1903. In 1929, New York Cardinal Patrick Hayes established a national headquarters in St. Jean Baptiste Church, a parish staffed by the Congregation of the Blessed Sacrament, and appointed the pastor its national director. The U.S. headquarters remain in New York.

(See also **CONFRATERNITY; FORTY HOURS DEVOTION**.)

NONE

The canonical prayer offered at or around the ninth hour of the day, that is, 3:00 P.M.

Before the revision of the Divine Office at Vatican II, None was obligatory. After the revision, None was required only among contemplative religious.

NOVENA

The public or private devotional practices over a period of nine consecutive days or, by extension, over nine weeks in which one day a week is set aside for the devotions.

The word *novena* is derived from the Latin word *novem*, meaning "nine." Usually, the prayers are for a particular intention, and are in honor of a particular saint or a particular facet of the life of Our Lord or Our Lady. The person making the novena is often praying to obtain special graces or favors. Any suitable prayers may be used in making a novena, but it is preferable to attend Mass and receive Holy Communion daily as practices of the novena.

Public novenas are made in churches, often in preparation for a specific feast. Other elements of the novena services may include the stations of the cross, litanies, and hymns.

Many of today's novenas first gained

popularity in the seventeenth century, but the spirit of the novena stretches farther back in history. The exact origin of novenas is difficult to pinpoint. The Old Testament does not record any nine-day celebration of the Jewish peoples. In the New Testament, Acts says that during the nine days between the Ascension of Our Lord and the descent of the Holy Spirit at Pentecost, the Apostles "with one accord devoted themselves to prayer, together with the women and Mary the mother of Jesus, and with his brothers" (see Acts 1:14). This is sometimes suggested as the basis for novenas.

In pre-Christian times, the ancient Romans and Greeks celebrated nine days of prayer to avert the wrath of the gods or when some wonder had been predicted by the soothsayers. Families held a nine-day mourning period at the death of a loved one with a special feast after the burial on the ninth day. The *parentalia novendialia* was celebrated annually to remember all departed family members. It is possible that Christianity simply adapted this pagan practice from Roman culture, although St. Augustine actually condemned it.

Nine days of mourning continued to be observed until the Middle Ages, when a novena of Masses became popular, especially in the case of prominent individuals. In medieval times, particularly in Spain and France, prayers were offered nine days before Christmas to prepare for the feast. The practice was seen as signifying the nine months Christ was in the womb. Over time, other novenas were composed to help the faithful prepare for a special feast or to invoke the aid of a favorite saint.

Today a novena in honor of Our Lady of Perpetual Help is known worldwide. Other prominent novenas include those focusing on the Holy Spirit, the Holy Trinity, the Sacred Heart, Christ the King, the Immaculate Conception, the Queen of Peace, the Seven Sorrows, the Sorrowful Mother, St. Joseph, St. Ann, St. Jude, and the souls in purgatory.

NOVENA FOR THE BLESSED SOULS IN PURGATORY

A popular devotion for the dead.

Originally the novena was made for the repose of a deceased person. This meaning is still used for the novena of Masses said after the death of a pope. There are a number of novenas for the souls in purgatory commonly in use throughout the world. This Spanish novena has, in addition to the prayers and reflections, *ejemplos*, or "examples." These are historical vignettes from the lives of the saints and holy persons regarding the subject matter of the novena, in this case the suffering souls.

To begin, the petitioner asks Christ's aid through the Precious Blood and the sorrows of Our Lady. He petitions for the grace to avoid sin and to persevere until death. He calls on the infinite kindness and mercy of God to console and to release suffering souls from purgatory.

Based on the Passion, the prayers and meditations in this devotion are directed to Jesus sweating blood in the garden of Gethsemane, Jesus prisoner for our love, Jesus taken before the tribunal, Jesus mistreated and detained while Barabbas is released, Jesus whipped at the column, Jesus crowned with thorns, Jesus carrying the cross, and Jesus nailed to the cross. The final day, the prayers and meditations are in favor of the blessed souls liberated from purgatory by the prayers and suffrages offered during the novena.

The *ejemplos* for this novena include the following: 1) A compassionate virgin named Christiana had a vision in which she was taken before God to contemplate the pains of purgatory. After she was shown the terrible sufferings of the souls, God gave her the choice to enter immediately into paradise or to return to earth to help the poor, suffering souls with her prayers. She was so moved by the vision that without hesitation she opted to return to earth in order to intercede for the souls of purgatory. She began a type of life so austere and strict that people began to criticize her. She responded that they only spoke that way because they ignored what happens in purgatory and that if they had shared her vision they, too, would do

penance. 2) Blessed John of Alvernia (1259-1322), of the Order of Minors, was accustomed to celebrate Holy Mass for the faithful departed on November 2 with so much fervor that he would appear to be completely consumed by continual grief. Once, precisely at the instant of the elevation, he directed to the Eternal Father a fervent prayer that through the merits of his Only Son, he would deign to free the holy souls from their pains. Blessed John then saw a vision where a great multitude of poor souls, like brilliant sparks that fly from a forge, were directed joyously to paradise. 3) A father, being close to death, commissioned his son to remember to offer prayers and Masses for his soul. This the son faithfully did. Thirty two years later, the son had a vision in which his father appeared to him completely surrounded by flames and lamenting bitterly about the lack of prayers for him. "How could you say such a thing," the son demanded. "I have commissioned Masses and prayers and I have personally fasted, prayed, and performed every type of good work on your behalf." Sadly the father replied, "My son, all the good you have done and are doing doesn't help me or you because you have done these things without love of God because you are constantly in a state of mortal sin. Your confessions were in vain because they were lacking in true sorrow and repentance. The goodness of God has sent me to you today to warn you, for your good and for mine." Having said this, the father disappeared. The son recognized his error, made a good confession and began prayers and good works that eventually aided his father's soul and saved his own. 4) Blessed Catherine Mattei (1486-1547), a virgin of the Third Order of St. Dominic, was sick in bed with a very high fever. She began to meditate on the flames of Purgatory and the Lord took her in spirit to view them. When she asked what the fire was really like, the Lord allowed a spark to touch her neck which was contorted for some time afterward. Later, she testified that there is no suffering in the world that will compare with the pain of purgatory. 5) A Dominican religious in the last days of his life begged a priest friend of his to offer Mass upon his death. This the friend did without delay. After the Mass while the priest was disrobing, the dead religious appeared to him in a vision, scolding him for leaving him in purgatory for thirty years. Startled, the priest pointed out that the religious had only died an hour before, and that his corpse was still warm. The deceased then said, "Learn from this how fierce is the fire of purgatory when only one hour seems to me like thirty years. Move yourself to pity and have mercy on all the souls in purgatory." 6) St. Malachy, Bishop of Ireland and the first canonized Irish saint (1095-1148), had a dream in which he saw his sister, who was

lamenting that although on various occasions the Mass had been offered for her she was still not at rest. The saint understood perfectly and began anew to offer Mass for the repose of her soul. Again she returned in his dreams, dressed in black at the door of the church. He continued to offer prayers and Masses for her and a later dream showed her in a lighter-colored dress inside the church but away from the altar. At last, in his dreams, he saw his sister in the company of other souls all dressed in brilliant white and near the altar. From this he understood that prayers and sacrifices had helped his sister complete what she owed God in purgatory. 7) One reads in the life of the Venerable Mary d'Antigna that a deceased nun of her monastery appeared to her and requested that the nuns pray the devotion of the Stations of the Cross for her and for the other souls. Maria then heard the voice of Jesus in her heart saying that the prayer of the way of the cross is very helpful to the poor souls and requesting her to tell her sisters how much good they do with this devotion and the treasures they store up when they offer it for the holy souls of purgatory. 8) A certain devotee of the Mother of God was accustomed to saying the litany of the Most Holy Virgin daily for the souls in purgatory. This man had enemies who swore to kill him. One day as he was resting, the enemies entered his house. Although they saw his clothes lying on the bed, God caused the pious man to become invisible to the eyes of his enemies. When the man awoke, he discovered the disorder in his house and guessed what had happened. Immediately he gave thanks to the Queen of Heaven for her intercession and for that of the poor souls. 9) In the book of Tobit, one reads that this pious man often buried the dead, even the enemies of the Hebrews. Once he even got up from his dinner in order to do so. The Archangel Raphael was so grateful for this mercy of Tobias that he assisted his son and restored the old man's sight. Further, he gave Tobias to understand that his tearful prayers and his mercy in burying the dead pleased him so much that Raphael himself would present Tobias's prayers to God. This final *ejemplo* reminds Christians that all service in favor of the dead is most pleasing to the angels of God. The novena ends with an *alabanza* (a chanted song/poem of praise) that extols the efficacy of the Rosary said in favor of the Poor Souls.

Novenas in favor of the souls in purgatory were indulgenced by Pope Pius IX in 1849 and have been enriched in several successive indults.

NOVENA IN HONOR OF OUR LADY QUEEN OF PEACE

A devotion to promote world peace associated with the Congregation of the Sacred Hearts of Jesus and Mary.

An ancient and miraculous statue of Our Lady Queen of Peace is venerated in the chapel of the Religious of the Sacred Hearts of Jesus and Mary in Paris, France. It is carved wood, eleven inches tall, and depicts the Virgin holding her divine Son on her left are. In her right hand she bears an olive branch, the symbol of peace. As early as the sixteenth century, there is a mention of the statue being a precious possession in the household of a noble French family. Eventually the statue was given to the Duke de Joyeuse, who later embraced the religious life in the Capuchin Order where he was known as Father Ange. He was devoted to Our Lady under this title because it was while praying in front of the image that he first felt the call to religious life. In appreciation for this great favor, he had a chapel built in her honor in the Capuchins' house in Paris. Later the oratory was opened to the public. Eventually the image was placed in the niche above the outside door of the monastery where it remained for nearly sixty years. For several years, a clear light illuminated the statue during the night. Many miracles began to be reported by intercession to Our Lady in front of the image.

The statue was moved to the chapel where Father Ange was buried and the miracles kept multiplying. The chapel proved too small to contain the crowds and a new chapel was built where the statue remained until 1790. During the

French Revolution, the Capuchins were forced to abandon their monastery and gave the image into the keeping of a pious woman named Madame Pepin. At her death, she willed the statue to her widowed sister, Madame Coipel. The statue then passed through many hands until it finally came to Madame Riolet Coipel. She gave the sacred image to Father Coudrin, the founder of the Congregation of the Sacred Hearts of Jesus and Mary. She was very moved by his sermons, and he became her spiritual director. She suggested that he give all rights of possession to his beloved order, which he did. The image was carried in procession to the chapel of the order, and since that day numerous favors have been showered on her clients. The image was given a papal crown by Pope St. Pius X. Prayers in her honor were indulgenced by Pius IX and St. Pius X. Through the efforts of the religious order founded by Father Coudrin, this title of Our Lady has spread worldwide, and shrines, public novenas, and copies of her image have reached the far corners of the earth.

Favors especially asked through the novena prayers to Our Lady of Peace are for the peace and concord among nations and the cessation of war, for peace of soul and strength and courage in the trials of life, for peace in families and reconciliation of enemies, for the cure of the sick, and for conversion of sinners.

NOVENA IN HONOR OF OUR LADY OF PERPETUAL HELP

A popular devotion long associated with the Redemptorist Congregation.

Fifty years after the icon had been given to the Redemptorists by Blessed Pope Pius IX (r. 1846-1878), the Redemptorists of St. Louis, Missouri, commemorated the event by having a solemn novena in her honor in their church. Later, monthly novenas were held, and in 1916 a perpetual novena, held weekly, was established. One version of the novena reads:

Behold at your feet, O Mother of Perpetual Help, a wretched sinner who has recourse to you. O Mother of Mercy, have pity on me. I hear you called by all, the Refuge and the Hope of sinners; be, then, my refuge and my hope. Assist me, for the love of Jesus Christ; stretch forth your hand to a miserable fallen creature who recommends himself to you, and who devotes himself to your service forever. I bless and thank Almighty God, who in his mercy has given me this confidence in you, which I hold to be a pledge of my eternal salvation. It is true, dearest Mother, that in the past I have miserably fallen into sin because I had not turned to you. I know that with your help I shall conquer. I know, too, that you will assist me, if I recommend myself to you; but I fear, dear Mother, that in time of danger, I may neglect to call on you, and thus lose my soul. This grace, then, I ask of you with all my soul, that, in all the attacks of Hell, I may ever have recourse to you. O Mary, help me; O Mother of Perpetual Help, never suffer me to lose my God.

(Three Hail Marys are then said.)

Mother of Perpetual Help, grant that I may ever invoke your most powerful name, which is the safeguard of the living and the salvation of the dying. O Purest Mary, O Sweetest Mary, let your name henceforth be ever on my lips! Delay not, O Blessed Lady, to help me whenever I call on you; for, in all my temptations, in all my needs, I shall never cease to call on you, ever repeating your Sacred Name: Mary, Mary! O what consolation, what sweetness, what confidence, what emotion fills my soul when I utter your Sacred Name, or even only think of you! I thank the Lord for having given you, for my good, so sweet, so powerful, so lovely a name. But I will not be content with merely uttering your name; let my love for you prompt me ever to hail you, Mother of Perpetual Help.

(Three more Hail Marys are said.)

Mother of Perpetual Help, you are the dispenser of all the gifts which God grants to us miserable sinners; and for this end He has made you so powerful, so rich, and so bountiful in order that you may help us in our misery. You are the advocate of the most wretched and abandoned sinners who have recourse to you; come to my aid, dearest Mother, for I recommend myself to you. In your hands I place my eternal salvation, and to you I entrust my soul. Count me among your most devoted servants; take me under your protection and it is enough for me. For, if you protect me, dear Mother, I fear nothing; not from my sins, because you will obtain for me the pardon of them from Jesus your Divine Son. But one thing I fear, that in the hour of temptation I may through negligence fail to have recourse to you and thus perish miserably. Obtain for me, therefore, the pardon of my sins, love for Jesus, final perseverance, and the grace to have recourse to you and (*mention your request here*), O Mother of Perpetual Help.

(Three final Hail Marys are said.)

Pray for us, O Mother of Perpetual Help, that we may be made worthy of the promises of Christ.

Let us pray:

Lord Jesus Christ, who gave us Your Holy Mother, Mary, whose renowned image we venerate, to be a Mother ever ready to help us, grant, we beseech You, that we who constantly implore her maternal aid may merit to enjoy perpetually the fruits of Your redemption, who lives and reigns with God forever and ever. Amen.

NOVENA IN HONOR OF ST. ANN

A devotion, promoted by the Passionists, using modern media.

A solemn novena in honor of St. Ann is held in July at the Basilica of the National Shrine of St. Ann in Scranton, Pennsylvania. This novena has made good use of the modern media. Those who cannot attend the novena at the church may watch it on television or pray along with it on the internet. Services on her feast day at this church are held in Italian, Slovak, Polish and Lithuanian as well as in English. In addition to the annual solemn novena, novena services are held every Monday throughout the year.

The novena concludes with a blessing with the relics of the saint: "Good St. Ann Pray for us. Through the Intercession of Saints Paul of the Cross and Gabriel, and especially St. Ann May Almighty God bless us with continual health of mind and body. In the Name of the Father, and of the Son, and of the Holy Spirit. Amen." Devotions conclude with Benediction of the Blessed Sacrament.

There has been a great devotion to St. Ann in Scranton since the founding of a Passionist monastery in 1905. The foundation, built over a coal mine, was dedicated to St. Ann. On August 15, 1911 the monastery shook, cracked and split due to a severe mine subsidence. The community of priests moved out. But they had complete confidence that they would be able to come back again. In their words, "St. Ann will take care of her own." In a short time, with repairs, all was safe and the Passionists returned.

Again on July 28, 1913, an even more menacing disturbance took place. A gigantic "squeeze" threatened to slide the whole monastery and church down the hill. Immediately the Passionists and the neighbors prayed for help through the intercession of St. Ann. The next morning, on an inspection of the mines that run under the monastery, it was found that the slide had suddenly stopped, turned back and settled solidly under the monastery.

The present St. Ann's Monastery Church was dedicated on April 2, 1929. Here, the weekly St. Ann's Novena has continued every Monday throughout the years. More than 10,000 people per day attend the annual ten day St. Ann's Solemn

Novena, which begins July 17 and ends on July 26, the Feast of St. Ann. There is also an annual solemn novena held at St. Anne's Church in Fall River, Massachusetts.

Making a novena to St. Ann is an indulgenced practice, but no particular formula or prayer is mandated. Simply make a devout supplication or say some prayers in honor of the saint for nine successive days.

NOVENA IN HONOR OF ST. JUDE

A devotion promoted by the Dominicans.

St. Jude, as patron of hopeless and impossible causes, is one of the most popular saints of the Church. Novenas are regularly held in his honor in a number of churches and shrines in the United States. One of these, a solemn novena, is held five times annually during the months of March, May, July, and October at the Shrine of St. Jude Thaddeus in Chicago. The saint's feast is October 28. This shrine is maintained by the Dominican fathers of the Province of St. Albert the Great. Here, the nine days of the solemn novena provide times of Eucharist, of Dominican preaching of special novena prayers, and of personal intentions brought to the intercessory power of St. Jude.

The following prayers to St. Jude may be prayed as a novena:

St. Jude by those sublime gifts which you received in your lifetime, namely, your kinship with our Lord Jesus Christ, and your vocation to be an Apostle; by that Glory which is now yours in heaven as the reward of your apostolic labors and your martyrdom; obtain for us from the Giver of every good and perfect gift all the graces whereof we stand in need in order to keep in our hearts the divinely inspired doctrines which you have transmitted to us in your Epistle; that is to say, to grow in grace, holding to the truths of our most holy Faith; to keep ourselves in the love of God, looking for the mercy of Jesus Christ unto eternal life; to strive by ail means to help them who go astray; exalting thus the glory and majesty, the dominion and power of him who is able to present us spotless with exceeding joy at the coming of our divine Savior, the Lord Jesus Christ. Amen.

The follow prayer may also be used:

St. Jude Thaddeus, relative of Jesus Christ, glorious Apostle and martyr, renowned for your virtues and miracles, faithful and prompt intercessor of ail who honor you and trust in you! You are a powerful patron and helper in great afflictions. I entreat you from the depths of my heart; come to my aid with your powerful intercession, for you have received from God the privilege to assist with your visible help those who almost despair of all hope. Look down upon me. Time and again I find myself discouraged and depressed by the troubles I must face. I know that others around me have burdens as heavy or heavier than mine but I sometimes come close to despairing that I will be able to continue carrying mine. Overwhelmed by these thoughts, I ask your help.

Do not forsake me in my sadness. Hasten to my aid. I will be grateful to you all my life and will honor you as my special patron. I will thank God for the graces bestowed upon you, and will encourage honor to you to the best of my ability. Amen.

NOVENA IN HONOR OF ST. ODILIA

A Crosier devotion for the blind and afflicted.

As patroness of the blind and afflicted, novenas in honor of St. Odilia are made at the Crosier Monastery in Onamia, Minnesota, and a national novena is held there from July 10 to July 18. In addition to the prayers, participants in the novena are asked to practice some form of self denial

or give an alms and receive Holy Communion at least once during the novena.

NOVENA IN HONOR OF THE HOLY SPIRIT

A devotion in preparation for Pentecost.

In the New Testament we read in the book of Acts that during the nine days between the Ascension of Our Lord and the descent of the Holy Spirit at Pentecost, the Apostles, Mary, and the others spent time in "constant prayer" (see Acts 1:12-14). This is sometimes suggested as the basis for all novena devotions and the novena to the Holy Spirit in particular.

This novena is usually prayed in preparation for the Feast of Pentecost. During this novena, no particular form of prayer is prescribed. Any prayer to the Holy Ghost will suffice. One indulgenced prayer that might be used is the following: "Holy Spirit, Spirit of truth, come into our hearts; give to all peoples the brightness of Thy light, that they may be well pleasing to Thee in unity of faith."

NOVENA IN HONOR OF THE IMMACULATE CONCEPTION

A devotion to the patroness of the United States, including an act of consecration.

In August of 1492 when Christopher Columbus set sail and eventually wound up in the new world, at the end of each day of the voyage he gathered his crew and they chanted the *Salve Regina*. Most Americans learn that he named the first place he landed "San Salvador" in honor of the Savior. However, the second place he named Santa Maria de la Concepción in honor of Our Lady. In 1640, Father Andrew White, an early Jesuit missionary, declared the Americas to be under the patronage of the Holy Redeemer and the Immaculate Virgin. In 1846, the bishops of the United States petitioned the Holy Father to name Mary as the patroness of the country under the title of the Immaculate Conception. The request was granted in 1847. The dogma of the Immaculate Conception and the visions of St. Catherine Labouré and St. Bernadette popularized this title throughout the world. In 1959, a national shrine of the Immaculate Conception was dedicated in Washington, D.C., and is one of the largest churches in the world.

To make a novena in honor of the Immaculate Conception, pray the following prayers daily for nine consecutive days:

Almighty Father, we offer this novena to honor the Blessed Virgin Mary. She occupies a place in the Church, which is highest after Christ and yet very close to us, for You chose her to give to the world that very Life which renews all things, Jesus Christ, Your Son and Our Lord.

And so we praise you, Mary, Virgin and Mother. After the Savior Himself, you alone are holy, free from all stain of sin, gifted by God from the first instant of your conception with a unique holiness. We praise and honor you.

Mary, free from all sin and led by the Holy Spirit, you embraced God's saving will with a full heart, and devoted yourself totally as a handmaid of the Lord to the fulfillment of his will in your life, and to the mystery of man's redemption. We thank you and love you.

Mary, your privileged and grace-filled origin is the Father's final step in preparing humanity to receive its Redeemer in human form. Your fullness of grace is the Father's sign of His favor to the Church and also his promise to the Church of its perfection as the Bride of Christ, radiant in beauty. Your holiness in the beginning of your life is the foreshadowing of that all-embracing holiness with which the Father will surround his people when his Son comes at the end of time to greet us. We bless you among all women.

Mary, we turn with confidence to you who are always ready to listen with a mother's affection and powerful assistance. Consoler of the Afflicted, Health of the Sick, Refuge of Sinners, grant us comfort in tribulation, relief in sickness, and liberating strength in our weakness. You, who are free from sin, lead us to combat sin. Obtain for us the victory of hope over anguish, of fellowship over alienation, of peace over anxiety, of joy and beauty over boredom and disgust, of eternal visions over temporal ones, of life over death. 0 Mary, conceived without sin, pray for us who have recourse to you. (*Mention your request here.*)

Let us pray:

God Our Father, we make these petitions through Mary. We pray most especially for the coming of Your kingdom. May You, together with Your Son and Holy Spirit, be known, loved, and glorified and Your law of love faithfully followed. We pray in faith through Jesus Christ, Your Son and Our Lord, in whom all fullness dwells, now and forever. Amen.

Act of Consecration

Most Holy Trinity: Our Father in heaven, who chose Mary as the fairest of Your daughters; Holy Spirit, who chose Mary as Your spouse; God the Son, who chose Mary as Your Mother; in union with Mary, we adore Your majesty and acknowledge Your supreme eternal dominion and authority. Most Holy Trinity, we put the United States of America into the hands of Mary Immaculate in order that she may present the country to You. Through her we wish to thank You for the great resources of this land and for the freedom which has been its heritage. Through the intercession of Mary, have mercy on the Catholic Church in America. Grant us peace. Have mercy on our president and on all the officers of our government. Grant us a fruitful economy born of justice and charity. Have mercy on capital and industry and labor. Protect the family life of the nation. Guard the innocence of our children. Grant the precious gift of many religious vocations. Through the intercession of our Mother, have mercy on the sick, the poor, the tempted, sinners — on all who are in need.

Mary, Immaculate Virgin, our Mother, Patroness of our land, we praise you and honor you and give ourselves to you. Protect us from every harm. Pray for us, that acting always according to your will and the Will of your Divine Son, we may live and die pleasing to God.

NOVENA IN HONOR OF THE MOST HOLY TRINITY

A trinitarian devotion.

No particular prayer is required to gain the indulgence of a novena to the Most Holy Trinity. The Doxology (Glory be to the Father) could be used in combination with some meditation or other prayer.

NOVENA IN HONOR OF THE SACRED HEART OF JESUS

A popular private devotion.

Any of the beautiful prayers to the Sacred Heart may be used to make a private novena. One prayer that could be used is:

My Jesus, I bless Thy most humble Heart and I give Thee thanks that, in giving it to me to be my example, not only dost Thou urge me with strong pleadings to imitate It, but even at the cost of Thine own great humiliations, Thou dost point out and make plain to me the way of salvation. fool and ingrate that I am, how far have I gone astray. Pardon me; no longer shall pride rule in me, but with a humble heart will I follow Thee through the midst of tribulations and thus obtain my peace and salvation. Do Thou give me strength and I will bless Thy Sacred Heart for ever. Amen

The chaplet of the Sacred Heart may also be recited daily for nine days for a novena.

NOVENA IN HONOR OF THE SEVEN SORROWS

A popular devotion promoted by the Servites and the Passionists.

A novena in honor of the seven sorrows may be prayed by meditating on each sorrow and following it with a Marian prayer. The seven sorrows of Mary, as traditionally listed are: 1) Mary accepts in faith the prophecy of Simeon [Lk 2:34-35]; 2) Mary flees into Egypt with Jesus and Joseph [Mt.2:13-14]; 3) Mary seeks Jesus lost in Jerusalem [Lk 2:43-45] 4) Mary meets Jesus on the way to Calvary [Lk 23:26-27]; 5) Mary stands near the cross of her Son [Jn 19:25-27]; 6) Mary receives the body of Jesus taken down from the cross [Mt 27:57-59]; 7) Mary places the body of Jesus in the tomb, awaiting the Resurrection [Jn 19:40-42].

St. Gabriel Possenti was devoted to Our Lady of Sorrows. His favorite prayer to her under this title could be used in a novena:

O Mother of Sorrows, by the anguish and love with which thou didst stand at the cross of Jesus, stand by me in my last agony. To thy maternal heart I commend the last three hours of my life. Offer these hours to the Eternal Father in union with the agony of our dearest Lord in atonement for my sins. Offer to the Eternal Father the Most Precious Blood of Jesus, mingled with your tears on Calvary, that I may obtain the grave of receiving Holy Communion with the most perfect love and contrition before my death, and that I may breathe forth my soul in the adorable presence of Jesus. Dearest Mother, when the moment of my death has at last come, present me to Jesus as your child. Beg Him to receive me into His Kingdom of glory to be united to Him forever. Amen.

Other novenas to the Mother of Sorrows may be obtained from the Servite fathers.

NOVENA OF CHRIST THE KING

A devotion to precede the November Feast of Christ the King.

A novena or triduum held immediately before the Feast of Our Lord Jesus Christ the King in honor of him is enriched with indulgences. No particular formula is prescribed. The following prayer and invocation could be used:

O Christ Jesus, I acknowledge Thee to be the King of the universe; all that hath been made is created for Thee. Exercise over me all Thy sovereign rights. I hereby renew the promises of my Baptism, renouncing Satan and all his works and pomps, and I engage myself to lead henceforth a truly Christian life. And in an especial manner do I undertake to bring about the triumph of the rights of God and Thy Church, so far as in me lies. Divine Heart of Jesus, I offer Thee my poor actions to obtain the acknowledgement by every heart of Thy sacred kingly power. In such wise, may the kingdom of Thy peace be firmly established throughout all the earth. Amen.

Jesus, King and center of all hearts, by the coming of Thy kingdom, grant us peace.

NOVENA OF GRACE

A Jesuit devotion in honor of St. Francis Xavier.

In 1633, Father Marcello Mastrilli, a Jesuit, was seriously injured in an accident. In a vision, he was urged by St. Francis Xavier to go to the East as a missionary. Although dying, he made a vow to do so. In a second vision, St. Francis told him that he would be cured. He also assured him that he would die a martyr's death. This came to pass in Japan in October 1637. Traditionally, the Novena of Grace is celebrated so that it ends on March 12, the day on which St. Francis Xavier was canonized. Part of the novena is to make a visit to a Jesuit church or chapel, although that is not required to obtain the indulgences.

The prayer for the novena is:

O Saint Francis Xavier, well beloved and full of charity, in union with thee, I reverently adore the Majesty of God; and since I rejoice with exceeding joy in the singular gifts of grace bestowed upon thee during thy life and thy gifts of glory after death, I give Him hearty thanks therefore; I beseech thee with all my heart's devotion to be pleased to obtain for me, by thy effectual intercession, above all things the grace of a holy life and a happy death. Moreover, I beg of thee to obtain for me... (*here mention the spiritual or temporal favor to be prayed for*). But if what I ask of thee so earnestly doth not tend to the glory of God, and the greater good of my soul, do thou, I pray, obtain for me what is more profitable to both these ends. Amen.

NOVENA, ROSARY

An extended devotion based on the private revelations of Fortuna Agrellie.

The devotion known as the Rosary Novena to Our Lady is of comparatively recent origin. In an apparition of Our Lady of Pompeii in 1884 in Naples, the heavenly Mother appeared to Fortuna Agrellie. The young woman had been extremely sick for more than a year, and her case had been given up by the doctors. On February 16, 1884, the afflicted girl and her relatives began a novena of Rosaries. She was favored with an apparition on March 3, 1884. The Queen of Heaven appeared holding the Christ Child and accompanied by St. Dominic and St. Catherine of Siena. Fortuna begged to be cured and Our Lady told her, "Since you have called me by the title so pleasing to me, 'Queen of the Holy Rosary,' I can no longer refuse the favor you have asked. Make three novenas and you shall obtain all." Later, in another apparition, Our Lady told her, "Whoever desired to obtain favors from me should make three novenas of the prayers of the Rosary, and three novenas in thanksgiving."

The novena consists of five decades of the Rosary each day for twenty seven days in petition; then immediately five decades each day for twenty seven days in thanksgiving, whether or not the request has been granted. Thus, the novena is actually fifty-four days long. The meditations — the joyful mysteries, the sorrowful mysteries, and the glorious mysteries — should be rotated each day during the novena.

NOVENA TO OUR SORROWFUL MOTHER

A Servite devotion.

The public novena to Our Sorrowful Mother can be made only in churches and chapels in which the *Via Matris* has been canonically erected. These stations are usually found in Servite churches and oratories. A private novena to Our Sorrowful Mother may be made by saying the official prayers of the novena and making the *Via Matris* for nine consecutive days or for nine consecutive Fridays. A perpetual novena would be held on every Friday throughout the year with the services being the same as the public novena, but with the substitution of the Desolata on Good Friday. The Desolata is a devotion in honor of the sorrows of Mary which was observed in many churches, especially those of the Jesuits, on Good Friday evening.

In 1937, George Cardinal Mundelein, Archbishop of Chicago, approved of the Perpetual Novena in honor of Our Sorrowful Mother for the Servite Church of Our Lady of Sorrows in Chicago, Illinois. The devotion was originated by the Reverend James R. Keane, O.S.M., who was then the prior of the Servite Community in Chicago. The first novena services were held on Friday January 8, 1937. They consisted of the *Via Matris*, six prayers from the ancient Servite Manual, two hymns, the Memorare and Benediction of the Most Blessed Sacrament. Within a year, there was a phenomenal record of attendance at the thirty-eight services held each Friday. By the end of the decade, more than a million people were attending the novena services by then held in churches all over the world. The novena prayer book was published in twenty-two foreign languages. The devotion to Our Sorrowful Mother is new only in its novena form. The *Via Matris,* and the other prayers, date back to the Middle ages. the devotion itself, devotion to Mary's Sorrows, is as old as the Catholic Church. The six official prayers of the novena are: 1) The prayer to Our Sorrowful Mother for a particular grace, 2) the prayer for a happy death, 3) the Hail Mary of Our Sorrowful Mother written by St. Bonaventure, 4) prayer for our sick relatives and friends, 5) prayer for our beloved dead, and 6) an act of consecration to Our Sorrowful Mother. The *Via Matris,* which is a part of this novena, is an indulgenced prayer.

NOVENA TO MARIA GORETTI

A devotion for purity, especially in favor of youth.

In 1951, Monsignor James P. Conroy of the Fort Wayne-South Bend Diocese wrote a novena booklet in honor of St. Maria Goretti based on the canonization homily of Pope Pius XII. The booklet was written to mark the first observance of the Feast of St. Maria Goretti following her canonization during the Holy Year, June 24, 1950. During the Jubilee year 2000, a new edition of Father Conroy's booklet was published through the efforts of the St. Maria Goretti Novena Apostolate and Salvator Mundi Communications of Navan, Ontario, Canada. The booklet is a tribute to St. Maria Goretti for the occasion of the fiftieth anniversary of her canonization. The novena is made annually at St. Maria Goretti church in Laflin, Pennsylvania. Although each day is dedicated to the attainment of a different virtue, the overall intention of the novena is for purity. The other virtues prayed for in the novena besides purity are: obedience, self-denial, contented living, confidence in God, respect for teachers, love of Holy Communion, charity to others, and love of Our Blessed Mother. Although the novena is designed for June 27 to July 5, the vigil of the Feast of St. Maria Goretti, it may be prayed on any other successive nine days of the year. The main prayer of the novena is:

> Oh, St. Maria Goretti who, strengthened by God's grace, did not hesitate even at the age of twelve to shed your blood and sacrifice life itself to defend your virginal purity, look graciously on the unhappy human race, which has strayed far from the path of eternal salvation. Teach us all, and especially youth, with what courage and promptitude we should flee, for the love of Jesus, any-

thing that could offend Him or stain our souls with sin. Obtain for us from our Lord victory in temptation, comfort in the sorrows of life, and the grace which we earnestly beg of thee (*insert daily intention here*) and may we one day enjoy with thee the imperishable glory of Heaven. Amen.

NOVENA TO ST. JOSEPH, SPOUSE OF MARY MOST HOLY

A popular devotion to St. Joseph.

In 1876, Pope Pius IX granted indulgences, on the usual conditions, to all the faithful who with contrite heart devoutly make at any time during the year the novena to St. Joseph, spouse of Mary Most Holy, with any formula of prayer approved by ecclesiastical authority. The prayer, indulged by the same pontiff, which is sometimes known as the Memorare to St. Joseph can be used as a novena. This prayer was indulged in 1863:

> Remember, O most pure spouse of the Blessed Virgin Mary, my sweet protector St. Joseph that no one ever had recourse to thy protection or implored thy aid without obtaining relief. Confiding therefore in thy goodness, I come before thee, and humbly supplicate thee. Oh, despise not my petitions, foster-father of the

Redeemer, but graciously receive them. Amen.

NOVENAS INDULGENCED IN HONOR OF THE BLESSED VIRGIN MARY

Eleven indulgenced devotions honoring the Virgin.

Pope Pius IX granted indulgences to all the faithful who devoutly and with contrite heart shall make at any time during the year any of the following novenas in honor of the Blessed Virgin Mary, with any formula of prayer, provided it be approved by competent ecclesiastical authority, on the usual conditions. This indult covered eleven novenas: In honor of the Immaculate Conception of the Blessed Virgin Mary, in honor of the Birth of Mary, in honor of the Presentation of Mary in the Temple, in honor of the Annunciation, in honor of the Visitation, in honor of Mary's holy delivery and of the birth of the Child Jesus, in honor of the purification of the Blessed Virgin Mary, in honor of the Dolors of Mary, in honor of the Assumption of Mary, in honor of the Sacred Heart of Mary and of her patronage, and in honor of the Feast of the Most Holy Rosary of the Blessed Virgin.

NUESTRO SEÑOR DE LOS MILA-GROS — See LORD OF THE MIRA-CLES.

NUN

A member of a religious congregation of women.

In Canon Law, nuns are categorized as *moniales*, or women religious in solemn vows. In popular use, the term nun generally refers to women religious who are cloistered and the term sister is used for those in active orders.

NUNC DIMITTIS

The canticle or hymn of the holy prophet Simeon upon seeing Jesus in the Temple at the Presentation, from the first two words of the prayer in Latin (literally, "Now dismiss").

Recorded in the Gospel of Luke (see Luke 2:29-32), it is an expression of joy and thanksgiving for the blessing of having lived to see the Messiah. It is used in the night prayer of the Liturgy of the Hours.

One version reads:

Lord, now let your servant go in
  peace;
your words have been fulfilled:
my own eyes have seen the salvation
which you have prepared in the sight
  of every people:
a light to reveal you to the nations
and the glory of your people Israel.

(See also LITURGY OF THE HOURS; PRESENTATION IN THE TEMPLE .)

NUPTIAL MASS AND BLESSING

A special Mass in the Roman Rite assigned to be celebrated in conjunction with a marriage.

A blessing to the married couple is imparted immediately after the Lord's Prayer. The blessing is never given outside Mass, nor is it bestowed on elderly couples.

O ANTIPHONS

Antiphons traditionally recited during Advent Liturgy of the Hours.

They are so named because each begins with "O"; they are also called the "Great Antiphons." The O Antiphons are also sometimes used to make private novenas from December 17 to December 23.

One version reads:

O WISDOM, Who didst come out of the mouth of the Most High, reaching from end to end and ordering all things mightily and sweetly: come and teach us the way of prudence.

O ADONAI and Leader of the house of Israel, Who didst appear to Moses in the flame of the burning bush, and didst give unto him the Law on Sinai: come and with an outstretched arm redeem us.

O ROOT OF JESSE, Who dost stand for an ensign of the people, before Whom kings shall keep silence, and unto Whom the Gentiles shall make their supplication: come to deliver us, and tarry not.

O KEY OF DAVID and Scepter of the house of Israel, Who dost open and no man doth shut, Who dost shut and no man doth open, come and bring forth from his prison-house the captive that sitteth in darkness and in the shadow of death.

O DAWN OF THE EAST, Brightness of the Light Eternal, and Sun of Justice, come and enlighten them that sit in darkness and in the shadow of death.

O KING OF THE GENTILES and the Desired of them, Thou Cornerstone that dost make both one, come and deliver man, whom Thou didst form out of the dust of the earth.

O EMMANUEL, our King and Lawgiver, the Expected of the Nations and their Savior, come to save us, O Lord our God.

In some local churches in the Middle Ages, two more were added to these seven: one to the Virgin Mary (*O Virgo virginum*); and the other to the Archangel Gabriel (*O Gabriel*); or to St. Thomas the Apostle, whose feast then fell on December 21 (*O Thoma Didyme*). There were even churches where twelve Great Antiphons were sung; besides the nine just mentioned were added one to Christ the King of Peace (*O Rex pacifice*), one to Mary (*O mundi Domina*), and one to Jerusalem, the city of the people of God (*O Hierusalem*).

(See also **ANTIPHON; LITURGY OF THE HOURS; NOVENA.**)

O SALUTARIS

Latin for the first two words of the hymn *O Salutaris Hostia* (O Saving Victim), attributed to St. Thomas Aquinas.

St. Thomas is thought to have written the hymn at the request of Pope Urban IV (r. 1261-1264), who instituted the Feast of Corpus Christi. The last two verses of this hymn are often used at the exposition of the Blessed Sacrament. The words of the hymn are:

O Saving Victim, op'ning wide
The gate of heav'n to men below:
Our foes press on from every side,
Thine aid supply, Thy strength
  bestow.

To Thy great Name be endless praise,
Immortal Godhead, One in Three,
O grant us endless length of days
In our true native land with Thee.
Amen.

(See also **BENEDICTION**.)

OBEDIENCE

The moral virtue by which one submits to the will or law of one in exercise of legitimate authority.

Obedience may be demanded for a variety of reasons: a vow, a contract, religious piety, or the office of one in authority. As a virtue, obedience is pleasing to God because the sacrifice of one's will is chosen out of love for God. In the Bible, to obey is really to "hear" the expressed will of God by responding to it completely and without hesitation.

OBERAMMERGAU

A Passion play performed every ten years in a small town south of Munich, Germany, in fulfillment of a vow made in 1633.

Community leaders pledged to stage the play if the town was spared from the plague, and it was. The performances now attract thousands of visitors from around the world.

OBLATES OF ST. BENEDICT

A form of association between laypeople and individual monasteries, similar to Third Orders.

In the early Middle Ages, an "oblate" was a boy or young man put under the full-time care of a monastery. The term came from the Latin for "offered." Parents presented a child with the pious intent that he would be cared for by the order and later become a member of it. The practice was stopped by the Council of Toledo (656). Now the term refers to members of particular orders (such as the Oblates of Mary Immaculate) and lay adults who have volunteered to serve a religious community, even for a limited time.

Oblates do not take vows and do not

make any permanent obligation. They are not, strictly speaking, members of Third Orders (Tertiaries) because their relationship extends to only one individual monastic house. Devotion to the liturgy is encouraged, and they are urged to pray the Liturgy of the Hours.

(See also **THIRD ORDER.**)

OBSESSION

An extraordinary state of mind in one who is seriously molested by evil spirits in an external manner more than simple temptation.

OCCASION OF SIN

A person, place, or thing that is an attraction and enticement to sin.

It may be either a situation that always leads to sin or one that usually leads to sin. One is obliged to avoid occasions of sin or, if they cannot be avoided completely, to make them as "remote" as possible.

OCOTLAN, OUR LADY OF

A Marian devotion and image based on the apparition reported by Juan Diego Bernardino in Tlaxcala, Mexico, in 1541.

The visionary said Mary brought him to an unknown spring by a ravine of oak trees. On the following day, the people noticed an ocote, a type of pine tree, burn-

ing, and an image of Mary was found inside the burnt trunk. It is now housed in a basilica there named in honor of Our Lady of Ocotlan. Miracles have been attributed to her intercession. The spring continues to flow.

OCTAVE

A celebration for a period of eight days, or a renewed celebration on the eighth day after a feast.

The first mention of such a custom is in the fourth century in connection with the dedication of basilicas in Tyre and in Jerusalem. After that, octaves are frequently mentioned in connection with Easter, Pentecost, and Christmas. The linking of octaves to feasts of saints began in the eighth century. The current liturgical calendar includes only the octaves of Christmas and Easter.

OCTAVE OF PRAYER FOR CHRISTIAN UNITY

Eight days of prayer beginning on the Feast of St. Peter's Chains in Rome (January 18) and concluding on the Feast of the Conversion of St. Paul (January 25) for the union of Christians.

The week of prayer for Christian unity was the inspiration of Father Paul Wattson, S.A., of Graymoor, New York in 1908, when it was established as the Chair of

Unity Octave. From 1926, the Faith and Order movement published suggestions for a similar octave to Wattson's to be held around the time of Pentecost. In 1935, Abbe Paul Couturier called for a universal week of prayer for unity. From the mid 1950s, the Faith and Order Commission of the World Council of Churches had been collaborating with a Roman Catholic ecumenical agency to produce guidelines for the celebration of the octave. Responsibility for the Roman Catholic participation in drafting the proposed texts for each year has, since 1966, been borne by the Pontifical Council for Promoting Christian Unity.

(See also **CHRISTIAN UNITY, WEEK OF PRAYER FOR**.)

OCTOBER

Along with May, one of the two months during which a particular devotion is shown to the Virgin Mary.

In October, she is invoked under the title of Our Lady of the Rosary and so it has been called the month of the Rosary. In 1868, Pope Pius IX indulgenced October devotions, and Pope Leo XIII extended the custom of such services to all parish churches to pray for the normalization of relations between the Holy See and the kingdom of Italy after the final disintegration of the Papal States. Although the Lateran Pacts of 1929 between

the Holy See and Italy brought an end to the stated obligation to hold such services, the custom continued.

ODOR OF SANCTITY — See **SANCTITY, ODOR OF**.

OFFICE

The full cycle of canonical Hours, called the Divine Office or any portion of the Divine Office.

It is also the entire day's liturgy (Mass and Liturgy of the Hours all together) or any public celebration of ecclesial prayer.

OFFICE FOR THE DEAD, RECITING THE

Special prayers for the departed.

Under the 1991 norms and grants of indulgences, a partial indulgence is granted to the Christian faithful who devoutly recite the morning prayer or evening prayer from the Office for the Dead.

OFFICE OF THE STAR

A favorite medieval mystery play.

"Office of the Star" was a pageant of the Magi's visit on Epiphany. It began during the eleventh century in France as part of the liturgical service in church, and spread throughout Europe. From its beginning as a devout religious ceremony, it degenerated into a boisterous affair. King Herod was introduced into the play as a raging maniac, throwing a wooden spear around, beating clergy and laity, and creating havoc by his antics. Because of the abuses, it was abolished as a part of the liturgical service and was replaced by an Epiphany play known as the "Feast of the Star." This play was performed partly inside the church and partly outside but was not associated with the Mass.

In more religious areas, the Epiphany celebrations kept their original character, although simplified such as the *Sternsingen* in Germany and the Festival of Los Tres Reyes in the Spanish speaking nations.

(See also **EPIPHANY; MAGI; MORALITY PLAY.**)

OIL OF ST. ANNE

Blessed oil from St. Anne's shrine based on the ancient custom of blessing oil for the sick at various pilgrimage sites.

In earlier times, pilgrims took oil from the lamps burning at the shrine, had it blessed, and brought it home for the sick.

(See also **ST. ANNE.**)

OIL OF ST. JOHN

A traditional medieval remedy made from plants collected on the Feast of the Nativity of St. John the Baptist.

On St. John's morning, the peasants of Piedmont and Lombardy went out to search the oak leaves for the "oil of St. John" which was supposed to heal all wounds made with cutting instruments. Originally, perhaps, this oil was simply mistletoe or a decoction made from it. In the French province of Bourbonnais, a popular remedy for epilepsy was a decoction of mistletoe that had been gathered on an oak on St. John's Day and boiled with rye flour.

(See also **ST. JOHN THE BAPTIST.**)

OILS, HOLY

Three types of oil used sacramentally for anointing; oil of the saints.

The followers of Jesus take their name — Christians — from his title as "the Christ": the anointed One (see Acts 10:38).

In ancient times, oil was a sign of abundance and joy. In the Old Testament, kings, priests, and, occasionally, prophets were anointed. It symbolized that person's goodness and healing presence in the community. Now the "oil of catechumens" signifies cleansing and strengthening. The anointing of the sick with the "oil of the sick" brings healing and comfort. And the use of sacred chrism for the post-baptismal anointing and at confirmation and ordination is a sign of consecration. Oil is also used for certain blessings, such as the dedication of churches and altars.

Each of the three can be olive or vegetable oil. Traditionally, they're blessed by the bishop on Holy Thursday (or, more recently, earlier during Holy Week). "Chrism" has balm mixed in with it. (Also called "balsam," balm is a thick, aromatic tree resin that was prized for both its pleasant smell and its assumed medicinal properties.) After Holy Thursday's Chrism Mass, all three kinds are distributed to parishes. Typically, they are stored in three urns by the altar or near the baptismal font. A lesser amount can be transferred to a smaller receptacle for use during the celebration of a sacrament. There was a time when the three oils were kept in an ambry, a locked wall cupboard. Some older church buildings still have a little door in the sanctuary wall that's marked *Olea Sancta* (Latin for "holy oils").

"Oil of the Saints" is an oily or other liquid which has exuded from the relics of certain saints, an oil which has been poured over the relics of certain saints and collected as a sacramental, or an oil blessed in honor of a certain saint. This oil is used for anointing with prayer for the intercession of the saint and faith in God for health of the soul and body.

The word *manna* is often used in place of the word oil when describing the liquids which exude from the relics of some saints. Possibly this is due to the fact that the formation of this oil is as mysterious as was the formation of the manna supplied to the Israelites during their wandering in the wilderness in Old Testament times. The oil that has been observed originating from the relics of saints generally takes the form of a colorless, odorless, tasteless fluid and has occurred in different countries with various atmospheric conditions and circumstances. Three major saints with whose relics this phenomenon is associated are St. Andrew, who died in the first century; St. Nicholas, who died in the fourth; and St. Walburga, who died in the eighth. Medical science cannot explain why their bones secrete a liquid which still collects at certain times that would seem unfavorable for the formation of any liquid. The relics of St. Gerard Majella exuded a fluid for a time, although this has not continued to the present, and the first miracle accepted for his beatification involved the cure of a dying man who applied this mysterious oil and was restored to complete health. Other saints whose relics or bodies gave off a fluid include St. Agnes of Montepulciano, St. Camillus de Lellis, St. Paschal Baylon, St. Julia Billiart, St. Mary Magdalene dei Pazzi, Venerable Mother Maria of Jesus, Blessed Matthia Nazzarei of Matelica, and, in our own times, St. Sharbel Makhlouf.

St. Sharbel died in 1898, and a mysterious fluid was first observed coming from the body about four months after his death. This fluid appeared to come from the pores and seemed a mixture of blood and sweat. The fluid continued to exude for more than half a century. At the ritual exhumation before beatification in 1965, the body had decomposed and the fluid had stopped its flow. There are numerous well-documented incidents of this phenomenon, but no natural explanation has been found for it.

From the middle of the fifth century, it was a custom to pour oil or water over the relics of martyrs and to collect this liquid as relics called *oleum martyris*. The custom was later extended to the relics of saints who were not martyrs. St. Paulinus of Nola and St. Martin of Tours are examples of saints whose relics have been thus treated.

In the fifth and sixth centuries, the tomb of the martyr St. Menas became a popular place of pilgrimage. As a souvenir, flasks of oil and of water were given to the pilgrims. The water probably came from a well near the tomb; the oil was taken from that burned in lamps before the tomb. This practice has continued as a part of the cultus of a number of saints through modern times. A special prayer for the blessing of oil in honor of St. Serapion, martyr, was found in the Roman Ritual. Originally this blessing had been reserved to the Order of Our Lady of Ransom.

OPLATKI (OPLATEK OBLATKY OPLATKY)

A thin wafer of unleavened bread used in Polish and Eastern European Christmas customs.

Similar to a host, the bread is stamped with sacred figures and blessed by the priest. The wafer is broken and eaten by all at the family table on Christmas Eve as they exchange good wishes and honor their family members who are away from home.

(See also **KUCIOS [TWELVE APOSTLES' DINNER]**.)

OPUS DEI

Latin for "work of God."

It is a worldwide institution founded by St. Josemaria Escrivá de Balaguer in Madrid in 1928. Its goal is spreading throughout all sectors of society a profound awareness of the universal call to holiness and the apostolate of Christian witness and action in the ordinary circumstances of life. Pope John Paul II established Opus Dei as a personal prelature in 1982 with the full title "Prelature of the Holy Cross and Opus Dei." The prelature operates the Pontifical University of the Holy Cross in Rome. In the United States, members of Opus Dei, along with cooperators and friends, conduct apostolic works corporately in major cities.

Also, the Benedictines, in fidelity to the Rule of St. Benedict, applied the term

Opus Dei to the Liturgy of the Hours as an affirmation that prayer was a special duty and privilege of monks and was especially pleasing to God.

ORANTE

A figure in early Christian art.

Depicted in the classical attitude of prayer, the *orante* has his or her hands lifted up, with palms facing outward, the elbows slightly bent. The physical demeanor of the *orante* is meant to convey an attitude of adoration and praise; as the hands are lifted up, so the *orante*'s mind and heart are raised to God. The palms are open to show an offering of thanks but also to keep the sacred at a distance, lest the *orante* be guilty of profaning the presence of the sacred by approaching too closely. The most famous depiction of the *orante* is seen in the fresco painting of the three praying men in the Catacombs of Priscilla in Rome.

ORATORY

A chapel.

An oratory is a place set aside by the bishop or a diocese for the celebration of all liturgical services unless the liturgical laws forbid them or the bishop limits them. Solemn public worship is not to be celebrated in an oratory. Oratories are classified as public, semipublic, and private.

ORDER

A religious community of men or women who have professed solemn vows or a prescribed form of worship.

ORDERS, SACRAMENT OF HOLY

One of the seven sacraments.

In this sacrament a bishop imposes hands and prays to confer spiritual power and grace to carry out the ordained ministry of the Church. Major orders are comprised of the offices of deacon, priest, and bishop.

ORTHODOX CHURCH

The body of Eastern Christian believers who have a valid sacramental and hierarchal system but became separated from full communion with the Catholic Church by not acknowledging the pope as Supreme Shepherd of the Church.

Separation from the Catholic Church is traced to July 16, 1054, when Cardinal Humbert, the head of a papal delegation in Constantinople, placed a document of excommunication on the altar of Hagia Sophia, the cathedral church of Constantinople. The excommunication resulted in part from a disagreement between East and West over the *filioque* phrase (Latin for "and the Son") in the Creed. This led to a schism between East and West that continues to the present day.

ORTHODOXY, FEAST OF

An observance in the Byzantine Rite on the first Sunday of Lent marking the definition of the Second Council of Nicaea (787), whereby the grounds for venerating images (icons) and relics was established.

The Second Council of Nicaea distinguished between adoration (which is due to God alone) and veneration (which can be given to an icon or relic).

OSTENSORIUM — See **MONSTRANCE**.

OUR FATHER — See **LORD'S PRAYER**.

OUR LADY

A familiar title of the Virgin Mary used as a prefatory to many other fuller titles given to the Blessed Virgin. (See also the following cross-references.)

OUR LADY HELP OF CHRISTIANS — See **HELP OF CHRISTIANS, OUR LADY**.

OUR LADY OF THE ANGELS — See **ANGELS, OUR LADY OF THE**.

OUR LADY APARECIDA — See **APARECIDA, OUR LADY**.

OUR LADY OF ATOCHA — See **ATOCHA, OUR LADY OF**.

OUR LADY OF BEAURAING — See **BEAURAING, OUR LADY OF**.

OUR LADY OF CARTAGO — See **CARTAGO, OUR LADY OF**.

OUR LADY OF THE CENACLE — See **CENACLE, OUR LADY OF THE**.

OUR LADY OF CHAPI — See **CHAPI, OUR LADY OF**.

OUR LADY OF CHARITY OF EL COBRE — See **CHARITY OF EL COBRE, OUR LADY OF**.

OUR LADY OF CHARTRES — See **CHARTRES, OUR LADY OF**.

OUR LADY OF CHINA — See **CHINA, OUR LADY OF**.

OUR LADY OF CHIQUINQUIRA — See **CHIQUINQUIRA, OUR LADY OF.**

OUR LADY OF CONSOLATION — See **CONSOLATION, OUR LADY OF.**

OUR LADY OF COROMOTO — See **COROMOTO, OUR LADY OF.**

OUR LADY OF EINSELDELN — See **EINSELDELN, OUR LADY OF.**

OUR LADY OF FÁTIMA — See **FÁTIMA, OUR LADY OF.**

OUR LADY OF GOOD COUNSEL — See **GOOD COUNSEL, OUR LADY OF.**

OUR LADY OF GOOD REMEDY — See **GOOD REMEDY, OUR LADY OF.**

OUR LADY OF GRACE — See **GRACE, OUR LADY OF.**

OUR LADY OF GUADALUPE — See **GUADALUPE, OUR LADY OF.**

OUR LADY OF HAL — See **HAL, OUR LADY OF.**

OUR LADY OF HOPE — See **HOPE, OUR LADY OF.**

OUR LADY OF KIBEHO — See **KIBEHO, OUR LADY OF.**

OUR LADY OF KNOCK — See **KNOCK, OUR LADY OF.**

OUR LADY OF LA CHAPELLE — See **LA CHAPELLE, OUR LADY OF.**

OUR LADY OF LA SALETTE — See **LA SALETTE, OUR LADY OF.**

OUR LADY OF LAVANG — See **LAVANG, OUR LADY OF.**

OUR LADY OF LOURDES — See **LOURDES, OUR LADY OF.**

OUR LADY OF LUJAN — See **LUJAN, OUR LADY OF.**

OUR LADY OF MEDJUGORJE — See **MEDJUGORJE, OUR LADY OF.**

OUR LADY OF MERCY — See **MOTHER OF MERCY.**

OUR LADY OF THE MOST BLESSED SACRAMENT — See **MOST BLESSED SACRAMENT, OUR LADY OF THE.**

OUR LADY OF MOUNT CARMEL — See **MOUNT CARMEL, OUR LADY OF.**

OUR LADY OF OCOTLAN — See **OCOTLAN, OUR LADY OF.**

OUR LADY OF PERPETUAL HELP — See **PERPETUAL HELP, OUR LADY OF.**

OUR LADY OF THE PILLAR — See **PILLAR, OUR LADY OF THE.**

OUR LADY OF PROMPT SUCCOR — See **PROMPT SUCCOR, OUR LADY OF.**

OUR LADY OF PROVIDENCE — See **PROVIDENCE, OUR LADY OF.**

OUR LADY OF THE RIVERS — See **RIVERS, OUR LADY OF THE.**

OUR LADY OF THE ROCKIES — See **ROCKIES, OUR LADY OF THE.**

OUR LADY OF THE ROSARY OF THE PHILIPPINES — See **LA NAVAL.**

OUR LADY OF THE ROSARY OF POMPEII — See **POMPEII, OUR LADY OF THE ROSARY OF.**

OUR LADY OF SAN JUAN — See **SAN JUAN, OUR LADY OF.**

OUR LADY OF SCHÖNSTATT — See **SCHÖNSTATT, OUR LADY OF.**

OUR LADY OF SILUVA — See **SILUVA, OUR LADY OF.**

OUR LADY OF THE SNOW — See **SNOW, OUR LADY OF THE.**

OUR LADY OF SOLEDAD — See **SOLEDAD, OUR LADY OF**.

OUR LADY OF SUYAPA — See **SUYAPA, OUR LADY OF**.

OUR LADY OF VICTORY — See **VICTORY, OUR LADY OF**.

OUR LADY OF WALSINGHAM — See **WALSINGHAM, OUR LADY OF**.

OUR LADY QUEEN OF THE APOSTLES — See **QUEEN OF THE APOSTLES, OUR LADY**.

OUR LADY QUEEN OF THE CLERGY — See **REGINA CLERI**.

OUR LADY QUEEN OF PEACE — See **QUEEN OF PEACE, OUR LADY**.

OUR LADY'S ROSARY MAKERS
A nonprofit organization.

Established in Louisville, Kentucky, in 1949 by Brother Sylan, it was dedicated to producing and supplying free rosaries to missionaries throughout the world. There are currently twenty-four thousand members.

OUR LADY'S THIRTY DAYS
The traditional name for August 15 to September 15 in some areas of central Europe.

(See also **ASSUMPTION**.)

OXFORD MOVEMENT
A movement begun in 1833 at Oxford to return the Church of England to apostolic Christianity.

The Oxford Movement was led by John Keble, Edward Pusey, John Henry Newman, and Richard Hurell Froude, all of whom were Anglican clergymen and Fellows of Oriel College; and by W. G. Ward, an Anglican layman who was a Fellow of Balliol College. The five men set out to recall the Church of England to the Catholic principles on which it had been founded.

In 1845, Newman and Ward became Catholics. Over the next twenty years, nearly a thousand Anglican clergy and laity followed in their lead. Among them was Henry Edward Manning, who, like Newman, went on to become a cardinal.

In the early nineteenth century the Church of England had largely lost its original ideals and had fallen increasingly under the power of the State. Holy Communion was generally celebrated only a few times a year, many of the clergy had grown lethargic and genuine piety was rare.

The influence of European Protestantism and the rationalist spirit which flowed from the Enlightenment had both contributed to this decline. In addition, Britain had been ruled by a succession of German monarchs each of whom, although officially head of the national church, neither understood it nor cared about it greatly. The Methodist movement founded by John Wesley, which soon broke away from the Church of England, was partly a reaction against the malaise which existed within it. The Methodist Church thus became one of the "nonconformist" or "dissenting" Protestant bodies, mainly evangelical and Bible-based, which rejected the authority of the national church. In addition, Anglicans felt threatened by the increase in the Catholic population as Irish immigrants flooded into the cities, by the new freedoms which Catholics gained from the Catholic Emancipation Act of 1829, and by the removal of other measures which had barred all but members of the established Church from public life.

Concerned for its future, a group of devout Anglican academics at Oxford University set out to recall the Church of England to the Catholic principles upon which it had been founded: a body of clearly-stated doctrine, sacramental worship, and government by bishops who saw themselves as successors of the Apostles, deriving their authority, not from the State, but from the commission which Christ gave to the Twelve. They regarded the Church of England as the local branch of the universal Church, treading a middle way (via media) between evangelical Protestantism on the one hand and Rome on the other.

John Keble, who had entered Oxford at fifteen, was a classical scholar and religious poet who in 1831 became Professor of Poetry in the university. Edward Pusey, a distinguished orientalist, had come into close contact with liberal theology during a two-year period of study in Germany and was repelled by its rationalistic temper. In 1828, aged twenty-eight, he was appointed Professor of Hebrew at Oxford, a post he held until his death in 1882. John Henry Newman, originally an evangelical, embraced the Catholic position after forming a close friendship with Pusey and Froude, and after becoming Vicar of St Mary's. the University Church. Richard Hurell Froude, dogged by tuberculosis, died a month short of his thirty-third birthday in 1836. Had he lived, he might well, like Newman and Ward, have become a Catholic. His diaries, published after his death, show a marked antipathy to the Protestant Reformers and their ideals. W. G. Ward, originally a liberal Protestant, became a disciple of Newman after hearing him preach. In *The Ideal of a Christian Church*, published in 1844, he urged the Church of England to ask pardon of Rome and to "sue humbly" for re-union. As a result, he was fired from his university post as a mathematics tutor and deprived of his degrees.

Newman dated the foundation of the Oxford Movement to a sermon which Keble preached at St. Mary's on July 14, 1833, in protest at a move by the British Government to suppress ten Irish bishop-rics. Under the title "National Apostasy," the sermon attacked this as an intolerable interference by the State in the rights of the Church. He warned his fellow-coun-trymen against turning away from the Church of England and admonished the many who had already turned away from God altogether. Salvation, he insisted, was possible only through the sacraments.

Although the government did suppress the bishoprics, Keble's sermon, preached before an influential congregation, had considerable impact. He and his colleagues followed it with *Tracts for the Times*, a se-ries of pamphlets designed to arouse the clergy to a sense of the Church of En-gland's divine origin and authority. Insist-ing on its Catholic character, they defined "Catholicism" as fidelity to the teachings of the early and undivided Christian Church. The *Tracts* attempted to make that Church live again.

Such was their influence that the Ox-ford group were often referred to as the Tractarians, a name still sometimes used as a synonym for the Oxford Movement

itself. Predictably, they attracted criticism from liberal-minded academics and from others who suspected them of nudging the Church of England in the direction of Rome. This was ironic, since they were originally conceived as an antidote to the twin dangers of "Romanism and Dissent."

The *Tracts* were edited by Newman, who himself wrote twenty-three of them. The most famous of these was *Tract 90*, which insisted that the Thirty-Nine Arti-cles — the Church of England's sixteenth-century doctrinal manifesto — was consistent with the teachings of the early Church and hence with Roman Catholi-cism in its original and genuine form. This aroused such a storm of controversy that publication of the *Tracts* ceased.

In preparing his case Newman had made an intense study of early Christian history and of the writings of the Fathers of the Church. This, together with the op-position which he encountered from much of the Anglican leadership, led him to the conviction that the Church of En-gland was in schism from the Catholic Church founded by Christ and that he could no longer remain within it. Ward came to a similar conclusion. In 1845 both men became Catholics. During the next twenty years, nearly a thousand Anglican converts, clergy and laity, followed in their wake. Among them was Henry Edward Manning, destined, like Newman, to be-come a cardinal. Along with many others, Pusey and Keble remained within the Anglican fold for the remainder of their lives. Pusey emerged as leader of the Anglo-Catholic party, whose ultimate vision was reunion between the Anglican and Roman Churches.

The Oxford Movement had a deep and lasting effect on both churches. In the Church of England Eucharistic worship was transformed, religious orders were revived and a new social conscience result-ed in much pastoral and charitable work, especially among the poor of the great cities. These fruits may be seen today not only in England but in churches belonging to the Anglican communion across the world.

To the Catholic Church, the Oxford Movement gave John Henry Newman, its greatest nineteenth century convert, whose thought had so profound an influence upon the Second Vatican Council.

P

PAGEANT — See **CORPUS CHRISTI PROCESSION**.

PAIN BÉNIT

In certain cultures, the bread that is blessed and distributed to the faithful during certain times of the year as a sign of belief in and love for Christ and as a symbol of the unity of Christ's Body, the Church.

It is a sacramental, not to be confused with the consecrated Host, which is the true body of Christ.

PALL

The piece of stiff linen, or cardboard covered with linen, usually between four and seven inches square, that covers the chalice at Mass so as to prevent dust and other foreign particles from landing in the chalice.

It is also the cloth spread over the coffin at funeral Masses. It is white, in imitation of the white robe given in baptism.

PALLIUM

A narrow circular band made of white wool with two pendants about a foot long that hang from the front and back.

The use of the *pallium* is reserved to the pontiff and archbishops, except that archbishops need permission from the Holy See to use it. Occasionally, bishops receive the *pallium* only as an indication of special favor, with no change in their status. The *pallium* is a symbol of authority.

Agnus is the Latin for "lamb." Annually, two lambs are blessed on St. Agnes's feast day at her church on the Via Nomentana in Rome. Since the fourth century, the lambs have been presented at a solemn Mass in the basilica, and they are carefully cared for by the Benedictine nuns of St. Cecilia's convent in Trastevere until the time of shearing. Wool from these lambs is woven by the nuns into the *pallia*.

St. Peter Giving the Pallium to Leo III

PALM SUNDAY— See HOLY WEEK.

PALMESEL (PALM DONKEY) — See HOLY WEEK; SACRAMENTALS.

PALMS (PALM BOUQUETS)

A sacramental connected with Passion Sunday.

(See also HOLY WEEK; SACRAMENTALS.)

The Blessing of Lambs on the Feast of St. Agnus

PAN BENDITO

Spanish for "blessed bread."

The custom developed in central Europe and the Latin countries of receiving *pan bendito* at church on St. Blaise's feast day, February 3. Pious tradition held that eating a small piece would heal a sore throat. In other regions, bread is also blessed in the name of St. Joseph, St. Anthony, and other saints.

PANGE LINGUA

A hymn written by St. Thomas Aquinas for the institution of the Feast of Corpus Christi in 1264 (literally "Sing, my tongue").

It is used during the Liturgy of the Hours and was often sung during Corpus Christi processions from the time of the Middle Ages. The final two stanzas, which begin with the words *Tantum ergo sacramentum*, are used at Benediction.

Pange Lingua

Sing, my tongue, the Savior's glory,
Of his Flesh the mystery sing;
Of the Blood, all price exceeding,
Shed by our immortal King,
Destined for the world's redemption,
From a noble womb to spring.

Of a pure and spotless Virgin
Born for us on earth below,
He, as man, with man conversing,
Stayed, the seeds of truth to sow;
Then he closed the solemn order

Wondrously his life of woe.

On the night of that Last Supper
Seated with his chosen band,
He, the Paschal Victim eating,
First fulfills the Law's command:
Then as Food to all his brethren
Gives himself with his own hand.

Word made flesh, the bread of nature
By his word to Flesh he turns;
Wine into his Blood he changes:
What though sense no change
    discerns?
Only be the heart in earnest,
Faith her lesson quickly learns.

Tantum Ergo
Down in adoration falling,
Lo! the Sacred Host we hail;
Lo! o'er ancient forms departing,
Newer rites of grace prevail;
Faith for all defects supplying
Where the feeble senses fail.

To the everlasting Father,
And the Son who reigns on high,
With the Holy Spirit proceeding
Forth from each eternally,
Be salvation, honor, blessing,
Might, and endless majesty.

Amen.

(See also **BENEDICTION; LITUR-
GY OF THE HOURS; TANTUM
ERGO**.)

PANNUCHIDA — See **ROYAL HOURS**.

PANNYKHIDIA
A service for the departed in the Byzantine Rite.

Originally, the *pannykhidia* was a vigil preceding a funeral. It could just as well be a separate memorial service today.

PANSY
A tricolor plant traditionally referred to as "the Trinity flower" in parts of Europe and used as symbol for the Trinity. Since medieval times, there have been many imaginative and symbolic ways to indicate the great mystery of the Holy Trinity. The Church has not officially accepted any of them, but has tolerated some and forbidden others. Three plants — the shamrock, the pansy (viola tricolor), and in Puerto Rico a delicately perfumed white flower with three petals called the Trinitaria —have traditionally been seen as symbols of the Trinity.

PANTOKRATOR
Greek for "Almighty."

It is an image of Christ as the ruler of heaven and earth used in the Eastern Church. Often it is located on one of the central domes of an Eastern Church building. In the West, the equivalent title is "Christ the King."

PAPAL BLESSING

A blessing given by the pope to the people of the world or by a bishop to the people under his care.

From the beginning of their pastoral office, diocesan bishops and those equivalent to them in law have the right to impart the papal blessing with a plenary indulgence in accord with its prescribed formulary three times a year in their own dioceses at the end of a Mass which has

Blessed John XXIII Giving a Papal Blessing

been celebrated with special liturgical beauty on solemnities or feasts that they will designate, even if they only assist at the Mass. This grant extends also to such blessings when given by means of radio or television.

PAPEL PICADO

Papel Picado is the Hispanic version of origami, or cut-paper work, a craft known all over the world. Fanciful and elaborate designs cut from paper are popular throughout Mexico on all feast days. They are used to decorate the churches with all their side altars, and are sometimes used as decorations in the home. The art is particularly prevalent on the Day of the Dead when elaborate skulls and skeletons are cut and used as fanciful decorations in the churches and on home altars and in decorations in the local cemeteries. In Poland, the art is known as *wycinanki* and the cuttings are often used as we would use wall paper. In Germany, the name is *scherenschnitte*; here, the decorative cut outs are backed with a contrasting paper and framed as decorations. Throughout the Orient, the decorative paper cutting is used in a number of ways and some of the most elaborate cuttings are quite expensive.

PARACLETE

A New Testament title for the Holy Spirit

as advocate and "Counselor" (see John 14:16-17, 26; 16:7-11).

PARALITURGICAL ACTIONS

Those rites, prayers, devotions, and ceremonies that are not part of the liturgy per se but are associated with it in spirit.

Devotions such as the Rosary, Stations of the Cross, and various novenas may be considered paraliturgical actions because they prepare us and dispose us to celebrate the Paschal mystery in the Holy Eucharist.

PARAY-LE-MONIAL

A shrine to St. Margaret Mary Alacoque.

It is located near Lyons, France, in the convent where she spent her religious life as a Visitation nun.

(See also ST. MARGARET MARY ALACOQUE.)

PARDON CRUCIFIX

A sacramental promoted by the Pious Union of the Pardon Crucifix, an association that began in France in the early twentieth century. Members were encouraged to seek pardon from God and neighbor.

The headquarters for this Pius Union were in Lyons, France. The faithful were recommended to carry or wear the crucifix on their person, and to devoutly kiss it with the following intentions: To testify love for Our Lord and the Blessed Virgin; gratitude towards the Holy Father, the pope; to beg for the remission of our sins; the deliverance of souls in purgatory; the return of the nations to the faith; forgiveness among Christians; reconciliation among the members of the Catholic Church. Two invocations which were to be said before the crucifix are: "Our Father who art in heaven, forgive us our trespasses as we forgive those who trespass against us," and "I beg the Blessed Virgin Mary to pray to the Lord our God for me." The front of the crucifix is ornately chased metal. The obverse is plain, and is centered with a design of the Sacred Heart. Along the length are found the words, "Behold this heart which has so loved men." On the crossbar are found the words, "Father forgive them."

PARDON OF LE PUY

A ceremony dating back to 992 in the cathedral at Le Puy, France, occasioned by the approach of the millennium and the fear that it induced.

PARTICULAR JUDGMENT — See JUDGMENT, PARTICULAR.

PASCHAL CANDLE — See EASTER CANDLE.

PASCHAL PRECEPT

A Church law requiring reception of the Eucharist in the Easter Season (also called the Easter Duty) unless, for a just cause, once-a-year reception takes place at another time.

PASSION SUNDAY

The fifth Sunday in Lent, so-called because the Gospel for that day tells of Christ beginning his sufferings by being stoned out of the temple.

(See also **HOLY WEEK**.)

PASSION WEEK

The traditional name once used for the week before Holy Week.

PASSIONIST EMBLEM

An emblem associated with St. Paul of the Cross (1694-1775), founder of the Passionists.

The emblem features a white heart, surmounted by a cross, bearing the title of the Passion of Jesus Christ. St. Paul explained the white color of the heart symbolizes that the heart, which has the Passion imprinted on it, ought to be already purified. He called the sign a "terror of hell" and a "sign of salvation." From this practice of the founder, the wearing of a small Passionist emblem gradually

Passionist Emblem

developed. The original emblems were of cloth; today, the emblems are more commonly made of metal. Those who wear a small sign of the Passion are encouraged to recite the pious aspiration "Passion of Christ, strengthen me."

PASSIONTIDE

The traditional name formerly used for the final two weeks of Lent.

PASSOVER SEDER

A major celebration of the Jewish people; sometimes celebrated in Catholic parishes.

The Passover was celebrated by the Jews on the fourteenth day of the month Nisan, which began about a week before the full moon of spring. It was instituted to commemorate the deliverance of the people of Israel the night before their departure from Egypt. The angel of death destroyed the firstborn of Egypt but passed over the houses of the Israelites. As announced by Moses, God commanded that each Hebrew family should slay a young lamb without blemish and sprinkle its blood on the frame of the door. In the evening the lamb was to be roasted, no bones were to be broken, and it was to be eaten with unleavened bread and bitter herbs by all members of the family. The rite was to be repeated every year in a solemn ceremony on the eve of the feast, and it is still one of the major celebrations of the Jewish people everywhere today. It was this feast that Our Lord observed on the night before he died. In recent years in the United States, it has become a custom in many parishes to hold a Passover seder as a parish celebration. In some places, this is arranged by, or for, the members of the R.C.I.A. who will be joining the church that season.

PASTERKA (SHEPHERD'S MASS) — See **MIDNIGHT MASS ON CHRISTMAS**.

PASTORAL VISITATION

The visiting of a church or oratory by the bishop and his presiding over a religious service there.

PASTORES — See **ADVENT PLAYS**.

PATER NOSTER — See **LORD'S PRAYER**.

PATRON OF THE HOLY SOULS, ST. MICHAEL

Traditionally, St. Michael the Archangel is charged to assist the dying and accompany their souls to their private judgment, bring them to purgatory, and afterward present them to God at their entrance to Heaven. Thus, he is the patron of the holy souls. This is the reason for dedicating cemetery chapels to him, and all over Europe thousands of such chapels bear his name. In past centuries, weekly Masses were offered in his honor and in favor of the departed ones in these chapels.

(See also **ST. MICHAEL THE ARCHANGEL**)

PATRON OF THE HOLY SOULS — ST. NICHOLAS OF TOLENTINO

Nicholas of Tolentino (1245-1305) was an Italian Augustinian priest famous for eloquent preaching and as a confessor. An ardent pastor and lover of the poor, he gained fame because of the many miracles he worked in his lifetime. The recipients of his benevolence were told by the saint, "Say nothing of this. Give thanks to God, not to me. I am only an earthen vessel, a poor sinner." The confidence of the faithful placed great trust in his intercession for the souls in purgatory. Many years after his death, he was officially designated Patron of the Holy Souls.

Toward the end of his life, the saint was suffering from a prolonged illness when the Blessed Virgin appeared to him in a vision and told him to ask for a small piece of bread, dip it in water, and eat it. She promised he would be cured by his obedience to her wishes. In gratitude for his immediate cure, he began blessing small pieces of bread and giving them to the sick. This custom is continued even today at the shrine of the saint.

Forty years after his death, the incorrupt body of the saint was exposed to the faithful in the wooden urn in which it was first buried. During this exhibition the arms of the saint became detached from his body, beginning the strange history of the bleeding arms.

There is no documented proof of the identity of the person who amputated the arms of the saint, although legend says it was a German monk named Teodoro who wanted to take the arms as relics to his native country. A large flow of blood followed the sacrilegious act. The guilty monk was apprehended and the body reburied. When exhumed a hundred years later, the arms were still intact and imbued with blood although the body of the saint had completely decomposed. The remains were again reburied beneath the pavement of a chapel adjoining the church where the body had first been buried, and the arms were encased in beautifully crafted silver reliquaries.

Toward the end of the fifteenth century, fresh blood again began to spill from the arms. This effusion was repeated twenty times before 1699.

At one point, the community of Tolentino discovered the bones of the saint had disappeared. Several recorded meetings were held between 1475 and 1515 regarding the mysterious disappearance but the motive and the location of the bones were not discovered. Five hundred years later, in 1926, the bones were located buried far beneath the pavement of the chapel. The bishop immediately petitioned the Vatican to examine the relics, and in 1929 a papal decree declared their authenticity.

PATRON SAINTS

Saints acknowledged to be special protectors and intercessors for persons, churches, dioceses, and the universal Church.

A patron saint is one who either by tradition or by conscious choice is venerated by the faithful as their special protector or intercessor. The notion of a patron or favorite intercessor for a particular place, class of people, trade, or pastime has existed from about the fourth century. A patron of a place may have been chosen because he was born, lived, or died there, or because his relics are preserved in that locality. Some were chosen as patrons of particular trades because they themselves practiced that trade. Other patrons have been selected as protectors against natural calamities. Many of the stories on which the selection of patrons has been made are wholly legendary, In some cases the reason a particular saint was chosen as a patron is incomprehensible. The first regulation of the selection of patrons was made by Pope Urban VIII in 1630 when he declared that they must be canonized (not just among the blessed), and that the choice by clergy and people must be approved by the bishop and confirmed by the Sacred Congregation of Rites. These prescriptions were included in the 1917 Code of Canon Law, and although new regulations were issued in 1973, the general lines remain unaltered. Today, the confirmation is required from the Congregation for Divine Worship. Attempts are made to ensure that the historical existence of patron saints is verified and where this is not possible that they be changed. In addition, the practice of having protectors against particular eventualities, such as the patron against being struck by lightening, is officially frowned on, but survives in the popular religiosity of the people. Although there are many official patron saints, there are equally as many unofficial ones whose intercession is credited and relied on by the people of a particular place or group. In addition, each person is at liberty to have a special patron to whom intercessory prayers are made for any number and kind of requests for heavenly aid.

(See also **Appendix A**).

PAX CHRISTI

The international Catholic peace organization begun in 1945 to reconcile France and Germany after World War II.

Today, it exhorts all nations to seek peace "based on the natural law and on the justice and charity of Christ."

PEACE, SIGN OF

A gesture of greeting exchanged by the celebrant and participants at Mass.

PENANCE

A spiritual change that enables a sinner to turn away from sin, or the virtue that enables human beings to acknowledge their sins with true contrition and a firm purpose of amendment.

Confidence in God's mercy and forgiveness is fundamental to the Christian virtue of penance, along with a determination to be conformed to the Passion, death, and

Resurrection of Christ through the practice of mortification.

PENANCE, SACRAMENT OF

Also called confession or the sacrament of reconciliation.

Catholics are required to confess all their mortal sins by species (type of sin) and number (approximate) to a priest. The current Code of Canon Law obliges Catholics to confess all mortal sins by species and number at least once a year and encourages the frequent reception of the sacrament for sins not judged to be mortal.

PENITENTES

Full name: *Los Hermanos Penitentes*, "The Penitent Brothers."

A lay religious organization in the southwestern United States, primarily northern New Mexico and southern California, originally organized for pious observances involving the expiation of sin through prayer and bodily penance, and for mutual aid.

In the harsh frontier areas, where priests were often scarce, the *penitentes* organized public worship and helped the faithful to prepare for a *Buena Muerte*, a death in the state of grace leading to entrance into heaven.

The brotherhoods evolved into a conservative cultural force, in many cases helping to preserve local customs and faith, especially in poorer rural and urban areas. In some places, they acquired political influence. Many of the brotherhoods evolved into secretive societies with restricted membership.

PENITENTIAL PSALMS

A category referring to Psalms 6, 32, 38, 51, 102, 130, and 143 because of their penitential nature.

PENTECOST

A movable feast held fifty days after Easter.

Pentecost commemorates the descent of the Holy Spirit on the Apostles, the preaching of Peter and the other Apostles to Jews in Jerusalem, and the baptism of those who heard the preaching (see Acts 2:1-41). It is considered the birthday of the Church. The observance dates back to the early Church. Since the twelfth century it has also been called Whitsunday (White Sunday) in England, a reference to the white garment worn at that time by infants upon being baptized.

The name Pentecost comes from the Greek *pentekoste* (the fiftieth) meaning the fiftieth day after Easter. On this day the Jews celebrated a great religious festival of thanksgiving for the harvest, called the Feast of First Fruits or the Feast of Weeks. The Jews used the word *Pentecost* to indicate the

Pentecost

pean races. The festival is called the "Green Holyday" in Poland and Ukraine. In Germany, it is called the "Flower Feast" or *Blumenfest*. In Latin countries a similar term is used: *Pascha Rosatum*, in Latin, meaning "Feast of Roses." The Italian name *Pascua Rossa* (Red Pasch) was inspired by the color of the priests' vestments. Pentecost was held annually from a very early date although the first mention of it as a great feast was made in the third century by Origenes and Tertullian. Tertullian mentioned it as a well-established feast and the second day for the baptism of catechumens, the first being Easter. Until the seventh century, only the day was celebrated in the Western Church. After that time the entire week began being celebrated as a festive observance. The vigil of Pentecost in the Eastern Churches is also devoted to special prayer for the souls of the departed. After a solemn blessing of a bowl of cooked cereal mixed with ground nuts, spices and honey, along with cakes and breads brought by the people, the foods called *Kollyba* are offered to friends and strangers as a symbol of the resurrection of the body. Then a

entire season of fifty days. The early Christians accepted the Jewish usage and called the season from Easter to Whitsunday "Pentecost." They kept it as a festive time of joy; no fasts were kept, and the faithful prayed standing up in honor of the Resurrection. Some countries named the feast after the ancient custom of decorating homes and churches with flowers and boughs. The custom dates back to the nature lore of the pre Christian Indo-Euro-

procession is made to the cemetery where the priest blesses the graves which have been decorated with flowers. A joyful meal often follows the ceremonies.

PENTECOST DEW

A pious superstition in rural northern Europe that ascribes special healing power to dew that falls during Pentecost night.

The custom was for people to walk barefoot through the grass on the early morning of the feast. The moisture was collected on bread that was then fed to livestock as a protection against disease and accidents.

PENTECOST TREE

A German custom in which, on Pentecost eve or Pentecost, a young man planted a tree in front of the house of a young woman he liked.

It was considered an honor to have a *Pfingstbaum*, or Pentecost tree, planted in front of one's house.

PERPEQ

A traditional Albanian Easter cake, usually prepared on Holy Saturday morning and taken that afternoon to the church to be blessed.

It is the first food eaten after attending the Easter Vigil.

Even during the communist persecution, this tradition was continued. The sturdy Albanian Catholics made their *perpeq* in spite of the fact that they would have been imprisoned if they had been found out. After the churches were destroyed in 1967, the people secretly brought the cakes to priests in hiding for the traditional blessing.

PERPETUAL ADORATION — See ADORATION, NOCTURNAL.

PERPETUAL HELP, OUR LADY OF

A Marian image and devotion.

The original icon is at the Church of St. Alphonsus, Rome, and has been under the care of the Redemptorists since the mid-nineteenth century, when Pope Pius IX charged the order to promote the devotion worldwide. The image is at least four centuries older. Our Lady of Perpetual Help is among the best known images of Mary.

The picture of Perpetual Help is similar in many ways to the Byzantine Madonna known as the *Hodegetria* which, tradition holds, St. Luke painted from life. However, the theme of the Perpetual Help image is a portrayal of sorrow, thus it falls into the "Passion type" of Byzantine Madonnas. Mary's head is titled maternally toward her Child. Her hand loosely clasps the tiny hand of her Son. The Christ Child has a look of fright and sorrow as he gazes into the future and sees the vision of his Passion and death awaiting him. Hastily he has run to find refuge in the arms of his Mother. So swiftly has he run to her that his little sandal has come loose. The background of the picture is a simple, unadorned field of gold. This symbolizes divinity. The Greek letters identify the persons portrayed in the picture. They are the Mother of God, Jesus Christ, and the Archangels Michael and Gabriel, who hold the symbols of the Passion. The Mother of God is the central figure of this picture.

On Mary's forehead is a simple eight-pointed star of gold and a four-pointed ornamental cross which may have been added to the original picture by a later artist. Around her head is a plain golden halo, while the halo of the Child is decorated with a cross to show his dignity and office. The tunic, visible at the neck and sleeves, is red and is fringed with golden stripes. A green inner veil holds back the hair. A cloak of rich blue covers her head and drapes over her shoulders. The folds of her clothing are indicated by thin gold lines.

The child's fingers hold his Mother's right hand, although they rest loosely. The features of the Child closely resemble those of the Mother. His head is covered with curly auburn hair and is surrounded with an embellished halo, a sign of his divinity.

He is clothed in a green tunic with full sleeves which is held in at the waist with a reddish sash. A yellow-brown mantle is draped over his right shoulder and covers most of his body. To the left of the picture is the Archangel Michael. The Archangel Gabriel is on the right. Both are clothed in purple tunics and their wings are green streaked with gold. The angels are carrying the instruments of the Passion in veiled hands. Inscriptions in Latin are found on some of the copies of this ancient picture.

The first documented part of the history of the image of Our Mother of Perpetual Help was written on a large piece of parchment affixed to a wooden tablet which hung, along with the picture, for many years in St. Matthew's Church in Rome. Later, the parchment was fastened to the picture itself. Written in both Latin and Italian, the document gives a history of the picture's arrival in Rome in 1499 and its enthronement in the Augustinian church of St. Matthew. Copies of this parchment are in the Vatican Library. A condensed translation of the document tells that a merchant, native to Crete, stole the picture of the Virgin which had been the instrument of many miracles on the island. He boarded a ship, and at sea, a wild storm arose. Although the sailors knew nothing of their precious cargo, their fervent prayers to the Mother of God were heard and they were saved from the storm. The merchant came to Rome and was stricken with a fatal disease. He asked a Roman friend to care for him, and he was taken into his friend's home and nursed tenderly. Before his death, the merchant begged his friend to fulfill a last request. He confessed the theft of the famous picture and asked his friend to put the picture in a church, where it could be properly venerated.

After the merchant's death, the picture was found among his belongings, but the Roman's wife fancied it and hung it in her bedroom. The Blessed Virgin, in a number of visions, told the Roman to put the picture in a more honorable place, but he ignored her requests. Finally, the Virgin appeared to the Roman's six-year-old daughter, telling her to warn her mother and her grandfather to take the picture out of the house. After further delays, she appeared to the child again and commanded her to have her mother place her picture between St. Mary Major and St. John Lateran in the church dedicated to St. Matthew. At last, the mother obeyed the heavenly injunction and called the Augustinian fathers who were in charge of that church. Thus, the picture was enshrined in the church of St. Matthew in March 1499. Here the image of the Mother of Perpetual Help remained for three centuries, until the destruction of the church by French invaders in 1798. During these centuries, the church of St. Matthew was one of the most important pilgrimage sites in Rome.

In 1798, the French military governor of Rome ordered that thirty churches, including that of St. Matthew, be destroyed and the land put to better use. The Augustinians hastily removed some of the artworks and the church furnishings, taking some items to St. John Laterans and some, including the miraculous image, to St. Eusebio's. The picture remained at St. Eusebio's until 1819, when the Augustinians were transferred to the small church and monastery of Santa Maria in Posterula on the other side of the city. Here there was already a picture of Our Lady in the church, so the image of Perpetual Help was put in the monastery chapel where it remained until 1865. One of the Italian lay brothers was transferred to this monastery in 1840. He recognized the picture and remembered his devotion to the picture when it was in St. Matthew's. Brother Augustine told the story of the picture to his favorite altar boy, Michael Marchi. The Congregation of the Most Holy Redeemer, also known as the Redemptorists, was founded by St. Alphonsus Mary Liguori in 1732 to minister to the most abandoned. The congregation grew rapidly, and in 1853 the pope commanded the vicar general of the order to establish a house in Rome to serve as their worldwide headquarters. The property they bought was on the Equiline Hill, and was shaped like a triangle. The estate lay along the base of the hill, and at the tip of the triangle were the ruins of the old St. Matthew's church.

As the Redemptorists built, they also began to research the history of their property. In 1859, their historian discovered some documents telling of a famous image of Our Lady which used to be enshrined in the church of St. Matthew. Father Michael Marchi, the former altar boy, told his Redemptorists brothers that he knew about the famous image and knew where it was. During 1862 and 1863, a Jesuit preacher named Father Francis Blosi delivered a series of sermons on some of the famous pictures of Our Lady that hung in the churches of Rome. One picture that he spoke about was the image of Perpetual Help. In his sermon he spoke of the previous fame of the picture and asked if any of his hearers knew where the picture was. He expressed the wish that the picture, if it could be located, be returned to Mary's chosen place on the Esquiline Hill so that all the faithful might come and pray before it.

When the Redemptorists heard of Father Blosi's sermon, and realized that Our Lady had designated a spot for her shrine, they recalled Father Marchi's account of the icon's hidden repose in the chapel of the Augustinian monastery. The community brought the news to the superior of the Redemptorists, Father Nicholas Mauron. Father Blosi was contacted, and he sent a copy of his sermon for the consideration of the superior. Most Reverend Father Mauron directed the men at St. Alphonsus to pray for the guidance of the Holy Spirit. In December 1865, Father Mauron obtained an audience with the Holy Father, Pope Pius IX during which he told the pope the story. After reading the statement of Father Marchi, the Holy Father, a great devotee of our Blessed Mother, took the paper and on the reverse wrote directions that the image of Perpetual Help be given into the care of the Redemptorists at the Church of St. Alphonsus, with the provision that the Redemptorist superior substitute a suitable picture to the Augustinians. The Augustianians chose a careful copy of the image, and rejoiced that the picture would receive the honor she deserved at the site which she herself had chosen almost four centuries before.

The image was brought to the Church of St. Alphonsus on January 19, 1866. Although the picture was more than four centuries old, and possibly four times that age, the colors were still bright and fresh. Only a small section of one of the sleeves had faded. The picture, painted on wood, had suffered some damage on the reverse from worms and there were a number of nail holes left in the picture. A Polish artist restored the picture, and a solemn procession to place the image on the high altar of the St. Alphonsus was held April 26, 1866. During the course of the procession, a number of miraculous events were reported. The image of Our Lady of Perpetual Help was solemnly crowned on June 23, 1867.

(See also **NOVENA TO OUR LADY OF PERPETUAL HELP.**)

PERPETUAL ROSARY FOR THE DEAD

A custom established by Dominicans Petronus Martini (Bologna) and Timothy Ricci (Florence) in the seventeenth century, in which individuals pray the entire Rosary at a set hour of the day once a month or once a year. Records of the Perpetual Rosary at the Dominican Basilica in Krakow, Poland, date from 1902.

The joyful mysteries are prayed for the conversion of sinners. The sorrowful ask help for the dying. The glorious are for the souls in purgatory. Members are asked to attempt to receive the sacrament of penance (confession) and the Eucharist on their chosen day of prayer.

PERSIGNARSE AND SANTI-GUARSE

A Hispanic custom in which two signs of the cross are used together, one following the other.

The thumb and forefinger are crossed to form a cross. First, the *persignarse*, or "signing yourself," is made by making the

sign of the cross on the forehead, the mouth, and the breast while praying the following: "By the sign of the Holy Cross, deliver us, Lord, from our enemies." Then the *santiguarse*, or "blessing yourself," is made, the traditional sign of the cross. At the conclusion, with thumb and forefinger still forming a cross, the person puts his hand to his lips and kisses the cross thus formed.

(See also **SIGN OF THE CROSS.**)

PETER'S CHAINS, FEAST OF

One of the feasts in honor of St. Peter and others.

Celebrated in the former Church calendar on August 1, this feast recalled the release of St. Peter from the bondage of chains. It was also celebrated to honor St. Paul and the martyrdom of the Seven Holy Maccabees. In the Middle Ages, this date was called "Lammas Day," when it was customary to consecrate bread baked from the first grain harvest or when the annual feudal tribute of lambs was due.

PETER'S CHAIR, FEAST OF

A feast tracing its origins back to Rome in the fourth century.

It is currently celebrated on February 22. Previously, it was celebrated on January 18. The feast highlights the unity of the Church founded upon St. Peter.

PETER'S PENCE

A collection made each year among Catholics for the maintenance of the Holy See and the pope's works of charity.

The custom originated in England in the eighth century and was originally a tax of a penny on each house that was collected on St. Peter's feast day (June 29).

PETITION

One of the four purposes of prayer.

In prayers of petition, persons ask of God the blessings they and others need.

PHOENIX AND FLAMES

An image used as a symbol in the early Church for Christ's Resurrection.

PIGS OF ST. ANTHONY

Animals associated with the Order of Hospitalers founded under the name of St. Anthony of Egypt (251-356) around 1100.

The order was located at La Motte, France, which became a destination for pilgrims. The pigs, each equipped with a bell, were allowed to roam freely in towns throughout western Europe and scavenge for food. The livestock provided income and food for the sick being cared for by the Hospitalers.

PILGRIM VIRGINS

A name referring to statues, icons, and other images of Mary transported from home to home, parish to parish, and country to country to promote devotion.

Among the best known are the images of Our Lady of Fátima, which travel throughout the world visiting parishes, a practice promoted by the Blue Army.

The image of the Virgin of San Juan de los Lagos also travels to visit her clients.

In 1995, under an initiative of the laity, 108 statues of Our Lady began traveling in France as a prelude to the Jubilee 2000. The initiative spread worldwide, inviting the faithful to renew their consecration to Jesus through the Immaculate Heart of Mary.

Phoenix

PILGRIMAGE

The practice of traveling to a holy place to obtain some spiritual benefit.

The purpose could be to venerate a sacred object or relic, to be in the presence of a holy person, to do penance, or to offer thanksgiving for graces received.

For as long as man has worshipped, he has felt the need to visit sacred places. There is evidence that prehistoric man journeyed to mountains or rivers where he believed the gods lived, to seek favors or to beg for protection from danger. This was necessary because the gods could only function within their own territory. With the dawn of civilization people began to worship gods who had once been human, or who possessed human characteristics — gods whose birth or death may have occurred at some identifiable spot, where devotees might go to pay homage.

As myths developed, sites favored by the gods were credited with wonder-working properties. Egyptians flocked to Ammon's oracle at Thebes and Greeks to the oracle at Delphi, where Zeus had located the center of the earth and where the god dispensed wisdom through the mouths of young women who went into a trance for the purpose.

The pilgrim impulse, so deeply implanted in human nature, quickly showed itself among early Christians, who ardently wished to visit the places where Jesus had lived and died.

The first recorded pilgrim was Bishop Alexander, who, around 212 A.D., traveled to Jerusalem from Cappodocia, in Asia Minor (Turkey). The historian Eusebius, who mentions Alexander's journey, says that the bishop made it "because of a vow and the celebrity of the place," which suggests that pilgrimages were already an established institution.

In fact, if we are to believe a letter written from Bethlehem at the end of the fourth century by St. Paula and her daughter St. Eustochium, two of the devout ladies who gathered there around St. Jerome, pilgrimages began in Apostolic

A Pilgrimage Site

times. By that time, large numbers were traveling from all over the known world to visit the Holy Places: Armenians, Indians, Persians, Ethiopians, Gauls and even pilgrims from the British Isles.

A Spanish nun named Etheria, who wrote an account of her own pilgrimage, describes the system of guides and lodgings provided during this period. Pilgrimages were planned by clerics who mapped out the route and indicated the various stopping-places, rather in the manner of modern travel agents.

The Holy Land was not the first pilgrims' sole destination. From the earliest times, so many Christians traveled to Rome to pray at the tombs of St. Peter and St. Paul that they gave the word *roam* to the English language. To make a pilgrimage to Rome during pagan days was to court martyrdom. Christian pilgrims were frequently arrested at their prayers and executed.

When the Emperor Constantine granted toleration to Christianity in 312, the flow of pilgrims swelled to include kings and princes. St. Bede, writing in the early eighth century, records that Caedwalla, King of the West Saxons, abdicated his throne and traveled to Rome, hoping to be baptized and then to die afterwards and go to heaven. "By God's grace, both of these hopes were realized," Bede adds.

During the Middle Ages shrines multiplied, and pilgrimage became truly an international industry. As readers of Chaucer's *Canterbury Tales* will recall, the medieval pilgrim was not always motivated by single-minded piety; all too often the holiday spirit vied with the journey's religious purpose.

Chaucer's pilgrims travel to St. Thomas Becket's shrine to thank the martyr for his intercession when they were sick, but this pious aim does not prevent them from getting drunk, quarrelling, and telling bawdy stories en route. Half a century later, in the *Imitation of Christ*, Thomas à Kempis observed gloomily: "They that go much on pilgrimage be seldom thereby made perfect and holy."

Apart from the moral dangers, it was soon realized that a pilgrimage might become an end in itself; the journey and the religious exercises a substitute for inner conversion. In the fourth century, St. Jerome reminded pilgrims that Christ could be worshiped as well in Britain as in Jerusalem. An eighth-century Irish poem warns: "To go to Rome means great labor and little profit; the king you seek can only be found there if you bring him within you."

These misgivings did nothing to stem the tide of pilgrims, who forged a network of important highways across Europe. When St. Thomas More declared: "It is certain that God wishes to be worshiped in particular places," he was expressing the mind of medieval man at its most devout. Confessors occasionally imposed a pilgrimage as a penance.

Throughout these centuries Rome and the Holy Land remained major destinations, but from the ninth century they were rivaled by the Spanish shrine of Compostella, where relics said to be those of St. James the Greater were discovered, confirming a tradition that the Apostle's body had long ago been taken from Jerusalem to Spain.

Those who made the pilgrimage to Compostella wore a scallopshell plucked from the neighboring seashore as proof of their journey. In time, the scallopshell became the universal badge of the pilgrim. Although doubt has been cast on the authenticity of the relics, many thousands of pilgrims continue to visit Compostella each year.

There is also much skepticism about the Holy House of Loreto, another shrine whose enormous popularity lasted well into modern times. As one Catholic scholar observed, it attracted "the ridicule of one half of the world and the devotion of the other half." Tradition held that in 1291 angels bore away from Nazareth the house of the Holy Family and carried it by stages to its present resting-place near Ancona, on Italy's Adriatic coast. Today the simple stone cottage may be seen inside the basilica in the little town of Loreto. Scholarly doubts notwithstanding, nearly fifty popes have honored the shrine in various ways. In 1920 Pope Benedict XV

declared Our Lady of Loreto the patron saint of aviators.

Whatever level of approval the Church may give to a particular shrine or pilgrimage, she is careful never to make belief in its authenticity an article of faith. Nor does papal approval place a shrine or a relic outside the sphere of scientific investigation. However, even where tradition is proved to be merely pious fable, there is no reason to doubt that the sincere faith of the pilgrim may often have been rewarded, perhaps even miraculously.

That relics may be false or evidence manufactured was understood by some observers even when fraud and gullibility flourished. One remembers Chaucer's Pardoner, with his glass of "pigges bones" and his shred of St. Peter's sail. Chaucer clearly exercised a healthy skepticism, and we may be sure that his was not unique.

On at least one occasion a medieval pope took action to correct what he saw as misguided piety. From the thirteenth century, Ireland's most famous pilgrim destination was Lough Derg in County Donegal. Christ was said to have revealed to St. Patrick that pilgrims to the island in the center of the lake would gain a plenary indulgence and be granted a vision of hell's torments and the joys of heaven. The story grew that a cave which penetrated far into the rock led to purgatory and thence to paradise. An intrepid German monk decided to investigate and found that the cave led nowhere in particular. In 1497 Pope Alexander VI had the entrance blocked and the pilgrimage to "St. Patrick's Purgatory" banned. In later centuries it was revived, and today crowds of pilgrims annually take the boat to the island for a purgatorial regime of prayer and fasting.

In addition to spiritual gains, the great pilgrimages of the Middle Ages brought mighty social and economic benefits. Those who normally never left their own towns or villages were, on pilgrimage, brought into contact with people of many nations and of different social classes. In this way pilgrimages were a great unifying force. Most shrines were governed by monasteries who were charged with the maintenance of roads and bridges, and who also provided for the poor and sick. The pilgrims' offerings largely financed these good works.

In England, the dissolution of the monasteries by Henry VIII destroyed such great pilgrimage centers as Canterbury, Durham, Glastonbury, and St. Albans. In consequence, the towns themselves dwindled in importance and thousands of poor and sick people were deprived of the help which the monks had once provided. In modern times, the eleventh-century shrine of Walsingham, Norfolk, has been revived with notable success.

In the New World the most famous shrine is that of Our Lady at Guadalupe, near Mexico City. During the past 150 years, reported apparitions by Our Lady have brought pilgrims flocking to a number of shrines in Europe, of which Lourdes and Fátima are the most prominent. At Knock, in Ireland, an airport has been built especially to cater for the thousands of pilgrims who come each year to visit the humble parish church where Our Lady, St. Joseph, and St. John the Baptist appeared in 1879.

Two recent Marian apparitions, at Garabandal, Spain and at Medjugorje, Bosnia-Herzegovina, although not condemned, are being treated with caution by the ecclesiastical authorities. Nevertheless, each continues to attract large numbers of pilgrims. In exercising caution when dealing with new phenomena, the Church remains alert to the possibility of fraud, self-deception, or demonic trickery. This caution protects the interests of pilgrims.

Meanwhile, as in the earliest days, Rome and the Holy Land remain among the most popular pilgrimage destinations, although the troubled political situation in the Middle East has inevitably curtailed the flow of pilgrims there.

From 1300 the popes have regularly proclaimed Jubilee years, in which pilgrims to Rome can gain a plenary indulgence upon the usual conditions. The custom had its origin in Old Testament days when, in seven yearly cycles, debts were cancelled and bondsmen freed. Today, jubilee years normally take place at each quarter of a century. The most recent Jubilee was in the year 2000, when millions of pilgrims traveled to Rome and millions more gained the indulgence by visiting designated churches in their home dioceses.

PILLAR, OUR LADY OF THE

A Marian image and shrine near Zaragoza, Spain.

The simple wooden statue features Our Lady holding the Christ Child, who holds a bird in his hand. It stands on a stone (jaspar) pillar about six feet high. An ancient tradition says St. James the Apostle journeyed to Spain in 40 A.D to spread the Gospel. The tradition maintains that as he paused to pray beside the River Ebro, Our Lady, who was still in Jerusalem, appeared to him and seven companions. She offered words of encouragement and requested a chapel to be built at that spot, leaving the column as a proof of her appearance. The present church dates from the seventeenth century. Although there is no evidence for the devotion before the twelfth century, it holds a treasured place in Spanish piety. The Feast of Our Lady of the Pillar is celebrated there on September 12.

PIOUS ASSOCIATION — See CONFRATERNITY.

PIOUS FOUNDATION

A collection of goods, including money, that is intended for the pastoral apostolate, charitable apostolate, or other work of the Church, established by competent authority.

PIOUS FUND

A special fund created by the seventeenth-century Jesuit missionaries, who evangelized northwestern Mexico.

The fund was eventually confiscated by the Mexican government and only paid back to the Church in the nineteenth and twentieth centuries.

PIOUS UNION — See CONFRATERNITY.

PIOUS UNION OF THE APOSTOLATE OF THE SICK — See APOSTOLATE OF THE SICK, PIOUS UNION OF THE.

PIOUS UNION OF PRAYER

An association established in 1898 that publishes the *St. Joseph's Messenger* and *Advocate of the Blind* quarterly.

The group counts some fifteen thousand members in both the United States and Canada and accepts prayer requests by mail or phone.

PIOUS UNION OF ST. JOSEPH — See **ST. JOSEPH, PIOUS UNION OF**.

PIOUS WILL

A donation of temporal goods, money, or other objects to the Church with a stipulation that it be used for a specific cause or that Masses or prayers be offered in return.

PLAIN CHANT

Also called "plain song."

It is an ancient monodic chant consisting of an unaccompanied melodic line, usually sung with Latin texts, used within the liturgy of the Church.

POINSETTIA

A plant associated with Christmas.

A native of Central America, the poinsettia has come to be widely used in churches and homes at Christmas because the flaming star of its red bracts is seen as symbolic of the star of Bethlehem. In Mexico, the flower is called the "flower of Holy Night."

Joel Roberts Poinsett (1851), the U.S. ambassador to Mexico from whom the flower received its name, brought this flower with him back to his home in South Carolina. Its origin is explained by a charming Mexican legend. A poor little boy went to church on Christmas Eve in sadness because he had no gift to bring to the Holy Child. He knelt humbly outside the church and prayed fervently and with tears, assuring Our Lord how much he wished to offer Him a lovely present, telling Him that he was poor and afraid to approach with empty hands. When the child rose from his knees, he saw a green plant with gorgeous blooms spring up at his feet. The Poinsettia is a prolific bloomer and has spread throughout the United States.

POMPEII, OUR LADY OF THE ROSARY OF

A Marian image and devotion dating to the late nineteenth century and Blessed Bartolo Longo, who commented: "There is something about that picture which impresses the soul not by its artistic perfection but by a mysterious charm which impels one to kneel and pray with tears."

While visiting the valley of Pompeii on business in 1872, Longo was shocked and filled with great pity at the ignorance, poverty, and lack of religion of the inhabitants of the area. He promised Our Lady to promote the faith and the devotion to her Rosary there.

In order to encourage the people, he determined to acquire a picture of Our Lady with her rosary. A Dominican sister offered him a large painting which had

Our Lady of the Rosary of Pompeii

na ... I hesitated whether to refuse the gift or to accept."

Seeing his hesitation, the sister urged him to take it, predicting that it would work miracles. Longo accepted the gift and made arrangements to transport it. It arrived wrapped in a sheet on top of a load of manure.

The first response was disappointment, so Longo had an artist refurbish it and ornament it with diamonds donated by the faithful. The Virgin was given a crown and the painting was mounted on marble. Immediately on its exposition, the picture became a veritable fountain of miracles. In less than ten years, more than 940 cures were reported at the shrine. Today, the pilgrims still flock to the shrine, around which one of the largest centers of social work in the world flourishes.

been bought at a junk shop for three francs.

Blessed Bartolo himself described the picture, which was dilapidated, wrinkled, soiled, and torn by saying: "Not only was it worm-eaten, but the face of the Madonna was that of a course, rough country woman ... a piece of canvas was missing just above her head ... her mantle was cracked. Nothing can be said of the hideousness of the other figures. St. Dominic looked like a street idiot. To Our Lady's left was a St. Rose. This latter I had changed later into a St. Catherine of Sie-

PONTMAIN, OUR LADY OF

A Marian devotion to Our Lady of Hope.

The devotion is based on apparitions of the Blessed Mother reported by six children near an old barn in Pontmain, France, in 1871. The children said Mary called herself the "Madonna of the Crucifix," and gave the world a message of hope through prayer and the cross. There is now a minor basilica on the spot.

The seers at Pontmain ranged in age from twenty-five months to twelve years. Although about sixty adults gathered, they were unable to see anything. The demeanor of the children made it plain that they did, indeed, see something. The Virgin appeared in a blue robe seeded with golden stars. Her hair was covered with a black veil and she wore a golden crown with a red line about the middle.

During the several phases of the three-and-a-half-hour apparition, writing appeared which the oldest children spelled out to the adults. The first sentence was "But pray, my children." The next writing spelled out "God will hear you in a short time." Then an invisible hand spelled out "My Son permits Himself to be moved."

Then, the beautiful Lady appeared sad and recollected, and a large bloody cross with the words "Jesus Christ" appeared in front of her. She took it in her hands and seemed to pass it to the children. The red crucifix disappeared and small white crosses appeared on each of her shoulders. Again, the Lady lowered her hands and smiled at the children. The children cried out, "Look, she is smiling — she is smiling." Slowly, the apparition dissolved.

In the United States, the Oblates of Mary Immaculate are in charge of this devotion.

(See also **HOPE, OUR LADY OF.**)

POOR BOX

Sometimes called the alms-box.

It is a slotted box to collect alms for the needy and was found in churches from the earliest days of Christianity.

POOR CHILD JESUS

An image of Christ and an emphasis on ministry to children in poverty dating back to nineteenth-century France and a dream by a girl named Clare Fey.

She reported that in it she saw "the Poor Child Jesus." As an adult, she founded the Order of the Sisters of the Poor Child Jesus.

POOR SOULS

A reference to the souls in purgatory, although the phrase "poor souls" has no official Church sanction.

The Church teaches that they cannot pray for themselves but can be helped through the prayers of the saints in heaven and the faithful on earth.

(See also **DULIA.**)

PORTABLE ICON

A small painting.

Portable icons were popular from the thirteenth to sixteenth centuries and are still common among members of the Eastern Church.

Some, carved from sandstone, slate, bone, or shale were made to be worn as pectoral amulets. Others were carved and enclosed in small metal protective coverings to be worn about the neck. Some of the portable icons were made in the form of a triptych (*skladen*). Folding icons consisting of a central panel with two, four, or more side leaves were widely used in medieval Russia, and were carried by their owners when traveling as a substitute for domestic iconostases. Miniature icons were made which were intended to be worn around the neck and were therefore fitted with loops on the headpieces. These were often donated to churches and monasteries, either as *ex voto* appendages to venerated icons or under the wills of their owners after their deaths.

(See also **ICON**.)

PORTIUNCULA

Francis Bernadone was praying in the church of San Damiano one day when he heard an image of the crucified Christ speak to him. "Go, Francis, and repair my house, which as you see if falling into ruin." Taking these words literally, Francis sold some of his father's goods and used the money to repair the church. The little chapel the saint restored, called the Portiuncula, stands today inside the great church of St. Mary of the Angels. The cell in which the saint died is preserved under the bay of this basilica's choir.

(See also **ST. FRANCIS OF ASSISI**.)

POSADAS — See **ADVENT PLAYS**.

POTTER'S FIELD

A common traditional name for the burial ground of paupers.

It is a reference to the land bought with the money Judas received to betray Jesus (see Matthew 27:3-10).

POWER OF THE KEYS

A term referring to Jesus' giving Peter authority over the Church.

In conferring the role of leadership upon Peter, Our Lord said, "I will give you the keys of the kingdom of heaven, and whatever you bind on earth shall be bound in heaven, and whatever you loose on earth shall be loosed in heaven" (see Matthew 16:19). The power of the keys thus refers to the supreme authority and jurisdiction vested by Christ in the Apostles and their successors.

PRAGUE, INFANT JESUS OF — See **INFANT JESUS OF PRAGUE**.

PRAYER

The raising of the mind and heart to God in adoration, thanksgiving, reparation, and petition.

Prayer, which is always mental because it involves thought and love of God, may be vocal, meditative, private or personal, and public, social, or official. Its highest form is contemplation, a foretaste of the beatific vision. The official prayer of the Church as worshiping community is called the liturgy.

PRAYER BEFORE A CRUCIFIX — See CRUCIFIX, PRAYER BEFORE A.

PRAYER BOOK — See HORARIA; LITURGY OF THE HOURS; MISSAL.

PRAYER FOR THE FAITHFUL DE-PARTED

A traditional prayer for the dead.

One indulgenced version reads:

Eternal rest grant unto them, O Lord, and let perpetual light shine upon them. May their souls and the souls of all the faithful departed through the mercy of God rest in peace. Amen.

PRAYER FOR A HAPPY DEATH

Prayers and pious exercises asking for a happy death.

Among the most common is the sim-ple: "Jesus, Mary, and Joseph, I give you my heart and my soul. Jesus, Mary, and Joseph, may I die in your blessed company."

PRAYER FOR MANKIND

A title of a prayer ending the letter to the Corinthians written by St. Clement around the year 95.

One translation reads:

God of all flesh, who gives life and death, you who cast down the insolence of the proud and turn aside the scheming of men, be our help!

O, Master, appease the hunger of the indigent; deliver the fallen among us.

God, good and merciful, forget our sins, our wrongdoing and backsliding; take no account of the faults of your servants.

Give us concord and peace, as to all the inhabitants of the earth.

It is from you that our princes and those who govern us here below hold their power; grant them health, peace, concord, stability; direct their counsels in the way of goodness.

You alone can do all this and confer on us still greater benefits.

We proclaim it by the high priest

and master of our soul, Jesus Christ, by whom to you be all glory and power, now and in endless ages. (See also **ST. CLEMENT**.)

PRAYER FOR PEACE

A popular prayer commonly attributed to St. Francis of Assisi.

One version reads:

Lord, make me an instrument of your peace.

Where there is hatred, let me sow love.

Where there is injury, pardon.

Where there is doubt, faith.

Where there is despair, hope.

Where there is darkness, light.

And where there is sadness, joy.

O Divine Master, grant that I may not so much seek to be consoled as to console,

To be understood, as to understand,

To be loved, as to love,

For it is in giving that we receive,

It is in pardoning that we are pardoned,

And it is in dying that we are born to eternal life.

(See also **ST. FRANCIS OF ASSISI**.)

PRAYER FOR THE POPE

Any of a number of prayers for the Holy Father.

One reads:

Let us pray for N., our pope. May the Lord protect him and grant him length of days. Amen. May the Lord be his shield and deliver him from all harm. Amen. May the Lord give him happiness and peace all the days of his life. Amen.

PRAYER FOR UNITY OF CHRISTIANS

A prayer specially said to bring about unity among all Christians.

It reads:

Almighty and eternal God, you gather the scattered sheep and watch over those you have gathered. Look kindly on all who follow Jesus, your Son. You have marked them with the seal of one baptism; now make them one in the fullness of faith and unite them in the bond of love. We ask this through Christ our Lord. Amen.

(See also **OCTAVE OF PRAYER FOR CHURCH UNITY**.)

PRAYER FOR VICTORY IN BATTLE

A prayer composed by Pope Leo XIII (r. 1878-1903) and formerly said after some Masses.

(See also **ANGELS**.)

PRAYER FOR VOCATIONS (PRIESTLY AND RELIGIOUS)

Any prayer said to foster vocations to the priesthood and the religious life.

One popular one reads:

Lord, in your love for the Church, you provide bishops, priests, and deacons as shepherds for your people, and you call men and women to leave all things to serve you joyfully in religious life. May those whom you have raised up as servants of the Gospel and ministers for your altars show forth dedication and compassion. May those whom you have chosen to serve you as religious provide by their way of life a convincing sign of your kingdom for the Church and the whole world. We ask this through Christ Our Lord. Amen.

PRAYER IN PRAISE OF CREATED THINGS

Also known as the "Song of Brother Sun" and the "Canticle of the Creatures."

It is a prayer attributed to St. Francis of Assisi.

One version reads:

Most High Omnipotent, Good Lord.
Thine be the praise, the glory, the
honor, and all benediction.
To Thee alone, Most High, they are
due,

and no man is worthy to mention
Thee.

Be Thou praised, my Lord, with all
Thy creatures,
above all: Brother Sun, who gives the
day and lightens us therewith.
And he is beautiful, and radiant with
great splendor
of Thee, Most High, he bears
similitude.

Be Thou praised, my Lord, of Sister
Moon and the stars,
in the heaven hast Thou formed them,
clear and precious and comely.

Be Thou praised, my Lord, of Brother
Wind,
and of the air, and the cloud, and of
fair and of all weather,
by which Thou givest to Thy
creatures sustenance.

Be Thou praised, my Lord, of Sister
Water,
which is much useful and humble
and precious and pure.

Be Thou praised, my Lord, of Brother
Fire,
by which Thou hast lightened the
night,
and he is beautiful and joyful and
robust and strong.

Be Thou praised, my Lord, of our
Sister Mother Earth,

which sustains and hath us in rule,
and produces divers fruits with
    colored flowers and herbs.

Be Thou praised, my Lord, of those
    who pardon for Thy
love and endure sickness and
    tribulations.

Blessed are they who will endure it in
    peace,
for by Thee, Most High, they shall be
    crowned.

Be Thou praised, my Lord, of our
    Sister Bodily Death,
from whom no man living may escape,
woe to those who die in mortal sin.

Blessed are they who are found in
    Thy most holy will,
for the second death shall not work
    them ill.

Praise ye and bless my Lord, and give
    Him thanks,
and serve Him with great humility.

PRAYER OF THE FAITHFUL

The intercessory prayers offered during Mass or at other liturgical functions.

Generally speaking, the proper formula of the Prayer of the Faithful consists of prayers for the Church, public authorities, the salvation of the world, the sick and deceased, and local needs.

PRAYER OF THE HEART — See JESUS PRAYER.

PRAYER OF QUIET — See QUIET, PRAYER OF.

PRAYER TO ST. JOSEPH FOR A HAPPY DEATH

A prayer said by the faithful to be prepared for death.

It reads:

St. Joseph, guide me on my way. Protect my soul from harm. And if this journey ends today, please come with Mary and her Son and take me to your Home to stay. Amen.

PRAYER TO ST. JOSEPH, PATRON OF THE CHURCH

A prayer of Blessed Pope John XXIII to St. Joseph as patron of the Church.

It reads:

O St. Joseph! Always be our protector. May your inner spirit of peace, of silence, of good work, and of prayer for the cause of Holy Church always be an inspiration to us and bring us joy in union with your blessed Spouse, our most sweet and gentle and Immaculate Mother, and in the strong yet tender love of Jesus, the glorious and immortal King of all ages and peoples. Amen.

PRAYER TO ST. JOSEPH, PATRON OF WORKERS

A prayer of Pope St. Pius X to St. Joseph as patron of workers.

It reads:

Glorious St. Joseph, pattern of all who are devoted to toil, obtain for me the grace to toil in the spirit of penance, in order thereby to atone for my many sins.

To toil conscientiously, putting devotion to duty before my own inclinations.

To labor with thankfulness and joy, deeming it an honor to employ and to develop, by my labor, the gifts I have received from Almighty God.

To work with order, peace, moderation, and patience, without ever shrinking from weariness and difficulties.

To work, above all, with a pure intention and with detachment from self, having always before my eyes the hour of death and the accounting which I must then render of time ill-spent, of talents unemployed, of good undone, and of my empty pride

in success, which is so fatal to the work of God.

All for Jesus, all though Mary, all in imitation of you, O Patriarch Joseph! This shall be my motto in life and in death. Amen.

PRAYER, ATTITUDES, AND STANCES

The traditional postures in which Christians pray, including kneeling, sitting, standing, and lying face down.

The earliest stances adopted by Christians seem to have been adopted from the Greek and Roman religions. The supplicant stood with his palms upward and arms outstretched either in front of the body or, more commonly, held upward. A variation of this was what is known as the *orans* position, where the arms are bent at the elbows but still held upward. By the third century, Christians were also praying with their arms crossed over the breast. Celtic monks sometimes lay prone on the floor with their arms outstretched in the form of a cross. Standing or kneeling with the arms outstretched was another posture for prayer and one that in many religious orders was done as a penitential exercise. The most common form today, in which the hands are placed flat against each other with the fingers pointing upward, seems to date from about the ninth century.

PRAYING AROUND THE CHURCH

A European custom of walking through the churchyard sprinkling the graves with holy water and saying prayers for the souls of the departed. This is a private and non-liturgical substitute for the ancient Asperges procession.

PRAYING FOR THE DEAD

A practice dating back to the early Church.

As the Second Vatican Council's "Dogmatic Constitution on the Church" explains: "In full consciousness of this communion of the whole Mystical Body of Jesus Christ, the Church in its pilgrim members, from the very earliest days of the Christian religion, has honored with great respect the memory of the dead; and, 'because it is a holy and a wholesome thought to pray for the dead that they may be loosed from their sins' (2 Maccabees 12:46) she offers her suffrages for them" (n. 50).

The Order of Christian Funerals affirms the value of praying for the departed: "The Church through its funeral rites commends the dead to God's merciful love and pleads for the forgiveness of their sins. At the funeral rites, especially at the celebration of the Eucharistic Sacrifice, the Christian community affirms and expresses the union of the Church on earth with the Church in heaven in the one great communion of saints. Though separated from the living, the dead are still at one with the community of believers on earth and benefit from their prayers and intercession."

Sacred Scripture provides the foundation for the Catholic custom of praying for the dead. In the second century before Christ, the Jews came to believe that even if someone died in a state of sin which merited punishment, the destiny of the deceased could be altered by the prayers of the living.

The Second Book of Maccabees recounts that Judas Maccabeus and his men arranged for the burial of fellow soldiers who had died in sin. Because they were wearing amulets forbidden by the Mosaic Law, God justly struck them down. Judas, however, believed that this punishment in the afterlife was not definitive. He and his warriors "turned to supplication, praying that the sin that had been committed might be wholly blotted out" (see 2 Maccabees 12:42).

Judas collected money for sacrifice in the temple and had prayers offered for the dead. "For if he were not expecting that those who had fallen would rise again, it would have been superfluous and foolish to pray for the dead. But if he was looking to the splendid reward that is laid up for those who fall asleep in godliness, it was a holy and pious thought. Therefore he made atonement for the dead, so that they might be delivered from their sin" (see 2 Maccabees 12:44-46).

According to this inspired author of the Old Testament, those who had led good lives, despite occasional sin, could still be purified after their death. Through the prayer and sacrifice of others they could be rewarded with resurrection from the dead.

In the New Testament, the single specific reference to the apostolic practice of praying for the dead is St. Paul's entreaty for Onesiphorus: "May the Lord grant him to find mercy from the Lord on that Day" (see 2 Timothy 1:18). Here a living Christian intercedes for a deceased brother, asking God to be merciful to him on judgment day.

Aristides of Athens provides the earliest testimony to this pious custom. About the year 140 A.D., he gave this advice to believers: "If one of the faithful dies, obtain salvation for him by celebrating the Eucharist and by praying next to his remains."

A half-century later, *The Passion of Perpetua and Felicitas* relates a story describing the practice of praying for the departed. Condemned to death, Perpetua had a vision of her dead brother Dinocratus, who was experiencing great suffering. Because of her faith, she was confident that she could relieve him from his state of pain. Perpetua "prayed for him night and day, wailing and crying that [her] prayers be granted." A few days later, in a second vision, she saw that her brother had been delivered from his torment. Not only had she prayed for her brother, her prayers for him had been instrumental in alleviating his suffering.

By the fourth and fifth centuries, witnesses to offering prayers for the faithful departed abound. St. Cyril of Jerusalem wrote about the well-established custom of praying for the deceased during the Eucharistic Prayer. Explaining this practice to the newly baptized, he said: "We believe that it will be of very great benefit to the souls of those for whom the petition is carried up, while this holy and most solemn sacrifice is laid out."

In describing his last conversation with his mother, St. Augustine records her last request to her two sons: "Bury my body wherever you will; let not care of it cause you any concern. One thing only I ask you, that you remember me at the altar of the Lord wherever you may be" (*Confessions*, Book 9,11).

St. Augustine's own entreaty for his holy mother is a touching example of the believer's trust in the effectiveness of prayers for the faithful departed: "Forgive her too, O Lord, if ever she trespassed against you in the long years of her life after baptism. Forgive her, I beseech you; do not call her to account. Let your mercy give your judgment an honorable welcome, for your words are true and you have promised mercy to the merciful" (*Confessions*, Book 9, 13). Though Augustine left Monica's destiny to God alone, he was convinced that his prayers could hasten the day when his mother's soul would enter the heavenly Jerusalem.

Innumerable graffiti and markings in the catacombs and other ancient places of Christian burial confirm the antiquity of the custom of praying for the dead. Engraved on these ancient stones are supplications in which the departed beg for the prayers of their loved ones who are still alive. These inscriptions not only give expression to faith and hope in eternal life but also show the belief that union with God is impeded by sin. The prayers of the living express the confidence that God will purify the departed according to their need.

According to our historical sources, this practice of praying for the dead began even before the reasons for doing so were clearly formulated. Christians assumed that the departed could be aided by the prayers of the faithful on earth. This custom necessarily implied belief in the possibility of some purification for the soul after death. "The early Church," writes Edmund Fortman, "Did not seem to be very clear about where these were or how prayer would help them, but she definitely knew that prayer and the Mass could be of benefit for these faithful Christians."

Official Church teaching on praying for the dead is most fully summarized in statements of the Council of Florence (1439) and the Council of Trent (1563). At Florence, the Church formulated her teaching on the value of praying for the faithful departed, linking this practice with the doctrine of purgatory. "But if they die [after Penance] truly repenting in charity before making satisfaction by worthy fruits for what they have done or omitted to do, their souls are purged after death ... by the punishments of purgation and purification. The intercession of the living faithful is effective in lessening this punishment, by the sacrifice of the Mass, prayer, almsgiving, and other pious works which the faithful are wont to do."

From the earliest centuries until the Protestant Reformation in the sixteenth century, praying for the dead went unchallenged. The Reformers, however, denied the doctrine of purgatory and the accompanying teaching of praying for the dead, holding them to be Catholic inventions. Deliberately opposing these denials, the Fathers at Trent reasserted official teaching by solemnly defining both the existence of purgatory and the value of prayer for the deceased. The Catholic Church teaches, they said, that "there is a purgatory, and that the souls detained therein are aided by the suffrages of the faithful and chiefly by the acceptable sacrifice of the altar."

The Fathers at Vatican II reaffirmed Catholic doctrine on the practice of praying for the departed.

According to Church tradition, how we pray tells us what we believe. In 1979, the Vatican's Letter "Certain Questions Concerning Eschatology" resolutely recalled that the Church's prayer life is a point of departure for doctrine. In examining new theories dealing with what happens between the death of a Christian and the general resurrection, the Congregation for the Doctrine of the Faith stated: "The Church excludes every way of thinking or speaking that would render meaningless or unintelligible her prayers, her funeral rites and the religious acts offered for the dead" *Recentiores episcoporum Syndoti*, n. 4). Praying for the dead is anchored in the Church's profession of faith (International Theological Commission, p. 425).

Such prayer sheds light on what the Church believes about the "possibility of a purification of the elect before they see God, a purification altogether different from the punishment of the damned" (*Recentiores episcoporum Syndoti*, n. 4). No binding doctrine exists, however, regarding purgatorial fire, its duration, or the kind and intrinsic nature of its punishment.

PRAYING TO THE DEAD

In earlier centuries, whenever the question was raised whether the faithful could pray not only for the souls in purgatory but also to them, theologians answered negatively. Yet the spiritual solidarity of the Mystical Body raises the question whether those in purgatory can pray for us, as the saints in heaven do. Can these souls, unable to help themselves, help those on earth?

Although the Church has no official prayers to the poor souls and has not officially encouraged them, she has never condemned this practice (Bastian, p. 569). Two theological arguments support this custom. First, the spiritual interchange within the communion of saints speaks in its favor. Second, though not yet in heaven, those in purgatory are truly friends of God. United as they are in the one body of Christ with many members (see Romans 12:4), it is reasonable to maintain that the departed can reciprocate the love shown to them by praying for those on earth.

PRECIOUS BLOOD

A reference to the blood of Christ.

The Feast of the Most Precious Blood (July 1) was instituted by Blessed Pope Pius IX in thanksgiving for his return to Rome from Gaeta after the revolution of 1848. In 1960, Blessed Pope John XXIII approved the Litany of the Precious Blood.

In the early 1800s, St. Gaspar del Bufalo began to preach and widely spread the devotion to the Precious Blood. This apostle of the Precious Blood founded an order of missionary preachers known as the Society of the Precious Blood. Under St. Gaspar's influence, Blessed Maria de Mattias founded an apostolic order of sisters under the title of Adorers of the Blood of Christ. Since that time, thirteen more Institutes have been established in the Church under the title of the Most Precious Blood of Jesus.

PRECIOUS BLOOD HEART

An emblem of the Confraternity of the Precious Blood.

It consists of a small heart made of red cloth. On one side, a sunburst haloes the crucified figure of Our Lord. Above the crucifix is the name of the confraternity; about the foot are the words "We beseech Thee help Thy servants whom Thou hast redeemed with Thy Precious Blood." On

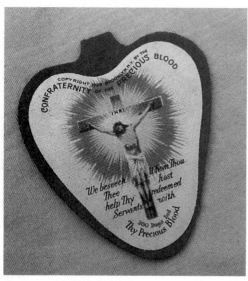

Precious Blood Heart

the back of the heart is a red drop of the Precious Blood on a white background with the saying of Pope Pius IX: "Place on thy heart one drop of the Precious Blood of Jesus and fear nothing." American headquarters for the Confraternity of the Precious Blood is at the cloistered monastery of the Precious Blood sisters in Brooklyn, New York.

(See also **CONFRATERNITY**.)

PRESENTATION IN THE TEMPLE

The February 2 feast commemorating the presentation of Jesus in the Temple, according to prescriptions of Mosaic law (see Leviticus 12:2-8; Exodus 13:2; Luke 2:22-32) and the purification of Mary forty days after his birth.

The Greek Church calls the feast *Hypapante*, "the Meeting" or "Encountering." In the Latin Church and in Rome during the seventh century, it ranked after the Assumption as the foremost Marian feast and was called the Purification of Mary. Its orientation today is more explicitly Christological. The feast is also called Candlemas, from the practice of blessing candles and carrying them in procession on that day, a custom that began around the eleventh century.

In a charming Mexican custom, this is the day the people literally bring Baby Jesus to the temple. Most Mexican Catholic homes have a treasured image of the

The Presentation — Dressing of Jesus

Child Jesus on the family altar. Annually, they sew or purchase new clothes for the statue. On February 2, the families take the image dressed in its new finery to the priest at church to be blessed

PRESENTS, CHRISTMAS

A Christian tradition adapted from the Roman custom, called *strenae*, of exchanging gifts at the beginning of the new year. This custom remained among the French peoples up to the present century under the name *etrennes*. In some countries, gifts are presented on St. Nicholas's Day (December 6), New Year's Day (January 1), or Epiphany (January 6).

At the advent of Christianity, like so many other pagan customs, the gift-giving custom was adapted, spread and became a part of the actual Christmas celebration. Christians presented gifts to their friends at Christmas in honor of the Baby Jesus. Thus, the gift became two — a gift for their friend and a gift for God because it was given in honor of his Son.

In Germany, the packages of Christmas gifts presented to children were called "Christbundles." They contained sweets, toys, and useful things. In medieval times in Britain, the priests emptied the alms boxes in all churches on the day after Christmas and distributed the gifts to the poor. In imitation of this practice, many people of the working class kept their own personal boxes of earthenware and stored their savings there all year. At Christmas, they received the last flood of coins from patrons, customers, and friends. The day after Christmas, they broke the boxes and counted the money. Eventually, this custom of giving and accepting presents became known as "boxing" and December 26 is still known as "boxing day" in Britain.

Christmas gift-giving in American is a combination of two old European customs: the gift giving of St. Nicholas, who left small gifts in stockings on the eve of his feast, and the gifts the children found under the tree on Christmas Day, which they believed were brought by the Christ Child.

In most European countries, the Child Jesus was the gift bringer. He came with angels during the night to decorate the tree and leave presents for the children of the household. Family celebrations included the reading of the Christmas Gospel, prayers and singing of hymns before the gifts were opened. In Spanish-speaking countries, a crib scene was set up with an empty manger. The Christ Child brought gifts for the children, and his image was found in the manger on Christmas morning. It Italy, Lady Befana, a sort of fairy queen, brings the children's presents on January 6, Epiphany.

In Russia, a legendary old grandmother named Babushka is the gift bringer. There, the children are told that when the Magi were on the way to Bethlehem, Babushka misdirected them on purpose, delaying their visit to the newborn Savior. She repented of her unkindness and on Christmas Eve goes about looking for the Christ Child and taking gifts to all the children in his name.

Christkindl is the diminutive name of the Christ child, gift bringer in Germany. this custom came to America with the German immigrants in the middle of the last century, but *Christkindl* was gradually adapted in the form of Kris Kringle, or Santa Claus.

St. Nicholas was one of the major, most popular and beloved saints of pre-Reformation Europe. The celebration of his feast, including his gift bringing, had spread to most parts of Europe. After the Reformation, many countries abolished his feast and forbade veneration of the saint. A "Christmas Man" was substituted for the saint, and soon the cult of St. Nicholas was forgotten in many countries.

The memory of St. Nicholas was impossible to obliterate in Holland, however, because for centuries this nation of seafarers had also venerated him as the patron of their ships. A statue of the saint was often the figurehead on the prow of Dutch ships. When the Calvinists tried to eradicate the saint and substitute the Nordic Christmas Man, they succeeded only in obliterating the religious details of his past. Sinter Klaus, dressed in his bishop's ornaments, still arrives mounted on a white charger to visit little children on the eve of his feast.

Sinter Klaus emigrated to America with the Dutch settlers and continued to visit the children, filling their wooden clogs with his presents. After British settlers founded New York, they found the kindly bishop more appealing than their own Father Christmas, especially because the bishop brought gifts for the children.

The Dutch pronunciation of his name became Americanized to Santa Claus, and he lost his bishop's robes and donned the secular dress of Father Christmas, although he kept his original colors. His visit was transferred from December 6 to Christmas

Eve, and he acquired his home and work factory at the North Pole, his sleigh, reindeer, and the custom of sliding down the chimney from the Christmas Man. He retained the practice of placing his gifts in the children's shoes or stockings.

In the nineteenth century, the Christmas custom of Santa Claus spread throughout the United States. As the country grew more prosperous and more secular, the presents at Christmas grew more expensive and elaborate.

Today, merchandizing, beginning at Thanksgiving, has obscured much of the holy and religious significance of Christmas. The holiday hysteria has so pervaded the season that many non-Christians have adapted their own religious celebrations at this time of year and have adopted the custom of Santa Claus and his gift-giving. Customs that crossed the ocean to our shores have been altered and by the middle of this past century were returned to Europe in their altered form, changing the face of the celebrations they initially stemmed from.

All the original Christian gift-giving customs denoted goodwill on the Christ Child's birthday. "Truly I say to you, as you did it to one of the least of my brethren, you did it to me." (see Matthew 25:40).

The Catholic heritage of Christmas customs began not with shopping and elaborate parties, but with simplicity and religious significance.

PRETZEL

A traditional Lenten food.

During Lent, Christians in the Roman Empire made a special dough with flour, salt, and water only, because fat, eggs, and milk were forbidden. This was shaped in the form of two arms crossed in prayer. The little breads were called "little arms." The Latin word was changed by the Germans to the term *brezel* or *prezel* which became in English "pretzel." The oldest known picture of a pretzel is found in a fifth-century manuscript. From medieval times to the present, these breads remained an item of Lenten food in many parts of Europe, and in some cities were distributed to the poor during Lent.

PRIE-DIEU

French for "pray God."

It is a kneeler or bench suitable for kneeling while at prayer.

PRIME

Literally "first," from the Latin title of this part of the Divine Office, *ad primam*, "at the first hour of the day."

Prime began in monastic communities as an additional prayer before the morning work period. In the reform of the Divine Office following Vatican II, Prime was suppressed and the obligation to pray it was removed. However, some monastic communities continue to use the Office of Prime.

PRINCE OF PEACE
A title for Christ.

It is based on the Old Testament: "For to us a child is born, / to us a son is given; / and the government will be upon his shoulder, / and his name will be called / 'Wonderful Counselor, Mighty God, Everlasting Father, Prince of Peace.' / Of the increase of his government and of peace / there will be no end, / upon the throne of David, and over his kingdom, / to establish it, and to uphold it / with justice and with righteousness / from this time forth and for evermore" (see Isaiah 9:6-7).

PRINCES OF THE APOSTLES
A traditional name for Sts. Peter and Paul, whose feast day is June 29.

Both were martyred during the persecution of Nero (r. 54-68). Their deaths have been commemorated since the early Church.

(See also ST. PAUL; ST. PETER.)

PRO MARIA COMMITTEE
A Marian organization.

It was established in 1949 to promote devotion to Our Lady of Beauraing. It's American headquarters are in Lowell, Massachusetts. It promotes an Association of Prayers called the Marian Union of Beauraing and distributes pamphlets, leaflets, a book, and medals.

(See also BEAURAING, OUR LADY OF.)

PRO SANCTITY MOVEMENT
An international organization.

It was begun in post-World War II Italy with the primary focus of spreading God's universal call to holiness.

PROCESSIONS
A traditional religious ritual.

Funeral processions may have originated in early Christianity before the end of the second century. Solemn processions are mentioned in the Roman liturgy of the fourth century. Processions for the translations of relics were common throughout the Middle Ages. Processions remain a part of Catholic life throughout the world today.

(See also TRANSLATION.)

PROFESSION OF FAITH
A public act by which personal belief is expressed through the recitation of a Creed.

By this means, a person attests to the

A Marian Procession in New York

Our Lady of Guadalupe Procession in Mexico

community his faith in the teachings of the Church. The recitation of the Nicene Creed at Mass is the most common form of profession of faith. On certain occasions, solemn professions of faith are required of persons who are about to undertake special responsibilities within the community of the Church.

PROMPT SUCCOR, OUR LADY OF

A Marian image and devotion; the principal patroness of New Orleans and Louisiana.

The Ursuline Monastery of New Orleans was founded under the auspices of Louis XV of France by a band of French Ursulines in 1727. Other sisters came from France, and in 1763 when Louisiana became a Spanish possession, Spanish sisters helped to carry on the work. In 1800, when Louisiana again became French territory, the Spanish sisters left for Cuba, and by 1803, only seven Ursulines remained to carry on the large number of social works the sisters managed. The superior appealed to a cousin of hers in France, Mother St. Michel, for aid and personnel.

Mother St. Michel was a zealous worker in her diocese, and her bishop did not want to lose her, so when she requested leave to go to the missions, he demanded she receive the directive to do so from the pope. This reply amounted almost to a definite "no" as the pope was in Rome, a virtual prisoner of Napoleon, and his jailors were under strict injunction not to allow him to correspond with anyone. Additionally, there was no reliable way of sending messages. Nonetheless, Mother St. Michel wrote her request.

One day at prayer, Mother felt inspired to call on the Queen of Heaven with these words, "O Most Holy Virgin Mary, if you obtain a prompt and favorable answer to my letter, I promise to have you honored in New Orleans under the title of Our Lady of Prompt Succor." Surprisingly, she received a prompt and favorable reply from the pope.

Mother and her companions arrived in New Orleans in December of 1810, bringing a statue she had commissioned in promise of her vow. The statue was installed in the convent chapel, and from that time veneration to Mary under the title of Our Lady of Prompt Succor has grown and spread across the country. Prayers before this statue are credited with saving the Ursuline convent from fire in 1812. The victory of Andrew Jackson's American forces over the British in the Battle of New Orleans, in 1815, is another favor attributed to the all-powerful intercession of Our Lady of Prompt Succor. By Papal decree in 1851, Pius IX authorized the celebration of the Feast of Our Lady of Prompt Succor. The statue was solemnly crowned by the papal delegate in 1895.

This was the first ceremony of this type in the United States. In l928, a new shrine in Our Lady's honor was consecrated and Our Lady of Prompt Succor was confirmed as the principal patroness of the City of New Orleans and the State of Louisiana.

PROPHECIES OF ST. MALACHY

St. Malachy was a twelfth-century monk (1095-1148) and bishop who reformed the Church in Ireland, linking it more closely with Rome. The saint, whose family name was O'Morgair, was born in Armagh in 1094. St. Bernard describes him as of noble birth and gives many interesting anecdotes about the saint, praising him for his zeal. Although not as well known as Nostradamus, he made a number of prophecies, including prophecies about the popes. According to tradition, he wrote his prophecy about the popes while in Rome and presented his vision to Pope Innocent II, but the prophecy was suppressed or forgotten in the papal archives. They were discovered and first published in Venice in 1595. Like those of Nostradamus, the prophecy of St. Malachy is in code. Only a few words, in Latin, are given for each pope. Serious doubts remain as to the true authorship of the prophecies and the prevailing view today seems to be that they are elaborate forgeries. The saint attempted a second journey to Rome

in 1148, but on arriving at Clairvaux he fell sick, and died in the arms of St. Bernard. Numerous miracles are recorded of him, and St. Malachy was canonized by Pope Clement (III), on July 6, 1199. His feast is celebrated on November 3, in order not to clash with the Feast of All Souls.

PROPHECY

The communication of divine revelation by inspired intermediaries, called prophets, between God and his people.

Old Testament prophecy was unique in its origin and because of its ethical and religious content, which included disclosure of the saving will of the Lord God for the people, moral censures, and warnings of divine punishment because of sin and violations of the Mosaic law and covenant, in the form of promises, admonitions, reproaches, and threats. Although Moses and other earlier figures are called prophets, the period of prophecy is generally dated from the early years of the monarchy to about a hundred years after the Babylonian Exile. From that time on, the written law and its interpreters supplanted the prophets as guides of the people.

Old Testament prophets are cited in the New Testament, with awareness that God spoke through them and that some of their oracles were fulfilled in Christ. John the Baptist is the outstanding prophetic figure in the New Testament. Christ never claimed the title of prophet for himself, although some people thought he was one. There were prophets in the early Church, and St. Paul mentioned the charism of prophecy in 1 Corinthians 14:1-6. Prophecy disappeared after New Testament times. The Book of Revelation is classified as the prophetic book of the New Testament.

In contemporary non-scriptural usage, the term is applied to the witness given by persons to the relevance of their beliefs in everyday life and action.

(See also **REVELATION**.)

PROVIDENCE, OUR LADY OF

A Marian image and devotion.

The original Our Lady of Providence was painted about the year 1580 by Scipione Pulzoni, a native of Gaeto, Italy. In 1664, it was placed in the Church of San Carlo ai Catinari, Rome and put in custody of the Barnabite Fathers. Our Lady of Providence is the patroness of Puerto Rico.

PSALTER, LAY — See HORARIA.

PURGATORY

A state of final purification following death and before entering heaven for those who have died in God's friendship but were only imperfectly purified.

Purgatory is a final cleansing of human imperfections before a soul is able to enter the joy of heaven. The souls in purgatory are members of the communion of saints.

(See also **ALL SOULS' DAY**.)

PURIFICATION

The previous title for the feast celebrated on February 2, the Presentation.

Under the old calendar, a feast of the Virgin Mary was held on February 2. It has now been replaced with the Feast of the Presentation in the Temple. The Law of Moses prescribed that every Jewish mother after giving birth to a boy child was to be excluded from attendance at public worship for forty days. At the end of that period, she had to present a yearling lamb for a holocaust and a pigeon for sin offering, thus purifying herself from ritual uncleanliness. In the case of poor people, two pigeons sufficed as an offering. The Gospel reports how Mary, after the birth of Jesus, fulfilled this command of the law, and how on the same occasion Simeon and Anna met the newborn Savior (see Luke 2: 22-38) The first historical description of the feast is given in the diary of Aetheria, about 390. From Jerusalem, the feast spread into the other churches of the Orient. The Armenians call it the Coming of the Son of God into the Temple. In the Coptic Rite it was termed Presentation of the Lord in the Temple. In the Greek Church it was known as the Meeting of the Lord, commemorating the meeting with Simeon and Anna. The Chaldeans and Syrians called it the Feast of the Old Man Simeon. In the Western Church it appeared first in the liturgical books of the seventh and eighth centuries under the title Purification of Mary. In 701, Pope Sergius prescribed a procession with candles for this and the other three feasts of Mary which were then annually celebrated in Rome. The ceremony of blessing the candles originated in the eighth century in the Carolingian Empire.

(See also **PRESENTATION IN THE TEMPLE.**)

PYSANKY — See **KRASHANKY, PYSANKY**.

Q

QUADRAGESIMA

The forty days of Lent, a penitential period in the Church.

QUADRAGESIMA OF ST. PHILIP

A pre-Christmas fast observed in the Eastern Church.

A custom since the Middle Ages, it begins in mid-November after the Eastern Feast of St. Philip. In the West, this Apostle's feast day is in May.

QUAESTOR

One designated to collect alms for the poor.

QUEEN OF ALL HEARTS MEDAL

A medal worn by the members of the Confraternity of Mary, Queen of All Hearts, a pious union established in 1899.

Pope St. Pius X erected the confraternity as an archconfraternity in 1913. The medal is heart-shaped. On the front is a design of the Queen of All Hearts Statuary group found in the Regina Dei Cuori Chapel in Rome. Mary is seated, holding the Child Jesus. Kneeling at her feet are St. Louis de Montfort and an angel. The book *True Devotion to Mary* is pictured under the group. On the obverse of the medal is a shield with a monogram of Mary surmounted by a crown. The shield is circled with a rosary entwined with a lily, symbolizing Mary's purity.

(See also **CONFRATERNITY**.)

QUEEN OF ALL SAINTS, MARY

A Marian title.

It is a reference to the place the Blessed Mother holds in heaven.

QUEEN OF THE AMERICAS GUILD, INC.

A guild founded in 1979 to establish an English-information center and retreat center near the Basilica of Our Lady of Guadalupe in Mexico City.

Mary, Queen of All Saints

QUEEN OF THE APOSTLES, OUR LADY

A Marian title and feast observed on the Saturday after the Ascension.

The title is first found in the oldest version of the Litany of Loreto about the end of the twelfth century. A feast requested by the Pallottine Fathers was approved in 1890. Under this title, Mary is venerated by a number of congregations that have special apostolic charisms; they include the Pallottines, the Claretians, and the Salvatorians.

QUEEN OF THE CLERGY, OUR LADY

A Marian title.

It is especially devoted to the Fraternity of Mary, a priestly association established to provide for the ongoing spiritual, intellectual, and fraternal formation and support of the local clergy under the patronage of Our Lady, Queen of the Clergy.

QUEEN OF PEACE, OUR LADY

A Marian image and devotion.

An ancient statue of Our Lady Queen of Peace is venerated in the chapel of the Religious of the Sacred Hearts of Jesus and Mary in Paris, France. It is of carved wood, eleven inches tall, and depicts the Virgin holding her Son on her left arm. In her right hand she bears an olive branch, the symbol of peace.

Sixteenth-century records indicate the statue was owned by a noble French family. It was later given to the Duke de Joyeuse, who joined the Capuchin Order where he was known as Father Ange. The priest was devoted to Our Lady under this title because it was while praying in front of the image that he first felt the call to religious life. In appreciation for this great favor, he had a chapel built in her honor in the Capuchin house in Paris. Later the oratory was opened to the public. Eventually the image was placed in the niche above the outside door of the monastery, where it remained for nearly sixty years. For several years, a clear light illuminated the statue during the night. Many miracles began to be reported by intercession to Our Lady in front of the image.

Following Father Ange's death, the statue was moved to the chapel where he had been buried and miracles continued to be reported. After the chapel proved too small to contain the crowds, a new one was built. The statue remained there until 1790. During the French Revolution, the Capuchins were forced to abandon their monastery and gave the image into the keeping of a pious woman named Madame Pepin. At her death, she willed the statue to her widowed sister, Madame Violet Coipel. The statue then passed through many hands until it finally came to Madame Coipel. She gave the sacred image to Father Coudrin, the founder of the Congregation of the Sacred Hearts of Jesus and Mary, who was also her spiritual director. On her suggestion, he gave all rights of possession to the order.

The image was given a papal crown by Pope St. Pius X. Prayers in her honor were indulgenced by Blessed Pius IX and St. Pius X. Through the efforts of Father Coudrin's order, devotion to Mary under the title "Our Lady Queen of Peace" has spread worldwide.

Visionaries who reported seeing Mary at Medjugorge said she introduced herself as the Queen of Peace.

QUEENSHIP OF MARY

A Marian title dating back to the early fourth century, a reference to her preeminence and power.

In 1954, Pope Pius XII instituted the liturgical Feast of the Queenship of Mary, and issued the encyclical *Ad Coeli Reginam*, which concerned the royal dignity of Our Lady. Mary's queenship is one of love and service. The feast is now observed on August 22.

QUIET, PRAYER OF

A form of contemplation that cannot be achieved by human effort but is a gift from God, although it presupposes a life of virtue.

It directs the human will toward God and brings an experience of peace and heightened awareness of God's presence.

QUINCEAÑERA

A traditional Hispanic family celebration on a daughter's fifteenth birthday.

At Mass, the young woman renews her baptismal vows, promising to remain faithful to God and to follow his will for her life, whether she marries, remains single, or becomes a religious. She also asks Our Lady to be her model, strength, and guide. The girl is traditionally dressed in a long dress almost as elaborate as a wedding gown but in her chosen colors.

During the ceremony, traditional gifts including a Bible, a rosary, a cross, a medal, and a crown are presented by the *padrinos* (godparents) and blessed by the priest. The girl's long lace mantilla is removed and replaced with a jeweled tiara or crown. Traditionally, there were fifteen attendants, but in recent years the number has been reduced in most places. Like weddings, *quinceañera* customs change from time to time.

After the Mass, a fiesta is held, with mariachi Musicians, an ample meal, and an elaborate cake. The girl who is celebrating her *quince años* dances the first dance with her father or another close male relative. Then all, from youngest to oldest, join in the fun and festivities.

The elaborate celebration has been cause for some controversy, primarily due to the costs. However, the system of *padrinos*, who shoulder the costs for various parts of the festivities, offsets the cost to the family.

QUINQUAGESIMA

The traditional name for the Sunday before the first Sunday in Lent.

The first Sunday in Lent was known as *Quadragesima*, "forty," to mark the forty-day fast. In the monastic communities there was apparently the wish to extend the fast, and the first evidence of this seems to be the Council of Orléans in 511. Later, the *Sexagesima*, or sixtieth, and the *Sep-tuagesima*, seventieth, were established. On that day the *Alleluia* ceased to be used at Mass until Easter. The custom spread throughout the Church in the eighth century.

QUMRAN HYMN BOOK

A testimony of the daily prayer life of the early Christians is found in one of the famous Dead Sea scrolls. In the Hymn Book of the Qumran community, first century B.C., the author mentions the daily exercise of prayer in the morning, about noon, and in the evening. In addition, he speaks of three additional prayer times during the night.

R

RACCOLTA

A book containing prayers and pious exercises to which the popes have attached indulgences.

The *Raccolta* was first published at Rome in 1807 by Telesforo Galli, one of the consultors of the Congregation of Indulgences. The editions of 1877, 1886, and 1898 were official publications of the Sacred Congregation of Indulgences and Holy Relics. The *Raccolta* contained, in an arranged, convenient order, the prayers, novenas, pious practices, etc., to which general indulgences had been attached, as well as the decrees and rescripts granting the indulgences, and the conditions requisite for gaining them.

Today, the *Raccolta* has been replaced by publication of the *Enchiridion Indulgentiarum*, or *Handbook of Indulgences: Norms and Grants*, just as the Apostolic Penitentiary carries on the work previously handled by the Congregation of Indulgences.

(See also **INDULGENCE**.)

RAISING OF THE CROSS

An ancient Mexican custom called *Levantamiento de la Cruz* in which a cross made of wood or iron is taken to the church, blessed, and then taken to the cemetery in order to conclude the rites and prayers that accompany the death of a beloved one.

This raising of the cross is a reminder that death is provisional and that Christ has conquered death.

RANDAN

The Christian population of Malta has adopted the Muslim term *Randan* for Lent.

READING SACRED SCRIPTURES

It is an indulgenced practice when the Christian faithful read Sacred Scripture with the veneration due God's Word and as a form of spiritual reading.

REAL PRESENCE

A reference to Christ in the Eucharist.

It is the dogma of the Catholic Church teaching that when the bread and wine (matter) are consecrated (form) by a duly ordained priest who has the proper intention, the body, blood, soul, and divinity of Jesus Christ becomes really, truly, and substantially present — still under the appearances of bread and wine. Adoration is to be given to the Sacred Species.

(See also **EUCHARIST**.)

RECITING THE OFFICE FOR THE DEAD — See **OFFICE FOR THE DEAD, RECITING THE**.

RECONCILIATION, RITE OF — See PENANCE, SACRAMENT OF.

RED CROSS OF ST. CAMILLUS

A symbol worn by members of the Order of the Servants of the Sick, founded by St. Camillus de Lellis (1550-1614).

At the time of the order's founding, the red cloth cross on the black habit was regarded as an inspiration for the sick by reminding them of Christ's Passion, death, and Resurrection. Additionally, it reminded the priests and brothers who wore the habit of their dedication and solemn commitment of service to those who were ill.

Today, the Servants of the Sick carry on the work of St. Camillus in three hundred fifty houses, hospitals, clinics, and other health facilities in almost thirty countries. Members distribute small simple red cloth crosses worldwide. A special blessing was included in the Roman Ritual for the crosses.

RED SCAPULAR (PASSION)

A scapular based on the apparitions of Christ reported by Sister Apolline Andriveau, a Sister of Charity of St. Vincent de Paul, in 1846, in France.

The front panel features a crucifix, embellished with the other instruments of the Passion. A hammer and pincers in the upper left-hand corner symbolize penance

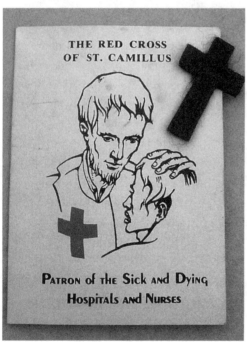

Red Cross of St. Camillus

Red Scapular of the Passion

and the need to pull sin from one's life to make room for the healing grace offered by the sacred wounds. In the upper right-hand corner three nails and the crown of thorns represent the mental and physical discipline that must go together in order for one to achieve integrity of spirit. Beneath the cross is a ladder that stands for the virtues by which one must ascend one's own cross in union with the redeeming cross of Christ. A crowing rooster symbolizes that the time for repentance is at hand. A spear reminds one of the need to pierce one's own heart and break it free from every attachment except God. Other symbols displayed are the scourges, the sponge, a water pot, and Veronica's veil. The red scapular of the Passion is promoted by the Archconfraternity of the Holy Agony.

(See also **SCAPULAR**.)

REGINA CAELI LAETARE

Latin for "Queen of Heaven, rejoice"; a hymn or prayer to Mary said or sung during the Easter season in place of the *Angelus*.

According to pious legend, Pope St. Gregory the Great (r. 590-604) heard angels singing the verses as the picture of Our Lady reputed to be painted by St. Luke reached the bridge crossing the Tiber River during a procession. The hymn, however, does not date from much before the year 1200. In 1743, Pope Benedict XIV instructed that it replace the *Angelus* as an Easter prayer.

One version reads:

O Queen of Heaven, rejoice, alleluia!
For he whom you were privileged to bear, alleluia!
Has risen as he said, alleluia!
Rejoice and be glad, O Virgin Mary, alleluia!
For the Lord has truly risen, alleluia!

Let us pray:

O God, you gave joy to the world through the Resurrection of your Son, our Lord Jesus Christ. Grant that we may obtain, through his Virgin Mother, Mary, the joys of everlasting life. Through the same Christ our Lord. Amen.

REGINA CLERI

Latin for "Queen of the Clergy."

Ancient title of Our Lady. An image under this title is at the graduate house of studies of the old North American College in Rome, now called Casa Santa Maria. A copy stands in the courtyard of St. Mary's Seminary in Houston, Texas.

RELICS

The physical remains and effects of saints, which are considered worthy of veneration inasmuch as they are representative of persons in glory with God.

In line with norms laid down by the Council of Trent and subsequent enactments, discipline concerning relics is subject to control by the Congregations for the Causes of Saints and for Divine Worship and the Discipline of the Sacraments.

The word *relic* come from the Latin *relinquo* for "I leave; abandon." There are three categories of relics. "First class" is a part of a saint's body. "Second class" is an item worn or used by a saint during his or her lifetime. And "third class" is an item that has been touched to a first-class relic. Usually, it is a bit of cloth. The document that accompanies a relic is often referred to as the authentics.

The earliest reference to relics is an account of the martyrdom of St. Polycarp, who was killed in 156.

After the fourth century, wherever possible, a church was erected over the grave of a martyr, with the altar immediately above. The space below and in front of the altar — generally beneath the level of the nave or sanctuary — was known as the *confessio*. With the construction of tomb-altars, the body or relics of the saint came to be placed immediately beneath the altar, or were built into a space between the supports. Today, the sepulcher is a small square or oblong opening or cavity of a fixed altar in which are placed relics of the saints.

By the fifth century, dismembering a body and dividing up the bones was considered an acceptable practice, because in the East, Christians believed the soul was totally present everywhere in the body and so every part was of equal worth. By the tenth century, relics were being placed in shrines and in receptacles (called *reliquaries*) in churches that became centers of pilgrimage.

Some relics, even among those that are well known, are of dubious origin. The veneration of a traditional relic can continue even if it cannot be authenticated. While some are almost certainly spurious, there is no need to assume deliberate fraud. Rather, honor given in good faith to a false relic is nevertheless profitable to the worshiper and in no way dishonors the saint. However, relics proven and known to be false must be withheld from the veneration of the people.

Relic of St. John Bosco

Various Relics

Abuses have occurred in all ages with regard to relics. In 1215, Canon 62 of the Fourth Lateran Council, inserted in the *Corpus Juris*, forbade relics to be sold or to be exposed outside of their cases or shrines, and prohibited the public veneration of new relics till their authenticity had been approved by the pope. Subsequent entries in Canon Law deal with abuses of the cult. The sale or traffic in relics is known as simony and is forbidden by Canon Law.

No Catholic is formally bound to the positive veneration of relics, but it was forbidden by the Council of Trent to say that such veneration ought not to be given.

RELICS OF CHRIST — See **CHRIST, RELICS OF**.

RELICS OF THE VIRGIN MARY — See **VIRGIN MARY, RELICS OF THE**.

RELIGIOUS RULE — See **RULE, RELIGIOUS**.

RELIQUARY

A receptacle, varying in size and shape, containing the relics of a saint or other sacred object.

Reliquaries date from the earliest Christian times. Small ampulae or jars which contained dust from the martyrs' graves or oil from the lamps which burned beside them are the first reliquaries. Rings and pendants hung about the neck, each containing relics, were also popular among the early Christians. Later, reliquaries in the form of cloth or metal purses came into style. Reliquaries in the form of a small house, church, or replicas of the part of the body of the saint enshrined in it were constructed of precious metal and ornamented with jewels. Sometimes an entire statue of the saint was constructed to hold a small relic.

During the Baroque period, entire bodies of saints were enclosed in glass or crystal reliquaries resembling caskets. Legislation by the Fourth Lateran Council in 1215 requires relics to be displayed in a reliquary. Today, most first class relics are enclosed in a small metal and glass container known as a theca.

A Casket Reliquary in a Church

A Crystal Casket Reliquary

RENEWAL OF BAPTISM PROMISES

The repeating of one's baptismal promises.

The renewal of baptismal vows is a part of the Easter Vigil liturgy.

REPARATION

To make amends to God for the ingratitude for and rejection of God by others.

REPARATION TO THE SACRED HEART, ACT OF

A prayer that reads:

Most loving Jesus,
how great is the love which you have
poured out upon the world.
How casual and careless is our
response!
Kneeling before you, we wish to atone
for the indifference and the slights
which pierce you to the heart.
R. Praise to the Heart of Jesus, our
Savior and our God.

We ask forgiveness for our own
shameful neglect.
We wish to make amends
for those who are obstinate in their
unbelief,
for those who turn away from the
light
and wander like sheep without a
shepherd,
and for those who have broken their
baptismal promises
and reject the gentle yoke of your law.
R. Praise to the Heart of Jesus, our
Savior and our God.

We wish to make amends for the sins
of our society:

for lust and degradation, for the
corruption of the young,
for indifference and blasphemy, for
attacks against your Church,
for irreverence and even sacrilege
against your love in this Blessed
Sacrament,
and for the public defiance of your
law.
R. Praise to the Heart of Jesus, our
Savior and our God.

These are the sins for which you died,
but now we share in your atonement
by offering on the altar in union with
you
the living sacrifice you made on the
cross,
joining to it the sufferings of your
Virgin Mother,
and those of all the saints and the
whole Church.
R. Praise to the Heart of Jesus, our
Savior and our God.

We promise faithfully
that by your grace
we shall make reparation for our own
sins
and for those of others
by a strong faith,
by holy living,
and by obedience to the law of the
Gospel,
whose greatest commandment is that
of charity.

R. Praise to the Heart of Jesus, our
Savior and our God.

We also promise to do our best
to discourage others from insulting
you
and bring those we can to follow you.
R. Praise to the Heart of Jesus, our
Savior and our God.

Jesus, Lord,
receive this loving act of homage
together with the prayers of our Lady,
who stood by the cross,
our model in reparation.
Keep us faithful, even to the point of
death,
give us the gift of perseverance,
and lead us all to our promised land
in heaven,
where you, with the Father and the
Holy Spirit,
live and reign for ever and ever.
Amen.
R. Praise to the Heart of Jesus, our
Savior and our God.

REQUIEM AETERNAM

Latin for "eternal rest."

It is a prayer that reads:

Eternal rest grant unto them, O
Lord. And let perpetual light shine
upon them. May their souls and the
souls of all the faithful departed,
through the mercy of God, rest in
peace. Amen.

REQUIEM MASS

The traditional name for the Mass of
Christian Burial.

It comes from the first words of an
opening prayer that begins with the Latin
words *Requiem aeternam dona eis, Domine* (Eternal rest grant unto him [her,
them], O Lord).

RESERVATION OF THE BLESSED
SACRAMENT

The practice of keeping the Blessed Sacrament in the tabernacle.

It is done for two reasons: 1) so that the
sick may receive Holy Communion, and 2)
for the adoration of the faithful. It also involves the removal of the Holy Eucharist
from the tabernacle at the conclusion of the
Mass of the Lord's Supper on Holy Thursday evening and the reposition of the Eucharist in a repository chapel.

RETABLOS

Traditional Mexican religious images
made by painting thin sheets of tin-plated
iron.

Anonymous artists produced thousands
of these paintings from the early nineteenth
to the early twentieth century.

The word *retablo* is derived from the
Latin *retro tabula* — "behind the (altar)
table." The artistic tradition of decorating the space behind the altar was import-

DOMENICO PONTICIELLO
MARIA MAJELLA
SANTANTIMO 26 SETTEMBRE
1902

Two Retablos

vow or in thanksgiving or petition for divine intervention, favors, or aid, and placed in a public shrine or church.

While the *retablo santo* ceased being produced around the beginning of this century, the *retablo ex-voto* tradition continues. Today, the *retablos* are considered highly collectible works of popular art.

(See also **EX VOTO**.)

RETREAT

Time taken for the purpose of devotion, prayer, and meditation to advance in the spiritual life. The word also designates a place where one can spend time in solitude to pray and reflect.

The practice of retreats predates Christianity. The forty days Christ spent in the

ed to the colonies along with the Catholic religious during Spain's conquests in the New World.

Retablos are of two types: *laminas* and *ex votos*. The *laminas*, or *retablos santos*, were intended for private devotion and were hung near home altars. A *retablo ex-voto* is a gift offered in completion of a

desert serves as the model for Christian retreats. Retreats were formally introduced during the Reformation era, and the Jesuits were the first to incorporate them into their rule of life. Sts. Francis de Sales and Vincent de Paul actively promoted retreats in the seventeenth century, and the practice of annual retreats became widespread in the nineteenth century. In recent years, the form and character of retreats have become more specialized and particular.

RETREAT OF ST. STANISLAUS — See ST. STANISLAUS, SPIRITUAL EXERCISES OF.

RETRIBUTION
The reward or punishment due to good or sinful actions.

However, retribution is normally associated with punishment for sin.

RETROUVAILLE
A weekend retreat for couples with troubled marriages.

Retrouvaille began in 1977 as a French-language weekend in Quebec, Canada. It was adapted into English in Ontario and revised to strengthen the content of the weekend and add post-weekend programs. It is now worldwide.

REVELATION
God's communication of himself.

It is through revelation that God makes known the mystery of his divine plan, a gift of self-communication that is realized over time by deeds and words, and most fully by the sending of his Son, Jesus.

Divine revelation is transmitted through two sources: Sacred Tradition and Sacred Scripture. As the 1965 "Dogmatic Constitution on Divine Revelation" (*Dei Verbum*) states: "Sacred Tradition and Sacred Scripture make up a single deposit of the Word of God, which is entrusted to the Church" (n. 10).

Number 9 of the same constitution summarizes clearly the relationship of these twin conduits of divine revelation and their importance for the life of the Church:

Sacred Tradition and Sacred Scripture, then, are bound closely together, and communicate one with the other. For both of them, flowing from the same divine well-spring, come together in some fashion to form one thing, and move toward the same goal. Sacred Scripture is the speech of God as it is put down in writing under the breath of the Holy Spirit. And Tradition transmits in its entirety the Word of God which has been entrusted to the Apostles by Christ the Lord and the Holy Spirit. It transmits it to the successors of the Apostles so that, enlightened by the spirit of truth, they may faithfully preserve, expound and spread it abroad by their preaching. Thus it comes about that the Church does not draw her certainty about all revealed truths from the holy Scriptures alone. Hence, both Scripture and Tradition must be accepted and honored with equal feelings and devotion and reverence.

The Church makes a clear distinction between divine revelation and private revelation. Private revelation is given by God to a person for his or her own benefit and the benefit of others as opposed to the universal revelation for all given to Israel and the Apostles.

Some private revelations have been approved by the Church. This only means they contain nothing contrary to faith and morals and that in addition there is sufficient evidence to justify belief in their authenticity. However, the Church does not and cannot impose belief in a private revelation and its contents either on an individual or on the faithful at large.

RING

Jewelry traditionally used to symbolize power or commitment.

The Christian use of wedding rings apparently developed from the Roman custom of betrothal rings. This custom was adapted in some religious orders of women who wear a ring indicative of their vows as a "bride of Christ." Their rings are conferred at the time of their solemn profession.

Episcopal rings are first mentioned as an official part of the bishop's insignia in the

Finger or Ring Rosary

early seventh century. The pope's ring is known as the Fisherman's Ring. It is a gold seal ring engraved with St. Peter in a boat and the pope's name around it. At the pope's death, it is ceremonially broken.

Rosary rings with ten beads to indicate a decade became popular in the fifteenth century; their popularity has revived in recent times. Today there are many styles of rings with Christian symbolism.

RINGS, JESUIT — See **JESUIT RINGS**.

RITE

A religious custom, usage, or ceremony.

In one sense, *rite* refers to the words and actions prescribed for a liturgical or sacramental act such as the Mass or baptism. In another, it has come to be synonymous with liturgy. In the Catholic Church, various rites have come about through the geographical, cultural, and political diversity that accompanied the spread and development of the Church. There are nine such rites in the Catholic Church: Roman, Mozarabic (Old Spanish), Ambrosian (Milanese), Byzantine, Chaldean, Alexandrian, Antiochene, Armenian, and Maronite.

RITE OF RECONCILIATION — See PENANCE, SACRAMENT OF.

RITUAL

A liturgical ceremony performed with words, gestures, and sacred objects under the auspices of the Holy See.

It is also a book authorized by the Holy See, containing the ceremonies and prayers used during sacred rites.

RIVERS, OUR LADY OF THE

A Marian image and devotion.

It dates back to the mid-twentieth century and Father Edward Schlattmann, pastor of St. Francis Church in Portage des Sioux, in the area just north of St. Louis, Missouri. Members of the Legion of Mary built a shrine to Our Lady of the Rivers as part of their invoking her aid to protect their area from flooding.

ROCKIES, OUR LADY OF THE

A Marian image and devotion.

The statue of Our Lady of the Rockies is ninety feet tall and is located outside Butte, Montana. The idea originated as an *ex voto* by Bob O'Bill in 1979, when he promised to erect the statue of Our Lady if Bob's wife, who was seriously ill at the time, recovered. Joyce O'Bill, Bob's wife, prefers that the monument's history be remembered as a symbol of all promises kept, not just one, a symbol of what can result when many people pool their talents and resources, and work in unity. Although the O'Bills are Catholic, many of the workers on the project were of other religions.

Finished in 1983, the statue is fabricated of sixty tons of steel. Painted white, her hands open wide as if in blessing on those in the town below. The statue is dedicated to Our Blessed Mother and to mothers everywhere.

(See also EX VOTO.)

ROGATION DAYS

Special days of penance and prayer, similar to ember days, that were replaced in 1969 by periods of prayer extending for one to several days.

The two times of rogation days were the Feast of St. Mark (April 25) and the Monday, Tuesday, and Wednesday before Ascension Thursday.

ROGATIONTIDE

The traditional name for three days following the fifth Sunday after Easter, a customary period to ask God's blessings on land and crops.

In earlier times, it consisted of the practice by a pastor and his parishioners of making a procession around the parish (known as the "beating of the bounds"). Typically, a statue of Our Lady was carried and stops were made at each cardinal point of the compass. This custom is now sometimes observed in Anglican parishes in the United States. Another name for Rogationtide was "gang week."

(See also EMBER DAYS.)

ROMAN RITE

A manner of celebrating the sacraments and other ecclesiastical ceremonies and the recitation of the Liturgy of the Hours authorized by the diocese of Rome and mandated for use in most dioceses of Western Catholicism.

The Roman Rite, altered somewhat by the Second Vatican Council, is the most widely used rite in Christendom.

ROMAN STATIONS

Churches within the city of Rome where the early popes celebrated Mass on special days, in time becoming a Lenten devotion.

Tradition has it that clergy and congregation assembled in one place and processed to another where the Holy Sacrifice of the Mass was offered. At the head of these processions, a relic of the true cross was carried aloft. This practice continues to the present day. Now, a list of which stational churches and on what days they will be used is published in advance.

RORATE MASS

An Advent custom in Austria, Switzerland, and Germany.

Families walked in the dark of the early morning, (carrying lamps, candles or, later, flashlights) to church, where Mass was celebrated and favorite Advent hymns were sung.

ROSARY

A form of mental and vocal prayer centered on mysteries or events in the lives of Jesus and Mary.

Its essential elements are meditation on the mysteries and the recitation of a number of decades of Hail Marys, each beginning with the Lord's Prayer. Introductory

Rosary Beads

The Five Sorrowful Mysteries
1. The Agony in the Garden
2. The Scourging at the Pillar
3. The Crowning of Thorns
4. The Carrying of the Cross
5. The Crucifixion

The Five Glorious Mysteries
1. The Resurrection
2. The Ascension
3. The Descent of the Holy Spirit
4. The Assumption
5. The Crowning of the Blessed Virgin

prayers may include the Apostles' Creed, an initial Our Father, three Hail Marys, and a Glory Be to the Father; each decade is customarily concluded with a Glory Be to the Father; at the end, it is customary to say the Hail Holy Queen and a prayer from the liturgy for the Feast of the Blessed Virgin Mary of the Rosary.

The mysteries of the Rosary, which are the subject of meditation, are:

The Five Joyful Mysteries
1. The Annunciation
2. The Visitation
3. The Nativity
4. The Presentation
5. The Finding in the Temple

The complete Rosary, also called the Dominican Rosary, consists of fifteen decades. In customary practice, only five decades are usually said at one time. Rosary beads are used to aid in counting the prayers without distraction. The Rosary originated through the coalescence of popular devotions to Jesus and Mary from the twelfth century onward. Its present form dates from about the fifteenth century. Carthusians contributed greatly toward its development; Dominicans have been its greatest promoters.

In 2002, Pope John Paul II marked the twenty-fourth anniversary of his election by signing the apostolic letter *Rosarium Virginis Mariae,* "The Rosary of the Virgin Mary." In it he suggested five new "mysteries of light": Christ's baptism in the Jordan, his self-manifestation at the wedding at Cana, his proclamation of the kingdom of God with his call to conver-

Indian Corn and Job's Tears Rosaries

the cross, at the beginning and the end of the chaplet. The *Requiem Eternam* and the Acts of Faith, Hope, and Charity are said on the large beads, and on the small beads is said "Sweet Heart of Mary, be my salvation."

(See also **CHAPLET; CONFRATERNITY.**)

sion, his Transfiguration, and his institution of the Eucharist.

ROSARY FOR THE DEAD

A chaplet dating back to the mid-nineteenth century and promoted by the Archconfraternity of Notre Dame du Suffrage. Also referred to as "Beads of the Dead."

The chaplet consists of four decades of ten beads commemorating the forty hours between Christ's death and his Resurrection. The rosary has a cross and a medal of the archconfraternity, representing the souls in purgatory. There may also be five introductory beads as found on the Dominican rosary.

Either the *De Profundis* (Psalm 130) or the Our Father and Hail Mary are said on

ROSARY OF OUR LADY OF SORROWS (SERVITE)

A chaplet focusing on the traditional Seven Sorrows of Mary.

Promoted by the Servite Order, it consists of seven groups of seven beads, each septet separated by a medal of one of the sorrows. At the end of the chaplet is a medal of Our Lady with her heart pierced with seven swords. A crucifixion scene is generally found on the obverse side.

Each mystery is introduced by a meditation to guide reflection as an Our Father and seven Hail Marys are prayed. The Rosary is concluded with three Hail Marys as an added petition for true sorrow and a desire to model one's life on the example of the life and faith of Our Lady.

(See also **CHAPLET; SEVEN SORROWS OF MARY.**)

ROSARY OF OUR LADY OF TEARS

A chaplet promoted by the Institute of the Missionaries of the Scourged Jesus since 1930, based on visions of Mary reported by the institute's co-founder, Sister Amelia.

The chaplet has forty-nine white beads, divided into seven parts by seven larger beads of the same color, similar to the Rosary of the Seven Sorrows of Mary. At the end, there are three more small beads and a medal of Our Lady of Tears.

One version of the chaplet prayers reads:

O crucified Jesus, we fall at Your feet and offer You the tears of the one who with deep compassionate love accompanied You on Your sorrowful way of the Cross. O good Master, grant that we take to heart the lessons which the tears of Your most holy Mother teach us, so that we may fulfill Your holy will on earth, that we may be worthy to praise and exalt You in Heaven for all eternity. Amen.

(On the large beads and the final three beads, say...)

V. O Jesus, look upon the tears of the one who loved You most on earth.
R. And loves You most ardently in heaven.

(On the small beads, say...)

V. O Jesus, listen to our prayers.

R. For the sake of the tears of Your most Holy Mother.

(On the medal, say...)

O Mary, Mother of Love, Sorrow, and Mercy, we beseech you to unite your prayers with ours so that Jesus, your Divine Son, to whom we turn, may hear our petitions in the name of your maternal tears, and grant us, not only the favors we now ask, but the crown of everlasting life. Amen. (See also **CHAPLET.**)

ROSE

A symbol of Mary.

This flower was long associated with Greek and Egyptian gods; during the Middle Ages, the Church began using it as a symbol for the Blessed Mother. A number of pious legends concerning Mary and roses date back to medieval times.

Our Lady of Guadalupe placed rare Castilian roses in St. Juan Diego's cloak as a sign of the truth of her presence. At Lourdes, France, St. Bernadette reported that Our Lady appeared to her, standing on a rosebush and with golden roses on her feet. Visionaries at LaSalette said Our Lady wore roses.

Roses and rose petals have often been blessed as sacramentals, a pious custom in Dominican churches on the Feast of the Holy Rosary. Roses are also associated with

St. Thérèse of Lisieux, the Little Flower, because of her promise to send a "shower of roses" from heaven. They are also associated with St. Rita of Cascia and St. Dorothy.

ROSEMARY

An herb associated with Mary since the Middle Ages.

In ancient Greece, students wore sprigs of rosemary in their hair to stimulate their memory. Later, the plant became symbolic of remembrance. Along with many other plants and herbs, during the middle ages the rosemary was rededicated to the Virgin. It became one of the best-loved herbs worldwide, is a symbol of love and fidelity, and was often worn at weddings. St. Thomas More wrote that he let this herb run wild all over his garden. It was the chosen emblem of English funeral wakes and burial grounds. In France, it was carried by mourners and thrown into the open grave on the coffin. The Spaniards revere the plant as one of the bushes that gave shelter to the Virgin on the flight to Egypt, and both in Spain and Italy it was considered a safeguard against witches and evil spirits. Legend holds that the Virgin dried her cloak on the plant, imparting the color of the sky to the flowers. The traditional Easter meal in Europe is lamb flavored with rosemary. The herb was laid in cradles to prevent nightmares. Rosemary was burned in churches as incense. Hungarian queen's water, a miraculous liquid for the cure of many illnesses including arthritis was an herbal cure popular for many years. Attributed to St. Elizabeth, Queen of Hungary, the recipe called for three parts of distilled brandy and two parts of the leaf and flower of rosemary.

ROSES, OUR LADY OF (BAYSIDE MOVEMENT)

A cult active near Bayside, New York, stemming from reported private revelations to Mrs. Veronica Leuken. The cult is prohibited by Church authorities.

ROYAL HOURS

A Holy Thursday night vigil celebrated in the East.

Originally known as the *Pannuchida* — meaning "all-night service" — it traditionally includes the reading or singing of the texts of the Passion arranged in twelve chapters with prayers, prostrations, and hymns after each chapter. Because the emperors in Constantinople attended the *Pannuchida*, it became known as the Royal Hours. In Russia, it was customary to carry home candles from the service and use them to light the lamps in front of family icons. Ukrainians traditionally celebrated the Royal Hours on Good Friday morning.

RUBRICS

Liturgical directives that guide the administration of the sacraments.

Rubrics may be either obligatory or directive (which allow for interpretation). The word *rubric* is derived from the Latin word meaning "red." The rubrics are written in red in the Missal so as to distinguish them from the text of the Mass.

RULE, RELIGIOUS

The basic regulations of a religious institute, encompassing its daily order and discipline.

S

SABBATINE PRIVILEGE

A reference to Mary's intercession associated with the Brown Scapular.

The Sabbatine Privilege contends that Mary will aid the souls of members of the Confraternity of the Blessed Virgin of Mount Carmel after their death by her continual intercession, by her suffrages and merits, and by her special protection, particularly on Saturday, which is the day especially dedicated by the Church to her. The pious tradition has often been misinterpreted to mean that scapular wearers, simply because they are wearing the scapular at the time of death, will be taken to heaven on the first Saturday after death. The Church teaches, and the Carmelite Rule affirms, that Jesus Christ is the only one who liberates a person from his or her sin.

In a recent letter to all the faithful, the provincial superiors of the Carmelites in the U.S. and Canada wrote: "Our Carmelite Family has been the custodian of one of the most popular sacramentals in Catholic devotional life, the Brown Scapular of Our Lady of Mount Carmel, for over seven hundred years. The connection between the Order of Carmel and the Brown Scapular is as indissoluble as it is ancient because the Brown Scapular is the signifying part of our Carmelite religious habit. Wearing the scapular signifies some degree of membership in our Carmelite Family."

While acknowledging that Carmelites for centuries have striven to make the Brown Scapular as accessible as possible, the Carmelite superiors added:

In our zeal to spread this devotion, perhaps we have not exercised sufficient care in the catechesis of the scapular. Well-meaning people have often spread the devotion with extravagant claims that have no historical background and which sometimes are difficult to reconcile with sound Christian Doctrine. In our catechesis of the Brown Scapular of Our Lady of Mount Carmel, we Carmelites accept the mandate to clearly teach the doctrine that the Church teaches and our Carmelite Rule affirms so well — that Jesus Christ is the only one who liberates us from our sin. The Universal Church has entrusted the Carmelite Order with the responsibility for guaranteeing the authenticity of this devotion as it has been revised by the Holy See.

The Carmelite superiors then pointed out that in the light of historical research, the document of the Holy See does not sustain the Sabbatine Privilege (Scapular wearers would be saved from hell and taken into heaven on the first Saturday after death). An authentic appreciation for this sacramental requires a living faith in Jesus Christ and to walk as his co-disciples with the Blessed Virgin Mary in the communion of saints.

(See also **SCAPULAR**.)

SACRAMENT OF THE ANOINTING OF THE SICK — See ANOINTING OF THE SICK.

SACRAMENT OF BAPTISM — See BAPTISM.

SACRAMENT OF CONFIRMATION — See CONFIRMATION.

SACRAMENT OF THE HOLY EUCHARIST — See EUCHARIST.

SACRAMENT OF HOLY ORDERS — See ORDERS, SACRAMENT OF HOLY.

SACRAMENT OF MARRIAGE — See MARRIAGE, SACRAMENT OF.

SACRAMENT OF PENANCE — See PENANCE, SACRAMENT OF.

SACRAMENTALS

Sacred signs that bear a resemblance to the sacraments, and by means of which spiritual effects are signified or obtained through the prayers of the Church.

A sacramental can be an object (such as a rosary) or an action (such as making the sign of the cross).

Sacramentals differ from the seven sacraments in several important ways. Christ instituted the sacraments; the Church institutes — and can abolish — sacramentals. A sacrament imparts grace in virtue of the rite itself (it is efficacious); the grace associated with sacramentals depends on the disposition of the recipient and the intercession of the Church. While sacramentals do not confer the grace of the Holy Spirit in the way the sacraments do, by the Church's prayer, they prepare a person to receive grace and dispose that person to cooperate with it.

Prior to the high Middle Ages, the term *sacrament* (*sacramentum*) was also used for rites, prayers, and objects other than the seven sacraments. Not until the thirteenth century did the Church draw a clear distinction between "sacraments" and "sacramentals." Theologians then defined sacraments as those seven actions instituted by Christ that cause what they signify. Sacramentals, they maintained, resembled the sacraments but were instituted by the Church and prepared the participants to receive grace.

First among the Church's sacramentals are blessings that invoke God's protection and beneficence. Praise of the God "who has blessed us in Christ with every spiritual blessing in the heavenly places" (see Ephesians 1:3) is necessary to every sacramental blessing. Sacramentals are primarily blessings or actions using the Church's prayer. Through simple gestures and prayer, the Church implores God's blessing on persons or things — from making the sign of the cross on the brow of a child, to wearing scapulars, to honoring holy pictures, to lighting blessed candles.

An object is a sacramental only because it has been so blessed by this intercessory prayer. Sacramentals are primarily prayers directed to God and secondarily, through his response, a sanctification of persons or objects.

When a blessing sets apart a particular object exclusively for God, it is commonly called a "consecration." These blessings withdraw certain persons, or more commonly, certain objects, from the everyday world and consecrate them totally to God and his service. The prayer offered asks that the objects be the bearers of a blessing for those who use them, occasions for encountering God.

The Church has no definitive list of sacramentals but, rather, multiplies them according to need. For sacramentals closely connected to the Church's public worship, it is appropriate that a minister of the Church, whether deacon, priest, or bishop, perform the blessing. The bishop presides at the most solemn blessings, and the priest presides over the more ordinary ones in the community to which he ministers. That the 1983 Code of Canon Law allows the laity to administer certain sacramentals reflects Vatican II's recognition of the faithful's common priesthood (see *Lumen Gentium*, n. 10). Because of their special responsibility, parents may bless their children and catechists bless their students. In these and other situations laymen and laywomen may bless, thereby ministering certain sacramentals.

The right to establish official sacramentals belongs to the Holy See (see Code of Canon Law, Canon 1167). Without hesitation, however, the pope grants requests to individual bishops and bishops' conferences to institute sacramentals appropriate to specific cultures and situations.

Whereas the seven sacraments confer sanctifying grace because they are actions of Christ himself, the sacramentals prepare us to cooperate with it. In traditional theological language, the sacramentals are efficacious *ex opere operantis Ecclesiae*; that is, they bring forth spiritual fruits by virtue of the Church's intercessory prayer and the recipient's willing cooperation in faith and love.

When a medal or a scapular is blessed, it does not itself become a cause of grace. What happens is that God responds to our petition to give special graces when the faithful use these things with the proper dispositions. The sacramentals provide actual graces that prepare the soul to receive an increase of sanctifying grace, an intensification of friendship between God and the individual.

SACRAMENTALS IN EASTERN RITES — See EASTERN RITES, SACRAMENTALS IN.

SACRAMENTARY

The English edition of the *Roman Missal* (*Missale Romanum*), containing the directives, prayers, and rubrics for the Sacrifice of the Mass.

The Lectionary possesses the readings used during the liturgy. Both volumes are available in Latin and the vernacular.

SACRAMENTS, SEVEN

The unique signs instituted by Christ that give the grace they signify.

They are baptism, penance, Holy Eucharist, confirmation, holy orders, matrimony, and anointing of the sick. As long taught by the Church, the sacraments are defined by name and number. They produce grace *ex opere operato* (literally, "from the work performed"); this means that any sacrament administered properly with no obstacles gives grace, regardless of the holiness of the minister.

SACRAMENTS OF INITIATION

The three sacraments that enable one to be fully prepared to spread the Gospel. They are: baptism (rebirth), confirmation (recommitment or "sealing"), and Holy Eucharist (nourishment).

SACRED ART — See ART AND DEVOTION.

SACRED HEAD OF JESUS

A devotion to and image of Christ as Divine Wisdom.

It is based on the writings of Teresa Helena Higginson, a nineteenth-century teacher in England.

The devotion bears a striking analogy to the one in honor of the Sacred Heart. Neither is simply a material object of worship; instead they are symbols of the love of Jesus Christ and the Divine Wisdom. Consideration, adoration, and love shown to the Sacred Head as the Seat of Divine Wisdom is particularly fitting in our day as a devotion to be used in reparation for all of the insults given to that Divine Wisdom by mankind's sins of intellectual pride.

SACRED HEART AUTO EMBLEM

A sacramental promoted by the Sacred Heart Auto League.

Father Gregory Bezy, S.C.J., began the apostolate of prayer in 1954 in Walls, Mississippi. To remind people that driving time could be prayer time, the priest had a statue of the Sacred Heart designed that could be placed on the dashboards of cars and other vehicles. When dashboards were metal, a small magnet in the base of the plastic statue was used to hold it in place. The statues were mailed to millions of people across the United States in an effort to get them to join the "apostolate of prayerful, careful, and reparative driving." Excess contributions collected were used to support the home mission effort in northern Mississippi.

In the late 1960s, Father Bezy and his assistant, Roger Courts, designed a symbol of the Auto League that was more appealing to Catholics at that time: a Sacred Heart Dashboard Medal. The medals were mailed out nationwide in an effort to con-

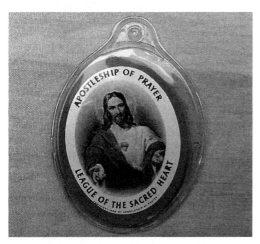

Sacred Heart Badge

tinue and expand the Auto League and the other apostolic works of the Sacred Heart League and Southern Mission.

As with any item which is mass produced and widely distributed, the dashboard medal lost its popularity as had the statue. Therefore, the league began to distribute a membership key ring. Every so often the design and type of the small reminder distributed by the league changes, in keeping with current ideas.

SACRED HEART BADGE

A sacramental promoted by St. Margaret Mary Alacoque (1647-1690) based on her reported visions of Christ.

The badge is oval. It shows Christ with his heart exposed on one side and the heart itself on the other. The badge was brought to the United States by the Apostleship of Prayer and is used as an external sign of the union of the members with Christ. On the front of the badge is "Apostleship of Prayer — League of the Sacred Heart." On the reverse: "Cease, the Heart of Jesus is with me" and "Sacred Heart of Jesus, Thy Kingdom Come."

(See also SACRED HEART OF JESUS.)

SACRED HEART ENTHRONEMENT

An acknowledgment of the sovereignty of Jesus Christ over the Christian family. It is expressed by the installation or picture of the Sacred Heart of Jesus in a place of honor in the home, accompanied by an act of consecration.

The great modern apostle of devotion to the Sacred Heart, especially of priestly and family consecration, was Father Mateo Crawley-Boevy (1875-1960). A priest of the Fathers of the Sacred Heart, he founded the Catholic University of Valparaiso, and then requested Pope St. Pius X to allow him to devote himself to bring the "entire world, home by home, family by family," to the Sacred Heart. Instead of granting permission, the pope commanded Father Mateo to dedicate his life's work to this aim. Father Mateo spoke five languages fluently. He traveled the world organizing the crusade for the enthronement of the Sacred Heart. Father Mateo saw the sanctification of the family as the ultimate goal of the apostolate. He believed the enthronement fulfilled all of the requests of the Sacred Heart made to St. Margaret Mary at Paray-le-Monial. To him, the family as a social cell must be the living throne of the King of Love.

The National Enthronement Center is the headquarters of the national Sacred Heart enthronement apostolate in the United States of America under the direction of the Congregation of the Sacred Hearts, East Coast Province, in Fairhaven, Massachusetts, USA.

SACRED HEARTS BADGE

A sacramental associated with devotion to the Sacred Heart of Jesus and the Immaculate Heart of Mary based on visions of Mary reported by St. Catherine Labouré (1806-1876).

In his encyclical on the Sacred Heart, *Haurietis Aquas*, Pope Pius XII enjoined the faithful to join devotion to the Immaculate Heart of Mary to that of the Sacred Heart of Jesus. His words echoed those of Our Lady at Fátima, "The Heart of Jesus wishes to be venerated together with the Heart of His Mother." In 1793, Father Mary-Joseph Courdin founded the Congregation of the Sacred Hearts for the promotion of this devotion.

SACRED HEART OF JESUS

A devotion to and image of Christ based on the private revelations of St. Margaret Mary Alacoque (1647-1690) at Paray-le-Monial, France.

There are five main elements to this devotion:

1. Adoration. Christ proposed his Sacred Heart for worship as the source of love, mercy, grace, sanctification, and salvation for all, and asked that its image be honored.
2. Belief in the merciful love of that heart for all.
3. A generous return of love for Jesus

Christ. Christ indicated his wish for all to love him.

4. Reparation. Christ asked his faithful to love him more and more to make up for those who do not love him.

5. Special love and reverence for the Blessed Sacrament.

In the early seventeenth century, devotion to the Sacred Heart was greatly promoted by St. John Eudes, who is known as the founder of its liturgical cult. By 1672, he had obtained the celebration of the feast to the Sacred Heart for all the seminaries of his order, and in 1765 the feast was approved by Rome at the request of the bishops of Poland. In 1856, Blessed Pius IX extended the feast to the universal Church. In the revised liturgical calendar, the Feast of the Sacred Heart of Jesus is observed on the second Friday after the Feast of Corpus Christi.

In recent years, the doctrine of mercy of the Sacred Heart has been confirmed through a series of private revelations to a humble Spanish lay sister of the Religious of the Sacred Heart, Sister Josefa Menendez. For a period of nearly ten years before her death in 1923, Our Lord favored her with almost daily conversations, and showed himself to her, dictating a message which he told her was for the benefit of all men. Much of the message was the same as at Paray, but his great appeal at Poitiers was for confidence and absolute blind trust in his merciful love.

In his 1956 encyclical on the Sacred Heart, *Haurietis Aquas*, Pope Pius XII explained the doctrinal foundations of the devotion in Scripture, tradition, and the liturgy, and recommended the practice of this devotion to all the faithful.

SACRED HEART ROSARY

One of several chaplets that focus on the Sacred Heart.

The best-known features a cross and thirty-nine beads.

Sacred Heart Rosary

One version reads:

(On the cross, say …)

Soul of Christ, sanctify me! Body of Christ, save me! Blood of Christ, inebriate me! Water from the side of Christ, wash me! Passion of Christ, strengthen me! O Good Jesus, hear me! Within Thy wounds hide me; permit me not to be separated from Thee; from the malignant enemy defend me; in the hour of death call me and bid me come to Thee, that with Thy saints I may praise Thee, forever and ever. Amen.

(On the large beads, say …)

O sweetest Heart of Jesus, I implore that I may ever love Thee more and more.

(On the small beads, say …)

Sweet Heart of Jesus, be my love.

(At the end of each decade, say …)

Sweet Heart of Mary, be my salvation.

(At the conclusion say …)

May the Heart of Jesus in the most Blessed Sacrament be praised, adored, and loved with grateful affection at every moment in all the tabernacles of the world, even to the end of time

(See also **CHAPLET**.)

SACRED HEART, TWELVE PROMISES OF THE

Twelve promises to persons having devotion to the Sacred Heart of Jesus, which were communicated by Christ to St. Margaret Mary Alacoque in a private revelation in 1675.

They are:

1. I will give them all the graces necessary in their state in life.
2. I will establish peace in their homes.
3. I will comfort them in all their afflictions.
4. I will be their secure refuge during life and, above all, in death.
5. I will bestow abundant blessing upon all their undertakings.
6. Sinners shall find in my Heart the source and the infinite ocean of mercy.
7. By devotion to my Heart tepid souls shall grow fervent.
8. Fervent souls shall quickly mount to high perfection.
9. I will bless every place where a picture of my Heart shall be set up and honored.
10. I will give to priests the gift of touching the most hardened hearts.
11. Those who promote this devotion shall have their names written in my Heart, never to be blotted out.

12. I will grant the grace of final penitence to those who communicate [receive Holy Communion] on the first Friday of nine consecutive months.

SACRED MEAL

A gathering around food possessing a religious meaning, which for Catholics culminates in the Holy Sacrifice of the Mass.

The sacred meal is, for Christians, the Last Supper. The Agape was a fellowship meal held immediately prior to the offering of the Holy Eucharist in early Christian times.

SACRED PLACES

Places such as churches or oratories designated by Church authority for divine worship or for the burial of the faithful.

SACRED TIMES

Sundays of the year, holy days of obligation, and days and seasons of penance that are so designated by Church authority.

SACRED VESSELS

Items associated with the Mass and the Eucharist.

They include: chalice (or cup); paten (or plate); ciborium (container for consecrated hosts); monstrance (used for displaying the consecrated host for Eucharistic adoration); and pyx (a small container used to bring the Blessed Sacrament to the sick and homebound).

SACRIFICE

The act of offering to God, and often the subsequent destruction or consumption of some gift.

It runs deep throughout the history of the world. Scripture is full of such offerings. The greatest sacrifice is the very offering of Christ himself to the Father through the Holy Spirit, which sacrifice is perpetuated at each Holy Mass.

SACRIFICE OF THE MASS

The offering of the combined Liturgies of the Word and the Eucharist at which bread and wine are changed into the body, blood, soul, and divinity of Jesus Christ.

SACRILEGE

The violent, disrespectful treatment of persons, places, and objects dedicated to God.

Receiving the sacraments unworthily (i.e., in mortal sin) is also sacrilegious.

SAINTS — For individual saints, see ST. [NAME].

SAINTS, CULT OF THE

The veneration, called *dulia*, of holy persons who have died and are in glory with God in heaven which includes honoring them and petitioning them for their intercession with God.

Liturgical veneration is given only to saints officially recognized by the Church. Private veneration may be given to anyone thought to be in heaven. Veneration of the saints is essentially different from *latria*, the adoration given to God alone; however, by its very nature, it leads to worship of God.

The traditional, rationalist explanation of the rise of the cult of the saints within Christianity is that these holy men and women replaced the heroes, or the gods, of classical religion. As evidence for this, it is possible to point to shrines of saints which are geographically identical with shrines of pagan gods. Even Pope St. Gregory the Great, when giving instructions to his missionaries to the Anglo-Saxons in England, suggested that where suitable, formerly-pagan buildings existed, the Christians should take them over. But though there are points of convergence, the differences are even more striking. As Peter Brown points out in his influential book, *The Cult of the Saints*, by the middle of the fourth century the Emperor Julian the Apostate was criticising the honor shown to saints precisely because they were dead human beings. Paganism — and Judaism — had a repugnance for

corpses; Christians, on the other hand, honored the bodies of the holy dead, and honored the tombs, or shrines, in which they lay. As early as 160 A.D., after the martyrdom of St. Polycarp, Christians respectfully gathered his remains. It was the control of these shrines, Brown has argued, that was one of the factors in the rise to power of the local bishops; communal pilgrimages to the shrines became one of the ways in which the Christian community achieved its identity.

The first saints recognised by Christians were martyrs such as Polycarp. Martyrs witness (the word *martyr* means "witness") to the Passion of Christ, and in suffering their own passion they have the courage to imitate Christ. This act is seen by the earliest theologians as a source of grace for the Church, and even those who have not paid for their Christianity with their lives but have suffered in prison, the *confessors* — another word meaning "witness" — come to share in the glory which is attributed to the martyrs. Because they survive imprisonment, confessors have a role to continue to play in the Church. Christians who had apostatized in time of persecution, especially in the great persecutions under Decian and Diocletian, could receive pardon, and re-entry to the Church, by appealing to the confessors for forgiveness.

Those who were still living could not, of course, be given liturgical recognition. Those who had died could, however, be commemorated: the day of death (or better, of birth into heaven, the *dies natalis*) was marked as early as the middle of the third century, and the day of death remains the most usual day on which a saint is honored. From at least 258 A.D., the Feast of Sts. Peter and Paul was celebrated in Rome on February 22. Toward the end of the third century and the beginning of the fourth Christians began to pray to the saints for their own needs. This development may have been influenced by the Roman system of patrons and clients: the Christian faithful being the clients, the saints their patrons, presenting their petitions to the Father. What was significant for petitioners was the saint's power with God, his or her ability, as it were, to sway the Almighty and, in later centuries and perhaps rather more crudely, to work miracles, chiefly if not entirely of healing. For instance the people in Gaul believed it was the intervention of the saints in 451 that prevented Attila the Hun from sacking Rome.

At least from the middle of the fourth century, local churches — Rome being the first which is known to have done so — began to produce calendars, or martyrologies. These listed the saint's day of death, the place of burial, and sometimes a brief account of the circumstances of the saint's death. Some of these accounts of martyrs' sufferings, the *Acta* (or "deeds" as they were called) had been preserved at length. In some churches, though Rome disapproved, they were read out during the liturgy. The martyrologies were not limited to local saints, but included those whose lives had been of especial importance for a particular church, no matter where they had died.

As time went by, the saint's death did not have to be a violent one. Athanasius, the great though controversial bishop of Alexandria who died in 373, wrote the life of St. Anthony of Egypt, who died in 356. Anthony was a hermit, not a martyr, and he battled on Athanasius' side in the controversy with those who followed the heresy of Arius. By Athanasius' account, St. Anthony was also subject to extraordinary temptations of the devil, which he overcame. The life, or *Vita*, of Anthony was enormously influential in the establishment of the style of Christian writing known as hagiography, in which the lives of holy men and women were recorded. These lives helped to spread devotion to the saints, and brought about the recognition of people as saints. There are acknowledged saints who do not have lives written of them (at least, whose *vitae* have not survived), but there was a period in the early middle ages when an effort was made to ban the veneration of any saint who did not have a *vita*.

Hagiographies were composed for many purposes. It is now commonly supposed that hagiographical works present a saint to the reader for imitation, but that has not always been the case. Indeed, in many instances even where a saint is ostensibly presented for imitation, there is an underlying purpose which is quite different, for example the exaltation of a particular monastery, or even diocese, through the composition and dissemination of the life — sometimes spurious — of its founder. Even Alban Butler, the compiler in the mid-eighteenth century of the collection still known as *Butler's Lives of the Saints*, was intending something more through his collection than simply to present the saints for admiration or imitation. He was attempting to demonstrate that the Catholic Church in England of his own day was a direct descendant of the Church of the martyrs of the middle ages. In other words, saints whose day of death came to be included in local calendars or martyrologies, although they were not themselves martyred, came to be recorded there for a wide variety of reasons which were of importance to the local church at the time, and not simply because of the outstanding holiness of their lives.

SAINTS, DEVOTION TO

The proper veneration of the Church's "holy ones," those who have led a life in union with God through the grace of Christ and received the reward of eternal life.

The Church teaches that within the communion of saints — the souls in heaven, the souls in purgatory, and the faithful on earth — there is a perennial link of charity and an abundant exchange of good things. The holiness of one profits another. Christians have shown a devotion to the saints since the earliest days of the Church.

The saints do not want or need veneration, nor is there retribution for not honoring them. "Clearly, if we venerate their memory, it serves us, not them," wrote St. Bernard of Clairvaux. "But I tell you, when I think of them, I am consumed by a tremendous yearning to be with them. The memory of the saints should inspire and encourage us to achieve the enjoyment of their hoped-for company," Bernard continued. "Let us love those who love us, hasten to those who await us" (*Sermo*, n. 2).

To venerate the saints by celebrating their feasts, naming children and churches after them, and invoking their support enriches Catholic life. It is also an act of gratitude for what the saints do for the faithful, a way of loving them as heavenly neighbors.

In her wisdom, the Church teaches that it is not necessary for the individual Christian to have devotion to any particular saint, except for the Blessed Virgin Mary. Respecting the liberty of individuals to choose saints for themselves is fundamental.

In matters of devotions, unlike matters of faith, a legitimate plurality should reign.

Preachers and devotees of certain saints must avoid monopolistic or imperialistic claims for their saint. It is, after all, possible "to get a man without St. Ann" or to find a lost article without St. Anthony. No particular devotion is obligatory for all Catholics. The faithful are free to pick Patrick or Catherine, Peter or Paul, John or Teresa as a role model and advocate. Different intellectual and cultural milieus encourage an enriching diversity.

It is the long-standing practice of the faithful piously to implore the heavenly aid of the saints in heaven who are closely joined with Christ. Why bother to ask the saints to pray to God for us rather than pray to him directly? Intercession "means that the blessed who are one with the risen Christ are still interested in us; they can and do pray for us" (American Bishops, *Behold Your Mother,* n. 84). Unlike veneration, which is something believers do for the saints, intercession is something the saints do for believers. Just as we continue to honor others despite the separation of death, so also can believers continue to solicit the prayers of the saints. Like the risen Christ, they are alive to the believer.

The happiness of the saints is not static enjoyment of a heavenly reward. Present in love to the Son, they know his mind. Since on earth they lived "for Christ" as his disciples, so now they are united with him in bringing the plan of redemption to completion. Saints intercede for the faithful with Christ, and through him to the Father. They want what their Lord wants — our salvation. To seek the intercession of the saints means that they are significant for me, as I am for them. Intercession is the language of the mystical body.

Among the most frequent intercessory prayers are requests to the saints or about-to-be saints for miracles, usually physical cures. Before canonization or enrolling an individual in the official list of saints, the Church takes as a divine sign a miracle performed through the intercession of the candidate. Miracles are the seal of approval upon the teaching and witness of the would-be saint. That people ask for such favors of those who have died renowned for their holiness testifies to Catholic belief in the saints' intercessory influence before the throne of God.

Nothing is clearer than the Scripture teaching that there is "one mediator between God and humanity, the man Christ Jesus" (see 1 Timothy 2:5). Christ alone is Lord and Savior. This unique mediation of Jesus can never compromised. Only Jesus Christ, through his Passion, death, and Resurrection, has re-forged the link with the Father by "making peace by the blood of his cross" (see Colossians 1:20).

The mediation of the saints "takes away nothing from Christ's all-sufficient mediatorship" but "rather shows its power" (*Lumen Gentium,* n. 60). The one mediator does not exclude secondary mediation, unquestionably subordinate to that of Christ. "There is nothing to prevent others in a certain way from being called mediators between God and man," wrote St. Thomas Aquinas, "insofar as they, by preparing or serving, co-operate in uniting men to God" (*Summa Theologiae*, III, q26 ,a 1c). Following St. Thomas Aquinas, the Fathers at Vatican II taught that Christ's unique mediation "does not exclude but rather gives rise to a manifold cooperation that is but a sharing in this one source" (*Lumen Gentium*, n. 62).

In 1969, Pope Paul VI published a revision of the calendar of saints: *Mysterii paschalis celebrationem* (February 14, 1969). Since the Second Vatican Council, liturgists had wanted to prune the Church's calendar of historical inaccuracies. The experts subjected to critical scrutiny the histories of the saints mentioned in it. The pope then included in the revised calendar only those saints who passed the exam of historical authenticity. St. Christopher failed the test. So did Philomena, Valentine, and a score of others. Many Catholics were enraged at having their favorite intercessors dethroned by Vatican authorities. Wisely, churches, schools, and religious organizations with these patrons were not required to change their names. But they did lose their official feast days in favor of saints who represented the Church's universality and whose lives were fully attested.

Although saints called Christopher, Philomena, and Valentine probably lived, nothing more than their names could be gleaned from a careful study of the Church's tradition. No one claimed they did not exist, only that careful historical study could not affirm their existence. These "ex-saints," moreover, had never been officially canonized, since devotion to them preceded this papal process introduced in the Middle Ages. It's not yet clear whether popular piety to them will cease. St. Christopher medals are still around. And where would lovers be without Valentine's Day?

Pruning the calendar also involved changing the date of celebration of many saints. A saint's day is usually that of his or her "birthday" into heaven. If, however, that conflicted with one of the Church's great liturgical seasons, such as Advent or Lent, another suitable date was used. Thus, for example, the Feast of St. Thomas Aquinas moved from March 7 (during Lent) to January 28. Other feasts had never been celebrated on the correct day. These, too, were changed. Despite the clamor, the new liturgical calendar better reflects the catholicity of the Church's saints.

Care should be taken to avoid the distortions that arise from time to time in well-meaning but misinformed Catholic devotional practices regarding the saints. The saints are not bridges over a gap that separates the faithful from a remote Christ, as if believers are unworthy to approach him directly. Most religions have supernatural figures that mediate between humanity and the inaccessible God.

Catholics do not need saints to get closer to the Lord. The Son of God himself has satisfied this need: "He who sees me, sees the Father" (see John 14:9). The mediation of the saints in no way interferes with direct union with Christ. The saints are not doors that have to be passed through before encountering Christ. Through grace, the faithful enter directly into union with Christ. To think of the saints as the middle link between the faithful and a distant Christ is to misunderstand the deepest meaning of the Incarnation, the fact that Christ became like us in all things but sin.

In the Church's history, the cult of saints has occasionally threatened to rival the worship of Christ. In their shrines and through their relics, the people thought the saints to be powerfully "present." Sometimes the poorly-catechized felt that the saints were closer to them than Christ, even in the Eucharist. This is simply erroneous.

At the Second Vatican Council, the Fathers were very aware that deviations had crept into the Church's devotional life. Popular devotions, including those to some saints, sometimes obscured the primary importance of the Mass as the center of all Catholic worship. The Fathers urged "all concerned to work hard to prevent or correct any abuses, excesses, or defects which may have crept in here or there, and to restore all things to a more ample praise of Christ, and of God" (*Lumen Gentium*, n. 51).

(See also **DULIA**.)

SAINTS, INVOCATIONS AND VENERATION OF

Calling upon the saints for help (invocation) and giving them praise and honor as holy people (veneration).

SAINTS, PATRON — See **PATRON SAINTS**.

SAINTS' EMBLEMS — See **APPENDIX D**.

SALT, LITURGICAL USE OF

The ritual use of salt in the liturgy.

Before the reform of the liturgy, salt had a more prominent usage. It was used during the scrutinies of catechumens and at the baptisms of infants. It was also used in the blessing of holy water and in the rite of consecration of a church and an altar. In the liturgy in use now, salt may be mixed with newly blessed holy water. This recalls the salt scattered over the water by the prophet Elisha. Salt in the Scriptures represents wisdom and integrity of life. Salt is no longer used in Christian initiation.

SALUTATIONS (GREETINGS)

An Eastern European custom.

Traditionally the greeting "Praised be Jesus Christ" is answered with "Forever and ever." Among the Slovaks, some other Eastern European groups, and certain religious orders, a customary salutation is given when meeting another on the street or entering the home. The customary Slovak greeting is "Praised be Jesus Christ," and the response is "Forever and ever." On Easter Sunday, the greeting is "Jesus Christ is risen from the dead," repeated three times, and the reply is "Indeed, He has risen," also repeated three times. If it is a priest or religious entering the house, their hand is always reverently kissed along with the greeting. On taking leave of a Slovak home, the expression used is always "Remain with God," to which is answered "And you with His Divine Son."

SALVE REGINA — See HAIL HOLY QUEEN.

SANCTIFICATION

The process by which one grows in holiness.

This occurs through the infusion of sanctifying grace, which enables one to be a friend of God. The seven sacraments are the primary means by which one experiences a more profound indwelling of the Holy Spirit.

SANCTIFYING GRACE

The "habitual" life of God given to one at baptism and reinforced when receiving the other sacraments, in prayer, and through the performance of charitable works.

Through sanctifying grace, God enlivens the whole person and enables one to be authentically converted to the Lord.

SANCTITY

Sacred state of blessedness, holiness, or sainthood.

SANCTITY, ODOR OF

A term using sweetness of smell metaphorically for the condition of sainthood but sometimes understood literally because of olfactory phenomena associated with the remains of some holy people.

SAN JUAN, OUR LADY OF

A Marian devotion and image; a pilgrim statue.

Devotion to the Virgin of San Juan de los Lagos dates back to the early seventeenth century when Antonio of Segovia, a Spanish Franciscan missionary, took a small statue of the Immaculate Conception to the town of San Juan Bautista Mezquetitlan, Mexico (later renamed San Juan de los Lagos). By 1623, many of the Nochixlecas Indians venerated Our Lady under the title of *Cichaupilli*, which simply means "Lady."

Today, the little statue stands in the church dedicated to the Immaculate Conception and is known as Our Lady of St. John of the Lakes. The statue depicts Mary with her hands folded in prayer. She stands on a half moon and two stars. The base is made of silver. Behind her, over her crown, are two angels holding a scroll with the inscription "Immaculate Mother, pray for us."

The pious legend of the devotion tells that the first miracle of the little statue was its self-preservation. In 1623, the statue appeared ragged, and the face was disfigured. The curate took it from the main church and put it in the sacristy. An old Indian woman, Ana Lucia, came daily to pray and to sweep and clean the church. Each morning, she found the statue back in the main church, in spite of the fact that she returned it daily to the sacristy by order of the curate.

In 1623, a troop of traveling acrobats came to the city. The family consisted of a man, his wife, and two daughters. While practicing a trick for their performance, the youngest daughter accidentally fell on some knives in the act, and died. One of the Indians, noticing the grief of the parents, went and got the old Indian Ana Lucia. In compassion for the mother of the girl, Ana told the parents to pray to Our Lady, and went and got the statue from the church. When Ana Lucia laid the image of the Virgin on the dead girl's breast, the young girl immediately returned to life. Her wounds healed instantly, leaving no trace or scar. The ecclesiastical authorities of the diocese conducted an official investigation, and confirmed the authenticity of the miracle after examining the eleven witnesses who gave sworn testimony to what they had seen.

In appreciation, the acrobat took the statue to Guadalajara in order to have it restored. There he found a sculptor who restored it quickly and brilliantly. When the acrobat went to pay the artist, however, he was missing. No one seemed to have any knowledge of the artist — who he was or where he had gone. The mystery surrounding the restoration of the statue caused its fame to spread even more quickly. Numerous miracles have been claimed through the intercession of Mary from prayers before the little statue. Today, the shrine of Our Lady of the Lakes is one of the favorite places of pilgrimage in Mexico. Pilgrims come from all parts of Mexico, and from those parts of the United States where those of Spanish and Mexican descent have migrated. The devotion to the Virgin of San Juan is a strong one. As all her devotees cannot come to her, from time to time she travels to them. Wherever she goes, she leaves behind her new and renewed devotion to the Immaculate Conception. In a number of places in the American Southwest, churches dedicated to her have been built, and replicas of the image enshrined.

SANTA RITA NO. 1
A famous Texas oil well.

The name originated with a group of Catholic women from New York who had invested in stock sold by the driller. They asked that the well be named for St. Rita, as a patron of the impossible. After the driller completed the derrick over the well, he climbed to the top, sprinkled dried rose petals that had been blessed in the saint's name and given him by the investors, and christened the well. It came in with a gusher. This well, drilled on state-owned lands, opened the field that pumped riches into the University of Texas, where the original pump is displayed today in Austin.

SANTEROS
Religious folk artists dating back to colonial New Mexico.

Because in its earliest years the region was isolated and few religious articles were imported, the Spainish there began to produce sacred art for themselves. Working almost exclusively with home-crafted local materials, the artists developed a dynamic iconic tradition. It was important that the painter be a holy man, and a *santo* made by a holy *santero* came to have a sacredness of its own. In other words, the art had a different relationship to the painter and viewer; it operated from the religious, rather than the aesthetic, plane. Once the coming of the railroad opened the area and the colony was less isolated, many priests brought in inexpensive copies of European art, and the *santos* were removed from the churches. In recent years, however, an appreciation of the art has developed and the *santos* have become highly collectible. In addition, Catholic artists in New Mexico have begun to revive the religious traditions of the *santeros* and their religiously inspired art.

(See also **ICON**.)

SANTO NIÑO DE ATOCHA — See ATOCHA, SANTO NIÑO DE.

SANTO NIÑO OF CEBU — See CEBU, SANTO NIÑO OF.

SATURDAY
The traditional day on which a particular

SCALA COELI

Latin for "stairway to heaven." According to legend, while saying a requiem Mass in the church of St. Mary at Scala Coeli in Rome, St. Bernard of Clairvaux had a vision of the souls he was praying for going up to heaven by means of a ladder. A special indulgence was given for Masses said at this church and for other, specially named, churches outside Rome.

SCALA SANCTA

Latin for "holy staircase."

A set of steps near the Lateran Basilica in Rome that, according to pious legend, were the stairs which Christ ascended into the Praetorium for judgment by Pilate. Tradition holds that the staircase was brought to Rome by St. Helena, mother of Constantine. Today, the white marble stairs have been enclosed in wood. It is an indulgenced practice for pilgrims to ascend the stairs on their knees.

Santos

devotion is paid to Mary.

The practice dates back to the eighth century. By the eleventh century, the custom of having a Mass in honor of Mary on Saturdays was widely practiced.

(See also **WEEKDAY DEVOTIONS**.)

SATURDAY OFFICE OF MARY —
See **MARY, SATURDAY OFFICE OF**.

SCAPULAR

A sacramental; part of a religious habit.

The scapular began in the Middle Ages as a narrow piece of cloth about the width of the shoulders with an opening in the center so that it could be slipped over the head and hang in equal lengths. Originally, it was a work garment meant to protect the tunic; through the years it became part of the habit. Later, an abbreviated form came into use and was given to the laity so that the wearer could share in the merits and good works of the particular group of which it served as a badge. Approved by the Church as sacramentals, these scapulars typically consist of two small squares of woolen cloth joined by strings that are worn about the neck. They are presented in a ceremony of investiture or enrollment. There are nearly twenty scapulars for devotional use.

SCAPULAR MEDAL

A medallion with a representation of the Sacred Heart on one side and of the Blessed Virgin Mary on the other.

Authorized by Pope St. Pius X in 1910, it may be worn or carried in place of a scapular by persons already invested with a scapular.

His decree reads:

> For the future all the faithful already inscribed or who shall be inscribed in one or other of the real scapulars approved by the Holy See (excepting those which are proper to the Third Orders) by what is known

as regular enrollment may, instead of the cloth scapulars, one or several, wear on their persons, either round the neck or otherwise, provided it be in a becoming manner, a single medal of metal, through which, by the observance of laws laid down for each scapular, they shall be enabled to share in and gain all the spiritual favors (not excepting what is known as the Sabbatine Privilege of the Scapular of Our Lady of Mount Carmel), and all the privileges attached to each.

The right side of this medal must show the image of Our Most Holy Redeemer, Jesus Christ, showing his Sacred Heart, and the obverse that of the Most Blessed Virgin Mary. It must be blessed with a separate blessing for each of the scapulars in which the person has been enrolled and for which the wearer wishes it to suffice. Finally, these separate blessings may be given by a single sign of the cross (*unico crucis signo*), whether in the act of enrollment or later at the convenience of those enrolled, it matters not how long after the enrollment or in what order they may have taken place; the blessing may be given by a priest other than the one who made the enrollment, as long as he possesses the faculty, ordinary, or delegated, of blessing the different scapulars — the limitations, clauses, and conditions attached to the faculty he uses still holding their force — all things to the contrary, even those calling for special mention notwithstanding.

(See also **SABBATINE PRIVILEGE**.)

SCAPULAR OF THE HOLY FACE

A sacramental associated with the Archconfraternity of the Holy Face.

Made of white cloth, it features the well-known image of Christ based on the pious legend of St. Veronica. Archconfraternity members may wear a medal with that image or a cross instead of the scapular.

The wearing of the scapular is also associated with Sister Marie de St. Pierre, a discalced Carmelite nun of Tours, France, said to have received special favors from Our Lord. She reported that Christ offered a number of promises to anyone who showed honor and reverence for his holy face.

SCAPULAR OF THE IMMACULATE CONCEPTION — See **BLUE SCAPULAR (IMMACULATE CONCEPTION)**.

SCAPULAR OF THE IMMACULATE HEART OF MARY

A sacramental that originated with the Sons of the Immaculate Heart of Mary in 1877, and was sanctioned by Blessed Pope Pius IX that same year. The sacramental owes its origins to a heavenly inspiration given to Bishop Joseph Xifre, C.M.F., co-founder and later superior general of the Missionary Sons of the Immaculate Heart.

The scapular is of white woolen cloth. The front part has a representation of the burning heart of Mary, out of which grows a lily. The heart is circled with a wreath of roses and pierced with a sword.

SCAPULAR OF THE MOST BLESSED TRINITY

A sacramental associated with a reported series of private revelations to St. John of Matha (1160-1213), founder of the Order of the Most Holy Trinity, the Trinitarians.

The first of these revelations came as St. John was celebrating his first Mass. An angel clothed in a white garment appeared at the altar. Across his breast and shoulder was a cross of red and blue. His arms were crossed and held over what appeared to be two captives — a Christian and a Moor. St. John understood that he was to found an order for the redemption of captives, Christian and non-Christian alike.

St. John retreated to the desert, where he met St. Felix of Valois. Together the two men lived, for a time, the eremitical life, fasting and praying fervently for guidance in their mission. At last, after a number of other apparitions, the two traveled to Rome in 1198 to seek the counsel of the Holy

Father. Pope Innocent III, while deliberating on their proposals, is reported to have had a vision of an angel wearing a red-and-blue cross. He approved the new institute and ordered it to be called the Order of the Most Holy Trinity for the Ransom of Captives. He gave the members a white habit with a red-and-blue cross (the upright bar being red, the crossbar blue).

This habit became the basis for the later Scapular of the Blessed Trinity. This scapular is the badge of the members of the Confraternity of the Most Holy Trinity.

SCAPULAR OF THE MOST PRECIOUS BLOOD

A sacramental associated with the Confraternity of the Most Precious Blood.

In Rome, members were invested with a red scapular or a red girdle. No special indulgences were connected with the wearing of this scapular, and its use was optional with the members of the confraternity. As used in Rome, the scapular had on the front portion a representation of the chalice with the Precious Blood adored by angels. The back segment was simply a small portion of red cloth.

SCAPULAR OF THE MOST SACRED HEART OF JESUS

A sacramental introduced in France in 1876.

This scapular consists of two segments of white woolen cloth connected by two strings. One segment of the scapular bears the usual representation of the Sacred Heart, and the other features a representation of the Blessed Virgin under the title of Mother of Mercy.

In 1876, a poor young woman named Estelle Faguette was dying of consumption in Pellevoisin, a small town in central France. Estelle had been the chief provider for her family, who were distraught at the thought of her impending death. The last rites had been administered, and all preparations for her death were concluded.

As Estelle lay dying, she reported an apparition of Our Lady, who announced her complete cure in five days. Overcome with gratitude, Estelle begged to be allowed to enter a cloistered community. Our Lady answered, directing her to become a lay apostle instead and telling her, "One can be saved in every state. Where you are, you can publish my glory."

During the next year, Estelle reported receiving ten more apparitions of Mary. Each visit emphasized a particular point. During one, Our Lady was seen by Estelle wearing a scapular, which she asked Estelle to make known.

On one side of the scapular is an image of Mary Immaculate. On the other is the pierced heart of Jesus, ringed with thorns and flames burning from the top. The burning heart is surmounted with a cross.

The bishop of Bourges appointed a commission to investigate, and in 1877 his report was taken to Rome. The Confraternity of Our Lady of Pellevoisin was established, and Pope Leo XIII gave approbation both to the confraternity and to the scapular.

of arms — the tiara and the keys of Peter. Underneath are written the words of Pope Leo XIII: "Son, follow Her counsel."

This scapular is worn by the members of the Pious Union of Our Mother of Good Counsel.

(See also **GOOD COUNSEL, OUR LADY OF.**)

SCAPULAR OF OUR LADY OF GOOD COUNSEL

A sacramental associated with a Marian devotion and image of Our Lady of Good Counsel.

In 1753, Pope Benedict XIV established the Pious Union of Our Lady of Good Counsel. More than any other pope, Leo XIII, who was himself a member of the pious union, was deeply attached to this devotion. He instituted the White Scapular of Our Lady of Good Counsel, added the title "Mother of Good Counsel" into the Litany of Loreto, declared the shrine a minor basilica, and placed a copy of the image over the altar in the Pauline chapel in the Vatican.

From this picture came the front panel of the White Scapular. This Madonna depicts the mother with her eyes closed, and the Child's right arm around her neck. His left hand is at the neck of her garment. Mary is shown as a queen and the Child's eyes are intent on her. The back panel of this scapular shows the papal coat

SCAPULAR OF OUR LADY OF MOUNT CARMEL

A sacramental associated with the Carmelite Order.

The Brown Scapular of Our Lady of Mount Carmel is the habit of the Carmelite Order. For the religious Carmelites, it takes

Scapular of Our Lady of Mount Carmel

the form of two long undecorated panels of brown cloth joined at the shoulders and falling, one panel to the front and the other to the back. For the laity it is in the form of two smaller pieces of brown or dark cloth, preferably plain, joined over the shoulders by ribbons and falling in the same manner as the larger scapular.

As the order's habit, the scapular signifies some degree of affiliation to the Carmelites such as the religious men and women of the order and aggregated institutes, including the Third Order (a secular, or lay, order), as well as members of public associations and confraternities of Our Lady of Mount Carmel such as active communities of the Scapular Confraternity. Those who have been invested in the scapular practice the order's spirituality and have been granted some association with the order; those who wear the scapular out of devotion, practice the order's spirituality, but have no formal association with the order; and, those who are committed to practice the Marian characteristics of Carmelite spirituality but use outward forms other than the Brown Scapular to express this devotion.

It should be noted, too, that the scapular is the common habit of all the branches of the Carmelite family and a sign of unity of that family. Therefore, the Scapular Confraternity and similar associations of the faithful centering around this sacramental belong not to any one branch of Carmel but to the entire Carmelite family. Thus there is only one common public association of the Scapular of Our Lady of Mount Carmel.

According to the Rite for the Blessing and Enrollment in the Scapular of the Blessed Virgin Mary of Mount Carmel, approved by the Holy See in 1996, any priest or deacon has the faculties for blessing the scapular. And a person given authority to act in the name of the order may receive people into the confraternity of the scapular.

The prayer for the blessing of a scapular reads:

> O God, author and perfection of holiness, who will call those who were born of water and the Holy Spirit to the fullness of the Christian life, look with kindness on those who are about to receive devoutly the Scapular of Carmel which they will wear faithfully as the sign of their commitment to the Virgin Mary of Mount Carmel. Grant that in surrendering to the love of the most tender Virgin, they may conform themselves to the image of Jesus Christ your Son, and having run the course of this life happily, may they enter into the joy of your house. Through Christ Our Lord. Amen.

The minister then places the scapular on each person who has requested it, and says:

Receive this scapular. (Through this scapular you become a member of the Confraternity of the Blessed Virgin Mary of Mount Carmel.) Full of faith in the love of such a great Mother, dedicate yourself to imitating her and to a special relationship with her. Wear this sign as a reminder of the presence of Mary in your daily commitment to be clothed in Jesus Christ and to manifest him in your life for the good of the Church and the whole of humanity, and to the glory of the Most Blessed Trinity. Amen.

(See also **MOUNT CARMEL, OUR LADY OF**; **SABBATINE PRIVILEGE**.)

SCAPULAR OF OUR LADY OF RANSOM

A sacramental associated with the Mercedarian Order.

St. Peter Nolasco (c. 1189-1258) devoted his life to the rescue of captives from the Moors, who were then occupying much of Spain. With this aim in mind, he founded the Order of Our Lady of Ransom (Mercedarians) between 1218 and 1234.

The faithful, on entering the confraternity erected by this order, are given a small scapular of white cloth. On the front of the scapular is the picture of Our Lady of Ransom. The back may depict the order's coat of arms.

SCAPULAR OF THE SACRED HEARTS OF JESUS AND MARY

A sacramental approved by the Sacred Congregation of Rites in 1900.

One panel features the two Sacred Hearts in their traditional representations: the heart of Jesus with the cross and fire, wreathed with thorns; and the heart of Mary pierced with a sword. Beneath these are the instruments of the Passion. The other panel of the scapular usually bears a simple red cross. A religious of the Daughters of the Sacred Heart in Antwerp, Belgium, convinced the bishop of Marseilles of the supernatural origin of this scapular. He, along with Cardinal Mazzella, cardinal-protector of the community, petitioned the Holy See for its approval. The Missionaries of the Sacred Heart and the Oblate Missionaries have custody of this scapular.

SCAPULAR OF THE SEVEN SORROWS

A sacramental associated with the Servite Order.

The community was founded, and members received their habit based on reported private revelations made to seven noblemen of Florence who were later can-

517

onized. These wealthy young merchants were members of a Marian confraternity known as the *Laudesi* (Praisers). In 1233, as they were meditating after ceremonies on the Feast of the Assumption, Our Lady appeared to them and, promising her protection and help, told them to leave the world and live entirely for God.

At first, the seven began a life of prayer and solitude. Later, they were joined by others, and their community evolved into a religious order today known in many parts of the world.

On Good Friday, 1240, the brothers were praying in their oratory, when suddenly they received a vision of the Mother of God surrounded by a radiant light. She was clad in a long black mantle and was holding a black habit in her hands. In this same vision, she gave the founders the name "Servants of Mary," presented them with the rule of St. Augustine, and told them that their black habit would serve as a reminder of the sorrows she endured.

Shortly after Pope Alexander IV had sanctioned the Servite Order, many of the faithful began to associate themselves with the order in confraternities honoring the Seven Sorrows of Mary. In later times, members also wore a scapular of black cloth.

Today's Scapular of the Seven Sorrows is made of black cloth and usually bears a picture of Our Lady of Sorrows on the front panel. The back panel may also have a picture of Our Lady.

SCAPULAR OF ST. BENEDICT

A sacramental associated with the Benedictine Order.

The small scapular of the Oblate is a reminder of the full habit worn by the monks. A person becoming an Oblate receives a small black scapular in the rite of investiture. In 1950, the Holy See gave permission for the Oblates of St. Benedict to wear the medal of St. Benedict in place of the Oblate scapular.

A little larger than most of the small scapulars, it is slightly more than two inches high and almost as wide. The scapular is black with the image of St. Benedict as an abbot with staff and rule book on one side. Also featured are the traditional chalice with the serpent, symbolizing the saint's miraculous deliverance from poison. On the other panel, St. Scholastica, Benedict's twin sister, is portrayed as a Benedictine abbess, with staff and book surmounted by a dove.

SCAPULAR OF ST. CAMILLUS (HELP OF THE SICK)

A sacramental associated with the order founded by St. Camillus of Lellis (1550-1614).

Today's universal symbol of aid and charity, the Red Cross first appeared on the black background of the Scapular of St. Camillus of Lellis. In 1576, this large, boisterous young man decided to serve the sick in the same hospital in Rome where he had previously been hospitalized for a painful infection of his leg. Eventually, he became the superintendent and, familiar with the deplorable conditions of the hospitals in that era, gathered faithful companions to assist him in his work.

Ordained in 1584, St. Camillus and his associates formed the nucleus of a new order in the Church, the Ministers of the Sick, later called the Clerks Regular of the Order of St. Camillus, or Camellians. The scapular was originally part of its habit.

In the Church of St. Magdalen at Rome, there is a picture of the Blessed Virgin said to be painted by the celebrated Dominican painter Fra Angelico, which is specially venerated under the title "Help of the Sick." Both panels of the scapular bear an image of the painting on one side and the red cross on the black field edged in red on the reverse.

The original purpose of the red cross, which was approved in 1586 by Pope Sixtus V (r. 1585-1590), was to inspire the sick and dying with confidence and contrition by reminding them of the cross of Christ, red with his blood that he shed for their redemption.

In 1860, a brother of the Order of St. Camillus, Ferdinand Vicari, founded a confraternity under the invocation of the Mother of God for the poor sick. At their reception, the members were given a scapular of black woolen cloth with the front portion bearing a copy of the famous Marian image and the back featuring a small red cross. This scapular is no longer available, and the confraternity has ceased to exist.

SCAPULAR OF ST. DOMINIC

A sacramental associated with the Order of Preachers, the Dominicans.

Blessed Reginald of Orléans (1183-1220) reported receiving the Dominican scapular from the hands of Mary. Made of white wool, it was approved by the order as the usual form of affiliation with the community. No images are necessary, but the scapular as given in the house of the Dominican general at Rome has on one side the picture of St. Dominic kneeling before the crucifix and on the other that of Blessed Reginald receiving the habit from the hands of the Mother of God.

SCAPULAR OF ST. JOSEPH

A sacramental associated with Blessed Pope Pius IX's declaration of St. Joseph as patron of the universal Church in 1870.

The use of a scapular honoring Jesus' foster father began in the diocese of St. Claude, France, in the late nineteenth century. The devotion was initiated by Mother Marie of Jesus, foundress of the Franciscan Sisters of the Immaculate Conception, and Father Peter Baptist of

Rheims, O.F.M. Cap. The scapular was approved for the universal Church by Pope Leo XIII in 1893, and its propagation was entrusted to the Capuchins.

The original scapular was white, but the version that received final approval is made in the colors traditionally assigned in Christian iconography to St. Joseph: white, purple, and gold. The purple, which forms the base of the rectangular scapular, stands for Joseph's humility and modesty, though it likewise suggests his royal ancestry traced to King David. Two rectangles of yellow or gold symbolize his justice and sanctity. The scapular's bands are white, indicating Joseph's purity.

The front panel shows St. Joseph carrying the Infant Jesus in one arm and a lily in the other hand. Beneath the image is this invocation: "St. Joseph, Patron of the Church, Pray for Us." The back panel features the papal arms (the tiara and two keys), a dove to symbolize the Holy Spirit, and a cross. An inscription, translated from the Latin, reads: "The Spirit of the Lord Is His Guide."

Wearing the scapular is seen as having a fourfold purpose:

1. To remind one of his or her dedication to the saint and of the need to imitate St. Joseph's purity, humility, and justice.
2. To ask his help to strengthen, guard, and gladden the Church.
3. To obtain, at the time of death, the help of him whom the Church has also proclaimed patron of a happy death.
4. To obtain from the saint the interior spirit, the fear of sin, and the grace necessary for one's state in life.

SCAPULAR OF ST. MICHAEL

A sacramental associated with the Archconfraternity of St. Michael the Archangel.

The two segments of cloth of this scapular are in the shape of a shield. One is blue and the other is black, as are the bands. Both sides of the scapular have the traditional representation of the Archangel St. Michael slaying the dragon, and carry the inscription *Quis ut Deus*, "Who is like God." Pious tradition attributes these words to St. Michael in the great battle at or near the beginning of time when Satan was cast out of heaven.

SCAPULAR OF ST. NORBERT

A sacramental associated with the Praemonstratensian Order.

St. Norbert (c. 1080-1134) reported receiving the direction to found his order, an indication of the place where the order should begin, and the holy habit from the hands of the Blessed Virgin in a vision. He and members of his order were known for promoting Eucharistic devotion.

Based on his devotion to both the

Blessed Sacrament and Mary, St. Norbert established the Church's first Third Order for laypeople. In 1128, he gave a little scapular of white wool to Count Theobald of Champagne and Blois as a proof and an emblem of the man's union with the Norbertine family. The Norbertine scapular ranks as one of the oldest scapulars in the Church.

SCHÖNSTATT, OUR LADY OF

A Marian title and image associated with the International Apostolic Movement of Schönstatt.

It traces its roots to 1914 and a German priest, Father Joseph Kentenich, and the members of the Marian Sodality under his care. Members strive for everyday sanctity and try to serve the universal apostolate of the Church in the world today. The eighteenth of each month is celebrated as "covenant day," a reference to their covenant of love with the Mother of God.

An image of Mary with the Child Jesus is honored in all Schönstatt shrines throughout the world. The original painting, by Luigi Crosio, has the title *Refugium Peccatorum*, "Refuge of Sinners," but is now better known as "Mother Thrice Admirable, Queen and Victoress of Schönstatt." Under this title, Mary is seen as the Mother of God, the Mother of the Redeemer, and the Mother of all. The image was placed in the shrine at Schön-statt, Germany, in 1915.

SCOURGE

A whip used during Christ's Passion.

The Abbey of Subiaco, Italy, claims to have this relic, but there is no extant account to explain how it came there.

SCRIPTURAL ROSARY

A form of Rosary combining customary prayers with passages from Scripture before each Hail Mary.

The Scripture passages progress so that the story of each mystery unfolds as the beads are prayed. The scriptural Rosary dates to the Middle Ages when the beads were prayed with a short thought or meditation for each rather than a decade-long meditation for each mystery. A nonprofit organization first known as the Scriptural Rosary Center and renamed the Christianica Center was founded in 1961 in Chicago to introduce the scriptural Rosary.

(See also **ROSARY**.)

SECULAR ORDERS, THIRD ORDERS — See **CONFRATERNITY**.

SEPTUAGESIMA

The traditional name for the third Sunday before Lent, seventy days before Easter.

SERENITY PRAYER

A prayer written by philosopher and theologian Reinhold Niebuhr (1892-1971).

It reads:

God, grant me the serenity
To accept the things I cannot change,
The courage to change the things I
    can,
And the wisdom to know the
    difference.

Living one day at a time,
Enjoying one moment at a time;
Taking as Jesus did,
This sinful world as it is,
Not as I would have it;
Trusting that He will make all things
    right if I surrender to His will;
So that I may be reasonably happy in
    this life
And supremely happy with Him
    forever in the next.
Amen.

SERVICE

The exercising of one's duty toward God and neighbor.

The first three commandments encompass one's responsibility of serving the Lord through prayer and worship. The final seven commandments are concerned with one's vocation to serve others through charitable works and good example. Also, it is any liturgical rite without the Mass (e.g., the Good Friday liturgy).

SEVEN DEADLY SINS

The traditional list is pride, anger, covetousness, lust, envy, sloth, and gluttony. They are often depicted in ecclesiastical art and in literature.

SEVEN DOLORS — See SEVEN SORROWS OF MARY.

SEVEN GIFTS OF THE HOLY SPIRIT — See GIFTS OF THE HOLY SPIRIT.

SEVEN HOUSES, VISIT OF THE

Latin American Holy Thursday custom.

It is a reenactment of the Last Supper in the church with the pastor presiding and twelve men or boys dressed as Apostles speaking the dialogue of the Gospels. Afterward, the faithful make the visit of the Seven Houses, stopping at seven churches in which they receive from the priests a piece of bread in remembrance of the Last Supper.

SEVEN JOYS OF THE BLESSED VIRGIN MARY

An ancient popular devotion that commemorates the principal joys of the Virgin Mary.

At first, there were only five, but later the number grew to seven to match that of the Seven Dolors, or Sorrows. This devotion was especially popular in England in the Middle Ages to the time of Henry VIII's breaking away from the Church. Forming a part of the Franciscan crown, or Rosary, the Seven Joys were propagated widely by the members of this religious order. The joys are: the Annunciation; the Visitation; the Nativity of Christ; the Adoration of the Magi; the Finding in the Temple; the Resurrection; and the Assumption of the Blessed Mother.

SEVEN LAST WORDS OF CHRIST

A reference to the seven last sets of words spoken by Christ from the cross.

They are:

1. "Father, forgive them; for they know not what they do" (see Luke 23:34).
2. "Truly, I say to you, today you will be with me in Paradise" (see Luke 23:43).
3. "Woman, behold, your son! . . . Behold, your mother!" (see John 19:26-27).
4. "My God, my God, why hast thou forsaken me?" (see Mark 15:34).
5. "I thirst" (see John 19:28).
6. "It is finished" (see John 19:30).
7. "Father, into thy hands I commit my spirit!" (see Luke 23:46).

(See also **GOOD FRIDAY**.)

SEVEN OFFERINGS OF THE PRECIOUS BLOOD

A devotion promoted by St. Gaspar del Bufalo in the early nineteenth century.

The prayer reads:

ETERNAL FATHER, I offer You the merits of the Most Precious Blood of Jesus, Your Beloved Son and my Redeemer, for the propagation and exaltation of my dear Mother the Holy Church for the safety and prosperity of her visible Head, the Holy Roman Pontiff, for the cardinals, bishops, and pastors of souls, and for all the ministers of the sanctuary.

Glory be to the Father, and to the Son, and to the Holy Spirit. As it was in the beginning, is now, and ever shall be, world without end. Amen. Blessed and praised forevermore be Jesus Who has saved us by His Precious Blood. Amen.

ETERNAL FATHER, I offer You the merits of the Most Precious Blood of Jesus, Your Beloved Son and my Divine Redeemer, for the peace and concord of nations, for the conversion of the enemies of our holy faith, and for the happiness of all Christian people.

(Glory be to the Father, etc.)

ETERNAL FATHER, I offer You the merits of the Most Precious

Blood of Jesus, Your Beloved Son and my Divine Redeemer, for the repentance of unbelievers, the extirpation of all heresies, and the conversion of sinners.

(Glory be to the Father, etc.)

ETERNAL FATHER, I offer You the merits of the Most Precious Blood of Jesus, Your Beloved Son my Divine Redeemer, for all my relations, friends, and enemies, for the poor, the sick, and those in tribulation, and for all those for whom You will I should pray, or know that I ought to pray.

(Glory be to the Father, etc.)

ETERNAL FATHER, I offer You the merits of the Most Precious Blood of Jesus, Your Beloved Son and my Divine Redeemer, for all those who shall this day pass to another life, that You may preserve them from pains of hell and admit them the more readily to the possession of Your Glory.

(Glory be to the Father, etc.)

ETERNAL FATHER, I offer You the merits of the Most Precious Blood of Jesus, Your Beloved Son and my Divine Redeemer, for all those who are lovers of this Treasure of His Blood, and for all those who join with me in adoring and honoring It, and for all those who try to spread devotion to It.

(Glory be to the Father, etc.)

ETERNAL FATHER, I offer You the merits of the Most Precious Blood of Jesus, Your Beloved Son and my Divine Redeemer, for all my wants, spiritual and temporal, for the holy souls in purgatory, and particularly for those who in their lifetime were most devoted to this Prince of our Redemption, and to the sorrows and pains of our dear Mother, most Holy Mary.

(Glory be to the Father, etc.)

Blessed and exalted be the Blood of Jesus, now and always, and through all eternity. Amen.

SEVEN PRIVILEGED ALTARS OF THE VATICAN BASILICA

A reference to St. Peter's altars dedicated to: the Blessed Virgin, Sts. Processus and Martinian, St. Michael the Archangel, St. Petronilla, Our Lady of the Pillar, Sts. Simon and Jude, and St. Gregory the Great.

It is an indulgenced act for the faithful piously to visit all and to recite a prayer of their own choosing in honor of the titular saint of each. Other indulgences are granted if the visit is accompanied by confession, communion, and prayers for the intention of the pope.

SEVEN SATURDAYS IN HONOR OF OUR LADY OF RANSOM

A custom associated with the Marian title and the founding of the Mercedarian religious order by St. Peter Nolasco in 1218.

Traditionally, the faithful took part in public exercises for seven Saturdays in honor of the Virgin. On one they were to visit a church associated with the Mercedarians.

St. Peter Nolasco founded the order based on a request from Mary during a reported apparition. Members took a vow to act as hostages, if necessary, to free Christian captives whose faith was in danger from the Moors. This was important at the time of the Crusades; the order's work has since been adapted to changing historical circumstances. Today, the main focus of the Mercedarians' apostolate is reconciliation. Although the feast was originally kept in honor of Our Lady of Ransom, in recent years the name was changed to Our Lady of Mercy.

(See also SCAPULAR OF OUR LADY OF RANSOM.)

SEVEN SACRAMENTS — See SACRAMENTS, SEVEN.

SEVEN SORROWS OF MARY

Also called the Seven Dolors of Our Lady.

The Seven Sorrows are an expansion upon the five sorrowful mysteries of the Rosary.

They are:
1. Mary accepts in faith the prophecy of Simeon (see Luke 2:34-35).
2. Mary flees into Egypt with Jesus and Joseph (see Matthew 2:13-14).
3. Mary seeks Jesus lost in Jerusalem (see Luke 2:43-45).
4. Mary meets Jesus on the way to Calvary (see Luke 23:26-27).
5. Mary stands near the cross of her Son (see John 19:25-27).
6. Mary receives the body of Jesus taken down from the cross (see Matthew 27:57-59).
7. Mary places the body of Jesus in the tomb, awaiting the Resurrection (see John 19:40-42).

In central Europe, the feast is known as *Schmerzensfreitag*. On this day, popular devotions are held and a special soup is served for dinner. The soup is made of seven bitter herbs and is called *Siebenkrautersuppe*. The herbs used are: watercress, parsley, leek, nettle, sour clover, primrose, and spinach.

Particular devotions of Our Mother of Sorrows, including the Scapular and the Rosary of the Seven Sorrows, are proper to the Servite Order.

Seven Sorrows of Mary

The liturgical calendar celebrates the memorial of Our Lady of Sorrows on September 15, appropriately the day following the Feast of the Triumph of the Cross.

SEVEN SUNDAYS OF ST. JOSEPH

A devotion that tradition says was begun by two Franciscans in the eighteenth century.

According to the legend, the Franciscans were saved from drowning by St. Joseph, who requested that they should spread the devotion of his seven sorrows and his seven joys.

The devotion is usually practiced during the seven Sundays before the saint's feast on March 19, but it may be made on any seven consecutive Sundays. It is simply made by meditating, on each of those Sundays, on the sorrowful and joyful experiences St. Joseph went through, in the order they happened. Other prayers can be added to the meditations.

The seven sorrows and joys are:

1. Joseph's sorrow when finding Mary was with child and he thought of separating from her; his joy in learning from the angel that the Child was the Son of God.

2. His sorrow at the birth in poverty in the stable; his joy when he witnessed the angels bow to the Child, and the visit of the Magi.

3. His sadness when he saw the blood shed at the circumcision; his joy when he followed the angel's instructions to name the Child "Jesus."

4. His sadness at the prophecy of Simeon; his joy at the realization that the Child was destined for the salvation of mankind.

5. His sadness on the flight to Egypt; his joy at seeing the pagan idols of Egypt fall in the presence of the true God, Jesus Christ.

6. His sadness on his return in finding the throne was still occupied by another cruel tyrant; his joy in settling in Nazareth.

7. His sadness when the Child Jesus

Sevenfold Flame

was lost for three days; his joy when the Boy was found in the temple.

SEVENFOLD FLAME

A common representation or symbol for the Holy Spirit.

The symbolism is found in the biblical description of the Day of Pentecost: "And there appeared to them tongues as of fire ... And they were all filled with the Holy Spirit" (see Acts 2:3-4). The seven flames signify the seven gifts of the Spirit.

(See also **GIFTS OF THE HOLY SPIRIT**.)

SEXAGESIMA

The traditional name for second Sunday before Lent, sixty days before Easter.

SEXT

That part of the Divine Office that is said at midday.

SHAMROCK

Wood sorrel (*Oxalis acetosella*) is a plant sometimes called "alleluia" because it springs forth during the time of year when the alleluia was sung in churches. It is considered by many to be the plant with which, by tradition, St. Patrick taught King Oengus and the ancient Irish pagans the mystery of the Trinity, although a tiny kind of clover is sometimes also accepted as the true shamrock. Fra Angelico often depicted this plant in his paintings.

(See also **ST. PATRICK**.)

Shamrock

SHIP

An early symbol and metaphor for the Church.

Ship

The Church is sometimes referred to as the "bark" or ship of St. Peter. The central part of a church building is called the "nave," coming from the Latin for "ship" (*navis*).

SHKODRA — See **GOOD COUNSEL, OUR LADY OF**.

SHOULDER WOUND OF CHRIST

A devotion based on visions of Christ reported by St. Bernard of Clairvaux.

Pious legend says the saint asked Jesus which was his greatest unrecorded suffering. Our Lord answered that he had on his shoulder while he bore the cross a wound that was more painful than the others.

A traditional prayer associated with the devotion reads:

O most loving Jesus, meek lamb of God, I, a miserable sinner, salute and worship the most sacred wound of Your shoulder. Alone You did bear Your heavy cross which so tore Your flesh and laid bare Your bones as to inflict on You an anguish greater than any other wound on Your Blessed Body. I adore You, O Jesus, Most Sorrowful, I praise and glorify You and give You thanks for this most secret painful wound, beseeching You by the merit and pain of Your heavy cross to be merciful to me a sinner and to forgive me my mortal and venial sins and to lead me on towards heaven along the Way of the Cross. Amen.

SHRID PYE — See **MINCE PIE**.

SHRINE

A holy place or building where a sacred image or relics are kept or where apparitions were reported to have occurred.

Shrines are generally the focus of devotion and pilgrimage. As defined in Canon Law, a shrine is "a church or other sacred place which, with the approval of the local Ordinary [bishop], is by reason of special devotion frequented by the faithful as pilgrims" (Canon 1230).

SHRINE, CROWNED

A shrine approved by the Holy See as an official place of pilgrimage.

A Roadside Shrine

A Yard Shrine

The designation permits public devotion at the shrine and implies that at least one miracle has been attributed to devotion there. Among the best known crowned shrines are those of Lourdes and Fátima.

SHRINE OF BEAUPRÉ — See BEAU-PRÉ, SHRINE OF.

SHROUD OF TURIN

Also known as the Holy Shroud (Italian: *Santa Sindone*), the Shroud of Turin is a worn, yellowed, and partially scorched linen cloth that has long been venerated as the burial sheet in which Jesus' body was wrapped immediately after he was taken down from the cross on Golgotha. It is best known for bearing a clear depiction of Christ's crucified body, although precisely how the image was imprinted upon the cloth remains even today a mystery. Additionally, the date of the shroud is the source of controversy among scientists and experts. Nevertheless, the shroud has been the source of private devotions since at least the middle of the fourteenth century, and there is evidence to indicate that it was known and revered for centuries before its sudden appearance in Western Europe.

The Shroud measures 14 feet 3 inches in length and 3 feet 7 inches in width. Upon the linen is the image of a Semitic man, with long hair and a beard, who bears the clear marks of crucifixion. All of the wounds described in the New Testament account of Jesus' Passion are present in the hazy brown pigmenting, including the stigmata, the marks from the crown of thorns on the head, bruises on the shoulders, and severe cuts or lacerations on the back where the flogging would have occurred.

The recorded history of the Shroud arguably begins with the accounts in the Gospels of Jesus' death. Mark (15:43-46) wrote: "Joseph of Arimathea, a respected member of the council, who was also himself looking for the kingdom of God, took courage and went to Pilate, and asked for the body of Jesus. And Pilate wondered if he were already dead; and summoning the centurion, he asked him whether he was already dead. And when he learned from the centurion that he was dead, he granted the body to Joseph. And he bought a linen shroud, and taking him down, wrapped him in the linen shroud, and laid him in a tomb which had been hewn out of the rock; and he rolled a stone against the door of the tomb."

The Shroud first became known in the West only in 1354, although there was a long history in the lands of the Eastern Empire of cloths bearing the image of Christ. In the second century, for example, there were accounts of a cloth bearing Christ's image in Edessa, modern Urfa, Turkey. It is possible that these were references to the veil of Veronica, another famed relic, but the cloth, known as the *Mandylion* (handkerchief) and termed *acheiropoietos* (not drawn by human hand), was found in 525 during a restoration of St. Sophia Church in Edessa. The *Mandylion* was not a mere handkerchief, but was, in fact, a cloth folded eight times so that only the face was visible. In 944 it was moved from Edessa to Constantinople during the struggle between the Byzantine Empire and Islam for control of Asia Minor. In the imperial capital, it was given a place of honor among the other relics in the imperial palace and was displayed unfolded, so that its entire length, presenting the image of a crucified man, was then visible. What became of the cloth after the brutal pillaging of Constantinople by Christian soldiers of the Fourth Crusade in 1204 was unknown, but it is possible that it was taken by a soldier from the fallen city back to Europe.

In 1354, a French knight, Geoffroi de

Charny, presented a cloth bearing Christ's crucified image to canons of Lirey, near Troyes. From this moment, the history of the Shroud was fully documented, and the cloth was the source of increasing veneration. The first official statement on the shroud came from antipope Clement VII (r. 1378-1394) who proclaimed that it could be used as an object of veneration as long as it was considered only a representation of the original shroud. The authenticity of the cloth was so widely accepted that it became a prized possession of the House of Savoy when, in 1453, Marguerite de Charny, granddaughter of Geoffroi, gave it to Anna of Lusignano, wife of Duke Ludovico of Savoy. The powerful rulers of Savoy built a chapel for the treasure at Chambéry. In 1506, Pope Julius II approved a Mass and Office for the relic, fulfilling the hopes of the House of Savoy that it might display the Shroud for public devotions.

In December, 1532, a fire broke out in the chapel, and the casket holding the Shroud was set aflame, melting the silver lining. The molten silver dripped onto a portion of the cloth, burning through layers of the folded linen and causing lines of carbonization that are still visible. Water stains, from the water used to extinguish the flames during the fire, are also still apparent. Soon after the fire, some nuns from the Chambéry Order of Poor Clares sewed patches to repair the damaged sections of the Shroud; the patches are still on the cloth.

War forced the Savoyards to move the Shroud to Turin in 1535, starting a period in which the cloth traveled to Turin, Vercelli, Milan, Nice, and then back to Chambéry. In 1578, it was sent permanently to Turin as a gesture to St. Charles Borromeo who had expressed a desire to venerate the Shroud following the cessation of a plague in Milan. The cloth remained in Turin from that time, and in 1694, a separate chapel was established to house it. Named after its architect, Guarino Guarini, the Guarini Chapel served ever after as the chief repository for the Shroud.

The first photographs of the Shroud were taken in May, 1898, by a lawyer, Secondo Pia, renewing public interest in the cloth and sparking efforts to determine its date and genuineness. The first photographs were taken during a public exposition. The Shroud proved to be a natural negative, meaning that when developed the photo revealed a positive image on the photographic negative. To the public excitement over this curious phenomenon was added the discovery in 1899 of a document purportedly written around 1389, in which the bishop of Troyes proclaimed it a fraud after an artist confessed to painting it. The document itself was called into question, however, becoming only one part of a debate that continued throughout the twentieth century.

In 1931, a new set of photographs was taken, by the professional photographer Giuseppe Enrie, during the public exhibition of the Shroud for the wedding of Umberto of Savoy. The first color photograph was taken in 1969 by Giovanni Battista Judica-Cordiglia at the same time that the Cardinal Custodian of the Shroud, Michele Cardinal Pellegrino of Turin, appointed a scientific commission to undertake a formal study of the Shroud. A new era of scientific investigation began, leading to the 1978 celebration of the Fourth Centenary of the transfer of the Shroud from Chambéry to Turin. Scientists from across the globe were given access to the cloth, including the American members of the so-called Shroud of Turin Research Project (STURP).

In 1988, radiocarbon dating (Carbon 14 testing) of the cloth was conducted in laboratories in Oxford, Tucson, and Zürich. With each laboratory using the same strip of cloth, scientists determined that the Shroud dates to between 1260 and 1390, a period consistent with the claims made in the document found in 1899. The radiocarbon tests, however, were questioned subsequently on the basis that the fire at Chambéry may have caused sufficient irradiation of the cloth to offset the correct radiocarbon dating by as many as 1,100 years. Further theories argued that the presence of both bacteria and fungus on the Shroud may have created additional inaccuracies in the carbon dating process.

Other scientific investigations have centered on examining the details of the image and the many physical properties of the Shroud, including the specific composition of the threads and the traces of myrrh, aloe, soil, pollens, plants, and grains that became imbedded in the fabric. The striking results found that the botanical traces on the cloth can be placed not only to Palestine but specifically to the area around Jerusalem. Soil and blood were found on the knees and peak of the nose on the image, reflecting closely where Jesus would have fallen while carrying the cross. Finally, the cloth is sprinkled with both myrrh and aloe, two elements consistent with Jewish burials shrouds from the time. of Christ. Objective examinations continue, including attempts to determine how the image was imprinted onto the cloth.

Scientific study has been encouraged by the Church for many decades. Assisting this work was the gift of the Shroud in 1983 to the Holy See by the terms of Umberto II of Savoy's will. In 1992, a committee was assembled to determine the most advisable means of preserving the Shroud for posterity. The cloth was subsequently placed in a crystal shrine in the Guarini Chapel to maintain control over the internal temperature and humidity.

On the night of April 11-12, 1997, a

fire threatened the destruction of the Shroud, just as in 1532. The flames damaged severely the Guarini Chapel, and the Shroud was saved only by the swift work of the Turin fire brigade. The next year, the cloth was placed in a new case, protected by bullet-proof glass and the most advanced forms of environmental monitors.

The Shroud remains today one of the best known of all relics, even though the Church has never formally certified it to be genuine. Pope John Paul II declared in 1998 that "Since it is not a matter of faith, the Church has no specific competence to pronounce on these questions. She entrusts to scientists the task of continuing to investigate, so that satisfactory answers may be found to the questions connected with this Sheet.... The Church urges that the Shroud be studied without pre-established positions that take for granted results that are not such; she invites scientists to act with interior freedom and attentive respect for both scientific methodology and sensibilities of believers."

Devotion to the Shroud has been expressed since the fourteenth century, growing in popularity as the cloth became better known throughout Europe. An actual feast for the Shroud has been celebrated on May 4 in Europe since 1506. On April 25, 1506 Pope Julius II issued the Bull *Romanus Pontifex* stipulating an Office and Mass *de Sancta Sindone*. The pope wrote in the bull of "that most fa-

mous shroud in which our Savior was wrapped when he lay in the tomb and which is now honorably and devoutly preserved in a silver casket." The Shroud remains the source of devotions, with international organizations fostering a deeper understanding of the relic and promoting wider devotion to the Redeemer whose image the Shroud represents. One of the best known devotional societies is the Holy Shroud Guild, established in 1951 and maintained by the Congregation of the Most Holy Redeemer (the Redemptorists).

Pope John Paul II has also stressed that for many reasons the Shroud is acceptable as an object of devotion. At the celebration of the one-hundredth anniversary of the first photograph of the Shroud on May 24, 1998, he proclaimed:

The Shroud is a challenge to our intelligence. It first of all requires of every person, particularly the researcher, that he humbly grasp the profound message it sends to his reason and his life. The mysterious fascination of the Shroud forces questions to be raised about the sacred Linen and the historical life of Jesus ... the Shroud is a mirror of the Gospel. In fact, if we reflect on the sacred Linen, we cannot escape the idea that the image it presents has such a profound relationship with what the Gospels tell of Jesus' passion and death, that every sensitive person feels inwardly touched and moved at beholding it....

The image of human suffering is reflected in the Shroud. It reminds modern man, often distracted by prosperity and technological achievements, of the tragic situation of his many brothers and sisters, and invites him to question himself about the mystery of suffering in order to explore its causes....

The Shroud is also an image of God's love as well as of human sin. It invites us to rediscover the ultimate reason for Jesus' redeeming death. In the incomparable suffering that it documents, the love of the One who "so loved the world that he gave his only Son" (Jn 3:16) is made almost tangible and reveals its astonishing dimensions.

The Shroud is also an image of powerlessness: the powerlessness of death, in which the ultimate consequence of the mystery of the Incarnation is revealed. The burial cloth spurs us to measure ourselves against the most troubling aspect of the mystery of the Incarnation, which is also the one that shows with how much truth God truly became man, taking on our condition in all things, except sin. The Shroud is an image of silence.

There is a tragic silence of incommunicability, which finds its greatest expression in death, and there is the silence of fruitfulness, which belongs to whoever refrains from being heard outwardly in order to delve to the roots of truth and life....

The Shroud shows us Jesus at the moment of his greatest helplessness and reminds us that in the abasement of that death lies the salvation of the whole world. The Shroud thus becomes an invitation to face every experience, including that of suffering and extreme helplessness, with the attitude of those who believe that God's merciful love overcomes every poverty, every limitation, every temptation to despair.

SHROVE TUESDAY

The traditional name for the day before Ash Wednesday.

It is a day on which the faithful went to confession to be "shriven," that is, to be absolved.

(See also **MARDI GRAS**.)

SIGN

Something that gives direction but, more importantly, points beyond itself to some spiritual reality that may not be attained easily or perceived readily.

In the Gospels, particularly the Gospel of John, Jesus refers to his miracles as signs. A rich theology of signs is present in the Church's liturgical and sacramental life. Signs may be gestures (standing, kneeling, bowing, prostrating oneself, etc.), actions (blessing oneself, anointing with chrism, etc.), liturgical vesture (alb, stole, chasuble, etc.), sacred vessels (chalice, ciborium, etc.), and ecclesiastical art (stained glass, bells, Book of the Gospels, etc.). Without these signs, the faith would be unknowable and opaque. With them, it is possible for Catholics to enter into the mysteries behind the signs and thereby be caught up into the life of Christ and the Church. We refer to the sacraments as signs because they both cause and effect grace through the act of signifying.

SIGN OF THE CROSS

A sign, ceremonial gesture, or movement in the form of a cross by which a person confesses faith in both the Holy Trinity and the Redemption wrought by Christ, while interceding for the blessing of himself or herself, other persons, and things.

In Roman Rite practice, a person making the sign touches the fingers of the right hand to the forehead, below the breast, left shoulder, and right shoulder while saying: "In the name of the Father [forehead], and of the Son [breast], and of the Holy [left shoulder] Spirit [right shoulder]." The sign can also be made with the thumb on the forehead, the lips, and the breast. For the blessing of persons and objects, a large sign of the cross is made by movement of the right hand. In Eastern Rite practice, the sign is made with the thumb and first two fingers of the right hand joined together and touching the forehead, below the breast, the right shoulder, and the left shoulder; the formula generally used is the doxology: "O Holy God, O Holy Strong One, O Immortal One." The Eastern manner of making the sign was general until the first half of the thirteenth century; by the seventeenth century, Western practice involved the whole right hand and the reversal of direction from shoulder to shoulder.

SIGN OF PEACE — See **PEACE, SIGN OF**.

SIGNING OF BREAD — See **BREAD, SIGNING OF**.

SILENCE, VIRGIN OF

A Marian title associated with Our Lady of Knock.

It got its name because, according to those who reported the vision, Our Lady did not speak.

(See also **KNOCK, OUR LADY OF**.)

SILENT NIGHT

An Austrian Christmas carol written by Josef Mohr, the parish priest in the small town of Oberndorf, near Salzburg, in 1818.

Later, it remained hidden among the manuscripts of the church choir for some time until it was discovered and brought to a family of singers known as the Rainers. They began to sing it at their concerts and it became widely used in Austria and Germany. They performed the song on their American concert tour from 1839 to 1843, and within a few years it was equally popular in the United States. Tradition holds that Father Mohr wrote the piece quickly as a substitute to be accompanied by guitar when the church organ failed.

SILUVA, OUR LADY OF

A Marian image and devotion dating back to the early seventeenth century.

A reported apparition of Mary in Siluva, Lithuania, led to the discovery of a deed to a church that had been buried for safekeeping some four decades earlier when the building had been confiscated by anti-Catholic forces. The deed's recovery led many to return to their lost practice of the faith.

SIMONY

The selling or purchasing of spiritual things, which is forbidden both by natural and ecclesiastical law.

The term is derived from the story of Simon Magus (see Acts 8:18-24), in which he attempted to purchase spiritual power from the Apostles.

SIMPLE FEASTS

A term used before the reform of the Church calendar and the Sacred Liturgy in the West, referring to the least important grade of feast.

By decree of the Sacred Congregation of Rites in 1961, simple feasts became commemorations. Now many of the former simple feasts are designated optional memorials.

SIN

The deliberate, free, knowledgeable transgression of Divine Law, which is a refusal to strive for sanctity and may either drive all charity from one's soul ("mortal sin") or partially expel charity ("venial sin").

Sin entered the world through the disobedience of Adam and Eve. The Old Testament considers sin to be "missing the mark," while sin in the New Testament is viewed as straying from the loving Father. The redemption wrought by Christ has conquered sin. All sins are forgivable, except the sin against the Holy Spirit (see Matthew 12:31-32).

SIN EATING

A superstitious custom in Wales and Hereford dating back to the eighteenth century.

After someone's death, the parish's "sin eater" — generally a very poor man — was brought to the house. He stood on one side of the corpse, and a crust of bread, a bowl of ale or milk, and a sixpenny coin were passed to him over the body. His eating and drinking were seen as signifying he had taken on himself the sins of the deceased (eaten that person's sins) and so the ghost of the deceased was prevented from haunting the home. This custom lingered in Wales until about the nineteenth century; in Herefordshire, the ceremonial drinking of port wine by visitors at the wake may be a remnant of the custom.

SINGING

The worship of God in song at liturgical functions by the celebrant, cantor, choir, congregation, or a combination of these.

Singing during the sacred functions has been a mainstay since the early Church.

SJUSOVARDAGEN

Swedish for "day of the sleepyhead."

The now-suppressed Feast of the Seven Sleepers of Ephesus is a medieval legend. The story maintained that a group of Christian martyrs were walled up in a cave near Ephesus during the Roman persecutions, woke up two centuries later, and were hailed as living proof of the resurrection of the dead.

In Swedish, the name for their feast was *Sjusovardagen*, which also means "the day of the sleepyhead," or "one who sleeps late in the morning." An amusing celebration to celebrate this feast grew up among the fennoswedish people of Southwest Finland about the turn of the last century.

Each town in the region has its own *sjusovare*, a "sleepyhead" who finds it difficult to arise before seven in the morning. This was often the mayor, but always a well known person in the town. On the morning of the feast, a group of men would capture him from his bed and throw him into the closest body of water. Many townspeople gathered to watch, and the local press mentioned it.

The children believe that the person is still asleep when he is thrown in the water. However, even the victim *sjusovare* is in on the prank, which is accompanied by much laughter and high spirits.

Sjusovardagen is still printed in all official fennoswedish calendars and almancs, even though most of the other Catholic days have been deleted, with the exception of Henrik (Henry, the patron of Finland), and Lucy.

SLAVERY OF LOVE, HOLY

A Marian devotion.

It is attributed to the writings of St. Louis Marie Grignon de Montfort (1673-1716).

(See also **CONSECRATION TO JESUS THROUGH MARY.**)

SNOW, OUR LADY OF THE

A Marian devotion that, tradition holds, dates back to an apparition in Rome in 352.

According to legend, an elderly, childless, noble couple asked the pope for guidance concerning the distribution of their estate after their deaths. He advised them to pray. During the night of August 4, 352, the Virgin Mary appeared in their dreams and expressed a desire that a church in her honor be built in Rome on the hill covered with snow. The next day, the citizens of Rome awoke to the astonishing sight of the Esquiline Hill draped in a blanket of snow. The husband and wife accepted this as Our Lady's answer to their prayers and provided funds for the construction of the church, now known as the Basilica of St. Mary Major and popularly known as the first Shrine of Our Lady of the Snow.

In the United States, a National Shrine of Our Lady of the Snows is located in Belleville, Illinois.

In 1941, the Oblates of Mary Immaculate introduced the devotion of Our Lady of the Snows to the American Midwest at Belleville, Illinois. An original painting of Our Lady of the Snows by J. Watson Davis of New York shows Our Lady of the Snows in the Artic sky above some kneeling Eskimos. This became the center of a small shrine in the corner of the Oblate seminary. The shrine has since been moved to a place in what is now known as the National Shrine of Our Lady of the Snows.

In l958, Navy chaplain Lt. Leon Darkowski took part in Operation Deep Freeze II. Before leaving for the Antarctic, Father Darkowski had a medal of Our Lady of the Snows struck and distributed to Catholic Seabees who placed themselves under the protection of Our Lady at a Mass in the Quonset Naval Air Station chapel, North Kingston, R.I.

SOCIAL FUNCTIONS OF CEMETERY — See **CEMETERY, SOCIAL FUNCTIONS OF** .

SOCIETY OF ST. MONICA

Reverend Dennis McNeil founded the Society of St. Monica in Cuyahoga, Ohio, in 1986, to promote confident, daily prayer for the return of inactive Catholics and Catholics who have left the Church. The society counts more than 10,000 members worldwide.

SOCIETY OF THE DIVINE ATTRIBUTES

Founded in 1974 as a contemplative

prayer society made up of lay, clerical, and religious. Their headquarters are in Pittsburgh, Pennsylvania.

SODALITY

An organization, usually of laypeople, that promotes pious or charitable acts.

(See also **CONFRATERNITY**.)

SOLEDAD, OUR LADY OF

The Virgin of Solitude, a Mexican Marian image and devotion dating back to the early seventeenth century.

One of the most beautiful images of Our Lady in Mexico is known as La Virgin de la Soledad, the Virgin of Solitude. Dressed in black, the image depicts Our Lady from the time of the crucifixion to the Resurrection. Here, the Mother of Christ is alone after her son's death. Dressed in a mantle of mourning, another variation of the *Mater Dolorosa* (Mother of Sorrows), she personifies the Church after the disciples have fled, left to shoulder the sorrows of the world alone. Under this title, she is especially honored in the state of Oaxaca.

According to an ancient legend, in 1620 a mule train camped outside the city of Oaxaca discovered an extra mule which did not belong to anyone in the group. The mule refused to move and when prodded, it rolled over and died. When the pack it carried was opened, a beautiful statue of the Virgin of Soledad was found inside. Taking this as a sign from heaven, the people first built a shrine, later a church and finally the imposing basilica which stands today on the spot where the statue first appeared. The statue was clothed in luxurious velvet robes embroidered with gold and pearls, and wore a golden halo.

La Soledad became the patron of the city, the state, and of the mariners who sailed to and from her ports. Traditionally the sailors walked, often barefoot, from the coast to the shrine, bringing pearls, gold, and precious stones as token of their devotion.

Our Lady of Soledad

During the mid-nineteenth century, many religious treasures were hidden rather than turned over to the state as required by law during the first persecution of the Church in Mexico. Some were forgotten and became lost. In 1888, a young man leased a portion of the Portal de la Claveria for his store which sold fine fabrics and imports. The Portal had once been part of the treasury of the archdiocese and the cathedral before the reform of the government. When an interior wall was knocked down during the renovations, the workers found a large iron chest and a smaller wooden box in a hollowed-out space in the floor under the wall. The box contained a totally rotten velvet robe of La Soledad, embroidered with gold and pearls. The chest contained a virtual treasure of pearls and stones which had been given to the Virgin through the years by the mariners. The store owner, Luis Bustamante, bought the finest French velvet available and had some nuns embroider a new robe, using the original pearls and gold. Then the treasures were returned to the Virgin at the basilica. In the late 1980s some of the Virgin's jewels were stolen. Unfortunately, the crime has not been solved.

In Colombia, on Good Friday, the faithful hold the *Descendimiento* and the *Procesion de la Soledad de Maria*. An immense image of Christ is taken down from the cross in the presence of Mary, all dressed in black as the Virgin de Soledad. A long procession begins through the barrios, finally arriving at the tomb, where in the presence of Mary, Christ is buried. Then Mary is enthroned and accompanied by the people in her mourning for several hours.

SOLEMNITY

The highest rank of liturgical celebration.

SOLEMNITY OF MARY, MOTHER OF GOD

A holy day of obligation and solemnity celebrated on January 1.

The Western calendar in effect since 1970, in accord with Eastern tradition, reinstated the Marian character of this commemoration on the octave day of Christmas. The former Feast of the Circumcision, dating at least from the first half of the sixth century, marked the initiation of Jesus (see Luke 2:21) into Judaism and, by analogy, focused attention on the initiation of persons in the Christian religion and their incorporation in Christ though baptism. The newly designated solemnity supplanted the Feast of the Motherhood of Mary, which was formerly observed on October 11. That feast was first approved for Portugal at the request of King Joseph Emmanuel in 1751 by Pope Benedict XIV, who composed the Mass himself. Pope Pius XI made it a universal observance to commemorate the 1500th anniversary of the Council of

Ephesus held in 431. It was this council that defended Mary's title of *Theotokos* (Greek for "God-bearer").

SON OF JOSEPH, JESUS

A title of Christ emphasizing his relationship to St. Joseph.

The genealogy of Our Lord is traced by the evangelists through St. Joseph as head of the house and family, from the line of King David. Having been chosen by God to be the foster father of Jesus, St. Joseph had a privileged association with the Divine Child. With Mary, Joseph was the first on earth to pay homage to the Incarnate Son of God.

What little is known of Joseph is found in the Gospels. He was a carpenter or builder by trade, an "upright man." As a good father, Joseph by his labor provided for his family. He did all in his power to protect and care for them and keep them from harm. St. Joseph carried Jesus in his arms, played with him, and later taught him his trade. Luke tells us that Jesus was obedient to his parents (see Luke 2:51).

As there is little mention of the life of Christ during the "hidden years," it is reasonable to suppose that the family led an average life at Nazareth.

A probable reconstruction of the daily life at Nazareth can be made from historical and archaeological research. If the traditional site of the holy house is accurate,

the home was probably a one-room building with a cave at the back which could be used as a storeroom. The house would be built of stone with a flat roof covered by stones or tiles which were covered with earth. The floor would have been made either of stone flags or beaten earth.

The village of Nazareth lies on a hilltop among the bare Mountains of Galilee. Here, in the humble home, the Holy Family lived in a framework of spiritual closeness.

The family would rise at dawn, roll up their bedding and stack it in a corner. They would begin their day with a prayer, the *Shemah Yisrael,* a confession of faith taken from several passages in the Pentateuch. This prayer was repeated again in the evening. During the saying of this prayer, the family would stand facing the temple in Jerusalem, and Jesus and Joseph would wear the *taliss,* a prayer shawl, and the phylacteries. The latter were little parchment boxes bound to wrist and forehead by a leather strap and containing the prayer. These served as reminders that God would not desert his people, as long as Israel obeyed him.

Next the family would eat a light breakfast of bread and wine, fresh fruit and preserved olives. A blessing was said before and after each meal, and before taking anything at all to eat or drink during the day. As Joseph and Jesus left for the day's work, they would turn and touch with their right hand the little wooden box called a *Mezuzah* nailed to the lintel of the door above the right doorpost, then kiss their hand. Inside the Mezuzah was a parchment scroll containing the same promises to Israel and commands of God that the *Shemah Yisrael* set forth.

Our Lady would spend her day performing the housewife's chores common to the Jewish homes of that day. She would wash the dishes and sweep the floor. Putting a shawl on her head, she would take a large earthen jug down the steep street to the public fountain. Here she would fill the jug and return with it on her head as the women of Nazareth still do to this day. The family wash was done at this same fountain. Our Lady ground wheat between two flat stones for the family bread. The loaves were not baked at home but were carried to a large public oven. Additionally, large pieces of meat were roasted in this oven. Cooking at home was limited as it was done over a charcoal brazier. Mary probably carded wool or flax and spun it into thread, but the weaving of the cloth probably was done by a professional weaver. The main meal of the day was at noon. In addition to the bread, fruit, and wine, there would be a dish of meat or fish from the Lake of Galilee. The evening meal, eaten about six o'clock, would consist of bread, wine, and a vegetable or cheese. After the evening meal, the family would recount stories of the

ways of God with Israel. Mary and Joseph would repeat from memory long passages from the Law of Moses, the Psalms, and the prophecies, and teach them to Jesus.

By nine o'clock, after evening prayers, the family would unroll the bedding for sleep. The light, a simple wick in a dish of olive oil, would be put out. On Fridays at sundown, the men assembled in the synagogue for the prayer service. Afterwards, Joseph and Jesus would walk home through the gathering dusk along streets where in every window the Sabbath candle was lighted. At home, the menorah would be burning on the table set with a clean linen cloth, with the Sabbath wine already poured.

On the Sabbath morning, the principal religious service of the week was held in the synagogue. The older men sat on the front benches, the younger men to the rear, and the women sat in a special section. The prayer *Shemah Yisrael* opened the service. During the prayer, all stood and faced toward Jerusalem. Then followed a reading of the section of the Law of Moses appointed for that Saturday. Next came a reading from one of the other books of the Old Testament and then a sermon. The readers and preachers were selected from the congregation, and if a visitor were present he was usually asked to speak.

The long service was over about noon, when the family returned home to eat the meal Our Lady had prepared the day before. In the afternoon, one was permitted to take a walk of a little more than a mile. Then it was time for the vesper service. The Sabbath ended at sundown, and the shopkeepers came out and took down the shelters from the front of their shops. Vendors commenced hawking their wares through the streets, and women hurried off to the fountain. The children played in the streets and the men stood around talking and visiting.

This simple lifestyle was the type lived by the Holy Family until the time for Jesus' public ministry. It was broken only by the pilgrimages to Jerusalem. So Jesus grew both tall and wise, and was loved by God and man (see Luke 2:52).

The following description of Jesus is written by Publius Lentulus, Governor of Judea, and is addressed to Tiberius Caesar, Emperor of Rome. It was found in an excavated city written in Aramaic on stone.

There lives at this time in Judea, a man of singular virtue whose name is Jesus Christ, whom the barbarians esteem as a prophet, but his followers love and adore him as the offspring of the immortal God. He calls back the dead from the graves, and heals all sorts of diseases with a word or a touch. He is a tall man, and well shaped, of an amiable and reverend aspect; his hair of a color that can hardly be matched, the color of chestnut full ripe, falling in waves about his shoulders. His forehead high, large and imposing; his cheeks without spot or wrinkle, beautiful with a lovely red; his nose and mouth formed with exquisite symmetry; his beard thick and of a color suitable to his hair reaching below his chin. His eyes bright blue, clear and serene, look innocent, dignified, manly, and mature. In proportion of body, most perfect and captivating, his hands and arms most delectable to behold. He rebukes with majesty, counsels with mildness, his whole address, whether in word or deed, being eloquent and grave. No man has seen him laugh, yet his manner is exceedingly pleasant; but he has wept in the presence of men. He is temperate, modest and wise; a man, for his extraordinary beauty and divine perfections, surpassing the children of men in every sense.

SONGS OF ASCENT

The category of Old Testament Psalms (specifically Psalms 120-134) that were probably used by pilgrims as they "went up" to the temple for the new year commemoration.

SORROWS OF THE BLESSED VIRGIN MARY — See SEVEN SORROWS OF MARY.

SORROWFUL AND IMMACULATE HEART OF MARY

Devotion based on private revalations of Berthe Petit (1879-1943), a Franciscan tertiary and mystic from Belgium.

The picture most representative of Mary under the title of the Sorrowful and Immaculate Heart is somewhat mysterious in origin. It is venerated at the Convent of Ollignies, Belgium. The picture was discovered at the time of the armistice of 1918 in the cellars of the boarding school conducted by the Bernardine Nuns where Berthe Petit had been educated. After the departure of the troops, one of the nuns was tidying up and putting the convent in order. She found a piece of cardboard on which was pasted a pornographic picture. She tore off the picture to throw it in the fire, and to her great astonishment discovered that the picture was covering a very beautiful representation of Mary. This picture of Our Lady was put in a place of honor, and soon many favors were attributed to prayers made before it.

A number of things indicate that the picture is of French origin. When Berthe saw it in 1919, she recognized in it the twofold symbol of the Virgin of the Sorrowful and Immaculate Heart. The picture shows Mary holding in her left hand a lily, symbolic of her immaculate purity. The index finger of her right hand points to her Sorrowful Heart, surrounded by flames and pierced by a sword. The features resemble those of the Pietà, or Sorrowful Virgin, so well known in many churches. Her far-seeing gaze seems to contemplate with sadness the sins of the world — the cause of the sufferings expressed on the gentle face.

Berthe and her friends lost no time in propagating this picture as representative of the devotion to the Sorrowful and Immaculate Heart of the Virgin. Soon copies of the picture were in demand everywhere in Belgium, and the devotion had begun to spread throughout Europe, worldwide. Since 1959, the Camaldolese religious in La Seyne-sur-Mer, France, where the first church dedicated to Our Lady under this title was erected, have been in charge of the devotion. Slowly, and surely, the devotion has spread around the world. In dioceses on every continent, aided by a number of religious orders and pious associations, the title of Sorrowful and Immaculate Heart of Mary is becoming known to those who honor Mary in order to give more honor to her Son.

SORROWS, OUR LADY OF

Marian title especially propagated by the Servite order.

On the feast of her Assumption, August 15, 1233, Our Lady appeared to seven noblemen of Florence, instructing them to establish a religious order which would preach her sorrows to the Christian world. She appeared again on Good Friday, April 15, 1240. In the second apparition, Mary presented the seven with a habit, indicated to them the rule for the order, and gave them the name "Servants of Mary." The seven holy founders of the Servites built their first monastery in Monte Senario. The Servite Order became the last of the five mendicant orders of the Catholic Church.

A number of devotions in honor of Our Sorrowful Mother grew out of the fervent preaching of the Servite Friars. The *Via Matris* and a number of prayers date back to the Middle Ages. Seven chief sorrows of Mary's life have been chosen to make up the Rosary of the Seven Dolors. The chaplet consists of seven sets of seven beads each. Between the sets are medals showing the seven sorrows. At the end are three beads and a medal of Our Lady with seven swords piercing her heart. The Rosary begins with an act of contrition, the Our Father, and seven Hail Marys in memory of Mary's tears, and it ends with three times the invocation "Virgin most sorrowful, pray for us." (See also **SEVEN SORROWS OF MARY**).

SOUL FOOD

A custom based on the pre-Christian tradition of placing food on graves in November when the spirits of the dead were believed to roam the earth.

The Christian tradition developed of baking special breads and "soul food." At the family meal in many places on this day, an extra place is set in remembrance of the departed and the extra food is later given to the poor. An ancient belief held that the dead came back to earth on this day; therefore, many central Europeans kept their windows open so that the souls in purgatory could hear the prayers said on their behalf.

(See also **DÍA DE LOS MUERTOS**.)

SPIRITUAL COMMUNION

A private devotion focusing on the Eucharist when one is unable to receive Christ in the Blessed Sacrament.
One suggested form is:

O Lord Jesus, since I am unable at this time to receive you in the holy sacrament of the Eucharist, I beg you to come spiritually into my heart in the spirit of your holiness, in the truth of your goodness, in the fullness of your power, in the communion of your mysteries and in the perfection of your ways. O Lord, I believe, I trust, I glorify you. I am sorry for all my sins. O Sacrament most Holy, O Sacrament divine, all praise and all thanksgiving be every moment thine.

SPIRITUAL EXERCISES OF ST. STANISLAUS — See **ST. STANISLAUS, SPIRITUAL EXERCISES OF**.

SPIRITUAL LIFE INSTITUTE OF AMERICA

An eremitical movement to foster the contemplative spirit in America, founded by Reverend William McNamara, O.C.D., in Crestone, Colorado, in 1960. A second foundation was made in Nova Scotia and a third hermitage was established in Sligo, Ireland.

SPIRITUAL WORKS OF MERCY

Seven Christian duties traditionally associated with the soul.

They are: instruct the ignorant, admonish the sinner, counsel the doubtful, comfort the sorrowful, bear wrongs patiently, forgive all injuries, and pray for the living and the dead.

(See also **CORPORAL WORKS OF MERCY**.)

SPIRITUALITY

The way an individual responds through grace to the call of Christ and his invitation to discipleship.

This always involves conversion, or change of heart, on the part of those called by Christ. Believers are called to renounce sin and unite themselves to the Lord's preeminent victory over sin and death, his Paschal mystery. While this call is intensely personal, it simultaneously brings the faithful into communion with the Church, the Body of Christ. Through baptism and the other sacraments, believers are linked ever more deeply to the Savior and to all those redeemed by the blood of his cross. Although the faith admits of many different spiritualities (e.g., Ignatian and Franciscan), a single spirituality can be discerned in the life of every believer. Traditionally, it rests on personal prayer, the sacraments, and the virtues. Engaged in these, it now becomes possible for those in the Catholic tradition to pursue holiness, the goal of everyone who bears the name Christian.

SPONSOR

A person who gives special assistance to one who is about to be baptized or confirmed; also called godparent.

SPOUSE OF CHRIST

A special title by which the Church is especially understood as the spouse of Christ (see Ephesians 5:22-33).

Also, a professed religious woman, by reason of her vowed chastity, is called a bride of Christ.

SPRING CLEANING

The tradition of giving one's home a thorough cleaning on the three days after Passion Sunday to prepare for the great feast of Easter.

The custom may have developed from the Jewish practice of ritually cleansing and sweeping the whole house as prescribed in preparation for the feast of Passover.

SPY WEDNESDAY

The Wednesday of Holy Week, referring to Judas Iscariot's agreeing to show the chief priests where they could easily capture Jesus (see Mark 14:10).

ST. AGATHA'S BREAD

A Sicilian custom.

Legend says St. Agatha's breasts were cut off during her martyrdom, around 250. This story is honored on her feast, February 5, by baking bread in round loaves. In the region near her birthplace of Catania in Sicily, little rounded marzipan confections meant to symbolize breasts are also eaten on her day as special treats. Catanese nuns make the sweets, which are called *minne de vergine*. The legend has led to her veneration today as a patroness in cases of breast cancer.

According to legend, Agatha miraculously freed her native city from starvation and stopped an eruption of Mount Etna, and so she is venerated as a "bread" saint and a patron of protection against fire. On her feast day, people bake Agatha loaves to which they attach little pieces of paper with her picture and handwritten prayers against fire. The loaves are taken to the church to be blessed, then kept in the home as a sacramental.

ST. AGNES

A virgin and martyr held in high esteem by the Church since her death (d.c. 304, feast day January 21). Agnes's name and

St. Agnes

The Martyrdom of St. Agnes

the date of her feast are listed in the calendar drawn up in 354.

While St. Agnes remains one of the most famous of the Roman martyrs, there is little known for certain about her. She was killed in Rome and was buried in the cemetery on the Via Nomentana, where a church was built in her honor about the year 350 by Constantia, the daughter of the Emperor Constantine. She was entombed in a silver shrine given by Pope Paul V in the early seventeenth century.

In liturgical art, she is depicted in flames with a sword at her feet (references to the pious legend that holds that fire failed to kill her and so she was decapitated). The lamb, symbolic of purity, represents her virginity.

On the Feast of St. Agnes, two lambs are blessed. The lambs, one crowned with a wreath of white roses, the other with red roses, represent the virginity and the martyrdom of the saint. The wool of the lambs is formed into *pallia* and distributed to archbishops.

(See also **PALLIUM**.)

ST. ANNE

The mother of Mary, also called Ann, Anna, and Hannah (the Hebrew for "grace"); wife of St. Joachim (d. first century, feast day July 26).

Information on Mary's parents comes from several apocryphal writings: the *Gospel of the Nativity of Mary*, the *Pseudo-Matthew*, and the *Protoevangelium* of James, all which profess to give an account of Mary's birth and life. This story bears a strong resemblance to the story of Hannah (see 1 Samuel 1 and 2).

St. Anne has been venerated in the East since the early Church, particularly in Constantinople (now Istanbul, Turkey). She was listed in one of the Church's oldest calendars. Her cultus became popular in the West in the thirteenth century and was instituted in the Roman Calendar in 1481. She is the patron of widows, pregnant women, plague victims, childless women, and nursemaids as well as other careers. She is the patron of Florence, Italy, because the city was freed from a tyrant on her feast day. She is also the patron of Naples and Innsbruck. St. Anne's water was considered a remedy for physical ailments. She is depicted in liturgical art as a matron, often teaching or holding the Blessed Virgin Mary as a child.

Sts. Anne and Mary

Sts. Anne and Mary

ST. ANNE'S SHELL CHAPEL

A small chapel on the grounds of the motherhouse of the Sisters of Providence at St. Mary-of-the-Woods, Indiana, dedicated to St. Anne.

The interior is walled with iridescent shells from the Wabash River. The shrine was developed from an *ex voto* by Blessed Mother Theodore Guérin, foundress of the order. A native of Brittany, and the daughter of a captain in the French navy, she was familiar with the tradition of sailors asking for St. Anne's intercession for protection while at sea. During a perilous crossing from Europe to the United States in 1842, Blessed Theodore prayed to St. Anne and promised to build a chapel in the saint's honor.

(See also EX VOTO.)

ST. ANTHONY OF EGYPT

One of the founders of monasticism (c. 251-356, feast day January 17).

St. Anthony lived as a hermit, often alone, from the time he was twenty. Gradually, other ascetics built a community in nearby huts or caves. At their request, he regulated their communal worship, work, and penance schedules. Laymen and laywomen also sought the saint's guidance. Among those who visited him was the Emperor Constantine. A good deal is known about St. Anthony because of a surviving biography written by St. Athanasius (296-373), bishop of Alexandria, who was acquainted with him. His influence was great during his life, and his reputation continued to be prominent into the Middle Ages. He is the patron of several orders of canons and knights and of the poor, the sick, swineherds, butchers, and domestic animals. He is invoked against fire and plague and is prayed to for good harvests. The pig and bell are associated with him because of the Order of Hospitalers of St. Anthony. He is depicted with a T-shaped staff and bells, symbolic of a hermit.

(See also KNIGHTS OF MALTA [HOSPITALERS].)

ST. ANTHONY OF PADUA

A Doctor of the Church (1195-1231, feast day June 13).

Born in Lisbon, Portugal, St. Anthony was the first theologian of the Franciscan Order and was renowned for his preaching; canonized shortly after his death, he is referred to as the Evangelical Doctor.

During his lifetime, St. Anthony was called the "Wonder Worker" because of many reported miracles. He is the patron of Padua and Lisbon, children, travelers, married couples, women, animals, and miners. He is invoked against infertility, demons, fevers, wars, shipwrecks, and plagues and is popularly known for finding lost articles. In iconography he is shown as a Franciscan, sometimes with the Child Jesus standing on a book.

The son of a Portugese nobleman, Martin deBoullion, and Theresa, a descendent of the Austrian kings, he was given the name Fernando. At fifteen, he joined the Regular Canons of St. Augustine where he devoted himself to prayer and study and became a Bible scholar.

In 1220, Anthony was accepted by the Franciscans and left for Morocco to preach the Gospel to the Moors. He fell ill, and was forced to return to Europe. A storm drove his ship to the shores of Italy where he lived for the rest of his life. Wherever he went, the gifted preacher drew large crowds. Often no church was large enough to contain his listeners, and he would preach in the open air. He traveled throughout France, Spain, and Italy. His greatest success was in Padua, where the entire city flocked to hear his sermons.

In 1226 Anthony was elected as the envoy from the Franciscans to Pope Gregory IX. Afterwards, he returned to Padua where he preached until his death on June 13, 1231, at the age of thirty six.

Even in his lifetime, Anthony was acclaimed as a miracle worker and a number of miraculous stories are related about him. At Rimini, the people refused to listen to him preach against the Catharist heresy. Therefore, he told them he would preach to the fish. So many fish crowded the banks that the people were struck by

St. Anthony of Padua with the Infant Jesus

the miracle and threw themselves at this feet, begging his pardon. At Bourges, a citizen challenged him by telling the people to watch as his mule chose either the pail of corn he was holding or the religion of the friar standing with a monstrance. As the people watched, the mule bypassed the feed and instead knelt in adoration in front of the Blessed Sacrament. Anthony had only been dead a short while when the people of Padua asked Pope Gregory IX to enroll him among the saints. A commission of cardinals studied his life and the miracles offered as proof of his holiness. Forty-six miracles were approved for his canonization, two of which were worked during his lifetime. He was proclaimed a saint in 1232.

Thirty-two years after his death his remains were taken to a basilica built in his honor. His tongue was found incorrupt. The tongue was removed by St. Bonaventure, who was present, and is now kept in a golden reliquary in the treasury chapel of the basilica in Padua where it is on constant display.

In 1981, the 750th anniversary of St. Anthony's death, his sarcophagus was opened for the first time since 1350. Three bundles wrapped in red damask with gold trimmings were found inside the double wooden caskets. One contained the saint's habit and the other two contained the bones and the skull. The saint's vocal cords were found to be perfectly preserved. These are now kept in a reliquary in the chapel beside the incorrupt tongue of the saint. These two great relics comprise a fitting memorial for the saint who was an outstanding preacher of Holy Scripture.

During the time of the wars against the Turks, the Christian land armies were under the special protection of St. Anthony, and his help was invoked by the troops before each battle. By a special royal order of 1668, the Spanish government made St. Anthony a soldier of the second infantry regiment. At every victory in which this regiment was involved, he was given an official promotion to a higher rank. After two hundred years he had attained the rank of colonel. In 1885 he was given the rank of general and retired from active service.

In Portugal, Italy, Spain, and France, St. Anthony is the patron of sailors and fisherman. His statue is often placed in a little shrine on the ship's mast and the sailors pray to him in storms and other dangers. Girls go to St. Anthony's shrines to pray for a husband. They light candles and drink from the fountain in the churchyard (Anthony's Well.) In Spain he is called *Santo Casamentero*, "the Holy Matchmaker." In former times, Basque girls went in pilgrimage on his feast day to Durango where they prayed in his shrine for a "good boy." Young Basque men often made the same journey and waited outside the church to ask the girls to dance after their devotions. In Portugal, when their wishes were not granted, or when they did not find a husband, the girls took their revenge by lowering the saint's statue down a well, turning him against the wall, or breaking a bottle of wine on his back.

St. Anthony is also the patron of animals. In the days before automobiles, everyone in Rome, from the pope to peasants, sent horses and mules to St. Anthony's Church on June 13 to be blessed.

The words "St. Anthony, guide !" were

often written on the envelopes of mail sent by the saint's devotees in hopes of heavenly intercession with the postal service.

Many explanations of why St. Anthony is particularly known for returning lost items have been attempted, but no one knows for certain. There is a report in an ancient Portuguese book which may be historical. A man had stolen a valuable volume of chants from a monastery. Later, while praying to St. Anthony, he became repentant for the theft and inspired with a great urge to return the book. He did so, telling that the saint had made him restore the volume. The custom of praying to the saint for lost articles is known to have actually started in Portugal and spread from there to the rest of Europe. Immigrants brought the custom with them to America.

ST. ANTHONY'S BREAD

A devotion dating to the thirteenth century.

Tradition holds that while the basilica in Padua was being built, a child fell into a barrel of water and drowned. In her grief,

Two renditions of St. Anthony's Bread

the mother called on St. Anthony for help and promised to donate the child's weight in grain for the poor if the child was restored to life. While the mother was still praying, the child arose as if from a deep sleep. This miracle gave rise to the pious practice of giving alms to the poor as a petition or in return for favors received through St. Anthony's intercession. In the nineteenth century, a pious French woman named Louise Bouffier promised loaves of bread for the poor in exchange for St. Anthony's help. Her shop in Toulon became a center of devotion to the saint; the alms of those whose favors were granted were given to the poor families of the city.

Many Franciscan institutions continue to bless and distribute loaves of bread for the poor or toward the education of a seminarian in honor of St. Anthony of Padua.

Also in the nineteenth century, Blessed Hannibal Mary Di Francia, the founder of the Rogationist Fathers of the Heart of Jesus and of the Daughters of the Divine Zeal, established the Anthonian Orphanages in the most poverty stricken area of Messina, Italy. In 1887, a cholera epidemic ravaged Messina. The devotion of St. Anthony's Bread also began independently at this time. In Blessed Hannibal's words:

As the cholera raged in Messina in 1887, the widow Susanna Consiglio Miceli, a pious and wealthy woman, vowed to St. Anthony that she would give sixty lira for bread for the orphans of [the great saint] housed in our Anthonian Orphanages. She pledged her donation in honor of the saint, providing he spared her and her family from disease. St. Anthony of Padua delighted in this vow that he himself inspired. Neither the widow nor her family caught the disease. One October day after the cholera had ceased, a young man came to me on behalf of anonymous people and gave me sixty lira to buy bread for the orphans…. The specification made an impression on my because I had never witnessed the giving of alms with such intention. Some time later, the same young man on behalf of the same unknown person, gave me the same offering and the same specification of buying bread for St. Anthony's orphans. These welcome visits were repeated over and over again during 1888 and in the years to come, but after a while the lady revealed herself to me and invited me to come to her home. There she requested that I ask the orphans of St. Anthony to remember her and her family in prayer. For the rest of her life, she sent alms for St. Anthony's bread both for the blessings already granted and for blessings yet to come. In about 1893, I heard a friend of mine speaking of St. Anthony's Bread, which he professed started in Tolone, France, in 1890. Amazed, I asked myself, 'haven't we received St. Anthony's Bread in our institutes longer than that?' To tell the truth I had never thought of encouraging this devotion to placate so many people who wait for favors, and at the same time to help our orphans and the poor who knock on our door daily. But when I became aware that this holy practice, already existing in my institute, had also started in Tolone and was spreading all over the world, I thought of encouraging it as a great means to foster faith in souls, to implore favors for so many afflicted, and to get charitable alms under the title of St. Anthony's Bread in favor of my Anthonian Orphanages. I began placing little boxes in churches, in shops, and in stores, specifying their purpose; soon after, people who were waiting for the Lord's favor from St. Anthony responded by promising alms. The orphans began saying prayers to obtain favors for the afflicted from the loving heart of Jesus and from the Immaculate Mary through St. Anthony of Padua. The great saint himself has presented the prayers of the innocent orphans before the throne of divine clemency

and has obtained many favors for his devoted followers who have promised bread to these orphans.

Like the Franciscans, today's Rogation Fathers use the alms donated as the devotion of St. Anthony's Bread for the poorest of the poor.

ST. ANTHONY'S FIRE
A disease of the skin named for the saint (St. Anthony of Egypt) who was invoked to help those afflicted with it. The disease has been identified with erysipelas or ergotism, but appears originally to have been a far more virulent and contagious disorder. The disease is produced by eating a poisonous fungus which grows on rye. It takes the form of an inflammation of the skin accompanied by fever, burning sensations, convulsions, and gangrene. Anthony is still invoked against diseases of the skin.

ST. APPOLONIA
A martyr of Alexandria (d. 249, feast day February 9).

At a time when mobs roamed the streets of Alexandria, Egypt, attacking Christians, St. Appolonia was captured. Because she refused to deny Christ, she was tortured by having her teeth pulled out with pincers, and then being burned to death. She is the patroness of dentists and invoked against toothaches. She is depicted with pincers.

ST. BARBARA

A legendary martyr who remains popular despite the suppression of her cult in 1969 (d. fourth century, feast day formerly on December 4).

St. Barbara

Pious tradition says Barbara's father, a pagan, had her locked in a tower when he discovered she was a Christian and later turned her over to Roman authorities who tortured her. Then he killed her and, the story goes, he was immediately struck and killed by lightning. She was regarded as the patron of stonemasons, fireworks makers, architects, and other construction businesses, as well as artillerymen, armorers, gunsmiths, and miners. She was invoked against fire, lightning, sudden death, and final impenitence. Barbara was depicted holding a tower or a palm.

St. Barbara is a popular image in the cult of Santaria. A representation of her has been corrupted to use as a hidden image of that cult's major diety, Chango.

ST. BARBARA TWIG (BRANCH)

A custom in some parts of Europe through the mid-twentieth century.

On the saint's December 4 feast, small branches were broken from fruit trees and put in a pitcher of water in the kitchen or other warm room of the house. The branches broke into bloom around Christmas. Many blossoms were considered good luck. A twig that bloomed on Christmas was thought to indicate that no family member would die in the coming year.

ST. BARTHOLOMEW

Bartholomew's name is found in the lists of the Apostles, but nowhere else in the New Testament. Because Bartholomew, meaning "Son of Talmai", is a surname, not a personal name, some scholars think that he may be the person mentioned as Nathanael whom the Lord praised for his innocence and simplicity of heart. If so, he was a devout resident of Cana who, upon hearing Jesus came from the rival town of Nazareth, asked, "Can anything good come from Nazareth?" After meeting Jesus, who amazed him by his wisdom, Bartholomew became among the first to declare Christ "the Son of God, the king of Israel."

Legend says he preached in Egypt, Persia, Mesopotamia, India, and was martyred in Armenia by being skinned alive and beheaded.

ST. BENEDICT

The founder of monasticism in western Europe (c. 480-547, feast day July 11).

In 500, St. Benedict, an abbot, left Rome to live the life of a hermit and lived alone in a cave in Subiaco for three years. As his holiness and austerities became known, monks at a nearby community asked him to become their abbot. After they balked at his strict rule (and even tried to poison him), St. Benedict returned to Subiaco and continued to attract others whom he organized into twelve monas-

teries. In 525, he moved to Monte Cassino, and in 530 began the monastery that became the birthplace of Western monasticism. His famous rule — which stressed common sense, moderate asceticism, prayer, study, work, and community life — affected spiritual and monastic life in the West for centuries.

His remains and those of his twin sister, St. Scholastica, are, with good evidence, believed to have been found during the assault on Monte Cassino in World War II. There is a tradition, now discredited, that they were translated to Fleury, France, in 703. Pope St. Gregory the Great (r. 590-604) wrote of Benedict's life, and in 1964, Pope Paul VI declared him a patron of

St. Benedict

Europe. Benedict is depicted in iconography as a monk sometimes accompanied by a raven holding a bun in its beak. Other depictions show him carrying an open book of his rule and the staff of an abbot.

ST. BENEDICT'S HERB

Avens (*Geum urbanum*).

Also known as city avens, colewort, clove root, goldy star, herb bennet, way bennet, and wild rye, it was called the "blessed herb" in the Middle Ages when it was worn as an amulet believed to stave off evil spirits.

A publication on herbals in 1491 states that "where the root is in the house, Satan can do nothing and flees." The original name was St. Benedict's herb, from the legend that an evil monk once presented the saint with a goblet of poisoned wine. The saint blessed the wine and the goblet shattered. In medieval times, the plant's graceful trefoil leaves and the five petals of its yellow bloom symbolized the Holy Trinity and the five wounds of Our Lord.

ST. BERNARD OF CLAIRVAUX

The founder of the Cistercian Order, Doctor of the Church (1090-1153, feast day August 20).

One of six brilliant sons of a Bergundian nobleman, Bernard decided to join the new monastery at Cîteaux in 1113. He convinced four of his brothers and twenty-seven of his friends to come with him. Within two years, he was sent to establish a new house at Clairvaux. This monastery prospered and grew, leading to nearly seventy other monasteries in France, England, and Ireland.

St. Bernard's personal fame spread quickly, in spite of his diffident nature, and he was drawn into public affairs. He attacked luxury among the clergy and persecution of the Jews. He preached against the Albigensian heresy and stirred up enthusiasm for the Second Crusade. In spite of his immense activity and chronic ill health, this abbot and theologian was a prolific writer. Two of his most famous writings are the treatise "On the Love of God" and his sermons to his monks, "On the Song of Songs." The popular Marian prayer, the *Memorare,* is attributed to him.

St. Bernard is the patron of the Cistercians, bees, and candles. He is invoked against children's diseases, animal epidemics, demonic possession, storms, and approaching death. He is depicted with a beehive.

(See also **MEMORARE**.)

ST. BERNARD OF MONTJOUX

An Augustinian canon (d. 1081, feast day May 28).

St. Bernard was probably born in Italy. To aid lost travelers, he founded Alpine hospices in the two passes that came to be named for him. The monks that operated the hospices became Augustinians, and the famed St. Bernard dogs can be tracked back to this saint. He is the patron of mountain climbers.

ST. BLAISE

A bishop, physician, and martyr (d.c. 316, feast day February 3).

St. Blaise was the bishop of Sebaste, Turkey, when persecutions broke out. He hid in a cave and took care of wild animals. Years later, hunters found him and turned him over to the Roman authorities. He was tortured with iron rods and spiked combs before being beheaded.

The custom of blessing throats on his feast day is based on the pious legend of St. Blaise healing a young boy who had a fish bone stuck in his throat. The candles used in the ceremony commemorate those brought to him in prison by the boy's mother. St. Blaise is the patron of doctors, tanners, plasterers, pets, hat makers, tailors, shoemakers, stone carvers, hosiery workers, wool dealers, weavers, and cattle. He is invoked against neck and throat problems. (See also **BLESSING OF THROATS**.)

ST. BRIGID OF KILDARE

The foundress of a religious community at Kildare, Ireland (c. 450-525, feast day February 1).

Also called "Bride" and known as "the Mary of the Gael," St. Brigid, a nun, was the daughter of an Irish chieftain and a slave, both of whom had been baptized by St. Patrick. In 470, she founded a double monastery at Cill-Dara, Kildare, and became the abbess of the community, the first in Ireland. Kildare became a center for learning and spirituality. St. Brigid also founded an art school that became famous for illuminated manuscripts, especially the *Book of Kildare*, reportedly lost in the 1600s.

There are numerous legends and traditions associated with St. Brigid. Most of the wonders related of Brigid emphasize her charity; her miracles were to meet the spiritual and physical needs of her neighbors. One miracle story the Irish love to tell about Brigid, who was called the "wonder worker," is that while sitting with a blind nun one afternoon, the sunset was so beautiful that Brigid was moved with pity that her companion could not see. She touched the blind nun's eyes and her sight was restored. Surprisingly, the nun was not pleased and asked Brigid to make her blind again, telling her that "when the world is so visible to the eyes, God is less clear to the soul."

In the highlands of Scotland, February first is St. Bride's Day (St. Brigid). Servants take a sheaf of oats and dress it up in women's clothes, put it in a basket, and lay a club by it to see if there is an imprint of the club the next morning. If so, St. Brigid came by in the night and there will be a good harvest. In other parts, the family makes a bed of corn and hay over which some blankets are thrown. They then go out and call three times "Brigid, Brigid, come in, thy bed is ready." They leave candles burning near it all night. This custom may stem from old superstitions connected with Brigit the Celtic goddess of fire and crops.

A woman's special privilege of proposing in leap years is traced to an old story about St. Brigid and St. Patrick. In their day, celibacy was not mandatory for either priests or nuns. Brigid came to Patrick in tears saying that there was much unrest and anxiety among her women because of the unfair custom that prohibited women from taking the initiative in matrimony. Patrick, sternly celibate himself, sympathetically offered to grant the ladies the right to do their own proposing one full year of each seven. Evidently a good bargainer, Brigid talked him into one year out of each four. As soon as the agreement was in effect, Brigid proposed to Patrick. He begged off on grounds he had taken a vow of celibacy, but his natural gallantry made him soften his refusal by giving Brigid a kiss and a silk gown. Up until the last century, it was an unwritten law in the British Isles that any man had to pay a forfeiture of a silk dress to the lady he turned down during leap year.

Brigid died at Kildare and was buried in Downpatrick with Sts. Columba and Patrick, all patrons of Ireland. Brigid's cultus spread far beyond her native land. In England and Scotland, churches were dedicated in her honor as St. Bride. In Wales she is known as *Ffraid Santes*.

ST. BRIGID'S CROSS

A cross made of rushes, straw, or wood.

In rural Ireland, a couple just taking possession of a farm or homestead would nail a St. Brigid's cross under the barn eaves. In some areas, it was placed in dwellings and on farm buildings on the eve of the Feast of St. Brigid, February 1. The legend of the cross is that Brigid, renowned for her charity, once acted as nurse to a pagan chieftain. While he slept, she made a cross with some rushes from the floor.

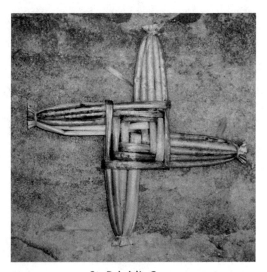

St. Brigid's Cross

On waking, the chieftain asked why she had formed the cross, and the saint told the story of Calvary. He was deeply impressed and his subsequent conversion, combined with a return to health, was attributed to her prayers.

ST. CHRISTOPHER

An early Christian martyr (d. third century, feast day July 25).

While St. Christopher was inscribed in the Roman Calendar about 1550, his feast is relegated to particular calendars because of the legendary nature of accounts of his life. One popular account appears in the thirteenth-century *Golden Legend* of Blessed James of Voragine (c. 1230-1298). It tells of a heathen king who, through the prayers of his wife to the Blessed Virgin, had a son whom he named Offerus. This young man grew to great size and strength. The boy decided to serve only the strongest lord in the world, and began in the service of an emperor. Discovering that the emperor was frightened of the devil, Offerus then served the devil for a while until he saw how the devil trembled at the sight of a crucifix. And so the young giant determined to serve Christ; asking advice from a hermit, he was instructed to make a home by a deep and treacherous river and carry Christian pilgrims across.

One night a little boy asked to be carried, so Offerus placed the child on his shoulders and entered the churning water. As they forded the river, the child became heavier and heavier until Offerus thought he would fail. When he reached the other side, he asked with surprise why the child was so heavy. The child replied that he had carried not only the whole world but him who made it. The child identified himself as Christ, then took Offerus into the water and baptized him, giving him the name of Christopher, meaning "Christ-bearer." He instructed

St. Christopher Carrying the Child Jesus

the saint to place his staff into the ground where it immediately burst forth into leaves and blossoms. The Christ Child then disappeared. Christopher later joyfully suffered persecution and death for his beloved Lord.

The legends inspired many devotions. St. Christopher was venerated as a patron against sudden and unexpected death, especially during the times of epidemics and plagues. The faithful believed that by praying before his picture in the morning, no harm would come to them that day. The custom began of hanging his picture over the door of the house, or painting it on the walls outside so that others could also venerate the saint. The saint is the patron of ferryboats, pilgrims, travelers, gardeners, and freight ships. He is also known as a patron of skiing.

ST. CHRISTOPHER MEDAL

A popular sacramental.

Although coins with the image of St. Christopher are from a much earlier period, medals and plaques date back to the sixteenth century. Their original purpose was to serve as a picture of the saint for travelers to gaze on in the morning and to protect them from sudden death that day.

ST. CLARE OF ASSISI

Mystic and foundress of the Poor Clares (1194-1253, feast day August 11).

Born in Assisi and a friend of St. Francis, St. Clare was joined in religious life by two of her sisters and her widowed mother. Clothed in rough habits of brown wool, the nuns went wherever Francis and his monks went, practicing penance, rejoicing in God's gifts, and living on alms.

Clare is usually represented in art holding a ciborium. This refers to the time when Saracens came to plunder the city of Assisi. The terrified nuns ran to Clare who, carrying only the Blessed Sacrament,

St. Clare of Assisi

stood firmly before the attackers and confidently called upon God to protect her nuns and to spare the city of Assisi. At the end of her prayer, she heard a voice say, *"Ego vos semper custodiam"* ("I will always protect you").

Clare is the patroness of embroidery workers, gilders, and washerwomen. She is invoked for good weather, and against eye disease. Her protection is sought against all evils of the soul and body. She is also the patron saint of television, based on the legend of her "seeing" in a vision Christmas Mass being celebrated when she was ill and could not attend the liturgy in the church.

ST. CLEMENT

The third successor of St. Peter, first of the Apostolic Fathers, and martyr (d.c. 100, feast day November 23).

St. Clement is commonly credited with writing an important letter to the Church in Corinth to settle a dispute there. Because his successes irritated the Roman emperor, he was sent to the mines of Crimea, Ukraine, where he established seventy-five churches. For this, he was tied to an anchor and thrown into the sea. His relics were discovered some seven hundred years later and translated to the Church of San Clemente in Rome, in the year 868.

He is the patron of the Crimean peninsula, children, stonemasons, marble workers, sailors, and hatters. He is invoked against disasters at sea, storms, and lightning. In art, he is depicted as a pope, sometimes with an anchor.

(See also **PRAYER FOR MANKIND**.)

ST. DISMAS

The traditional name given to "the Good Thief," crucified with Christ (see Luke 23:39-43). His feast day is March 25.

Dismas is the patron of persons condemned to death and of prisoners in general. In the United States, the American Catholic Correctional Chaplains Association, by special permission from Rome, observes the second Sunday in October as Good Thief Sunday and celebrates Masses in American prisons in honor of St. Dismas.

St. Dismas

ST. DUNSTAN

Archbishop of Canterbury and great figure in English history (900-988, feast day May 19)

All that is known of Dunstan's early years is that he was related to the royal family of Wessex and received a good education at Glastonbury. Later he became a monk and priest. King Edmund I commissioned him to restore monastic life at Glastonbury, and from this began his revival of organized monasticism in England which had ceased to exist after the Scandanavian invasions. Dunstan founded or re-founded many abbeys and helped to draw up a national code of monastic observance, in line with the Rule of St. Benedict. He was a principal adviser to all the Wessex kings of his time, and in 959 was made archbishop of Canterbury. The present coronation rite of the English sovereign derives from the one compiled and used by Dunstan for the coronation of Edgar as king of all England at Bath in 973.

Dunstan was also credited with being a skilled metal worker, a skilful scribe, and a musician. As an old man, he delighted in teaching the boys of the cathedral school at Canterbury, and the students returned his affection as he was a gentle master. St. Dunstan is the patron of blacksmiths. Many fanciful legends are related about Dunstan, a favorite saint of the English Catholics. One of the most famous, especially beloved by children, tells that St. Dunstan was so good that from worry the devil constantly watched his activities. Once, when Dunstan was working at the monastery forge, he looked up and saw the devil peering at him through the window. Quick as a flash he pulled his red hot tongs from the coals and grabbed the devil's nose with them. Howling and writhing, the devil ran and dipped his nose in nearby Tunbridge Wells to cool it off. To this day, the water in Tunbridge Wells, according to the English, is sulfur water.

ST. DYMPHNA

An Irish maiden (dates of birth and death unknown, mid-seventh century, feast day May 15).

According to legend, St. Dymphna was murdered by her pagan father at Gheel near Antwerp, Belgium, where she had fled to escape his advances. In the thirteenth century, her relics were discovered there, and since then there have been reported cures of mental illness and epilepsy attributed to her intercessions. She is the patron of people with mental illness.

During the Middle Ages, those who visited Gheel to invoke the saint were encouraged to make a nine-day novena at the shrine, and many participated in seven ceremonies called penances. There is a novena in honor of St. Dymphna for preservation from nervous disorders through her intercession and for true wisdom through imitation of her virtues. The virtues mentioned on successive days of this novena are: faith, hope, charity, piety, prudence, justice, fortitude, temperance, and chastity. The prayers in the form of a novena were approved by Pope Urban VIII in 1635.

The shrine at Gheel has drawn thousands of pilgrims through the centuries. Many miraculous cures have been reported, with one of the greatest miracles being the calm and caring attitude of the citizens toward the poor disturbed folk who visit the shrine. This friendly accep-

tance may be one big factor in the many cures that are effected at the shrine. The mentally ill are welcome in Gheel, and many are taken into the homes of the townsfolk to be cared for.

In the United States, devotion to this lovable girl saint is promoted by the Franciscan Mission Associates, and they conduct a perpetual novena of prayer every Monday in the Franciscan seminaries. There is a national shrine of St. Dymphna on the grounds of the Massillon State Hospital at Massillon, Ohio. This chapel was the first church in the U.S. to be dedicated to the saint in 1939. The shrine is the national headquarters for the League of St. Dymphna.

St. Dymphna

ST. EGIDIO COMMUNITY

An ecclesial community of laypeople founded in Rome in 1968 by Andrea Riccardi, a history professor.

Members come together to live the Gospel and give special charitable attention to the poor. The community has several thousand members who work in Europe, North America, Africa, and Asia.

ST. FIACRE

Patron of Gardeners (d. c. 670, feast day August 30).

In spite of the abundance of statues of St. Francis seen in American gardens, the patron of gardeners is St. Fiacre, a seventh-century hermit priest and a hotheaded Irishman.

A shrine in the saint's honor was established near Paris, France, over a rock where the saint had waited for an audience with the bishop. Because of the number of pilgrims passing through Paris on their way to this shrine of St. Fiacre, an enterprising Parisian put up a tavern, calling it the Hotel de St. Fiacre. Soon there was a thriving cab business going between the hotel and the shrine. The cabs became known as fiacres, and St. Fiacre by extension became patron of cabdrivers.

Little is known of the origins of this saint. His original Irish name may have been Fiachra. Coming into France, he was kindly received at Meaux by St. Faro who gave him a piece of land on which to build a hermitage. Fiacre built a cell for himself and a large hospice for travelers. He spent his time in prayer, working with his hands, and caring for the travelers and the poor of the area. Fiacre's fame for miracles was widespread. All manner of diseases were cured by his touch — blindness, fevers, and especially tumors. For many centuries, his chapel and his shrine drew the sick, and his intercession was especially asked for by persons suffering from hemorrhoids. Fiacre is looked on as the patron saint of gardeners because of the fine vegetables he grew around his hermitage. His emblem in art is a spade.

ST. FRANCIS OF ASSISI

The founder of the Franciscans (1181 or 1182-1226, feast day October 4).

St. Francis of Assisi remains one of the Church's most popular saints and is also admired by non-Catholics.

The son of a wealthy merchant, Francis, whose baptismal name was actually Pietro Bernadone, was a leader among his carefree, pleasure-seeking peers. In 1205 he went off to war, was taken hostage, and, later, became seriously ill. Twice Francis experienced a vision of Christ that prompted him to change his lifestyle. At the Portiuncula, a small chapel, he heard an image of the crucified Christ speak to him: "Go, Francis, and repair my house, which as you see is falling into ruin." Taking these words literally, Francis sold some of his father's goods and used the money to repair the church. He began to spend his time among the poor and the sick. His father thought Francis was insane and publicly disowned him.

The happy personality that had made Francis so popular when he was a wealthy young man about town remained with him, and people flocked to hear him preach. Eleven of his boyhood friends left home and joined him in his poverty. The Franciscan Order was founded on April 16, 1209. In 1210, Francis and his friends went to Rome to receive the approval of Pope Innocent III. In 1212, Francis and St. Clare founded the first community of

"Poor Ladies," now known as Poor Clares. By 1219, when a general chapter was held, there were five-thousand Franciscans at the meeting.

On Christmas 1223, Francis built a life-size crèche and began the custom of placing Nativity scenes in churches and homes. On September 17, 1224, while praying at a hermitage, he received the stigmata. Two years later he died. Francis was canonized in 1228.

While Francis was ordained only to the diaconate, considering himself unworthy of the priesthood, his impact on religious life was profound. His life and ministry were characterized by joyous worship, a reverence for nature, and concern for the poor and sick. He is the patron of Italy, Catholic Action, and ecologists. In art he is depicted in his habit, with the stigmata and sometimes with a winged crucifix. He is also shown preaching to birds or other animals.

(See also **PRAYER FOR PEACE**; **PRAYER IN PRAISE OF CREATED THINGS**.)

Two Renditions of St. Francis of Assisi

ST. GABRIEL THE ARCHANGEL

Gabriel is the angel of the annunciation to Mary (feast day September 29)

Gabriel is mentioned as the angel sent to Zechariah (see Luke 1: 11-19), in the book of Daniel (8:16; 9:21), and to proclaim the Annunciation (see Luke 1:26-38).

Gabriel's cult began very early in Rome. In art, he is usually depicted holding a scroll with the Ave Maria. He is patron of telecommunications and of the postal service. His emblem is a spear and shield emblazoned with a lily.

ST. GEORGE

Martyr (d.c. 300, feast day April 23).

St. George was killed for the faith in Lydda, Israel, before the reign of Emperor Constantine, and may have been a soldier in the imperial army. Some accounts of his life are pious legend or mere myth that began to circulate in the sixth century. Tales of his slaying a dragon trace their history to the twelfth century and became popular after being included in the *Golden Legend* in the thirteenth. That text portrayed him a model knight and protector of women. It held that, after his slaying of a dragon saved not only a damsel but a whole town, all the residents converted to Christianity.

St. George was venerated in England as early as the eighth century and was named patron of the Crusades. "St. George's Arms," a red cross on a white background, later became the basis for British military uniforms, the country's Union flag, and decorations of the Order of the Garter. Henry VII of England was especially devoted to St. George.

St. George is the patron of England, Portugal, Germany, Aragon, Spain, Genoa, and Venice. He is also patron of the Order of the Garter and the Boy Scouts. In art he is depicted as a young knight in mortal combat with a dragon, a medieval symbol of evil.

St. George

Many pious customs worldwide developed around this popular saint. Among the South Slavonians, a barren woman who desired a child placed a new chemise on a fruitful tree on the eve of St. George's Day. Next morning before sunrise she examined the garment and if she found that some living creature had crept on it she hoped that her wish would be fulfilled within the year. Then she put on the chemise confident that she would be as fruitful as the tree. In the Ukraine on St. George's Day (April 23) the priest in his robes accompanied by acolytes went out to the field where the crops were beginning to show green and blessed them. Then young married people lay down in couples on the fields and roll on them to promote the growth of crops. In some parts of Russia, the priest himself was rolled over the crops.

In medieval mystery plays, St. George was always represented killing the dragon. The actor playing the saint's part made certain his spear pierced a bag filled with "blood" attached to the inside of the dragon's skin, making the red liquid flow copiously while the monster "died" to the great delight of the spectators. In the legendary folklore of the Middle Ages, St. George had the task of driving demons and witches away from the homes and fields. Much of this lore survived in parts of Europe to the present century.

In Germany and Austria, on the eve of St. George's feast boys cracked whips to help the saint drive demons away. In Poland, farmers lighted fires in their yards to frighten evil spirits away. On the morning of the feast, the dew was mixed into the fodder to make the animals immune from attacks of demons or witches. Polish farmers have a fairy tale that St. George

St. George

lives in the moon, which the Blessed Mother gave him as a reward for his great deeds. From there he comes down on his feast day with a "key" to open the earth and free plants and flowers from the shackles of winter. In Alpine countries and among the Slavic nations, it was customary to drive the domestic animals to spring pastures on St. George's Day. The farm hands blew merrily on their trumpets (*Georgiblasen*) while they marched with the cattle out into the open. In Austria, a traditional spring hike was made into the countryside on the saint's feast.

St. George is the most popular saint in philately and he is honored on more stamps by more countries than any other saint. In most of the stamp designs, he is shown on horseback in battle with the dragon.

ST. ISIDORE THE FARMER

A miracle worker (1070-1130, feast day May 10).

St. Isidore was born in Madrid, Spain, to a poor family and worked as a hired hand on an estate outside the city. Noted for a life of devotion and for generosity to the poor despite his own lack of material goods, St. Isidore also gained a reputation for performing miracles.

While there are many pious legends about St. Isidore, it is quite clear that he was a dutiful laborer, a kind neighbor, and a devout Christian. His life became a model of Christian perfection lived in the world. His wife, Maria Torribia, resembled him in character. In Spain, where she is known as Maria de la Cabeza, she, too, is regarded as a saint.

Forty years after St. Isidore's death, his body was transferred from the cemetery to a shrine in the Church of St. Andrew and his cult began to spread with reports of many miracles and favors attributed to his intercession. Over the centuries, several Spanish monarchs sought his help and reported having received aid. He is the patron of farmers and the city of Madrid. In art he is depicted with a sickle or plow.

ST. JOHN THE BAPTIST

An eremitical prophet and martyr (d. first century, feast days June 24 [birth] and August 29 [death]).

Referred to as "the man sent by God," St. John was the son of Zechariah and Elizabeth and therefore was a relative of Jesus. After living as a recluse in the desert in Judea, he began preaching at the River Jordan and baptizing penitents. Christ came to John to be baptized before going to preach in Galilee. St. John remained near the river until he was arrested by King Herod Antipas and beheaded.

Patristic tradition says St. John was freed from original sin and sanctified in his mother's womb. Since the earliest

St. John the Baptist

times, the Church has celebrated his birth liturgically. He is considered the forerunner of the early Desert Fathers and is the patron of monastic life. He is also the patron of missionaries and farriers. In art he is shown as an ascetical hermit, sometimes holding a lamb. Other depictions feature the saint carrying a staff that ends in a cross or holding his own head.

ST. JOHN BOSCO

Founder of the Salesian order (1815-1888, feast day January 31)

"Enjoy yourself as much as you like, if only you keep from sin!" What John Bosco realized and what some people sadly never learn is that many will be attracted to Christ if those who represent Him have an attractive disposition. Rigid, rude, grumpy people who also claim to be religious are a scandal to the Church. The joy of Christ as shown in the life of this nineteenth-century wonder-worker is a hallmark of the truly religious.

As a youth, John Bosco practiced his skills as a juggler, tightrope walker, ventriloquist, and acrobat in order to attract

571

the attention of his peers. After gaining their admiration and respect, he encouraged them to pray with him. As an adult, the saint's reflection of God's joy was passed on to one of the greatest of the armies of religious in the Church — the Salesian order. Sympathetically attracted to abandoned and neglected boys, this humble Italian priest established a teaching apostolate that would transform the boys into good and industrious citizens. His work has spread throughout the world. From the age of nine, the saint was favored with a series of visionary dreams which guided his actions. Pope Pius XI once remarked that, "In John Bosco's life the supernatural became the natural and the extraordinary ordinary." In addition to his dreams, the saint was favored with many mystical phenomena, such as the gift of prophecy and the ability to multiply food. Having to make night calls in the city of Turin in a time of anti-clericalism and in dangerous parts of the city, the saint was often accompanied by a large gray dog which disappeared when the priest returned safely to the rectory. In spite of all the miraculous and mystical facets of his life, by the testimony of all who knew him, the saint maintained a joyful, warm, and loving humanity that attracted those around him and allowed him to accomplish his mission of leading them to God. In spite of his prodigious work of founding institutions for his boys,

building churches, and raising funds for these endeavors, he found time to author more a hundred books and pamphlets. In recognition of this accomplishment, he was declared the patron saint of Catholic publishers and editors.

ST. JOHN'S FIRES

A custom adapted by the Church based on the traditional fire festivals generally held throughout Europe during the summer solstice. A Christian perspective was given to them by renaming them after St. John the Baptist.

A writer from the first half of the sixteenth century wrote that in almost every village and town of Germany public bonfires were kindled on the Eve of St. John and young and old of both sexes gathered about them and passed the time in dancing and singing. The people wore chaplets of mugwort and vervain and looked at the fire through bunches of larkspur which they held in their hands, believing that this would preserve their eyes in a healthy state throughout the year. As each departed, he threw his mugwort and vervain into the fire to burn up his bad luck. The fires were connected to the harvest, and around Baden, the people jumped over the fires to prevent backache at the time of harvest.

In Norway, the fires were said to banish both sickness and witches. In Sweden, the Eve of St. John was the most joyous night of the whole year. It was celebrated by the frequent discharge of firearms as well as the bonfires. Here the festival is one of water as well as of fire, and certain holy springs are then supposed to be endowed with wonderful medicinal virtues. In the lower valley of the Inn, an effigy called the "Lotter," which has been corrupted into "Luther," is carried about the village and then burned. At Ambras, one of the villages where Martin Luther was burned in effigy, those who went through the village between eleven and twelve on St. John's Night and washed in three wells would see all who were to die in the following year. The Estonians believed that the St. John's fire kept witches from the cattle and said that he who did not come to the bonfire would have thistles and weeds in his harvest.

In Brittany, the custom of the midsummer bonfires was kept up to the middle of this century. Here the ritual was slightly more Christian — when the flames from the bonfire died down, the whole assembly knelt round the bonfire and an old man prayed aloud. Then all rose and marched thrice around the fire; at the third turn they all stopped, picked up a pebble, and threw it into the flames

At Jumièges, in Normandy, through the first half of the nineteenth century, the festival was marked by certain singular features which bore the stamp of antiqui-ty. Every year the Brotherhood of the Green Wolf chose a new chief or master. The new head assumed the title of the Green Wolf and donned a peculiar costume consisting of a long green mantle and a very tall, green, cone-shaped hat without a brim. Thus arrayed, the new Green Wolf chief stalked solemnly at the head of the brothers, chanting the hymn of St. John and carrying a crucifix and holy banner to a place called Chouquet. Here the procession was met by the priest, precentors, and choir, who conducted the brotherhood to the parish church. After hearing Mass, the company adjourned to the house of the Green Wolf where a simple meal was served. At night, a bonfire was kindled to the sound of handbells by a young man and a woman decked with flowers. Then the Green Wolf and his brothers, with their hoods down on their shoulders and holding each other by the hand, ran round the fire after the man chosen to be the Green Wolf of the following year. Though only the first and last man in the chain had a free hand, they attempted to thrice seize the future Green Wolf, who in his efforts to escape hit the brothers with a long wand he carried. Once captured, the man was carried to the burning pile and the brothers pretended to throw him in. After the ceremony, the brothers returned to the house of the Green Wolf where another simple supper was set out. Until midnight, a sort of religious solemnity prevailed. At the stroke of midnight, constraint gave way to license, pious hymns were replaced by Bacchanalian ditties, and the shrill quivering notes of the village fiddle hardly rose above the roar of voices of the merry brotherhood of the Green Wolf. The celebration continued the next day, and included parading an enormous, tiered loaf of consecrated bread surmounted by a pyramid of verdure adorned with ribbons. Hand bells, deposited on the steps of the altar, were entrusted as insignia of office to the man who was to be the Green Wolf the next year.

(see also ST. JOHN THE BAPTIST).

ST. JOHN'S WINE — See LOVE OF ST. JOHN.

ST. JOSEPH

The husband of Mary and foster father of Jesus (d. first century, feast days March 19 [principal feast] and May 1 [St. Joseph the Worker]).

A descendant of the house of David and a "just man" (see Matthew 1:18-21), St. Joseph is written about in the infancy narratives in Matthew and Luke, including Mary's pregnancy, Jesus' birth in Bethlehem, the Holy Family's flight into Egypt to escape King Herod, and their returning to Nazareth. He is last men-

St. Joseph

tioned when he and Mary find the lost Jesus in the Temple. It is believed that he died before the crucifixion.

Veneration of St. Joseph began in the East, where apocryphal writings presented biographies of Christ's foster father. In the ninth century, the Irish writer Oengus the Culdee in his *Felire of Oengus* commemorated him; but it was not until the fifteenth that veneration of St. Joseph became widespread in the West. His feast was placed on the Roman Calendar in 1479. Both St. Francis of Assisi and St. Teresa of Ávila helped spread devotion to him. Through a series of official acts, pontiffs from the late nineteenth through the mid-twentieth centuries promoted veneration to St. Joseph. Blessed Pope Pius IX declared him patron of the universal Church. Pope Leo XIII ranked him next to Mary, and Pope Benedict XV declared him protector of workers. Pope Pius XI named him patron of social justice, and Pope Pius XII established the Feast of St. Joseph the Worker on May 1. Blessed Pope John XXIII inserted the name of St. Joseph in the Roman Canon and named him co-patron of Vatican II.

There is a paradox about St. Joseph. Though we know he was most singularly chosen, because of his hidden life and humble occupation we think of him as being very common and ordinary. He is the highest of saints, yet always approachable. Churches named after him are everywhere, his altars and statues abound, yet he is referred to and often seems to be the forgotten saint. At Christmas, Joseph is always depicted at the nativity, yet the songs sing of the Child and Mother, the star, wise men, angels, and shepherds. Joseph is there, yet hardly noticed. Multitudes carry his name as their own. His name is common among those who do not honor him as a saint, and the English language even uses it to designate the common man — "Good old Joe." In the army, again, the common man is referred to as "G.I. Joe." In the past century, just as the recognition of the common man's role is coming to the center of the world stage, more and more, Joseph's role in the Church is being brought forward.

Pope Leo XIII points out in simple words the reason for honoring and invoking St. Joseph. He was the husband of Mary and was looked on as the father of Jesus Christ. The dignity of the Mother of God is so high that no created being can be above her. But Joseph was joined to her in marriage and he comes nearer than anyone else to the height of that dignity. When God

St. Joseph with the Child Jesus

gave Joseph as husband to the Virgin, he gave her a companion in life, a protector and guardian, and one to share in her most high dignity. Although it is plain from Scripture that St. Joseph was not the biological father of Jesus, it is equally plain that Joseph really acted as a father to Jesus and was accepted as such by all. Most importantly, Jesus, the Son of God, accepted Joseph as His earthly father, and He obeyed him and learned from him. What St. Joseph once did for Jesus and Mary, he now does for the Church, and his work is essentially a continuation of that begun in Bethlehem. St. Joseph stands ready to provide for all who call on him. Poor on earth, he is rich in heaven, and stands ready to help all who request his intercession.

In art, St. Joseph is shown as a man with a lily blossoming from a staff and sometimes with the Christ Child or with a carpenter's tool. Medieval depictions of St. Joseph as an elderly man were designed to underscore the absence of conjugal relations between him and the Blessed Virgin. While maintaining the truth of Mary's perpetual virginity, modern illustrations generally portray St. Joseph as a younger man.

Customs connected to the devotion to St. Joseph are known worldwide. When the devotion to this saint began to spread rapidly in the sixteenth and seventeenth centuries, Wednesday became a special day associated with St. Joseph. First, Wednesday was the only weekday dedicated by the Church in the votive Masses to saints other than the Blessed Virgin. Therefore, St. Joseph obviously "belonged" on Wednesday. Second, in the popular mind the ancient Station Days were considered of higher distinction than the other weekdays, and since Saturday was already devoted to the Blessed Virgin and Friday to the Passion of Christ, the only day left on which to honor St. Joseph in a special way was Wednesday. For whatever reason, the custom was approved and confirmed by the Church.

In the Alpine sections, a custom known as Josephstragen is popular. St. Joseph is known as a patron of the married and of families. In past centuries it was a widespread custom for newlywed couples to spend the first night of matrimony, called St. Joseph's Night, in abstinence, and to perform some devotion in honor of the saint that he might bless their marriage.

A popular Spanish custom is known as *Merienda del Cordero,* meaning "Repast of the Lamb." On the east coast of Spain in the Valencia region, fires are burned in honor of St. Joseph. The custom was started by the carpenters of past centuries who cleaned their workshops before March 19 and burned all the litter on the evening of their patron's feast. Today, wooden structures made of wood by boys and men during the weeks before the feast are collected and exhibited at street crossings. These structures represent houses, figures, and scenes, many of which are symbolic of some political event of the past year. They are admired and then judged, and on the eve of St. Joseph's Day, the best one receives a prize and is put aside. All the rest are burned in joyful bonfires. The celebration includes music, dancing and fireworks (traca). In some parts of Italy, ancient nature lore rites are still performed on St. Joseph's Day. One is the "burial of winter," where a *scega vecchia* (a symbolic figure) is sawed in half. In central Europe the day is celebrated by farmers as the beginning of spring. They light candles in honor of the saint and put little shrines with his picture in their gardens and orchards. Then they have their fields blessed by the priest. In many sections of Europe, small round breads called St. Joseph's loaves (*fritelli*) are baked and eaten on March 19 to honor the heavenly "bread father." From the seventeenth century on it was customary to have a statue of the saint on the table during the main meal and to "serve" it generous portions, which afterward were given to the poor.

(See also **JOSEPHSTRAGEN; MERIENDA DEL CORDERO.**)

ST. JOSEPH MEDAL

A sacramental.

The medal officially promoted today was created in 1971 to mark the centenary of Blessed Pope Pius IX declaring St. Joseph the patron of the universal Church.

Father Christopher Rengers, O.F.M.Cap. is the originator of the St. Joseph Medal. The design for the medal was carved by Norbert Schrader, and the medal was struck in Germany. It is enameled in purple and white. The medal is rectangular in shape to preserve the memory of the St. Joseph Scapular which was approved by Pope Leo XIII in 1893 and given to the Capuchin order to promote. On the face of the medal, St. Joseph is shown in a protective stance, with his arms about the child Jesus and Our Lady. The petition inscribed on the face of the medal reads: "That all may be one; St. Joseph Our Protector Pray for Us." The letters GIJM stand for Joseph's fidelity to grace in his interior life and his love for Jesus and Mary. The obverse of the medal has the words: "Feed my lambs, feed my sheep. The spirit of the Lord his guide." It depicts sheep underneath the shepherd's staff and crossed keys, a symbol of the papacy; the whole is surmounted by a dove symbolizing the Holy Spirit.

ST. JOSEPH, REALTOR

The tradition of asking St. Joseph's intercession when buying or selling property.

An old, if bizarre, custom regarding St. Joseph is still popular today in the United States. It involves burying a statue of St. Joseph in order to sell a piece of property. Religious goods stores all across the U.S. report high sales of inexpensive statues of the saint which people then bury in the backyard and pray for a speedy and successful sale of their property. Perhaps St. Joseph's role in selling real estate arose from his being patron saint of carpenters, but the exact origin of this custom is clouded in history. Although the custom seems to border on superstition, many persons with true devotion to the saint have acted in good faith to request his aid. St. Brother André of Montreal is one who appealed to St. Joseph in the matter of property over and over. Herbert Cardinal Vaughn, Archbishop of Westminster, London, was trying to purchase property to begin his new religious community, the Millhill Josephites. Having been refused by the owner of the desired property, the cardinal asked the owner to keep a package for him and put it in a closet under the staircase. The owner complied with the request, little knowing the package contained a statue of St. Joseph. Soon after, the owner changed his mind and sold the property to the cardinal. Dorothy Day is another who had a great devotion to St. Joseph and who asked his help in obtaining property. She buried a medal of the saint on the land she wished to acquire.

Although these are concrete instances of persons who used a sacramental of the saint in order to acquire property, the origin of the use of a sacramental to sell property is unknown.

ST. JOSEPH, PIOUS UNION OF

An association founded in Italy in 1913 by Blessed Louis Guanella, founder of the Servants of Charity.

The association's two aims are to promote devotion to St. Joseph, as patron of a happy death, and to promote prayer and good works for the benefit of the dying. Pope St. Pius X approved the Pious Union and was one of the first members. He enriched membership in the association with a number of indulgences. Today, there are nearly a million registered members of the Pious Union of St. Joseph worldwide. Among them are thousands of priests who promised to celebrate one Mass per year for the intentions of the Pious Union, so daily hundreds of Masses are celebrated in every part of the world for the salvation of the dying and for the repose of the souls of all deceased members. All members pray daily for the dying. The universal ejaculation of the Pious Union is: "O St. Joseph, foster Father of Jesus Christ and true spouse of the Blessed Virgin Mary, pray for us and for the dying of this day (night)." The primary center is at the Church of St. Joseph in Rome. One of the first Guanellian priests to come to the U.S., Father Germano Pegoraro S.C., upon retirement, began the Pious Union of St. Joseph in the United States. The American headquarters are in Grass Lake, Michigan.

In 1995, Bishop Kenneth Joseph Povish

of Lansing visited Grass Lake. He counseled Father Germano to build a church and assisted in obtaining the designation for it of the National Shrine of St. Joseph, Patron of the Dying.

ST. JOSEPH'S ALTAR

A Sicilian custom.

The custom of St. Joseph's altar was brought by the Sicilian immigrants to the United States. Originally, the tables or altars were family affairs, but as the Italian-American population grew, the celebrations became more public. The custom is prevalent in America today wherever there are Italian-Americans.

The St. Joseph altar originated in a region of Sicily many centuries ago during a period of drought and famine. The people turned to St. Joseph, asking his help and intercession. Rains came and their crops prospered. In thanksgiving, the community brought their prized food as an offering to their patron. Today, the altar is generally large and has three levels to represent the Holy Trinity. The statue of St. Joseph is given the most prominent place, although representations of the Holy Family and the Blessed Virgin are often also displayed. The altar is draped in white and adorned with flowers. The finest grains, fruits, vegetables, seafood, and wine are prepared and all are invited to share in the prayers and festivity.

The St. Joseph altar is an offering of love, labor, and sacrifice. Reasons for erecting the altar vary. For many, it is to fulfill a promise or give thanks for a favor. For others, the altar is a petition. For all it is an opportunity to share with those less fortunate. Preparations begin weeks in advance of the feast, and much hard work is involved, but all participants accept this as a form of sacrifice and a labor of love. Many hours are spent making the elaborate loaves of bread, cakes and cookies which adorn the altar. Many of these are symbolic — shapes include the crown of thorns, hearts symbolizing the Sacred Hearts of Jesus and Mary, the cross, the chalice, a monstrance, St. Joseph's staff, fish, birds, flowers, and many more.

St. Joseph's Altar

The meals served for the St. Joseph altar include fruits, vegetables, seafood, and pasta dishes. Often, children are dressed as members of the Holy Family, sometimes with angels or favorite saints accompanying them. The children are served first, a portion of each of the delicacies from the altar. This ritual is solemnly observed and accompanied by prayer and hymns. Guests are invited to dine after the Holy Family have completed their meal.

Originally, in Sicily, the families would go out to the poor in the community and bring them into their houses. The master of the house and his family would bathe the feet of the poor, just as Christ had done to his disciples before the Last Supper. Then the visitors would be seated at the table. The poor would be served first, following which the family and invited guests would eat. At the end of the feast, the remains would be gathered and distributed to the poor. When the Sicilian immigrants reached the United States, most could speak no English and felt awkward about choosing people who did not understand the language or their custom.

Consequently, they selected children of the family and friends to represent the Holy Family or Christ and his Apostles. Instead of the foot-washing ceremony, the children would stand on benches or chairs and those present would kiss their hands and feet as an act of humility. Afterward, the host, his family, and friends would carry baskets of food to those in need. There is often a bowl of green fava beans on the altar, which guests take home as a "lucky bean." The custom stems from one of the famines in Sicily. At that time, the fava bean was used as cattle fodder. In order to survive, the farmers cooked and ate them. Today, it is considered a delicacy and used in numerous recipes. When dried, and blessed, it is used as a sacramental. An old Sicilian saying is that if you carry a blessed fava bean in your purse, your purse will never be empty. (And, of course, it is not. It always contains at least the bean.)

Another custom that prevalent among Italian-Americans is to save blessed bread from the St. Joseph's altar as a sacramental. The saint is invoked in cases of danger from storms, and some people keep pieces of it in their cars to protect against harm from collisions.

ST. JOSEPH'S BREAD — See BREAD, ST. JOSEPH'S.

ST. JUDE THADDEUS

An Apostle and martyr (d. first century, feast day October 28).

According to custom, St. Jude is the brother of another Apostle, St. James the Less, and the reputed author of the Epistle of St. Jude. Pious legend holds that he went to Persia with St. Simon where he was martyred.

According to ancient tradition, the story of the Apostle Jude is tied in with the history of the Holy Shroud. King Abgar of the city of Edessa in northwestern Mesopotamia, about 350 miles north of Galilee, was stricken with a dread disease, probably leprosy. He had heard of Jesus and His healing miracles, and sent a message begging Jesus to cure him. When the message arrived, Jesus had already ascended into heaven. The Apostles, impressed with the king's faith, decided to send Jude with the Holy Shroud. It could not be brought and shown as a shroud because all people have a natural revulsion toward objects which have been in close contact with the dead. Therefore, before being brought to the king, the cloth seems to have been folded and decorated so that it showed only the portrait-like image of the Holy Face of Jesus. Jude brought the shroud to Edessa and the king was cured and baptized. Jude then established Christianity in Edessa.

The origin of devotion to St. Jude as patron of difficult or hopeless cases is obscure. Because of confusion over his name and that of the traitor Judas, veneration was effectively discouraged for many centuries but began to gain popularity in the Middle Ages. In art, St. Jude is pictured carrying the image of Jesus on a disk in his hand, carrying a staff, and with a flame over his head.

One person who experienced the effect of St. Jude's patronage was the Catholic entertainer Danny Thomas. As a young comedian in Detroit, he found himself one day without a job, with a pregnant wife, and flat broke. Sitting in a church pondering whether to quit show business and get some sort of menial job in order to pay the bills, he saw a pamphlet about St. Jude. He asked himself what case could be more hopeless than his own. He put his last $7 in the prayer box, asking the saint to return his money ten-fold. On his return home, there

St. Jude Thaddeus

was a message asking him to do a radio commercial for a fee of $75, five dollars more than he had asked for. In 1943, Thomas asked St. Jude's help in making a big decision. He promised that if the saint would give him a sign, he would build a shrine where the poor, helpless, and homeless could come for comfort and aid. He received his sign that night; again his prayers were answered.

Two years later in Chicago, Thomas remembered the vow he had made. He got the idea for a hospital where children would be cared for regardless of race, creed, or the ability to pay; a place where no suffering child would be refused. He talked to his friends about his idea, and formed a committee and a board of directors. They decided the hospital would care for children with catastrophic, often fatal diseases. It would be devoted to research and would share the benefits of its knowledge with medical facilities worldwide. St. Jude's hospital opened February 4, 1962, in Memphis, Tennessee. Today, the hospital offers care to thousands of sick children and has drastically increased the survival rate for childhood cancers.

The major relics of this saint are enshrined in St. Peter's Basilica in Rome. Small relics have been distributed worldwide but a major relic, the forearm, is kept at the St. Jude Shrine in Chicago. This relic is kept in a silver reliquary shaped as a life-size forearm. A glass section exposes the relic to view. Another major shrine in the U.S. dedicated to the saint is in Baltimore, Maryland. St. Jude is the titular patron for many churches in this country, many of which have a shrine in his honor.

Two customs that cross from true piety into superstitious practice have been popularized in connection with devotion to St. Jude. One is the belief that a petitioner is obliged to publish in a newspaper a classified advertisement giving thanks to the saint. The superstition lies in the misguided belief that such a pledge and its fulfillment guarantee that the prayers will receive the desired answer. The second is a chain letter purportedly associated with devotion to St. Jude. It carries a promise of reward if the conditions are met or a threat of punishment if explicit instructions are not followed.

ST. JULIAN THE HOSPITALER

The patron of boatmen, innkeepers, and travelers (date unknown, feast day February 12).

Veneration paid to St. Julian was very popular in the Middle Ages though based on doubtful tales reported in the *Golden Legend*. That text claimed that Julian killed his noble parents in a case of mistaken identify. Later, as an act of penance, he and his wife built an inn and opened a hospital for the poor.

ST. LAWRENCE

A deacon, chief assistant to Pope Sixtus II, and martyr (d. 258, feast day August 10).

One of seven deacons serving the pontiff at that time, Lawrence was probably born in Huesca, Spain. When authorities of the Roman Empire demanded the treasures of the Church, St. Lawrence showed them the poor and disabled. Tradition holds that he was killed by being placed on a red-hot gridiron and that, as he lay dying, he joked that he was roasted on one side and should be turned over. St. Lawrence was buried near Campo Verano in Rome, and a basilica was built over his grave. His *Passio* was written a century after his death. St. Lawrence is mentioned in the first Eucharistic Prayer or Roman Canon. He is invoked by those suffering from lumbago and rheumatism and is known as the patron of cooks, chefs, and restaurant owners. In art he is shown as a deacon with a gridiron or grill.

ST. LUCY'S CROWN

A Swedish custom associated with the Feast of St. Lucy, December 13.

The custom involves a daughter impersonating the saint by dressing in white with a red sash and wearing a wire crown on her head covered with bilberry twigs. In her crown are nine lighted candles. She goes through the house very early in the morning waking the family and giving each member a cup of coffee or a sweet drink and offering a platter of pastries. Although Sweden is most famous for celebrating the custom, it actually began in Sicily. The name Lucy comes from the Latin for "light" (*lux*).

ST. MARGARET MARY ALA-COQUE

A French religious of the Visitation Order.

St. Margaret (1647-1690) instigated the spreading of devotion to the Sacred Heart after Our Lord appeared to her and told her of his desire to be loved by all and to encourage everyone to seek sanctification and salvation.

(See also SACRED HEART OF JESUS.)

ST. MARTIN OF TOURS

A bishop and pioneer of Western monasticism (c. 316-397, feast day November 11).

Born the son of a pagan army officer in what is now Hungary, St. Martin moved with his family to Italy. At fifteen he was inducted into the army. In 337, in Amiens, France, he cut his cloak in half to clothe a freezing beggar and that night had a vision of Christ wearing what he had given away. Converting to Christianity, he left the army and returned to Italy. Around 360, he joined St. Hilary of Poitiers and became a hermit in Ligugé, the first monastic community in France. Against his own wishes, he was made bishop of Tours in 371. While a bishop, he founded Marmoutier Abbey. Martin was an extremely popular saint in France, and his shrine at Tours became a major pilgrimage site. He is the patron of France, soldiers, conscientious objectors, beggars, tavern keepers, winegrowers, and alcoholics. In art he is shown cutting his cloak. In Spain, he is known as San Martín de Caballero.

In the early Middle Ages, before the

St. Martin of Tours and the Beggar

season of Advent had been firmly established, the time of spiritual preparation for Christmas in France began on his feast and was referred to as *Quadragesima Sancti Martini*, or "Forty Days' Fast of St. Martin." Later, "St. Martin's Summer" was popularly used to describe a short period of unseasonably warm weather in November. It was on his feast day in 1918 that the Armistice was signed, thereby putting an end to the First World War.

Some customs connected with this saint which arose in different areas had more of the magical, as opposed to devotional, elements in them. A statue of the saint in Eure gained a reputation for curing stomach disorders. Pilgrims to the shrine took two ribbons; one was left hanging on the statue and the other, after having been touched to the image, was worn for nine days and then burned. Even today, among the Spanish speaking who have a great devotion to San Martin, there are remnants of these magical elements connected to the devotion. In a Mexican *yerbaria* there is always a variety of perfumes, incenses, and waters labeled with the saint's name. Wondrous properties are claimed for these.

ST. MARTIN'S GOOSE

A traditional menu item for Martinmas, the feast day of St. Martin of Tours, November 11.

Legend says that when Martin heard

he had been elected bishop he was so horrified that he ran and hid in a barn. A meddlesome goose found him and made so much noise that his searchers found him. The goose's descendants continue to this day to pay the price for its disservice.

ST. MARTIN'S LAMP

A German custom in which children make or buy lanterns of sugar beets or paper to carry in a procession on November 11.

In the early evening, a man dressed as the saint but wearing only half a cloak rides in the streets near the parish church. He carries a burlap sack filled with soft pretzels or soft rolls and leads the procession. The children follow, holding up their lanterns on sticks and singing a song about feeding the hungry beggar. The children follow the saint as he rides through the old part of town and back to the church. Then they circle around the saint and he passes out the contents of his sack. The laughing, happy children fight to get close enough to the saint to make certain of receiving a pretzel or roll.

ST. MICHAEL THE ARCHANGEL

One of the three archangels mentioned in Scripture (feast day, September 29).

St. Michael was the leader of the angels in battling Satan and his followers and evicting them from heaven: "Now war arose in heaven, Michael and his angels fighting against the dragon; and the dragon and his angels fought, but they were defeated and there was no longer any place for them in heaven. And the great dragon was thrown down, that ancient serpent, who is called the devil and Satan, the deceiver of the whole world — he was thrown down to the earth, and his angels were thrown down with him" (see Revelation 12:7-9).

Christian tradition assigns four offices to him: l) to fight against Satan, 2) to rescue the souls of the faithful from the power of the devil, especially at the hour of death, 3) to be the champion of God's people, and 4) to call away from earth and bring men's souls to judgment. He was venerated from earliest Christian times as an angelic healer. There is evidence for the honor in which he was held from the beginnings of Christian history, and he was also venerated by the Jews.

St. Michael's feast was originally combined with the remembrance of all angels, and had been celebrated in Rome from the early centuries. In 813, his feast day was introduced in all the countries of the Carolingian Empire and was celebrated as a public holiday. All through medieval times, St. Michael's Day was kept as a great religious feast and one of the annual holiday seasons as well. Two apparitions of the archangel, at Mont-Saint-Michel (France) and on Mount Gargano (Italy)

St. Michael the Archangel

at one time had special feast days assigned to commemorate them. From the early centuries, a favorite practice in the Oriental Church was to build shrines to the saint on the tops of mountains and hills, and the custom carried over to the West where his shrines often replaced the pagan cult shrines of the god Woden.

In northern Spain, Michael was acclaimed as the national patron of the Basques. Here his feast was kept with great celebration. His statue was brought from the national shrine to all churches of Navarre for a short visit annually so he could be honored and venerated by the faithful in their home towns. Some of the ancient lore of the Germanic nations has come down to our time in the form of St. Michael's parades, fairs, plays, and other customs. St. Michael's patronages include policemen and the military.

ST. MICHAEL'S LOVE

A traditional name in northern Europe and England for wine consumed on the Feast of St. Michael.

ST. NICHOLAS

A bishop of Myra in Asia Minor (d. fourth century, feast day December 6).

Although a true historical figure, St. Nicholas is best known in legends, including the famous tradition that he threw bags of gold through the window of three destitute young women who needed dowries to get married; otherwise, their desperate father was prepared to put them on the streets as prostitutes.

From this, stories of his acts of charity became popular in the East. There was a church dedicated to St. Nicholas at Constantinople from the sixth century. From the ninth century in the East and the eleventh in the West, St. Nicholas has been one of the most popular saints of Christendom. He is celebrated in pious custom and folklore, represented countless times in paintings and carvings, innumerable churches are named for him, and yet little factual information is known about him. He is also known as St. Nicholas of Bari because in 1087 Italian merchants moved his relics from Myra to Bari, in Apulia. His shrine became one of the great pilgrimage sites of the Middle Ages.

Legends about St. Nicholas, far fetched and often childish, abound. One holds that he brought to life three children who had been murdered and hidden in a brine vat. Others say he miraculously saved three unjustly condemned men and rescued sailors in distress off the Lycian coast. Thus

St. Nicholas of Myra

his patronage of children, criminals, and sailors. In the United States, St. Nicholas, is one of the threads of the origin of Santa Claus. The name is derived from the Dutch dialect form of his name, *Sinte Klaas*.

In Europe, St. Nicholas does not come on Christmas Eve as he does in America, but on the eve of his own feast, the night before December 6. Instead of coming down the chimney, he rings the doorbell. He carries a bag on his back containing cookies and fruits. St. Nick questions the youngsters about their behavior and their future intentions. If he is pleased, he gives them a treat with the promise of something more on Christmas, when the Christ Child, not the saint, will bring the promised gifts. In some countries he is accompanied by a helper, a frightening figure, whose job it is to punish those children who have not been good. Because Nicholas was quite young when he became a bishop, a custom arose in medieval England of celebrating St. Nicholas' Day by selecting a boy from the cathedral choir to be a mock-bishop for a term of office from December 6-28. In full Episcopal regalia and followed by a magnificent entourage, the boy-bishop put on a hilarious burlesque of the pomp and dignity of the real bishop. This custom was revived in several English cathedral towns in the middle of this century. In 1034, when the shrine at Myra fell into the hands of the

Saracens, several Italian cities vied for possession of the relics because of the saint's popularity and the phenomenon that attended his remains. The relics were removed in secret and enshrined at Bari in Apulia, where they remain today. A new basilica was built to enshrine the relics with Pope Urban II presiding over its consecration. A liquid exuded from the saint's bones which was first observed at Myra and which continued at Bari. The liquid, according to examinations made by scientists from the University at Bari, is a combination of hydrogen and oxygen with an extremely low content of bacteria, and is considered biologically pure. This liquid collects only on the bones of the saint and not on the walls or other surfaces of the tomb. Although there are five periods when the liquid was not observed for a few years at a time, the saint's bones have given off this miraculous fluid continuously for centuries, and still do today. Other patronages of the saint include those of Russia, Greece, Apulia, Sicily, and Lorraine, France.

ST. NICHOLAS'S BREAD — See **BREAD, ST. NICHOLAS**.

ST. ODILIA WATER — See **WATER OF ST. ODILIA**.

ST. PATRICK

A bishop and missionary to Ireland (c. 389-461, feast day March 17).

A Roman citizen born in Roman Britain, Patrick was captured at age sixteen by Irish raiders and sold into slavery. During the six years of his captivity during which he worked tending flocks, he underwent a profound religious transformation. In 407, Patrick was commanded in a dream to escape. He traveled two hundred miles to board a ship and return to the continent.

In Gaul, St. Patrick became associated with several monastic institutions, and he began a theological training that would allow him to return to Ireland as a missionary bishop. He served for twenty-nine years in Ireland, where his achievements included the promotion of native clergy and the integration of the Christian faith with the Irish-Celtic culture. He is the author of a work called *The Confession*, but there are also a large number of legends (including his driving the snakes out of Ireland) and generally unreliable sources about his life (among them the *Life of St. Patrick* by Muirchu, the *Irish Annals*, and Tirechan's *Breviarium*).

The cult of St. Patrick began soon after his death, and he remains immensely popular worldwide. The patron of Ireland, his feast is celebrated as a holiday in many countries. He is shown in art as a bishop, often holding a shamrock, since, according to legend, he used the plant to teach about the Trinity.

One of the largest celebrations in honor of St. Patrick is held each year in New York City. Thousands of worshipers crowd into the century-old St. Patrick's Cathedral to attend the Solemn Mass in honor of Ireland's patron, which is celebrated by the Cardinal-Archbishop of New York and a host of clergy, Outside the cathedral on Fifth Avenue in Manhattan, more than a million people of various ethnic origins and religious beliefs, as either marchers or onlookers, express their affection for St. Patrick with a parade. The first St. Patrick's Day parade was held in New York on March 17, 1762. That celebration has been carried out each year since, with both religious and civic dignitaries reviewing the proceedings. Similar celebrations are held in cities, towns, and villages in many parts of the world, especially in the U.S.

In France, at Marmoutier and St. Patrice, devotion to St. Patrick is ascribed to the tradition that Patrick himself visited these spots. The place known as "*le trou de St. Patrice*" at La Neuville appears to have once enjoyed the reputation, similar to St. Patrick's Purgatory on Lough Derg, of being an entrance to the underworld. St. Patrick's Purgatory on Lough Derg is in County Donegal, Ireland. This is one of the few truly penitential places surviving in Western Europe from the Middle

St. Patrick

Ages, and, according to legend, is an entranceway to the underworld associated with a promise made to St. Patrick that he would be the one to judge the Irish after death. This legend helps explain other legends associating St. Patrick with purgatory and especially with the winning of freedom for souls in that place.

ST. PAUL

The Apostle to the Gentiles, theologian, and martyr (d.c. 67; feast days June 29 [with St. Peter] and January 25 [his conversion]).

A Roman citizen who was born at Tarsus in Asia Minor, Saul (his preconversion name) was a Jew of the tribe of Benjamin, a pupil of the great rabbi Gamaliel, a Pharisee. Paul was also a learned rabbi and a scrupulous observer of the Mosaic law. As recorded in the Acts of the Apostles, Paul considered the new Christian faith an abomination, and he promoted and joined in the persecution of the followers of Christ. While heading to Damascus to continue that work, he underwent a profound conversion (see Acts 9:3-5; 22:6-8; 26:13-15) and went on to share the Good News with non-Jews on three missionary journeys. He is especially known for his letters, or epistles, to Christian communities: Romans, 1 and 2 Corinthians, Galatians, Ephesians, Philippians, Colossians, 1 and 2 Thessalonians, 1 and 2 Timothy, Titus, and Philomen.

St. Paul was martyred about 67 at the command of the Emperor Nero. Owing to his possession of Roman citizenship, Paul was beheaded. He was said to have been buried in a cemetery on the Via Ostia owned by a Christian named Lucina. Years later, it became the site of the Basilica of St. Paul-Outside-the-Walls.

Paul is the patron of preachers and theologians, ropemakers, weavers, and tentmakers. Throughout his career, he financed his ministry by practicing the tentmaker's trade. Paul's aid is invoked against snakebites, hail, and for acceptance of the circumstances of daily living, and for a holy death.

An old English folksong tones: "If St. Paul's Day be fair and clear, it does betide a happy year." St. Paul's day gives advance information about the weather and more. The rest of the song refers to the condi-

St. Paul

tions of rain, clouds, and wind, and tells that it is possible to foretell what will be the price of grain, the health of livestock, and the prospects of war. The song was already old when it was translated from Latin to English, and most of western Europe had believed it for many centuries. In Hungary, grain was blessed after Mass on Peter and Paul's Day. People wove crowns, crosses, and other religious symbols from straw, had them blessed, and then carried them on wooden poles in procession around the church. Afterward, these were taken home and kept suspended from the ceiling over the dining table. There is also a special blessing of bread in Hungary on this day.

In art, St. Paul is depicted with a sword or book; both are his traditional symbols.

ST. PAUL MIKI AND COMPANIONS

Japanese martyr saints (d. 1597, feast day February 6).

St. Francis Xavier first took Christianity to Japan in 1549, and for a generation the new faith flourished there. In 1588, under the angry leadership of the Emperor Tagosama, an era of persecution began. Thousands of Christians were tortured and killed. They were burned, beheaded, crucified, and suspended head downward over pits of burning sulphur. St. Paul Miki and twenty five companions were crucified at Nagasaki in 1597. Of the group, six were European Franciscan missionar-

ies led by the Spanish St. Peter Baptist. St. Paul Miki was a Japanese Jesuit priest and St. Leo Karasuma was a Korean layman. The remainder were Japanese laymen, of whom three were young boys. They were executed simultaneously by a sort of crucifixion, being raised on crosses and then stabbed with spears.

The persecutions continued for many years and finally it appeared that there were no Christians left in Japan. Three hundred years later, when Christianity was again permitted in Japan, a priest saying Mass was startled when a stranger came and knelt by him whispering, "My heart is with your heart." Startled, the priest questioned the stranger and learned that Christians in Japan had gone underground, and for three centuries, this lovely statement had been the secret password by which Christians recognized each other, and kept the faith alive.

ST. PEREGRINE

A Servite friar and mystic (c. 1260-1345, feast day May 1).

Born in Forli, Italy, into a wealthy family, he led a dissolute youth, and according to tradition, was so enraged during some public disturbance that he struck St. Philip Benzi on the face. When St. Philip calmly turned and offered the other cheek, Peregrine was deeply impressed, and later went on to join the Servites in Siena. Following training, he returned to his hometown and remained there for the rest of his life. Because he suffered cancer of the foot until, as the result of a vision, he was miraculously cured, St. Peregrine is the patron of those with cancer. In more recent times, he has also been called a patron of those with AIDS. St. Peregrine is a patron of Spain and is particularly beloved in Austria, Hungary, Bavaria, and Italy. Promoting devotion to St. Peregrine Laziosi has become a central apostolate of the Servites.

ST. PETER

The first Vicar of Christ, Prince of the Apostles, and founder of the see of Rome (with St. Paul), martyr (d.c. 64, feast days June 29 [with St. Paul] and February 22 [Chair of Peter]).

From Bethsaida, near Lake Tiberias, Simon Peter (also called *Cephas*) was a fisherman like his brother, St. Andrew. It was Andrew who introduced Simon to Jesus, who then called him to become a disciple. Jesus gave Simon a new name: *Cephas* or "the rock." It is the Greek translation of that, *petros*, from which the name Peter derives.

Peter is listed first of the Apostles in all New Testament accounts and was among the select few (with John and James the Greater) at the Transfiguration. He is mentioned more than any other disciple, and played a major role in the events of the Passion (including cutting off the ear of a slave in the garden and, as Christ had predicted, denying knowing Christ). Following the Resurrection, Peter went to the tomb with the "other disciple" (probably St. John) and the risen Lord appeared to Peter before the other disciples. Immediately following the Ascension, Peter was clearly the head of the Apostles. He was also instrumental in bringing the Good

St. Peter

News to the Gentiles, established a local church in Antioch, presided over the Council of Jerusalem in 51, and wrote two epistles to the Church in Asia Minor. Along with St. Paul, he established his see in Rome where, tradition holds, he was crucified in the circus of Nero on Vatican Hill, requesting to be executed upside down because he was not worthy to die as Christ had. He was buried on Vatican Hill, and excavations under the basilica named for him have unearthed his probable tomb. His relics are enshrined in the *confessio* under the high altar of the basilica.

Possibly stemming from the ancient Germanic mythology of the gods Thor and Woden, after their conversion the Christianized Germanic people seem to have invested St. Peter and St. Paul with the function of "weather makers." Many legends ascribe thunder and lightning to some activity of Peter in heaven such as bowling. When it snows, St. Peter is "shaking out his feather bed." In France, also, St. Peter is known as a rainmaker.

In the rural sections of the Alpine countries when the church bells ring the Angelus on June 29, people step under the trees in their gardens and kneel down to pray. After the prayer, they bow and make the sign of the cross, believing that on St. Peter's Day the blessing of the Holy Father in Rome is carried by angels throughout the world to all who sincerely await it. The faithful traditionally have visited the tomb of St. Peter in the Vatican Basilica. Here there is a bronze statue of the saint and pilgrims devoutly kiss the foot of the statue and pray for the intentions of the Holy Father.

With Paul, Peter is invoked against snake bites, and custom has it that one who prays especially well on St. Peter's and St. Paul's feast day will not be bitten by a snake during the coming year.

St. Peter is the patron of fishermen, sailors, leather merchants, locksmiths, shoemakers and cobblers, and watchmakers. He is invoked against fever because Christ cured his mother-in-law. He is prayed to particularly for strength and for forgiveness of sins. From the tenth century, Peter has been venerated as the gatekeeper who guards the entrance to heaven, admitting or turning away souls. In art, he is shown carrying two keys, symbolic of his primacy in the Church.

ST. PETER'S PLANT

Any flower or herb traditionally associated with St. Peter, including *primula hirsuta,* which was used as a medicinal tea, especially as a remedy for snake or dog bite.

ST. RAPHAEL THE ARCHANGEL

Archangel of healing. (feast day September 29).

Raphael was sent in human form as the

593

traveling companion of the young Tobias who was on his way to be the eighth husband of Sara, whose seven previous husbands had been slain by a demon. Raphael bound the demon, Asmodeus, "in the desert of upper Egypt." Thus, Sara was delivered from the devil and her marriage to Tobias was blessed. On this same journey, Raphael restored sight to Tobias' father who was blind.

Raphael, or "Healer of God," is assumed to be the angel who, as told in John 5:4: "troubled the water" and "whosoever then first after the troubling of the water stepped in was made whole of whatsoever disease he had."

Raphael is invoked against all sickness — physical, mental, or spiritual — and against possession by spirits. With Michael, he is known for his healing of the sick. He is the patron of doctors and nurses, lovers, travelers, and young and innocent people.

ST. RITA OF CASCIA

Augustinian nun, stigmatic, patroness of the impossible (d.1457, feast day May 22).

Born at Spoleto, Italy, in 1381, as a young girl St. Rita dreamed of entering a convent, and begged her parents for permission. They denied her, and arranged a marriage for her at the tender age of twelve. Rita (sometimes called Marguerita) was married to Paolo Ferdinando, a man of violent and abusive temperament. After nearly twenty years of marriage, Rita's husband was murdered. In his last years, he had repented because of Rita's constant prayers for him. Shortly after the death of her husband, both of her sons died. Rita filled her days with prayer, fasting, penances of many kinds, and charitable works.

At last, she was admitted to the convent of the Augustinian nuns at Cascia in Umbria, where she lived a life of perfect obedience and great charity. At first, Rita was denied entrance, but she was accepted after the bolted doors and gates of the monastery were miraculously opened for her by her patron saints.

Especially devoted to the passion of Christ, Rita prayed to participate in some way with Our Lord in His suffering. In a mystical experience, one of the thorns from the crucifix struck her on the forehead, leaving a deep wound that did not heal. It festered and produced such an offensive odor that for the next fifteen years she stayed in virtual seclusion. A number of other supernatural happenings are reported in her life, although these cannot be well substantiated because the only extant biography of her was written 150 years after her death.

She died on May 22, 1457. At her death, her cell was filled with an extraordinary perfume and a light emanated from the wound on her forehead. The bells of the city began ringing of their own volition. The body was placed in the church and the miracles reported by the many pilgrims to her bier were so numerous and the perfume that filled the church was so intense, that the civil and ecclesiastical authorities allowed the body to be placed in a position between the cloister and the church, where the body could be venerated by both pilgrims and cloistered nuns. The body remained in this position for over 150 years without a proper entombment. When the remains were examined prior to her beatification, the body was discovered to be in a good state of preservation. A report from this time, 1627, states that the eyes of the relic opened unaided and remained open for some time as paintings done during that time indicate. The body seemed to move to one side and after a lapse of some years returned to its original position. One recorded observation said that the body elevated to the top of the sarcophagus.

Rita was canonized in 1900, and her devotion spread rapidly beyond Italy to Europe and the Americas. A new basilica was built in her honor at Cascia in 1946. Here, the saint's miraculously preserved body is housed in a golden shrine. A heavenly sweet smell is frequently noticed at the shrine.

An interesting relic is growing in the courtyard of the convent. In order to test her obedience, her superior handed Rita a piece of dry wood and ordered her to plant it and water it daily. The stick sprouted into a healthy grapevine that still bears fruit. Every year the harvest of grapes is divided among high ranking ecclesiastics. The leaves are dried, made into a powder, and sent to the sick around the world.

(See also **SANTA RITA**.)

ST. SCHOLASTICA

Twin sister of Benedict (c.480-543, feast day February 10). Little is known of the early life of Scholastica and Benedict. Their parents were Christian patricians; the love of order, seclusion, prayer, charity and hospitality which characterizes the lives of these twin saints was apparently fostered in a Christian home. Scholastica was apparently dedicated to God at an early age, although she probably continued living at home. There is a tradition that in collaboration with her brother, she founded and governed a community of nuns at Plombariola about five miles from his own monastery, although no historical documents or ruins remain to confirm its location. Some scholars believe her convent was a kind of hermitage with only a few religious near the base of Monte Cassino where an ancient church dedicated to her now stands.

St. Scholastica apparently had a joyous nature and lived simply in an intense mystical union with God. The last antiphon for the vespers of her feast announced: "She could do more because she loved more !" According to the writings of St. Gregory, it was customary for St. Benedict and St. Scholastica to meet once a year at a house about halfway between the monastery and the convent to spend a day together in prayer and spiritual conversation. This was an occasion of mutual encouragement and support. On one such occasion, which proved to be the last, the saintly pair had spent the day as usual and together with their companions had just finished their evening meal. The time for parting was at hand, and Scholastica, perhaps sensing her impending death, asked her brother to continue the discussion and postpone his return to the monastery until the next morning. Benedict, disciplined monk that he was, refused. Thereupon, Scholastica had recourse to a higher power. She bent her head and prayed that God would answer her petition. As soon as she raised her head, a torrential storm began, making it impossible for Benedict and his monks to leave.

In astonishment, Benedict looked at his sister and exclaimed, "What have you done?"

Laughingly, Scholastica replied, "I asked a favor of you and you refused. I asked my Lord and He has granted my petition ! Go now, brother ! Go, if you can !"

Needless to say, Benedict had no alternative but to yield to his sister's wishes and they resumed their discourse, spending the entire night in delightful conversation on spiritual things.

Three days later, the significance of this miracle was understood more clearly when he was favored with a vision in which he saw the soul of his sister winging its flight to heaven in the form of a dove. He announced her death to his community, thanking God for the eternal happiness of his sister.

Benedict arranged for Scholastica's burial in the tomb he had prepared for himself, and where he himself was laid only a few weeks later. Thus, in death as in life, the brother and sister remained closely united.

In art, Scholastica is represented as a Benedictine Abbess, with the dove as her emblem. She is also shown with a crosier in recognition of her authority over her first spiritual daughters, and she is counted as the foundress of the Benedictine nuns. Sometimes she is shown with a book representing the Holy Rule, or with a lily and a crucifix. Occasionally she is pictured with a small child at her feet because she is invoked against convulsions and colic. She is also invoked by expectant mothers for a happy delivery and against storms.

ST. STANISLAUS, SPIRITUAL EXERCISES OF

The pious participation in the Rosary, hearing of a sermon, prayers, blessing, and a prayer for the intention of the pope as part of an observance of the November 13 Feast of St. Stanislaus Kostka (1550-1568).

ST. STEPHEN'S HORSES

A custom associated with the tradition of St. Stephen the martyr as the patron of horses.

It was a general practice among the farmers in central Europe to decorate their horses on St. Stephen's Day and bring them to church to be blessed by the priest. Afterward, the horse was ridden three times around the church. Hay and oats, were blessed on this day, December 26, and the people threw kernels of these blessed oats at one another and at their domestic animals. Water and salt were also blessed and kept to be fed to the horses in case of sickness. Women baked special breads in the form of horseshoes to be eaten on the feast.

ST. SYLVESTER'S NIGHT

The name of a New Year's Eve festival held on the Feast of St. Sylvester, December 31.

Besides the traditional reveling, a number of ancient customs are still practiced in many European countries, especially in rural areas. In Spanish-speaking sections, it is a tradition to eat twelve grapes at midnight, one at each stroke of the tower bell. In central Europe, the new year is greeted with the cracking of whips, the shooting of guns, and the making of banging and clanging noises inside the home. The noise is a remnant of the pre-Christian ritual of driving away demons. Sylvester night was a traditional night of superstitious practices aimed at predicting what the new year would bring. To give these oracles a character of devotional practice instead of merely superstition, prayers were asked of St. Sylvester in traditional rhymes.

ST. TERESA'S BOOKMARK

A maxim by St. Teresa of Ávila.

The great Carmelite reformer and mystic, Teresa de Ahumada y Cepeda (1515-1582), was known for here charming wit and common sense as well as for her mystical experiences. Teresa's spiritual maturity was recognized as her books and letters became known; today her works are regarded as classics of spiritual literature. She combined a life of mystical contemplation with one of dazzling activity. Teresa died in 1582 and was canonized in 1622 by Pope Gregory XV. She was declared a Doctor of the Church in 1970. Her feast day is October 15. One of her maxims, commonly known as St. Theresa's bookmark, reads:

Let nothing trouble you, let nothing frighten you. All things are passing; God never changes. Patience obtains all things. He who possesses God lacks nothing: God alone suffices.

ST. THÉRÈSE OF LISIEUX

A Carmelite nun, mystic, and Doctor of the Church (1873-1897, feast day October 1).

Born in Alençon, France, St. Thérèse entered the convent in Lisieux in 1888 and died of tuberculosis nine years later. Using a spirituality that she called the "little way," she lived the seemingly ordinary life of a nun; but her spiritual advancement was so profound that her superior (who was also her older sister) instructed her to write her autobiography (*The Story of a Soul*) in 1895. Canonized in 1925, she became one of the most popular saints of the twentieth century. In 1927, Pope Pius XI declared her (along with St. Francis Xavier) patron of foreign missions. In 1944, Pope Pius XII named her (along with St. Joan of Arc) protector of France. In 1997, Pope John Paul II declared her the third female Doctor of the Church (along with St. Catherine of Siena and St. Teresa of Ávila).

St. Thérèse is also known as the Little Flower, based on her self-description as the "little flower of Jesus." Near death, she held that her mission — to make God loved — was about to begin, that she would "spend my heaven doing good on earth" and "let fall a shower of roses." Devotees consider the unexpected appearance of a rose as a sign of her intercession.

Images of St. Thérèse are usually based on photographs that were taken of her in Carmel. Often, however, she is portrayed in art holding a crucifix amid a bouquet of roses.

St. Thérèse of Lisieux

ST. URSULA

Popular saint of the Middle Ages (c. fourth century, feast day formerly October 21)

The legend of Ursula tells of a beautiful princess of Cornwall whose fame reached a Scottish prince named Conan. He sent for her to come and marry him, requesting her to bring other girls to marry Christian soldiers with him. She immediately set sail with 11,000 eligible young ladies, but their boats were driven off course up the Rhine river where they were all killed by the barbarian Huns against whom they defended their virtue at Cologne in 383.

It is far more likely that Ursula was accompanied by eleven companions. The large number mentioned in her legend probably stems from the twelfth century discovery of a vast quantity of human bones at Cologne. What was found was probably an old Roman cemetery, but popular opinion made the bones the remains of the ill-fated bridal party.

An interesting sequel to this story is found in the state of Louisiana. In the seventeenth century, Louisiana belonged to France, and the king sent boatloads of girls to marry the lonely settlers. Each girl was given the "King's dowry," a small chest containing one blanket, four sheets, two pair of stockings, six headdresses and a "pelisse." The arrival of these "casket girls" in New Orleans was celebrated with a procession in honor of St. Ursula, and they were housed in the Ursuline convent while waiting for the young men to make their choices.

Ursula's cult was suppressed in 1969.

ST. VALENTINE

A priest, physician, and martyr (d. 269, feast day February 14).

The legend of St. Valentine tells of a young priest who lived in Rome in the thirrd century. He was jailed for refusing to renounce his Christian faith. In prison, Valentine sent letters to his loved ones via a dove that came and sat on his cell window. The message simply said, "Remember your Valentine."

Valentine, along with St. Marius and his family, assisted the martyrs who suffered during the reign of Claudius II. According to his "Acts," after his arrest the Prefect of Rome first imprisoned him, then had him beaten with clubs and beheaded. While in prison, he restored sight to the little blind daughter of his judge, Asterius, who thereupon was converted with all his family and suffered martyrdom with the saint. The date of his martyrdom is thought to be about 270.

A medieval version of the legend says that shortly before his execution, Valentine had sent a note to the kind daughter of his prison master. This legend was obviously intended to provide a belated reason for the already existing custom of the day.

There was a church of St. Valentine on the Flaminian Way in Rome which was built in the middle of the fourth century. It is possible that Valentine was of Persian descent. Records of a martyred bishop at Terni may simply refer to the priest-martyr Valentine.

The custom of choosing a partner and sending "Valentines" on February 14 apparently arose from the old idea that birds begin to pair on that day. There is no doubt however, that the historical origin of the Valentine lore is based on a coincidence of dates. The pagan Romans celebrated Lupercalia, a great feast, on February 15. The feast was in honor of the pastoral god Lupercus, who is an equivalent of the Greek god Pan. On the eve of the feast, and as part of it, he young people held a celebration of their own, declaring their love for each other, proposing marriage, or choosing partners for the following year. In some places, the boys drew billets to choose their partners. These names were worn pinned to the sleeves of the young men. (Even today, it is said that a man "wears his heart on his sleeve" when he shows his interest in a young lady.) The couples sometimes exchanged presents. The Roman youth festival was under the patronage of the goddess Juno Februata. After the Roman Empire became Christian, the feast was changed to the patronage of the saint whose feast was celebrated on February 14, the priest and martyr Valentine.

Proof of the Roman origin of the Valentine lore is the fact that in countries of Roman historical background even small details like the games of chance and other customs were continued into the late Middle Ages, while in other countries, these details are missing and St. Valentine as patron of young lovers is the only observance.

In Germany, Austria, and among the western Slavs, Laetare Sunday used to be the day to announce the engagements of young people. In Bohemia, the boys would send messengers to the homes of their girl friends to deliver the proposal. In Austria, the girls of each village lined up in front of the church after Mass and their boy friends would take them by the hand and lead them back into the house of God, thus "proposing" to them by a silent act of religious import. After the couple prayed together, they would seal the engagement with a special meal. These engagement customs were called "Valentine," although they did not take place on St. Valentine's Day. The name is explained by the fact that St. Valentine was already considered the heavenly patron of young lovers and engaged couples.

In the seventeenth century, a hopeful maiden ate a hard-boiled egg and pinned five bay leaves to her pillow before going to sleep on Valentine's Eve, believing this would make her dream of her future husband.

The American custom of sending Valentine cards is unknown in the countries of northern Europe. This custom came from England. The traditional words actually imply: "You are my Valentine and I offer you my companionship, my affection and love for the next twelve months and am willing to consider marriage if this companionship proves satisfactory for both of us."

The Duke of Orléans is believed to have

made the first valentine card while imprisoned in the Tower of London in 1415. He wrote love poems to his wife in France. Sweethearts exchanged handmade cards in some places during the seventeenth and eighteenth centuries. In France, these were huge paper hearts trimmed with yards of real lace. In the United States, Valentine cards became popular during the Civil War. Elaborate cards trimmed with spun glass, satin ribbons, and sometimes mother-of-pearl ornaments were sold. For a time, Valentine's Day was as big an event as Christmas.

November 10, 1836, St. Valentine's relics were placed in the Carmelite Church on Whitfriars Street in Dublin, Ireland. A humble Carmelite priest, Father John Spratt, had been tireless in his efforts for the stricken poor of the Dublin Liberties. On a brief visit to Rome, he was surprised by a gift from Pope Gregory, given as a mark of the pope's esteem for the hardworking priest. The gift was the remains of St. Valentine, who also, in life, had a wide reputation for holiness and self-denial. The relics were removed from the cemetery of St. Hippolytus in Rome and dispatched on the long journey to Dublin. Here they were enshrined in the church on Whitefriars Street for the glory of God and the veneration of the faithful.

Today, St. Valentine's feast is still celebrated on February 14. The crocus, which blooms around this time of the year, is St. Valentine's flower. To this day, St. Valentine is honored as a patron for lovers and sweethearts. For Catholics, he remains a symbol not only for our love for each other, but for the love between God and man.

ST. VINCENT DE PAUL SOCIETY — See **VINCENT DE PAUL SOCIETY**.

ST. VITUS

A martyr (d.c. 300, feast day June 15).

The details of St. Vitus's life are unknown, but there was an early martyr with that name and the cult of St. Vitus is ancient. There are various explanations how his name came to be associated with the nervous disorder chorea, at one time commonly referred to as "St. Vitus's Dance." One legend holds that visitors to a German shrine bearing his name believed that anyone who danced in front of the church on his feast day would be assured of good health for the coming year. Some moved with such tremendous enthusiasm that their spasmodic movements were seen to resemble those of chorea patients.

In the eighth century, St. Vitus's relics were brought to France and later to the Abbey of Corvey. At that time, the abbey was a center of great missionary activity and the monks there introduced the veneration of St. Vitus to the Germanic and

Slavic tribes. His cult soon spread throughout France, Germany, England, Scandinavia, and eastern Europe. His feast was celebrated with pilgrimages, a holiday from work, and festivals.

In the strange "epidemics" of dancing mania that swept western Europe at various times from the fourteenth to the sixteenth centuries, St. Vitus's patronage grew to gigantic proportions. The victims of that mass hysteria were brought to his shrines and led three times around his altar or statue to obtain relief or cure.

Originally, St. Vitus's patronage was sought only to help those with medical or emotional disorders associated with movement. Over time, it was extended to include true performances and he became known as the patron of dancers and actors.

In art, St. Vitus is often pictured with a chicken, reflecting the medieval custom of bringing roosters, hens, and eggs as gifts to his shrines. He is also often pictured with a dog.

ST. WINEFRIDE'S WELL

A shrine located at Clwyd in North Wales.

According to pious legend, in 634 St. Winefride rejected a suitor who then beheaded her. A miraculous fountain sprang up where her head hit the ground. Her uncle, the holy abbot St. Beuno, raised her to life again and she became abbess of a convent at the place known as Holywell.

Her life was written at the Abbey of Shrewsbury in the twelfth century. The abbey claimed to have her relics, and devotion to her was popular during the Middle Ages and survived to recent times, although mining activity diverted the original spring in the early part of the twentieth century. Pilgrims bathe in the waters, asking for St. Winefride's favors.

STABAT MATER

A traditional Marian prayer and hymn.

Although its authorship is disputed, it is commonly attributed to Jacopone da Todi (c. 1228-1306). The poem was well known in Europe by the end of the fourteenth century and appeared in several local missals in the fifteenth. It was inserted as a sequence into the *Roman Missal* and as a hymn into the Breviary in 1727 for recitation on the Feast of the Seven Sorrows of the Virgin Mary (Friday before Good Friday). After changes were introduced by Pope Pius XII, it now appears on the Feast of Our Lady of Sorrows (September 15).

One version reads:

At the Cross her station keeping
Stood the mournful Mother weeping,
Close to Jesus to the last.

Through her heart his sorrow sharing,
All his bitter anguish bearing,
Lo! the piercing sword had passed.

For his people's sins rejected,
Saw her Jesus unprotected,
Saw with thorns, with scourges rent.

Saw her Son from judgment taken,
Her beloved in death forsaken,
Till his spirit forth he sent.

Jesus, may your Cross defend me,
And your Mother's prayer befriend
　me.
Let me die in your embrace.

When to dust my dust returns
Grant a soul, which for you yearns,
In your Paradise a place. Amen.

STAINED GLASS

An art form, dating from the twelfth century, used to decorate churches, buildings, and homes.

By using colors and the arrangement of the pieces, stained glass provides an eloquent and descriptive means of expressing God's presence.

STAR

A symbol traditionally associated with the Epiphany.

(See also **EPIPHANY**; **MAGI**.)

STAR OF THE SEA

A Marian title.

The hymn *Ave Maris Stella* (Latin for "Hail, Star of the Sea") presents Mary as the gate of heaven and also has her guiding travelers into port. It has been known from the ninth century but may have been written earlier. From that time the image of Mary as the Star of the Sea became a popular one in Western devotion. A wooden statue of Our Lady, Star of the Sea, has been venerated in Maastricht, Netherlands, since the late Middle Ages. About four feet tall, it was given to the Franciscan church there in 1400 by Nicholas von Harlaer when he joined the order. She holds the Infant Jesus in her left hand and a small vase in her right hand. The vase was originally intended as an inkpot, a remnant of a devotion popular in Flanders known as Our Lady of the Inkpot, but the vase is now used to hold a lily. The Child, sculpted without clothes, is usually dressed in a brocade outfit while the Virgin wears a matching cloak.

Star

STATION

A Latin term that seems to have arisen from the military meaning of sentry duty and has come to mean the place where the liturgy will be held.

During the Middle Ages, the liturgies were accompanied by processions, and the term came also to mean the stopping points along the processional routes. In Rome, there are stational churches to which indulgences have been attached, making them prominent on the route of churches visited by pilgrims.

STATIONS OF THE CROSS

A form of devotion commemorating the Passion and death of Christ, consisting of a series of meditations (stations); also called "Way of the Cross."

The traditional fourteen are:

1. Jesus is condemned to death.
2. Jesus takes up his cross.
3. Jesus falls for the first time on the way to Calvary.
4. Jesus meets Mary, his Mother.
5. Simon of Cyrene helps Jesus carry his cross.
6. Veronica wipes Jesus' face with a veil.
7. Jesus falls the second time.
8. Jesus meets the women of Jerusalem.
9. Jesus falls the third time.
10. Jesus is stripped of his clothes.
11. Jesus is nailed to the cross.
12. Jesus dies on the cross.
13. Jesus' body is removed from the cross.
14. Jesus is buried.

Images of these scenes are mounted in most churches, chapels, and in some other places, beneath small crosses. A person making the Way of the Cross passes before these stations, or stopping points, pausing at each for meditation. If the stations are made by a group of people, only the leader walks from station to station. (A plenary indulgence is granted to the faithful who make the stations, under the usual conditions: freedom from all attachment to sin, reception of the sacraments of penance and the Eucharist, and prayers for the intentions of the pope.)

The stations originated remotely from the practice of Holy Land pilgrims who visited the actual scenes of incidents in the Passion of Christ (Jerusalem's *Via Dolorosa*). Representations elsewhere of at least some of these scenes were known as early as the fifth century. Later, the stations evolved in connection with and as a consequence of strong devotion to the Passion in the twelfth and thirteenth centuries. Franciscans, who were given custody of the holy places in 1342, promoted the devotion widely; one of them, St. Leonard of Port Maurice, became known as the greatest preacher of the Way of the Cross in the eighteenth century. The general features of the devotion were fixed by Pope Clement XII in 1731.

STATIONS, IRISH

An Irish devotion during which Mass is celebrated in a family home.

The historical origin of the Irish "station Masses" is uncertain. They may have begun in the practice of priests celebrating Mass secretly in homes during post-Elizabethan times when Catholic worship was banned in Ireland. Today, the station Masses continue mostly in the rural areas of the country. The homes selected are often repainted and redecorated in honor of the event. Neighbors are invited, and a rather elaborate breakfast follows the Mass.

STEWARDSHIP

The proper and profitable management of that with which a person is entrusted.

In Christian terms, this would refer to both physical and spiritual things, which are to be used and administered responsibly, because all things ultimately belong to God.

STICHON

A scriptural quotation, often from the Psalms, used in the East.

It is also the prayer inspired by the scriptural quotation.

STIGMATA

Marks of the wounds suffered by Christ in his crucifixion, in his hands and feet by nails, and in his side by the piercing of a lance.

Some persons, called stigmatists, have been reported as recipients or sufferers of marks like these. The Church has never issued any infallible declaration about their possession by anyone, even in the case of St. Francis of Assisi, whose stigmata seem to be the best substantiated and may be commemorated in the Roman Rite liturgy. Ninety percent of some three hundred reputed stigmatists have been women. Judgment regarding the presence, significance, and manner of causation of stigmata would depend, among other things, on irrefutable experimental evidence.

St. Pio Forgione of Pietrelcina (1887-1968), better known as Padre Pio, is the only priest to have borne the stigmata.

STIPEND

A common term for the offering given to a priest for celebrating a Mass or performing some other sacramental ceremony.

STOCK

The term usually applied to a container for oils used for the various sacraments.

The oil stocks are generally three in

number, corresponding to the types of holy oil: chrism, oil of catechumens, and oil of the sick.

STOUP

A vessel used to contain holy water.

STRIKING THE BREAST

A gesture of repentance since the early Church.

The custom is still practiced by some at Mass during the praying of the *Confiteor* and *Lamb of God*.

SUB TUUM PRAESIDIUM

The earliest known prayer to the Virgin Mary whose text has survived; from the Latin for "under your protection."

The earliest text is written in Greek on an Egyptian papyrus and constitutes the first documentary evidence of the existence of devotion to Mary. The papyrus was discovered in Egypt in 1917, and dates to the second half of the third century. The date of the composition of the prayer is unknown. The *Sub Tuum* is used in Litanies to the Blessed Mother and as a concluding prayer in the Liturgy of the Hours. One translation reads:

We fly to your patronage, O holy Mother of God; despise not our petitions in our necessities, but deliver us always from all dangers, O glorious and blessed Virgin. Amen.

SUFFRAGES

Prayers or Masses offered for special intentions, particularly for the dead.

"By the hidden and kindly mystery of God's will," wrote Pope Paul VI, "a supernatural solidarity reigns among men and women." Just as we are interdependent during this life, so are we beyond death. Without this communion of saints, praying for the dead would be senseless. The Church is the communion of the "holy ones" or "saints" who dwell on earth, in heaven, and in purgatory.

A link of grace and mutual concern ties together those who have reached their heavenly home, those who are being purified, and those who are still pilgrims on earth. All are branches engrafted onto the single vine that is Christ (see John 15:1-8)

For Christ and those united in his Body, the dead are alive. Death does not dissolve the relational and social nature of humanity. The supernatural fellowship of charity that unites members of the one Body of Christ (see 1 Corinthians 12:27) includes those in the state of purgation. Human solidarity reaches even beyond the confines of death.

Because in the communion of saints all share the profound fellowship of grace "with the Father and with his Son Jesus Christ" (see 1 John 1:3), they also experience a solidarity in the spiritual goods flowing through the whole Body of Christ — on earth, in heaven and in purgatory. In the Church no one lives for himself alone, just as no one dies for himself alone (see Romans 14:7). Everyone suffers and rejoices together (see 1 Corinthians 12:26). Each act of love profits all those who are united in Christ, just as every sin harms them.

After death, therefore, those in purgatory do not stand alone before God. The Church's faith tells us that the saving power of love transcends the grave. The bonds forged during life are indestructible. Consequently, the prayers and the merits of the living can help the departed in obtaining salvation from "God, who is rich in mercy" (see Ephesians 2:4).

Our prayers for the dead are efficacious because we are "in Christ," in the Body of which he is the head (see Ephesians 1:22-23). Such petitions are often called suffrages; that is, they are intercessory prayers and good works. As intercessory, they make a request through Christ, imploring God to free those in purgatory so that they will be cleansed from whatever still needs purification.

These prayers are made with filial confidence. Catholics believe that the Father knows what we need before asking him (see Matthew 6:8) and that "the Spirit helps us in our weakness; for we do not know how to pray as we ought, but that very Spirit intercedes with sighs too deep for words" (see Romans 8:26).

To intercede on behalf of others through prayer is a practice that goes back to Abraham's intercession for Sodom and Gomorrah (see Genesis 18:16-33). In the New Covenant, Christ himself is our intercessor before the Father: "He is able for all time to save those who approach God through him, since he always lives to make intercession for them" (see Hebrews 7:25). Since Christians are united to Christ in "one body" (see Ephesians 4:6), praying for the brethren was part and parcel of early Church life (see Acts 12:5). In the communion of saints, the pilgrims on earth look not only to their own interests, but to the interests of others (see Philippians 2:4), joining their prayers to those of Christ.

As a testimony to their supernatural solidarity with those in purgatory, the living may request that God apply to the purgatorians the spiritual "fruits" of their own good works and prayers. The love underpinning such actions releases the infinite love of Christ for the beloved deceased.

Likewise, the more individuals have the mind "which you have in Christ Jesus" (see Philippians 2:5), the more their prayers will be efficacious for others. Precisely how this is accomplished is not known. Without dictating to God how their good works can be "applied" to the faithful departed,

Catholics trust that his love and mercy will prompt God to speed the purification of the faithful departed.

Praying for the dead does more than retain their presence in the thoughts of the living. It is also an act of mercy. The ministry of consolation falls to each of the faithful when a fellow member of Christ's Body dies. Catholics are called to comfort the bereaved, but also, and more importantly, to pray for the deceased. Suffrages for the faithful departed help them to purify their love so that every trace of sin and its remnants will be erased. Sustained by this supernatural solidarity, those in purgatory will receive their citizenship in heaven, from where they await the resurrection of the body (see Philippians 3:20). Such generosity will surely be rewarded. "Blessed are the merciful, for they shall obtain mercy" (see Matthew 5:7).

SUNDAY

The day on which members of the Church have gathered for the celebration of the Eucharist since apostolic times.

While Jews who had become Christians continued to observe the Sabbath each Saturday, they also celebrated Sunday as the new Christian day of worship because it was the day of Christ's Resurrection.

In apostolic times, the Mass was held within the frame of a ritual meal (an agape) held on Saturday night after sunset. Soon after the close of the first century, the Eucharistic celebration was separated from the meal in many places and transferred to the early morning hours of Sunday and made part of a service according to the Jewish custom of worshiping on the Day of the Lord. The service was held in the form of a vigil or night watch before dawn on Sunday and usually consisted of a sermon, prayers, singing of Psalms, and readings from Holy Scripture. The earliest testimony concerning this Christian Sunday celebration comes from the poet Pliny the Younger (c. 62-113). In a letter to the emperor he reported on the Christians in his province and described their Sunday service. A detailed description of the Sunday Mass is found in the *Apologia* of St. Justin Martyr, who died for the faith about 165: "We meet on Sunday because it is the first day, on which God created the world, and because our Savior, Jesus Christ, rose from the dead on the same day."

By the end of the fourth century, this morning celebration on Sunday had replaced in all Christian communities the original Saturday night meal and Eucharist. After the Church obtained freedom under Constantine in 313, the hour of Sunday Mass was changed from dawn to nine o'clock in the morning, the time the Romans customarily assigned for important business.

The early Christians referred to Sunday as the "Day of the Lord." In 1998, Pope John Paul II issued an Apostolic Letter, *Dies Domini*, "The Lord's Day," on the importance of keeping holy the Lord's Day.

(See also **EASTER**.)

SUNDAY OBLIGATION

The duty of the faithful to participate in the Eucharistic Sacrifice on Sundays and holy days of obligation.

SUPEREROGATION

Actions that go beyond the obligations of duty and the requirements enjoined by God's law as necessary for salvation.

Examples are the profession and observance of the evangelical counsels of poverty, chastity, and obedience, as well as efforts to practice charity to the highest degree.

SUPERSTITION

A violation of the virtue of religion by which God is worshiped in an unworthy manner or creatures are given honor that belongs to God alone.

SUYAPA, OUR LADY OF

A shrine to the Virgin Mary in Honduras.

According to pious legend, in 1747 two Indian farm workers had to sleep by the roadside when returning home late from work one Saturday. As one of them, Alejandro Colindres, lay down, he felt something hard in the ground. In the morning, he dug it out and discovered it to be a small statue of the Virgin, standing on a golden globe. For twenty years, the family and neighboring farm families venerated the image in the Colindres home and miracles were attributed to its intercession. After being cured of kidney problems, a wealthy landowner build a small chapel on his property to house the image. From that time the indigenous people made the image an object of special devotion. The festival for the Virgen de Suyapa, the patroness of Honduras, is celebrated February 1-3. The festivities begin with a nine-hour pilgrimage from El Piliguin, where legend says the tiny wooden statuette was found, to the Suyapa Basilica, where the image is housed today. Thousands of pilgrims line up to see Our Lady, who believers say has been a source of countless miracles. The discovery of the Virgin is reenacted and masses and concerts are held.

SVIACHENE DINNER

A customary Ukrainian Christmas Eve meal.

When Ukraine under King Volodymyr (St. Vladimir) accepted Christianity from Byzantium in 988, many pagan traditions were in existence which were adapted by the Church to the new religion. The *Svi-ata Vechera*, or "Holy Supper," is the central tradition of the beautiful Christmas Eve celebrations in Ukrainian homes. The dinner table sometimes has a few wisps of hay on the embroidered table cloth as a reminder of the manger in Bethlehem. Many Canadian and American families wear their Ukrainian embroidered shirts on this occasion. The meal begins when the first star in the eastern evening sky is seen. In farming communities, the head of the household brings in a decorated sheaf of wheat called the *didukh*. Originally a pagan custom, it now represents the Christian belief in an afterlife as well as a bountiful harvest. A prayer is said and the father says the traditional Christmas greeting, "*Khristos rodyvsya!*" (Christ is born!) which is answered by the family with "*Slavite Yoho!*" (Let Us Glorify Him!) After the meal, the family gathers to sing carols.

SWEETHEARTS OF ST. JOHN

A Sardinian and Sicilian midsummer tradition and festival.

In Sardinia, there was a great midsummer festival which bore the name of St. John. At the end of March or on the first of April, a young man of the village presented himself to a girl and asked her to be his *comare* (sweetheart),offering to be her *compare*. The invitation was consid-ered an honor by her family and was gladly accepted. At the end of May the girl made a pot of the bark of the cork-tree, filling it with earth and sowing a handful of wheat and barley in it. The pot was placed in the sun and watered, and the plant had a good head by St. John's Eve (June 23, also called Midsummer's Eve). The pot was then called *Erme* or *Nenneri*.

On St. John's Day, the young man and the girl, dressed in their best and accompanied by a large retinue, walked in procession to the local church. Here they threw the pot against the door of the church, after which they sat and ate eggs and herbs to the music of flutes. Wine was mixed in a cup and passed round, each one drinking as it passed. Then all joined hands and sang "Sweethearts of St. John," over and over again after which they finished the evening with a dance. This was the general custom in Sardinia. As practiced at Ozieri, on the Eve of the feast, the window sills were draped with rich cloths on which the pots were placed, gaily adorned with red and blue silk and varicolored ribbons. Each pot held a statuette or cloth doll dressed as a woman or a Priapus-like figure. This custom was rigorously forbidden by the Church. The boys walked about together to look at the pots and then wait for the girls who assembled on the public square for the festival. Here they kindled a great bonfire. Those who wished to be "Sweethearts of St. John" grasped the ends of a long stick which they then passed through the fire to seal their relationship to each other.

Similar customs were observed at the same time in Sicily. Pairs of boys and girls became gossips (sweethearts) of St. John on St. John's Day by each drawing a hair from his or her head and performing various ceremonies over them. They tied the hairs together and threw them up in the air or exchanged them over a potsherd which they afterwards broke in two with each person preserving a fragment with pious care. The tie formed in this way is supposed to last for life. In some parts of Sicily the gossips of St. John presented each other with plates of sprouting corn, lentils, and canary seed that had been planted forty days before the festival. The one who received the plate pulled a stalk of the young plants, bound it with a ribbon and preserved it among his or her greatest treasures, restoring the platter to the giver. At Catania, the gossips exchanged pots of basil and great cucumbers. The girls tended the basil and the thicker it grew the more it was prized. In these midsummer customs of Sicily and Sardinia, it is possible that St. John has replaced the pagan Adonis. Basil and garlic are also important plants in his cult in Portugal.

SYMBOL

A token, pledge, or sign by which we can experience some reality through another reality.

Most often, symbols are used in connection with the liturgy. Through symbols, we can participate in the saving mysteries of Christ's Passion, death, and Resurrection. This is preeminently true in the celebration of the Eucharistic Sacrifice. The Word of God and the bread and wine are symbols that make present again the redemption won for us on Calvary by Christ. A symbol, in the religious sense, is cognitive and evocative. As such, it bids us look beyond what our senses tell us is present and available to us, and elicits from us a belief in a more transcendent, mysterious reality that the senses cannot apprehend.

T

TANTUM ERGO

The Latin title of a hymn sung at Benediction.

It is from the composition by St. Thomas Aquinas, *Pange Lingua* (Latin for "Sing, my tongue"). The words translate literally as "therefore so great."

One translation reads:

Down in adoration falling,
Lo! the Sacred Host we hail;
Lo! o'er ancient forms departing,
Newer rites of grace prevail;
Faith for all defects supplying
Where the feeble senses fail.

To the everlasting Father,
And the Son who reigns on high,
With the Holy Spirit proceeding
Forth from each eternally,
Be salvation, honor, blessing,
Might, and endless majesty.
Amen.

Another translation, by John Mason Neale and others, reads:

Therefore we, before him bending,
This great Sacrament revere;
Types and shadows have their ending,
For the newer rite is here;
Faith, our outward sense befriending,
Makes the inward vision clear.

Glory let us give, and blessing
To the Father and the Son;

Honor, might, and praise addressing,
While eternal ages run
Ever too is love confessing
Who from both, with both is one.
Amen.

(See also **BENEDICTION**; **PANGE LINGUA**.)

TARCISIANS

A Catholic children's group devoted to the Eucharist, the Sacred Heart of Jesus, and the Rosary.

Members are encouraged to enter into the mission of the Church by "earning golden pennies for the Lord" through prayer, acts of self-sacrifice, and Eucharistic exercises. The last may be visits to the Blessed Sacrament or reception of Holy Communion. The group was named after St. Tarcisius, who was martyred while protecting the Eucharist during a persecution in the early Church. Pious legend holds that he was an adolescent.

The National Enthronement Center is the headquarters of the national Sacred Heart enthronement apostolate, which includes the Tarcisians, in the United States of America under the direction of the Congregation of the Sacred Hearts, East Coast Province, in Fairhaven, Massachusetts.

TE DEUM LAUDAMUS

Latin for "We praise you as God"; the title of a hymn dating back to the early fifth century.

A song of praise and thanksgiving, the *Te Deum* is prescribed for use in the Office of Readings and Liturgy of the Hours on Sundays, solemnities, and feasts.

The hymn dates from the late fourth or early fifth century, and some scholars attribute it to St. Ambrose, thus it is sometimes known as the Ambrosian hymn. It is often used at times of particularly solemn celebrations such as jubilees.

One translation reads:

You are God: we praise you; you are the Lord: we acclaim you; you are the eternal Father: all creation worships you.

To you all angels, all the powers of heaven, Cherubim and Seraphim, sing in endless praise:

Holy, holy, holy Lord, God of power and might, heaven and earth are full of your glory. The glorious company of Apostles praise you. The noble fellowship of prophets praise you. The white-robed army of martyrs praise you.

Throughout the world the holy Church acclaims you: Father, of majesty unbounded, your true and only Son, worthy of all worship, and the Holy Spirit, advocate and guide. You, Christ, are the king of glory, the eternal Son of the Father.

When you became man to set us free, you did not spurn the Virgin's womb. You overcame the sting of death, and opened the kingdom of heaven to all believers. You are seated at God's right hand in glory.

We believe that you will come, and be our judge. Come then, Lord, and help your people, bought with the price of your own blood, and bring us with your saints to glory everlasting.

V. Save your people, Lord, and bless your inheritance.

R. Govern and uphold them now and always.

V. Day by day we bless you.

R. We praise your name for ever.

V. Keep us today, Lord, from all sin.

R. Have mercy on us, Lord, have mercy.

V. Lord, show us your love and mercy.

R. For we put our trust in you.

V. In you, Lord, is our hope.

R. And we shall never hope in vain.

TEACHING CHRISTIAN DOCTRINE

A partial indulgence is granted the Christian faithful who either teach or study Christian doctrine.

TEMPTATION

Any incitement to sin arising from the world (the actions or inducements of others), the flesh (our own weaknesses and desires), and the devil (suggestions by fallen angels).

According to Scripture, God allows us to be tempted but never beyond our powers to resist with the help of his grace. The trial of temptation provides the occasion for moral and spiritual growth. Fidelity to the practices of the faith and perseverance in prayer afford the chief means by which one is strengthened against temptation.

TENEBRAE

Latin for "darkness"; a name that once applied to the public chanting of Matins and Lauds on Wednesday, Thursday, and Friday of Holy Week.

In medieval practice, the Tenebrae services were recited in total darkness. A candle stand holding fifteen candles, known as a hearse, stood before the altar. At the end of each of fifteen Psalms read daily, one candle was extinguished until only a single candle at the top remained lighted. Finally, this lighted candle was hidden behind the altar until the end of the service when it was brought forward again. The former action symbolized the Apostles deserting Christ, his Passion, and his descent to the dead. The latter, the reappearance of the last candle, represented the Resurrection. A din at the end of the service was originally the sound of chant books being closed, but later symbolism attached to the noise the chaos following the crucifixion at the "sixth hour." The services in a modified form continued until the liturgical reforms of Pope Pius XII in 1955. Since the further revision of the liturgical books in 1970, Tenebrae has emerged in many places as a paraliturgical observance marked by readings, motets, and hymns on the Wednesday of Holy Week.

TERCE

The third hour of the Divine Office, prayed at midmorning.

TERTIARY

Sometimes called "Third Order," referring to laity living in the world seeking Christian perfection in their state of life in accordance with the spirit of a particular religious order.

Although Tertiaries are not religious, they may be full members of a religious order and are subject to the superior general of the institute. Tertiaries of the various Orders of Friars Minor are now called Secular Franciscans.

(See also **CONFRATERNITY**.)

TESTAMENT OF ST. FRANCIS

A response sometimes used at Stations of the Cross credited to St. Francis of Assisi.

One version reads:

> We adore you, O Christ, and we bless you because by your holy cross you have redeemed the world.

THANKSGIVING

An expression of gratitude to God for his goodness and the blessing he grants; one of the four ends of prayer.

THAUMATURGE

From the Greek word for "wonder-worker"; a title given to saints who became known for the number and magnitude of the miracles attributed to them.

Among them are St. Gregory Thaumaturgus, St. Nicholas of Bari, St. Anthony of Padua, St. Vincent Ferrer, and Blessed Brother André of Mount Royal. The word is also sometimes applied to images some consider miraculous by virtue of the miracles attributed to the intercession of the person depicted.

THECA

A sheath or cloth-covering in which relics are kept.

The term also designates the metal holder in which first-class relics are distributed.

(See also **RELICS**.)

THEOLOGICAL VIRTUES

The supernaturally infused "good habits" of faith, hope, and charity, having God as their object and motive.

Faith enables one to accept the truths revealed by God on the basis of his authority. Hope allows one to anticipate eternal life by trusting God and his grace. Charity impels one to love God, oneself, and others for his sake. Acts of faith, hope, and charity assist one in growing in holiness and in becoming more cooperative by obeying God and his plan.

THEOTOKION

A commemoration for the Mother of God in the Byzantine liturgy.

THEOTOKOS

Greek for "God-bearer."

The Council of Ephesus (431) was called to settle a dispute concerning the teachings of the patriarch of Constantinople, Nestorius, who held that Mary was the Mother of Christ but not the Mother of God. More than two hundred bishops attended and held that tradition had always used the term *Theotokos* for the Blessed Virgin. In so defining Mary as Mother of God, the council reaffirmed the divinity of Christ. In the Eastern Churches, *Theotokos* is the most commonly used title for Mary.

(See also **MARY, MOTHER OF GOD.**)

THERESIANS OF THE UNITED STATES

An organization for women founded by Monsignor Elwood C. Voss and Virginia Siegle O'Donnell in Pueblo, Colorado, in 1961.

Named for St. Thérèse of Lisieux, it encourages its members to focus on prayer, education, vocation, community, and ministry. While the original communities were designed primarily for women religious it quickly became evident that both lay and women religious could benefit from taking part. In 1969, the mission statement was revised to reflect this change. The organization became international in 1970.

THIRD ORDER

Generally, an association of laypeople connected to consecrated religious who fol-

low a particular rule and spirituality in either the First or Second Order (respectively, male and female religious).

The most famous of those are the Franciscans, Dominicans, and Carmelites.

(See also **CONFRATERNITY.**)

THIRTEEN COINS (LAS ARRAS)

A keepsake in a Mexican-American wedding.

Traditionally, the groom presents the bride with the coins as a symbol of giving her everything he has and vowing to support her.

THREE HAIL MARYS

The praying of three Hail Marys — one each in honor of the Father, the Son, and the Holy Spirit.

It is based on reported private revelations of St. Mechtilde of Helfta (d. 1298).

The Franciscan preacher St. Leonard of Port Maurice (d, 1751) advised that people practice the devotion of the Three Hail Marys morning and evening in honor of Mary Immaculate in order to obtain the grace of avoiding all mortal sin both day and night. St. Alphonsus Liguori (d.1787) suggested that the devotion should be said kneeling and wrote an ejaculation to be said after each prayer. The devotion was also promoted by Father John Baptist du Bois who founded the Confraternity of

Three Hail Marys. The devotion was indulgenced by Pope Leo XIII.

THREE HOURS DEVOTION

Traditionally, this devotion begins at twelve noon on Good Friday. Every fifteen minutes, a priest mounts the pulpit to preach short sermons to prepare the minds and hearts of the people for the three o'clock hour commemorating Christ's death on the cross. These messages are usually based on the seven last words of Christ. In some places, shortly before three o'clock, the altar boys light up flashing powder to simulate lightening, and noise will be made to simulate the earthquake. After the final sermon, the priest mounts to the crucifix and detaches the body of Christ. He takes it down and places it in a position on a platform or in an elaborate casket for the people to venerate. This popular devotion, also known as *Tre Ore*, was first performed in Lima, Peru, by Father Alphonso Messia, S.J. (1732). It quickly spread to all the Latin-speaking countries. From Italy, it spread to England and to the United States where it has grown in popularity even among some Protestant churches.

(See also **SEVEN LAST WORDS OF CHRIST; GOOD FRIDAY**.)

THREE KINGS DAY — See EPIPHANY.

THURIBLE

A metal vessel capable of holding burning charcoal.

When incense is added to the burning charcoal, it produces rising smoke, which signifies prayer ascending to heaven. A thurible can be used at the Holy Sacrifice of the Mass, the recitation of the Divine Office, and Benediction of the Blessed Sacrament. It also goes by the name of "censer."

TITHE

A percentage of one's income given as an offering to God.

The traditional amount of ten percent is based upon the law found in Leviticus 27:30, which prescribed that one tenth of all produce, animals, and plants be set aside and given back to the Lord. It is one of the precepts of the Church that all members must give support, in accordance with their circumstances, to the Church's work and ministry.

TICKET TO HEAVEN

In 1982, Father Paul Thomas, a priest of the Altoona- Johnstown diocese (Pennsylvania), told his congregation, "I have been telling people how to get to heaven for forty years. I am gong to put it in a nutshell for you."

Father Paul composed a meditation that

begins, "Lord Jesus, Your holy will be done ... first, last, and always. But it is Your holy will that I go to heaven when I die. Therefore, may this be my ticket to Heaven." He mimeographed copies for the Sunday bulletin, never dreaming it would go outside his own congregation. At the urging of a visitor to the Mass when they were distributed, Father Paul had a local printer make 5,000 copies and began to distribute them. More than 2.5 million copies of the ticket-sized booklet have been distributed worldwide. Father Paul continued distributing the booklets until his death. The booklet is not copyrighted, and those who receive them have permission to reproduce them, or translate them into other languages.

TITLE

A relic reputed to be the board used for the inscription atop Christ's cross.

It is kept in the Church of the Holy Cross in Jerusalem, Rome. The relic is nine inches by five inches with the inscription in Greek and Latin. It is speculated that the section with the text in Hebrew was separated before St. Helena brought the relic to Rome in the fourth century.

(See also **I.N.R.I.**; **RELICS**.)

TLAXCALA, CHILD MARTYRS OF

Cristobalito, Antonio, and Juan, three child martyrs (twelve to thirteen years old), known as the martyrs of Tlaxcala, were the first native Christian martyrs of the New World. They were witnesses to and participants in the Spanish evangelization of Mexico; they served as catechists and translators for the missionary priests. All three gave their lives for the faith between 1527 and 1529, when they refused to recant their commitment to Christ. Cristobalito's pagan father, a tribal chief, had his son beaten with clubs and finally set on fire for his faith. Antonio and Juan were clubbed to death two years later.

The three child martyrs of Tlaxcala were beatified by Pope John Paul II at the shrine of Our Lady of Guadalupe in Mexico City in May, 1990.

TONGUE OF ST. ANTHONY

St. Anthony died in 1231 and was proclaimed a saint within a year of his death. In 1263 when the body of the great orator and Doctor of the Church was transferred to the basilica in Padua built in his honor, the sarcophagus was opened and the tongue was found incorrupt. It was removed by St. Bonaventure, who was present at the translation of the relics, and is now kept in a golden reliquary in the chapel of the basilica where it is on constant display.

(See also **ST. ANTHONY OF PADUA**.)

TOSSING OF THE CROSS

A Byzantine Rite ceremony during which water is blessed to be used as holy water for the coming year.

Traditionally the ceremony is held on the Feast of the Epiphany, also known as Theophany or the Feast of the Jordan and the Feast of Holy Lights.

The blessing takes place preferably at streams, lakes, bays, or gulfs. In Greece, the Aegean, the Adriatic, the Mediterranean, the Gulf of Mexico and holy water fonts are all blessed. In Russia, holes in the form of crosses are cut in the frozen rivers, and the blessing is performed over these. The service is lengthy and includes the ceremony of tossing of the cross into the blessed body of water, to be retrieved by swimmers who receive a prize for their efforts.

TOWELS

Among the Ukrainians, beautiful towels of linen are hand-embroidered and draped around the tops of the ikons, both at home and in the church.

TRADITION

In the religious sense, the teachings and practices handed down, whether in oral or written form, separately from but not independent of Scripture.

Tradition is divided into two areas:

1. Scripture, the essential doctrines of the Church, the major writings and teachings of the Fathers, the liturgical life of the Church, and the living and lived faith of the whole Church down through the centuries.
2. Customs, institutions, and practices that express the Christian faith.

TRANSFIGURATION OF THE LORD

The August 6 feast commemorating the revelation of his divinity by Christ to Peter, James, and John on Mount Tabor (see Matthew 17:1-9).

The feast may have originally commemorated the dedication of the original basilica there. The Transfiguration has been observed in the East since the fifth century, but it did not enter the West until the middle of the ninth.

Pope Callistus III formally included it in the Roman Calendar in 1457 as a thank-offering for the victory of Christian troops over the Turks near Belgrade in 1456. In the Eastern Churches, it is still observed as one of the most important feasts of the year.

TRANSLATION

The moving of a saint's body or relics to another location.

In the early Church and early Middle Ages, the translation was seen as the saint's canonization. The term is also used to describe a feast being transferred to a new date as well as the transfer of a cleric to a more important post.

TRANSUBSTANTIATION

A theological term adopted by the Fourth Lateran Council in 1215 to describe the change of the substance of bread and wine into the substance of the body and blood of Christ, so that only the bread and wine remain, when consecrated by a validly ordained priest.

TREASURY OF THE CHURCH

The superabundant merits of Christ and the saints from which the Church draws to confer spiritual benefits, such as indulgences.

TRIDUUM

Latin for "three days"; a three-day series of public or private devotion.

(See also **HOLY WEEK**.)

TRIDUUM, PASCHAL

A period of three days for the most exalted liturgical celebration of the year.

It begins with the Mass of the Lord's Supper on Holy Thursday evening and concludes with Vespers on Easter Sunday, recalling the Passion, death, and Resurrection of Christ, along with his institution of the Holy Eucharist and holy orders.

TRINITARIAN FORMULA

The words "In the name of the Father, and of the Son, and of the Holy Spirit."

TRINITY COLUMNS

Columns erected in central European city and town squares in the seventeenth and eighteenth centuries in honor of the Holy Trinity.

Typically made of marble or granite, they feature Trinitarian symbols and statues of saints who were patrons against epidemics.

TRINITY RAIN

There is a superstition that no matter what the weather is on Trinity Sunday, it is good and wholesome. Trinity rain is credited with special powers of health and fertility, and the superstitious save it for drinking and bathing. Ghosts and witches are prevented from doing harm and magic flowers blossom at midnight; their finders receive all kinds of miraculous benefits. On the other hand, in popular fantasy, the neglect or desecration of this great Sunday is punished with dire misfortune. This superstition derives from the ancient lore of the death demons roaming the earth at this season of the year.

TRINITY SUNDAY

A movable observance celebrated on the Sunday after Pentecost to commemorate the mystery of the Trinity: Three Persons in One God (see Matthew 28:18-20).

A votive Mass for the Trinity dates from the seventh century; an office was composed in the tenth. Pope John XXII extended the feast to the universal Church in 1334.

TRINITYTIDE

The traditional name for a period in the Church year from Trinity Sunday to Advent Sunday.

TRIPLE CANDLE

A type of three-branched candle.

It was used at the Easter Vigil liturgy on Holy Saturday night until 1955, when the Paschal candle currently in use was restored to its original and preeminent position.

TRIPTYCH

Three painted panels joined by hinges.

The central panel is the most important scene and usually displays a signifi-cant event from the life of Christ, Mary, or a saint. The two side panels feature other participants in the event shown in the center. During the Middle Ages, triptychs were often placed above the high altar of a church. Triptychs have been made in a variety of sizes, including some small enough to be worn on a necklace or carried by a person who is traveling.

TRIQUETRA

A Trinitarian symbol made from three equal arcs that are interwoven so that they have a continuous flow.

The arcs express equality; the interwoven patterns express indivisibility; the continuous movement expresses eternity. The center forms an equilateral triangle, which is one of the oldest representations of the Trinity. When the triquetra is formed with two parallel lines, it is known as a Celtic Tyrone Knot.

Triquetra

TRIUMPH OF THE CROSS

The feast observed every September 14.

It recalls two events:

1. The exposition for veneration of the true cross in Jerusalem by Emperor Heraclius in 629.
2. The dedication of the Basilica of the Resurrection, built by Emperor Constantine over the Holy Sepulcher.

TROPARION

In the Byzantine liturgy, a commemoration for a saint or feast day.

It is variable and is sung.

TUNIC, HOLY

A relic said to be the seamless robe taken from Christ at his crucifixion. Churches in both Germany and France claim to have the holy tunic.

Two traditions tell how a tunic came to be in Trier, Germany. The first holds that it was brought there by St. Helena. The second maintains that it was a gift to the city from Pope Sylvester in the early fourth century. Records prove that the relic has been at Trier at least since the twelfth century, except for a brief time during the Napoleonic wars. It has been put on display only rarely, the last time in the 1950s.

There is also a relic claimed as Christ's tunic at Argenteuil near Paris, which has been attested from 1156. At one point, for safekeeping, this tunic was cut into parts and hidden, but eventually it was reclaimed and sewn together again. In 1983, this relic was stolen by an extremist group but was returned two months later and put on display at Easter.

(See also **RELICS**.)

TWELFTH NIGHT — See **EPIPHANY**.

TWELVE PROMISES OF THE SACRED HEART — See **SACRED HEART, TWELVE PROMISES OF THE**.

TWENTY-FOUR GLORY BE TO THE FATHER NOVENA

Novena to St. Thérèse of Lisieux.

It includes reciting the Glory Be twenty-four times daily for nine days in thanksgiving to the Trinity for the twenty-four years of St. Thérèse's life. The practice dates back to 1925 and a Jesuit priest named Putigan.

The novena can be said at any time, but from the ninth to the seventeenth of each month, the petitioner joins in prayer with others making the novena. The following or a similar prayer begins the novena:

Holy Trinity, God the Father, God the Son and God the Holy Ghost, I thank

Thee for all the blessings and favors Thou hast showered upon the soul of Thy servant Theresa of the Child Jesus during the twenty-four years she spent here on earth, and in consideration of the merits of this Thy most beloved Saint, I beseech Thee to grant me this favor if it is in accordance with Thy most Holy Will and is not an obstacle to my salvation.

After this prayer, follows the twenty four "Glory be to the Father" prayers between each of which may be included this short ejaculation: "St. Theresa of the Child Jesus, pray for us."

U

ULTREYA — See **CURSILLO MOVEMENT**.

UMBRELLA

The word umbrella is derived from the Latin word *Umbra*, which means shade. The first umbrellas were for protection from the sun and were possibly inspired from the canopy of a tree, which would offer a cool shade from the heat of the day. Umbrellas probably originated in China about the eleventh century B.C., although ancient sculptures from Neneveh, Persepolis, and Thebes have been found depicting their use. There is also evidence of their use about the same time period in India. The first umbrellas were probably a converted branch or leaf from a tree, or a hat on a stick.

The word *Parasol* comes from the Latin words *papare*, (to prepare), and *sol* (sun). Today we tend to use the word parasol for protection against the sun and umbrella for that against rain. The original difference in the terms was that umbrellas were carried by the person being shaded and parasols were carried by others to provide shade for someone else.

The first umbrellas (or, more correctly, parasols) were associated with rank and status. They were used in early pagan religious practice. The Coptic Church traditionally used parasols in some of their ceremonies, and continues to do so today.

The parasol or umbrella can symbolize the vault of heaven. In its symbolic and protective role the umbrella can be compared to the *baldachin* (canopy) in many of its forms.

During the middle ages, an umbrella was used in ceremonial regalia for the pope. The custom may have originated from a parasol given to Pope Sylvester I by Constantine.

The striped canopy of an umbrella depicted in the papal colors of red and gold above the crossed keys of St. Peter was once used on a papal badge. Known as an *ombrellino*, it is still worn by the Cardinal Camerlengo as acting head of the Catholic Church during an interregnum in the papacy.

Christians in India celebrate their festivals broadly on the pattern adopted worldwide. However some influence of local Indian tradition is evident among Syrian Christians, who use elephants, umbrellas, and traditional music as accessories to their festivities and celebrations.

(See also **BASILICA**.)

UNCTION, EXTREME

One of the seven sacraments.

It is the former name for the sacrament of the anointing of the sick.

(See also **ANOINTING OF THE SICK; OILS, HOLY**.)

URBI ET ORBI

Latin for "to the city and to the world."

It is the title of blessing given by the pope immediately after his election and annually at Christmas and Easter.

V

VANITIES

Images and objects that remind one of the swift passage of time, the illusions of this world, and even the tedium of life.

Vanities became popular in the sixteenth century, and their use became rarer but continued through the early nineteenth. Today, the practice finds remnants in the folk art and celebrations of a number of countries.

Symbols of the end of life were not relegated to paintings and sculpture, but spilled over to furniture and clothing. Girolamo Savonarola, an Italian reformer, recommended that everyone carry with him a small death's head made of bone and look at it often. Death-head rings were popular and were later distributed, along with mourning gloves, to those who attended burial services in New England. Watches and brooches were made in the shape of death's heads or coffins. Furniture was marked with skulls and skeletons.

As late as the mid-nineteenth century, the skeleton was still a favorite subject for earthenware dishes. Engravings recalling the uncertainty and brevity of life were commonly found over fireplaces.

VENERABLE

The canonical title given to a deceased person who, though not beatified or canonized, has been judged to have lived the heroic virtues.

VENERATION OF THE SAINTS — See DULIA.

VENI CREATOR SPIRITUS

Latin for "Come, Creator Spirit."

It is the title for a widely used hymn or sequence: "Come Holy Spirit, Creator Come." It is commonly believed to have been composed by Rabanus Maurus (c.776-856), abbot of Fulda and archbishop of Mainz. The devout recital of the hymn is an indulgenced prayer.

One translation reads:

Come, O Creator Spirit, come
And make within our hearts thy
    home;
To us thy grace celestial give,
Who of thy breathing move and live.

O Comforter, that name is thine,
Of God most high the gift divine;
The well of life, the fire of love,
Our souls' anointing from above.

Thou dost appear in sevenfold dower,
The sign of God's almighty power;
The Father's promise, making rich
With saving truth our earthly speech.

Our senses with thy light inflame,
Our hearts to heavenly love reclaim;
Our bodies' poor infirmity
With strength perpetual fortify.

Our mortal foe afar repel,
Grant us henceforth in peace to
dwell;
And so to us, with thee for guide,
No ill shall come, no harm betide.

May we by thee the Father learn,
And know the Son, and thee discern,
Who art of both; and thus adore
In perfect faith for evermore.

All glory to the Father be,
All glory, risen Son, to thee,
Who with the Paraclete art one,
Reigning while endless ages run.
    Amen.

VENI SANCTE SPIRITUS

Latin for "Come, Holy Spirit."

A prayer to the Holy Spirit, it is also the sequence (or hymn) sung on Pentecost immediately before the reading of the Gospel. It came into universal use, replacing another sequence, in the liturgical reforms that followed the Council of Trent. In the Middle Ages, it was known as "the golden sequence." It began to be used in France about the year 1200 and it is usually attributed to Stephen Langton, archbishop of Canterbury. A devout recitation of the hymn is an indulgenced prayer.

One translation of the prayer reads:
V. Come, Holy Spirit, fill the hearts of
    your faithful.

R. And kindle in them the fire of your
love.
V. Send forth your Spirit and they shall
be created.
R. And you will renew the face of the
earth.

Let us pray:

Lord, by the light of the Holy Spirit you have taught the hearts of your faithful. In the same Spirit help us to relish what is right and always rejoice in your consolation. We ask this through Christ our Lord. Amen.

One translation of the sequence reads:

Holy Spirit, Lord of light,
From the clear celestial height,
Thy pure beaming radiance give.

Come, thou Father of the poor,
Come with treasures which endure:
Come, thou Light of all that live!

Thou, of all consolers best,
Thou, the soul's delightsome guest,
Dost refreshing peace bestow.

Thou in toil art comfort sweet;
Pleasant coolness in the heat;
Solace in the midst of woe.

Light immortal, Light divine,
Visit thou these hearts of thine,
And our inmost being fill.

If thou take thy grace away,
Nothing pure in man will stay;
All his good is turned to ill.

Heal our wounds, our strength renew;
On our dryness pour thy dew;
Wash the stains of guilt away.

Bend the stubborn heart and will;
Melt the frozen, warm the chill;
Guide the steps that go astray.

Thou, on those who evermore
Thee confess and thee adore,
In thy sevenfold gifts descend.

Give them comfort when they die;
Give them life with thee on high;
Give them joys that never end. Amen.
Alleluia.

VENIAL SIN

Disobedience to God involving light moral matter or done without adequate knowledge, freedom, and full consent of the will.

God detests all sin; however, the love of God can exist in one who has committed venial sins (but not mortal sins). Venial sin is remitted through the sacrament of penance, Holy Communion, acts of charity and penance, etc.

VENITE, EXULTEMUS DOMINO

Latin for "Come, let us sing unto the Lord."

It is a canticle derived from Psalm 95, which was said or sung in church services at Matins.

VERONICA

The story of Veronica does not occur in the Bible, though the apocryphal Acts of Pilate gives this name to the woman with a blood flow who was cured by touching the hem of Jesus' cloak. Critics of the tradition point out that the very name of the saint is a combination of Latin and Greek words meaning "true image." Nonetheless, the story has been a part of popular Christian culture for centuries.

VERONICA'S VEIL

Pious tradition since about the forth century holds that Veronica wiped Jesus' face on his way to Calvary. Veronica's veil refers to the cloth on which he caused an imprint of his face to appear. The veneration at Rome of a likeness depicted on cloth dates from about the end of the tenth century; it figured in a popular pilgrimage devotion during the Middle Ages and in the Holy Face devotion practiced since the nineteenth century. A faint, indiscernible likeness said to be of this kind is preserved on cloth in St. Peter's Basilica. The origin of the likeness is uncertain, and the identity of the woman is unknown.

A custom developed of sending copies

of the veil to Rome to be touched to the original, thus making the copies objects of special devotion as well. The relic has been exhibited at intervals during its history. In 1849, Pope Pius IX allowed the relic to be publicly exposed between the feasts of Christmas and Epiphany. On the third day of the showing, the veil became engulfed with a soft light while the face assumed a tinge of color and shone forth as though it were alive. It appeared to be more distinctly in relief, its eyes deeply sunken while it wore an expression of profound severity. The canons of the basilica immediately ordered the bells to be rung, attracting crowds of people who witnessed the three-hour manifestation. An apostolic notary subsequently composed a document attesting to the fact of the manifestation. A 1993 reference states that the image on this cloth has completely faded.

As with many relics, there are a number of stories which make it difficult to pin down the true historical facts. In June of 2000, a news report came out stating that the relic had disappeared in 1608 when the part of the basilica housing it was remodeled. Jesuit Father Heinrich Pfeiffer, a professor of Christian Art History at the Pontifical Gregorian University, announced that he had found the relic in the abbey of Monoppello, Italy. A small piece of stained pale cloth had been kept in the Capuchin monastery of this tiny

Veronica's Veil

village and revered as a sacred icon with wondrous properties. The almost transparent veil measures about 6.5 by 9.5 inches and bears dark red features of a bearded man with long hair and open eyes. Depending on the angle from which the cloth is viewed, the image becomes invisible. Ultraviolet examinations of the cloth confirm that the image is not paint. Enlarged digital photographs of the image reveal that it is identical on both sides of the cloth, and it bears a striking resemblance to the face on the Shroud of Turin.

According to records in the monastery,

the veil was donated to the Capuchins in 1608 by a nobleman of Monoppello who had bought it from a woman who needed money to get her husband out of jail. In 1618, it was placed in a walnut frame between two sheets of glass. It has remained in the custody of the monastery since that time.

There are stories about the veil having been either moved for protection during the sack of Rome in 1527, or robbed and profaned at a later date, but none of this has been documented. The presence of the veil in the basilica has been documented since the eighth century.

The veil played a key part in the convocation of the first Holy Year in 1300. At that time, it was being shown in the basilica, and this led to huge spontaneous pilgrimages, which convinced the pope to declare the first Holy Year.

VESPERS

The evening service of the Divine Office, also known as "Evening Prayer."

VESTMENTS, MASS

Garments worn by the priest and deacon during the celebration of the Eucharist.

In the early Church, vestments worn for liturgies were the same as the clothes in ordinary popular use. They became distinctive when their form was not changed to match changes in popular style. Liturgical vestments symbolize sacred ministry and add appropriate decorum to divine worship.

Mass vestments include:

Amice: A rectangular piece of white cloth worn about the neck, tucked in the collar and falling over the shoulder. It is secured by two long ribbons or tapes wound about the waist. It is prescribed for use when the alb does not completely cover the ordinary clothing at the neck.

Alb: An ankle-length tunic of white fabric. The alb is common to all ministers in divine worship.

Cincture: A cord that serves as a belt, girding the alb so as to prevent tripping over the alb.

Stole: A long, band-like vestment worn by a priest about the neck and falling to about the knees. A deacon wears a stole over his left shoulder and fastened at his right side.

Chasuble: In Latin, *casula* (little house). Originally, a full, circular cloak, like a poncho covering the body, it is the outer garment of a priest or bishop celebrating Mass.

Chasuble-alb: A vestment combining the features of the chasuble and the alb. It is used with a stole by concelebrants and, by way of exception, by celebrants in certain circumstances.

Dalmatic: The outer garment worn by a deacon in place of a chasuble.

Cope: In Latin, *pluviale* (raincoat). It is worn for ceremonies other than Mass itself. Made in a semicircular shape it is worn draped around the shoulders full length and fastened across the upper chest by a clasp called the *morse.* The cope usually has a hood, either real or stylized, falling nearly to the waist.

The material, form, and ornamentation of vestments have been subject to variation and adaptation, according to norms and decisions of the Holy See and conferences of bishops. Tradition has associated the vestments with spiritual qualities and virtues: the amice with the helmet of salvation; the alb with the white robes of joy, which true Christians have washed in the blood of the Lamb of God; the cincture with chastity and continence; the stole with priestly authority; the chasuble with charity.

VIA LUCIS

Latin for "the Way of the Light"; a recent devotion proper to the post-Easter liturgical period.

The new practice has characteristics similar to the Way of the Cross (*Via Crucis*) and can be prayed personally or in community. A Paschal candle or icon of the Resurrection is carried, rather than a cross.

The *Via Lucis* includes fourteen stations for reflection on Christ's Pasch, from his Resurrection to Pentecost. The service may include readings of the biblical narratives corresponding to each station, followed by silence, meditative prayer, and a hymn.

One suggested set of stations for the *Via Lucis* is:

1. Jesus rises from the dead.
2. The disciples find the empty tomb.
3. Jesus appears to Mary Magdalen.
4. Jesus walks with the disciples to Emmaus.
5. Jesus reveals himself in the breaking of bread.
6. Jesus appears to the disciples.
7. Jesus confers on his disciples the power to forgive sins.
8. Jesus confirms Thomas in faith.
9. Jesus appears to his disciples on the shore of Lake Galilee.
10. Jesus confers primacy on Peter.
11. Jesus entrusts his disciples with a universal mission.
12. Jesus ascends into heaven.
13. Mary and the disciples await the Holy Spirit.
14. Jesus sends the Spirit promised by the Father to his disciples.

Promotion of the devotion began in 1994 by a group called TR2000 (TR standing for *Testimonio del Risorto*, Italian for "The Witness of the Risen [Christ]"). Its primary function is to remind the faithful to live the Easter spirituality according to 2 Timothy 2:8.

The *Via Lucis* was presented in 1989 to Don Egidio Vigano, the seventh successor to Don Bosco as head of the Salesian Order, who offered his support and help to TR2000. In 1990, the *Via Lucis* was first solemnly celebrated by Don Vigano in Rome at the catacomb of St. Calixtus during the general chapter of the Salesians. The stations, sculpted by the artist Dragoni, were erected in the catacomb in 1996, and they were celebrated there during a World Youth Day in Rome.

VIA MATRIS

Latin for "the way of the mother."

It is a devotion known as "The Way of the Sorrowful Mother," based on private revelations reported by the founders of the Servants of Mary in the thirteenth century.

The *Via Matris* is among the many devotions that grew out of the fervent preaching of the Servites. One historical study indicates that the devotion existed as early as the fourteenth century in Flanders.

Patterned on the Stations of the Cross, the *Via Matris* is a set of seven stations commemorating the Seven Sorrows of Our Lady. The stations are canonically erected in churches, although the blessing and erection of these stations used to be reserved to the Servite Order. Since Vatican II any priest may perform the ritual. They were first indulgenced by Pope Gregory XVI.

The stations of the *Via Matris* are:

1. Simeon prophesies that a sword would pierce Mary's soul.
2. Joseph flees with Mary and Jesus into Egypt.
3. Mary and Joseph search for Jesus in the Temple.
4. Mary meets Jesus on the way to Calvary.
5. Jesus dies on the cross.
6. Mary receives the body of Jesus in her arms.
7. Jesus is laid in the tomb.

(See also **SEVEN SORROWS OF MARY**.)

VIATICUM

The administration of the Holy Eucharist to those about to die.

VICTORY, OUR LADY OF

An ancient Marian title of undetermined origin.

Our Lady of Victory is venerated independently in Constantinople, Paris, Sicily, Prague, and elsewhere. The title may have resulted from prayers to Our Lady during times a region was being threatened, attacked, or invaded. A famous victory over the Turks in the naval battle of Lepanto (1571) was attributed entirely to Our Lady's intercession; as a result, Pope Pius V established the day of the battle, October 7, as a Feast of Our Lady of Victory. Two years later, the name of the feast was changed to Our Lady of the Rosary. Father Nelson Baker of New York was devoted to Our Lady under the former, and placed his works, homes of charity for children, under her care. He inaugurated the Spiritual Association of Our Lady of Victory to support the institutions and spread devotion to Our Lady of Victory.

VIGIL

Literally, a vigil means to "keep watch." In Catholic usage, this came to mean the eve of certain important feasts. It had its origin in the early Christian practice of beginning the celebration of Sundays, of Easter, and of some other major feasts on the evening before and continuing until the Mass at dawn. The practice either died out entirely (as in the case of having a Saturday vigil for every Sunday) or was moved back until the previous day. On the pre-1970 calendar, the vigil remained simply as a way of beginning a major feast on the previous evening, and no overnight services were held.

VIGIL FOR THE DEAD

A custom begun by the Hebrews to ensure against premature burial.

In the Middle Ages, the vigil for the dead was considered a Christian act of piety.

(See also **WAKE**.)

VIGIL LIGHT

A candle burned as an act of devotion, or for a particular intention, in a shrine or before a holy image.

The flame is said to "keep vigil" when the person cannot be present.

VINCENT DE PAUL SOCIETY

A charitable organization founded by Blessed Frederick Ozanam (1813-1853) in Paris in 1833 and originally intended to instruct young men in the Catholic faith to help them counter attacks on the Church.

Ozanam soon came to the conclusion that the best way to demonstrate Catholic commitment was through works of charity, and so he chose St. Vincent de Paul, known for his works of mercy, as the patron of the society that grew rapidly and now is worldwide. Members study Catholicism, put it into practice with works of charity, and provide one another with mutual support. The sanctification of its members is part of the purpose, and each regular meeting includes prayers, spiritual reading, and instruction, as well as the assignment of charitable tasks.

VINE AND BRANCHES

An image used as a symbol for Christ and his Church.

It is based on the Gospel of John: "I am the vine, you are the branches" (5:15).

Vine and Branches

VIRGIN MARY, RELICS OF THE

Major relics associated with Mary.

The cathedral in Prado, Italy, keeps in a crystal-and-gold reliquary a strip of green ribbon said to have been worn by Our Lady as a belt. A relic claimed to be her veil has been kept in the Cathedral of Chartres for more than a thousand years. What some believe to be her shroud is kept at the cathedral in Aachen, Germany. And a blue velvet chair is venerated as a Marian relic in the chapel of the motherhouse of the Daughters of Charity in Paris, France. St. Catherine Labouré reported it was the chair in which the Blessed Mother sat during an apparition in 1803. Other churches have claimed to have strands of her hair and vials of her breast milk.

VIRGIN OF THE POOR (BANNEUX)

A Marian image and devotion.

It is based on apparitions reported by eleven-year-old Mariette Beco in Banneux, Belgium, in 1933.

Sunday, January 15, 1933, Mariette, the oldest of the seven Beco children, looked out the window to see if she could see her brother, who was late coming home. Instead, she saw the luminous figure of a young woman in the garden. Thinking it was a reflection from the oil lamp, she moved the lamp, but the figure was still there. The woman was very beautiful, about five feet tall. She was dressed in a white gown with a blue sash. A rosary hung from her right hand. Only her right foot was visible, and it was adorned with a golden rose. Her head was inclined a little to the left, and she appeared to be smiling at Mariette.

Mariette called to her mother, who could only see a white shape and who cautioned Mariette to shut the curtain, thinking it might be a witch.

Mariette picked up a rosary and began praying it, and as she watched the lips of the lady moved although Mariette could hear nothing. The lady beckoned to Mariette to come outside but her mother forbade it. When she returned to the window, the lady had disappeared.

The following Monday, Mariette confided the story to her school chum Josephine Leonard who suggested they go and tell the parish priest, Father Louis Jamin. Believing the girls must have heard of the recent apparition in Beauraing, Father Jamin advised the girls to remain silent about the vision.

On Monday and Tuesday night, Mariette looked for the lady but could not see her. She was, however, convinced that she had seen Our Lady, and there was a great change in her behavior. She began to study her catechism, and the next day she attended Mass and said her prayers.

Wednesday night, just before seven, Mariette went outside. Her father followed her and found her kneeling with her rosary before the spot where she said she had seen the lady three days before. Suddenly Mariette stretched out her arms. She could see the figure of her lady floating toward her through the pines. The figure came to a halt about a yard and a half in front of Mariette. Her feet didn't touch the ground, but rested on a grayish cloud about a foot off the ground. The lady appeared the same, except this time Mariette noticed that she had a halo. Mariette continued to pray. Her father jumped on his bike and went to tell the priest what was happening. The priest was not in, so he persuaded a neighbor and his son to come back with him. As they arrived, Mariette walked out of the garden and approached them on the road. When they asked where she was going, Mariette simply said, "she is calling me."

Twice, Mariette dropped to the ground, kneeling. Then she continued. Abruptly she turned right, and knelt at the brink of a small stream. The lady stood on the other bank and spoke for the first time, telling Mariette to put her hands in the water. Mariette obeyed. Then the lady told Mariette that the spring was reserved for her, and said "*au revoir*" (goodbye for the present). Although only Mariette could hear the words, she repeated them aloud. The lady then slowly withdrew into the sky, growing smaller and smaller until she disappeared.

Later that evening Father Jamin returned home and was told what had happened. In company with a Benedictine monk and a friend, he went to the Beco household and had a long conversation with Mr. Beco. Mariette was sleeping, and they did not disturb her. When the priest asked Mr. Beco, a lapsed Catholic, if he believed Mariette had seen the Virgin, he answered yes, and asked to come to confession the next day.

The following evening, Mariette experienced a third apparition. Again, she returned to the spring at the insistence of the figure. Here she asked the apparition about her statement that the spring was reserved for her. The smiling lady said, "For all the nations … for the sick … I come to relieve the sick." Following the advice of the priest's Benedictine friend, Mariette asked the lady, "Who are you, Madame?" The lady said to her, "I am the Virgin of the Poor."

In all, there were eight appearances. During the fourth apparition, Mariette asked if the Lady wanted anything and was told she would like a little chapel. In the other apparitions, the message was given "I come to relieve suffering." Asked for a sign, the lady replied, "Have faith in me … I shall trust you…. Pray earnestly."

At the sixth appearance, Mariette was entrusted with a secret which she never revealed. At the final apparition, the Virgin said, "I am the Mother of the Savior, Mother of God. Pray hard." Then, she spoke the parting word "*adieu*" and imposed a blessing on Mariette. Mariette fainted, and did not see Our Lady's departure. She knew, however, that this would be her final sight of the beautiful lady from the choice of the word "*adieu*" (goodbye) instead of the previously used "*au revoir.*"

For several years, Mariette was subject to every kind of test. She was examined by panels of doctors and psychiatrists. None could find any trace of hysteria or untruth.

As with any reported apparition, those at Banneux were investigated thoroughly. A number of miraculous medical cures were claimed through the prayers and the use of the water at Banneux. Although not accepted as proofs, these are accepted as presumptions in favor of the apparitions. Within a year of the apparitions, the bishop approved the establishment of the worldwide "International Union of Prayers." Today, this group has more than two million members throughout the world, each pledged to say a prayer of their own choice daily in union with those sent up from Banneux for the poor, the suffering, and for peace on earth. In 1942, as a result of the unanimous verdict of the Ecclesiastical Commission, supported by rescripts of approval from the Holy See, the bishop authorized by Pastoral Letter the cult of Our Lady of Banneux, Our Lady of the Poor. This approval was renewed and confirmed in 1947, and again in 1949.

VIRGIN OF SILENCE — See **SILENCE, VIRGIN OF**.

THE VIRGIN WHO UNTIES KNOTS — See **KNOTS, THE VIRGIN WHO UNTIES**.

VIRTUE

A good habit of the intellect or will that enables one to perform an action with ease.

Some are infused (e.g., theological virtues: faith, hope, charity) while others are developed by practice (e.g., cardinal virtues: prudence, justice, fortitude, temperance). Virtue brings to fulfillment the powers and abilities that one possesses.

VISIONS

A charism through which an individual perceives someone or something that is naturally invisible; not to be confused with illusions or hallucinations.

Several of the saints (among them St. Teresa of Ávila and St. John of the Cross) claimed to have had visions. St. Thomas divided visions into corporeal, imaginative, and intellectual. Like other charisms, visions are for the spiritual good of people. However, they are not necessary for salvation or holiness.

VISIT OF THE SEVEN HOUSES — See SEVEN HOUSES, VISIT OF THE.

VISITATION OF MARY

The feast celebrated on May 31 to commemorate Mary's visit to her cousin Elizabeth after the Annunciation and before the birth of John the Baptist, the precursor of Christ (see Luke 1:39-45).

The feast began in the Middle Ages and was observed in the Franciscan Order before being extended throughout the Church in 1389 by Pope Urban VI (r. 1378-1389). Originally kept on July 2, in the 1969 reform of the calendar, the date was changed to May 31 so that it falls in line with the other events of the Gospel of Luke, between the Annunciation and the Nativity of John the Baptist.

(See also MAGNIFICAT [CANTICLE OF MARY].)

VISITING A CEMETERY

An indulgenced act applicable only to the souls in purgatory to devoutly visit a cemetery and pray, if only mentally, for the dead.

An indulgence is also gained for visiting a catacomb or cemetery of the early Christians.

VISITING CHURCHES — See CHURCHES, VISITING.

VISITING THE SACRED CRIB IN ST. MARY MAJOR

An indulgenced act to visit and pray at the relic venerated as Christ's crib kept in the Basilica of St. Mary Major, Rome.

The prayer to be recited to gain the indulgences is:

I adore Thee, O incarnate Word, the true Son of God from all eternity, and the true Son of Mary in the fullness of time. As I adore Thy divine Person and the sacred Humanity thereto united, I feel myself drawn to venerate likewise the poor Crib that welcomed Thee when Thou wast a little Child, and which was, in very truth, the first throne of Thy love. Would that I could fall prostrate before it with the simplicity of the shepherds, with the faith of Joseph, and the love of Mary! Would that I too could bend low to venerate this precious memorial of our salvation with the spirit of mortification, poverty and humility, with which Thou, the Lord of heaven and earth, didst choose a manger to be the resting place of Thy dear limbs. And do Thou, O Lord, who didst deign in Thine infancy to be laid in this manger, pour into my heart a drop of that joy which must have been experienced at the sight of Thy lovely infancy and of the wonders that accompanied Thy birth; by virtue of this Thy holy birth, I implore Thee to give peace and goodwill to all the world, and in the name of all mankind to render perfect thanksgiving and infinite glory to Thine eternal Father, with whom in the unity of the Holy Spirit, Thou livest and reignest one God, world without end. Amen.

VISITING THE SCALA SANCTA

An indulgenced act to ascend the *Scala Sancta* (Holy Staircase) in Rome while devoutly meditating on the Passion of Our Lord.

The "Holy Stairs" are near the Lateran Basilica and lead up to the *Sancta Sanctorum*, a chapel which is the only remaining part of the old Lateran palace which was otherwise almost entirely destroyed by fire in 1308. Originally these were known as the *Scala Pilati*, or Stair of Pilate, because it was believed that these steps in their original location had been those up which Christ had walked into the Praetorium for judgment by Pilate. Tradition claims that the stairs were brought to Rome by St. Helena after her visit to the Holy Land in 327. They are twenty-eight steps of white marble. They have been much worn and are now encased in wood, although pilgrims can see the original steps through some gaps which have been intentionally left in the covering. Many pilgrims ascend the stairs on their knees to gain the indulgence granted by Pope Pius VII.

(See also **SCALA SANCTA.**)

VISITING THE SEVEN CHURCHES OF ROME

An indulgenced act to visit and pray in the so-called "Seven Churches" in Rome: St. Peter's Basilica, St. Paul-Outside-the-Walls, St. John Lateran, St. Mary Major, St. Sebastian's, St. Lawrence-Outside-the-Walls, and Holy Cross in Jerusalem. In each of the Basilicas, the supplicant recites Our Father, Hail Mary and Glory Be five times before the altar of the Blessed Sacrament and the same prayers once more for the intentions of the pope. Also, the pilgrim is to recite some prayer to the Blessed Virgin and to the titular saint of the respective basilica. In the Basilica of the Holy Cross in Jerusalem, he prays the Apostles' Creed and the versicle "We Adore Thee, O Christ," for the prayer to the titular saint. It is also an indulgenced pious act to visit the churches of the stations in Rome. According to the *Handbook of Indulgences, Norms and Grants* revised in 1991, the faithful may also gain an indulgence by visiting any one of the four patriarchal basilicas in Rome and reciting an Our Father and the Creed.

VISITING THE SICK

An indulgenced act to accompany the Blessed Sacrament when the Eucharist is being brought to the sick.

(See also **CORPORAL WORKS OF MERCY**.)

VISITING ST. PETER'S TOMB

An indulgenced act to visit the tomb of St. Peter in the Vatican Basilica in gratitude for the privileges granted by Almighty God to the holy Apostle, praying an Our Father, Hail Mary, and Glory Be three times before the tomb.

VOCATION

The calling from God to follow a particular way of life.

Specifically, the term "vocation" is understood as God's call to a distinctive state of life, namely, married, single, religious, or priestly; the sacraments of matrimony and holy orders are thus designated sacraments of vocation.

VOTIVE MASS

A Mass offered for a special intention.

In general, this term refers to Mass formularies in the Roman Missal for special occasions or in honor of aspects of the mystery of God or the saints.

VOTIVE OFFERINGS

Freewill gifts of money or other goods in light of some spiritual request.

They are also the donation made when candles or vigil lights are lit to signify an intention.

VOW

A free and deliberate promise made to God concerning a possible and better good to be fulfilled by the person making it.

W

WAKE

The traditional gathering of the deceased's family and friends on the evening before a funeral. An ancient custom throughout the world, extant records of wakes in Europe go back over a thousand years.

Wakes before the mid-1800s in Ireland, as in much of Europe, were a mixture of Christian devotion and traditional magic, ritual observance, and festive celebration. In 1778, one writer observed: "The old people amuse themselves in smoking tobacco, drinking whiskey and telling stories in the room with the corpse; whilst the young men, in the barn or some separate apartment, exhibit feats of activity; or, inspired by their sweethearts, dance away the night to the melodious pleasing of a bagpipe."

At the ancient festive wake, the diversions for the most part consisted of party games. There were competitions involving riddles, tongue-twisters, and extempore versifying, games of competition involving feats of strength, agility, or endurance, and elaborate practical jokes which could, and often did, include the corpse. There are reports in which the deceased, usually laid out on a table and in full view, was dealt a hand of cards, had a pipe inserted in his mouth, or was taken onto the floor for a dance. Impoverished members of the lower classes were willing to endure extra hardships in order to set aside enough money for a "proper wake"

when their time was come. Funds had to be available for food, tobacco and pipes, snuff, and plenty of Irish whiskey.

Festive wakes of this type existed in most of Ireland and much of Europe in the late eighteenth and early nineteenth centuries.

Some wake games were in the form of mimes. Particularly condemned by the Church were mimes involving fake weddings, mock confessions, and other satires directed at Catholic teaching and religious practice. A popular kissing game called Frimsy Framsy was singled out for special mention in clerical condemnations of wakes on at least three occasions during the eighteenth century, being denounced as a "most disgraceful ceremony and the cause of a multitude of sins." Other repeated condemnations by the Church authorities were against obscene songs, scurrilous talk, and excessive consumption of alcohol. The record of Church condemnations paints a picture of a general atmosphere of ribaldry at wakes.

The Irish historian Prim pointed out that many of the activities at the festive wakes were remnants of Pagan rites. Others argued that the festive wake was primarily intended to comfort and placate the spirit of the deceased person by means of a last great feast at which he was present as the guest of honor.

In addition to the festivities, the wakes also involved a recognition that the occasion was one of mourning. The Irish *keen*, a traditional part of the wake, was a eulogy in verse on the qualities of the dead person and a lament for his passing, interspersed with loud wailings and cries of grief. This keen was pronounced at intervals over the corpse, first at the wake and later during the funeral procession and burial. Although a keen could be performed by a friend or relative of the deceased, as late as the nineteenth century it was a frequent practice to hire specialist keeners, and keening developed into an art.

The festive wake was a body of procedures which enabled the community to come to terms with the death of one of its members. By the display of vitality and gaiety, the members of the community responded to a reminder of general mortality; by the keen, the bereaved found a means to express their feelings in a controlled and manageable form. By the end of the eighteenth century, the opposition of the Church to the practices of the festive wake had a long history. Public penances were imposed on those who engaged in lewd songs or games and profane tricks. Time and again the Church condemned the practice of distributing alcoholic drink at funerals, and young persons, especially the unmarried, were charged not to attend. The main reason for the clerical opposition was practical, rather than ideological. The Church did not condemn the wake as a survival of pre-Christian practices or as a ritual response to death, but rather condemned them because they were seen as occasions of undesirable behavior. There was a marked hostility to keening, however, based on the commands of St. Paul, who had forbidden displays of immoderate grief for the dead. In 1806, Archbishop Bray of Cashel condemned "all unnatural screams and shrieks and fictitious tuneful cries and elegies at wakes, together with the savage custom of howling and bawling at funerals." By the early decades of the nineteenth century, clerical prohibitions began to have an effect on the wake practices. The keen gradually was replaced by hymns and Gregorian chant. Toward the end of the nineteenth century, a trend toward Anglicization changed many attitudes and many of the old Gaelic customs passed into history. Although wake games were still being played as late as the 1920s in some counties, today's wake is generally more sedate with talking, visiting, and storytelling replacing the more boisterous recreations. The use of alcohol at wakes and funerals has never been completely stamped out, but today its use is more moderate.

In 1623, hundreds of horsemen and twice that many on foot attended funerals and joined in the feasting that sometimes impoverished the relatives of the dead person. A description of a 1778 wake mentioned that guests came from far and near to pass the time in smoking and drinking whiskey. In 1841, a Mrs. S.C. Hall reported that at wakes "disreputable things occurred as there was no shortage of whiskey and both men and women drank to excess." It is no wonder that the attention of the Church came to be directed on the use of alcohol at wakes and funerals and that every effort was made to curb the abuses. The drinking of alcohol did not stop at the wake. In some places, a man stood with a bottle of whiskey at the entrance to the graveyard. He offered the funeral participants a drink as they passed by.

Only about twenty years ago, many traditional customs remained in the wakes and funerals of Ireland that seem odd or superstitious to today's American observers. Even today, remnants of these can be found in the Irish countryside. According to Irish actor and storyteller Eamon Kelly, if chided about these superstitions or *piseoga*, the people murmur, " 'Tis the custom' and it is a brave man indeed who would defy them beyond the teeth."

The advent of funeral homes gradually changed the character of wakes, and they became more solemn occasions in most areas. Today, people attend to pray for the dead and console the grieving. A remnant of the festivities remains in the gathering for a meal after the funeral either in the church hall, the family home, or a local restaurant.

WALSINGHAM, HOLY HOUSE OF (See WALSINGHAM, OUR LADY OF.)

WALSINGHAM, OUR LADY OF

A Marian image and devotion based on apparitions reported by Lady Racheldis de Faverches in Walsingham, England, in 1061.

The widow of a Norman landowner, Lady de Faverches reported that Mary instructed her to build a replica of Mary's house in Nazareth, where she had received the visit of the Archangel Gabriel and promised that pilgrims who visited this shrine would receive the same graces as if they had made the long and dangerous journey to Palestine. Our Lady made no requirement that the architecture reproduce the Palestinian original; but she was precise about the length and width of the structure, which Richeldis had built in the local vernacular style. This probably resembled a small log cabin with vertical, rather than horizontal split logs. Some time later, a seated statue of the Madonna and Child came to be in the house; its appearance was believed to be miraculous; but the focus of the shrine was the Holy House itself, not the image within it. Richeldis's son Geoffrey gave the shrine into the custody of the Augustinian Canons. They established a priory there, built a protective masonry structure over the original wooden Holy House, and later, a magnificent church for the thousands of pilgrims, from kings to peasants, who came for five centuries to ponder the joy of Mary and all mankind in the wonder that God should become man, and taking flesh, delight to dwell among us.

"The Holy House" — referred to as "England's Nazareth" — became the fourth great shrine of medieval Christendom, joining those of Jerusalem, Rome, and St. James's in Compostela, Spain. The Feast of Our Lady of Walsingham is celebrated on the Feast of the Annunciation, March 25.

The devotion was interrupted for 350 years when the English Reformation destroyed the Norfolk shrine. In 1538 King Henry VIII confiscated and razed the Walsingham shrine, selling its lands into private ownership, along with all other monastic holdings in England.

In the nineteenth century Charlotte Pearson Boyd, a devout Anglican, developed great personal devotion to Our Lady of Walsingham. Around 1863, Miss Boyd noticed a small stone building used as a barn which appeared to be a late medieval chapel, located about a mile from the site of the original shrine at Walsingham. She discovered it had been "The Slipper Chapel," the last place pilgrims visited before leaving their shoes to walk the last mile barefoot as a penance. Miss Boyd purchased the building in the 1890s and

began extensive renovation to restore it to religious use. During this process, Miss Boyd was received into the Roman Catholic Church. Eventually the chapel was given to the local Catholic bishop. In 1934, the site was declared the Roman Catholic National Shrine of Our Lady of Walsingham. Marist Fathers and Marist Sisters administer and care for the Norfolk shrine today.

In the 1920s the Anglican vicar of Walsingham, Alfred Hope Patton, erected a shrine to Our Lady of Walsingham in his parish church, which he later moved to its own nearby site. Eastern Orthodox Christians maintain their own shrine in the village. Modern pilgrims often visit all three of these shrines.

Today, Our Lady of Walsingham is again venerated as patroness of England. As such, she inspires in Roman Catholics, Anglicans, and English-speaking Orthodox Christians a genuine ecumenism based on hope for eventual unity. Devotion to Our Lady of Walsingham was brought to American shores by military personnel stationed in England during the Second World War. The first shrine dedicated to her was at St. Bede Catholic Church in Williamsburg, Virginia.

In 2000, A pilgrimage shrine of Our Lady of Walsingham was founded in Houston, Texas. It was built and is maintained by the Pastoral Provision personal parish of Our Lady of Walsingham (Anglican use) in the diocese of Galveston-Houston. In 1980, a papal Pastoral Provision was instituted, allowing for the entrance of former Episcopalians (American Anglicans) into the Roman Catholic Church while preserving elements of the Anglican liturgy. Houston's Our Lady of Walsingham Church, founded in 1984 by a former Episcopalian priest and parishioners, is one of several Pastoral Provision parishes in the United States. The inspiration of the parish's former Episcopalians to erect the pilgrimage shrine is a tribute to Mary as the Mother and Queen of Christians of all nationalities.

WASHING OF THE ALTAR

A ceremonial washing of the main altar in St. Peter's Basilica on Holy Thursday.

In general, the practice of washing altars according to a prescribed ritual goes back to the seventh century; it came to Rome in the early eleventh.

WASSAILING

An English New Year tradition of going house to house singing and offering good wishes. The participants go from house to house singing and offering God's blessings to the occupants of the houses for the forthcoming year. At the houses they visit they are treated to bowls of spiced ale made with ale, apples, sugar and spices.

The Wassail Cup is a large wooden bowl, often a family heirloom, which was used on this occasion. The word comes from the Saxon *Waes Hael*, a greeting signifying good health. The group going wassailing carries a Wassail-branch. This is an evergreen branch tied to a tall stick such as a broom handle and decorated with silvered baubles, tinsel, and red bows.

WATER, HOLY

A sacramental used for blessings.

There were many pre-Christian water rites. Our pre-Christian ancestors observed the effects of rain, and for them, water assumed a magical property of fertility and new growth. The Church elevated this pre-Christian symbolism of nature into a Christian sacramental.

Water is used many ways liturgically. At Mass, the priest's mingling a few drops of water with the wine to be consecrated symbolizes the union of two natures in Christ, the unity of Christ and his people, and the water that came out with blood from his side. This is possibly based on the Jewish custom of taking water with their wine. In baptism, water represents death to one's old self and a new life in Christ.

A ceremony of blessing water originated in the eighth century in the Carolingian Empire. In the ninth century, the words of St. Paul that through baptism we rise with Christ into newness of life (see Romans 6:4-11) seem to have prompted some bishops of the Frankish realm to introduce the custom of sprinkling holy water on the congregation before Mass to remind them of the grace of baptism. A century later, the same practice was prescribed at Verona, Italy, and soon afterward it was accepted by Rome. Called the rite of the *Asperges*, it became a part of the solemn service on Sunday. In many places during the Middle Ages a procession around the church was held, and holy water was sprinkled on the graves.

It is customary to have a holy water font at the entrance of a church and for one to use the sacramental while making the sign of the cross. Holy water is ordinary water sanctified by the blessing of the Church. The blessing consists of exorcisms of water and salt; the salt is added to the water in the form of a cross to signify that this water is now preserved from corruption. The practice of putting salt into the water comes from the incident of the miraculous cure of the poisonous well where the prophet Eliseus used salt to purify the water of the well (see 2 Kings 19-22).

In the Roman ritual, the priest prays, "May this creature of yours, when used in your mysteries and endowed with your grace, serve to cast out demons and to banish disease. May everything that this water sprinkles in the homes and gatherings of the faithful be delivered from all that is unclean and hurtful; let no breath of contagion hover there, no taint of corruption; let all the wiles of the lurking enemy come to nothing. By the sprinkling of this water may everything opposed to the safety and peace of the occupants of these homes be banished, so that in calling on your holy name they may know the well-being they desire, and be protected from every peril; through Christ our Lord. Amen."

Christ's faithful are permitted to take holy water home with them to sprinkle the sick, their homes, fields, etc. It is recommended that they put it in fonts in the rooms of their homes and use it to bless themselves daily and frequently. Water blessed during the Easter Vigil is known as Easter Water. It is customary for millions the world over to obtain for their homes this Easter water which has been blessed on Easter Saturday.

A special blessing of water on the Eve of the Epiphany was approved for the Roman ritual in 1890. This blessing comes from the Orient, where the Church has long emphasized the mystery of our Lord's baptism in her celebration of Epiphany. Years before the Latin Rite officially adopted the blessing of Epiphany water, diocesan rituals in lower Italy had contained such a blessing. Water is specially blessed and is a part of the cultus of a number of the saints. A papal brief of 1628 authorizes the blessing of water for the sick in honor of the Blessed Virgin Mary and St. Torellus. This water is drunk by the sick. Water is blessed in the name of St. Peter the Martyr asking through his intercession that all who drink it or are sprinkled with it may be delivered from evil spirits, illness, and suffering of both body and spirit. The blessing for the water in honor of St. Vincent Ferrar asks that in the name of God the Father and of St. Vincent, the water may "heal the sick, strengthen the infirm, cheer the downcast, purify the unclean, and give full well-being to those who seek it." This water is blessed with a relic or image of the saint. The blessing for water in the name of St. Raymond Nonnatus asks that "all who suffer from fever may be delivered from every infirmity of body and soul when they bathe in this water, or drink it, or are sprinkled with it, and so deserve to be restored unharmed to your Church where they will always offer their prayers of gratitude." This water is then sprinkled with holy water. In the blessing of the water in honor of St. Albert, Confessor, the exposed relics of the saint are immersed in the water. The prayer for this blessing asks that through the prayers of Blessed Albert, the faithful who reverently drink this water may regain health of body and soul and so persevere in God's holy service. The same is true of water blessed in honor of St. Ignatius, Confessor, and St. Vincent de Paul, except the relics are left in the reliquary

and a medal may be substituted for the actual relics. In some churches, the people bring water, wine, bread, and fruit to church on St. Blaise's feast day to be blessed. The blessing of these items that are sprinkled with holy water asks that all those "who eat and drink these gifts be fully healed of all ailments of the throat and of all maladies of body and soul, through the merits of St. Blaise, bishop and martyr."

Water is often a feature at locations where Marian apparitions have been reported.

WATER OF ST. ODILIA

A sacramental associated with St. Odilia (d.c. 720).

Popular tradition says she was born blind at Obernheim, in the Vosges Mountains, in Alsace, to a local nobleman. Because of her disability, he gave her away. Later, miraculously cured, she reconciled with her father. She eventually served as an abbess, and her shrine was a popular place of pilgrimage during the Middle Ages.

According to John Novelan, a lay brother of the Crosier Order in Paris, St. Odilia appeared to him in 1287 and told him that she had been appointed to be patroness of his order. She is also patroness of the blind and of those afflicted with eye disease. For centuries it has been the practice in the Crosier Order to bless water in honor of St. Odilia, dipping her relic in it and asking God to give it a "power against all diseases and bodily infirmities." Many cures, especially of diseases of the eyes, are credited to her intercession.

WAY OF THE CROSS — See STATIONS OF THE CROSS.

WAYSIDE SHRINES

The custom of erecting small shrines and chapels along roads, often as an *ex voto*. The custom is worldwide and is of long standing tradition in many countries. It is not limited to Christianity, and the orient is replete with examples from Buddhism and Shinto.

In the Middle Ages, chapels were built for private devotion, to commemorate some special event or to enshrine a treasured relic. Some became famous places of pilgrimage. Wayside and bridge chapels, intended for the use of travelers, were often found on the way to important shrines of pilgrimage. While the Church has specific regulations for private chapels where Mass is to be said, there are no restrictions on the construction of a small building or in setting aside a portion of a home to be used for private prayer and devotion.

During the twelfth and thirteenth cen-turies, there were a number of religious associations founded for the purpose of building bridges. This work, which aided travelers, particularly pilgrims, was regarded as a work of piety as well as one of public utility. Bishops customarily granted indulgences to those who by donations of money or by their actual labor contributed to the building of a bridge. In the south of France, brotherhoods for this purpose wore a common habit with a distinctive badge but were not religious in the sense of taking vows. In some cases, the associations consisted of three parts: knights who provided most of the funds and were known as *donati*; clergy, who might in the strict sense be monks; and the artisans who completed the actual work. Women were sometimes members of these associations. Besides the construction of bridges, the lodging and entertainment of travelers as well as the collection of alms commonly entered into the scope of the brotherhoods. The origin of these associations is wrapped in obscurity although one, the Fratres Pontifices (bridge builders) is commonly said to have been founded by St. Benezet, a youth who was divinely inspired to build the bridge across the Rhone at Avignon. Although the old bridge at Avignon dates from the end of the twelfth century, and St. Benezet was a historical person, the rest of the legend is not proved. There are still some remains of chapels connected to the bridges built about this time.

The countryside in the Bavarian region of Germany is covered with small wayside stopping places or shrines. These range from shrines as elaborate as small chapels to simple religious images, pictures or statues, in small shelters on poles along the roadside.

Many street corners in Mexico are ornamented with glass-fronted boxes containing a picture or statue of Mary. Personal piety, whether in payment of a manda (vow) or in supplication, or as a memorial to a loved one, has put them there. Small chapels are scattered along the roadsides for the same reason. One special type of roadside memorial is connected with the death observances in the country.

(See also **DESCANSOS**.)

WEDDING RING

As a sacramental, a symbol of the love and union of husband and wife.

In the archdiocese of Westminster, England, an indulgence may be gained by a married couple who kiss the blessed ring and recite with contrite heart the following prayer: "Grant us, O Lord, that loving You, we may love each other and live according to Your holy law."

The earliest betrothal rituals involved an exchange of gifts or property, usually from the groom to the bride's family. Gold rings date back to the early days of marriage by purchase when gold rings were often used as currency. During medieval times, the groom-to-be placed a ring on three of the bride's fingers to represent the Holy Trinity.

WEEK OF PRAYER FOR CHRISTIAN UNITY — See CHRISTIAN UNITY, WEEK OF PRAYER FOR; OCTAVE OF PRAYER FOR CHRISTIAN UNITY.

WEEKDAY DEVOTIONS

Designating a particular devotion or theme for a particular weekday Mass when a major feast is not celebrated.

The practice began in the Middle Ages when, for example, the English monk Alcuin (c. 735-804) chose the Passion for Friday and Mary for Saturday. Customarily, Monday was the Trinity; Tuesday, angels; Wednesday, Apostles; and Thursday either the Holy Spirit or the Eucharist and Christ the High Priest. Another common listing was: Sunday, Holy Trinity; Monday, Holy Spirit and souls in purgatory; Tuesday, angels; Wednesday, St. Joseph; Thursday, Blessed Sacrament; Friday, Passion and Sacred Heart; Saturday, Mary.

WELL-DRESSING

A medieval custom usually held on or near the Feast of the Ascension.

The practice dates back to the time of plagues and the people at Tissington, England, were spared, a fact they attributed to the purity of the water supply. There and at a number of locations in the area, boarded frames covered with damp soil were placed over wells. For well-dressing, a variety of beautiful designs, all with religious themes, were created from flowers, berries, and leaves. A short service was held at each well, and the well was solemnly blessed.

WELLS, HOLY

Any of a number of wells or springs associated with devotion to Mary or a saint.

WHITE SCAPULAR

A popular name for the Scapular of the Immaculate Heart of Mary.

(See also **SCAPULAR**.)

WHITSUNDAY — See **PENTECOST**.

WIENIEC — See **ASSUMPTION**.

WITNESS

One who testifies.

In its Christian sense, witness refers to the Apostles, martyrs, and the first disciples of Christ who bore witness to his Resurrection. More widely, it describes every Christian who is called to bear witness, by word and deed, to the hope that comes from Our Lord, Jesus Christ.

WORLD MARRIAGE DAY

A celebration on the second Sunday in February.

World Marriage Day began in Baton Rouge, Louisiana, in 1981 when couples encouraged the mayor, governor, and bishop to proclaim St. Valentine's Day as "We Believe in Marriage Day." The idea was presented to and adopted by Worldwide Marriage Encounter's national leadership the following year. In 1983, the name was changed to World Marriage Day and designated to be celebrated on the second Sunday in February. In 1993, Pope John Paul II imparted an apostolic blessing on the event. It has adopted the theme "Love One Another" to echo the commandment given by Jesus in the Gospel of John.

WORLD MISSION ROSARY

A sacramental and method of praying the Rosary introduced by Archbishop Fulton J. Sheen in the mid-twentieth century to encourage prayers for the missions and missionaries.

As the beads are prayed, the supplicant is encouraged to offer those prayers for the missionary efforts of the Church in each continent. Each decade of the rosary beads consists of a different color to symbolize the continents: green for Africa, red for the Americas, white for Europe, blue for Oceania, and yellow for Asia.

WORLD YOUTH DAY
Annual and biannual celebrations devoted to young people.

Most dioceses host a World Youth Day each year. In the United States it is celebrated on the last Sunday in October; in other countries, it is generally on Palm Sunday, when the pope meets with the youth of the diocese of Rome and delivers a "Message to the Youth of the World." Each message has a scriptural text as its theme.

Since the Jubilee Year of 1983-84, a biannual worldwide gathering of teens and young adults has been hosted by a number of countries. The pope has attended the celebrations, which typically draw hundreds of thousands of participants.

In 1985, which the United Nations had declared to be the International Year of Youth, there was a second gathering in Rome. On that occasion the pope entrusted the young people with a large wooden cross, which he asked them to carry across the world as a sign of Christ's love for mankind. Other gatherings have been held in Argentina, Spain, Poland, the United States, the Philippines, France and Canada. Two million young people attended the Jubilee Year gathering in Rome in August 2000, when the wooden cross returned, having been carried across the world during the previous fifteen years. On this occasion, for the first time, pilgrims from China took part.

Not all attendees are Catholics; Jews, Muslims, and other Christians have also taken part.

WORLDWIDE MARRIAGE ENCOUNTER
An organization that brings couples together for a weekend program of events directed by a team of several couples and a priest to develop each participant couple's abilities to communicate with each other as husband and wife. The worldwide headquarters is in San Bernardino, California.

WREATH
A common symbol of victory adopted by the Church for popular use.

Circular wreaths woven of flowers and greenery have been popular since pre-Christian times. Wreaths of bay laurel were awarded to the victors in the Olympic Games and to heroes returning from war, and are still today known as a symbol for victory. In the middle ages, the monks wove wreaths of flowers which the priests wore on feast days. A number of pagan groups, especially the worshipers of Baal, used wreaths of Marsh marigold to ward off evil spirits. During the Middle Ages, the plant was "Christianized" and dedicated to the Virgin. In Poland, young girls carried large wreaths made of the recently harvested rye or wheat, intertwined with poppies and bachelor button during the annual *Dozynki* or harvest walk and celebration. The fruit of the orchard — plums, apples and pears — was tied to the wreaths with yellow, red, blue, and purple ribbons. In France and many sections of central Europe, the Feast of Corpus Christi was known as the Day of Wreaths. Huge bouquets of flowers were borne on the top of wooden poles, and wreaths and bouquets of exquisite flowers in various colors were attached to flags and banners, houses, and green arches that spanned the streets. The men wore small wreaths on their left arms in the processions and the girls wore them on their heads. The monstrance containing the Blessed Sacrament was adorned with a wreath of choice flowers. In Poland, the wreaths were blessed on the eve of the feast. After the feast, the people decorated their homes with them. these wreaths were hung on the walls, windows and doors of the houses and were put up on poles in the gardens, fields and pastures with a prayer for protection and blessing upon the growing harvest. Ever-green wreaths, of course, are common at Christmas, and solemn wreaths are part of the funeral customs of many countries.

WREATH, ADVENT — See ADVENT WREATH.

WWJD

During the 1990s, many Catholic youth wore woven band bracelets sporting the initials WWJD. The initials stand for the question "What would Jesus do?" and the popular slogan appeared not only on bracelets, other jewelry, key chains, t-shirts, and other merchandise. Although the concept was begun by a Protestant group, Catholics as well as other Christians adopted it as it rode a giant wave of prosperity through much of the decade.

The youth group at Calvary Reformed Church in Holland, Michigan, had studied the Charles Sheldon book, written in 1896, called *In His Steps*. In the novel, a tramp dressed in rags disrupts the status quo in a midwestern church Sunday service by posing a shocking statement. He had made repeated pleas for help which were disregarded by the townspeople. One Sunday, when they arrived for church, well-dressed and reverent, the tramp enters the church and rocks their world by saying "It seems to me there's an awful lot of trouble in the world that somehow wouldn't exist if all the people who sing such songs went and lived them out." With that, he collapsed and died. The shocked congregation pledged to live the following year by constantly asking themselves one question — "What Would Jesus Do?"

The Holland youth group also pledged to ask, "What Would Jesus Do?" To remind themselves tangibly, they found someone to make woven bracelets that bore four letters: WWJD. The idea caught on, the manufacturer began to release the bracelets nationwide, and millions of the bracelets were sold.

WYPOMINKI

A black-bordered paper used in a Polish custom of bringing paper to the parish priest on All Souls' Day.

The names of their beloved dead are written on the sheets. During November at evening devotions and Sunday Masses, the names are read from the pulpit and prayers are offered for the repose of their souls.

Y

YAHWEH

The Hebrew name of God.

God's proper name revealed to Moses during the Exodus.

(See also **JEHOVAH [J-H-V-H]**.)

YEW TREE

An ancient symbol of death.

Yew trees are often found in European churchyards, especially in the south of England. The yew was used in Ireland as a substitute for palms on Passion Sunday.

Z

ZACHARY, CANTICLE OF — See ZECHARIAH, CANTICLE OF.

ZAPOPAN, ANNUAL PROCESSION OF OUR LADY OF

A custom based on devotion to a small image of the Immaculate Conception dating back to Spanish Franciscan Fray Antonio de Segovia during his apostolic journeys among the Indians of Jalisco, Mexico, beginning in the year 1530.

Fray Antonio was having little success in converting the Indians or making peace

Our Lady of Zapopan

until he begged Our Lady's help. While he was preaching, luminous rays began to issue from the statue which so impressed the Indians that they laid down their arms, agreed to peace, and asked for Baptism. Fray Antonio called the image *La Pacificadora*, "She Who Makes Peace," and gave the little image to the village of Zapopan.

The statue is twelve inches tall and made of a mixture of corn and cornstalk mixed with glue. Her hands are made of wood and are clasped in prayer. She holds a scepter, golden keys to the city, and a *bastón* (Spanish for "cane" or "walking stick"), in this case a golden stick that indicates her military rank as "General of the Army of the State." The image was honored by a papal coronation in 1919, and since 1940 her sanctuary has been designated a minor basilica.

Beginning in 1734, and to the present day, the great devotion to Our Lady under this title is demonstrated each year when the statue leaves its sanctuary in Zapopan on June 13, the Feast of St. Anthony of Padua, and travels northwest to the capital city of Guadalajara. She visits every church in the city until October 4, the Feast of St. Francis of Assisi. On that day she is brought back to Zapopan in a procession with all the pomp and celebration worthy of a queen. Dressed in a medieval costume with a cloak and a broad-brimmed hat, she is borne along the way on her silver base protected by uniformed members of a society known as the Guards of Our Lady of Zapopan. Native Indian dancers in colorful costumes from remote villages, mariachi singers, military bands, choirs, and jugglers are all part of the procession. In the past, airplanes have been used to strew flowers along the path of the procession. At night, fireworks, lights, music, dancing, and various celebrations salute the little queen. Thousands take part in the annual procession.

ZEAL

A motive of love and the resulting action that urges one to serve God.

It may be disturbed by scrupulosity or misdirected by self-righteousness.

ZECHARIAH, CANTICLE OF

Also known as the *Benedictus* (from the Latin for "blessed").

It is found in Luke 1:68-79, which begins, "Blessed be the Lord God of Israel, for he has visited and redeemed his people."

ZUCCHETTO

The small, circular skullcap worn by bishops, abbots, and other prelates.

Usually made of fine leather covered with silk, it is also called a *pileolus* (Latin for "skullcap"). The zucchetto is doffed in the presence of a higher prelate; hence the pope's skullcap is called a *Soli Deo* because he removes it for God alone.

Appendix A

Patron Saints

A patron saint is one chosen as a special advocate with God, one who receives a special honor by a place, association, or person, in accordance with Catholic teaching that angels and saints have special spheres of activity. The choice must be confirmed by the Holy See and must include those saints who are recognized as canonized saints, unless by special indult, an individual who is beatified is chosen. There may be a principal and a lesser patron, but a mystery of religion cannot be a patron in the proper sense.

Trades and professions, states of life, diseases, and places in old Christian countries also have their patrons, usually by ancient or local tradition. It is common for an individual to take as patron the saint whose name is assumed at Confirmation, putting himself under the saint's protection, studying his or her life and attempting to profit by the saint's example. The patron saint of a church gives his or her name to the church and is technically called its titular. Although there are thousands of saints considered by custom as patrons, only a few of them are officially recognized by the Church.

The Roman practice of patronage, whereby someone of wealth and influence extended protection and support to less influential and wealthy clients, apparently carried over to the cult of the saints from about the third or fourth century. Many of the stories on which some early patrons were selected are now considered only legendary. The entire social life of the Catholic world before the Reformation was animated with the idea of protection from heavenly patrons. In England alone there were more than 40,000 religious groups, each with their own patron.

The selection of patrons was first recognized by Pope Urban VIII in 1630, when he declared that the individual must be among the canonized, must be chosen by the clergy and people with the approval of the bishop, and that the choice must be confirmed by the Sacred Congregation of Rites. These regulations were included in the 1917 Code of Canon Law, and their general ideas have remained. New regulations were issued in March 1973, and since the changes in the Roman Curia, the confirmation is now required from the Congregation of Divine Worship. Some attempts have been made to change patronages where the saint's historicity cannot be verified, and the practice of having protectors against particular eventualities is now officially frowned on, although the custom still survives.

The Third Eucharistic Prayer contains a place where the "saint of the day or the patron saint" may be named. This list of patron saints contains both those patrons officially designated, and those acknowledged as patrons by long tradition.

Acacius • Headache

Adelaide • Empresses; princesses

Adelard • Gardeners

Adjutors • Swimmers; yachtsmen

Agatha • Blood disorders; breast cancer; Catania; hemorrhages; Malta; nurses

Agnes • Children of Mary; young girls

Alban • Refugees; torture victims

Albert • Scientists

Albert the Great • Medical technicians

Aloyisus • Boys

Aloysius Gonzaga • Youth

Alphonsus Liguori • Arthritis; confessors; rheumatism; theologians; vocations

Amand • Wine merchants

Ambrose • Candle makers; learning

Anastasia • Weavers

Anastasius • Fullers

Andrew • Fishermen; Russia

Andrew Apostle • Scotland

Andrew Avellino • Sudden death

Andronicus • Silversmiths

Angsar • Denmark; Scandinavia

Ann • Brittany; cabinet makers; Canada; childbirth; childless couples; domestic workers; housewives; miners; women in labor

Anthony • Gravediggers; skin diseases

Anthony Abbot • Herdsmen

Anthony of Egypt • Basket makers; brush makers; butchers

Anthony of Padua • Animals; barren women; loss of material goods; lost articles; poor; Portugal; travel hostesses; travelers

Appolonia • Dentists; lightening; toothache

Armand • Innkeepers

Augustine • Brewers; theologians

Augustine of Hippo • Printers

Balbina • Lymph grand diseases

Balthasar • Epilepsy

Barbara • Artillery men; gunners; lightening; miners; sudden death

Basil the Great • Hospital administrators

Bede, the Venerable • Scholars

Benedict • Fever; kidney disease; poison; skin disease

Benedict Joseph Labre • Homeless

Benedict of Nursia • Europe; monks; speliologists

Benedict the Black • Black missions

Bernard of Clairveaux • Candle makers

Bernard of Siena • Advertisers

Bernardine • Communications personnel

Bernardine of Siena • Public relations

Blaise • Doctors; goiters; neck ailments; sore throat; whooping cough

Blandina • Girls

Bona • Travel hostesses

Boniface of Crediton • Brewers; tailors

Boris and Gleb • Princes

Brendan • Sailors

Bridget • Dairy workers; Ireland; nuns; scholars; Sweden

Bernard of Montjoux • Mountaineers; skiers

Bruno • Possessed

Camillus de Lellis • Hospital workers; hospitals; nurses; sick

Canute • Denmark

Casimir of Poland • Kings; Lithuania; princes

Cassian • Stenographers

Castrius • Sculptors

Catherine of Alexandria • Philosophers; single women; wheelwrights; women students

Catherine of Bologna • Artists

Catherine of Siena • Fire prevention; Italy; nursing services; philosophers

Catherine of Sweden • Miscarriage

Cecilia • Musicians; singers; organ builders; poets

Charles Borromeo • Catechists; seminarians

Charles the Good • Counts; crusaders

Christina • Mental problems

Christopher • Accidents; bookbinders; gardeners; infections; motorists; plague; porters; sailors; storms; sudden death; travelers; contagious fevers

Clare • Eye problems

Clare of Assisi • Television

Clement • Sick children

Clement I • Marble workers; stonecutters

Clothilde • Queens; adopted children

Cloud • Nail makers

Columba • Ireland

Contardo Ferrini, Blessed • universities

Cosmos and Damien • Barbers; doctors; pharmacists; physicians; surgeons

Crispin and Crispinian • Saddle makers; shoemakers; tanners

Cuthbert • Sailors

Cuthman • Shepherds

Cyriacus • Eye problems; possession

Cyril and Methodius • Bohemia; ecumenists; Europe; Moravia

Dagobert • Kings

David • Poets; Wales

Denis • France; Possessed; possession

Devota • Monico

Dionysius • Headache

Dismas • Funeral directors; prisoners; the condemned (to death); thieves

Dominic • Astronomers; Dominican Republic

Dominic Savio • Choirboys; youth

Dorothy • Gardeners

Drogo • Shepherds

Dunstan • Armorers; goldsmiths; jewelers; locksmiths; musicians

Dymphna • Mental problems; princesses

Edgar • Kings

Edmund • Kings

Edward • England

Edward the Confessor • Kings

Edwin • Kings

Eligius • Jewelers

Eligius (Eloi) • Blacksmiths; metalworkers

Elizabeth • Childless couples

Elizabeth of Hungary • Countesses; nurses; nursing services

Elizabeth of Portugal • Queens

Eloi • Carpenters; workers with hammers

Erasmus • Children's intestinal diseases; colds; colic; stomach diseases

Eulalia • Sailors

Eustace • Fire; hunters

Eustachius • Torture victims

Felicity • Barren women

Ferdinand III • Engineers

Fiacre • Cabdrivers; gardeners; hemorrhoids; tumors

Florian • Firemen

Fra Angelico, Blessed • Artists

Frances of Rome • Motorists

Francis Borgia • Portugal

Francis de Sales • Authors; Catholic press; deaf; editors; journalists; animals

Francis of Assisi • Catholic Action; ecologists; Italy; merchants

Francis of Paola • Seamen

Francis Xavier • Australia; Borneo; foreign missions; New Zealand; plague

Francis Xavier Cabrini • Emigrants; hospital administrators; immigrants

Gabriel • Messengers; postal employees; radio workers; telecommunications workers; television workers

Gabriel Possenti • Clerics; youth

Gemma Galgani • Pharmacists

Genesius • Actors; comedians; lawyers; secretaries

Genevieve • Blindness; fever; women's army corps

Gengulphus • Knights

George • Boy scouts; dry skin; eczema; England; farmers; Germany; itch; Portugal; skin diseases; soldiers; sores; Venice; virus diseases (herpetic)

Gerald of Aurilla • Counts

Gerard Majella • Childbirth; pregnancy

Germaine Cousin • Shepherdesses

Gertrude • Fever; West Indies

Gertrude of Nivelles • Accommodations

Gervase and Protase • Haymakers

Giles • Cancer; crippling diseases; delirium; epilepsy; mental problems; nightmares; panic; sterility in women

Gomer • Hernia

Gotteschalc • Linguists; princes

Gregory • Scholars; singers

Gregory I the Great • Popes

Gregory of Neocaesarea • Desperate situations

Gregory the Great • Musicians; teachers

Gregory the Illuminator • Armenia

Gummarus • Courtiers

Guntrammus • Guardians

Guy of Anderlecht • Sacristans

Hadrian • Soldiers

Hallvard • Innocence

Hedwig • Queens; Silesia

Hedwig, Queen of Poland • Duchesses

Helena • Converts; divorce; empresses

Henry II • Dukes

Henry of Uppsala • Finland

Holy Family • Christian families

Holy Innocents • Choirboys; foundlings

Homobonus • Tailors

Hubert • Dog bites; hunters; rabies

Ignatius • Soldiers

Ignatius Loyola • Retreats

Imelda, Blessed • First Communicants

Immaculate Conception • Equatorial Guinea; U.S.A;

Immaculate Heart of Mary • Angola; Lesotho

Isidore • Farmers; laborers

James the Greater • Chile; laborers; pilgrims; rheumatism; Spain

James the Less • Fullers; hatters

Januarius • Blood banks

Jerome • Librarians

Jerome Emiliani • Deserted children; orphans

Joan of Arc • France; soldiers

John Baptist de la Salle • Teachers

John Baptist Vianney • Priests; secular clergy

John Berchmans • Altar boys; youth

John Bosco • Editors; laborers; youth

John Chrisostom • Orators

John Gualbert • Forest workers

John Nepomucene • Bridges; confessors; Czech Republic

John of Bridlington • Childbirth

John of Capistrano • Chaplains; jurists, juries; military chaplains

John of God • Alcoholism; booksellers; dying; heart problems; hospital workers; hospitals; nurses; printers

John of the Cross • Mystics

John Regis • Medical social workers

John the Apostle • Asia Minor

John the Baptist • Ferriers

John the Divine • Friendship

Joseph • Belgium; Canada; carpenters; China; dying; laborers; Mexico; Peru; sudden death; Universal Church

Joseph Cafasso • Prisoners

Joseph Calasanz • Catholic schools; students

Joseph of Arimathea • Funeral directors; tin workers

Joseph of Cupertino • Aviators

Joseph of Palestine • Guardians

Jude • Tanners

Jude Thaddeus • Desperate situations; hospital workers; hospitals

Julian • Ferrymen; innkeepers; knights

Julian the Hospitaler • Hospitalers

Justin Martyr • Philosophers

King Louis IX of France • Grooms

Lawrence • Cooks; lumbago; poor; rheumatism; Sri Lanka

Leonard • Childbirth

Leonard of Port Maurice • Home missions; parish missions

Louis Bertrand • Colombia

Louis IX • Crusaders; Kings

Louise de Marillac • Social workers

Lucy • Diarrhea; dysentery; eye problems; hemorrhages; writers

Lucy Philippini • Teachers

Ludmila • Bohemia; duchess

Luke • Artists; butchers; glassworkers; notaries; painters; physicians; surgeons

Lydia • Dyers

Lydwine of Shiedam • Skaters

Madonna of St. Luke • Italy

Mamas • Guardians

Margaret • Birth

Margaret Clitherow • Business women

Margaret of Antioch • Pain in childbirth; pregnancy

Margaret of Cartona • Midwives; homeless; single mothers

Margaret of Scotland • Queens

Marguerite Bourgeoys • Teachers

Maria Goretti • Children of Mary

Mark • Notaries; Venice

Martha • Cooks; dieticians; domestic workers; innkeepers

Martin de Porres • Race relations; hairdressers

Martin of Tours • Beggars; poison; soldiers

Mary • Korea

Mary, Blessed Virgin • Bodily health; spiritual health

Mary, Help of Christians • Australia

Mary, Queen of Africa • Africa; Uganda

Matilda • Queens

Matthew • Accountants; bankers; bookkeepers; tax collectors

Matthias • Alcoholism; smallpox

Maurice • Arthritis; cramp; dyers; gout; infantrymen; inflammation of the joints; metabolic diseases; muscle problems; soldiers; swordsmiths

Maurice d'Agaune • Dyers; weavers

Maurinus • deacons; Coppersmiths

Maximilian Kolbe • Drug addiction

Michael • Sick

Michael, Archangel • Grocers; holy souls; mariners; paratroopers; police officers; radiologists; Papua New Guinea

Monica • Alcoholism; mothers

Nicholas of Flüe • Councilmen; magistrates

Nicholas of Myra • Bakers; brides; children; coopers; Greece; merchants; pawnbrokers; Russia; sailors; Sicily; travelers

Nicholas of Tolentino • Lost souls; mariners; poor souls

Notburga • Fieldworkers

Notre Dame de Chartres • France

Odilia • Alsace; blindness; eye problems

Olaf • Carvers

Olaf II • Norway

Our Lady, Aparicio • Brazil

Our Lady Help of Christians • New Zealand

Our Lady, Mt. Carmel, Ayelsford • England

Our Lady of Africa • Algeria

Our Lady of Bandra • India
Our Lady of Banneux • Belgium
Our Lady of Beauraing • Belgium
Our Lady of Cartago • Costa Rica
Our Lady of Charity of Cobre • Cuba
Our Lady of Chinquinquira • Colombia
Our Lady of Copacabana • Bolivia
Our Lady of Coromoto • Venezuela
Our Lady of Czestochowa • Poland
Our Lady of Fátima • Portugal
Our Lady of Grace • Motorcyclists
Our Lady of Guadalupe • Mexico; The Americas
Our Lady of Guadalupe of Estremadura • Spain
Our Lady of High Grace • Dominican Republic
Our Lady of Hungary • Hungary
Our Lady of Japan • Japan
Our Lady of Knock • Ireland
Our Lady of La Vang • Vietnam
Our Lady of LaSalette • France
Our Lady of Limerick • Ireland
Our Lady of Loreto • Airmen; aviators; Italy
Our Lady of Lourdes • France; illness and pain
Our Lady of Lujon • Paraguay; Uruguay
Our Lady of Madhu • Sri Lanka
Our Lady of Mariazell • Austria
Our Lady of Montserrat • Spain
Our Lady of Nazareth • Brazil
Our Lady of Peace • El Salvador
Our Lady of Perpetual Help • Italy
Our Lady of Pompeii • Italy

Our Lady of Pontmain • France
Our Lady of Prompt Succor • New Orleans
Our Lady of Providence • Puerto Rico
Our Lady of Ransom • Spain
Our Lady of Safe Travel • Philippines
Our Lady of Shongweni • South Africa
Our Lady of Tears • Italy
Our Lady of the Assumption • India; Paraguay
Our Lady of the Cape • Canada
Our Lady of the Immaculate Conception • Tanzania
Our Lady of the Milk and Happy Delivery • U.S.A.
Our Lady of the Miraculous Medal • France
Our Lady of the Pillar • Spain
Our Lady of the Snows • Italy
Our Lady of the Turumba • Philippines
Our Lady of Victory • U.S.A.
Our Lady of Walsingham • England
Our Lady of Bandel • India
Our Lady of Lujon • Argentina
Our Lady of the Hermits • Switzerland
Pantaleon • Endurance; paralysis; physicians; tuberculosis
Paschal Baylon • Eucharistic congresses; Eucharistic societies
Patrick • Ireland
Paul • Snakebite
Paul the Apostle • Hospital public relations; Malta
Peregrine • Cancer
Peter • England

Peter Claver • Black missions; Colombia

Peter Gonzalez • Sailors

Peter of Alacántara • Watchmen; Brazil

Philemon • Dancers

Phocas • Gardeners

Pulcheria • Empresses

Raphael • Blindness; happy meetings; lovers; nurses; physicians; possession; travelers

Raymond Nonnatus • Childbirth; falsely accused; pregnancy

Raymond of Peñafort • Medical records librarians; canonists

Raymong Nonatus • Midwives

Regina • Shepherdesses; torture victims

René Goupil • Anesthetists

Rita • Cancer

Rita of Cascia • Desperate situations

Robert Bellarmine • Catechists

Roch • Contageous diseases; epidemic infections; invalids; knee troubles; lameness; plague; skin disease

Rose of Lima • South America; the Americas

Sabas • Lectors

Sacred Heart • The entire world

Sacred Heart of Jesus • Ecuador

Sacred Heart of Mary • Philippines

Santo Niño of Cebu • Philippines

Scholastica • Convulsions, especially of children; rain

Sebastian • Archers; athletes; plague; soldiers

Seraphina • Spinners

Servatus • Leg problems

Solangia • Shepherdesses

Solomon • Kings

St. Francis Xavier • Propagation of the Faith

St. John • Puerto Rico

St. Mary of the Hurons • Canada

Stanislaus of Cracow • Poland

Stephen • Masons; Mass servers

Stephen of Hungary • Kings; stonemasons

Stephen the King • Hungary

Tarcisius • First Communicants

Teresa of Ávila • Spain

Theobaldus • Church cleaners

Theodore the Great Martyr • Tempests

Theresa of Ávila • Headache

Thérèse of Lisieux • Aviators; florists; foreign missions; Russia; France

Thomas Aquinas • Catholic schools; chastity; colleges, philosophers; schools; students; universities

Thomas More • Adopted children; lawyers; politicians

Thomas the Apostle • East Indies; Malabar; architects

Thorlac Thorhallsson • Iceland

Tryphon • Gardeners

Ubald • Evil spirits

Valentine • Epilepsy; blindness; fainting spells; incurable disease; lovers; plague

Venerius • Lighthouse keepers

Viator • Catechists

Victor of Marseilles • Torture victims

Vincent • Portugal; Torture victims

Vincent (de Paul) • Charitable societies

Vincent Ferrer • Builders

Vincent Martyr • Vintners (winegrowers)

Vincent of Zaragoza • Portugal

Vitus • Chorea; comedians; epilepsy; lethargy; motor diseases; rabies; sleeping sickness; snakebite

Vladimir • Converts

Walter of Portnoise • Stress

Wenceslas • Czech Republic; Bohemia

Wilgefortis • Anxiety; (legendary) unsatisfactory husbands

Willebroard • Holland

Willibrord • Epilepsy; Luxembourg; motor diseases

Wolfgang • Apoplexy; hardening of the arteries; paralysis

Yves (Ivo) • Lawyers

Zita • Domestic servants

Appendix B

✑

Shrines and Places of Historic Interest in the U.S.

Listed below, according to state, are shrines, other centers of devotion, and some places of historic interest with special significance for Catholics. The list is necessarily incomplete because of space limitations.

Information includes: name and location of shrine or place of interest, date of foundation, sponsoring agency or group, and address for more information. E-mail address are included where available.

Alabama

- St. Jude Church of the City of St. Jude, Montgomery (1934; dedicated, 1938); Mobile Archdiocese. Address: 2048 W. Fairview Ave., Montgomery 36108; (334) 265-1390.

- Shrine of the Most Blessed Trinity, Holy Trinity (1924); Missionary Servants of the Most Blessed Trinity. Address: Holy Trinity 36859.

Arizona

- Chapel of the Holy Cross, Sedona (1956); Phoenix Diocese: P.O. Box 1043, W. Sedona 86339.

- Mission San Xavier del Bac, near Tucson (1692); National Historic Landmark; Franciscan Friars and Tucson Diocese; Address: 1950 W. San Xavier Rd., Tucson 85746-7409; (520) 294-2624.

- Shrine of St. Joseph of the Mountains, Yarnell (1939); erected by Catholic Action League; currently maintained by Board of Directors. Address: P.O. Box 267, Yarnell 85362.

California

- Mission San Diego de Alcala (July 16, 1769); first of the 21 Franciscan missions of Upper California; Minor Basilica; National Historic Landmark; San Diego Diocese. Address:

10818 San Diego Mission Rd., San Diego 92108; (619) 283-7319.

- Carmel Mission Basilica (Mission San Carlos Borromeo del Rio Carmelo), Carmel by the Sea (June 3, 1770); Monterey Diocese. Address: 3080 Rio Rd., Carmel 93923; (831) 624-1271.

- Old Mission San Luis Obispo de Tolosa, San Luis Obispo (Sept. 1, 1772); Monterey Diocese (Parish Church). Address: Old Mission Church, 751 Palm St., San Luis Obispo 93401.

- San Gabriel Mission, San Gabriel (Sept. 8, 1771); Los Angeles Archdiocese (Parish Church, staffed by Claretians). Address: 537 W. Mission, San Gabriel 91776.

- Mission San Francisco de Asis (Oct. 9, 1776) and Mission Dolores Basilica (1860s); San Francisco Archdiocese. Address: 3321 Sixteenth St., San Francisco 94114.

- Old Mission San Juan Capistrano, San Juan Capistrano (Nov. 1, 1776); Orange Diocese. Address: P.O. Box 697, San Juan Capistrano 92693; (949) 248-2026; www.missionsjc.com.

- Old Mission Santa Barbara, Santa Barbara (Dec. 4, 1786); National Historic Landmark; Parish Church, staffed by Franciscan Friars. Address: 2201 Laguna St., Santa Barbara 93105; (805) 682-4713.

- Old Mission San Juan Bautista, San Juan Bautista (June 24, 1797); National Historic Landmark; Monterey Diocese (Parish Church). Address: P.O. Box 400, San Juan Bautista 95045.

- Mission San Miguel, San Miguel (July 25, 1797); Parish Church, Monterey diocese; Franciscan Friars. Address: P.O. Box 69, San Miguel 93451; (805) 467-3256.

- Old Mission Santa Inés, Solvang (1804); Historic Landmark; Los Angeles Archdiocese (Parish Church, staffed by Capuchin Franciscan Friars). Address: P.O. Box 408, Solvang 93464 (805) 688-4815; www.missionsantaines.org.

- Shrine of Our Lady of Sorrows, Sycamore (1883); Sacramento Diocese. Address: c/o Our Lady of Lourdes Church, 745 Ware Ave., Colusa 95932.

Colorado

- Mother Cabrini Shrine, Golden; Missionary Sisters of the Sacred Heart. Address: 20189 Cabrini Blvd., Golden 80401.

Connecticut

- Shrine of Our Lady of Lourdes, Litchfield (1958); Montfort Missionaries. Address: P.O. Box 667, Litchfield 06759.

- Shrine of the Infant of Prague, New Haven (1945); Dominican Friars. Address: P.O. Box 1202, 5 Hillhouse Ave., New Haven 06505.

District of Columbia

- Mount St. Sepulchre, Franciscan Monastery of the Holy Land (1897; church dedicated, 1899); Order of Friars Minor. Address: 1400 Quincy St. N.E., Washington, D.C. 20017.

- Basilica of the National Shrine of the Immaculate Conception. National Shrine honoring Mary; founded by Bishop Thomas J. Shahan, Fourth Rector of the Catholic University of America in 1913; 400 Michigan Avenue NE, Washington, D.C. 20017. www.nationalshrineinteractive.com.

Florida

- Mary, Queen of the Universe Shrine, Orlando (1986, temporary facilities; new shrine dedicated, 1993); Orlando diocese. Address: 8300 Vineland Ave., Orlando, 32821; (407) 239-6600; www.maryqueenoftheuniverse.org.

- Our Lady of La Leche Shrine (Patroness of Mothers and Mothers-to-be) and Mission of Nombre de Dios, Saint Augustine (1565); Angelus Crusade Headquarters. St. Augustine Diocese. Address: 30 Ocean Ave., St. Augustine 32084.

Illinois

- Holy Family Log Church, Cahokia (1799; original log church erected 1699); Belleville Diocese (Parish Church). Address: 116 Church St., Cahokia 62206; (618) 337-4548.

- Marytown/Shrine of St. Maximilian Kolbe and Retreat Center, Libertyville; Our Lady of the Blessed Sacrament Sanctuary of Perpetual Eucharistic Adoration (1930 and Archdiocesan Shrine to St. Maximilian Kolbe (1989), conducted by Conventual Franciscan Friars, 1600 West Park Ave., Libertyville 60048; (847) 367-7800.

- National Shrine of Our Lady of the Snows, Belleville (1958); Missionary Oblates of Mary Immaculate. Address: 442 S. De Mazenod Dr., Belleville 62223.

- National Shrine of St. Jude, Chicago (1929); located in Our Lady of Guadalupe Church, founded and staffed by Claretians. Address: 3200

E. 91st St., Chicago 60617; (312) 236-7782.

- National Shrine of St. Thérèse and Museum, Darien (1930, at St. Clara's Church, Chicago; new shrine, 1987, after original destroyed by fire); Carmelites of Most Pure Heart of Mary Province. Address: Carmelite Visitor Center, 8501 Bailey Rd., Darien 60561; (630) 969-3311; www.saint-therese.org.

- Shrine of St. Jude Thaddeus, Chicago (1929) located in St. Pius V Church, staffed by Dominicans, Central Province. Address: 1909 S. Ashland Ave., Chicago 60608; (312) 226-0020; www.op.org/domcentral/places/stjude.

Indiana
- Our Lady of Monte Cassino Shrine, St. Meinrad (1870); Benedictines. Address: Saint Meinrad Archabbey, Indiana State Highway 62, St. Meinrad 47577; (812) 357-6585; www.saint meinrad.edu/abbey/shrine.

- Old Cathedral (Basilica of St. Francis Xavier), Vincennes (1826, parish records go back to 1749); Evansville Diocese. Minor Basilica, 1970. Address: 205 Church St., Vincennes 47591; (812) 882-5638.

Iowa
- Grotto of the Redemption, West Bend (1912); Sioux City Diocese. Life of Christ in stone. Mailing address: P.O. Box 376, West Bend 50597; (515) 887-2371; www.aw-cybermail.com/grotto.htm.

Louisiana
- National Votive Shrine of Our Lady of Prompt Succor, New Orleans (1810); located in the Chapel of the Ursuline Convent (a National Historic Landmark). Address: 2635 State St., New Orleans 70118.

- Shrine of St. Ann. Mailing address: 4920 Loveland St., Metaire 70006; (504) 455-7071.

- Shrine of St. Roch, New Orleans (1876); located in St. Roch's Campo Santo (Cemetery); New Orleans Archdiocese. Address: 1725 St. Roch Ave., New Orleans 70117.

Maryland
- Basilica of the National Shrine of the Assumption of the Blessed Virgin Mary, Baltimore (1806). Mother Church of Roman Catholicism in the U.S. and the first metropolitan cathedral. Designed by Benjamin Henry Latrobe (architect of the Capitol) it is considered one of the finest

examples of neoclassical architecture in the world. The church hosted many of the events and personalities central to the growth of Roman Catholicism in the U.S. Address: Cathedral and Mulberry Sts., Baltimore, MD 21201.

- National Shrine Grotto of Our Lady of Lourdes, Emmitsburg (1809, Grotto of Our Lady; 1875, National Shrine Grotto of Lourdes); Public oratory, Archdiocese of Baltimore. Address: Mount St. Mary's College and Seminary, Emmitsburg 21727; (301) 447-5318; www.msmary.edu/grotto/.

- National Shrine of St. Elizabeth Ann Seton, Emmitsburg. Religious/Historical. Foundation of Sisters of Charity (1809); first parochial school in America (1810); dedicated as Minor Basilica (1991); Address: 333 South Seton Ave., Emmitsburg 21727; (301) 447-6606; www.setonshrine.org.

- St. Francis Xavier Shrine, "Old Bohemia," near Warwick (1704), located in Wilmington, Del., Diocese; restoration under auspices of Old Bohemia Historical Society, Inc. Address: P.O. Box 61, Warwick 21912.

Massachusetts
- National Shrine of Our Lady of La Salette, Ipswich (1945); Missionaries of Our Lady of La Salette. Address: 251 Topsfield Rd., Ipswich 01938.

- Our Lady of Fatima Shrine, Holliston (1950); Xaverian Missionaries. Address: 101 Summer St., Holliston 01746; (508) 429-2144.

- St. Anthony Shrine, Boston (1947); downtown Service Church with shrine; Boston Archdiocese and Franciscans of Holy Name Province. Address: 100 Arch St., Boston 02107.

- Saint Clement's Eucharistic Shrine, Boston (1945); Boston Archdiocese, staffed by Oblates of the Virgin Mary. Address: 1105 Boylston St., Boston 02215.

- National Shrine of The Divine Mercy, Stockbridge (1960); Congregation of Marians. Address: National Shrine of The Divine Mercy, Eden Hill, Stockbridge 01262.

Michigan
- Cross in the Woods-Parish, Indian River (1947); Gaylord diocese; staffed by Franciscan Friars of Sacred Heart Province, St. Louis. Address: 7078 M-68, Indian River 49749; (231) 238-8973; www.rc.net/gaylord/crossinwoods.

- Shrine of the Little Flower, Royal Oak (c. 1929, by Father Coughlin); Detroit archdiocese. Address: 2123 Roseland, Royal Oak 48073.

Missouri

- Memorial Shrine of St. Rose Philippine Duchesne, St. Charles; Religious of the Sacred Heart of Jesus. Address: 619 N. Second St., St. Charles 63301; (314) 946-6127.

- National Shrine of Our Lady of the Miraculous Medal, Perryville; located in St. Mary of the Barrens Church (1837); Vincentians. Address: 1811 W. St. Joseph St., Perryville 63775; (573) 547-8343; www.amm.org.

- Old St. Ferdinand's Shrine, Florissant (1819, Sacred Heart Convent; 1821, St. Ferdinand's Church); Friends of Old St. Ferdinand's, Inc. Address: No. 1 Rue St. Francois, Florissant 63031.

- Shrine of Our Lady of Sorrows, Starkenburg (1888; shrine building, 1910); Jefferson City Diocese. Address: c/o Church of the Risen Savior, 605 Bluff St., Rhineland 65069; (573) 236-4390.

Nebraska

- The Eucharistic Shrine of Christ the King (1973); Lincoln diocese and Holy Spirit Adoration Sisters. Address: 1040 South Cotner Blvd., Lincoln 68510; (402) 489-0765.

New Hampshire

- Shrine of Our Lady of Grace, Colebrook (1948); Missionary Oblates of Mary Immaculate. Address: R.R. 1, Box 521, Colebrook 03576-9535; (603) 237-5511.

- Shrine of Our Lady of La Salette, Enfield (1951); Missionaries of Our Lady of La Salette. Address: Rt. 4A, P.O. Box 420, Enfield 03748.

New Jersey

- Blue Army Shrine of the Immaculate Heart of Mary (1978); National Center of the Blue Army of Our Lady of Fatima, USA, Inc. Address: Mountain View Rd. (P.O. Box 976), Washington 07882-0976; (908) 689-1701; www.bluearmy.com

- Shrine of St. Joseph, Stirling (1924); Missionary Servants of the Most Holy Trinity. Address: 1050 Long Hill Rd., Stirling 07980; (908) 647-0208; www.STShrine.org

New Mexico

- St. Augustine Mission, Isleta (1613);

Santa Fe Archdiocese. Address: P.O. Box 463, Isleta, Pueblo 87022.

- Santuario de Nuestro Senor de Esquipulas, Chimayo (1816); Santa Fe archdiocese, Sons of the Holy Family; National Historic Landmark, 1970. Address: Santuario de Chimayo, P.O. Box 235; Chimayo 87522.

New York

- National Shrine of Blessed Kateri Tekakwitha, Fonda (1938); Order of Friars Minor Conventual. Address: P.O. Box 627, Fonda 12068.

- Marian Shrine (National Shrine of Mary Help of Christians), West Haverstraw (1953); Salesians of St. John Bosco. Address: 174 Filors Lane, Stony Point, NY 10980-2645; (845) 947-2200;www.MarianShrine.org.

- National Shrine Basilica of Our Lady of Fatima, Youngstown (1954); Barnabite Fathers. Address: 1023 Swann Rd., Youngstown 14174; (716) 754-7489. Designated a national shrine in 1994.

- Original Shrine of St. Ann in New York City (1892); located in St. Jean Baptiste Church; Blessed Sacrament Fathers. Address: 184 E. 76th St., New York 10021; (212) 288-5082.

- Our Lady of Victory National Shrine, Lackawanna (1926); Minor Basilica. Address: 767 Ridge Rd., Lackawanna 14218.

- Shrine Church of Our Lady of Mt. Carmel, Brooklyn (1887); Brooklyn Diocese (Parish Church). Address: 275 N. 8th St., Brooklyn 11211; (718) 384-0223.

- Shrine of Our Lady of Martyrs, Auriesville (1885); Society of Jesus. Address: Auriesville 12016; (518) 853-3033; www.klink.net/~jesuit.

- Shrine of Our Lady of the Island, Eastport (1975); Montfort Missionaries. Address: Box 26, Eastport, N.Y., 11941; (516) 325-0661.

- Shrine of St. Elizabeth Ann Seton, New York City (1975); located in Our Lady of the Rosary Church. Address: 7 State St., New York 10004.

- Shrine of St. Frances Xavier Cabrini, New York (1938; new shrine dedicated 1960); Missionary Sisters of the Sacred Heart. Address: 701 Fort Washington Ave., New York 10040; (212) 923-3536; www.cabrinishrineny.org

Ohio

- Basilica and National Shrine of Our Lady of Consolation, Carey (1867);

Minor Basilica; Toledo Diocese; staffed by Conventual Franciscan Friars. Address: 315 Clay St., Carey 43316; (419) 396-7107.

- National Shrine of Our Lady of Lebanon, North Jackson (1965); Eparchy of Our Lady of Lebanon of Los Angeles. Address: 2759 N. Lipkey Rd., N. Jackson 44451; (330) 538-3351; www.nationalshrine.org.

- National Shrine and Grotto of Our Lady of Lourdes, Euclid (1926); Sisters of the Most Holy Trinity. Address: 21281 Chardon Rd., Euclid 44117-2112; (216) 481-8232.

- Our Lady of Czestochowa Shrine, Garfield Heights (1939); Sisters of St. Joseph, Third Order of St. Francis. Address: 12215 Granger Rd., Garfield Hts. 44125; (216) 581-3535.

- Our Lady of Fatima, Ironton (1954); Old Rt. 52, Haverhill, Ohio. Mailing address: St. Joseph Church, P.O. Box 499, Ironton 45638-0499; (740) 429-2144.

- St. Anthony Shrine, Cincinnati (1888); Franciscan Friars, St. John Baptist Province. Address: 5000 Colerain Ave., Cincinnati 45223.

- Shrine and Oratory of the Weeping Madonna of Mariapoch, Burton (1956); Social Mission Sisters. Parma Diocese (Byzantine). Address: 17486 Mumford Rd., Burton 44021.

- Shrine of the Holy Relics (1892); Sisters of the Precious Blood. Address: 2291 St. Johns Rd., Maria Stein 45860; (419) 925-4532.

- Sorrowful Mother Shrine, Bellevue (1850); Society of the Precious Blood. Address: 4106 State Rt. 269, Bellevue 44811; (419) 483-3435.

Oklahoma
- National Shrine of the Infant Jesus of Prague, Prague (1949); Oklahoma City Archdiocese. Address: P.O. Box 488, Prague 74864.

Oregon
- The Grotto (National Sanctuary of Our Sorrowful Mother), Portland (1924); Servite Friars. Address: P.O. Box 20008, Portland 97294; www.thegrotto.com.

Pennsylvania
- Basilica of the Sacred Heart of Jesus, Conewago Township (1741; present church, 1787); Minor Basilica; Harrisburg Diocese. Address: 30 Basilica Dr., Hanover 17331.

- National Shrine Center of Our Lady of Guadalupe, Allentown (1974); located in Immaculate Conception Church; Allentown Diocese. Address: 501 Ridge Ave., Allentown 18102; (610) 433-4404.

- National Shrine of Our Lady of Czestochowa (1955); Order of St. Paul the Hermit (Pauline Fathers). Address: P.O. Box 2049, Doylestown 18901.

- National Shrine of St. John Neumann, Philadelphia (1860); Redemptorist Fathers, St. Peter's Church. Address: 1019 N. 5th St., Philadelphia 19123.

- National Shrine of the Sacred Heart, Harleigh (1975); Scranton Diocese. Address: P.O. Box 500, Harleigh (Hazleton) 18225; (570) 455-1162.

- Old St. Joseph's National Shrine, Philadelphia (1733); Philadelphia Archdiocese (Parish Church). Address: 321 Willings Alley, Philadelphia 19106; (215) 923-1733; www.oldstjoseph.org.

- St. Ann's Basilica Shrine, Scranton (1902); Passionist Community. Designated a minor basilica Aug. 29, 1996. Address: 1230 St. Ann's St., Scranton 18504; (570) 347-5691.

- St. Anthony's Chapel, Pittsburgh (1883); Pittsburgh Diocese. Address: 1700 Harpster St., Pittsburgh 15212.

- Shrine of St. Walburga, Greensburg (1974); Sisters of St. Benedict. Address: 1001 Harvey Ave., Greensburg 15601; (724) 834-3060.

Texas

- National Shrine of Our Lady of San Juan Del Valle, San Juan (1949); Brownsville Diocese; staffed by Oblates of Mary Immaculate. Mailing address: P.O. Box 747, San Juan 78589; (956) 787-0033.

Vermont

- St. Anne's Shrine, Isle La Motte (1666); Burlington Diocese, conducted by Edmundites. Address: West Shore Rd., Isle La Motte 05463; (802) 928-3362.

Wisconsin

- Holy Hill — National Shrine of Mary, Help of Christians (1857); Discalced Carmelite Friars. Address: 1525 Carmel Rd., Hubertus 53033.

- National Shrine of St. Joseph, De Pere (1889); Norbertine Fathers. Address: 1016 N. Broadway, De Pere 54115.

- Shrine of Mary, Mother Thrice Admirable Queen and Victress of Schoenstatt (1965), Address: W284 N698 Cherry Lane, Waukesha 53188-9402; (414) 547-7733.

(**PRINCIPAL SOURCE**: CATHOLIC ALMANAC SURVEY.)

Appendix C

⟨⟨⟨⟩⟩⟩

Emblems of the Saints

Animate and inanimate objects are often connected with the saints, especially in their iconography.

Some of the more popular ones include:

St. Acatius: Bearded, on a cross, wearing crown of thorns or roses

St. Agatha: Tongs, veil, shears, pincers, palm, plate with breast

St. Agnes: Lamb, olive, palm

St. Ann: With small girl

St. Augustine: Dove, shell, bishop's crozier

St. Ambrose: Beehive, dove, ox, pen, scourge, as bishop, book in hand, knotted scourge

St. Andrew: Saltire (or X-shaped) cross, fish

St. Angela Merici: Ladder, cloak

St. Anne, Mother of the Blessed Virgin: Door

St. Anthony, Hermit: Bell, hog, Egyptian cross

St. Anthony of Padua: Infant Jesus, bread, book, lily, flame of fire, mule kneeling, flowering branch, heart

St. Apollonia: Tooth, pincers, shears

St. Augustine of Hippo: Flaming heart pierced by arrow, as bishop, book in hand, books at feet, dove, shell, child, pen

St. Barbara: Cannon, chalice with wafer, palm, tower, feather, sword, crown with plumes

St. Barnabas: Ax, lance, stones

St. Bartholomew: Curved knife, flayed skin

St. Benedict: Bell, broken cup, bush, crozier, raven

St. Bernard of Clairvaux: Pen, bees, instruments of the Passion

St. Bernardine of Siena: Tablet or sun inscribed with IHS

St. Blaise: Iron comb, two crossed candles

St. Bonaventure: Communion, cardinal's hat, ciborium, red staff

St. Boniface: Ax, book, fox, fountain, oak, raven, scourge, sword

St. Brigid of Kildare: Cross, candle, flame over head

St. Brigid of Sweden: Book, pilgrim's staff

St. Bruno: Chalice

St. Catherine of Alexandria: Lamb, sword, wheel, crown, apple, pear, pomegranate, book, palm

St. Catherine of Ricci: Crown, crucifix, ring

St. Catherine of Siena: Crucifix, lily, ring, stigmata, crown of thorns, jeweled scepter

St. Cecilia: Organ, musical instruments, cauldron, roses, palm, attending angel, crown

St. Charles Borromeo: Communion, coat of arms with sword

St. Christina: Arrows

St. Christopher: Staff, with Christ Child, as giant, torrent, tree

St. Clare: Monstrance

St. Colette: Birds, lamb

Sts. Cosmas and Damian: Box of ointment, vial, lancet, mortar and pestle

St. Cyril of Alexandria: Blessed Virgin holding the Child Jesus, pen

St. Cyril of Jerusalem: Book, purse

St. Dominic: Rosary, star, lily

St. Dorothy: Flowers, fruit

St. Edmund the Martyr: Arrow, sword

St. Elias: Staff, raven

St. Elizabeth of Hungary: Bread, red and white roses, crown, with beggar, flowers, pitcher, alms

St. Eustace: Roman soldier, stag with crucifix between its antlers, oven

St. Ferdinand, King: crown, pennant, flowering staff

St. Flora: Dress with crossed sash, wound on neck

St. Francis of Assisi: Birds, deer, fish, skull, stigmata, wolf, lily, lamb, crucifix

St. Francis Xavier: Bell, crucifix, ship, flame, lily

St. Gabriel Archangel: monstrance, trumpet, chalice, lily, palm, crowned

St. Genevieve: Bread, candle, herd, keys, breviary, demon with bellows

St. George: Dragon, shield, emblem of order of the garter, on white horse

St. Gertrude: Crown, lily, taper, heart circled with thorns

Sts. Gervase and Protase: Club, scourge, sword

St. Giles: Crozier, hermitage, doe

St. Gregory I the Great: Crozier with double or triple cross, dove by head, papal tiara

St. Helena: Cross

St. Hilary: Child, pen, stick

St. Hubert: Stag with the crucifix

St. Ignatius of Loyola: Communion, chasuble, book, apparition of Our Lord, plaque marked I.H.S.

St. Isidore: Bees, pen, broad-brimmed hat, plow with two oxen

St. James the Greater: Sword, pilgrim's staff, shell, key

St. James the Less: Halberd, fuller's club, square rule

St. Jerome: Lion, skull, raven, cardinal's hat, church in hand, book and pen, with angel dictating, as a penitent

St. Joan of Arc: Armor, banner of France, fleur-de-lis

St. John the Baptist: Head on platter, lamb, skin of animal, shepherd's crook

St. John the Evangelist: Chalice with snake, eagle, eagle crowned with stars, kettle, armor, cauldron

St. John of Berchmans: Rule of St. Ignatius, cross, rosary

St. John Chrysostom: Bees, dove, pen

St. John Climacus: Ladder

St. John Nepomucene: In cassock, cross and palm

St. John of God: Alms, crown of thorns, heart

St. Josaphat: Chalice, crown, winged deacon

St. Joseph, Spouse of the Virgin Mary: Infant Jesus, lily, rod, plane, carpenter's square, yellow clothes, flowering staff

St. Jude: Sword, lance, halberd, club

St. Julian: Hart

St. Justin Martyr: Ax, sword

St. Justina: Unicorn

St. Lawrence: Book of Gospels, cross, gridiron, dalmatic, coins, palm

St. Leander: Pen

St. Liberata: Shown as crucified and bearded female. (legendary)

St. Liberius: Pebbles, peacock

St. Longinus: Lance

St. Louis IX of France: Crown of thorns, nails, crusader's cross, fleur-de-lis

St. Lucy: Cord, eyes on salver, lantern, crown, poniard, palm, wound in throat

St. Luke: Ox, book, brush, palette

St. Margaret: Dragon, pearl, cross, palm, daisy

St. Margaret of Cortona: Carries cross and handkerchief

St. Mark: Winged lion, book and pen

St. Martha: Dragon, holy water jar

St. Martin of Tours: Cloak shared with beggar, goose, on horseback

St. Mary Magdalene: Alabaster box of ointment, cross, skull, scourge, crown of thorns

St. Mary Magdalene dei' Pazzi: Stigmata

St. Matilda: Alms, purse

St. Matthew: Lance, purse, winged man (cherub)

St. Matthias (Apostle): Ax, open Bible, lance

St. Matthias: Lance

St. Maurus: Crutch, scales, spade

St. Meinrad: Two ravens

St. Michael the Archangel: Banner, dragon, scales, sword, in armor, crowned

St. Monica: Girdle, tears

St. Nicholas: Anchor, as bishop, three children, ship, three purses or balls

St. Pantaleon: Olive

St. Paschal Baylon: Holding a monstrance, surrounded by sheep

St. Patrick: Shamrock, baptismal font, cross, harp, serpent

St. Paul: Two swords, fish, book, scroll

St. Peter: Inverted cross, keys, boat, cock, fish, yellow clothes

St. Peter Claver: Bell, vessel, black slave

St. Peter Nolasco: Angel puts book on head

St. Philip: Column, serpent, three loaves of bread, Egyptian cross, crosier ending in a cross

St. Philip Neri: Altar, chasuble, vial, dove, rosary, book

St. Philip of Jesus: Two crossed lances

St. Procopius: Deer

St. Raymond Nonnatus: Holds monstrance and stick with three crowns

St. Raphael: Pilgrim's garb, staff with gourd, fish.

St. Reparata: Banne

St. Rita: Crucifix and skull, rose, thorn on forehead

St. Roch (Rocco): Angel, bread, dog

St. Rose of Lima: Anchor, city, crown of thorns, roses

St. Rose of Viterbo: Wears crown of thorns, carries basket and staff or cross

St. Rose of Palermo: Wears crown of roses; cross and skull, book, scourge.

St. Scholastica: Lily, crucifix, dove at her feet

St. Sebastian: Arrows, crown

Sts. Sergius and Bacchus: Military uniform, palm

St. Simon (Apostle): Saw, book with fish, cross

St. Simon Stock: Scapular

St. Stephen: Dalmatic, stones, palm, Gospel

St. Sylvester: Dragon

St. Teresa of Ávila: Arrow, book, heart, banner with I.H.S.

St. Theodore: Crocodile

St. Thérèse of Lisieux: Roses entwining a crucifix

St. Thomas (Apostle): Lance, ax, carpenter's square

St. Thomas Aquinas: Chalice, monstrance, dove, ox, person trampled underfoot, sun

St. Thomas à Becket: Altar and long swords

St. Ursula: Arrow, clock, ship, white banner with red cross, staff, crown, dove

St. Veronica: Veil with imprint of Christ's face and the crown of thorns

St. Vincent: Boat, gridiron

St. Vincent de Paul: Children

St. Vincent Ferrer: Captives, cardinal's hat, pupil, trumpet, rosary around neck, skull in background

Appendix D

Sacred Symbols

Alpha and Omega • First and last letters of the Greek alphabet; Christ as beginning and end of all.

Anchor • Symbol of hope from earliest Christian times (Hebrews 6:19). An anchor was frequently used in the catacombs and sometimes associated with another common symbol, the fish. Although the cross was not used in early Christian art, the cross-piece and shaft of the anchor were sometimes drawn in such a way as to suggest a cross.

Butterfly • A symbol of Christ's resurrection.

Candle • Symbol for Christ, the light of the world.

Chalice and cross • Symbol for the Eucharist.

Chi Rho • First two letters of the Greek word for Christ.

Chi Rho anchor • Christ our hope.

Chi Rho with Alpha and Omega • Christ, the beginning and the end.

Cross • Premier symbol of Christianity.

Cross and orb • Symbolizes the worldwide spread of the Gospel; mission of the Church.

Cross and shroud • Symbolizes the descent from the cross. Often a ladder is shown leaning against the cross.

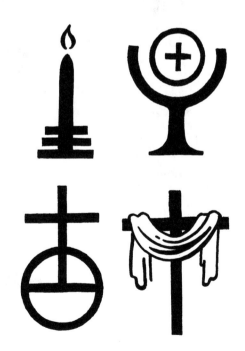

clockwise from top left: Candle; Chalice and Cross; Cross with Orb; Cross with Shroud

Cross with rising sun • Easter and Christ's victory.

Crown • Symbol used by Church for victory and sovereignty.

Crown and Cross • Symbol for Christ the King; victory over death.

Crown of thorns and nails • Symbol of Lent; three nails symbolize the Trinity; sometimes the sacred monogram is added.

Descending dove • Represents the Holy Spirit.

Didukh • Sheaf of water or grain used as Christmas symbol in Russia.

clockwise from top left: Cross with Rising Sun; Crown of Thorns and Nails; Heart with Flames; Evangelists

Dove • Ancient symbol of Holy Spirit based on Luke's account of Christ's baptism (3:21-22).

Equalateral triangle • Trinity.

Evangelists • Matthew — winged man; Mark — winged lion; Luke — winged ox; John — eagle.

Eye of God • Symbol of God's power to see all.

Fish • Symbol for Christ as savior; a rebus using the Greek words "Jesus Christ God Son Savior."

Hand of God • Symbol for God's blessings.

Heart with flames, crown of thorns and cross • Sacred Heart of Jesus.

Holy Name of Jesus • Devotion apparently begun in the eleventh century although invoking the name as a means of dispelling demons had been popular since early Christian times. A meditation of St. Anselm (1033-1109) in which he dwells upon the name itself was important in the development of this devotion. The custom of bowing the head on hearing the name was established before the thirteenth century and was commanded by a decree of the Second Council of Lyons in 1274. The Franciscan Guibert of Tournai (c. 1200-1284) wrote a treatise on the Holy Name, and the Franciscans and Dominicans were active in spreading the devotion.

Icon • Sacred art based more on symbolism than reality; example: three-handed

Mother of God is symbolic of favor granted to St. John of Damascus.

IHC • The abbreviation for the Greek word for Jesus.

INRI • The abbreviation for the Latin words which mean "Jesus of Nazareth, King of the Jews." It was placed on Christ's cross.

J.H.V.H. • Hebrew for Jehovah; Lord.

J.M.J. • Jesus, Mary, and Joseph.

Lamb of God • Symbol of sacrificial role of Christ.

Lily • Purity.

Messianic rose • Based on Isaiah; symbol for the advent of God in Jesus Christ.

"M" surmounted with a cross surrounded with stars • Mary.

clockwise from top left Crown and Palm; Rainbow; Three Crowns; Three Interlocking Circles

clockwise from top: J.M.S.; Lamb of God; Lily; Messianic Rose; "M" with Stars

Palm; crown and palm • Symbol of martyrdom.

Phoenix and flame • Symbol for the Resurrection — out of the ashes of death, Christ arose.

Rainbow • Symbolizes God keeping his covenants.

Seven fold flame • Pentecost; seven gifts of the Holy Spirit.

Shamrock • The Trinity.

Ship • Symbol for the Church.

Star • Symbol of the Epiphany.

Three crowns • The magi.

Three interlocking circles • Trinity.

Triquetra • Trinity symbol representing equality, indivisibility, and eternality.

Selected Bibliography

Abbot, Walter M., S.J., ed. *The Documents of Vatican II: Constitution on the Sacred Liturgy,* "Sacred Music." New York: Herder and Herder Association Press, 1966.

Apel, Willi. *Gregorian Chant.* Bloomington, Ind.: Indiana University Press, 1958.

Awalt, Barbe, and Paul Rhetts. *Our Saints Among Us: Four Hundred Years of New Mexican Devotional Art.* Albuquerque, N.M.: LPD Press, 1998.

Baker, Kenneth. "Preaching about Purgatory Today." *Homiletic and Pastoral Review,* 93:5.Translated editorial in *Civilta Cattolica.* February 1993.

Ball, Ann. *A Handbook of Catholic Sacramentals.* Huntington, Ind.: Our Sunday Visitor Publishing, 1991.

———. *A Litany of Mary.* Huntington, Ind.: Our Sunday Visitor Publishing, 1988.

———. *A Litany of Saints.* Huntington, Ind.: Our Sunday Visitor Publishing, 1993.

———. *Catholic Book of the Dead.* Huntington, Ind.: Our Sunday Visitor Publishing, 1995.

———. *Catholic Traditions in Cooking.* Huntington, Ind.: Our Sunday Visitor Publishing, 1993.

———. *Catholic Traditions in Crafts.* Huntington, Ind.: Our Sunday Visitor Publishing, 1997.

———. *Catholic Traditions in the Garden.* Huntington, Ind.: Our Sunday Visitor Publishing, 1998.

———. *Holy Names of Jesus.* Huntington, Ind.: Our Sunday Visitor Publishing, 1990.

Bastian, R.J. "Poor Souls." *New Catholic Encyclopedia.* vol. 11. New York: McGraw-Hill Book Co., 1967.

———. "Purgatory." *New Catholic Encyclopedia.* vol. 11. New York: McGraw-Hill Book Co., 1967.

Benedictines of Solesmes, ed. *The Liber Usualis.* Boston: McLaughlin and Reilly Co.,1950.

Bernard of Clairvaux. *Sermo.* no. 2.

Blaher, Father Damian, O.F.M. *The Little Flowers of St. Francis.* New York: E.P. Dutton and Co., 1951.

Bogle, Joanna. *A Book of Feasts and Seasons.* Leominster: Gracewing, 1992.

Bouyer, Louis. *Rite and Man.* Notre Dame, Ind.: University of Notre Dame Press, 1963.

Brett, Laurence F.X. *Redeemed Creation: Sacramentals Today.* Wilmington: Michael Glazier, 1984.

Bryan, David Burton. *A Western Way of Meditation: The Rosary Revisited.* Chicago: Loyola University Press, 1991.

Bunson, Matthew, ed. *Our Sunday Visitor's Catholic Almanac.* Huntington, Ind.: Our Sunday Visitor Publishing, 1999.

Bunson, Matthew, Margaret Bunson, and Stephen Bunson. *John Paul II's Book of Saints.* Huntington, Ind.: Our Sunday Visitor Publishing, 1999.

——— *Our Sunday Visitor's Encyclopedia of Saints.* Huntington, Ind.: Our Sunday Visitor Publishing, 1998.

Carola, Leslie Conton. *The Irish.* New York: Macmillan, 1993.

Catechism of the Catholic Church, Second Edition. nos. 946-962, 1459, 953, 2634-2636.

Catholic Word Book. New Haven: Knights of Columbus, 1973.

Civilta Cattolica. "Preaching about Purgatory Today." 15.

Code of Canon Law (1983). canona 1167:1; 1168.

Congregation for the Doctrine of the Faith. *Recentiores episcoporum Synodi.* nos. 4, 7. 1979.

Council of Trent. 1563. DS 1821, DS 1304, DS 1820.

Cruz, Joan Carroll. *Miraculous Images of Our Lady.* Rockford, Ill., TAN Books, 1993.

——— *Prayers and Heavenly Promises.* Rockford, Ill., TAN Books, 1989.

——— *Relics.* Huntington, Ind.: Our Sunday Visitor, 1984.

——— *The Incorruptibles.* Rockford, Ill., TAN Books, 1977.

Cummings, Patrick. *Life Everlasting.* Translated by Reginald Garrigou-Lagrange. New York: Herder, 1952.

De Breffny, Brian. *In the Steps of St. Patrick.* London: Thames and Hudson, 1982.

Dubruiel, Michael. *Mention Your Request Here: The Church's Most Powerful Novenas.* Huntington, Ind.: Our Sunday Visitor Publishing, 2000.

Eckel, Frederick L. *A Concise Dictionary of Ecclesiastical Terms.* New York: Abingdon Press, 1960.

Eucharistic Prayer I.

Eucharistic Prayer II.

Eucharistic Prayer III.

Eucharistic Prayer IV.

Evano, Jean. *"Blessings and Popular Religion." The Church at Prayer. Vol. 3. The Sacraments.* Edited by A.G. Martimort. Collegeville: The Liturgical Press, 1987.

Family Life Bureau. *Customs and Traditions of the Catholic Family.* Long Prairie, Minn.: The Neumann Press, 1994.

Fink, Peter E., ed. *The New Dictionary of Sacramental Worship.* Collegeville: The Liturgical Press, 1990.

Forsyth, Charlotte E. and Grace B. Branham. *The Last Things.* Translation Romano Guardini. New York: Pantheon Books, 1954.

Fortman, Edmund J. *Everlasting Life Towards a Theology of the Future Life.* New York: Alba House, 1986.

Freeze, Michael, S.F.O. *Patron Saints.* Huntington, Ind.: Our Sunday Visitor, 1992.

Giffords, Gloria Frasier. *The Art of Private Devotion: Retablo Painting of Mexico.* Essays by Yvonne Lange, Virginia Armella de Aspe, and Mercedes Meade. Austin, Texas: InterCultura, 1991.

Gilligan, W. Doyle. *Devotion to the Holy Spirit.* Houston: Lumen Christi Press, 1998.

Grierson, Roderick, ed. *Gates of Mystery: The Art of Holy Russia.* Ft. Worth, Texas: InterCultura, 1995.

Handbook of Indulgences: Norms and Grants. New York: Catholic Book Publishing Co., 1991.

Hayes, Zachary. *Visions of a Future: A Study of Christian Eschatology.* Wilmington: Michael Glazier, 1989.

Howard, Thomas. *Evangelical Is Not Enough.* San Francisco: Ignatius Press, 1984.

Hughes, Serge. *Purgation and Purgatory, The Spiritual Dialogue.* Translated St. Catherine of Genoa. New York: Paulist Press, 1979.

International Committee on English in the Liturgy. *The Roman Ritual: Book of Blessings.* New York: Catholic Book Publishing Co., 1989.

International Theological Commission "*De quibus quaestionibus actualibus circa eschatologiam.*" 1990. no. 8. *Gregorianum,* 73:3. 1992.

Jelly, Frederick, O.P. *Madonna: Mary in Catholic Tradition.* Huntington, Ind.: Our Sunday Visitor, 1986.

Johnson, Kevin Orlin. *The Rosary.* Dallas: Pangaeus Press, 1997.

Joyce, Timothy. *Celtic Christianity.* New York: Orbis Books, 1998.

Kern, Rev. Walter. *Updated Devotion to the Sacred Heart.* Canfield, Ohio: Alba House Communications, 1975.

Klinger, Elmar. "Purgatory." *Sacramentum Mundi.* vol. 5.Edited by Karl Rahner. New York: Herder and Herder, 1970.

Kreeft, Peter. *Fundamentals of the Faith: Essays in Christian Apologetics.* San Francisco: Ignatius Press, 1988.

Lasance, Rev. F.E. *My Prayer Book: Happiness in Goodness.* New York: Benzinger Brothers, 1938.

Maloney, George A. *The Everlasting Now.* Notre Dame, Ind.: Ave Maria Press, 1980.

Meally; Victor, ed. *Encyclopedia of Ireland.* Dublin: Allen Figgis, 1968.

Molinari, Paolo. "Saints, Intercession of." *New Catholic Encyclopedia.* vol. 12. New York: McGraw-Hill Publishing Co., 1967.

National Conference of Catholic Bishops. *Behold Your Mother: Woman of Faith.* no. 84. 1973 pastoral letter.

A New Catechism. New York: Seabury, 1971.

Nicholson, Eric. *Sin and Fear: The Emergence of a Western Guilt Culture, 13th-18th Centuries.* Translation of Jean Delumeau. *Le peche et la peur.* New York: St. Martin's Press, 1990.

O'Connell, Rev. John P. *The Prayer Book.* Chicago: The Catholic Press, 1954.

O'Donoghue, Rev. Noel Dermot. *Patrick of Ireland.* Wilmington: Michael Glazier, 1987.

Order of Christian Funerals. no. 6.

Osende, Victorino, O.P. *Pathways to Love.* St. Louis, Mo: B. Herder Book Co.,1958.

The Passion of Perpetua and Felicitas. Cited in *The Birth of Purgatory.* Le Goff. 49.

Phan, Peter C. *Eternity in Time.* Cranbury, N.J.: Associated University Press, 1988.

Pope Paul VI. *Indulgentiarum Doctrina.* (Apostolic Constitution on the Revision of Indulgences). nos. 2-3, 4. 1967.

———— *Marialis Cultus.* (Apostolic Exhortation for the Right Ordering and Development of Devotion to the Blessed Virgin Mary.) nos. 29-38. February 1974.

———— *Marialis Cultus.* (Apostolic Exhortation for the Right Ordering and Development of Devotion to the Blessed Virgin Mary.) February 1974. In *Cross and Crown Series of Spirituality.* vol. 12.

———— *Mysterii paschalis celebrationem.* (Apostolic letter.)February 14, 1969.

———— *Inter Plurimas Pastoralis* November 22, 1903.

Quinn, J.R. "Sacramentals." *New Catholic Encyclopedia.* vol. 12. New York: McGraw-Hill Publishing Co., 1967.

Quintiliani, Patricia. *My Treasury of Chaplets.* Worcester, Mass.: Patricia Quintiliani, 1995.

The Raccolta. Boston: Benziger Brothers Inc., 1943.

Rahner, Karl, and Johann B. Metz. "Prayer to the Saints." *The Courage to Pray.* New York: Crossroad, 1981.

Roccasalvo, Joan L. *The Eastern Catholic Churches.* Collegeville, Minn.: Liturgical Press, 1992.

Sacrosanctum Concilium. nos. 13, 60-62, 79.

St. Augustine. *Sermon.* 104: PL 39, 1947.

St. Augustine. *Confessions.* Book 9.11, 9:13.

St. Cyril of Jerusalem. *Catechetical Lectures.* 23.9-10.

St. Thomas Aquinas. *Summa Theologiae III.* q 86, a 5;III, q 26, a 1c.

Shaw, J.G. *The Story of the Rosary.* Milwaukee: Bruce Publishing Co., 1954.

Sheed, F.J., trans. *The Confessions of St. Augustine.* New York:. Sheed and Ward, 1943.

Steele, Thomas J., S.J. *Santos and Saints: The Religious Folk Art of Hispanic New Mexico.* Santa Fe: Ancient City Press, 1992.

Stravinskas, Rev. Peter M.J., ed. *Our Sunday Visitor's Catholic Dictionary.* Huntington, Ind.: Our Sunday Visitor Publishing, 1991.

Stravinskas, Rev. Peter M.J., ed. *Our Sunday Visitor's Catholic Encyclopedia.* Huntington, Ind.: Our Sunday Visitor Publishing, 1991.

Vagaggini, Cyprian. *Theological Dimensions of the Liturgy.* Translated by Leonard J. Doyle and W.A. Jurgens. Collegeville, Minn.: The Liturgical Press, 1976.

Varghese, Roy Abraham. *God-Sent: A History of the Accredited Apparitions of Mary.* New York: Crossroad Publishing Co., 2000.

Vatican II. *Lumen Gentium.* nos. 10, 49-51, 60, 62.

von Balthasar, Hans Urs. *You Crown the Year with Your Goodness.* San Francisco: Ignatius Press, 1989.

Walsh, Michael. *Dictionary of Catholic Devotions.* San Francisco: Harper San Francisco, 1993.

Weigle, Marta. *The Penitentes of the Southwest.* Santa Fe: Ancient City Press, 1970.

Weiser, Francis X. *Handbook of Christian Feasts and Customs.* New York: Harcourt, Brace, and World, 1958.

———— *Religious Customs in the Family.* Rockford, Ill.: TAN Books, 1998.

———— *The Easter Book.* New York: Harcourt, Brace, and Co., 1954.

———— *The Holyday Book.* New York: Harcourt, Brace, and Co., 1956.

Woodward, Kenneth L. *Making Saints.* New York: Simon and Schuster, 1990.

Wright, J.H. "Dead, Prayers for the." *New Catholic Encyclopedia.* vol. 4. New York: McGraw-Hill Publishing Co., 1967.

Yzermans, Vincent A., ed. *All Things in Christ,* encyclicals and selected documents of Saint Pius X. Westminster, Md.: The Newman Press, 1954.

Index

◎‿‿◎

A

Aachen, 25, 641
Abbey of Cluny, 34
Abbey of Corvey, 601
Abbey of Monoppello, 636
Abbey of Shrewsbury, 602
Abbey of Subiaco, 521
Absolution, 140, 259
Abstinence, 26, 62, 187, 198, 214, 294,
    305, 376-377, 576
Abuse, 13, 82, 250, 322
Acheiropoietos, 530
Acolouthia, 26, 163
Acolyte, 62, 82
Act of Acceptance of Death, 27
Acta Sanctorum, 27-28, 89, 353
Acta, 27-28, 89, 353, 503
Acts of Pilate, 635
Acts of the Apostles, 590
Acts, 27-28, 55, 59, 89, 99, 118, 140,
    168, 176, 209, 233, 245, 257, 267,
    277, 361, 381, 389, 405, 428, 453,
    487, 527, 536, 539, 574, 586, 590,
    599, 607, 615, 618, 635
Ad Coeli Reginam, 469
Ad Limina Apostolorum, 28
Ad Primam, 457
Adam and Eve, 136, 210, 277, 288-289,
    536
Adieu, 643
Adonai, 28, 271, 401
Adonis, 611
Adoration, 11, 28-29, 39, 58, 124, 153,
    168, 190, 204-205, 213, 244-245,

248, 254, 323, 359, 361, 379-380,
408-409, 421, 430, 444, 473, 480,
496, 498, 501-502, 523, 551, 615,
685, 688
Adoremus, 323
Adorers of the Blood of Christ, 454
Adriatic, 438, 622
Adultery, 357
Advent calendar, 29, 99
Advent candle, 30, 209, 624
Advent play, 30, 230
Advent wreath, 30, 662
Advent, 29-30, 99, 104, 130, 133, 136,
    138, 163, 209, 230-231, 272, 289,
    320, 332, 366, 401, 425, 444, 455,
    485, 506, 584, 624, 653, 662, 699
Advocate of the blind, 440
Aegean, 622
Aeterna Christi Munera, 30
Africa, 31, 228, 347, 565, 661, 678-679
Agape, 31-32, 206, 501, 608
Agnus Dei, 32, 298
Agnus, 32, 298, 419-420
Agreda, 296-297
Agrellie, Fortuna, 394
AIDS, 230, 250, 592
Airplanes, 672
Akathist Hymn, 32
Akita, 342
Alabama, 187, 683
Alabanza, 33, 384
Alb, 38, 145, 535, 637-638
Albania, 192, 211
Albertini, Canon Francesco, 125

Albigensian heresy, 558

Alcohol, 651-653

Alcoholics Anonymous, 100

Alcuin, 659

Alexander Sfirzo, 157

Alexandria, 33, 77, 95, 149, 204, 503, 550, 555, 675, 694

Alexandrian Rite, 145, 484

Alfred the Great, 230

Alice of Holland, 226

All Hallows Eve, 226

All Healer, 358

All Saints, 33-34, 46, 102, 111, 138, 140, 226, 239, 309-311, 314, 316, 462, 467, 479, 606

All Souls, 33-34, 48, 92, 168, 216, 232, 242, 383, 445, 461-462, 480, 523, 578, 663

All Souls' Day, 33-34, 48, 92, 168, 242, 462, 663

Allegoria, 266

Alleluia, 34, 184, 203, 229, 231, 470, 475, 527, 635

Alms, 34, 307, 389, 443, 455, 467, 554-555, 562, 658, 694-695

Alpha and Omega, 35, 697

Alpine, 82, 104, 210, 558, 570, 576, 593

Alsace, 94, 657, 678

Altar linens, 36

Altar, 35-37, 46, 56, 73, 76, 93, 100-101, 104, 127, 148, 153-154, 169-170, 175, 200, 210, 212, 237, 245-247, 264, 273, 296, 303-304, 320, 322, 346, 351, 361, 383, 406, 408, 432-433, 451-452, 455, 476, 479-480, 507, 513, 515, 574, 579-580, 593, 602, 617, 620, 624, 646, 655, 677, 696

Altarcitos, 246

Altotting, 78

Ambras, 573

Ambrosian hymn, 616

Ambrosian Hymn, 616

Ambrosian Rite, 37

Ambrosian, 118, 217, 484

Amen, 27-28, 37, 41, 45-46, 67, 122, 125, 141, 143, 149-150, 158, 166, 172, 177, 215-216, 225-226, 266, 288, 310-313, 315, 317, 328, 352, 357, 387-389, 391-394, 396-397, 402, 421, 445-449, 475, 480, 488, 500, 516-517, 522-524, 528, 603, 606, 615, 634-635, 645, 656

American Anglicans, 655

American Catholic Correctional Chaplain's Association, 563

Amice, 38, 637-638

Amiens, 38, 583

Amos, 39

Ampulae, 478

Amulet, 155, 558

An Paidrin Beag, 267

Anagogia, 266

Analecta Bollandiana, 90

Anathema, 38

Anawim, 38-39

Ancestor worship, 129

Anchor, 39, 152, 563, 695-697

Anchorite, 39, 232

Ancona, 438

Andachtsbilden, 234

Andriveau, Sister Apolline, 474

Angel Monday, 184

Angel of Death, 43-44, 176, 425

Angelic Choirs, 41

Angelic Warfare Confraternity, 146

Angelitos, Los, 168, 329

Angels of Death, 42-43, 164, 329, 366

Angels, 10, 39-46, 57-58, 60-61, 104,
120, 123, 134-135, 138, 140, 154,
164, 175, 177, 187, 192, 221, 256,
271, 303, 310-311, 314, 328-329,
366, 384, 409, 431, 438, 444, 446,
456, 475, 509, 514, 526, 575, 580,
585, 593, 616-617, 659, 673

Angels, our Lady of the, 44-45, 104, 187,
409

Angelus, 45, 76, 294, 475, 593, 685

Angers, 117

Anglican Church, 21, 133

Anglo-Catholic Party, 415

Anglo-Saxons, 102, 502

Anima Christi, 46

Anima Sola, 46-48, 168

Anitos, 115

Anjou, 250

Ann, 381, 387-388, 505, 549, 674, 686-
687, 689, 691, 693, 701

Anna, 308, 462-463, 531, 549

Annacata, 256

Annapolis, 342

Annointing of the Sick, 48-49

Annunciation bread, 49

Annunciation, 44, 48-49, 66-67, 99, 121,
205, 285, 296, 307, 328, 342-343,
397, 486, 523, 568, 644, 654

Anthonian orphanages, 554-555

Anthony's Well, 552

Anti-clerical, 278

Antioch, 50, 63, 95, 118, 143, 145, 158,
593, 678

Antiochene Rite, 484

Antiochene, 50, 484

Antiphon, 50, 61, 326, 337, 344, 401

Antipope Clement VII, 531

Antonio of Segovia, 509

Antwerp, 89, 234, 517, 564

Aparecida, Our Lady, 51, 409

Apocalyptic literature, 51

Apologia of St. Justin, 608

Apostatized, 502

Apostle spoon, 52

Apostle to the Gentiles, 590

Apostles, 28, 52, 60, 85, 117, 124, 138,
148, 158, 227, 243, 259, 284, 289,
300, 310-311, 373, 381, 389, 407,
412-413, 428, 444, 458, 468, 482-
483, 486, 522, 536, 557, 580-581,
590, 592, 616-617, 646, 659-660

Apostleship of Prayer, 52, 361, 497

Apostleship of the Sea, 53, 305

Apostolate of Prayerful, Careful, and
Reparative Driving, 497

Apostolate of Suffering, 52-53

Apostolate of the Sick, Pious Union of
the, 53, 440

Apostolate, 21, 53, 108-109, 163, 187,
204, 262, 264, 276, 304-305, 396,
407, 440, 497-498, 521, 525, 572,
592, 615

Apostolic blessing, 54, 259, 660

Apostolic Fathers, 563

Apostolic penitentiary, 15, 473

Apostolicam Actuositatem, 109

Appalachian Mountains, 231

Apparition, 54, 74, 146, 198-199, 220,
294-296, 303, 350, 394, 403, 443,
514, 525, 536, 538, 545, 641-643,
694

April, 113, 129, 211, 265, 273, 296, 304, 354, 359-360, 387, 433, 485, 532-533, 545, 566, 568-569, 610

Apulia, 587-588

Aquileia, 55

Aracoeli, Holy Child of, 56, 237

Aragon, 568

Aramaic, 26, 253, 543

Archangels, 40-42, 57, 431, 585

Archbishop of Mexico, 237

Archbishop of Zacatecas, 237

Archconfraternity (See Confraternity)

Archconfraternity of Christian Mothers, 57

Archconfraternity of Notre Dame du Suffrage, 487

Archconfraternity of St. Michael the Archangel, 520

Archconfraternity of the Holy Agony, 475

Archconfraternity of the Holy Face, 513

Archconfraternity of the Holy Ghost, 57

Archepiscopal cross, 153

Arequipa, 118-120

Argenteuil, 625

Argentina, 131, 287, 329, 332, 661, 679

Arian heresy, 149

Aristides of Athens, 451

Arma Christi, 168

Armenia, 83, 557, 676

Armenian Rite, 484

Arrevillaga, Rosario, 173

Artane Oratory of the Resurrection, 342

Artes Moriendi, 59

Arvel, 206

Ascension Thursday, 485

Ascension, 19, 42, 59-60, 99, 239, 366, 381, 389, 468, 485-486, 592, 659

Asceticism, 60, 557

Ash Wednesday, 26, 137, 187, 306, 337, 366, 534

Ashes, 60, 150, 171-172, 699

Asia Minor, 57, 436, 530, 586, 590, 593, 677

Asmodeus, 594

Asperges, 60, 450, 656

Aspergillum, 60

Aspiration, 61, 350, 424

Association of Holy Family Guilds, 197

Assumption, 49, 61-62, 82, 175-176, 192, 205, 239-240, 288, 293, 340, 342, 397, 412, 454, 486, 518, 523, 544, 660, 679, 686

Asterius, 599

Asylum, 116

Athanasius, 33, 77, 149, 314, 503

Atocha, Our Lady of, 62-65, 409

Atocha, Santo Nino De, 65

Atonement, 65-66, 121, 174, 213, 276, 316, 393, 450, 479

Atonement, Our Lady of, 65-66

Attila the Hun, 503

Augsburg, 102, 234, 288, 319, 348

August, 14, 61-62, 82, 118, 121, 288, 298, 304, 342, 359, 376, 387, 389, 412, 434, 469, 538, 544, 558, 562, 565, 570, 583, 622, 661

Augustinian Friars, 211

Augustinian rosary, 146

Augustinian, 75, 113, 115, 146, 211, 425, 431-433, 558, 594, 653

Ault, Henri, 131

Aureole, 226

Australia, 10, 229, 676, 678

Austria, 62, 88, 148, 213, 306, 485, 536,

569-570, 592, 600, 679
Authentics, 476
Auxiliaries of Our Lady of the Cenacle, 305
Avars, 33
Ave Maria — Hail Mary, 226
Ave Maria, 39, 66-67, 226, 568, 704
Ave Maris Stella, 67-68, 603
Averil, 206
Aves, 94
Avignon, 658

B

Baal, 662
Babushka, 456
Babylonian exile, 461
Bacca Lauri, 301
Baccalaureate, 301
Bacchanalian, 574
Bacchus, 191, 267, 696
Baconthorpe, John, 363
Baden, 572
Badge, 71, 267, 438, 497-498, 512, 514, 629, 658
Baker, Father Nelson, 640
Balbulus, Notker, 225
Baldachin, 629
Ball, Eldon, 19
Balliol College, 412
Balm, 104, 337, 406
Balsam, 406
Balthasar, 82, 335, 674, 706
Bambino, 56
Banyon tree, 303
Baptism of catechumens, 185, 429
Baptism, 34, 71-72, 76, 143, 146, 148, 150, 176-177, 185, 188, 198, 201,

304, 314, 344, 348, 354, 372, 375, 393, 419, 428-429, 446, 451, 478, 484, 486, 494, 496, 508, 540, 546, 655-656, 671, 698
Baptismal candles, 72
Barcelona, 360
Barnabite Fathers, 462, 689
Baroque Period, 478
Barrios Baez, Sister Josephine Carmen, 272
Basel, 339
Basil (the herb), 229-230, 355, 611
Basil, the Great, 33, 72, 145, 230, 314, 611, 674
Basilian, 88
Basilica of Our Lady of Lavang, 304
Basilica, 73
Basque, 552
Bataan Death March, 65
Bath, 564
Bathsheba, 357
Baton Rouge, 660
Batterham, Forster, 110
Battle of Lepanto, 73, 228, 307, 640
Battle of New Orleans, 460
Battle of Vienna, 228
Bavaria, 54, 60, 228, 592
Bay Laurel, 73, 301, 661
Bayside, 489
Beads of the Dead, 487
Beads, 13, 120-125, 127, 146, 156-157, 272, 274, 283, 317-318, 339, 483, 486-488, 499-500, 521, 545, 660-661
Beatification, 102, 159, 341, 406-407, 595
Beating of the bounds, 485

Beauduin, Dom Lambert, OSB, 320

Beaumont, Archbishop Francisco Lizana, 238

Beauraing, Our Lady of, 73-74, 409, 458, 679

Beco, Mariette, 71, 641-642

Bees of St. Rita, 74

Bees, 74-75, 100, 558, 693-695

Beeswax, 100

Befana, 75, 456

Behold Your Mother, 385, 505, 523, 704

Belgium, 67, 71, 88-89, 114, 226, 293, 309, 320, 517, 544, 564, 641, 677, 679

Belgrade, 622

Belleville, 538, 685

Bells, 76, 134, 167, 182, 249, 535, 550, 574, 593-594, 636

Benavides, Father Alonso, 293

Benedictine, 33, 111, 113, 186, 189, 230, 307, 351, 360, 419, 518, 596, 642-643

Benediction, 62, 76, 81, 83, 101, 142, 175, 190, 193, 204, 359, 387, 395, 402, 420-421, 447, 615, 620

Benedictus, The, 104, 326, 672

Benjaminite, 271

Benziger Brothers, 235, 705

Berdyaev, Nicholas, 112

Bergoglio, Archbishop Mario, 287-288

Bermuda, 184

Bernardino, Juan Diego, 219-220, 403

Bethlehem, 30, 136, 148, 188, 241, 271, 335, 436, 441, 456, 574, 576, 610

Bethsaida, 592

Betrothal rings, 483

Bezy, Father Gregory S.C.J., 497

Bible, 33, 41, 44, 59-60, 77, 197, 277, 336, 356, 373, 402, 469, 551, 635, 695

Biblical harmony, 77, 227

Biblical interpretation, 34, 77, 266

Biloxi, 84

Birthday of the Sun, 133

Bishop of Alexandria, 77, 149, 503, 550

Bishop of Rome, 300-301, 371

Bishop of Tours, 583-584

Bishop Ulrich of Augsburg, 319

Bisqueyburu, Sister Justine, 217

Black Fast, 77-78, 214

Black Madonna, the (Czestochowa), 79

Black Madonnas, 78, 360

Black Scapular (Passion), 79

Blessed Bartolo Longo, 441

Blessed bread, 92-93, 419-420, 580

Blessed candles, 80-81, 85, 495

Blessed dresses, 80-81

Blessed herb, 558

Blessed magnolia leaf, 81

Blessed roses, 81

Blessed Sacrament, 29, 76, 88, 142, 147, 164, 174-175, 187, 189-190, 193, 209, 213, 239-240, 244-245, 298, 318, 339, 361-362, 379-380, 387, 395, 402, 411, 479-480, 499-501, 521, 545, 551, 562, 615, 620, 646, 659, 662, 685, 689

Blessed Virgin, 41, 48, 56, 71, 80, 82, 89-90, 94, 125-126, 128, 138, 140-141, 175, 192, 204-205, 214, 242, 256, 258, 275, 309-310, 312, 317, 319, 329, 331-332, 342-343, 359, 363, 365, 383, 390, 396-397, 409, 423, 426, 432, 486, 493-494, 504,

512, 514, 516-517, 519-520, 522, 524, 543, 549, 561, 576, 578-579, 606, 619, 646, 657, 678, 686, 693-694, 705

Blessing before meals, 82

Blessing boat, 84

Blessing of animals, 82

Blessing of chalk and incense, 82

Blessing of Easter baskets (Sviachenia), 83

Blessing of grapes, 83

Blessing of herbs, 62

Blessing of horses, 83

Blessing of lambs, 184, 420

Blessing of roses, 81

Blessing of the shrimp fleet, 83-84

Blessing of the three kings, 82-83

Blessing of throats (St. Blaise), 92

Blessing of water, 34, 81, 185, 507, 655-657

Blessing yourself, 434

Blessing, 34, 49, 54, 56, 60, 62, 80-85, 90, 92, 101, 113, 137, 164-165, 181-182, 184-185, 192, 200, 211, 225, 243, 245, 256, 259, 263, 265, 299, 307, 332, 336, 347, 373, 377-378, 387, 397-398, 405, 407, 420-422, 426, 429-430, 434, 454, 463, 474, 484, 495, 500, 507, 512, 516, 535, 541, 559, 591, 593, 596, 615, 618, 622, 630, 639, 643, 655-657, 660, 662

Blessings for the cemetery, 85

Blinni, 337

Blood miracles, 86-88, 190

Blue Army, the, 89, 435, 688

Blue scapular (Immaculate Conception), 89, 513

Blum, Father Virgil, 305

Blumenfest, 429

Bogota, 130

Bohemia, 263, 600, 675, 678, 681, 687

Bolivia, 119, 679

Bolland, Rev. John, 90

Bollandist Delahaye, 28

Bollandists, 28, 89

Bologna, 378, 434, 675

Bolsena, 87

Bonaparte, Napoleon, 228

Bonfires, 572-573, 577

Book of Armagh, 329

Book of Blessings, 82, 85, 90, 137, 704

Book of Healing Herbs, 230

Book of Isaiah, 272

Book of Kildare, 559

Book of Revelation, 157, 273, 462

Books of Blessings, 90

Bosio, Antonio, 108

Bosnia-Herzegovina, 352, 439

Boston College, 236

Botanicals, 230-231

Botanicas, 48, 278

Botta, Antonio, 362

Bouffier, Louise, 554

Bourbonnais, 405

Bourges, 515, 551

Boveda, 167

Bowing the head, 241, 698

Bowing, 62, 90-91, 185, 241, 535, 698

Boxing Day, 91, 455

Boy bishop, 91, 199

Boy Scouts, 568, 676

Boyd, Charlotte Pearson, 654

Brandea, 91

Bread Father, 577

Bread, 35, 37, 49, 64, 78, 83, 87-88, 92-93, 111, 134, 170, 172, 181-182, 214, 248, 266, 289, 294, 298, 314, 328, 330, 407, 419-421, 425-426, 430, 434, 473, 501, 522, 535, 537, 541-542, 547, 553-555, 574, 577, 579-580, 588, 591, 611, 623, 638, 657, 693-694, 696

Bread, Signing of, 93, 535

Bread, St. Anthony's, 93, 552-555

Bread, St. Joseph's, 93, 580

Bread, St. Nicholas's, 93, 587-588

Breast plate, 329, 693

Brenham, 127

Breviarium, 588

Breviary, 66-67, 93, 190, 319, 323, 325, 602, 694

Brezel, 457

Bridal cincture, 93

Bride, 114, 390, 483, 546, 559-560, 619, 659

Bridge chapels, 658

Brigittine rosary, 94

Britain, 124, 135, 358, 413, 437, 455, 588

British Isles, 437, 560

Brittany, 550, 573, 674

Brooklyn, 454, 689

Brothers of the Blessed Virgin of Mount Carmel, 363

Brothers of the Christian Schools, 94

Brown scapular, 94, 365-366, 493, 515-516

Bruges, 94

Brussels, 73, 274, 293

Budapest, 61

Buddhism, 658

Buena Muerte, 428

Buenos Aires, 287, 332

Buga, Miraculous Christ of, 94, 356

Bunson, Matthew, 19, 702

Burial Ground of Paupers, 444

Burial of winter, 577

Burning bush, 191, 233, 401

Burns Library of Rare Books, 236

Bustamante, Luis, 540

Butler, 102, 371-372, 504

Butler's Lives of the Saints, 102, 504

Butte, 484

Butter Week, 337-338

Butterfly, 697

Byzantine Empire, 61, 530

Byzantine Rite, 26, 32, 72, 95, 127-128, 145, 163, 166, 185-186, 190, 232, 284, 289, 297, 301, 353, 409, 421, 622

Byzantine, 26, 32-33, 51-52, 57, 61, 72, 78, 95, 127-128, 145, 153, 158, 163, 166, 185-186, 190, 197, 202, 213, 225, 228, 232, 255, 284, 288-289, 297, 301, 342, 353, 359, 409, 421, 430, 484, 530, 618, 622, 625, 690

Byzantium, 95, 609

C

Cacella, Father Joseph, 350

Caedwalla, 437

Caguas, 274

Calafata, Andres, 114

Calaveras, 170

Calendar, 12, 26, 29, 49, 99-100, 116, 118, 137, 164, 181, 184, 203-204, 231, 239, 242, 340, 343, 366, 375-376, 403, 434, 462, 499, 506, 526,

536, 540, 548-549, 561, 574, 622, 640, 644

California, 142, 380, 428, 661, 683

Caliph, 63

Calix Society, 100

Calkin, John Baptist, 134

Calvary Reformed Church, 662

Calvat, 294, 296

Calvinists, 135, 456

Camaldolese, 156, 544

Camellians, 519

Camerlengo, Cardinal, 629

Campo Verano, 583

Camposanto, 166

Camus, Juan, 113

Cana, 121, 188, 486, 557

Canada, 20, 73, 110, 184, 380, 396, 440, 482, 493, 661, 674, 677, 679-680

Cancer, 111, 358, 547, 592, 674, 676, 679-680

Candelaria, 118-119

Candelieri, 62

Candlemas, 100-101, 454

Candles, 30, 47-48, 60, 62, 72, 78, 80-81, 85, 100-101, 115, 134, 167, 170, 185, 191, 214, 227, 246, 261, 278, 361, 454, 463, 485, 489, 495, 552, 558-560, 577, 583, 617, 646, 693

Canon, 26, 28, 76-77, 125, 139, 141-142, 150, 172, 183, 239, 259, 289, 298, 337, 397, 427-428, 477, 495, 528, 558, 575, 583, 673, 702

Canonical hours, 90, 102, 380, 404

Canonically crowned, 130

Canonization, 99, 102, 113, 142, 232, 236, 341, 350, 380, 395-396, 505, 552, 623

Canterbury Tales, 437

Canterbury, 102-104, 191, 437, 439, 564, 634

Canticle of Mary, 104, 336, 644

Canticle of the Creatures, 447

Canticle of Zechariah, 104, 325, 671-672

Canticle, 104, 275, 325-326, 336, 397, 447, 635, 644, 671-672

Capitoline Prison, 144

Capuchin Order, 384, 468, 577

Capuchin, 124, 384, 468, 577, 636, 684

Cardinal virtues, 232, 361, 644

Carey, 144, 689-690

Caribbean, 235

Carl Benziger and Sons, 235

Carmel of Tours, 319

Carmelite nun, 198, 513, 598

Carmelite Rule, 141, 365, 493

Carmelite water, 104

Carmelite, 21, 104, 123, 141, 198, 209, 216, 237, 318, 327, 364-366, 380, 493, 513, 515-516, 597-598, 601, 686, 691

Carnelevarium, 337

Carnem Levare, 337

Carnival, 104, 337-339

Carolingian Empire, 463, 585, 655

Carolingian, 12, 55, 117, 463, 585, 655

Carroll House, 342

Carrying of St. Joseph, 275

Carrying the Virgin, 104, 126, 210, 299

Carthusians, 486

Cascarones, 105, 338

Cascia, 75, 489, 594-595, 680

Cashel, Archbishop Bray of, 652

Casket girls, 599

Caspar, 82, 335

Castilian roses, 220, 488

Castro, 127

Casula, 637

Catacomb, Visiting, 105, 644

Catacombs of Priscilla, 408

Catacombs of St. Sebastian, 135

Catacombs, 39, 57, 101, 105-108, 135, 215-216, 346-347, 408, 452, 697

Catalonia, 360

Catania, 354, 547, 611, 674

Catching the Holy Ghost, 108

Catecheses, 271

Catechesis, 59, 355, 377, 493

Catechism of the Catholic Church, 4, 39, 58, 702

Cathedral of Naples, 271

Cathedral of Valencia, 158

Catherine Mattei, Blessed, 383

Catholic Action, 108-109, 567, 676, 683

Catholic Central Union of America, 305

Catholic Charismatic Renewal, 336

Catholic Emancipation Act, 413

Catholic League, 110, 305, 683

Catholic Medical Mission Board, 305

Catholic Movement for Intellectual and Cultural Affairs, 305

Catholic Network of Volunteer Service, 305

Catholic Total Abstinence League of the Cross, 305

Catholic University of Milan, 139

Catholic University of Valparaiso, 498

Catholic Worker Movement, 21, 110-113

Catholic Worker, 21, 110-113, 236

Catholic worship banned in Ireland, 605

CCD, 142

Celebration of Christmas forbidden, 133

Celestina Abdenago, 47

Celibacy, 560

Celtic Goddess, 560

Celtic Monks, 449

Celtic Tyrone Knot, 624

Celtic, 21, 76, 116, 152-153, 226, 358, 449, 560, 624, 704

Celts, 358

Cemetery of St. Hippolytus, 601

Cemetery, 44, 85, 105, 116-117, 129, 146, 151, 166, 168, 206, 425, 430, 473, 538, 548, 570, 590, 599, 601, 644, 686

Cemetery, Visiting, 85, 117, 644

Cena, 300

Cenacle, 117-118, 125, 300, 305, 409

Cenacle, Our Lady of, 116-117, 305, 409

Censer, 197, 260-261, 620

Center for Applied Research in the Apostolate (CARA), 305

Central America, 95, 104, 188-189, 305, 380, 441

Cephas, 592

Chain letter, 582

Chair of Unity Octave, 132, 403

Chaldean Rite, 118

Chaldean, 50, 118, 373, 484

Chalice, 36, 52, 79, 87, 158, 185, 209, 266, 351, 419, 501, 514, 518, 535, 579, 693-697

Challenge of Peace, 113

Chalma, 192

Chambery, 121, 245

Chambon, Sister Mary Martha, 121, 245

Chamorro, 378

Chango, 556

Chapi, Our Lady of, 118-119, 409

Chaplet of Divine Mercy, 121

Chaplet of Mary, Model for Mothers, 121

Chaplet of Mercy of the Holy Wounds of Jesus, 120-122, 246

Chaplet of St. Anthony, 122

Chaplet of St. Michael, 123

Chaplet of St. Paul, 123

Chaplet of St. Raphael, 120

Chaplet of St. Therese, 123

Chaplet of the Five Wounds (Passionist), 122-123

Chaplet of the Holy Spirit, 124

Chaplet of the Holy Spirit, 124

Chaplet of the Precious Blood, 125

Chaplet of the Sacred Heart, 124-125, 392, 500

Chaplets, 17, 120, 202, 499, 572, 705

Charismatic, 31, 336

Charity of El Cobre, Our Lady of, 126, 409

Charlemagne, 25, 230

Charles V of Spain, 63

Charles VII of France, 202

Charnel House, 46

Charny, Geoffroi De, 530-531

Chartres, 127, 409, 641, 678

Chartres, Our Lady of, 127, 409

Chastity, 127, 147, 205, 276, 308, 311, 375, 546, 565, 609, 638, 680

Chasuble, 535, 637-638, 694, 696

Chasuble-alb, 637

Chatky, 127-128

Chaucer, 437-438

Chekhov, 373

Chelsea, 266

Cherubim, 41, 44, 616

Chestnuts, 83

Chi Rho, 128, 153, 236, 697

Chicago, 20, 143, 327, 388, 395, 521, 582, 685-686, 702, 704

Child death, 329-330

Children of Mary, 73, 128, 198, 240, 352, 674, 678

Chile, 131, 677

Chimayo, 64-65, 192, 689

China, 128-129, 409, 629, 661, 677

China, Our Lady of, 128-129, 409

Chiquinquira, Our Lady of, 128-130, 409-410

Choraulein, 134

Chorea, 601, 681

Chortis, 189

Chouquet, 573

Chrism, 140, 244-245, 366, 405-406, 535, 606

Chrismation, 201

Chrismons, 130

Christ bundle, 130

Christ of St. John of the Cross, 130

Christ of the Agony of Limpias, 308

Christ of the Andes, 131

Christ of the Cross, 53, 130-131, 153, 155, 167, 214, 257-258, 313, 358, 366, 424, 443, 475, 500, 519, 523, 540, 697, 699

Christ of the Shadow of the Cross, 131

Christ seated on Calvary, 131-132

Christ the Divine Healer, 191

Christ the King, 27, 121, 132, 165-166, 274, 381, 393, 401, 422, 557, 616, 688, 698

Christ, Relics of, 94, 132, 155, 477

Christ's Second Coming, 29, 50, 277

Christian Brothers, 94, 110

Christian doctrine, 11, 142, 148, 259, 493, 617

Christian Family Movement (CFM), 109, 305

Christian initiation, 172, 185, 377, 508, 540

Christian Life communities, 305

Christian name, 109, 300, 372-373, 480, 546

Christian personalism, 111

Christianica Center, 521

Christianized, 229, 354, 593, 662

Christmas angel, 134

Christmas bells, 134

Christmas boxes, 91, 455

Christmas candle, 134, 136

Christmas carols, 134-135

Christmas crib, 135, 148, 150, 337, 371

Christmas Eve, 134, 136, 167, 275, 289, 407, 441, 456, 587, 609-610

Christmas letter, 136

Christmas light, 136

Christmas man, 456-457

Christmas Masses, 132, 136, 376

Christmas ship, 136

Christmas tree, 130, 136, 183, 210, 272, 455

Christmas, 29, 56, 82, 91, 99, 104, 130, 132-138, 148, 150, 167, 170, 181, 183, 188, 191, 198, 209-210, 233, 239, 246, 268, 271-272, 275, 289, 293, 301, 321, 332, 337, 343, 354-355, 358-359, 371, 375-376, 381, 403, 407, 425, 441, 455-457, 536, 540, 556, 563, 567, 575, 584, 587, 601, 609-610, 630, 636, 662, 698

Christmastide, 137

Christological, 49, 285, 342, 364, 454

Christopher Columbus, 389

Chromolithography, 234

Church of England, 44, 104, 412-415, 504

Church of Hagia Sophia, 299, 408

Church of St. Clare in Assisi, 158

Church of St. Peter am Perlach, 287

Church of St. Praxedes in Rome, 138

Church of the Most Holy Savior, 300

Churches, Visiting, 137, 440, 644, 646

Ciborium, 501, 535, 562, 693

Cichaupilli, 509

Cill-Dara, 559

Cincinnati, 235, 690

Cincture, 93, 144-145, 637-638

Cinerary Urns, 138

Circumcision, Feast of, 137, 199, 540

Circus of Nero, 593

Clairvaux, 352, 461, 504, 511, 528, 558, 693, 702

Claretian Fathers, 154

Claretians, 468, 684-685

Claudius II, 599

Clerks Regular of the Order of St. Camillus, 519

Clwyd, 602

Cockleshell, 137

Code of Canon Law (1917), 427, 673

Code of Canon Law (1983), 26, 495, 702

Code of Canon Law, 13, 26, 28, 141, 150, 239, 427-428, 495, 673, 702

Co-heirs, 9

Cohen, Father Hermann, 380

Coins, 192, 339, 347, 378, 455, 562, 619, 695

Cold War, 109

Colgan, Father Harold, 89

Colindres, Alejandro, 609

Collops, 138, 337

Cologne, 335, 599

Colonna, Cardinal John, 139

Color, Liturgical, 138, 188, 320

Colorado, 95, 546, 619, 684

Colossians, 41, 253, 505, 590

Columbarium, 138

Columbia University, 111

Column of the Scourging, 138

Comare, 610

Come Holy Ghost, 124, 176

Come Holy Spirit, 125, 389, 633-634

Come, Creator Spirit, 633

Comforter of the Afflicted, 139, 143, 192, 284, 310

Coming of the Son of God into the Temple, 462

Commemoration of the living and the dead, 139

Commemorative Medals, 346, 348

Commonweal, 111

Communal worship, 550

Communion and liberation, 139

Communion of Saints, 34, 149, 168, 267, 450, 453, 462, 494, 504, 606-607

Communione E Liberazione, 139

Communist, 78, 110, 127, 302, 350, 430

Commutative justice, 277

Compare, 610

Completorium, 139

Compline, 27, 51, 102, 139, 225, 326

Compostela, 137, 139, 218, 654

Compostella, 438

Conceptionist Convent, 297

Conceptionist, 173, 297

Concupiscible, 55

Confessio, 476, 593

Confession, 140, 200, 266, 383, 428, 434, 534, 541, 588, 642

Confessors, 99, 310-311, 313, 373, 437, 502, 674, 677

Confetti, 105, 338

Confirmation name, 140, 372, 673

Confirmation, 64, 140, 185, 189, 271, 299, 304, 372, 375, 405, 427, 494, 496, 673-674

Confiteor, 140, 606

Confraternity of Blessed Junipero Serra, 142

Confraternity of Catholic Clergy, 142

Confraternity of Christian Doctrine, 142

Confraternity of Mary, Queen of All Hearts, 467

Confraternity of Our Lady of Pellevoisin, 515

Confraternity of Our Lord of the Miracles, 327

Confraternity of the Blessed Virgin Mary of Mount Carmel, 493, 517

Confraternity of the Immaculate Conception, Our Lady of Lourdes, 142

Confraternity of the Most Holy Rosary, 142

Confraternity of the Most Holy Trinity, 514

Confraternity of the Most Precious Blood, 514

Confraternity of the Passion, 79, 124

Confraternity of Three Hail Marys, 619

Confraternity, 141

Congregation for Divine Worship and the Discipline of the Sacraments, 14

Congregation for Divine Worship, 14, 427

Congregation for the Causes of Saints, 102, 341

Congregation for the Doctrine of the Faith, 54, 453, 702

Congregation of Divine Worship, 674

Congregation of Indulgences, 79, 473

Congregation of the Blessed Sacrament, 362, 380

Congregation of the Most Holy Redeemer, 432, 533

Congregation of the Sacred Hearts of Jesus and Mary, 385, 469, 517

Congregation of the Sacred Hearts, 385, 469, 498, 615

Connecticut, 187, 285, 685

Conquistadors, 293, 297

Conroy, 395-396

Conscience, Examination of, 143, 193

Conscientious objection, 113

Consecrated ground, 85

Consecrated Host, 76, 86, 298, 419, 501

Consecrated Species, 225

Consecration to Jesus through Mary (De Montfort), 538

Consolata Missionaries, 144

Consolation, Our Lady of, 139, 143-144, 146, 284, 410, 689

Consoler of the Afflicted, 143

Constantia, 548

Constantinople, 33, 38, 78, 95, 139, 144, 149, 155, 213, 299, 371, 408, 489, 530, 549, 586, 639

Constitution on the Sacred Liturgy, 10,

12, 36, 99, 321, 323, 701

Conventual Franciscan Friars, 144, 685, 690

Conversions, 87, 130, 356

Cope, 638

Coptic, 33, 145, 153, 462, 629

Cord of St. Joseph, 145-146

Cord of St. Thomas, 146

Cord, 153, 637, 695

Cordoba, 332

Corinth, 563

Corinthians, 445, 462, 590, 606-607

Cornwall, 598

Coromoto, Our Lady of, 145-146, 410, 679

Corona — Crucita, 146

Corona of Our Mother of Consolation, 66, 146-147

Coronas, 339

Coronel, Maria Fernandez, 296

Corporal Works of Mercy, 35, 126, 145-146, 353, 546, 646

Corporal, 34-36, 126, 145-146, 353, 546, 646

Corpus Christi procession, 147, 190, 419

Corpus Christi, 12, 147, 163-164, 190, 200, 239, 402, 419-420, 499, 662

Corpus Juris, 477

Corregidor, 65

Corso, 338

Cospes Tribe, 146

Costa Rica, 104, 679

Council of Agde, 133, 376

Council of Florence, 452

Council of Jerusalem, 593

Council of Lyon, 249-250

Council of Rouen, 117

Council of Saragossa, 29
Council of Toledo, 402
Council of Tours, 133
Council of Trent, 99, 142, 147, 452, 476-477, 634, 702
Council, 9-12, 14, 26, 36-37, 53, 57, 77, 99, 109,149, 159, 182, 225, 227, 236, 241-242, 254, 300, 307, 321, 325, 352, 404, 409, 415, 450, 470, 478, 485, 506-507, 530, 540-541, 618-619, 623, 698
Counsels, Evangelical, 147, 190, 609
Count Theobald of Champagne and Blois, 521
Counterreformation, 339
Counters, 348
County Donegal, 438, 589
Courdin, Father Mary-Joseph, 498
Couturier, Abbe Paul, 404
Couturier, Marie-Alain, 236
Covenant, 77, 174, 310, 461, 521, 607
Cradle herb, 148
Cradle rocking, 148
Crawley-Boevey, Father Mateo Ss.Cc., 124
Credo, 94
Creed of Nicaea-Constantinople, 148
Creed of Pius IV, 148
Creed, 37, 52, 72, 121, 124, 148-150, 377, 408, 458, 460, 486, 582, 646
Creed, Apostles', 52, 124, 148, 486, 646
Creed, Athanasian, 148-149
Creed, Nicene, 148-149, 377, 460
Cremains, 138
Cremated, 138, 150
Cremation, 150
Crestone, 546

Crib, 135, 148, 150, 289, 337, 371, 456, 644-645
Crimea, 563
Cristeros, 132
Cristobalito, Antonio and Juan, 621
Croagh Patrick, 150
Crocus, 601
Crosier Order, 657-658
Crosier, 389, 596, 696
Crosio, Luigi, 521
Cross of Caravaca, 151-152, 154-155
Cross of Life, 154-155
Cross of Souls, 168, 487
Cross, 11-12, 15, 20, 29, 36, 39, 45, 53, 62, 79-82, 85, 93, 95, 114, 116, 122, 124-126, 128, 130-131, 141, 143, 150-158, 163, 167-168, 182, 185-189, 192, 197, 199, 204, 206, 212-214, 229, 232, 244-245, 247-248, 253, 257-258, 260, 263, 272-273, 279, 283, 295, 305, 313-314, 318-319, 326, 331, 345, 348-349, 351, 357-358, 366-367, 371-372, 380, 382-383, 387, 392, 407, 423-424, 431, 434, 442-443, 449, 469, 473-475, 479-480, 485-488, 494-495, 499-500, 505, 512-515, 517-520, 523, 525-526, 528-529, 532, 535, 540, 546, 560-561, 568, 571, 579, 582, 593, 602-604, 618, 620-622, 625, 638-639, 644, 646, 656, 658, 661, 677, 683, 687, 693-699, 705
Cross, Adoration of, 29, 153, 213
Cross, Constantine, 152, 155
Cross, Greek, 151-152
Cross, Latin, 151-152, 185-186
Cross, Orthodox, 152

Cross, Pectoral, 152-153

Cross, Relics of, 154-156, 371

Crowdie, 337

Crown and Cross, 156, 469, 696, 698, 705

Crown of Our Lord (Camaldolese), 156

Crown of Thorns, the, 25, 79, 156, 191, 230, 233, 273, 475, 530, 579, 696, 698

Crown of Twelve Stars, 157, 317

Crown, 25, 61, 79, 85, 114, 120, 156-157, 191, 204-205, 216, 230, 233, 263, 265, 273, 295, 303, 311, 317-318, 366, 385, 442-443, 467, 469, 475, 488, 509, 523, 530, 579, 583, 693-696, 698-699, 705-706

Crucifix, 85, 94-95, 101, 121, 131, 153, 157-158, 184, 188-189, 192, 212-213, 245, 247, 249, 257, 267, 272, 295, 308, 357, 423, 442-443, 445, 454, 474, 519, 561, 567, 573, 594, 596, 598, 620, 694, 696

Crucifix, Prayer Before a, 157, 445

Crucifixion, 47-48, 121, 125, 132, 153-154, 157, 201, 229, 235, 299, 312, 358, 486-487, 530, 539, 574, 591, 605, 617, 625

Cruz de Animas, 168

Crypt, 47, 106, 186, 297

Cryptographic writing, 106, 216

Cuba, 126, 460, 679

Cuban exiles, 127

Cubilete, 274

Cuenceme de Ceniceros, 378

Cult of saints, 80, 158, 249, 501-503, 507, 673

Cults, 47-48, 173

Cup — Holy Grail, 158

Curandero (Curandera), 158, 378

Curanderos, 159, 231

Curar, 159

Cursillistas, 159

Cursillo Movement, 32, 159, 305, 629

Cursing Psalms, 159, 259

Cuyahoga, 538

Cyprian of Carthage, 299

Cyprus, 363

Cyrillic alphabet, 373

Cyrillus of the Mother of God, 264

Czar Nicholas, 83

Czech kingdom, 263

Czechoslovakia, 88

Czestochowa, 78-79, 679, 690-691

D

Da Fabriano, Gentile, 212

Daily Worker, 110

Dali, Salvador, 130-131

Dalmatic, 638, 695-696

Damascus, 590, 699

Danes, 104

Daniel, 20, 568

Danville, 130

Dark Ages, 229

Dark Night of the Senses, 163

Dark Night of the Soul, 163

Daughter of Charity, 217

Daughters of the Divine Zeal, 554

Daughters of the Immaculate Conception, 239

Daughters of The Sacred Heart, 517

David, 7, 20, 51, 158, 171, 285, 301, 310, 314-315, 357, 401, 458, 520, 541, 574, 675, 702

Davis, J. Watson, 538

Day Hours, 27, 90, 102, 163, 266, 324

Day of Atonement, 276

Day of Indiction, 163

Day of the Lord, 21, 59, 163, 308, 608-609

Day of the Sleepyhead, 537

Day of Wreaths, 147, 163, 200, 662

Day, Dorothy, 21, 110-111, 113, 578

Days of Prayer, 132, 164, 276, 381, 396, 403, 446, 484, 594

Days of Precept, 239

De Antunano y Rivas, Sebastian, 327

De Benedictionibus, 90

De Bruillard, Bishop, 296

De Caussade, 25

De Charny, Marguerite, 531

De Cheminot, Jean, 363

De Faverches, Lady Racheldis, 653

De Joinville, Sire, 275

De la Vega, Enrique, 19

De Lara, Maria Manriquez, 263

De Mena, Pedro, 308

De Narvaez, Alonso De, 129

De Ojeda, Alonso, 126

De Profundis, 164, 487

De Rossi, 108

De Saint-Pierre, Sister Marie, 209

De Santana, Don Antonio, 129

De Urdaneta, Fray Andres, 113

Deacon, 31, 71, 172, 197, 408, 495, 516, 583, 637-638, 695

Dead Sea Scrolls, 470

Death cart, 164, 176

Death crier, 165

Death demons, 624

Death mask, 164-165

Death watch, 165

Deboullion, Martin and Theresa, 551

December, 14, 29, 48, 83, 91, 110, 128, 130, 132-133, 138, 163, 187, 210, 219-221, 241, 258, 321, 332, 338, 342-343, 359, 375-376, 401, 433, 455-456, 460, 531, 556, 583, 586-587, 597

Decian, 502

Decree on the Apostolate of the Laity, 109

Dedication of a Church, 101, 165, 218

Dedication to Christ the King, Act of, 27, 165

Dei Verbum, 77, 482

Deisis, 166

Deism, 259

Del Rizzo, Father Juan, 186

Delphi, 436

Dentelles, 234

Denver, 327

Deos, 261

Descansos, 166-167, 659

Descendimiento, 167, 540

Descent into hell, 227

Desert Fathers, 127, 571

Desolata, 167, 212, 395

Detroit, 581, 688

Devil, 41-42, 167, 288, 312, 351, 355, 503, 561, 564, 585, 594, 617

Devil's funeral, 167

Devotes, 385

Devotion of the Three Hours, 214, 619

Devotion to the souls in purgatory, 168

Devotional objects, 263, 347

Dia de Muertos, 168, 170

Diary of Aetheria, 462

Didache, 198

Didascalia Apostolorum, 50

Didukh, 170, 610, 698

Dies Domini, 16, 609

Dies Irae, 170-171

Dies Natalis, 99, 503

Dikeron, 185

Dinocratus, 451

Diocletian, 502

Dionisi, Annibale, 345

Directory on Popular Piety and the Liturgy, 14

Dirge cakes, 93, 172

Dirge, 93, 172, 298

Discalced Carmelite, 216, 513, 691

Disciplina Arcani, 172

Dismas, 47, 215, 563, 675

Distributive justice, 277

Divina Infantita, 71, 172

Divine compassion, 173-174

Divine liturgy, 26, 172, 175, 186, 323

Divine Mercy Sunday, 175, 353

Divine mercy, 21, 47, 121, 174-175, 353, 687

Divine praises, 26-27, 175

Divine revelation, 366, 461, 482-483

Divine wisdom, 496

Divining rods, 377

Divino Afflante Spiritu, 77

Doctor of the Church, 550, 558, 597-598, 621

Dogma of the Immaculate Conception, 340, 390

Dogma, 61, 172, 258, 340, 390, 473

Dogmatic Constitution on the Church, 450

Domestic Church — Home Church, 36, 175

Domestic shrines, 246, 681

Dominations, 41

Dominican rosary, 94, 434, 441, 486-487

Dominicans, 63, 135, 141, 146, 200, 241-242, 294, 326, 388, 434, 486, 519, 619, 686, 698

Domitian, 105

Don Pedrito Jaramillo, 159, 231, 378

Dona Sebastiana, 44

Donati, 658

Dormitio, 61

Dormition of Our Lady, 176

Dos Santos, Lucia, 198

Double Nine Day, 129

Dove, 176-177, 237, 240, 518, 520, 577, 596, 599, 693-696, 698

Downpatrick, 560

Doxology, 177, 250, 319, 392, 535

Dozynki (harvest walk), 662

Dragon, 44, 520, 568-570, 585, 694-696

Dragoni, 639

Druids, 127, 191, 203, 230, 358

Drumgoole, Father John, 146

Drunkenness, 32

Dublin, 10, 305, 342, 601, 704

Duc Me La Vang, 302

Duff, Frank, 305

Duke De Joyeuse, 384, 468

Duke Ludovico of Savoy, 531

Duke of Alba, 154

Dulia, 29, 177, 250, 254, 258, 301, 343, 443, 502, 507, 633

Dunkards, 32

Durango, 378, 552

Durham, 439

E

Earliest Dedication of a Christian Church, 165

Earliest known English Christmas carol, 135

East Syrian Rite, 118

Easter bells, 182

Easter bread - Paska - Babka, 182, 289

Easter carols, 182

Easter eggs, 183, 289

Easter kiss, 183

Easter lamb, 182-183, 489

Easter lily, 184, 308

Easter Monday, 184, 187

Easter parade, 184

Easter Triduum, 99, 181, 212, 244

Easter vigil, 72, 100, 181-182, 184-185, 242, 321, 430, 478, 624, 656

Easter walk, 187

Easter water, 34, 185, 656

Easter, 34, 42, 45, 59, 61, 71-72, 77, 83, 99-100, 105, 138, 175, 181-185, 187-188, 198, 203-204, 212, 225, 229, 231, 242, 244-245, 275, 289, 298-299, 306, 308, 314, 321, 338, 366, 377, 403, 423-424, 428-430, 470, 475, 478, 485, 489, 508, 521, 527, 547, 609, 623-625, 630, 639-640, 656, 698, 706

Eastern Rites, 34, 62, 185, 285, 377, 496

Eastertide, 184

Eastre, 181

Easy Essays, 110

Ecce Homo, 139, 186

Ecclesia De Eucharistia, 10, 14

Echarri, Father Vicente, 173

Echternacht, 186

Ecstasy, 54, 186

Ecuador, 88, 680

Ecumenism, 186, 654

Edessa, 530, 581

Edgar, 564, 676

Effigy, 165, 573

Egeria, 151, 298

Ego Vos Semper Custodiam, 563

Egypt, 106, 127, 191, 229, 392, 425, 435, 489, 503, 525-526, 550, 555, 557, 574, 594, 606, 639, 674

Egyptian hieroglyphics, 260

Eighteenth century, 48, 135, 234, 240, 264, 274, 302, 329, 363, 526, 537, 604, 651-652

Eighth century, 32, 57, 76, 139, 148, 202, 230, 258, 403, 435, 437, 463, 470, 511, 568, 601, 637, 655

Eight-pointed star, 431

Eikon, 253

Eikones, 253

Einseldeln, 186, 410

Einseldeln, Our Lady of, 186, 410

Einsiedeln, 79, 235

Ejaculations, Aspirations, Pious invocations, 186

Ejemplos, 381-382

Ektenes, 186

El Cobre, 126, 409

El Lazo, 93

El Piliguin, 609

El Sayid Abu-Ceit, 154

Elder bush, 206

Elegy, 298

Elevation, 76, 382

Eleventh century, 48, 52, 60, 88, 91, 187, 199, 210, 225, 241, 339, 360, 404, 454, 511, 629, 698

Elijah, 363-364

Elisha, 363, 508

Elizabeth, 66, 91, 226, 336, 489, 570, 644, 676, 687, 689, 694

Eluere, Perrine, 209

Ember days, 164, 168, 187, 484-485

Emblem, 71, 73, 125, 206, 286, 424, 454, 489, 496, 521, 566, 568, 596, 694

Emmaus walk, 184, 187

Emperor Augustus, 56

Emperor Aurelian, 133

Emperor Constantine, 57, 78, 152-153, 155-156, 324, 335, 371, 437, 511, 548, 550, 568, 608, 625, 629

Emperor Heraclius, 151, 154, 156, 625

Emperor Julian the Apostate, 502

Emperor Justinian, 133

Emperor Mauricius Flavius, 61

Emperor Nero, 458, 590, 593

Emperor Tagosama, 591

Emperor Valerian, 106

Empress Helper, 228

Empress Irene, 57

Enchiridion Indulgentiarum, 15, 262, 473

Encolpia, 347

Encyclicals, 20, 111-112, 706

Enflorar a Los Ninos, 206

England, 20, 44, 49, 60, 65-66, 76, 91, 102, 104, 116, 133-135, 137, 165, 203, 206, 214, 233, 248, 268, 308, 323, 337, 340, 342, 345, 358, 363, 412-415, 428, 435, 439, 496, 502, 504, 523, 558, 560, 564, 568, 586-587, 600, 602, 620, 633, 653-654, 659-660, 667, 673, 676, 678-679

England's Nazareth, 654

English Reformation, 654

Enlightenment, 413

Enrie, Giuseppe, 532

Enthronement of the Sacred Heart, 53, 187, 497-498, 615

Entierro, 273

Ephesians, 10, 41, 495, 546, 590, 607

Epiclesis, 259

Epidemics, 130, 558, 562, 602, 623

Epiphany carols, 188

Epiphany water, 656

Epiphany, 56, 75, 133, 137, 188, 239, 284-285, 335, 367, 404-405, 455-456, 603, 620, 622, 625, 636, 656, 699

Epiphanytide, 82, 188

Episcopal coronation, 294

Episcopal rings, 483

Episcopalians, 655

Epistle of St. Jude, 580

Equiline Hill, 432

Equivalent canonization, 102

Erba Santa Maria, 229

Erme, 610

Erysipelas, 555

Eschatology, 188, 300, 453, 703

Esquiline Hill, 433, 538

Esquipulas, Black Christ of, 76-77, 155, 188-189

Eternal rest, 445, 480

Eternal Word Television, 187

Etheria, 437

Ethiopians, 437

Etrennes, 455

Etymology, 181

Eucharist, 37, 51, 56, 76, 86, 88, 140, 142, 147, 181, 185, 189-190, 197-

198, 200-201, 204, 238, 243-246,
249, 258, 266, 297-298, 300, 308,
312, 343, 359, 361, 379, 388, 423-
424, 434, 451, 473, 480, 487, 494,
496, 501, 507, 545, 604, 608, 615,
623, 637, 639, 646, 659, 697
Eucharistic adoration, 11, 323, 501, 685
Eucharistic Congress, 143, 189-190
Eucharistic miracles, 86, 88, 190, 348
Eucharistic Prayer, 139, 451, 583, 615,
674, 703
Eucharistic processions, 190
Euchologion, 190
Euchology, 190
Eure, 584
Europe, 13, 16, 19, 34, 46, 49, 60, 62,
83, 93, 104, 132-135, 144, 147-148,
150, 156, 163, 165, 177, 183, 186,
188, 190-191, 199-200, 203-204,
210, 213-214, 217, 231, 234, 236,
242, 244, 275, 289, 307, 321, 328,
338-341, 345, 348, 354, 358, 379,
404, 412, 420-421, 425, 430, 435,
437, 439, 456-457, 489, 525, 530,
533, 544, 550-551, 553, 556-558,
565, 569, 572, 577, 586-587, 589,
591, 595, 597, 600, 602, 651, 661-
662, 674-675
European-Asia, 114
Evangelical counsels, 147, 190, 609
Evangelical Doctor, 550
Evangelismos, 49
Evangelization, 30, 191, 306, 355, 621
Eve of St. John, 354, 572-573
Eve, 51, 91, 134, 136, 164, 167, 200,
210, 225-226, 229, 275, 277, 288-
289, 294, 343, 354-355, 377, 407,

425, 430, 441, 455-457, 536, 560,
569, 572-573, 577, 587, 597, 600,
609-610, 640, 656, 662
Evenson, Rev. Dennis D., 19
Evergreen wreath, 30, 84
Evergreen, 30, 84, 301, 655
Ex Opere Operantis Ecclesiae, 495
Ex Opere Operato, 496
Ex Voto, 191-192, 355, 378, 444, 481,
484, 550, 658
Exaltation of the Cross, 154, 192
Examination of Conscience, 143, 193
Excommunication, 38, 75-76, 101, 117,
408
Exodus, 173, 260, 454, 667
Expectation of Birth of the Blessed Virgin
Mary, 48
Exposition of the Blessed Sacrament, 142,
193, 402
Exposition, 76, 142, 190, 193, 271, 402,
442, 531, 625
Exsultet, 185
Exul Familia, 53
Eye of God, 192-193, 698
Ezekiel, 44, 61

F
Faguette, Estelle, 514
Fairhaven, 187, 498, 615
Faith and Order Commission, 404
Faith healer, 158, 378
Faith, hope, and charity, 27, 71, 232,
487, 618
Fall River, 388
Fallen angels, 41, 617
Family Guild Movement, 197
Family icons (icon corner), 254-255

Family rosary, 197, 310

Fasching, 337

Fassnachstollen, 338

Fassnacht, 337

Fast, Eucharistic, 190, 197

Fastelavnsboller, 337

Fasting, 26, 29, 35, 197-198, 212, 214, 242, 245, 306, 321, 439, 513, 594

Father Ange, 384, 468

Father Bonaventure, 221

Father Christmas, 293, 456, 610

Father Clemente of St. Joseph, 237

Father Coudrin, 385, 469

Father of Christian archaeology, 108

Father Paul of Moll, O.S.B., 67

Fathers of the Sacred Heart, 498

Fatima, 687-690

Fatima, Our Lady of, 687-690

Fava Beans, 93, 580

Feast of Children, 75, 91, 455-456

Feast of Corpus Christi, 12, 147, 163, 190, 200, 402, 420, 499, 662

Feast of First Fruits, 428

Feast of Fools, 91, 199, 240

Feast of Holy Innocents, 91, 128

Feast of Holy Lights, 622

Feast of Matronalia, 362

Feast of Our Lady Help of Christians, 228

Feast of Our Lady of Chapi, 119

Feast of Our Lady of Charity of El Cobre, 126

Feast of Our Lady of Guadalupe, 299

Feast of Our Lady of Herbs, 62

Feast of Our Lady of Sorrows, 198, 294, 602

Feast of Our Lady of the Rosary, 200, 294, 307, 640

Feast of Our Lady of Victory, 307, 640

Feast of Our Lady of Walsingham, 654

Feast of Roses, 429, 488

Feast of St. Agnes, 548

Feast of St. Andrew, 29

Feast of St. Anthony of Padua, 307, 671

Feast of St. Blaise, 85, 101

Feast of St. Francis of Assisi, 671

Feast of St. John the Baptist, 231, 354, 405

Feast of St. John the Evangelist, 332

Feast of St. Joseph the Worker, 575

Feast of St. Lucy, 187, 583

Feast of St. Mark, 211, 395, 485

Feast of St. Martin of Tours, 340, 584

Feast of St. Michael, 203, 231, 586

Feast of St. Nicholas, 91, 586

Feast of St. Philip, 467

Feast of St. Rita, 75, 595

Feast of St. Stanislaus Kostka, 597

Feast of St. Stephen, 91, 597

Feast of St. Sylvester, 597

Feast of St. Thomas Aquinas, 506

Feast of Sts. Peter and Paul, 503

Feast of Swallows, 49

Feast of the Ascension, 659

Feast of the Assumption, 62, 240, 340, 342, 518, 544

Feast of the Birth of Mary, 48, 342, 375

Feast of the Chains of St. Peter, 298, 403, 434

Feast of the Circumcision, 137, 199, 540

Feast of the Conversion of St. Paul, 403

Feast of the Divine Mercy, 175

Feast of the Dormition, 61

Feast of the Epiphany, 56, 75, 284, 405, 622

Feast of the Holy Innocents, 91, 128

Feast of the Holy Rosary, 81, 397, 488

Feast of the Immaculate Conception, 219, 376

Feast of the Jordan, 622

Feast of the Most Holy Name of Mary, 242

Feast of the Most Precious Blood, 453

Feast of the Motherhood of Mary, 540

Feast of the Nativity of Mary, 120, 173, 375-376

Feast of the Nativity of St. John the Baptist, 375-376, 405

Feast of the Nativity, 120, 173, 241, 354, 375-376, 405

Feast of the Old Man Simeon, 463

Feast of the Presentation of Our Lord, 342

Feast of the Purification, 101

Feast of the Seven Sleepers of Ephesus, 537

Feast of the Seven Sorrows, 198-199, 525-526, 602

Feast of the Star, 405

Feast of the Triumph of the Cross, 156, 526, 625

Feast of Weeks, 62, 428, 579

Feast, 199 (See entries for individual feasts)

February, 85, 92, 101, 138, 308, 330, 342, 359, 394, 420, 434, 454-455, 462, 503, 506, 547, 555, 559-560, 582, 591-592, 595, 599-601, 609, 660, 701, 705

Felici, Luigi, 175

Felire of Oengus, 574

Ferdinand and Isabella, 64

Ferdinand III of Castile, 154

Ferdinando, 594

Festival of Los Tres Reyes, 405

Festival of Wreaths, 200

Festive wakes, 651

Fey, Clare, 443

Ffraid Santes, 560

Fiacres, 566

Fiesta, 30, 114, 378, 469

Fifteen Saturdays, 200

Fifteen Tortures of Our Lord, 200

Fifteenth birthday, 469

Fifteenth century, 56, 117, 135, 204, 210, 242, 255, 426, 483, 486

Fifth century, 32, 34, 36, 48, 59, 61, 133-134, 144, 148-149, 157, 177, 241, 274, 407, 476, 604, 616, 622

Filioque, 148, 408

Filipina, 294

Final Judgment, 50, 171

Finder of Lost Items, 200

Finigan, John Mary, 124

Finland, 537, 677

Fiorenza, Bishop Joseph, 121

Fireworks, 115, 330, 556, 577, 672

First American carol, 135

First Canadian bishop, 240

First canonized Irish saint, 383

First century, 32, 45, 135, 158, 234, 348, 358, 363, 406, 470, 535, 540, 549, 570, 572-574, 580, 608

First Christian martyr, 83

First Christian retreat, 117

First Communion, 32, 72, 140, 181, 185, 200-201, 346, 501

First Council of Constantinople, 149

First Council of Nicaea, 149

First crusade, 286, 319

First Friday, 200, 378, 501

First Holy Communion, 32, 140, 181, 185, 200-201, 501

First Holy Roman Emperor, 230

First holy year, 246, 637

First Mass of newly ordained priests, 201

First millennium, 373

First native Christian martyrs of the New World, 621

First plant to be used as a Christmas decoration, 191

First Saturday, 201, 493

First Third Order, 521

First World War, 584, 654

Firstfruits, 201

Fish, 39, 201, 236, 542, 551, 559, 579, 693-698

Fisherman's ring, 483

Five wounds, 123-124, 201, 245-246, 558

Flagellation, 201

Flaminian Way, 599

Flanders, 114, 348, 603, 639

Flax, 229, 542

Fleury, 151, 557

Flora, 345, 694

Floral wreath, 330

Florence, 80, 87, 434, 452, 517, 544, 549

Flower Feast, 429

Flower of Carmel, 202

Flower Sunday, 244

Flowers, 60, 62, 81-82, 129, 146, 163-164, 167, 170, 177, 184, 199-200, 202-204, 206, 229, 235, 241, 244, 257, 308, 330, 341-342, 345-346,
361, 429-430, 448, 489, 570, 573, 579, 623, 660-662, 672, 694, 702

Folk saints, 159, 231, 378, 705

Forli, 591

Fornari, 366

Fort Wayne-South Bend Diocese, 395

Forty Days' Fast of St. Martin, 584

Forty Hours Devotion, 204, 339, 379-380

Forty Hours of Carnival, 339

Fossores, 106

Fountain of Elijah, 363

Four-pointed cross, 431

Fourteen Holy Helpers, 204

Fourth century, 29, 33, 35, 50, 57, 106, 127, 132-133, 143, 148, 155, 177, 182, 187-188, 197, 211-212, 229, 242-244, 300-301, 306, 327, 347, 376, 403, 419, 426, 434, 436-437, 458, 469, 476, 502-503, 556, 586, 598-599, 608, 616, 621, 625, 673

Fourth Lateran Council, 182, 477-478, 623

Fra Angelico, 519, 527, 676

France, 38, 44, 47, 52, 61-62, 88, 110, 112, 121, 127, 134, 137, 143, 146, 149, 163, 176-177, 190, 200, 202-203, 206, 209, 234-235, 240, 245, 247, 266, 275, 294, 319, 326, 331, 340, 363, 373, 381, 384, 404, 423, 427, 435, 442-443, 460, 468, 474, 488-489, 498, 513-514, 519, 544, 551-552, 555, 557-558, 566, 583-585, 588-589, 593, 598-599, 601-602, 625, 634, 641, 658, 661-662, 675, 677-680, 695

Franciscan Apostolate of the Way of the Cross, 204

Franciscan Capuchin, 124, 684

Franciscan crown rosary, 204-205, 523

Franciscan Mission Associates, 565

Franciscan Mission Service of North America, 305

Franciscan Order, 141, 158, 204, 296, 550, 566, 644

Franciscan Sisters of the Immaculate Conception, 519

Franciscan, 7, 56, 66, 124, 141, 144, 158, 168, 170, 204-205, 219, 221, 241, 293, 296, 305, 378, 509, 519, 523, 544, 546, 550-551, 554, 565-566, 591, 603, 619, 644, 671, 683-685, 687, 690, 698

Frankincense, 260-261

Fratres Pontifices, 658

Fray Antonio de Segovia, 671

Frederick Ozanam, Blessed, 640

French Revolution, 294, 299, 379, 385, 468

Fresnillo, 64-65

Friars, 56, 66, 142, 144, 211-212, 297, 355, 359, 545, 618, 683-685, 687, 689-691

Frimsy Framsy, 651

Fritelli, 577

Froude, Richard Hurrell, 412-413

Fruits of the Holy Spirit, 205, 209

Funeral feast, 205-206

G

G.I. Joe, 575

Gabriel (Archangel), 41-42, 44, 66, 67, 68, 123, 240, 307, 387, 392, 401, 431, 568, 653, 676, 684, 694

Gaeta, 453

Galatians, 26, 205, 590

Galilee, 131, 541-542, 570, 581, 638

Galli, Telesforo, 473

Gallican, 118

Gallows, 144

Galveston, 338

Gamaliel, 590

Gang Week, 485

Garabandal, 439

Garden of Eden, 136

Garden of Our Lady, 341

Garlic, 229, 231, 355, 611

Gaudete Sunday, 30, 138, 209, 297

Gaul, 29, 503, 588

Gautrelet, 52

Gautrelet, Father Francis Xavier S.J., 52

Gelasian Sacramentary, 342

Genazzano, 211

General Examen, 143

General Instruction on the Liturgy of the Hours, 266-267

General Judgment, 209, 277

Generous Eve, 136

Genesis, 41, 607

Genoa, 192, 568, 703

Gentiles, 401, 590, 593

Genuflection, 91, 209, 245

George, Cardinal Mundelein, 395

Germany, 19, 25, 29-30, 46, 60, 78, 88, 91, 93, 134-135, 144, 148, 183, 188, 192, 203-204, 210, 221, 233, 235, 240, 284, 340, 373, 376-377, 402, 405, 413, 422, 427, 429, 455-456, 485, 521, 536, 568-569, 572, 577, 600, 602, 625, 641, 659, 676

Gesta, 47

Gethsemane, 42, 61, 79, 240, 382

Gheel, 564-565

Gifts of the Holy Spirit, 71, 124, 177, 205, 209, 256, 298, 522, 527, 699

GIJM, 577

Gillett, Sister Mary Jeremiah, O.P., 20

Gilligan, W. Doyle, 20, 703

Giraud, Maximin, 294, 296

Girdle, 145, 225-226, 275, 514, 695

Giussani, Monsignor Luigi, 139

Given name, 145, 275, 297, 300, 358, 372, 374, 510, 551, 563

Glasgow Art Gallery and Museum, 131

Glasgow, 53, 131

Glastonbury, 439, 564

Glory Be, 45, 53, 67-68, 121-125, 166, 177, 283-284, 311, 314, 318-319, 357, 388, 392-393, 446-447, 486, 523-524, 625-626, 634, 646

Gloss, 328

Glossolalia, 209

Gluttony, 32, 522

Gnostic, 284

God-bearer, 541, 618

Godparents, 52, 330, 469

Golden Bough, 358

Golden Counsels of St. Francis de Sales, 210

Golden fleece, 114

Golden Legend, 210, 306, 561, 568, 582

Golden Militia, 286

Golden nights, 210

Golden pennies, 615

Golden rose, 203, 205, 210, 331, 641

Golgotha, 529

Good Counsel, Our Lady of, 211-212, 410, 515, 528

Good Friday, 26, 29, 36, 80, 99, 138, 151, 153, 167, 204, 212-214, 244- 245, 248, 256, 260, 273, 361, 395, 489, 518, 522-523, 540, 545, 602, 620

Good luck, 105, 155, 233, 238, 338, 556

Good Old Joe, 575

Good Shepherd, The, 215, 311

Good Thief, the (Dismas), 215

Gorzkie Zale, 215

Gospel book, 185

Gospel of Luke, 397, 644

Gospel of the Infancy, 32, 335

Gospel of the Nativity of Mary, 549

Gospel, 32, 93, 101, 109-110, 127, 139, 176, 185, 191, 203, 229, 231, 253, 305, 317, 319, 335, 340, 355, 397, 424, 440, 447, 456, 462, 479, 496, 533, 535, 549, 551, 565, 634, 641, 644, 660, 696-697

Gossips of St. John, 354, 611

Goths, 106

Grace at Meals, 82, 215

Grace, Our Lady of, 215-216, 410, 679, 688

Graffiti, 106, 216, 452

Grail, the Holy, 158, 305

Grass Lake, 578-579

Graymoor, 66, 132, 350, 403

Great antiphons, 401

Great Britain, 124

Great Lent, 339

Great Schism, 95

Greatest Commandment, 479

Greccio, 135

Greece, 106, 301, 489, 588, 622, 678

Greek, 26, 31, 33, 35, 38-39, 49-52, 73, 77, 79, 114-115, 127-128, 134, 151- 153, 166, 177, 188, 191, 201, 203,

213, 225, 228, 230, 241, 253-254, 266, 284, 288-289, 298, 301, 309, 337, 343, 373, 421, 428, 431, 449, 454, 463, 488, 541, 592, 600, 606, 618, 621, 635, 697-699

Green Holyday, 429

Green Scapular (Immaculate Heart), 217

Green Thursday, 217

Greenwich Village, 110

Gregorian Calendar, 181

Gregorian Chant, 37, 217-218, 322-323, 652, 701

Gregorian Masses, 218

Gregorian music, 217

Gregorian water, 218

Gregorian, 37, 118, 181, 217-218, 289, 322-323, 636, 652, 701

Gregory of Sinai, 274

Griffin, 132

Grotto of the Anastasis, 298

Grotto, 218, 298, 331, 377, 686-687, 690

Grottoes of St. James, 218

Gruta, 218, 377

Guadalajara, 509, 671

Guadalupe, Our Lady of, 19, 26, 55, 65, 79, 219-221, 299, 342, 349, 377, 410, 439, 459, 467, 488, 621, 679, 685, 691

Guam, 378

Guard of Honor of the Immaculate Heart, 221

Guard of Honor, 213, 221

Guardian angels, 41, 221

Guards of Our Lady of Zapopan, 671-672

Guarini Chapel, 531-533

Guarini, Guarino, 531

Guatemala, 188-189, 329

Guibert of Tournai, 241, 698

Guild, 197, 221, 467, 533

Gulf of Mexico, 622

H

Haarlem, 53

Habit, 79-80, 127, 217, 225, 296, 326-327, 364-365, 474, 493, 511-512, 514-520, 545, 552, 567, 644, 658

Hagia Sophia, 299, 408

Hagiography, 75, 503

Hahilky and Vesnyanky, 225

Haifa, 363

Hail Holy Queen, 125, 146, 225, 486, 508

Hail Mary, 45, 66-67, 120-124, 146, 165, 205, 226, 283, 311, 319, 343, 395, 487, 521, 545, 646

Hair shirt, 226

Hal, 226, 348, 410

Hal, Our Lady of, 226, 348, 410

Halloween, 115, 226

Hanceville, 187

Hand of God, 4, 42, 149, 226-227, 698

Handbook of Indulgences: Norms and Grants, 473, 646, 703

Hannah, 549

Hannibal Mary Di Francia, Blessed, 554

Happiness of the Saints, 505

Hark, the Herald Angels Sing, 135

Harris, W.K., 184

Harrowing of Hell, 227

Haurietis Aquas, 498-499

Hawthorn tree, 73

Hawthorne, Rose, 111

Healer of God, 594

Health of Our Souls, Divine Healer, 265

Hearing of the Children, 227

Hearse, 206, 227, 617

Heart of Mary, 187, 200, 221, 228, 258, 309, 340, 343, 359, 361, 378, 397, 435, 487, 498, 500, 512-513, 517, 543-544, 660, 677, 680, 686, 688

Hebrews, 39, 384, 607, 640, 697

Help of Christians, Our Lady of, 80-81, 128-129, 228-229, 409, 678

Help of The Sick, 49, 221, 310, 439, 518-519

Hemp, 145

Henrik, 537

Henry VIII, 203, 267, 439, 523, 654

Herbal lore in Christian tradition, 229

Herbals, 230, 558

Herbergsuchen, 30, 230

Herbert, Cardinal, 578

Herbs, Holy, 230, 240

Hereford, 537

Heresy, 75, 149, 254, 379, 503, 551, 558

Hermeneutics, 266

Hermit, 39, 231-232, 503, 550, 557, 561, 566, 571, 584, 691, 693

Hernandez — Rivera, Bishop Enrique, 274

Heroic Act of Charity, 231-232

Hesychasm, 232

Hesychast, 232

Hidden years, 541

Higginson, Teresa Helena, 496

High Middle Ages, 248, 494

Hildegard of Bingen, 230

Hill of Crosses — Lithuania, 232

Hippolytus, 31, 601

Historical authenticity, 506

Hodegetria, 430

Holland, 53, 88, 226, 340, 456, 662-663, 681

Holly, 191, 203, 230, 233, 358

Holy Child Jesus, 64, 113, 237

Holy Child of Atocha, 64

Holy Child of Good Luck, 237-238

Holy Child of the Doves, 236-237

Holy childhood, 238, 318

Holy City, 271, 338

Holy cloths, 36

Holy Communion and Worship of the Eucharist Outside Mass, 190

Holy Communion, 32, 50, 56, 133, 140, 142, 149, 181, 183, 185, 190, 197, 200-201, 209, 238, 244, 248, 255, 266, 320-322, 328, 360, 380, 389, 393, 396, 412, 480, 501, 606, 615, 635

Holy crib, 289, 371

Holy Cross Father, 197, 351

Holy Cross in Jerusalem, 154-155, 372, 621, 646

Holy door, 73, 348

Holy face, 239, 513, 581, 635

Holy Ghost Fathers, 57

Holy Ghost hole, 49, 176-177, 240

Holy Ghost, 49, 57, 108, 124, 129, 176-177, 240, 357, 389, 625

Holy Grail, 158

Holy hour, 113, 197, 240, 617

Holy House of Loreto, 241, 328, 438

Holy house, 241, 328, 438, 541, 653-654

Holy Innocents, the, 91, 128, 241

Holy Land, 151, 242, 262, 286, 363, 437-439, 604, 645, 685

Holy matchmaker, 552

Holy Mother of Tonglu, 128

Holy Name of Jesus, 241-242, 253, 274, 309, 311-312, 319, 698

Holy Name Society, 109, 242

Holy ones, 504, 606

Holy Sacrifice of the Mass, 189, 244, 361, 485, 501, 620

Holy Saturday, 167, 184, 201, 213, 242-245, 321, 430, 624

Holy See, 14-15, 17, 20, 50, 53, 61, 71, 102, 108, 128, 140, 146, 175, 192, 199-200, 205, 209, 214, 237-243, 253, 262, 274, 286, 306, 318, 323, 345, 360, 371, 404, 419-420, 424, 435, 475, 484, 493-496, 507-508, 512, 516-518, 522, 527-528, 532, 536, 609, 623, 638, 643, 653, 673

Holy Shroud Guild, 533

Holy souls, 124, 242, 311, 359, 382-383, 425-426, 524, 659, 678

Holy staircase, 511, 645

Holy Supper, 245, 306, 345, 480, 610, 623

Holy Thursday, 36, 99, 181, 213, 217, 243-245, 306, 328, 337, 345, 361, 366, 406, 480, 489, 522, 617, 623, 655, 659

Holy water, 60-62, 81-82, 84, 142, 177, 185, 197, 218, 243, 450, 507, 516, 606, 622, 655-657, 695, 698

Holy Week, 75, 214, 227, 242-244, 273, 298, 306, 321, 345, 406, 420, 424, 547, 617, 623, 659

Holy wounds, 121-123, 245-246, 279, 558

Holy year, 75, 184, 246, 276, 395, 501, 622, 637

Holywell, 602

Home Altar, 36, 169-170, 246-247, 580

Honduras, 609

Hope, Our Lady of, 247, 410, 442-443

Horaria, 247, 445, 462

Horseshoes, 83, 597

Hosanna, 248

Hospice, 111, 566

Hospitalers, 286, 435, 550, 677

Host, 248

Hot Cross Buns, 214, 248

Hotel de St. Fiacre, 566

House of Savoy, 531

Houses of Hospitality, 110, 112-113

Houston, 19-21, 475, 654-655, 703

Huayana Putina Volcano, 119

Hue, 79

Huesca, 583

Hugo, Father John, 21, 111

Humabon, Rajah, 114

Humbert, Cardinal, 408

Humiliation of Relics (Ritual of Clamour), 249

Humiliation of Relics, 248-250

Hummel, Sister Mary Innocentia, 236

Hungarian Queen's Water, 489

Hungary, 61, 226, 489, 583, 591-592, 676, 679-680, 694

Huns, 348, 599

Huron Indians, 135

Hymn, 30, 32-33, 52, 67, 135, 149, 225, 241, 250, 284, 289, 325-326, 336, 397, 402, 420, 470, 475, 573, 602-603, 615-616, 633-634, 638

Hypapante, 454

Hyperdulia, 177, 250

Hyssop, 60

I

I.C.X.C., 185

I.H.C., 241, 251, 253

I.H.S., 241, 251, 253, 694, 696

I.N.R.I., 253, 256, 621

ICEL, 322-323

Icon corner, 197, 254-255

Iconoclasm, 57-58, 254

Iconoclastic controversy, 57

Iconography, 42, 226, 520, 550, 558, 693

Iconostasis, 255

Icons, 57, 185, 197, 253-255, 257, 378, 409, 435, 443-444, 489

Idaho State Penitentiary, 342

Ideal of a Christian Church, 413

Ignatius water, 256

IHC, 699

IHS, 693

Il Processione in Trapani, Sicily, 256

Illinois, 21, 395, 538, 685

Iluminar, 332

Imitation of Christ, 257-258, 437

Immaculate Conception, 80, 89, 94, 142, 175, 219, 221, 238-239, 258, 319, 330-332, 340, 342, 374, 376, 381, 389-391, 397, 509-510, 513, 519, 671, 677, 679, 685, 691

Immanence, 259

Immigrants, 85, 134, 136, 231, 238, 327, 339, 359, 372-373, 413, 456, 553, 579-580, 676

Immutability, 259

Imposition of Hands, 259

Improperia, 260

In Articulo Mortis, 260

In Danger of Death, 49, 260, 300, 314

In His Steps, 662

Incarnate Word, The, 260, 352, 645

Incarnation, 32, 41, 45, 48-49, 99, 149, 173, 254-255, 260, 284, 312, 507, 534

Incense, 78, 82-83, 129, 182, 185, 260-261, 367, 489, 620

Incorrupt, 297, 426, 552, 621

India, 20, 214, 557, 629, 679

Indiana, 3, 142, 550, 686, 701

Indians, 126, 135, 283, 297, 437, 509, 671

Indifferentism, 261

Indo-European, 338

Indulgence, 29, 33, 73, 105, 117, 201, 246, 262, 275-276, 309, 319, 348, 392, 404, 422, 438-440, 473, 511, 604, 617, 644-646, 659

Indulgenced Devotions Honoring the Virgin, 397

Indulgences of the Holy Land, 262

Indult, 121, 397, 673

Indwelling of the Holy Spirit, 262, 508

Infant Communion, 52

Infant Jesus of Prague, 263-264, 318, 444, 690

Infant Jesus Shrine, 262, 264, 690

Infant Jesus, 20, 64, 66, 75, 262-264, 285, 318, 335, 339, 444, 520, 551, 603, 690, 693, 695

Infant mortality, 330

Infant of Good Health, 264-265

Inkpot, Our Lady of the, 603

Innsbruck, 549

Inquisition, 278, 297

Institute of the Missionaries of the Scourged Jesus, 488

Institute of the Visitation, 121

Institution of the First Monks, 363-364

Intention, 27, 51, 146, 205, 246, 259, 265, 267, 361, 380, 396, 449, 473, 525, 554, 596, 640, 646

Intercession, 39, 57, 65, 73, 85, 102, 106, 130, 216, 219, 226, 228, 236, 242, 259, 266-267, 288, 294, 339, 352, 356, 384, 387, 389, 391, 394, 403, 406, 426-427, 437, 450, 452, 460, 468, 493-494, 502, 505, 509, 550, 553-554, 565-566, 570, 576-577, 579, 598, 607, 609, 618, 640, 657-658, 704

Intercessory prayers, 427, 448, 495, 505, 607

Internal forum, 266, 337

International Commission on English in the Liturgy, 322

International Institute of the Heart of Jesus, 266

International Union of Prayer, 71

International Year of Youth, 661

Intinction, 266

Invitatorium, 266

Invitatory, 266-267

Invocation of Saints, 267

Iota Eta Sigma, 241

Irascible, 55

Ireland, 10, 116, 134, 248, 258, 267, 287, 305, 342, 353, 358, 373, 383, 438-439, 461, 546, 558-560, 588-589, 601, 605, 651, 653, 667, 675, 679, 704

Irish annals, 588

Irish Penal rosary, 267

Isabel, 115, 130

Isaiah, 41, 209, 211, 272, 458, 699

Islam, 530

Israel, 26, 77, 164, 174, 242, 336, 363, 397, 401, 425, 483, 541-542, 557, 568, 672

Istanbul, 95, 549

Italian Revolution, 278

Italy, 20, 55, 62, 75, 79, 83-85, 88, 93, 105, 128, 135, 142, 144, 167, 173, 184, 202-203, 211, 239, 246, 328, 339-340, 362, 366-367, 373, 378, 404, 438, 456, 458, 462, 489, 521, 549, 551-552, 554, 558, 567, 577-578, 583, 585, 591-592, 594-595, 620, 636, 641, 656, 675-676, 678-679

Ite, Missa Est, 343

Itinerarium, 267

Ivy, 191, 233, 267-268, 358

J

J H V H, 699

J.O.C., 274

Jackson, Andrew, 460

Jacopone Da Todi, 602

Jalisco, 671

James of Voragine, Blessed, 561

January, 29, 71, 75, 99, 130, 132, 137-138, 188, 242, 308, 342, 359, 395, 403, 433-434, 455-456, 506, 540, 547, 550, 571, 590, 641

Japan, 88, 91, 184, 261, 342, 393, 591, 679

Japanese, 65, 138, 304, 375, 591

Jaramillo, Don Pedrito, 159, 231, 378

Jaricot, Pauline, 326

Jaslickare, 271

Jasna Gora, 78

Jasper, 138

Jebusites, 271

Jehovah, 271, 667, 699

Jerusalem liturgy, 50, 271

Jerusalem, 38, 47, 50, 95, 101, 118, 139,
    151-157, 203, 213, 230, 243, 271,
    286, 298-300, 363, 372, 392, 401,
    403, 428, 436-438, 440, 451-452,
    462, 525, 532, 541-543, 593, 604,
    621, 625, 646, 654, 694, 705

Jesous Ahatonnia, 135

Jesse Tree, 271-272

Jesse window, 271-272

Jesu Xpi Passio, 79

Jesuit rings, 272, 483

Jesuit University of El Salvador, 287

Jesuit Volunteer Corps, 305

Jesuit, 25, 111, 135, 175, 214, 234, 272,
    287, 305, 345, 390, 393-394, 433,
    440, 483, 591, 625, 636, 689

Jesus — Name, 66-67, 81, 175, 232,
    241-242, 253, 274, 309, 311-312,
    317, 319, 374, 405, 526, 543, 592,
    698

Jesus beads, 122, 272, 274, 488, 500

Jesus King of All Nations, 20, 273

Jesus Nazarenus Rex Iudaeorum, 253

Jesus Prayer, 31, 86, 128, 232, 272, 274,
    311-312, 314-315, 361, 388, 444,
    448, 479, 542

Jesus, Doctor of the Sick, 273

Jesus, I Trust in You, 175

Jetons, 348

Jewish, 51, 118, 137, 150, 253, 298, 324,
    381, 424-425, 429, 462, 532, 542,
    547, 608, 655

Jews, 198, 253, 298, 309, 424, 428, 450,

558, 585, 608, 661, 699

J-H-V-H, 271, 667

Joan of Arc, 117, 598, 677, 695

Jocists, 274

Johanneskraut, 377

John Baptist Calkin, 134

John Henry Newman, 11, 412-413, 415

John of Alvernia, Blessed, 382

John Vercelli, Blessed, 242

Jordan River, 188, 570

Joseph Cardinal Cardijn, 274

Joseph of Arimathea, 158, 530, 677

Joseph, Relics of St., 275

Joseph, St., 13, 67, 80, 92-93, 145-146,
    175, 237, 239-240, 275, 287, 307-
    309, 314-315, 319, 330, 341, 352,
    354, 359, 381, 396, 420, 439-441,
    448-449, 519-520, 526, 541, 574-
    580, 659, 683, 688, 690-691, 695

Josephstragen, 210, 275, 576-577

Joss, 129, 261

Journey of the Blessed Mother of God
    into Heaven, 61

Joy, 30, 34, 110, 138, 183, 200, 205,
    209-210, 276, 296, 299, 310-312,
    329-330, 357, 388, 391, 394, 397,
    405, 429, 446, 448-449, 462, 475,
    516, 526-527, 571-572, 638, 645,
    654

Joyful penance, 29

Jubilate Deo, 275, 289

Jubilee celebrations of priestly ordination,
    275

Jubilee celebrations of religious vows, 276

Jubilee indulgence, 73, 246, 276

Jubilee, 73, 155, 246, 275-277, 348-349,
    351, 395, 435, 439-440, 661

Judaism, 177, 198, 260, 271, 502, 540

Judas Iscariot, 547

Judas Maccabeus, 450

Judas, 444, 450, 547, 581

Judea, 543, 570

Judgment of God, 277

Julian calendar, 181

July, 130, 204, 288, 312, 330, 342, 359, 387-389, 396, 408, 414, 453, 461, 549, 557, 561, 644, 683-684

June, 16, 138, 312, 323, 354, 359, 375-376, 395-396, 434-435, 458, 550-552, 570, 590, 592-593, 601, 610, 636, 671, 684

Junipero Serra, Blessed, 142

Juno Februata, 600

Just Judge, Jesus the, 277-279

Justification, 26, 277

Justin Martyr, 28, 52, 608, 677, 695

Justo Juez, 277-279

K

Kateri Indian rosary, 283

Kateri Tekakwitha, 283, 374, 689

Kathisma, 284

Keane, Rev. James M., O.S.M., 395

Keble, John, 412-415

Keen, 16, 652

Kelly, Eamon, 653

Kempis, 258, 437

Kenosis, 173, 284

Kentenich, Father Joseph, 521

Kentucky, 412

Kerygma, 284

Keys of the kingdom of heaven, 444

Khristos Rodyvsya, 610

Kibeho, Our Lady of, 284, 410

Kildare, 559-560, 693

Kindelwiegen, 148

King Abgar, 581

King Charles III, 114

King Chostoes II, 156

King David, 357, 520, 541

King Edmund I, 564

King Gustavus Adolphus, 264

King Herod Antipas, 570

King Herod, 241, 386, 405, 574

King James II, 267

King Joseph Emmanuel, 540

King Oengus, 527

King of Love, 187, 498

King of the Franks, 230

King of the West Saxons, 230, 437

King Volodymyr, 609

King's dowry, 599

King's Lynn, 124

Kiss of peace, 285

Kissing sacred objects, 185

Kissing the foot of St. Peter's statue, 285

Kissing the hands of a newly ordained priest, 285

Kissing the ring, 285

Kissing under the mistletoe, 358-359

Kissing, 26, 122, 148, 257, 263, 651

Knight (Knighthood), 286, 530, 568

Knights of Santiago, 154

Knights Templar, 154

Knights, 154, 229, 285-286, 350, 550, 658, 676-677, 702

Knock, 342, 410, 439, 555

Knock, Our Lady of, 287, 410, 535, 679

Knots, 128, 146, 166, 287-288, 643

Knowles, Leo, 7, 20

Koimesis, 288

Koinonia, 288
Koinos, 288
Kollyba, 429
Konbologion, 127
Konboskienon, 127
Konnersreuth, 88
Kontakion, 289
Korea, 88, 678
Korean, 374-375, 591
Krakow, 434
Krashanky, 183, 289, 463
Kreitzberg, 20
Krewes, 338-339
Kris Kringle, 456
Kucios — Twelve Apostles Dinner, 289, 407
Kyriale, 289
Kyrie Eleison, 289

L
L'art Sacre, 236
L'art St. Sulpice, 235-236
La Chapelle, Our Lady of, 293, 410
La Conquistadora, 293
La Morenita, 221, 360
La Motte, 435, 691
La Naval (Our Lady of the Rosary of the Philippines), 294, 411
La Neuville, 589
La Pacificadora, 671
La Salette, Our Lady of, 294-295, 410, 687-688
La Seyne-Sur-Mer, 544
La Soledad, 167, 539-540
La Virgen Desatanudos, 287
Ladder, 475, 511, 693, 695, 697
Lady Befana, 75, 456

Lady Chapel, 296
Lady day, 49, 295-296, 408, 542
Lady in blue, 81, 296
Laetare Sunday, 138, 202, 210, 297, 362, 600
Laflin, 396
Laicism, 297
Lake Tiberias, 592
Laly, Father Campion, 151
Lamb of God, 32, 181, 183, 298, 310, 312-313, 315-316, 528, 606, 638, 699
Lambs of St. Agnes, 298, 548
Lamentations, Book of, 90, 298
Lammas Day, 434
Lamp ministries, 305
Lamp-lighting, 298
Lance, Holy, 299
Lanciano, 87-88
Lansing, 579
Lapse, 33, 595
Las Arras, 619
Las Mananitas, 299
Las Posadas, 30
Last Judgment, 36, 146, 188
Last Supper, 117, 158, 243, 245, 300, 328, 343, 421, 501, 522, 580
Last Things, 188, 300, 703
Lateran Basilica, 300, 511, 645-646
Lateran Pacts, 404
Laterani Family, 300
Latin Mass, 300-301, 343
Latin Rite, 31, 38, 78, 140, 300-301, 656
Latin, 300
Latria, 28, 177, 254-255, 301, 502
Laudesi, 518
Lauds, 102, 301, 326, 345, 379, 617

Laura, 301

Laurel, 73, 191, 301, 661

Lavabo, 302

Lavang, Our Lady of, 302-304, 410

Lavender, 229

Law of Moses, 201, 462, 542

Laws of the Reform, 173

Laxism, 304

Lay brothers, 248, 304, 428, 432

Lay Mission-Helpers Association, 305

Lay reader, 305

Le Puy, 52, 423

Le Sillon, 110

Le Trou de St. Patrice, 589

League of St. Dymphna, 565

League of the Cross, 305

Lebel, Bouassee, 235

Lectio Divina, 10

Lectionary, 496

Lector, 305

Leeks, 355

Legazpi-Urdaneta Expedition, 113

Legend, 56, 63, 78, 92, 95, 134, 153-
154, 167, 191, 210, 218, 229, 248,
283, 306, 328, 332, 335, 341, 354,
358, 371, 426, 441, 475, 489, 509,
511, 513, 526, 528, 537-539, 547-
548, 557-561, 563-564, 568, 580,
582, 584, 589, 598-599, 601-602,
609, 615, 658

Legends of the Saints, 210

Legion of Mary, 21, 109, 305-306, 484

Lent, 26, 29, 33, 60, 138, 183, 198, 202,
210-211, 306, 338-339, 347, 362,
366, 377, 409, 424, 457, 467, 470,
473, 506, 521, 527, 698

Lenten mourning, 306

Leon, 538

Leonard, Josephine, 642

Leopoldine Association, 306

Lepanto, 73, 228, 307, 640

Leper window, 307

Lepers, 117, 230, 307

Leprosy, 581

Letter to artists, 58

Letter, Certain questions concerning
eschatology, 453

Levantamiento de la Cruz, 473

Leviticus, 137, 276, 454, 620

Liber Pontificalis, 108, 307

Liber Usualis, 307, 701

Life of St. Patrick, 588

Light of the World, 30, 71, 100, 133-
134, 376, 697

Lignum Crucis, 154, 358

Lilies, 229, 307-308, 330

Lilium Candidum, 307

Lille, 143, 190

Lillie, Mrs. Frances Crane, 341

Lily of the Mohawks, 283

Lily, 44, 67, 184, 202, 205, 283, 307-
308, 467, 513, 520, 544, 568, 576,
596, 603, 693-696, 699

Lima, 19, 326-327, 620, 680, 696

Limpias, 308

Lincoln Cathedral, 342

Linden, Mrs. M., 309

Linen, 36, 38, 50, 145, 229, 419, 529-
531, 533, 542, 622

Lirey, 531

Lisbon, 550

Lisieux, 111, 123, 235, 318, 320, 489,
598, 619, 625, 680, 696

Listening to preaching, 309

Litaneia, 309

Litany — Precious Blood, 312-313, 453

Litany — Sacred Heart, 315-316

Litany of Loreto — Litany of the Blessed Virgin Mary, 312, 329

Litany of Loreto, 228, 309, 312, 329, 468, 515

Litany of St. Joseph, 309, 315

Litany of the Precious Blood, 312-313, 453

Litany of the Saints, 185, 309, 314

Litany, 121, 175, 185-186, 228, 249, 309-316, 329, 383, 453, 468, 515, 701

Lithography, 234

Lithuania, 192, 232, 536, 675

Little Arms, 200, 295, 303, 457

Little blind boy, 85

Little Crown of the Blessed Virgin, 316-317

Little Crown of the Infant Jesus of Prague, 317-318

Little crown, 120, 317-318

Little Flower (St. Thérèse), 318, 489

Little Flower, 123, 318, 489, 598, 688

Little Office of St. Joseph, 319

Little Office of the Blessed Virgin Mary, 319

Little Rosary of St. Anne, 319

Little sachet, 319

Little Way, 123, 319-320, 598

Liturgical art, 236, 548-549

Liturgical blessing, 81, 243

Liturgical calendar, 99, 116, 118, 137, 164, 184, 204, 239, 343, 366, 375-376, 403, 499, 506, 526

Liturgical Movement, 113, 320-323, 325

Liturgy and life collection, 236

Liturgy of Hours, 31, 50, 90, 93, 102, 104, 113, 139, 147, 163, 175, 190, 225, 247-249, 266-267, 275, 301, 307, 318-320, 323-325, 336, 343, 357, 361, 397, 401, 403-404, 408, 420-421, 445, 485, 606, 616

Liturgy of St. Basil, 33, 72

Liturgy of St. James, 50, 271, 326

Liturgy of St. John Chrysostom, 72

Liturgy of the Eucharist, 185

Living rosary, 61, 267, 326

Living Rosary, Association of, 61, 326

Lobkowitz, Princess Polyxena, 263

Loculi, 106

Lombardy, 405

London, 11, 21, 44, 192, 365, 380, 578, 601, 702

Longanimity, 326

Longfellow, Henry Wadsworth, 134

Lord of Miracles, 95, 326-327, 397

Lord's Prayer — Pater Noster, 425

Loreto — Holy House of Nazareth, 241, 328

Loreto, 79, 228, 241, 309, 312, 328-329, 438, 468, 515, 679

Lorica, 329

Los Angelitos, 168, 329

Los Hermanos Penitentes, 428

Lotter, 573

Lough Derg, 438, 589

Louis Guanella, Blessed, 578

Louis XV, 460

Louisiana, 81, 83, 460-461, 599, 660, 686

Louisville, 412

Lourdes water, 142, 331

Lourdes, 54-55, 80-81, 142, 192, 258, 330-332, 342, 410, 439, 488, 529, 679, 684-685, 687, 690

Lourdes, Our Lady of, 55, 80-81, 142, 258, 329-332, 342, 410, 679, 684-685, 687, 690

Love of St. John, 332, 574

Love of the Beautiful, The, 274

Lowell, 458

Lubich, Chiara, 203

Lucky bean, 580

Lucky mojo charms, 278

Lujan, Our Lady of, 332, 410

Luke, 26, 41, 48, 59, 63, 78, 104, 132, 137, 173-174, 176, 181, 184, 204, 209, 229, 243, 285, 289, 327, 336, 378, 397, 430, 454, 462, 475, 523, 525, 540-541, 543, 563, 568, 574, 644, 672, 678, 695, 698

Lumen Gentium, 352, 495, 505-507, 706

Luminarios, 332

Luminous, 295, 641, 671

Lunedi Dell' Angelo, 184

Lupercalia, 600

Lupercus, 600

Luther, Martin, 135, 573

Lutheran, 30, 130

Lux, 351, 583

Luxembourg, 144, 186, 681

Lydda, 568

Lyons, 234, 241, 423, 698

M

Maasmechelen, 309

Maastricht, 603

Maccabees, 434, 450

Macedonia, 274

Madonna Del Lume, 84

Madonna Della Guardia, 192

Madonna lily, 202, 307

Madonna of the Crucifix, 247, 442

Madrid, 62, 64, 380, 407, 570

Mafia, 56

Magdalena, Sister, 173

Magellan, 114

Magi, 75, 188, 205, 261, 284-285, 335, 355, 404-405, 456, 523, 526, 603, 699

Magic, 159, 623, 651

Magisterium, 266, 277

Magnificat — Canticle of Mary, 104, 326, 336, 644

Mainz, 633

Major Basilica, 342, 538, 644

Malta, 213-214, 286, 350, 473, 550, 674, 679

Man sent by God, 570

Manda, 218, 377, 659

Mandatum, 244, 337, 345

Mandylion, 530

Manhattan, 589

Manna, 51, 337, 406

Manning, Cardinal, 305

Manning, Henry Edward, 412, 414

Mantilla, 469

Manuals of Piety, 15

Maratta, Carlos, 366

March, 4, 48-49, 65, 71, 88, 91, 99, 308, 342-343, 354, 359, 388, 393-394, 432, 506, 526, 563, 574, 576-577, 588-589, 610, 654, 674

Mardi Gras, 104, 115, 138, 337-338, 534

Marguerita, 594

Maria Bambina, 173, 339

Maria de la Cabeza, 570

Maria De Mattias, Blessed, 454

Maria Hilf, 228

Maria Stein, 339, 690

Mariachi singers, 672

Marialis Cultus, 14, 705

Marian Movement of Priests, 340

Marian Union of Beauraing, 458

Marian year, 340, 343

Marist Fathers, 654

Marist Sisters, 654

Maritain, Jacques and Raissa, 112

Maritime industry, 53

Marjoram, 229

Mark, 14-15, 21, 26, 33, 50, 59, 139, 145, 156, 164, 166, 174, 176, 181, 211, 218, 243, 276, 285, 340, 372, 375, 395, 470, 485, 523, 530, 536, 547, 577, 601, 678, 695, 698

Marmoutier Abbey, 584

Marmoutier, 584, 589

Maronite, 484

Martin V, 212, 307

Martini, Petronas, O.P., 434, 584

Martinmas, 340, 584

Marto, Francisco, 198

Marto, Jacinta, 198

Martyr for chastity, 375

Martyrdom, 28, 121, 231, 388, 434, 437, 476, 502, 547-548, 599, 699

Martyrologies, 108, 374, 503-504

Martyrologium Romanum, 14

Martyrology, 102, 340, 353

Mary Garden, 341-342

Mary Magdalen Martinengo, Blessed, 200

Mary of the Gael, 559

Mary, Blessed Virgin, 48, 71, 80, 82, 90, 126, 128, 138, 140-141, 175, 204, 242, 258, 275, 309-310, 312, 319, 329, 331, 342-343, 359, 365, 390, 396-397, 423, 486, 494, 504, 512, 516-517, 522, 543, 549, 578, 619, 657, 678, 686, 705

Mary, Help of Christians, 80, 228, 678, 689, 691

Mary's Canticle, 326

Mary's dowry, 65

Mary's tears, 308, 487, 545

Maryland, 20, 342, 582, 686

Marymas, 343

Mass of Chrism, 244-245, 366

Mass of Christian Burial, 480

Mass of the Lord's Supper, 36, 243, 245, 306, 345, 480, 623

Mass of the Penitents, 245

Mass, 705

Massachusetts, 21, 204, 266, 341-342, 388, 458, 498, 615, 687

Massillon State Hospital, 565

Masslianitsa, 338

Mastrilli, 393

Matachines, 344

Matins, 27, 31, 102, 326, 345, 379, 617, 635

Matthew, 4, 11, 19, 26, 50, 72, 100, 112-113, 146, 156, 174, 176, 181, 188, 241, 243, 273, 277, 285, 306, 327, 335, 431-433, 444, 457, 525, 536, 574, 607-608, 622, 624, 678, 695, 698, 702

Matthia Nazzarei of Matelica, Blessed, 406

Maundy Thursday, 14, 243, 345

Maurin, Peter, 110, 112

Maurus, Rabanus, 633

May Altar, 101, 346

May crowning, 346

May pole, 345

May queen, 345

Mayer, Verlag Von Carl, 235

McGivney, Father Michael, 285

McKenna, Father Charles H., 242

McNamara, 546

McNeil, Rev. Dennis, 538

McTague, Edward A., 341

Mea culpa, 140

Meaux, 566

Medal of St. Benedict, 349-351, 518

Medal, 121-123, 125, 128, 146, 157, 239, 256, 283, 317-318, 346-352, 356, 467, 469, 487-488, 495, 497, 512-513, 518, 538, 545, 562, 577-578, 657, 679, 688

Mediatrix of All Graces, 352

Medicine men, 231

Meditation, 60, 124, 136, 163, 205, 240-242, 256, 297, 342, 352-353, 360, 367, 392, 481, 485-487, 521, 604, 620, 698, 702

Meditations and devotions, 11

Mediterranean, 622

Medjugorje, 352, 411, 439

Medjugorje, Our Lady of, 352, 410-411

Meeting of the Lord, 463

Melchior, 82, 288, 335

Melted cannons, 131

Memento Mori, 44, 176, 352

Memorare of St. Bernard, 121, 558

Memorare, 352, 395-396

Memorial of Mary, 61, 343

Memorial, 32, 38, 61, 84, 99, 106, 167, 172, 199, 242, 258, 329-330, 343, 353, 421, 526, 552, 645, 659, 688

Memphis, 582

Men of the Sacred Hearts, 187

Menendez, Sister Josefa, 499

Mennonites, 32

Mental prayer, 11, 352-353, 445, 485

Menthe de Notre Dame, 229

Mercedarian Order, 141, 517, 525

Mercedarian, 141, 517, 525

Mercy, 21, 28, 34-35, 47, 110-112, 121-122, 126, 128, 140, 145-147, 157, 165, 168, 171-175, 225, 246, 274, 278, 285, 289, 309-316, 318, 336, 352-353, 357, 362, 382-385, 388, 391, 411, 427, 445, 451, 480, 488, 498-500, 514, 525, 546, 607-608, 616, 640, 646, 687

Mercy, Works of, 35, 110-112, 126, 145-147, 168, 352-353, 546, 640, 646

Merienda Del Cordero, 354, 576-577

Mesopotamia, 557, 581

Messia, Father Alphonso S.J., 620

Messiah, 261, 298, 358, 397

Messina, 554

Mestizo, 220

Metanoia, 354

Metany, 354

Methodist, 32, 135, 413

Metropolitan Museum of Art, 158

Mexican Revolution, 173

Mexico City, 85, 173, 192, 214, 219-220, 238, 439, 467, 621, 705

Mexico, 19, 47, 64-65, 85, 92, 95, 121, 131-132, 146, 159, 166-168, 170, 173, 192, 214, 218-220, 237-238,

264-265, 272-274, 277, 293, 297, 329-330, 378, 403, 422, 428, 439-441, 459, 467, 509-510, 539-540, 621-622, 659, 671, 677, 679, 688, 703, 705

Mezquetitlan, 509

Mezuzah, 542

MFC, 305

Miami, 127, 327

Michael Pini, Blessed, 156

Michael the Archangel, 40-42, 44, 123, 354, 425, 431, 520, 524, 584-586, 678, 695

Michael, St. 146, 192, 203, 231, 520, 594

Michaelmas daisies, 203, 231

Michaelmas, 44, 203, 231

Michele Cardinal Pellegrino, 532

Michigan, 578, 662, 685, 687

Middle Ages, 30, 38-39, 48-49, 58, 60, 62, 75-76, 82, 94, 99, 141, 145, 147, 165, 168, 190-191, 199, 201-202, 206, 210, 218, 225-226, 229-230, 243-244, 248, 255, 258, 286, 325, 337, 343, 345, 347, 352, 381, 395, 401-402, 420, 434, 437, 439, 458, 467, 488-489, 494, 503-504, 506, 511, 521, 523, 545, 550, 558, 564, 569, 581-582, 584, 587, 589, 598, 600, 602-604, 622, 624, 629, 634-635, 640, 644, 656-659, 661-662

Midsummer's Eve — St. John's Eve, 354, 377, 610

Milagros, 187, 192, 355, 377, 397

Milan, 37, 139, 142, 204, 239, 339-340, 531

Milanese Rite, 37

Milanese, 37, 484

Military Hospitaler Order of St. John of Jerusalem, 286

Militia of Our Lord Jesus Christ, 286

Miller, Rev. J. Michael, C.S.B., 17, 20

Millhill Josephites, 578

Mince Pie — Shrid Pye, 355, 528

Miners, 64, 119, 550, 556, 674

Minims, 355

Minne De Vergine, 547

Minnesota, 19, 389

Minor Basilica, 73, 95, 442, 515, 671, 683, 686-687, 689-691

Miracle plays, 356

Miracle worker, 237, 551, 570

Miracles, 56, 86-89, 95, 114, 122, 130, 144, 154, 157, 187-188, 190, 211, 216, 226, 236, 257, 264, 294, 326-327, 331-332, 339, 346, 348, 355-356, 384, 388, 397, 403, 425, 431, 442, 461, 468, 503, 505, 509, 535, 550, 552, 559, 565-566, 570, 581, 595, 609, 618

Miraculous Medal, Our Lady of, 679, 688

Miraculous Responsory, 122-123, 356

Miserere, 357

Missa, 343

Missal, 190, 266, 309, 357, 445, 490, 496, 602, 646

Missale Romanum, 14, 496

Mission cross, 357, 697

Mission Doctors Association, 305

Missionaries of the Nativity, 173

Missionaries of the Sacred Heart, 517

Missionaries, 115, 119, 133-134, 144, 168, 173, 203, 230-231, 234, 256,

272, 302, 374, 412, 440, 488, 502, 517, 571, 660, 685, 687-689
Missionary Sons of the Immaculate Heart, 513
Mississippi, 84, 497
Missouri, 385, 484, 688
Mistgerion, 136
Mistletoe, 191, 358-359, 405
Mohr, Josef, 536
Monarchy, 133, 461
Monastic communities, 230, 249, 276, 457, 470
Monastic habit, 127
Monastic life, 557, 564, 571
Monasticism, 324, 550, 557, 564, 583
Moniales, 397
Monk, 76, 127, 359, 380, 426, 438, 461, 558, 564, 596, 642, 659
Monogram, 35, 128, 241, 253, 467, 698
Monstrance — Ostensorium, 359, 409
Monstrance, 76, 164, 173, 193, 204, 359, 409, 501, 551, 579, 662, 694-696
Monstrare, 76
Montana, 484
Monte Cassino, 351, 557, 595, 686
Monte Figogna, 192
Monte Senario, 545
Monterrey, 142
Month's Mind Mass, 360
Monthly devotions, 359
Monthly Mass, 360
Monthly period of recollection, 360
Montreal, 380, 578
Mont-Saint-Michel, 585
Montserrat, Our Lady of, 79, 360, 679
Monumento, 273, 361

Moorish conquest, 154
Moorish, 63, 154
Moors, 63-64, 154, 345, 517, 525, 551
Moquegua, 119
Moravian Germans, 135
Moravians, 32
Morelia, 264-265
Morning Offering, 53, 361
Morning Prayer, 102, 275, 301, 324-325, 327, 361, 404, 457, 470
Morocco, 551
Morse, 638
Mortal sins, 49, 140, 428, 528, 635
Mortification, 60, 145, 256, 361, 428, 645
Mosaic Law, 450, 454, 461, 590
Moses, 34, 51, 173, 191, 201, 233, 260, 401, 425, 461-462, 542, 667
Most Blessed Sacrament, Our Lady of, 360-362, 411
Most widespread devotion, 46
Mother Angelica, 187
Mother Marie of Jesus, 519
Mother of God, 45, 51, 58, 61, 66-67, 80, 89, 127, 130, 137, 144, 175, 219-220, 225, 239, 255, 264, 288, 294, 309-310, 314-315, 336, 342-343, 362, 365, 383, 431, 518-519, 521, 540, 575, 606, 618-619, 643, 699
Mother of Mercy — Mercy, Our Lady of, 128, 353, 362, 411
Mother of the Light, 30, 84, 315
Mother St. Michel, 460
Mother Thrice Admirable, 362, 521, 692
Motherhood of Mary, 32, 361-362, 540
Mothering Sunday, 362

Mounier, Emmanuel, 112

Mount Athos, 274

Mount Carmel, Our Lady of, 80, 94, 104, 168, 342, 362-366, 411, 493, 512, 515-517

Mount Gargano, 585

Mount Sinai, 260, 274

Mount Tabor, 622

Mourning angels, 44, 366

Mourning gloves, 633

Movable feast, 132, 181, 428

Movable observance, 59, 239, 624

Movimiento Familiar Cristiano, 305

Mozarabic, 118, 484

Muire, 374

Muller, Gerald, C.S.C, 20

Munich, 234, 402

Music in Catholic worship, 250

Muslim, 154, 214, 307, 379, 473

My Heart Is With Your Heart, 591

Myron, 185, 366

Myrrh, 260-261, 337, 367, 532

Mysteries of the Rosary, 94, 142, 275, 310, 367, 486, 525

Mysteries, 32, 81, 94, 99, 124-125, 142, 172, 205, 260, 275, 302, 310, 342, 346, 363, 367, 394, 434, 485-486, 525, 535, 545, 611, 656

Mysterii Paschalis Celebrationem, 506, 705

Mystery plays, 49, 136, 147, 356, 569

Mystic, 74, 173, 186, 308, 367, 544, 562, 591, 597-598

Mystical Body, 111, 325, 450, 453, 505

Mystical City of God, 296

Mystical death, 367

Mystical life, 256, 572, 597

Mystical marriage, 163

Mystics, 11, 245, 256, 677

N

Nacimiento - Precipio - Portal, 371

Nacimientos, 136

Nagasaki, 591

Nails, Holy, 371-372

Name Day, 226, 296, 375, 534, 547, 600

Nantes, 117

Naples, 46, 106, 271, 394, 549

Napoleon, 228, 379, 460

Napoleonic Wars, 625

National Apostasy, 414

National Catholic Conference for Seafarers, 305

National Enthronement Center, 498, 615

National Shrine to the Infant Jesus of Prague, 264

Native American, 221, 231, 297, 374

Nativity of Mary, 120, 126, 173, 339, 375-376, 549

Nativity of St. John the Baptist, 375-376, 405

Nativity of the Mother of God, 51

Nativity scene, 29, 135-136, 230

Nave, 249, 255, 476, 528

Nazareth, 241, 253, 328, 438, 526, 541-542, 557, 574, 653-654, 679, 699

Neneveh, 629

Nenneri, 610

Nero, 458, 590, 593

Nerra, Count Fulk, 250

Nestorian, 153

Nestorius, 619

Netherlands, 236, 603

Neumann, Theresa, 88

New Covenant, 77, 174, 607

New Eve, The, 288, 343, 597

New Haven, 285, 685, 702

New Mexico National Guard, 65

New Mexico, 64-65, 95, 131, 192, 220, 293, 297, 378, 428, 510, 688, 705

New Orleans, 336, 338, 460-461, 599, 679, 686

New Spain, 129, 219, 481

New Testament, 26, 34, 37, 41, 51, 77, 112, 209, 255, 259, 313, 325, 354, 381, 389, 422, 451, 461-462, 530, 536, 557, 592

New Year's Day, 455

New Year's Eve, 597

New York, 11, 15, 20, 110-112, 132, 146, 158, 262, 272, 322, 327, 355, 380, 403, 454, 456, 459, 489, 510, 538, 589, 640, 689, 701-706

Nicaean Council, 57

Nice, 531

Nicene Creed, 148-149, 377, 460

Nicene-Constantinopolitan Creed, 149

Nicho, 377

Nickname, 372-373

Niebuhr, Reinhold, 522

Night Prayer, 139, 163, 225, 299, 324, 326, 379, 397, 470

Nimbus, 226

Nine First Fridays, 378

Nine Fridays, 378, 395

Nine Tuesdays devotion, 378

Nineteenth century, 29, 91, 131, 134-135, 151, 214, 217, 234-235, 297, 302, 319-320, 360, 412, 415, 441, 457, 480, 482, 519, 523, 537, 554, 573, 635, 652, 654

Nino Fidencia, 231

Ninong, 115

Ninth century, 57, 72, 145, 230, 243, 258, 375, 438, 449, 574, 586, 603, 655

Nisan, 424

Nochixlecas Indians, 509

Nocturnal Adoration Society, 379-380

Nokotsudos, 138

None, 64, 102, 163, 249, 287, 326, 380, 637, 643

Nonviolence, 113

Norfolk, 439, 654

Normandy, 573

North Kingston, 538

North Tonawanda, 262

Nossa Senhora Aparecida, 51

Nostradamus, 461

Notre Dame Cathedral, 157

Notre Dame, 20, 44, 142, 157, 192, 229, 487, 678, 702, 704

Nova Scotia, 546

Novelan, John Brother, 657

November, 29, 33-34, 92, 117, 138, 168, 170, 206, 340, 342, 359, 382, 393, 461, 545, 563, 583-585, 597, 601, 663, 705

Novena for the Blessed Souls in Purgatory, 381-383

Novena in honor of Our Lady of Perpetual Help, 381, 385-386

Novena in honor of the Immaculate Conception, 388-391

Novena in honor of the Most Holy Trinity, 392

Novena in honor of the Sacred Heart of Jesus, 392

Novena in honor of the Seven Sorrows, 392

Novena of Christ the King, 393

Novena of Grace, 393

Novena, 30, 115, 226, 265, 293, 380-396, 401, 434, 564-565, 625-626

Nuestra Comadre Sebastiana, 44, 176

Nunc Dimittis, 104, 326, 397

Nuremberg, 234

O

O Salutaris Hostia, 76, 402

O'Bill, Bob, 484

O'Bill, Joyce, 484

O'Donnell, Virginia Siegle, 619

Oaxaca, 539

Oberammergau, 402

Oberndorf, 536

Obernheim, 657

Oblate Missionaries, 517

Oblates of Mary Immaculate, 402, 443, 538, 685, 688, 691

Oblates of St. Benedict, 402, 518

Obsession, 403

Occasion of Sin, 403

Octave of Prayer for Christian Unity, 403, 659

Octave, 52, 132, 188, 218, 244, 403-404, 446, 540, 659

October, 41, 51, 81-82, 84, 170, 198, 220, 226, 294, 307, 322-323, 326-327, 342, 359, 388, 393, 404, 540, 554, 563, 566, 580, 597-598, 640, 661, 671

Oengus the Culdee, 574

Offerus, 561

Office for the Dead, 164, 404, 473

Office of the Star, 404

Official language of the Latin Rite, 300

Ofrenda, 170

Ohio, 19-20, 144, 342, 352, 538, 565, 689-690, 704

Oil of catechumens, 405, 606

Oil of St. John, 405

Oil of the Saints, 337, 405-406

Oil of the sick, 405, 606

Oils (Holy Oil), 405-406

Old believers, 185

Old Testament, 26, 28, 41-42, 51, 77, 81, 185, 259, 272, 309, 324-325, 381, 405-406, 439, 451, 458, 461, 536, 542-543

Oldest Christian basilica, 300

Oldest Marian feast in the West, 342

Olea Sancta, 406

Oleum Martyris, 407

Ollignies, 544

Olympic Games, 661

Ombrellino, 73, 629

On the Love of God, 558

On the Song of Songs, 558

Onamia, 389

Onesiphorus, 451

Ontario, 396, 482

Operation Deep Freeze II, 538

Oplatek Oblatky Oplatky, 407

Optional memorial, 242, 330, 343

Opus Dei, 407-408

Orange blossoms, 330

Orans, 449

Orante, 408

Oratory, 33, 80, 90, 237, 264, 342, 363, 384, 408, 425, 468, 518, 687, 690

Order of Carmel, 141, 365, 493, 515

Order of Christian Funerals, 450, 704

Order of Hospitalers of St. Anthony, 435, 550

Order of Hospitalers, 286, 435, 550

Order of Minors, 382

Order of Oddfellows, 206

Order of Our Lady of Mercy, 157

Order of Our Lady of Ransom, 407, 517

Order of Pius IX, 286, 385, 469

Order of Pope St. Sylvester, 286

Order of Preachers, 453, 519

Order of St. Augustine, 144, 211

Order of St. Gregory the Great, 286

Order of the Garter, 568, 694

Order of the Golden Spur, 286

Order of the Most Holy Trinity for the Ransom of Captives, 514

Order of the Most Holy Trinity, 214, 513-514

Orders of Friars Minor, 618

Ordinary and Propers of the Mass, 307

Oriel College, 412

Origenes, 429

Original justice, 277

Orthodox, 58, 72, 78, 95, 127, 145, 149, 152-153, 181, 232, 255, 408, 654

Ossi Dei Morti, 92

Ostensorium, 359, 409

Ottoman Turks, 211

Our Father, 26, 94, 120-121, 123-125, 146, 156, 165, 205, 283, 311, 314, 317-319, 327-328, 350-351, 385, 390-391, 409, 423, 433, 486-487, 545, 607, 638, 640, 646

Our Lady of Hal, 226, 348, 410

Our Lady of Hope, 247, 410, 442-443

Our Lady of Knock, 287, 410, 535, 679

Our Lady of Loreto, 328, 438, 679

Our Lady of Mercy, 128, 157, 174, 353, 362, 411, 525

Our Lady of Pontmain, 247, 442, 679

Our Lady of Shkodra, 211, 528

Our Lady of Silence, 287

Our Lady of the Angels, 44-45, 104, 187, 409, 475

Our Lady of the Bowed Head, 216

Our Lady of the Poor, the Sick, and the Indifferent, 71

Our Lady of the Rosary, 65, 81, 129, 168, 198, 200, 228-229, 293-294, 307, 342, 359, 394, 404, 411, 441-442, 486-487, 640, 689

Our Lady Underground, 127

Our Lady's Bedstraw, 148

Our Lady's Rosary Makers, 412

Our Lady's Thirty Days, 62, 412

Our Mother of Mercy, 128, 225, 353, 362, 391, 411

Oxalis, 229, 527

Oxford Declaration, 323

Oxford Movement, 323, 412-415

Oxford, 21, 323, 412-415, 532

Ozark, 231

Ozieri, 610

P

Pachacamilla, 326-327

Pacifism, 111, 113

Padre Pio, 605

Padrinos, 469-470

Padua, 129, 200, 307, 357, 378, 550-555, 618, 621, 671, 674, 693

Pagan, 31, 33, 52, 100, 116, 126, 133, 191, 202-203, 206, 220, 229-231,

248, 253, 260-261, 267, 299, 338, 347, 354, 358, 381, 437, 455, 502, 526, 556, 560, 564, 583, 586, 600, 609-611, 621, 629, 651, 662
Pageants, 61, 147, 190, 214, 338
Palermo, 106, 696
Palestine, 242, 253, 532, 653, 677
Pall, 36, 419
Pallia, 419, 548
Pallium, 298, 419, 548
Pallottines, 262, 468
Palm bouquets, 245, 420
Palm donkey, 243, 420
Palm Sunday, 243-244, 306, 420, 661
Palmesel — Palm Donkey, 243, 420
Palomitas, 237
Pan Bendito, 420
Pan Benito, 92
Pan de los Muertos, 92
Pan, 92, 420, 600
Pange Lingua, 420, 615
Pannuchida, 421, 489
Pansy, 421
Pantheism, 259
Pantheon, 33, 703
Pantokrator, 421
Papal altar, 73
Papal arms, 73, 515, 520
Papal blessing, 263, 422
Papal coronation, 294, 671
Papal cross, 152-154, 694
Papal curia, 49
Papal knights, 286
Papare, 629
Papel Picado, 170, 422
Paraclete, 124-125, 175, 422, 634
Paradise tree, 136, 210

Paradises, 202
Paraguay, 332, 679
Paraliturgical, 11, 187, 423, 617
Parasite, 358
Parasol, 629
Paray-Le-Monial, 187, 423, 498
Parchment, 234, 431, 541-542
Pardon crucifix, 423
Pardon of Le Puy, 423
Parentalia Novendialia, 381
Paris, 57, 106, 157, 234-235, 299, 380, 384, 468, 566, 625, 639-641, 657
Parsley, 206, 229, 525
Particular Examen, 143
Particular Judgment, 277, 423
Pasch, 181, 429, 638
Pascha, 181, 429
Paschal candle — Easter candle, 423
Paschal candle, 32, 76, 100, 423, 624, 638
Paschal Lamb, 181, 183
Paschal mystery, 189, 239, 423, 546
Paschal Sacrifice, 343
Pascua Florida, 244
Pascua Rossa, 429
Pasello Da Mercogliano, 203
Paska, 83, 182, 289
Passau, 228
Passio, 79, 583
Passion of Perpetua and Felicitas, 451, 704
Passion Sunday, 138, 243-244, 306, 420, 424, 547, 623, 667
Passion Week, 243, 420, 424
Passionist Emblem, 424
Passionist Order, 79, 367
Passionists, 387, 392, 424

Passiontide, 424

Passover Seder, 183, 424-425

Passover, 181, 183, 198, 300, 424-425, 547

Pasterka — Shepherd's Mass — Midnight Mass, 425

Pastoral visitation, 425

Pastorelas, 30

Pastores, 425

Paten, 185, 501

Pater Noster — Our Father, 327

Patriarch Robert of Jerusalem, 154

Patriarchal cross, 152-153

Patrick Hayes, Cardinal, 380

Patristic writers, 34

Patron of a Happy Death, 520, 578

Patron of Hopeless Cases, 581

Patron of the Holy Souls — St. Michael, 425

Patron of the Holy Souls — St. Nicholas, 425

Patron of the Impossible, 388, 510

Patron of the Universal Church, 519, 575, 577

Patron of the Universal Church, Joseph, 519, 577

Patron of Workers, Joseph, 449

Patron saints, (See specific entries for patrons)

Patronage, 83, 94, 228, 365, 390, 397, 468, 581, 587, 600, 602, 606, 673

Patroness of the United States, 258, 389

Patroness, 51, 61, 78, 104, 123, 126, 129, 146, 211, 221, 229, 258, 343, 363, 389-391, 460-462, 547, 556, 563, 594, 609, 654, 657, 685

Pax Christi, 305, 427

PAX, 305, 351, 427

Peace, Sign of, 285, 427, 535

Pectoral amulets, 443

Pectoral cross, 152-153

Pegoraro, Father Germano, S.C., 578

Pellevoisin, 514-515

Penal times, 267

Penance rocks, 120

Penance, 26, 29-30, 35, 78, 120, 128, 138, 140, 189, 198, 201, 226, 246, 259, 295, 299, 327, 337, 359, 382, 427-428, 434, 436, 438, 449, 452, 474, 484, 494, 496, 501, 550, 562, 582, 604, 635, 654

Penitentes, 428, 706

Penitential Psalms, 428

Pennsylvania, 57, 342, 387, 396, 539, 620, 690

Pentateuch, 541

Pentecost dew, 430

Pentecost Sunday, 125, 176, 182, 240, 258, 343, 624

Pentecost —Whitsunday, 429, 660

Pentecost, 12, 34, 59, 99, 108, 117, 125, 138, 176-177, 182, 184, 187-188, 198, 240, 258, 340, 343, 366, 381, 389, 403-404, 428-430, 527, 624, 634, 638, 660, 699

Pentekoste, 428

People of God, 9, 173, 188, 314, 325, 401, 461, 585

Per Grazia Ricevuta, 192

Perfumes of the gods, 260

Periera, Juana, 104-105

Perpeq, 430

Perpetual Help, Our Lady of, 381, 385-386, 411, 430-434, 679

Perpetual Rosary for the Dead, 433-434

Persecutions of the Church, 85, 106, 132, 191

Persecutions, 85, 105-106, 132, 191, 231, 244, 261, 302-303, 502, 559, 591

Persepolis, 629

Persia, 106, 557, 581

Persignarse and Santiguarse, 434

Persona Christi, 302

Personal prelature, 407

Peru, 19, 118-120, 214, 279, 326-327, 620, 677

Peter De Honestis, Blessed, 128

Peter's Pence, 434-435

Petit, Berthe, 544

Petros, 592

Petruccia, 211-212

Peyton, Father Patrick, 197

Pfeiffer, Father, 636

Pfingstbaum, 430

PGR, 192

Pharisee, 590

Phelan, Anne C., 20

Philadelphia, 143, 338, 341, 691

Philately, 570

Philippians, 72, 284, 590, 607-608

Philippines, 30, 113-114, 294, 411, 661, 679-680

Philokalia, 274

Philomen, 590

Philomena, 506

Phoenician alphabet, 128

Phoenix and flames, 435

Phylacteries, 347, 541

Pia, Secondo, 531

Piedmont, 405

Pierina, Sister Maria, 239

Pigs of St. Anthony, 435

Pilate, 149-150, 186, 253, 511, 530, 635, 645

Pileolus, 672

Pilgrim virgins, 435

Pilgrimage, 25, 28, 64-65, 78, 104, 108, 137, 139, 186, 192, 226, 238, 246, 276, 294, 304, 328, 340, 347, 405, 407, 432, 436-439, 476, 509, 528, 552, 584, 587, 609, 635, 654-655, 657-658

Pillar, Our Lady of, 411, 439-440, 524, 679

Pious associations, 141, 347, 544

Pious custom, 72, 80-83, 85, 150, 285, 311, 451, 488, 586

Pious legend, 78, 95, 154, 248, 328, 332, 335, 354, 371, 475, 509, 511, 513, 528, 548, 559, 568, 580, 602, 609, 615

Pious Union of Our Lady of Good Counsel, 515

Pious Union of Prayer, 440

Pious Union of the Pardon Crucifix, 423

Piseoga, 653

Pittsburgh, 57, 539, 691

Pius IX, Blessed, 385, 453, 469, 499, 513, 519, 575, 577

Pius Union, 423, 578

Plague medals, 348

Plainchant, 118, 217

Plainsong, 118, 217

Plateros, 64

Plenary indulgence, 33, 117, 201, 246, 262, 275-276, 309, 422, 438-439, 604

Pliny the Younger, 608
Pliny, 358, 608
Plombariola, 595
Pluviale, 638
Poinsett, Joel Roberts, 441
Poinsettia, 441
Poitiers, 499, 583
Poland, 16, 61, 78-79, 88, 164, 183, 200, 422, 429, 434, 499, 569, 661-662, 675, 677, 679-680
Polixena, 263
Pompeii, Our Lady of the Rosary of, 200, 229, 411, 441-442
Pontifical Commission, 108
Pontifical Council for Migrants and Itinerant Peoples, 53
Pontifical Council for Promoting Christian Unity, 404
Pontifical Council for the Laity, 159
Pontifical Gregorian University, 636
Pontifical University of the Holy Cross, 407
Pontius Pilate, 149-150
Pontmain, 247, 442, 679
Poor Child Jesus, 443
Poor Clare Nuns, 127
Poor Clare, 127, 200
Poor Clares, 339, 531, 562, 567
Poor Ladies, 567
Pope Alexander III, 102
Pope Alexander IV, 80, 518
Pope Alexander VI, 246, 439
Pope Alexander VII, 304
Pope Benedict XIV, 339, 351, 475, 515, 540
Pope Benedict XV, 66, 240, 328, 438, 575

Pope Boniface VIII, 246
Pope Callistus III, 622
Pope Clement II, 200
Pope Clement VIII, 309, 379
Pope Clement X, 89
Pope Clement XII, 605
Pope Gelasius, 187
Pope Gregory IX, 551
Pope Gregory VII, 187
Pope Gregory XV, 597
Pope Gregory XVI, 125, 173, 639
Pope Innocent II, 461
Pope Innocent III, 514, 566
Pope Innocent VIII, 299
Pope Innocent XI, 212, 242, 304
Pope Innocent XIII, 242
Pope John Paul II, 10, 16, 19, 33, 58, 78, 112, 130, 155, 174, 176, 199, 232, 242, 246, 323, 340, 374, 407, 486, 533, 598, 608, 621, 660
Pope John XV, 102
Pope John XXIII, 102, 109, 312, 448, 453, 575
Pope John XXIII, Blessed, 448, 453, 575
Pope Julius II, 531, 533
Pope Leo IX, 351, 404
Pope Leo XI, 278
Pope Leo XII, 124
Pope Leo XIII, 56, 108, 240, 264, 275, 278, 404, 446, 515, 520, 575, 577, 620
Pope Paul I, 106
Pope Paul II, 10, 16, 19, 33, 58, 78, 99, 112, 130, 155, 174, 176, 199, 212, 232, 242, 246, 323, 340, 374, 407, 486, 533, 598, 608, 621, 660
Pope Paul V, 82, 548

Pope Paul VI, 36, 99, 145, 304, 344, 506, 557, 606, 705

Pope Pius IX, 80, 123, 258, 278, 297, 384-385, 396-397, 404, 430, 433, 453-454, 513, 519, 575, 577, 636

Pope Pius IX, Blessed, 385, 453, 513, 519, 575, 577

Pope Pius V, 307, 319, 348, 640

Pope Pius VII, 125, 130, 228, 379, 645

Pope Pius XI, 108-109, 132, 198, 274, 285, 540, 572, 575, 598

Pope Pius XII, 51, 61, 77, 108-109, 221, 259, 340, 395, 469, 498-499, 575, 598, 602, 617

Pope Sixtus II, 583

Pope Sixtus V, 102, 519

Pope St. Damasus, 34

Pope St. Gregory I, 191

Pope St. Gregory the Great, 29, 72, 137, 217-218, 371, 475, 502, 557

Pope St. Pius V, 307

Pope St. Pius X, 109, 200, 385, 449, 467, 469, 498, 512, 578

Pope St. Sergius I, 375

Pope Sylvester I, 629

Pope Sylvester II, 34

Pope Sylvester, 34, 286, 625, 629

Pope Urban II, 319, 588

Pope Urban IV, 147, 402

Pope Urban VI, 644

Pope Urban VIII, 228, 244, 427, 565, 673

Popular devotions, 11, 14, 16-17, 199, 212, 486, 507, 525

Por un Favor, 192

Portable icon, 254, 443

Portage des Sioux, 484

Porticello, 84

Porticoes, 202

Portiuncula, 444, 566

Portugal, 62, 84, 88-89, 189, 198, 350, 355, 540, 550, 552-553, 568, 611, 674, 676, 679-681

Posada, Jose Guadalupe, 169-170

Posadas, 30, 230, 444

Poverty, Chastity, Obedience, 147, 276, 609

Powers, 41-42, 99, 230, 249, 259, 377, 616-617, 623, 644

Prado, 641

Praemonstratensian Order, 520

Praetorium, 511, 645

Prague, 234, 639, 685

Prague, Infant Jesus of, 263-264, 318, 444, 690

Praised be Jesus Christ, 508

Prayer book, 67, 197, 233, 248, 357, 395, 445, 704

Prayer for a Happy Death, 395, 445, 448

Prayer for Mankind, 445, 563

Prayer for Peace (St. Francis), 446

Prayer for the Faithful Departed, 445

Prayer for the Pope, 246, 446, 578, 596

Prayer for Unity of Christians, 403, 446

Prayer for Victory in Battle, 446

Prayer for Vocations (Priestly and Religious), 447

Prayer of St. James, 50

Prayer of the Heart, 31, 52-53, 74, 274, 314-315, 352, 361, 383, 392, 444, 448, 479, 497

Prayer to St. Joseph for a Happy Death, 448

Prayer to St. Michael, 123

Prayer, attitudes and stances, 449

Praying around the church, 449-450

Praying for the dead, 450-453, 606, 608

Praying in tongues, 31

Precept, 183, 239, 424

Pre-Christian, 62, 83, 127, 211, 226, 230, 338, 345, 381, 545, 597, 652, 655, 661

Precious Blood Heart, 71, 175, 359, 454

Precious Blood, 47, 66, 71, 94, 122, 125, 146, 174-175, 233, 278-279, 312-313, 359, 381, 393, 453-454, 514, 523-524, 690

Prelature of the Holy Cross and Opus Dei, 407

Presbyter, 31

Presence of God, 288, 469, 526, 603

Presentation in the Temple, 100, 121, 205, 397, 454, 462-463, 486

Pretzel, 457, 585

Prezel, 457

Prie-Dieu, 457

Priestly vestments, 263

Prim, 651

Prime, 102, 235, 249, 457-458

Primula, 593

Prince Juan Carlos, 114

Prince of Peace, 75, 311, 458

Prince of the Apostles, 592

Princess Polixena, 263

Principalities, 41

Private revelation, 54, 80, 318, 366, 483, 500

Pro Maria Committee, 458

Pro Sanctity Movement, 458

Procesion de la Soledad de Maria, 167, 540

Processions, 12, 37, 49, 62, 101, 147, 163, 167-168, 190, 214, 273, 327, 345, 355, 420, 458, 485, 604, 662

Profession of Faith, 147-149, 185, 205, 242, 453, 458-460

Promesa, 219, 355

Prompt Succor, Our Lady of, 411, 459-461, 679, 686

Prophecies of St. Malachy, 461

Prophecy, 199, 298, 392, 461-462, 525-526, 572

Prostration, 128, 354

Protestantism, 234, 413

Protestants, 58

Protoevangelium of James, 549

Proverbs, 35, 200

Providence, Our Lady of, 411, 462, 679

Province of Latium, 300

Prudentius, 241

Psalm, 26, 32, 35, 37, 60-61, 164, 249, 266-267, 275, 284, 301, 305, 357, 487, 635

Psalms 100, 267

Psalms, 31, 35, 50, 60, 104, 118, 159, 239, 247, 249, 259, 267, 284, 299, 319, 324-326, 379, 428, 542-543, 605, 608, 617

Psalmus in Nativitate, 135

Psalter, Lay, 462

Psalters, 248

Pseudo-Matthew, 549

Publius Lentulus, 543

Puebla, 85

Puerto Rico, 47, 274, 355, 421, 462, 679-680

Purana, 214

Purgatory, 34, 44, 46-48, 117, 168, 231-

232, 267, 277, 311, 313, 381-384, 423, 425-426, 434, 438-439, 443, 452-453, 462, 487, 504, 524, 545, 589, 606-608, 644, 659, 701-704
Purification of Mary, 342, 397, 454, 463
Purification, 101, 163, 205, 342, 397, 452-454, 462-463, 607-608
Purificator, 36
Puritans, 133-135
Purity, 118, 121, 138, 145-146, 202, 229, 259, 307-308, 311, 317, 374, 395-396, 467, 520, 544, 548, 660, 699
Pusey, Edward, Newman, John Henry, 412
Putigan, 625
Putz, 135
Pysanky, 183, 289, 463
Pyx, 56, 501

Q
Quadragesima of St. Philip, 467
Quadragesima Sancti Martini, 584
Quadragesima, 470
Quaestor, 467
Quas Primas, 274, 285
Quebec, 73, 482
Queen Elizabeth I, 91
Queen Hatshepsut, 260
Queen of All Saints, Mary, 467
Queen of Heaven, Rejoice, 475
Queen of Peace, Our Lady of, 128-129, 384, 412, 468-469
Queen of the Americas Guild, Inc., 467
Queen of the Apostles, Our Lady, 412, 467-468
Queen of the Clergy, 412, 468, 475

Queenship of Mary, 342, 469
Quezon City, 294
Quinquagesima, 469-470
Quirio Catano, 188
Quis Ut Deus, 520
Qumran Hymn Book, 470
Quonset Naval Air Station, 538

R
Rabbinic literature, 34
Raccolta, 15, 473, 705
Rainmaker, 593
Raising of the Cross, 473
Ramos, Maria, 130
Ranchos de Taos, 131
Randan, 473
Raphael (Archangel), 41-42, 44, 120, 123, 384, 593-594, 680, 696
Raptures, 297
Ravasio, Sister Eugenia Elizabetta, 209
Reading Sacred Scriptures, 473
Real estate, 578
Real Presence, 12, 88, 147, 298, 473
Recentiores Episcoporum Syndoti, 453
Red Cross of St. Camillus, 474
Red Cross, 474, 513-514, 517-519, 568, 696
Red Pasch, 429
Red Scapular (Passion), 474-475
Redemptorist Congregation, 385
Redemptorists, 385, 430, 432-433, 533
Reformation, 58, 82, 133, 135, 184, 188, 355, 375, 452, 456, 481, 654, 673
Refugium Peccatorum, 521
Regina Caeli Laetare, 45, 475
Regina Cleri, 412, 475
Reginald, Blessed, 519

Regular Canons of St. Augustine, 551

Relics, 21, 25, 35-38, 91, 94, 99, 104-105, 132, 144, 151, 155-157, 186, 235-236, 249-250, 257, 262, 275, 299, 335, 337, 347, 371-372, 387, 406-407, 409, 426-427, 438, 458, 473, 475-478, 507, 528, 530, 533, 552, 563-564, 582, 587-588, 593, 601-602, 618, 621-622, 625, 636, 641, 657, 690, 702

Religious of the Cenacle, 118

Religious Persecution in Ireland, 267

Reliquaries, 154, 249, 426, 476, 478

Renewal of baptismal promises, 185, 478

Rengers, Father Christopher, O.F.M., Cap., 577

Rennet, 148

Reparation to the Sacred Heart, Act of, 479

Reparation, 85, 128, 175, 201, 239, 361, 444, 479-480, 496, 499

Repast of the Lamb, 354, 576

Requiem Aeternam Dona Eis, Domine, 480

Requiem Eternam, 487

Requiem Mass, 344, 480, 511

Rerum Novarum, 275

Resurrection, 38, 45, 59, 85, 99, 121, 149-150, 181-182, 184, 205, 238, 244, 246, 298, 310, 316, 324, 342-343, 352, 392, 428-429, 435, 451, 453, 474-475, 486-487, 505, 523, 525, 537, 539, 592, 608, 611, 617, 623, 625, 638, 660, 697, 699

Retablo Ex-Voto, 481

Retablo Santo, 481

Retablo, 47, 64, 168, 192, 480-481, 703

Retreat of St. Stanislaus, 481-482

Retreat, 111, 117, 276, 304, 467, 685

Retro Tabula, 480

Retrouvaille, 482

Revelation, 35, 51, 54, 58, 77, 80, 157, 174, 217, 260, 273, 317-318, 366, 461-462, 482-483, 500, 585, 622

Revised Standard Version Bible, 336

Rhodes, 286

Rhone, 658

Riccardi, Andrea, 565

Ricci, Timothy, 434

Richard of St. Victor, 34

Right of Sanctuary, 117

Rimini, 551

Ring, 127, 138, 285, 483, 497, 593, 659, 694

Rite for the Christian Initiation of Adults, 377

Rites, 34, 62, 100, 102, 105-106, 114, 137, 150, 185, 213, 285, 320-321, 323, 329, 338, 344, 377, 421, 423, 427, 450, 453, 473, 484, 494, 496, 514, 517, 536, 577, 615, 651, 655, 673

Ritual of Clamour, 249

River Ebro, 440

River Jordan, 188, 570

Rivers, Our Lady of, 411, 484

Roam, 435, 437, 545

Rockies, Our Lady of, 411, 484

Rogation Days, 164, 484-485

Rogation, 164, 484-485, 555

Rogationist Fathers of the Heart of Jesus, 554

Rogationtide, 485

Rohault de Fleury, 151

Roman calendar, 12, 100, 340, 549, 561, 574, 622

Roman martyrology, 102, 340

Roman Missal, 266, 496, 602, 646

Roman Ritual, 81-82, 90, 190, 407, 474, 656, 704

Romanus Pontifex, 533

Rome, 20-21, 28-29, 32-33, 35, 44, 49, 53, 56-57, 60-61, 66, 73, 89, 99, 105-106, 108, 113, 116, 118, 124, 132, 135-136, 138-139, 141, 154-155, 159, 191, 200, 211, 220, 243, 246, 262, 267, 277-278, 285, 296, 300-302, 309, 338, 345, 354, 371, 375, 377, 379-380, 403, 407-408, 413-414, 419, 430-434, 437-440, 453-454, 460-463, 467, 473, 475, 485, 499, 503, 511, 513-515, 519, 538, 543, 548, 552, 557, 563, 565-566, 568, 578, 582-583, 585, 592-593, 599, 601, 604, 621, 635-637, 639, 644-646, 654-656, 661, 676

Rood Screen, 255

Rooster, 278, 475

Rorate Coeli Desuper, 210

Rorate Mass, 210, 485

Rosarium Virginis Mariae, 14, 486

Rosary for the Dead, 433-434, 487

Rosary of Our Lady of Sorrows (Servite), 487

Rosary of Our Lady of Tears, 488

Rosary of Our Lord, 156, 200

Rosary of the Seven Joys, 204, 275, 523

Rosary priest, 197

Rosary rings, 483

Rosary, 31, 61, 65-66, 71, 74, 81, 89, 94, 120-122, 124, 129, 142-143, 146, 156, 168, 197-198, 200, 204-205, 225, 228-229, 248, 267, 275, 283, 293-294, 303, 307, 310, 319-320, 326, 331, 342-343, 359, 367, 384, 394, 397, 404, 411-412, 423, 434, 441-442, 467, 469, 483, 485-488, 494, 499, 521, 523, 525, 545, 596, 615, 640-642, 660-661, 689, 694-696, 702, 704-705

Rose petals, 488, 510

Rose, 30, 60, 67, 81, 111, 138, 149-150, 192, 202-203, 205, 209-211, 225, 229-230, 255, 310, 331, 367, 441-442, 488, 510, 573-574, 598, 608, 641, 680, 688, 696, 699

Rosemary, 191, 206, 229, 489

Roses, Our Lady of (Bayside Movement), 489

Rosweyde, 89

Rouen, 117

Roy, Rev. Neil J., 7, 16

Royal door, 255

Royal hours — Pannuchida, 421

Royal hours, 213, 421, 489

Rule of St. Albert, 365

Rule of St. Augustine, 80, 518

Rule of St. Benedict, 407, 558, 564

Russia, 83, 170, 185, 198-199, 214, 255, 338, 444, 456, 489, 569, 588, 622, 674, 678, 680, 698, 703

Russian emigrees, 127

Rwanda, 284

S

Sabbath, 298, 542-543, 608

Sabbatical, 276

Sabbatine privilege, 366, 493, 512-513, 517

Sacramentals, 17, 32, 72, 81-82, 92, 100, 127, 153-154, 185-186, 197, 199, 217, 246, 253, 256, 258, 262, 285, 323, 332, 350, 366, 420, 488, 493-496, 512, 701-702, 705

Sacramentum, 420, 494, 704

Sacred art, 58, 496, 510, 698

Sacred chrism, 244-245, 405

Sacred Congregation of Indulgences and Holy Relics, 473

Sacred Congregation of Rites, 102, 320, 427, 517, 536, 673

Sacred Head of Jesus, 496

Sacred Heart auto emblem, 496

Sacred Heart Auto League, 496

Sacred Heart badge, 71, 497

Sacred Heart rosary, 499, 615

Sacred Heart Society, 125

Sacred Heart, 12, 16, 53, 55, 71, 125, 165, 175, 187, 200, 210, 228, 259, 309, 315-316, 318-319, 330, 359, 361, 378, 381, 392-393, 397, 423, 479, 496-500, 512, 514, 517, 583, 615, 625, 659, 680, 684, 687-691, 698, 704

Sacred images, 26, 256-257

Sacred penitentiary, 15, 121

Sacred Scripture, 10, 34, 77, 266, 273, 305, 450, 473, 482

Sacred symbols — See Appendix D

Sacred Tradition, 482

Sacred vessels, 37, 501, 535

Sacred wounds, 245, 279, 475

Sacromonte, 192

Sacrosanctum Concilium, 10-12, 14, 705

Sainte-Chapelle, 299

Saints — See individual names

Saints, cult of, 502-540

Saints, devotion to, 504-507

Salesian, 186, 571-572, 639

Salutations - Greetings, 508

Salvatorians, 468

Salve Regina, 225, 390, 508

Salzburg, 536

Samuel (book of), 549

San Antonio, 189, 197

San Bernardino, 661

San Francisco de Asis, 131, 684

San Francisco, 84, 703-704, 706

San Juan Bautista, 509, 684

San Juan de Los Lagos, 435, 508-509

San Juan, Our Lady of, 411, 508-509, 691

San Salvatore In Onda, 262

Sancta Crucis Lignum, 358

Sancta Sanctorum, 645

Sanctifying grace, 71, 233, 354, 495-496, 508

Sanctuary of Consolation in Turin, 144

Sanctuary, 73, 100, 116-117, 144, 167, 220, 245, 255, 298, 303, 406, 476, 523, 671, 685, 690

Santa Claus, 115, 456-457, 587

Santa Fe, 65, 293, 689, 705-706

Santa Rita #1, 510

Santa Sindone, 529

Santarem, 87

Santeria, 47, 278

Santero, 95, 510

Santiago, 126, 154

Santo Casamentero, 552

Santo Domingo, 294

Saracens, 562, 588

Sardinia, 62, 354, 610-611

Saturday, 12, 33, 50, 167, 184, 187, 201, 213, 219, 242-245, 258, 321, 343, 378, 430, 468, 493, 510-511, 542, 576, 608-609, 624, 640, 656, 659

Saturnalia, 338

Saturnus, 338

Saul, 590

Savona, 362

Savonarola, Girolamo, 633

Saxon, 655

Scala Coeli, 511

Scala Pilati, 645

Scala Sancta, 511, 645

Scandinavia, 602, 674

Scapular medal, 495, 512

Scapular of Our Lady of Good Counsel, 212, 515

Scapular of Our Lady of Ransom, 517, 525

Scapular of St. Benedict, 518

Scapular of St. Camillus (Help of the Sick), 518

Scapular of St. Dominic, 519

Scapular of St. Joseph, 519, 577

Scapular of St. Michael, 519-520

Scapular of St. Norbert, 520

Scapular of the Blessed Virgin Mary, 79-80, 365, 494, 516-517

Scapular of the Holy Face, 513

Scapular of the Immaculate Heart of Mary, 513, 660

Scapular of the Most Blessed Trinity, 512-513

Scapular of the Most Precious Blood, 513-514

Scapular of the Most Sacred Heart of Jesus, 514

Scapular of the Sacred Hearts, 517

Scapular, 79-80, 89, 94, 202, 212, 217, 225, 364-366, 474-475, 493-495, 511-521, 525, 577, 660, 696

Scega Vecchia, 577

Scepter, 85, 129, 265, 307, 401, 671, 694

Scherenschnitte, 422

Schlattmann, Father Edward, 484

Schmerzensfreitag, 525

Schmittdner, 288

Schoenstatt Lay Movement, 305

Scotland, 53, 133, 559-560, 674, 678

Scott, David, 20

Scourge, 521, 693-696

Scranton, 387, 691

Scripture, 4, 10, 31, 34, 38, 50, 59, 77, 124, 184, 236, 266, 273, 276, 305, 317, 322, 324, 328, 355, 450, 473, 482-483, 499, 501, 505, 521, 552, 576, 585, 608, 617, 622

Scrutinies of Catechumens, 507

Scutari, 211

Seafarers, 53, 305, 456

Seamless robe, 625

Seashell, 139

Sebaste, 559

Second century, 31, 99, 143, 148, 155, 204, 272, 450, 458, 530, 606

Second Coming, 29, 50, 277

Second Council of Lyon, 250

Second Council of Nicaea, 26, 57, 409

Second Crusade, 558

Second Vatican Council, 9, 14, 77, 99, 236, 242, 300, 307, 321, 325, 352, 415, 450, 485, 506-507

Secretariats, 53

Secular Franciscans, 141, 618

Secular Orders — Third Orders, 141, 521
Seder, 183, 424-425
Seelen Brot, 93
Seissen, 236
Self-discipline, 60, 361
Seligenstadt, 376
Semana Santa, 214
Semitic, 26, 530
Senefelder, Aloys, 234
Senko, 261
Sensus Fidelium, 323
September, 41, 44, 51-52, 62, 92, 120, 126, 129, 146, 153, 156, 163, 173, 187, 242, 294, 296, 342, 359, 375, 412, 440, 526, 567-568, 585, 593, 602, 625
Septuagesima Sunday, 188
Septuagesima, 188, 521
Septuagint, 33, 298
Serafin, Thomas J., 21
Seraphim, 41, 616
Serenity Prayer, 522
Servant of God, 113, 232, 267
Servants of Charity, 578
Servants of Mary, 80, 141, 518, 545, 639
Service to the Poor, 158
Servite Order, 80, 487, 517-518, 525, 544-545, 639
Servites, 141, 392, 545, 591-592, 639
Serz, Verlag von, 235
Seven Altars of the Vatican Basilica, 523-524
Seven Canonical Hours, 90
Seven Dolors, 522-523, 525, 545
Seven Gifts of the Holy Spirit, 124, 298, 522, 699
Seven Holy Maccabees, 434

Seven Houses, Visit of, 522, 644
Seven Last Words of Christ, 214, 523, 620
Seven Privileged Altars, 524
Seven Sacraments, 71, 140, 189, 408, 494-496, 508, 525, 629
Seven Saturdays in honor of Our Lady of Ransom, 525
Seven Sorrows of Mary, 79-80, 199, 392, 487-488, 518, 522, 525-526, 543, 545, 602, 639
Sevenfold Flame, 527
Seventeenth century, 12, 46, 54, 67, 104, 114, 116, 124, 154, 216, 234, 240, 272, 288, 304, 308, 326, 332, 381, 434, 440, 481, 499, 535-536, 539, 548, 577, 599-600
Seventh century, 31, 61, 66, 100, 145, 184, 202, 227, 260, 375, 429, 454, 483, 624, 655
Sexagesima, 470, 527
Sext, 102, 163, 249, 326, 527
Shadow of the Cross, 131
Shamrock, 231, 421, 527, 588, 695, 699
Shanley, Rev. Dr. Kevin, O. Carm, 21
Sheen, Archbishop Fulton J., 660
Sheldon, Charles, 662
Shemah Yisrael, 541-542
Shinto, 658
Ship of St. Peter, 528
Ship, 91, 136, 431, 527-528, 551-552, 588, 694-696, 699
Shoulder wound of Christ, 528
Shrid Pye, 355, 528
Shrimp King and Queen, 84
Shrine of Our Lady of Lavang, 302-303
Shrine of Our Lord of the Miracles, 326

Shrine, 528 (See individual listings for shrines)

Shrine, Crowned, 528

Shriven, 534

Shroud of Turin, 529-533, 636

Shrove Tuesday, 138, 337, 534

Shuster, George, 111

Siauliai, 192, 232

Sicilian, 84, 256, 547, 579-580, 610

Sicily, 256, 354, 363, 547, 579-580, 583, 588, 611, 639, 678

Siebenkrautersuppe, 525

Sign of the Cross, 80-81, 85, 93, 122, 124, 153-154, 185-186, 272, 319, 434, 494-495, 512, 535, 593, 656

Sign, 100-101, 106, 120, 144-145, 183, 219-220, 228, 257285, 289, 364-365, 390, 405-406, 419, 424, 427, 431, 447, 488, 497, 505, 516-517, 534, 582, 593, 598, 611, 633, 643, 661

Signacula, 348

Signing yourself, 434

Silence, Virgin of (See Knock)

Silent Night, 536

Sillar, 118

Siluva, Our Lady of, 411, 536

Simeon, 104, 392, 397, 462-463, 525-526, 639

Simeon's Canticle, 326

Simila, 362

Simnel Cake, 363

Simon Magus, 536

Simony, 477, 536

Simple feasts, 536

Sin eating, 537

Sinibaldi, Father Giacomo, 379

Sinte Klaas, 587

Sinter Klaus, 456

Sinulog, 115

Sister Amelia, 488

Sister Apolline, 474

Sister Josefa Menendez, 499

Sister Marie de Jesus Agreda, 296

Sister Marie de St. Pierre, 319, 513

Sister of Charity of St. Vincent de Paul, 474

Sister of St. Dorothy, 198

Sister, 20, 121, 173-174, 209, 217, 236, 239, 245, 272-273, 297, 318, 363, 365-367, 383, 385, 397, 441-442, 447-448, 468, 518, 557, 595-596, 598

Sisters of Charity in Milan, 339

Sisters of Our Lady of Mercy, 174

Sisters of Providence, 550

Sisters of the Poor Child Jesus, 443

Sit Semper in Cordibus Nostris, 79

Sixteenth century, 25, 61, 114, 119, 126, 129, 133, 141, 148, 188, 210, 228, 240, 242, 273, 311, 345, 348, 384, 452, 562, 572, 633

Sixth century, 29, 33, 35, 44, 66, 76, 136, 148, 153, 202, 274, 299, 335, 337, 540, 568, 586

Skladen, 444

Skull and crossbones, 165

Slavery of love, 537

Slaves of the Immaculate Child, 173

Slavic, 83, 134, 182, 188, 570, 602

Slavite Yoho, 610

Sleepless monks, 26

Sligo, 546

Slipper Chapel, 654

Slovaks, 136, 508

Snow, Our Lady of the, 410-411, 538

Social justice, 109, 277, 575

Social teachings of the Church, 111

Socialist, 110

Society for Catholic Liturgy, 323

Society of St. Monica, 538

Society of the Catholic Apostolate, 262

Society of the Divine Attributes, 538

Society of the Precious Blood, 454, 690

Sodalities, 15, 128, 141

Sodality, 128, 327, 521, 539

Sodom and Gomorrah, 607

Sol, 629

Soledad, Our Lady of, 411-412, 539

Solemnity of Mary, 137, 342, 362, 540

Solemnity of the Annunciation, 342

Solemnity of the Assumption, 342

Solemnity, 16, 48, 59, 61, 132, 134, 137, 199, 258, 342, 362, 540, 574

Solesmes, 307, 701

Soli Deo, 672

Somalia, 260

Son of Joseph, Jesus, 540-542, 576

Son of Justice, 133, 311

Song of Brother Sun, 447

Sons of the Immaculate Heart of Mary, 513

Sopocko, Father Michael, 174-175

Sorrowful and Immaculate Heart of Mary, 543-544

Sorrowful Mother, 167, 199, 226, 352, 381, 394-395, 545, 639, 690

Sorrows, Our Lady of, 57, 80, 294, 342, 359, 374, 381, 392, 395, 487, 518, 525-526, 544, 602, 639, 684, 688

Soubirous, Bernadette, 330

Soul bread, 93

Soul food, 545

South America, 62, 95, 134, 147, 199, 326, 332, 338, 380, 680

South Carolina, 441

Souvenirs, 60, 348

Soviet Union, 78, 85, 199

Spain, 29-30, 48, 62-64, 79, 84, 88, 114, 129-130, 137, 139, 151, 154, 158-159, 199, 214, 218-220, 240, 244, 263, 273, 294, 296-297, 308, 327, 340, 344, 360, 380-381, 438-440, 481, 489, 517, 551-552, 568, 570, 576, 583-584, 586, 592, 654, 661, 677, 679-680

Spanish Civil War, 132

Spanish empire, 326

Spear, 7, 278, 299, 405, 475, 568-569

Spearmint, 229

Spencer, Mrs. Harry W., 130

Spikenards, 330

Spiritans, 57

Spiritual Association of Our Lady of Victory, 640

Spiritual communion, 453, 545

Spiritual Institute of America, 546

Spiritual wake, 213

Spiritual Works of Mercy, 147, 168, 353, 546

Spiritualist, 47

Spoleto, 594

Sponge, 475

Spratt, Father John, 601

Spy Wednesday, 547

St. Agatha, 46, 547, 693

St. Agatha's bread, 547

St. Agnes of Montepulciano, 406

St. Agnes, 298, 314, 406, 419, 547-548, 693

St. Alban's Abbey, 248

St. Albans, 20, 439

St. Albert, 365, 388, 657

St. Alphonsus Liguori, 432, 619

St. Ambrose, 31, 37, 75, 182, 371, 616, 693

St. Anastasia, 136

St. Andrew the Apostle, 337

St. Andrew, 29, 129, 152-153, 314, 337, 406, 570, 592, 693

St. Ann, 381, 387-388, 505, 686-687, 689, 691, 693

St. Anne, 67, 73, 122, 288, 319, 388, 405, 549-550, 691, 693

St. Anne's water, 549

St. Anselm, 241, 698

St. Anthony Guide!, 552

St. Anthony Maria Claret, 235

St. Anthony of Egypt, 435, 503, 550, 555

St. Anthony of Padua, 129, 200, 307, 378, 550-552, 554-555, 618, 621, 671, 693

St. Anthony Zaccaria, 204

St. Anthony, soldier, 552

St. Anthony's bread, 93, 552-555

St. Anthony's fire, 555

St. Appolonia, 555

St. Aquinas, 19-20, 30, 146-147, 174, 402, 420, 506, 615, 696, 705

St. Athanasius, 77, 149, 314, 503

St. Augustine of Canterbury, 191

St. Augustine, 80, 102, 143-144, 174, 182, 191, 211, 314, 381, 432, 451, 518, 551, 685, 688, 693, 705

St. Barbara Twig, 556

St. Barbara, 556, 684, 693

St. Bartholomew, 556-557, 693

St. Basil, 33, 72, 145, 230, 314

St. Basil, Bishop of Caesarea, 230

St. Bede the Venerable, 181

St. Bede, 181, 437, 654

St. Benedict, 111-112, 240, 314, 325, 349-351, 402, 407, 518, 556-558, 564, 595-596, 691, 693

St. Benedict's herb, 557-558

St. Benezet, 658

St. Bernadette, 54, 331, 390, 488

St. Bernard dogs, 559

St. Bernard of Clairvaux, 352, 504, 511, 528, 558, 693

St. Bernard of Montjoux, 558

St. Bernard, 121, 352, 461, 504, 511, 528, 558-559, 693

St. Bernardine of Siena, 241, 693

St. Beuno, 602

St. Blaise sticks, 92

St. Blaise, 85, 92, 101-102, 420, 559, 657, 693

St. Bonaventure, 226, 356, 395, 552, 621, 693

St. Bride's Day, 559

St. Bridget of Sweden, 94

St. Brigid — Mary of the Gael, 559

St. Brigid's Cross, 560, 693

St. Calixtus, 639

St. Camiillus of Lellis, 406, 474, 51

St. Catherine of Alexandria, 694

St. Catherine of Siena, 111, 174, 374, 394, 598, 694

St. Charles Borromeo, 204, 531, 694

St. Christopher medal, 349, 561-562

St. Christopher, 234, 349, 506, 560-562, 694

St. Clare, 158, 562, 566, 694

St. Claude, 519

St. Clement, 445-446, 563, 687

St. Cyril of Jerusalem, 151, 271, 451, 694, 705

St. Cyril, 33, 145, 151, 271, 451, 694, 705

St. Dismas, 215, 562-563

St. Dominic, 46, 75, 314, 383, 394, 442, 519, 694

St. Dorothy, 111, 198, 489, 694

St. Dunstan, 563-564

St. Dymphna, 349, 351, 564-565

St. Egidio Community, 565

St. Elizabeth of Hungary, 226, 489, 694

St. Elizabeth, Queen of Hungary, 489

St. Eustace, 694

St. Eustochium, 436

St. Faro, 566

St. Faustina Kowalska, 174

St. Felix of Valois, 513

St. Fiacre, 565-566

St. Francis de Sales, 210

St. Francis of Assisi, 44, 46, 75, 82, 111, 112, 135, 141, 146, 157-158, 170, 245, 273, 308, 314, 444, 446-447, 484, 562, 565-567, 574, 680, 605, 618, 671, 690, 702

St. Francis of Paola, 146, 355

St. Francis Xavier, 314, 393, 591, 598, 680, 686, 687, 694

St. Gabriel (Archangel), 42, 44, 67, 307, 387, 392, 401, 567-568, 694

St. Gaspar Del Bufalo, 453, 523

St. George, 568-570, 694

St. George's arms, 568

St. George's Day, 569-570

St. Gerard Majella, 406

St. Gertrude, 694

St. Giles, 694

St. Gregory Barbarigo, 102

St. Gregory Nazianzen, 33, 145, 182

St. Gregory of Tours, 337

St. Gregory Thaumaturgus, 618

St. Gregory the Great, 29, 34, 72, 91, 137, 217-218, 286, 371, 475, 502, 524, 557, 694

St. Helen, 78, 229

St. Helena, 151, 153, 155-156, 335, 371, 511, 621, 625, 645, 694

St. Hilary of Poitiers, 583

St. Ignatius of Antioch, 143

St. Ignatius of Loyola, 46, 256, 694

St. Ignatius, 46, 143, 256, 314, 657, 694-695

St. Irenaeus, 288

St. James the Apostle, 271, 440, 580

St. James the Greater, 139, 438, 694

St. James the Less, 580, 694

St. Januarius, 89, 271, 356

St. Jerome, 182, 436-437, 694

St. Joachim, 67, 549

St. Joan of Arc, 598, 695

St. John Baptist, 38, 166, 231, 300, 314, 354, 375-376, 405, 439, 570-572, 574, 690, 695

St. John Berchmans, 695

St. John Bosco, 229, 296, 476, 571, 689

St. John Chrysostom, 72, 155, 206, 695

St. John De Brebeuf, 135

St. John Eudes, 67, 258, 499

St. John Lateran, 73, 220, 246, 300, 432, 646

St. John Neumann, 235, 691

St. John of Matha, 214, 513

St. John of the Cross, 130, 141, 163, 644

St. John the Baptist, 38, 166, 231, 300, 314, 354, 375-376, 405, 439, 570-572, 574, 695

St. John the Evangelist, 138, 287, 332, 695

St. John's Day, 229, 354, 377, 405, 610-611

St. John's Eve, 229, 354, 377, 573, 610

St. John's fires, 377, 572-573

St. John's Night, 354, 573

St. John's wine, 574

St. John's Wort, 231

St. Joseph realtor, 577

St. Joseph scapular, 519, 577

St. Joseph the Worker, 574-575

St. Joseph, 67, 80, 92-93, 145-146, 175, 237, 239-240, 275, 287, 307-309, 314-315, 319, 330, 341, 352, 354, 359, 381, 396, 420, 439-441, 448-449, 519-520, 526, 541, 574-580, 659, 683, 688, 690-691, 695

St. Joseph, Pious Union of the, 441, 577-578

St. Joseph's altar, 93, 578-580

St. Joseph's loaves, 577

St. Joseph's messenger, 440

St. Joseph's union, 146

St. Juan Diego, 219, 378, 488

St. Jude Shrine, 388, 582, 685-686

St. Jude Thaddeus, 388, 580-581, 686

St. Jude, 381, 388, 524, 580-582, 683, 685-686, 695

St. Jude's Hospital, 582

St. Julia Billiart, 406

St. Julian, 296, 361, 581-582, 695

St. Justin Martyr, 608, 695

St. Lawrence, 314, 583, 695

St. Lawrence-Outside-the-Walls, 646

St. Leo Karasuma, 591

St. Leonard of Port Maurice, 604, 619

St. Louis De Montfort, 143, 467, 538

St. Louis IX, 299, 695

St. Louis, 132, 143, 299, 385, 467, 484, 538, 687, 695, 704

St. Lucy's crown, 583, 695

St. Luke the Evangelist, 63

St. Luke, 63, 78, 209, 229, 289, 430, 475, 678, 695

St. Luke's Day, 229

St. Malachy, 383, 461

St. Margaret Mary Alacoque, 54, 67, 187, 200, 240-241, 378, 423, 497-498, 500, 583

St. Margaret, 678, 695

St. Maria Goretti, 349-350, 395-396

St. Marius, 599

St. Mark's Cathedral, 139

St. Martin of Tours, 38, 102, 249-250, 340, 407, 583-584, 695

St. Martin's goose, 340, 584

St. Martin's lamp, 585

St. Martin's Lent, 29

St. Martin's summer, 584

St. Martin's wine, 340

St. Mary Magdalene Dei Pazzi, 406, 695

St. Mary Major, 73, 136, 246, 342, 432, 538, 644, 646

St. Mary-of-the-Woods, 550

St. Mechtilde of Helfta, 619

St. Meinrad, 186, 686, 695

St. Menas, 407

St. Michael (Archangel), 40-42, 354, 425, 520, 524, 584-586, 695

St. Michael's Day, 585

St. Michael's feast, 585

St. Michael's love, 586

St. Monica, 143-145, 538, 695

St. Nicholas of Bari, 587, 618

St. Nicholas of Myra, 367, 586-587

St. Nicholas of Tolentino, 92, 168, 425

St. Nicholas, 91-93, 168, 367, 406, 425, 455-456, 586-588, 618, 695

St. Nicholas's Day, 455

St. Norbert, 520-521

St. Odilia water, 588, 657-658

St. Odilio, 34

St. Pantaleon, 695

St. Paschal Baylon, 406, 695

St. Patrice, 589

St. Patrick, 150, 231, 329, 438-439, 527, 559-560, 588-589, 695, 702

St. Patrick's Day Parade, 589

St. Patrick's Purgatory Lough Derg, 589

St. Patrick's Purgatory, 439, 589

St. Paul Miki, 591

St. Paul of the Cross, 367, 424

St. Paul, 20, 73, 105, 123, 138, 239, 253-254, 314, 354, 367, 403, 424, 434, 437, 451, 458, 462, 474, 590-593, 601, 640, 652, 655, 657, 691, 695-696

St. Paula, 436

St. Paulinus of Nola, 155, 407

St. Paul-Outside-the-Walls, 246, 590, 646

St. Peregrine Laziosi, 592

St. Peregrine, 590-592

St. Peter Baptist, 314, 519, 591

St. Peter Julian Eymard, 296, 361

St. Peter Nolasco, 141, 517, 525, 696

St. Peter the Martyr, 563, 657

St. Peter, 73, 105, 118, 136, 138, 141, 206, 239, 246, 277, 285, 287, 296, 298, 309, 314, 361, 403, 419, 434-435, 437-438, 458, 483, 517, 519, 524-525, 528, 563, 582, 590-593, 629, 635, 646, 655, 657, 691, 695-696

St. Peter's Basilica, 524, 582, 635, 646, 655

St. Peter's plant, 593

St. Peter's sail, 438

St. Peter's in Rome, 136, 403, 582, 646

St. Petronilla, 524

St. Philip Benzi, 591

St. Philip Neri, 204, 240, 345, 696

St. Pierre, Sister Marie de, 319, 513

St. Pio of Pietrelcina, 605

St. Polycarp, 476, 502

St. Raphael the Archangel, 42, 592-593

St. Raymond Nonnatus, 657, 696

St. Rita of Cascia, 489, 594

St. Rita, 74-75, 489, 510, 594-595, 696

St. Roch, 348, 686, 696

St. Scholastica, 518, 557, 595-596, 696

St. Sebastian, 135, 348, 646, 696

St. Serapion, 407

St. Sharbel Makhlouf, 406

St. Simon Stock, 46, 202, 365, 696

St. Simon, 46, 202, 365, 524, 581, 696

St. Stephen, 61, 83, 91, 314, 597, 696

St. Stephen's Day, 597

St. Stephen's horses, 597

St. Sylvester, 286, 597, 696

St. Tarcisius, 615

St. Teresa, 111, 141, 314, 574, 597-598, 644, 696

St. Teresa's Bookmark, 597

St. Thérèse of Lisieux, 123

St. Thomas Aquinas, 19-20, 30, 146-147, 174, 402, 420, 506, 615, 696, 705

St. Thomas Becket, 104, 437, 696

St. Thomas More, 203, 206, 437, 489

St. Torellus, 657

St. Uldaric, 102

St. Ulrich of Augsburg, 102, 348

St. Ursula, 598-599, 696

St. Valentine, 598-601, 660

St. Veronica, 513, 696

St. Vincent de Paul, 474, 601, 640, 657, 696

St. Vincent Ferrer, 618, 696

St. Vincent Pallotti, 262

St. Vitus dance, 601

St. Vitus, 601-602

St. Vladimir, 609

St. Walburga, 406, 691

St. Willibrord, 186

St. Winefride, 602

St. Winefride's well, 602

Stabat Mater, 602

Stackpole, Robert, 21

Stair of Pilate, 645

Stairway to Heaven, 511

Star of Bethlehem, 188, 441

Star of the Sea, 53, 67, 202, 374, 602-603

Star of the Sea, Our Lady, 374, 603

Star, 53, 67-68, 188, 202, 216, 310, 374, 404-405, 431, 441, 558, 575, 603, 610, 694, 699

Station days, 576

Station Masses, 605

Station, 538, 576, 602, 604-605, 638

Stational Churches, 485, 604

Stational Churches, Days, 485

Stations of the Cross (Way of the Cross), 326, 604, 658

Stations, Irish, 605

Stedry Vecer, 136

Stella Maris Program for Seafarers, 53

Sternsingen, 405

Stichon, 605

Stigmata, 530, 567, 605, 694-695

Stipend, 605

Stock, 46, 82, 202, 365, 510, 605, 696

Stokes, John S., Jr., 341

Stole, 431, 535, 637-638

Story of a Soul, The, 598

Stoup, 606

Strawberries, 229

Strenae, 455

Striking the breast, 606

Sts. Processus and Martinian, 524

Sts. Simon and Jude, 524

Sturolite, 283

Sub Tuum Praesidium, 606

Subiaco, 521, 557

Suffrages, 382, 450, 452, 493, 606-608

Sulog, 115

Summa Theologiae, 506, 705

Sunday, 12, 16, 19-21, 29-31, 50, 93-94, 99, 112, 125, 132-133, 136, 138, 147, 149, 163, 168, 175-176, 181-183, 188-189, 202, 209-210, 227, 239-240, 243-244, 258, 265, 275, 294, 297, 306, 343, 353, 362, 379, 409, 420, 424, 428, 470, 485, 508, 521, 527, 547, 563, 600, 608-609, 621, 623-624, 640-641, 656, 659-663, 667, 701-706

Supererogation, 609

Supernatural solidarity, 606-608

Superstition, 13, 49, 82, 233, 347, 355, 430, 578, 582, 597, 609, 623

Suppression laws, 133

Supreme Order of Christ, 286

Supreme Shepherd of the Church, 408

Surname, 372, 374, 557

Sutamarchan, 129

Suyapa, Our Lady of, 412, 609

Sviachene Dinner, 609

Sviachenia, 83

Sviata Vechera, 610

Swaddling clothes, 25, 132

Sweden, 94, 264, 373, 572, 583, 675, 693

Sweethearts of St. John, 354, 610-611

Switzerland, 44, 79, 186, 235, 339, 485, 679

Sword of the Spirit, 127

Sybil of the Rhine, 230

Sylan, Brother, 412

Syllabus of Errors, 297

Symbol, 29, 31, 39, 59, 75, 79, 100, 118, 128-129, 134, 137, 145, 150, 153-154, 156, 170, 176, 182-184, 191, 193, 201, 203, 210, 226, 229-231, 233, 241, 254, 259, 277-278, 289, 294, 298, 347, 365, 384, 419, 421, 429, 435, 468, 474, 484, 488-489, 497, 518, 527, 544, 568, 577, 601, 603, 611, 619, 624, 641, 659, 661, 667, 697-699

Synagogue, 118, 324, 542

Syracuse, 106

Syria, 106

Syrian Christians, 629

Syrian Jacobites, 186

T

Tacubaya, 238

Taigi, Anna Maria, 308

Taliss, 541

Tantum Ergo, 76, 420-421, 615

Tarcisians, 615

Tarsus, 590

Tasseled, 145

Tau, 151

Te Deum Laudamus, 616

Teaching Christian doctrine, 617

Tekakwitha League, 283

Tenebrae, 227, 298, 617

Tennessee, 582

Tenth century, 31, 60, 133, 164, 228, 249, 319, 476, 593, 635

Teodoro, 426

Tepeyac, 219-221

Teramo, 167

Terce, 102, 163, 249, 326, 617

Terni, 599

Tertiary, 544, 617

Tertullian, 31, 429

Testimonio Del Risorto, 639

Teutonic goddess, 181

Texas, 19-21, 83, 127, 159, 189, 197, 297, 380, 475, 510, 654, 691, 703

Thaumaturge, 237, 618

Theatines of the Immaculate Conception, 89

Thebes, 436, 629

Theca, 478, 618

Theodore, 550, 680, 696

Theotokos, 343, 541, 618-619

Theresians of the United States, 619

Thessalonians, 10, 41, 50, 590

Third century, 141, 188, 234, 324, 429, 449, 503, 561, 606, 673

Third Eucharistic prayer, 674

Third millennium, 16, 125, 246

Third Order of St. Dominic, 383

Third Order, 141, 403, 516, 521, 617, 619, 690

Third Order, Carmelites, 141

Third Order, Dominicans, 141

Third Order, Franciscans, 141

Thirteen coins, 619

Thirteenth century, 12, 60, 75-76, 78, 80, 90, 128, 141, 164, 177, 190, 226, 240-241, 249-250, 298, 348, 360, 365, 373-374, 438, 494, 535, 549, 553, 564, 639, 698

Thomas Kempis, 258, 437

Thomas of Celano, 170

Thomas, Danny, 581

Thomas, Father Paul, 620

Three Hail Marys, 45, 94, 122-124, 386, 486-487, 619-620

Three Hours Devotion, 214, 620

Three Kings Day, 188, 620

Thrones, 41, 336

Thurible, 260-261, 620

Thurificati, 261

Thyme, 206, 229

Tiara and two keys, 520

Tiberius Caesar, 543

Ticket to Heaven, 620-621

Tilma, 220

Timothy, 254, 434, 451, 505, 590, 639, 704

Tishri, 276

Tissington, 660

Titular, 524, 582, 646, 673

Tlaxcala, 403, 621

Tobit, 42, 384

Todi, 339, 366, 602

Toison De Oro, 114

Tokyo, 151

Toledo, 63, 402, 690

Tolone, 555

Tomb burial, 105, 596

Tombs of St. Peter and St. Paul, 437

Tongue of St. Anthony, 621

Tonsured, 127

Torribia, Maria, 570

Tossing of the Cross, 621-622

Touraine, 250

Tours, 38, 102, 133, 209, 249-250, 319, 337, 340, 407, 513, 583-584, 678, 695

Towels, 622

Tower of London, 601

TR2000, 639

Traca, 577

Tract 90, 414

Tractarians, 414

Tracts for the times, 414

Traileros, 218

Trani, 87

Transfiguration, 487, 592, 622

Translation, 4, 13-14, 39, 90, 145, 171, 320, 431, 445, 458, 592, 606, 615-616, 621-622, 633-634, 703-704

Traveler, 64

Tre Ore, 620

Treaty of Limerick, 267

Trent, 99, 142, 147, 203, 267, 452, 476-477, 634, 702

Trental of St. Gregory, 218

Tridentine Mass, 140

Triduum, 99, 181, 212, 214, 242, 244, 393, 623

Trier, 625

Trikerion, 185

Trinitaria, 421

Trinitarian formula, 623

Trinitarians, 214, 513

Trinity columns, 623

Trinity flower, 421

Trinity rain, 623

Trinity Sunday, 12, 147, 183, 623-624, 659

Trinity, 67, 122-123, 134, 147, 149, 173, 183, 185, 209, 214, 227, 231, 260, 309, 311-312, 315, 318, 336, 381, 391-392, 421, 513-514, 517, 527, 535, 558, 579, 589, 623-625, 659, 683, 688, 690, 698-699

Trinitytide, 624

Triptych, 444, 624

Triquetra, 624, 699

Triumph of the Cross, 154, 156, 187, 526, 625

Tropologica, 266

Troyes, 531

True Devotion to Mary, 467

Tuberculosis, 175, 413, 598, 679

Tunbridge Wells, 564

Tunic, Holy, 625

Tupas, Rajah, 114-115

Turgis, L., 235

Turin, 144, 529-533, 572, 636

Turkey, 436, 530, 549, 559

Tutankhamen, 260

Twelfth century, 29, 34, 100, 108, 140, 230, 271, 335, 347, 360, 363, 428, 440, 468, 486, 568, 599, 602-603, 625, 658

Twelfth night, 188, 625

Twelve Apostles' Dinner, 289, 407

Twelve grapes, 597

Twelve promises of the Sacred Heart, 499-500, 625

Twentieth century, 46, 88, 174, 190, 205, 238, 260, 264, 274, 325, 423, 480, 531, 598, 602

Twin, 414, 482, 518, 557, 595

Two natures of Christ, 149, 655

Two thieves crucified, 47

Tyre, 165, 403

Tyrolian, 136

U

Ubi Arcano, 109

Uganda, 375, 678

Ukraine, 83, 183, 429, 563, 569, 609

Ultreya, 629

Umbra, 629

Umbrella, 73, 629

Umbria, 594

Unction, 193, 322, 337, 629

Unico Crucis Signo, 512

United Nations, 661

United States Bishops' Committee on the Liturgy, 250

United States Conference of Catholic Bishops, 142

Unity, 101, 112, 132, 186, 286, 289, 389, 403-404, 419, 434, 446, 484, 516, 645, 654-655, 659

Universal Church, 95, 102, 175, 239, 413, 426, 493, 499, 519-521, 575, 577, 624, 677

Universal Vocation to Holiness, 9

University of St. Thomas, 20, 294

Upper Room, 300

Urfa, 530
Ursuline, 460, 599, 686
Uruguay, 332, 679
Uspallata Pass, 131

V

Valencia, 158, 576
Valentine cards, 170, 600-601
Valentine, 170, 506, 599-601, 660, 680
Valentine's Day, 506, 600-601, 660
Vanities, 633
Varghese, Roy Abraham, 21, 706
Varietates Legitimae, 14
Vatican hill, 593
Vatican library, 431
Venerable Benedict Holzhauser, 54
Venerable Dominic of Jesus and Mary, 216
Venerable Margaret of the Blessed Sacrament, 318
Venerable Mary D'Antigna, 383
Venerable Mother Maria of Jesus, 406
Venerable Ursula Benincasa, 89
Venezuela, 88, 146, 679
Veni Creator Spiritus, 633
Veni Sancte Spiritus, 176, 634
Venial sins, 49, 140, 528, 635
Venice, 139, 274, 338, 461, 568, 676, 678
Venite, Exultemus Domino, 635
Venus, 211
Vercelli, 242, 531
Vernal equinox, 181
Veronica, 26, 79, 278, 475, 489, 513, 530, 604, 635-636, 696
Veronica's Veil, 26, 79, 278, 475, 635-636

Vesnyanky, 225
Vespers, 26, 67, 102, 182, 225, 244, 298-299, 326, 596, 623, 637
Vess, 305
VFGA, 192
Via Crucis, 638
Via Dolorosa, 604
Via Matris, 395, 545, 639
Via Nomentana, 419, 548
Via Solaria, 108
Viana Do Costelo, 84
Vicar of Christ, 592
Vicari, Ferdinand, 519
Victorian Era, 235, 358
Victorian, 235, 358
Victory, Our Lady of, 228, 263-264, 412, 639-640, 679, 689
Vidi Aquam, 61
Vienna, 216, 228, 234, 242
Vietcong, 304
Vietnam, 302-304, 679
Vietnamese, 85, 302-304, 375
Vigano, Don Egidio, 639
Vigil for the Dead, 640
Vigil, 72, 100, 181-182, 184-185, 213, 226, 242, 321, 396, 421, 429-430, 478, 489, 608, 624, 640, 646, 656
Vincent de Paul Society, 601, 640
Vincentian Fathers, 128
Vincentian nun, 356
Vine and branches, 641
Viola Tricolor, 421
Virgin Mary, Relics of, 477, 641
Virgin of Solitude, 539
Virgin of the Poor (Banneux), 641-642
Virgin of the Poor, 71, 127, 641-643
Virginia, 130, 619, 654, 703

Virgins, 67-68, 145, 309-311, 313, 315, 352, 435

Virgo Paritura, 127

Virtues, 27, 41, 71, 174, 232, 256-257, 297, 317, 330, 361, 388, 396, 475, 546, 565, 573, 618, 633, 638, 644

Vision, 38, 44, 54, 56, 80, 109-110, 126, 153, 173, 204-205, 218, 240, 308, 331, 365, 382-383, 393, 415, 426, 431, 438, 445, 451, 461, 511, 514, 518, 520, 535, 563, 566, 583, 592, 596, 615, 642

Visionary, 54, 403, 572

Visitation of Mary, 121, 336, 342, 397, 583, 644

Visitation Order, 245, 583

Visitation Sister, 121, 245

Visiting St. Peter's tomb, 646

Visiting the Sacred Crib in St. Mary Major, 644

Visiting the Seven Churches of Rome, 646

Visiting the Sick, 646

Viva Cristo Rey, 132

Voluntary poverty, 110-112, 158

Volunteer Missionary Movement, 305

Volunteers for Educational and Social Services, 305

Von Harlaer, Nicholas, 603

Voragine, Bishop James of, 210

Voss, Monsignor Elwood C., 619

Votive pictures, 44

Votum Fecit Gratiam Accepit, 192

Vow, 65, 126, 191-192, 218, 232, 363, 377-378, 393, 402, 436, 460, 481, 525, 554, 560, 582, 647, 659

Vratislav of Pernstyn, 263

Vulgate, 298

W

Wabash River, 550

Waco, 159

Wadding, 204

Wadding, Father Luke, 204

Waes Hael, 655

Wake, 76, 167, 213, 330, 414, 537, 640, 651-653

Wales, 116, 206, 537, 560, 602, 675

Walls, 75, 105-106, 117, 138, 164, 211, 216, 242, 327, 342, 378, 497, 562, 588, 662

Walsh, Michael, 7, 21, 706

Walsingham, 21, 412, 439, 653-655, 679

Walsingham, Holy House of, 653

Walsingham, Our Lady of, 21, 412, 653-655, 679

Waltham, 134

Ward, W.G., 412-413

Wars Against Turks, 552

Warsaw, 61, 174

Washing of the Altar, 655

Wassail cup, 655

Wassail-branch, 655

Water (holy water), 60-62, 81-82, 84, 142, 177, 185, 197, 218, 243, 450, 507, 516, 606, 622, 655-657, 695, 698

Water of St. Vincent, 657

Water pot, 475

Water, 34, 46, 60-62, 64, 71, 78, 81-84, 104, 118-119, 126, 142, 159, 170, 177, 185, 197, 199, 214, 218, 243, 256, 294, 302, 331, 407, 426, 447, 450, 457, 475, 489, 500, 507, 516, 531, 537, 549, 553, 556, 561, 564, 573, 588, 594-595, 597, 606, 622, 642-643, 655-658, 660, 695, 698

Wattson, Father Paul James Francis, S.A., 132

Wattson, Father Paul, 66, 132, 403

Way of the Cross, 204, 326, 383, 488, 528, 604, 638, 657-658

Way of the Light, 638

Wayside shrines, 166, 658-659

Weather makers, 593

Wedding ring, 659

Week of Prayer for Christian Unity, 132, 403-404, 659

Weekday devotions, 511, 659

Wells, Holy, 660

Wenner, Raven, 21

Wesley, Charles, 135

Wesley, John, 413

Wessex, 564

Western-Orthodox Schism, 148

Westminster Cathedral, 192

Westminster, 192, 578, 659, 706

What Would Jesus Do?, 662-663

White Scapular (Immaculate Heart), 513

White Sunday, 428

White, Father Andrew, 390

White, Mother Lurana Mary Francis, 66

Whitefriars Street, 601

Whitsunday, 308, 428-429, 660

Wieniec, 61, 660

Williamsburg, 654

Wilson, Mary, 21

Witchcraft, 233

Woden, 586, 593

Woman Clothed With the Sun, 157, 317

Wonder worker, 550, 559

Wood sorrel, 229, 231, 527

Woodcut, 59

Woods Hole, 341

Wool, 127, 419, 519, 521, 542, 548, 559, 562

Word of God, 10, 13, 261, 284, 298, 305, 309, 313, 325, 473, 482, 611, 645

Works of Mercy, 35, 110-112, 126, 145-147, 168, 352-353, 546, 640, 646

World Council of Churches, 404

World Mission Rosary, 660

World War II, 65, 109, 113, 115, 212, 236, 294, 304, 427, 557

World Youth Day, 639, 661

World's Fair, 132

World's Oldest Marian Shrine, 127

Worldwide Marriage Encounter, 660-661

Wreath, 30, 84, 164, 205, 330, 513, 548, 661-662

Wreaths of Flowers, 200, 661-662

WWJD, 662-663

Wycinanki, 422

Wypominki, 663

X

Xifre, Bishop Joseph, C.M.F., 513

Xylographs, 234

Y

Yahweh, 28, 173, 201, 271, 667

Yankee Stadium, 322

Yerbaria, 584

Yew tree, 667

Yodeling, 136

Z

Zacatecas, 64, 237

Zapopan, 671-672

Zapopan, Annual procession of Our Lady of, 671

Zaragoza, 440, 681
Zechariah, 104, 326, 568, 570, 671-672
Zechariah's Canticle, 326
Zephaniah, 38
Zeus, 436

Zizyphus Spire Christi, 157
Zumarraga, Fray Juan de, 219
Zwick, Louise, 21
Zwick, Mark, 21

Complete Your Catholic Reference Shelf with...